America's Courts and the Criminal Justice System

SECOND EDITION

America's Courts and the Criminal Justice System

SECOND EDITION

David W. Neubauer
University of New Orleans

Brooks/Cole Publishing Company
Monterey, California

Consulting Editor: *George F. Cole*

Brooks/Cole Publishing Company
A Division of Wadsworth, Inc.

Printed in the United States of America
10 9 8 7 6 5 4 3 2 1

Library of Congress Cataloging in Publication Data

Neubauer, David W.
  America's courts and the criminal justice system.

  Includes bibliographies and index.
  1. Criminal courts—United States. 2. Criminal
procedure—United States. I. Title.
KF9619.N4 1983   345.73′01   83-15167
                  347.3051

Sponsoring Editor: *Henry Staat*
Production Editor: *Jane Stanley*
Manuscript Editor: *Adrienne Mayor*
Permissions Editor: *Mary Kay Hancharick*
Interior Design: *Debbie Wunsch*
Cover Design: *Koney Eng*
Art Coordinator: *Judith Macdonald*
Interior Illustration: *Ryan Cooper*
Chapter Opening Illustrations: *Ron Grauer*
Typesetting: *TriStar Graphics*
Printing and Binding: *Halliday Lithograph*

For Jeffrey, Kristen, and Amy

Preface to the Second Edition

Writing a second edition is much like attending a class reunion. One meets a lot of old friends. It is comforting to catch up on recent events and find out that things are proceeding as before. In terms of writing, this means updating some materials but leaving the original analysis unaltered. At reunions one also brushes shoulders with people who are only vaguely familiar. The world has changed and some people have changed more than others. The same holds for the second edition of a text. The author finds that the issues have shifted, new events have intervened, and recent literature calls into question the old. Thus there is a need to provide major changes. Chapter 17, for example, has been totally recast and parts of other chapters have been rewritten from scratch. Finally, at a reunion one invariably rubs shoulders with some classmates that one might prefer to avoid. Alas, in revising I have encountered some materials that were either wrong or at best somewhat misleading. The broadening of one's experiences leads to rethinking some materials, in this case the materials on European justice. Extending the analogy further, class reunions along with revised editions end up evoking positive feelings. To an author, the highest accolade is the knowledge that enough people used the first edition to make a second edition a worthwhile endeavor. Revising also reawakens the importance of effectively communicating ideas, underscoring the responsibility to present up-to-date materials in a readable and coherent form.

Throughout the updating, revising, and recasting of the second edition, however, the basic thrust and organization of the book remains unaltered.

Acknowledgments

In writing this second edition, I have had the assistance and encouragement of people who deserve special recognition. As always, colleagues from a number of schools have offered valuable critiques and shared their thoughts. They include James Alfini (American Judicature Society), Larry Berkson (American Judicature Society), Warren Billings (University of New Orleans), George Cole (University of Connecticut), Roy Flemming (Wayne State University), David O. Friedrichs (University of Scranton), Mark Gertz (Florida State University), Edward Heck (University of New Orleans), Frank Höpfel (University of Innsbruck), John Paul Ryan (American Judicature Society and University of Illinois—Chicago), Paul Wice (Drew University), and Nancy Wolfe (University of South Carolina).

Preparation of the manuscript has been greatly aided by my research assistant John Fenasci and ably typed by Rosemary Griggs, Muriel Murphy, and Gail White. Throughout the revising process Henry Staat, Criminal Justice editor at Brooks/Cole, provided useful help and encouragement. As before, my wife and children deserve a special note of thanks for their love and continuing support. The dedication of the book to my children is a reflection of their perplexity and sometimes bemusement that Daddy was busy writing a book.

David W. Neubauer

Preface

This book is written for undergraduate courses that deal with America's criminal courts. That these courses (or parts of courses) are taught in departments as varied as criminal justice or police science, political science, sociology, psychology, and social welfare highlights not only the pivotal role of the criminal courts within the criminal justice system but also their importance and impact upon society as a whole.

There has been only a limited range of teaching materials suitable for these classes. To be sure there are a number of case books, but these are written for law students and do not meet the needs of undergraduates. A few books are aimed at undergraduate students, but these often resemble their law school counterparts and are heavy with discussions of the history, structure, and philosophy of courts. Although these are important matters, the books project a rather sterile image of courthouse justice and omit what courts do in practice (and not in theory), how they do it, and, most importantly, why they do it.

This book is intended to fill the gap. Its focus is on the dynamics of the courthouse. The emphasis grows out of my own field research. Over the last decade I have spent considerable time in state and federal courts in all parts of the nation. I have interviewed numerous judges, prosecutors, defense attorneys, probation officers, jailers, police officers, bail bondsmen, and occasionally defendants. I have also observed these officials in action and discussed with them their problems and their views of possible solutions. Throughout this book I have tried to convey to the reader this sense of being in the courthouse.

Just a few years ago it would not have been possible to write this book because relatively little was known about the operations of the criminal courts. But in the last decade a growing volume of literature authored by social scientists, lawyers, and law professors has begun to probe the workings of these important governmental bodies. Much of this literature, however, has not been incorporated into a text suitable for undergraduates. Thus, along with a stress of the dynamics of courthouse justice, this book is intended to provide students with an overview of current research.

Given the potential breadth of the material under discussion, I have had to focus on certain topics to the exclusion of others. First, this book focuses on the trial courts, not the appellate courts, although we will examine how the appellate courts affect the trial court process. Second, this book concentrates on the courts for adult offenders, not the juvenile courts. Because the structure, philosophy, and method of operation of the juvenile courts march to a drummer different from courts that deal with adult offenders (typically seventeen years old or older, although the exact age varies from state to state), juvenile courts are best left to a separate discussion.

Using the Book

All too often American higher education is treated as a spectator sport. Students read the text, take notes on the lecture, and then take an exam. This book tries to involve the readers as participant observers, not just passive spectators. To those interested in personally observing how their government operates, the courts provide excellent opportunity. Courts are located in every town in the nation, and they are also open to the public. Thus a number of discussion questions provide ideas on how best to observe the government—courts—in action. In addition, discussion questions suggest topics for interviews with those who take part in the criminal court process.

Crime and the courts also are steady sources of newspaper copy. Students are encouraged to read the local papers and relate these stories to the material in the book. To aid this process, some of the discussion questions suggest topics often covered in the media.

To encourage students to be active participants, this book uses some special features. *In the News* reprints news stories from around the nation on matters directly tied to the topic under examination. *Close-ups* look at the dynamics of justice. Finally, points of view that illustrate important topics are set within boxes. In selecting these special features, I have tried to include varying viewpoints and perspectives. I do not agree with all the assessments I offer. Neither should the reader. But they should prompt both of us to consider the position presented.

To the Student

Law and Structure

The starting point of this text is to provide readers with a working knowledge of the major structures and basic legal concepts that underlie the criminal courts. In deciding guilt or innocence and determining the appropriate punishment, the courts apply the criminal law through a complicated process termed *criminal procedure*. The structure of the courts, the nature of the criminal law they apply, and the type of the procedures followed all have important consequences for how the courts dispense justice. But to understand the legal system one needs to know more than the legal rules. One also needs to understand the assumptions underlying these rules, the history of how they evolved, and the goals they seek to achieve. A discussion of the assumptions, history, and goals highlights why America's criminal justice process is not a unitary process but consists of a number of separate and sometimes competing units. It also points out conflicts over the goals the criminal courts are expected to achieve.

Although America's criminal court process is complicated, it is useful to focus on three essential issues. When presented with someone alleged to have violated the law—a defendant—the court process seeks to answer three questions. First, is the defendant guilty? That is, did the defendant violate the legal rules? If the defendant is found guilty, the court must then confront a second question: what penalty should be applied to the wrongdoer? The third question often precedes the first two: have the governmental officials—police and prosecutors, primarily—followed the rules for investigating crimes and convicting defendants? If the courts determine that the defendant's rights have been violated, they may either directly penalize the law enforcement officials (which is rarely done) or indirectly penalize them by letting the defendant escape punishment. Throughout this book we will be examining how the various stages of the criminal process are geared to provided answers to these three basic questions.

Dynamics of the Process

All too many books leave the false impression that an understanding of the formal law and major structures of the court is all that one needs to know about the criminal courts. This kind of analysis provides only a limited description of how the courts administer justice. The law is not self-executing. It is a dynamic process of applying abstract rules to concrete situations. Decisions about whether charges should be filed, the amount of bail to be required, and the sentence the convicted will receive call for judges, prosecutors, and defense attorneys to make choices for which the formal law provides few precise guidelines. Thus the second objective of this book is to examine law in action—the dynamics of the criminal court process.

Invariably an examination of the law in action reveals a gap between how the law is supposed to operate and how it actually does operate. For example, the law in theory suggests that the guilt of defendants should be decided by a jury trial. Yet in practice, trials are rare. Most defendants plead guilty before any trial.

Problems

No treatment of the criminal courts would be complete without a discussion of the problems confronting the courts. Are the courts too slow? Are judges too soft in sentencing? Does the criminal court process discriminate against the poor? These are just a few of the questions being raised about the operations of the criminal courts and the types of questions this book will consider.

We can group the numerous problems under three general propositions. One goal of the courts is to protect society. To some, the courts are not properly fulfilling this role because they hamper efforts to fight crime. A second goal of the courts is to protect individual rights. To some the courts have failed to provide fair and impartial justice by discriminating against the poor, the ignorant, and members of minority groups. Finally, many contend that the courts are so poorly managed that justice is delayed and innumerable inconveniences are experienced by witnesses, jurors, victims, and others.

Reform

Many organizations, groups, and individuals have probed the problems facing the criminal courts and proposed reforms. The fourth objective of this book is to discuss and analyze the reforms that have been suggested for what ails the courts.

Not all agree on the types of changes needed. Some argue that certain reforms will produce greater difficulties without solving the original problems. Therefore, this book will discuss competing perspectives on the types of changes and reforms that are being proposed.

Organization of the Book

In writing this book I have used a spiral approach. I have begun with the basic building blocks of knowledge and then proceeded to use these building blocks for a deeper analysis. Within each chapter, the initial emphasis is on the basics; the later material emphasizes more complicated issues.

The book is divided into five parts. After the introductory chapter, which examines the controversies surrounding the criminal courts, the three chapters of part 1 provide the reader with an overview of the legal basis of the criminal courts: criminal procedure, criminal law, and the organization of courts. Part 2 introduces the legal actors—judges, prosecutors, and defense attorneys—who on a day-to-day basis must make the decisions. The emphasis is on how the working relationships among these actors structure their exercise of discretion.

Part 3 follows the general stages cases pass through from arrest to the determination of guilt or innocence. Why cases are removed from the process and why cases are bargained out are prime concerns of this section.

Part 4 focuses on the most important question in the criminal process: what sentence should be given to the guilty. While most of popular attention as well as legal analysis centers on the questions of legal guilt or innocence, the dynamics of the courthouse are geared to sentencing.

Part 5 identifies problems with the system and discusses several key aspects of reforming the criminal court process. Should the lower courts be abolished? Are the courts too slow? Should discretion be abolished?

Contents

4 What Is a Crime?   61

PART 2   The Legal Actors   81

5 The Dynamics of Courthouse Justice   83

6 The Prosecutor   103

10 After the Arrest: Case Attrition   187

11 Freedom for Sale   211

12 Preparing for Trial   237

13 Negotiated Justice and the Plea of Guilty   255

14 Trial   283

America's Courts and the Criminal Justice System

SECOND EDITION

CHAPTER 1

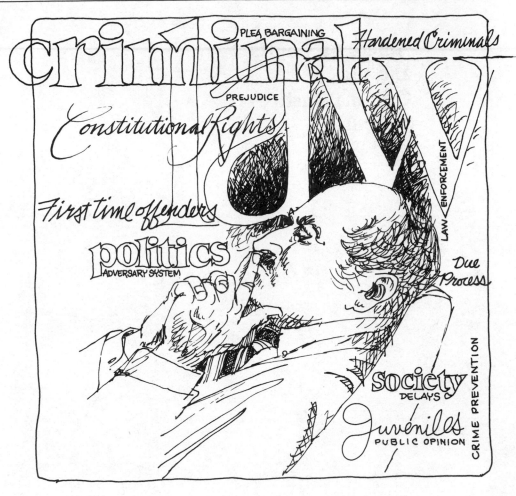

The Criminal Courts in Controversy

This is a book about America's criminal courts. It is about the history, values, traditions, and philosophy underlying the complex, sometimes contradictory, and often fragmented process by which defendants are found guilty—and sentenced to prison or placed on probation—or declared innocent. It is about the widespread controversy surrounding how the courts make these decisions and solutions proposed to correct the problems. It is about the defendants caught up in the process and what happens to the three-time losers, the scared young first offenders, and the business executives who are before the court to answer an indictment. But most of all, it is a book about the prosecutors, judges, defense attorneys, juries, and probation officers who on a day-to-day basis must make the decisions about guilt or innocence, probation or prison, and the factors that guide the selection among often hard choices. Throughout the book, attention is directed to the process by which the law is applied.

Until recently, there was little interest in the criminal courts. Courts, like police and corrections, were treated by the public with an unhealthy dose of "out of sight and out of mind." No longer. Increasing crime rates and controversial Supreme

Court decisions have focused attention on the judicial branch of government. Local newspapers and television news broadcasts carry stories about crime and courts almost every day. Thus in a basic sense, the criminal courts need no introduction. We all know something about how they operate and some of the problems they face. The purpose of this introductory chapter is to build upon the public concern about the criminal courts by considering some basic topics. We will discuss why the courts are important, some of the problems they face, and the debate over their operations. Finally, we will suggest that courts are not mysterious separate entities but part of the larger social and governmental process.

The pivotal role of the courts

criminal justice system

The term *criminal justice system* refers to the various agencies and institutions that are directly involved in the implementation of public policy concerning crime. The criminal justice system is composed of three principal components: police, courts, and corrections. The courts play a pivotal role within this system because after a crime has been committed any formal action must be funneled through the courts. Only the courts can detain a person prior to trial. Only the courts can find a person guilty. Only the courts can sentence a person to prison. Alternatively, of course, the courts may release the suspect prior to trial, find him or her not guilty, or decide not to send the guilty to prison. The decisions that courts make (and how they make them) have important consequences for other components of the crimi-

criminal courts

nal justice system. The reverse is equally true: the operations of police and corrections have major impacts on the *criminal courts*.

A fragmented criminal justice system

Although the three components of the criminal justice system are separate organizations, they are also tied together. Each component must interact with the other. This process is best visualized as three overlapping circles, one representing the police, another the courts, and the last corrections (see figure 1-1). All three circles operate within a wider circle representing the general public (National Advisory Commission on Criminal Justice Standards and Goals:5).

While police, courts, and corrections must by necessity work together, the criminal justice system is neither uniform nor coordinated.

> The major components of the law enforcement and criminal justice system do not comprise a system in the sense of a smoothly functioning, internally consistent organization. Not only is there fragmentation and lack of coherence within each element; there is also a serious lack of coordination among the elements even though the operation of each component has a direct bearing on the functioning of the others. [Advisory Commission on Intergovernmental Relations]

These interrelationships, however, are often marked by tension, a point made by the National Advisory Committee on Criminal Justice Standards and Goals:

> The interaction among the components of the system and the relationships underlying it—the interfacing of the components—are often characterized by conflict and even hostility. In part, this is because of competition for attention and funds from outside the

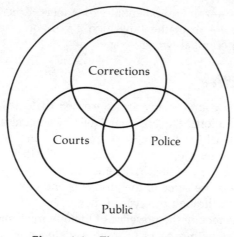

Figure 1-1. The overlapping circles of the criminal justice system.

system. But it also is the result of viewing the common task of processing accused persons from different perspectives. [p. 5]

The competing perspectives of police, courts, and corrections (to say nothing of differing views within the court community itself) toward processing the accused have caused some to question whether America has a system—or a nonsystem—of criminal justice. Some argue that the process is so fragmented, splintered, divided, and decentralized that there is no overall coordination in the American justice process. Others disagree, arguing that it is still useful to view criminal justice as a system. They point out that the system has some overall purpose and an interrelationship among the various components; moreover, the term *system* does not necessarily mean that all actions must be rationally ordered. The criminal justice process is a living system composed of a number of parts characterized by competing goals. Tensions and conflicts among police, courts, and corrections therefore are not necessarily undesirable. Tensions arising from competing goals can provide important checks on other organizations. This friction is particularly evident in the criminal justice system, where the work of each component is evaluated by others: the police make arrests, yet the decision to charge is made by the prosecutor; the judge and jury rate the prosecutor's ability. The very essence of the adversary process emphasizes conflict. Such contention ensures that multiple information sources will be considered.

Symbols of justice

The importance of the courts cannot be measured solely in terms of their role within the criminal justice system. The courts also play a meaningful symbolic role. The public looks to them as a forum of fairness and impartiality. Public confidence in any democratic system of justice depends on the public perceptions of the process as fair and just. Every citizen accused of a crime expects to have a day in court. At the same time, the public looks to the courts to punish wrongdoers. A conviction at trial is a public dramatization that those who violate society's rules will be punished. It also serves as a warning to potential wrongdoers. Americans believe that no one is above the law—no matter how high a position one occupies, a person may be convicted for criminal wrongdoing.

The courts: a consumer's perspective

consumer's perspective

Given the pivotal role of the courts, many are concerned that these institutions have fallen far short of expectations. The National Advisory Commission on Criminal Justice Standards and Goals, for example, found that there are "too many defendants for the existing system to handle effectively and efficiently. Backlogs are enormous; workloads are increasing. The entire court system is underfinanced." A useful way to examine some of the problems and criticisms surrounding the courts is to view them through the eyes of their users.

On a daily basis the courts require the presence of literally thousands of citizens to serve as jurors, to testify as witnesses, or to stand as defendants. These people who use governmental services have been labeled *consumers of justice*. Viewing the criminal court process through the eyes of these consumers—police officers, jurors, victims, witnesses, and defendants—highlights not only the importance of courts but also why many are so dissatisfied with their operations.

In a democracy a government is expected to be responsive to the wishes and demands of its citizens. The satisfaction or dissatisfaction citizens find as consumers of court services plays an important role in shaping their views and attitudes toward the government in general and the legal system in particular. Increasingly these consumers are critical of court operations.

The police

The police are the most regular users of the criminal courts. On a daily basis they must appear to request that charges be filed against those they have arrested, to testify at hearings, and to serve as witnesses during trial. To law enforcement personnel, the criminal courts represent a legal maze over which they have little control. Often they believe the process gives all the advantage to the guilty.

The police believe that bail turns the jail into a revolving door. Often those arrested are back on the streets within hours, some committing more crimes. It takes too long to get a case to trial. Evidence (heroin, for example) is thrown out of court on a technicality. Defendants are eventually allowed to plead guilty to a charge less serious than the one they allegedly committed. The sentences handed out are much too light. Thus, the police have come to believe that the courts frustrate their efforts to control crime. A Los Angeles cop had this to say:

> . . . The only people protected and served are criminals. They get the breaks, not the victims, not the witnesses, not the good people. Sit in a courtroom sometime and see who gets fucked around—cases continued, witnesses harassed and insulted, victims made out to be criminals, and plea bargaining. That's the worst! We could catch some dude coming out of a liquor store with a smoking gun in one hand and a bag of money in the other, and he'd walk out of court with ten days suspended for trespassing. Let me ask you. Who gets protected? Who gets served? The whole thing pisses me off. [Carter:122]

Ordinary citizens

Victims, witnesses, and jurors often come away from their brief encounter with the criminal courts with negative attitudes. Most of them are ordinary citizens, who consider their role a chance to serve their government. But to others their participation is an unwanted interruption of their daily lives. Often their appearance is postponed. When the case is finally heard, they still face long waits in crowded corridors deprived of simple amenities like a cup of coffee or a chair to sit on. During the trial (particularly if the charge is rape) the victims may feel they are on trial. It is no wonder that these consumers feel like unwelcome intruders in a system they find inefficient and mismanaged.

Defendants

Millions of Americans appear each year as defendants in a lower tribunal to answer charges as varied as driving too fast, creating a disturbance, or violating a city zoning ordinance. To many, their day in court consists of a long wait on hard benches, a brief appearance before the judge, the pronouncement of a fine, and a quick calling of the next case. Such "cash register justice" often shatters the textbook image of justice.

The reactions of defendants accused of serious crimes reveal some contrasting images of the American criminal courts. Unlike their middle-class brethren, typical felony defendants hold no illusions about the courts. Educated not by the lofty premises of civics textbooks but instructed by their street peers, many view the courts as a game not much different from life on the streets. They see the behavior of the police, prosecutors, judges, and defense attorneys as essentially the same as the behavior of law violators: conning, manipulating, and lying (Casper). Indeed, in the minds of many defendants their major adversary is not the judge, police, or prosecutor but their own defense attorney.

IN THE NEWS: CRIMINAL JUSTICE CUBE

It's long been understood that criminal justice is a Rubik's Cube: what the police do will affect what happens in court, which will affect what happens in the jails and prisons. You can't hope to deal with crime better by focusing on any single part—any more than you can solve the cube by concentrating on one square at a time.

Yet for years criminal justice officials have responded to public frustration by focusing blame on each other—regarding small matters as well as large. We could hold speedier trials, say court administrators, if only the corrections people would get the prisoners to court on time. We could keep more men on the street, say the police, if only the courts wouldn't tie them up so long when they bring people in. We could send convicts to prison faster, say judges, if only the probation department would prepare pre-sentencing reports on time.

There is certainly plenty of blame to go around—and that's the real point. It's time the various officials involved began turning such complaints into questions, and holding each other accountable for the answers.

New York Times, Dec. 9, 1981, p. 30 © 1981 by The New York Times Company. Reprinted by permission.

The general public

Ultimately all citizens are consumers of the criminal courts. They perceive that they might need the protection of the courts, they view the courts in symbolic terms, and, of course, as taxpayers they pay the expenses of the courts. Public dissatisfaction with the performance of the criminal courts is disclosed in several recent public opinion polls. To begin with, the fear of crime is pervasive in American society.

- 68 percent of Americans in 1981 perceived that crime increased in their neighborhood in the last year (Harris). Moreover, many blame the courts, at least partially, for this problem.
- 43 percent of the respondents in 1978 believed that ineffective courts are a serious/frequent cause of growing crime rates (Yankelovich, Skelly and White, Inc.). More specifically, citizens identified sentencing practices as a major factor.
- 83 percent of respondents in 1980 stated that the courts in their area do not deal harshly enough with criminals (National Opinion Research Center). Nor are the courts perceived as being well managed.
- Over half of those surveyed by the Yankelovich, Skelly and White polling organization in 1978 rated the inefficiency of courts as a "serious" or "very serious" problem.

Debate over the courts

While a consensus has emerged that the criminal courts require change, there is no agreement over what types of changes are in order. Even a brief review of the critical comments about the criminal courts discussed so far should indicate the varying and often conflicting views about what is wrong. Broadly, two differing diagnoses have been presented. One is that the courts have hindered effective law enforcement and therefore have produced inadequate protection of society. The other is that the court system is fundamentally unfair to defendants.

The public dialogue on these issues is between proponents of "law and order" and those who approve of the relatively liberal decisions of the Warren Court (named after former Chief Justice Earl Warren). But these terms, although they draw our attention to disagreements over the goals of the criminal courts, are not useful for systematic inquiry because they are too ambiguous and too emotional. More constructive in understanding the controversy over the criminal courts are the crime control and due process models developed by Herbert Packer. Although these models somewhat distort reality because they concentrate on extreme (polar) positions, they are quite useful because they examine in an unemotional way the competing values over the proper role of the criminal courts.

Crime control model

*crime con-
trol model*

The most important value in the *crime control model* is the repression of criminal conduct. Unless crime is controlled, the rights of the law-abiding citizens will not be protected, and the security of society will be diminished.

In achieving this goal of repressing crime, the courts must process defendants efficiently. They should operate like an assembly line—rapidly removing defendants against whom there is inadequate evidence and quickly determining guilt according to evidence. The crime control model holds that informal fact finding—initially by the police and later by the prosecutor—not only is the best way to determine if the defendant is in fact guilty but is also sufficiently foolproof to prevent the innocent from being falsely convicted. Accordingly, the crime control model stresses the necessity of speed and finality of the courts in order to achieve the priority of crime suppression.

Due process model

due process model

In contrast, the *due process model* emphasizes protecting the rights of the individual. Although adherents of the due process model do not downgrade the need for controlling crime, they believe that the sole pursuit of such a goal threatens individual rights and poses the threat of a tyrannical government. Thus, the key function of the courts is not the speed and finality projected in the crime control model but an insistence on a careful consideration of each case. The dominant image is one of the courts operating as an obstacle course. The due process model stresses the possibility of error in the informal fact-finding process and therefore insists on formal fact finding to protect against mistakes made by the police and prosecutors. In short, the proponent of the due process model believes the prime role of the courts is to protect the rights of the individual. Any resulting decrease in the efficiency of the courts is the price paid in a democracy based on individual liberties.

Law and politics

The criminal courts do not stand in splendid isolation, removed from the rest of society; their activities are intimately intertwined with other social institutions, community norms, public opinion, and the actions (or inactions) of other members of the criminal justice system. Unfortunately the belief of many Americans that law and politics are (or at least should be) separate obscures the larger social context that affects the criminal courts. Judicial reformers, for instance, believe that the cure to court ills lies in removing *politics* from the process. In these contexts politics is a dirty word, standing for corruption, undue personal influence, dirty tricks, or partisan affairs. Such partial views of politics, however, cloud what is a vital process. The criminal "courts are part of the political process, by which authoritative decisions are made about who gets what in society" (Easton:50).

politics

Applying this definition of politics to the activities of the criminal courts highlights some essential features of their operations. Certainly the decisions of the courts must be considered *authoritative;* only the courts have the legal power to detain suspects before trial or send those found guilty to prison. Because laws are unclear and resources limited, court officials must make important *decisions* about innocence or guilt, the nature of the charge, and the sentence. At times these decisions require choosing between competing values such as rights of the individual and protections for society. Finally, Easton's definition, by stressing *who gets what*, calls our attention to the importance of the authoritative decisions the courts make for defendants, victims of crimes, other components of the criminal justice system, and the general public.

Viewed from this perspective, criminal justice personnel engage in the same type of authoritative allocation of values as other governmental decision makers. The actions of legislators and mayors, for example, are generally viewed as political. The same holds true for the courts. At times these political considerations are direct—for example, in the involvement of political parties in selecting members of the criminal justice community. At other times these political influences are indirect. For example, the officials who staff the courts—judges, prosecutors, and defense attorneys—are typically lifelong members of their community and are therefore intimately acquainted with local values. Local community values are also transmitted to the criminal courts through decisions made by juries.

CLOSE-UP: REVOLVING DOOR JUSTICE: WHY CRIMINALS GO FREE

The following article from *U.S. News and World Report* provides a useful overview of the many problems and controversies surrounding America's criminal courts. Note that although the article appears to begin with the view that it is the courts that let the criminals go free, the article reaches a different conclusion. In particular, it finds that some of the problems the public blames the courts for are not their fault at all. Moreover the article highlights the conflict over the goals that the criminal courts should pursue. Viewed in this light, the fact that two out of three suspects arrested are never convicted may not be an indication that the criminal courts are failing.

Americans, for years, have been frightened by the constant rise in crime. Now, along with that fear, is a growing anger. The anger is about the way the nation's system of criminal justice handles criminals.

Almost everywhere you go, you hear people complain: Criminals arrested one day are often back on the street the next day, committing new crimes even before they can be tried for their past crimes. Many arrested as criminals are never brought to trial. When tried, relatively few are convicted. Even when convicted, few are sent to prison.

Almost every day, in their local newspaper, people read about a crime being committed by someone with a long criminal record, who has been arrested time after time and then, each time, soon set free.

To people it seems that criminals move in and out of the criminal-justice system as though it had a revolving door.

A Look at the Capital.   As a sample of what angers people, take a look at what happens to criminals in Washington, D.C.

In the nation's capital, 2 out of 3 persons arrested for serious crimes are not convicted. Of the one third who are convicted, only a little more than half spend any time in jail or prison. And, if they are convicted of two separate crimes, one right after the other, the chances are their sentences will be set to run concurrently. In effect, they commit their second crime "for free."

Six out of 10 persons who are arrested for serious felonies in Washington have prior criminal records. Between 1971 and 1975, a mere 7 percent of all those arrested for serious crimes accounted for 24 percent of all such arrests. Each had been arrested at least four times in that period, some as many as 10 times.

About one fourth of all persons arrested for felonies in Washington are either out on parole or probation for some previous crime, or else are free on some form of pretrial release on a pending charge.

Appalling as they are, these figures do not mean that Washington has an unusually bad system of criminal justice. In fact, official figures indicate that Washington does about an average job of prosecuting and punishing criminals. . . . What happens in the nation's capital is typical

(continued)

of what happens in major cities all across the country. So Washington was chosen by *U.S. News and World Report* as the subject of an intensive study to see how and why so many criminals go free.

One case found in this study illustrates how rapidly a criminal can go in and out of the "revolving door" of criminal justice. The man has been arrested at least seven times. Here is his record for just last year:

On May 25, 1975, he was arrested for robbery at gun point. While free on bond, he was arrested on July 22 for illegal possession of a gun. Again he was released, this time without bond. The next day he was arrested on a charge of petty larceny. The charge was reduced to attempted petty larceny, and he was released without bond.

On July 31, this man was rearrested for armed robbery. This time, bond of $2,000 was required. He made the bond and was released. On October 9, while still out on bond, he was arrested again—for armed robbery. On November 20, his gun-carrying charge was dropped by the prosecutor. On December 4, he was arrested for "unauthorized use" of an automobile. But that charge was also dropped. On January 26 of this year, the man finally pleaded guilty to the attempted-petty-larceny charge of last July 23, and was released to await his sentencing.

The Underlying Problem. Talk to police in any major city and they will cite similar cases. These cases represent the extremes—not the rule. But they point up the underlying problem that weakens all U.S. systems of criminal justice—the inability to keep known criminals off the streets.

Who's to blame for this? Study official records, talk to police, prosecutors and other authorities, and you find there is not just one culprit. Many are to blame.

Police, for example, make some bad arrests, frequently fail to come up with hard evidence or reliable witnesses. And, nationwide, police are able to make arrests in only about 1 of 5 serious crimes reported. Prosecutors, often overburdened, drop some cases that might have been won.

Favorite targets of public criticism are judges. They are accused of being "too lenient." Some undoubtedly are. But, in the over-all picture, they play a relatively small role in letting criminals go free. In Washington, for example, only 1 arrested criminal in 3 ever comes before a judge for sentencing. Parole boards, another popular target, frequently turn dangerous prisoners loose on society. The high crime rate among parolees shows that.

Even the American public itself must share a portion of the blame, because so many citizens refuse to "become involved" by testifying. A high percentage of prosecutions fail for lack of cooperative witnesses.

"'Revolving Door' Justice: Why Criminals Go Free." Reprinted from *U.S. News & World Report*, May 10, 1976, pp. 36–37. Copyright 1976 U.S. News & World Report, Inc.

Conclusion

For decades the public was indifferent to the needs and problems of the criminal courts. Even the legal community seemed unconcerned with whether the criminal courts lived up to the lofty ideal of providing equal protection under the law. But in a few short years how America's criminal courts dispense justice has become a high-priority item. The courts, because of their pivotal position within the criminal justice system, became the focal point of much of this public concern. Particularly in the nation's largest cities, the rising crime rate is swelling the dockets of the criminal courts, thus taxing already inadequate facilities. Jails are overcrowded. Delay is a major problem. The quality of justice dispensed by the criminal courts is being questioned as well. Some say the courts coddle criminals; others believe the courts have failed to protect the rights of the accused. While some argue that legal technicalities needlessly free the guilty, others are alarmed that the courts dispense one type of justice to the rich and a different variety to the poor.

As citizens experience delay, inconveniences, frequent rescheduling of cases, and confusion—when they appear as victims, witnesses, jurors, or defendants—they are increasingly voicing their dissatisfaction with the courts. For too long, they charge, the courts have been run as if they were a private club of judges and lawyers and not an important public body. This public dissatisfaction has forced courts to reexamine as well as alter many ways they do business. In turn, the criminal justice practitioners—the judges, prosecutors, and defense attorneys—have often been at the forefront in pointing out problems and deficiencies that require change.

For discussion

1. Discuss with several friends any personal contacts they have had with the criminal justice system as victim, witness, juror, or defendant. Were their experiences positive or negative? Why?
2. What are the most important problems facing the criminal courts? Why? What values do your choices of problem areas reflect?
3. How do the local papers cover the crime issue? For a week, count the number and type of crimes reported in the newspapers. How do these compare with official FBI crime statistics?
4. If you were a defendant in court, do you think you would be treated fairly and properly? Would your classmates feel the same way?
5. Do the local and state newspapers indicate any tensions among the principal criminal justice agencies (police, prosecutor, judge, defense attorney, corrections officials)?
6. Do you think that the criminal justice system in your community is fragmented? Are there any major gaps? For example, how easy is it to find information about a given case or defendant? Who benefits or suffers when the system is fragmented?

References

Advisory Commission on Intergovernmental Relations. *State–Local Relations in the Criminal Justice System.* Washington, D.C.: Government Printing Office, 1977.

Carter, Robert, "The Police View of the Justice System." In Malcolm Klein, ed., *The Juvenile Justice System.* Beverly Hills, Calif.: Sage Publications, 1976.

Casper, Jonathan. *American Criminal Justice: The Defendant's Perspective.* Englewood Cliffs, N.J.: Prentice-Hall, 1972.

Easton, David. *A Systems Analysis of Political Life.* New York: John Wiley, 1965.

Harris, Louis. *The Harris Survey.* New York: The Chicago Tribune-New York News Syndicate, February 23, 1981.

National Advisory Commission on Criminal Justice Standards and Goals. *Report on Courts.* Washington, D.C.: Government Printing Office, 1973.

National Opinion Research Center. *General Social Surveys.* Chicago: University of Chicago, 1980.

Packer, Herbert. *The Limits of the Criminal Sanction.* Palo Alto, Calif.: Stanford University Press, 1968.

Yankelovich, Skelly and White, Inc. *The Public Image of Courts: Highlights of a National Survey of the General Public, Judges, Lawyers and Community Leaders.* Williamsburg, Va.: National Center for State Courts, 1978.

For further reading

Balbus, Isaac. *The Dialectics of Legal Repression.* New Brunswick, N.J.: Transaction Books, 1977.

Casper, Jonathan. *American Criminal Justice: The Defendant's Perspective.* Englewood Cliffs, N.J.: Prentice-Hall, 1972.

Downie, Leonard, Jr. *Justice Denied.* New York: Praeger Publishers, 1971.

Harris, Richard. *The Fear of Crime.* New York: Praeger Publishers, 1969.

James, Howard. *Crisis in the Courts.* New York: David McKay Company, 1971.

National Advisory Commission on Criminal Justice Standards and Goals. *Report on Courts.* Washington, D.C.: Government Printing Office, 1973.

President's Commission on Law Enforcement and Administration of Justice. *Task Force Report: The Courts.* Washington, D.C.: Government Printing Office, 1967.

Silberman, Charles. *Criminal Violence, Criminal Justice.* New York: Random House, 1978.

Skoler, Daniel. *Organizing the Non-System.* Lexington, Mass.: D. C. Heath, Lexington Books, 1977.

1

The Legal System

Part 1 provides an introduction to basic legal concepts underlying the criminal courts.

Chapter 2 presents an overview of common law, the adversary system, and the twelve stages of the criminal court process. Its purpose is to tie together the various stages of a case that the remainder of the book analyzes individually.

Chapter 3 focuses on the organization of American courts. The consequences of America's diverse number of judicial bodies is the primary concern.

Chapter 4 centers on how the criminal law defines certain acts as illegal. An understanding of these definitions is an important first step in understanding discretion.

CHAPTER 2

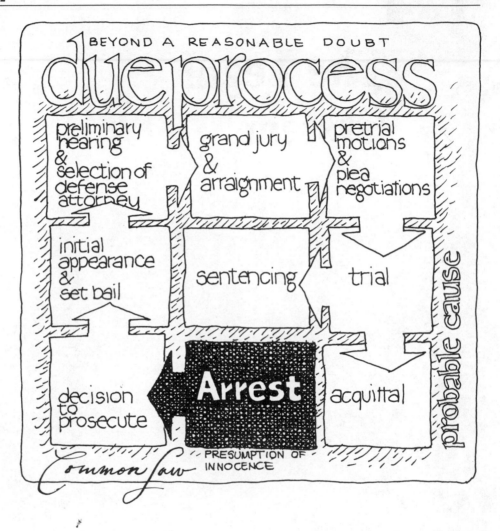

How (and Why) Cases Move from Here to There

Most Americans possess an elementary knowledge about the criminal courts. They learned in high school civics courses that a person is presumed innocent until proven guilty. Press coverage of dramatic criminal cases has made them aware of the number of varying steps and procedures involved in a criminal prosecution. Television shows portray some of the difficulties that detectives, prosecutors, and defense attorneys face in fulfilling their responsibilities. But beyond these basics, the average American only dimly perceives how the courts actually dispense justice.

It is useful to begin with a broad overview of the nature and basis of the criminal law, the agencies charged with applying that law, and the steps in the criminal process. We can begin best by asking some basic questions. Why do we have law and courts? What functions and purposes does society assign to courts and law? What are the major agencies of the criminal courts? What tasks do they perform? What procedures are used in the criminal court process? Why are they used? Answering these questions will provide the reader with a common core of knowledge that will avoid some (but certainly not all) of the confusion and misunderstanding about the criminal courts. It will also show how the numerous agencies and steps fit together. Throughout this book, we will be dissecting each of the actors and steps individually, so this broad overview is helpful in showing how all the pieces fit together.

A knowledge of the law, the agencies for applying that law, and the steps involved, however, are only the beginning point in examining the operations of the criminal court process. Equally as important is an examination of how these legal powers and legal procedures actually operate. A legal and structural analysis of the criminal courts omits the dynamics of the process. The interrelationship of judges, prosecutors, and defense attorneys has a major bearing on how the courts dispense justice. And each of these actors must make choices about how to dispense justice. These choices, far from being totally determined by the law, involve discretion. Thus, an additional purpose of this chapter is to introduce some of the major concepts and analytical tools we will need to analyze the dynamics of the criminal court process.

The basis of law

The fundamental basis of criminal law can be summarized in two words: human conflict. A controversy over how much money is owed, a quarrel between husband and wife, a collision at an intersection, a stolen television set are just a few examples of the wide range of disputes that arise in and threaten to disrupt the normal activities of society. Business, transportation, and everyday activities are dependent upon mechanisms for mediating these inevitable human conflicts. Without such a mechanism, individual parties might seek private, nonpeaceful means of settlement. The proverbial feud between the Hatfields and the McCoys illustrates the disruptive effects the blood feuds, motivated by revenge, have not only on the individual parties directly involved but also on the larger society.

law   *Law* is a body of rules. These rules are found in a variety of sources: statutes, constitutions, court decisions, and administrative regulations. A key function of such rules is to prevent or at least minimize human conflict. By specifying the rules ahead of time, most people and organizations are able to conform their actions to the law. But if they do not, the law fulfills a second function; it provides a basis for resolving disputes.

> Courts exist to settle arguments. Before there were courts, disputes had to be resolved by force. One tribe carried on a feud with another. Or, in medieval times, there was a formal combat between two armored knights. Around 750 years ago in England, courts began to take the place of combat. People had come to see that it would be better to have disputes settled without violence, and settled according to some logical rules. Judges were sent out from London, traveling a circuit on horseback, to decide arguments and maintain "the King's peace." And they slowly started to develop the rules that we call law.
>
> Anthony Lewis, *Clarence Earl Gideon and the Supreme Court* (New York: Random House, 1972), p. 18.

Common law

common law

The American legal system traces its origins to England and is therefore referred to as Anglo-American law. Beginning in the twelfth century, judges traveled around England settling disputes by applying the norms and rules common to that area. Eventually these rules emerged into a national set of rules known as the *common law*. Common law is often referred to as judge-made law because initially the rules were determined by judges, not by legislative or executive bodies. Although today law is increasingly the product of statutes passed by legislative bodies or administrative regulations announced by executive agencies, judges still play a major role in determining the rules of society for they interpret and apply that law. In turn there are two principal divisions of common law: civil and criminal.

Civil law

civil law

Most disputes that come to courts' attention involve private parties. Conflicts over ownership of property, failure to live up to the terms of a contract, or injuries suffered in an automobile accident are settled on the basis of the body of rules collectively known as *civil law*. A civil suit is brought by a private party to enforce a right or to seek payment for a wrong committed by another private party. These suits are brought because the courts possess powers that private parties do not: they can order a business to pay another business money owed under a contract,

monetary damages

grant a husband and wife a divorce, award *monetary damages* suffered for an injury received in an automobile accident, and so forth. The powers courts possess for settling disputes reveal an important difference between law and other societal rules (such as norms or informal rules) for settling disputes: only law has the binding power of the state behind it. Thus civil cases are basically means by which private parties borrow government power for private ends.

plaintiff defendant

Most civil cases involve a request for monetary damages. The *plaintiff* (the person who starts a lawsuit) demands that the *defendant* (the person against whom a lawsuit is brought) pay money for violating the plaintiff's legal rights (termed injury). For example, in a case involving an automobile accident, the injured party may request a sum of money to pay for hospital expenses, doctors' fees, lost wages, and general "pain and suffering." But in some instances, a suit for monetary damages cannot repair potential damages. If Farmer Jones' property is about to be flooded by a dam that Farmer Smith is building, Farmer Jones does not want to wait until his land is damaged to attempt to recover monetary damages; he wants to go on farming his land. Therefore, a second form of remedy, termed *equity*,

equity remedy chancery injunction

developed in Anglo-American law. (Equity was originally a *remedy* requested from the king of England and therefore was termed *chancery*.) Equity requests an *injunction* (a court order) requiring the defendant either to perform a certain action or to stop a specified action. Thus Farmer Jones could seek a court order prohibiting Farmer Smith from building the dam. Equitable relief is more flexible and broad-based than requests for monetary damages. Jury trials are not available in equity cases.

Civil law is having an increasing impact on the criminal justice system. Civil suits alleging police brutality, charging discrimination in hiring, or arguing that prison facilities are cruel and unusual punishment are just three examples. In turn, some requests for police or criminal court action are attempts to invoke criminal sanctions for essentially private disputes.

Criminal law

criminal law

Although virtually all disputes are potentially disruptive to the overall functioning of society, some are viewed as so disruptive that they require special treatment; civil law remedies are not enough. Through the criminal law, societies define certain acts as public wrongs and specify penalties to be imposed on violators. One of the goals of the *criminal law* is to prevent and control crime. Unlike the civil law, in which private parties file suit in court alleging an infringement of private rights, violations of public wrong are prosecuted by the state. Thus, criminal law differs from civil law in that a crime is a public wrong, prohibited by law, for which a punishment is provided. The common law insists that crime be carefully and narrowly defined.

Courts

courts

Courts and law go hand in hand; they provide a forum for resolving disputes through application of law. Obviously not all disputes in society are brought to the court. Some are privately resolved, sometimes in anticipation of what courts would do if they were brought to their attention. Certain types of conflicts—lovers' quarrels or disagreement over church doctrine, for instance—are not allowed to come

jurisdiction

to court. *Jurisdiction* is the legal term for matters that courts are authorized to hear. Still other disputes are mediated by arbitration panels, insurance adjusters, marriage counselors, student grade appeal boards, and the like. While many of these alternative tribunals function somewhat like the courts, they are not courts.

Four characteristics distinguish courts from other dispute-resolving institutions: courts "(1) resolve disputes, (2) by *applying* to them the society's *legal norms* and (3) to do so *impartially* and (4) *independently*" (Wheeler and Whitcomb:5). Each of these is critical for understanding how courts adjudicate criminal cases.

The first characteristic, courts resolve disputes, is a basic one. Courts formulate law on the basis of actual disagreements. Thus courts are passive. They do not seek out matters but wait for other parties to bring disputes to their attention. The second characteristic is that courts apply legal rules in solving disputes. They are thus different from marriage counselors, arbitrators, or student grade appeal committees who may use a variety of standards in their work. The third characteristic, impartiality, means that each side will have an opportunity to present its case in court and that the court's decision will be fair, unbiased, and just. The fourth distinguishing characteristic of courts is independence. Courts are expected to resolve disputes free from outside pressures. This means no matter how much an accused criminal has outraged the public or governmental officials, a court is expected to judge the case dispassionately and on its individual merits.

America's courts, of which there are almost 17,000, represent a bewildering array of names, types, functions, and geographical jurisdictions. Although we commonly speak of *the* American judiciary or *the* American court system, the United States does not have a single uniform court structure. Rather it has fifty-one separate court systems, one in each of the fifty states, plus one for the national government. As a result, each state differs from its neighbor. And even within a given state there is often little uniformity. (Chapter 3 will provide a detailed discussion of the organization and structure of America's courts.)

Rights of the accused

In addition to preventing and controlling crime, the courts seek to protect the individual rights of each citizen.

A key feature of a democracy is the insistence that the prevention and control of crime must be accomplished within the framework of law. The criminal process embodies some of society's severest sanctions: detention before trial, confinement in prison after conviction, and, in certain situations, execution of the offender. Because the powers of the criminal courts are so great, there is concern that those powers not be abused or misapplied. Moreover, the Christian-Hebraic tradition places a high value on the worth of each individual citizen and therefore respects the individual liberty of each citizen.

> In a free society you have to take some risks. If you lock everybody up, or even if you lock up everybody you think might commit a crime, you'll be pretty safe, but you won't be free.
>
> Senator Sam Ervin quoted in Richard Harris, *Justice* (New York: Avon, 1969), p. 162.

Restrictions on the use and application of governmental power take the form of rights granted to the accused. One of the most fundamental protections is the right to be considered innocent until proven guilty. Another is the right to remain silent. Still another is the right to a trial by jury. These protections—found in the U.S. Constitution, the Bill of Rights, and the common law heritage—exist not to free the guilty but to protect the innocent. A criminal justice process based on the necessity of protecting individual liberties (of both the innocent and the guilty alike) obviously reduces the effectiveness of that process in fighting crime. The ideological foundations of Anglo-American criminal law have always recognized that freeing some of the guilty is the price willingly paid to ensure that too many innocent persons are not found guilty.

The American tradition of instituting limits on the use of governmental power flows from three basic concerns. The primary justification for providing constitutional safeguards for those caught in the net of the criminal process is to ensure that innocent persons are not harassed or wrongly convicted. The American legal system is premised on a distrust of human fact finding. Because it fears human errors, the criminal court process provides multiple review points, believing that errors made at one step will be spotted during a later stage. The possibility of wrongly convicting an innocent person arises out of a situation in which honest mistakes are made by honorable people. But it also arises out of the possibility of dishonorable officials using the criminal justice process for less-than-honorable ends. Without built-in checks, the criminal justice process provides a quick and easy way for government leaders to dispose of their enemies. A common ploy in a totalitarian government is to charge persons with the ill-defined crime of being an "enemy of the state." The possibility of political misuse of the criminal justice process by tyrannical governments or tyrannical officials is a major concern in the Anglo-American heritage.

The third reason that democracies respect the rights of those accused or suspected of violating the criminal law is the need to maintain the respect and support of the community. Democratic governments derive their powers from the consent of the governed. Such support is undermined if power is applied arbitrarily. Law enforcement practices that are brutal, random, or overzealous are likely to produce fear and cynicism among the people, law breakers and law abiders alike. Such practices undermine the respect that law enforcement officials must have to enforce the law in a democracy. Even in a dictatorship efforts are often made to portray an image of a fair trial.

rule of law

A hallmark of American law, then, is that governmental officials must follow a regularized set of procedures in making decisions. The phrase *rule of law* stands for the idea that those who make decisions will do so by following the law. Although there is no precise definition of the rule of law, "its essential element is the reduction of arbitrariness by officials" (Skolnick:8). In short, we expect our leaders to make decisions according to an agreed-upon set of legal procedures.

Due process and the Bill of Rights

due process

The principal legal doctrine for limiting the arbitrariness by officals is *due process*. Due process of law is mentioned twice in the Constitution, once in the Fifth Amendment—"No person shall . . . be deprived of life, liberty or property without due process of law"—and in the Fourteenth Amendment—"No state shall deprive any person of life, liberty or property without due process of law." But due process, like the rule of law, has a broad meaning. Generally it stands for the rights of the accused, most of which stem from the *Bill of Rights*.

Bill of Rights provisions dealing with criminal procedure

Amendment IV.   The right of the people to be secure in their persons, houses, papers, and effects, against unreasonable searches and seizures, shall not be violated, and no warrants shall be issued, but upon probable cause, supported by oath or affirmation, and particularly describing the place to be searched, and the persons or things to be seized.

Amendment V.   No person shall be held to answer for a capital, or otherwise infamous crime, unless on a presentment or indictment of a Grand Jury, except in cases arising in the land or naval forces, or in the Militia, when in actual service in time of War or public danger; nor shall any person be subject for the same offence to be twice put in jeopardy of life or limb, nor shall be compelled in any criminal case to be a witness against himself, nor be deprived of life, liberty, or property, without due process of law; nor shall private property be taken for public use, without just compensation.

Amendment VI. In all criminal prosecutions, the accused shall enjoy the right to a speedy and public trial, by an impartial jury of the state and district wherein the crime shall have been committed, which district shall have been previously ascertained by law, and to be informed of the nature and cause of the accusation; to be confronted with the witnesses against him; to have the compulsory process for obtaining witnesses in his favor, and to have the Assistance of Counsel for his defence.

Amendment VIII. Excessive bail shall not be required nor excessive fines imposed, nor cruel and unusual punishment inflicted.

Bill of Rights

Bill of Rights. The major obstacle to the ratification of the U.S. Constitution was the absence of specific protections for individual rights. Several of the most prominent leaders of the American Revolution opposed the adoption of the Constitution, fearing that the proposed national government posed as great a threat to the rights of the average American as had the king of England. Therefore shortly after the adoption of the Constitution, ten amendments, collectively known as the Bill of Rights, were adopted. Many of these protections—particularly the Fourth, Fifth, Sixth, and Eighth amendments—deal specifically with criminal procedure. Some have aptly referred to the Bill of Rights as a constitutional code of criminal procedure.

Duh! But True point

Presumption of innocence

presumption of innocence

One of the most fundamental protections recognized in the American criminal justice process is the right to be presumed innocent (termed *presumption of innocence*). The state has the burden of proving defendants guilty of alleged crimes; defendants are not required to prove themselves innocent. This difference is a fundamental one. A moment's reflection will indicate the difficulty in proving that something did not happen or that a person did not do the alleged criminal act. Therefore a defendant is cloaked with the legal shield of innocence through the criminal justice process.

beyond a reasonable doubt

In meeting the obligation to prove the defendant guilty, the prosecution is required to prove the defendant guilty *beyond a reasonable doubt*, a legal yardstick measuring the sufficiency of the evidence. This burden of proof does not require that the state establish absolute certainty by eliminating all doubt whatsoever. Rather, beyond a reasonable doubt means just that: eliminating a reasonable doubt. The criterion of proof beyond a reasonable doubt is more stringent than the burden of proof in a civil case (involving two or more private parties) in which the yardstick is the preponderance of the evidence, meaning a slight majority of the evidence for one side or the other.

The adversary system

A system of criminal justice is more than rules on paper (definitions of crime and rights granted to the accused, for example); it is also a plan for distributing power among judges, jurors, prosecutors, legislators, and so on. Thus, under Anglo-

adversary system

American law, only the legislature has the power to define crimes. In turn, the courts are entrusted with applying and interpreting that law in specific cases. The premise of the Anglo-American legal system is that the best way for courts to apply the law is through *the adversary system*, a battle between two differing parties. This system is viewed as the best way to determine guilt or innocence and at the same time protect the rights of the accused. Under the adversary system the burden is on the prosecutor to prove the defendant guilty beyond a reasonable doubt. The defense attorney is charged with arguing for the client's innocence and asserting legal protections. The judge serves as a neutral arbitrator who stands above the fight as a disinterested party to ensure that each side battles within the established rules. Finally, the decision is entrusted to the jury (although in some instances a judge alone may decide).

The adversary system builds three different types of safeguards into the criminal court process. First, it provides a forum for testing evidence. The reasoning is that the two parties will approach "the facts from entirely different perspectives and objectives . . . [they] will uncover more of the truth than would investigators, however industrious and objective, seeking to compose a unified picture of what had occurred" (American Bar Association:3). Because American law views informal methods of fact finding as subject to errors, it therefore insists on a formal adversarial fact-finding process. Through cross-examination, each side has the opportunity to examine witnesses' truthfulness, to probe for possible biases, and to test what witnesses actually know, not what they think they know. The right to cross-examination is protected by the Sixth Amendment: "In all criminal prosecutions, the accused shall enjoy the right . . . to be confronted with witnesses against him."

The adversary system imposes a second type of safeguard by putting power in several different hands. Each actor is granted only limited powers and has limited powers to counteract the others. If the judge is biased or unfair, the jury has the ability to disregard the judge and reach a fair verdict. The opposite is also true. If the judge believes the jury has acted improperly, then the judge has the power to set aside the jury verdict and order a new trial. This diffusion of powers in the adversary system incorporates a series of checks and balances aimed at curbing political misuse of the criminal courts.

In diffusing power, the adversary system provides a third safeguard: it charges a specific actor—the defense attorney—with asserting the rights of the accused. Defense attorneys search out potential violations of the rights of the accused. They function as a perpetual challenger to the criminal court process and, in theory at least, are ready at every juncture to challenge the government by insisting that the proper procedures be followed.

The dispositional process

An important first step in understanding how American courts dispense justice is to learn the basic legal concepts underlying the process. The common law heritage, the differing purposes of civil and criminal law, the structure of the courts, the reasons why protecting the rights of the accused is so valued, and the presumption of innocence within the adversary system are all basic to an understanding of the legal model of the criminal court process. But mastering these legal concepts is just the first step. They provide only an imperfect road map of the day-to-day realities of the courthouse.

The formal adversarial model is present only in a limited degree. Few cases ever go to trial. Most defendants either plead guilty or have their cases dismissed before trial. Instead of conflict projected by the adversary model, judges, prosecutors, and defense attorneys cooperate on a number of matters. Whereas the main goal of the adversary model is to discover truth and decide guilt, a great deal of the court's attention is directed toward determining the appropriate penalty.

In short, there is a major gap between legal theory (law on the books) and how that law is applied on a daily basis (law in action). Although many persons find such a gap shocking, actually it is not; after all, no human institution ever lives up to the high ideals held out for it. If you spend five or ten minutes observing a stop sign on a well-traveled street, you will find that not all cars come to a complete stop, and some do not seem to slow down much at all. Yet at the same time, the stop sign (the law on the books in this example) clearly does affect the behavior of drivers (law in action). Realizing that law on the books is not the same as the law in action is only the second step in understanding how the courts dispense justice. The crucial task is trying to understand and explain why the law as practiced differs from the seeming intent of the formal rules. Toward this end a wide variety of studies of the criminal courts at the trial level have highlighted several important features about how the criminal courts operate. Assembly line justice, discretion, and the courtroom work group are concepts that describe how these institutions operate. These concepts also begin to suggest reasons for the deviations from the idealized version of the law.

Assembly line justice

A basic principle of the American legal system is that the courts will consider each case and each defendant individually. This expectation of individual attention is reinforced by fictionalized television prosecutors, judges, defense attorneys, and police officers who always have ample time to devote to a single case. To many, however, *assembly line justice* is a more realistic description of how the criminal courts operate. Particularly in the misdemeanor and traffic courts of large cities, dispositions are usually made with lightning speed. A person's day in court to answer a charge of speeding may consist of less than a minute before the judge.

assembly line justice

Assembly line justice is partially a reflection of the large number of cases that reach the court. Every year approximately one million felony cases and perhaps as many as ten million misdemeanor cases are begun. While accurate and complete court statistics do not exist in the United States, these estimates provide some idea of the volume of cases requiring processing each year. Add to this the large number of ordinance violations (city criminal laws) and even larger numbers of traffic cases, and it becomes obvious that the criminal caseload of the courts is indeed staggering. Because of the large volume of cases, overworked officials often become more interested in moving the steady stream of cases than in individually weighing each case on the scales of justice. Particularly in the large cities, there are tremendous pressures to move cases lest the backlog become worse and delays increase. Thus, unlike the trial model described by the law books, an administrative process geared to disposing of a large volume of cases dominates the law in action.

Discretion

discretion Underlying the administrative nature of justice is *discretion*. Although the textbook image of justice portrays a mechanical process of merely applying rules of law to given cases, a closer examination shows that each of the actors possesses ample discretion: the prosecutor in charging and plea bargaining, the defense attorney in negotiating over a sentence, and the judge in imposing a sentence.

One reason actors in the criminal court community exercise discretion is that the law provides only minimal guidance for making decisions. The clearest example is sentencing. The criminal law specifies a potential range of penalties for each criminal offense: probation, prison, or a fine. The law, however, provides only the broadest standards for deciding where in the range of penalties a defendant should be placed. Such discretionary decisions are required at virtually every step of the criminal court process. Judges, prosecutors, and defense attorneys also exercise discretion in an attempt to make the system fair. They seek individualized justice.

The courtroom work group

courtroom work group An important part of discretion in the criminal court process is the key role of the *courtroom work group*. Although we usually think of the criminal courts in terms of a conflict at trial, a more realistic appraisal is one of limited cooperation among the major participants. While defendants come and go, the judges, prosecutors, and defense attorneys work together daily. They are tied together by more than a shared workplace, the courtroom; each is dependent on the others. For example, defense attorneys seldom have resources for investigating a case. They are dependent on the prosecutor for access to police reports and the like. Because prosecutors have more cases to try than time to try them, they are dependent on guilty pleas from the defense to secure convictions. Judges are dependent on prosecutor and defense negotiating pleas to prevent a backlog of cases from developing. Such cooperation is a two-way street. Those who work within the system can expect to receive some benefits. Defense attorneys who do not needlessly make additional work for the others are sometimes able to secure a lighter than normal sentence for their clients. On the other hand, those who challenge the system can expect sanctions. Defendants represented by uncooperative defense counsel sometimes receive longer prison terms than they would otherwise.

This courtroom work group is best described as a social organization. No individual actor works in social isolation; each can accomplish tasks only by interacting with the others. The network of cooperation underlying the courtroom community produces a commonly understood set of practices. Courts develop rules of thumb about how certain types of cases will be handled and the penalties to be applied.

The criminal court process

The criminal court process is complicated. From the initial arrest to the final sentencing, a defendant's case passes through numerous stages. American law maintains that numerous—and sometimes redundant—steps in the criminal process are the best way to ensure that individual rights are protected. Analytically, the criminal court trial process can be broken down into twelve stages: arrest, the decision to prosecute, initial appearance, the setting of bail, holding a preliminary hearing, selecting a defense attorney, convening of the grand jury, holding the arraignment, deciding pretrial motions, engaging in plea negotiations, conducting a trial, and imposing sentence.

These twelve steps provide only a basic overview, however. Criminal procedure varies from state to state. The U.S. Supreme Court has ruled that certain steps are so vital—jury trial, for example—that they are required in all states, and for the federal government as well. Other procedures, however—most notably the grand jury—have been held by the Court to be less essential to the concept of "ordered liberty," and therefore states are not required to have them. To complicate matters even further, individual courts often adopt local rules that spell out additional details of criminal procedure. Procedural requirements also vary according to the severity of the offense.

These twelve stages do not have to occur in a set order. For instance, a defendant may have an attorney even before arrest or may delay hiring one until almost the day of trial. Just as important, these twelve separate steps are interrelated. The decision to charge, the outcome of the preliminary hearing, and the nature of the plea bargain all anticipate a jury verdict.

In outline form the steps of criminal procedure seem to suggest a streamlined process with defendants entering at the arrest stage and steadily moving through the various stages until conviction and eventually sentencing. This is not the case. The criminal process is filled with numerous detours. At each stage officials must decide either to advance the defendant's case to the next step, reroute it, or terminate it. Thus the twelve steps are actually the forums for observing and analyzing the effects of discretion, assembly line justice, and the courtroom work group. Figure 2-1 provides a schematic representation of this funneling effect, showing that the criminal process acts as a series of screens. Much like a set of sieves that sorts rocks into various sizes, the steps of the criminal process sort defendants into various categories. The result is that many cases that enter the criminal court process are eliminated during early stages.

Arrest. The criminal process typically begins with a police decision to arrest a suspect. In a small percentage of cases the police make arrests based on an *arrest warrant*, a court document authorizing the police to take a person into custody. Most arrests, however, are made in the field without a warrant. Under common law, police officers have the power to take a person into custody if they believe the person committed a felony (a major crime). But if the crime is a misdemeanor (an offense less serious than a felony and usually punishable by a fine or less than a

arrest
warrant

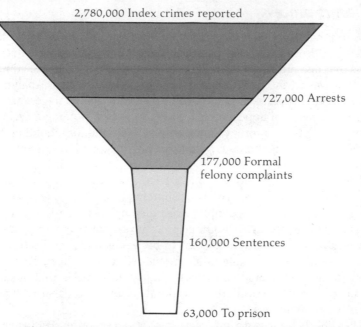

2,780,000 Index crimes reported

727,000 Arrests

177,000 Formal
felony complaints

160,000 Sentences

63,000 To prison

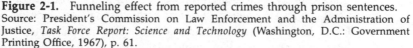

Figure 2-1.   Funneling effect from reported crimes through prison sentences.
Source: President's Commission on Law Enforcement and the Administration of
Justice, *Task Force Report: Science and Technology* (Washington, D.C.: Government
Printing Office, 1967), p. 61.

year in jail), most states allow the police to arrest only if they personally witness
the crime.

The police are able to arrest in only a small proportion of crimes. Nationwide,
they make arrests in only 19 percent of serious crimes. As a result, only 10 to 20
percent of the nation's major crimes potentially reach the court.

Decision to Prosecute.   After a suspect has been arrested and booked, the police must seek legal authority to continue detaining the person. If the charge is a
minor one, the police may apply to a lower court judge for a complaint. If the case
is a serious one, however, the police are usually required to request prosecution
from the district attorney. The prosecutor acts as the key link between the police
and the courts. This actor is the most important figure in the criminal courts process, controlling which defendants will be charged with a crime, influencing bail
setting, entering into plea bargains, and at times influencing the sentence as well.
Prosecutors possess wide discretion in deciding whether criminal charges should
be filed. During this initial evaluation a major consideration is the strength of the
evidence. On the other hand, factors other than the strength of the evidence may
also play a role.

In almost every part of the country, the charging decision results in a significant
number of arrested persons being released without the filing of criminal charges.
Estimates place the number of cases never resulting in prosecution as high as 33 to
50 percent of those referred by the police to the prosecutor (Kamisar, LaFave, and

Israel:7). Even when charges are accepted, the prosecutor may file a charge less serious than the police initially requested (for example, filing a misdemeanor rather than a felony).

Initial Appearance. An arrested person must be brought before a judge without unnecessary delay. In the United States the police are not allowed to detain a suspect for an indefinite period of time.

The initial appearance is the defendant's first encounter with the courts. At this time he or she is given a formal notice of the charges and the judge advises the defendant of the right to remain silent, the right to counsel, the right to bail, and the right to a preliminary hearing if applicable. In practice, judges make little effort to determine whether the defendant understands what is being explained. For felony defendants the initial appearance is a formality, because a defendant cannot enter a plea (guilty or innocent). For misdemeanor defendants, however, this step may be the only courtroom encounter. Roughly three out of four misdemeanor defendants plead guilty at the initial appearance and are sentenced immediately.

Bail. Bond is usually set at the initial appearance. Because a defendant is considered innocent until proven guilty, American law allows all defendants (except those charged with a capital offense, a crime for which the death penalty is possible) to remain at liberty before trial. Bail is a guarantee that the defendant will later appear for trial. Judges have wide latitude in setting the amount of bail.

bail

The most common form of *bail* is a cash bond. For felony defendants, bonds range from $1,000 to over $100,000. Because most defendants do not have that much cash on hand, they hire a bail bondsman who, in return for a 10 to 15 percent cash fee, will secure the defendant's pretrial release. An alternative to the cash bail system is release on recognizance. Defendants with strong ties to the community are viewed as unlikely to flee so they are released on their promise to return to court; no monetary bond is required. Defendants who cannot meet the bail bondsman's fees or qualify for release on recognizance must await trial in jail. In 1978 (the most recent date for which figures are available), 67,000 adults were being held in jail awaiting trial (U.S. Department of Justice, p. 38).

Preliminary Hearing. The preliminary hearing (termed a preliminary examination in some states) is designed to protect defendants against unwarranted prosecutions. It is the first time that a non-law-enforcement official (a judge) evaluates

---

IN THE NEWS:

It is 3 P.M. now, and Alvin, who was arrested for burglary at 11:30 the previous night, has not slept for 31 hours. He hunches forward and hides his face in his hands to shut out the sight of the iron bars, the guard and the door to the courtroom.

"I don't know," he mutters when someone asks him what the next step in his case will be. "I don't know," he mutters again when asked the name of his lawyer. Alvin has just been arraigned in Manhattan Criminal Court, and like many other defendants who filter each week through the same procedure, he understands almost nothing of what has happened to him.

New York Times, May 11, 1970, p. 29 © 1970 by The New York Times Company. Reprinted by permission.

probable
cause

the strength of the evidence against the accused. At a preliminary hearing the prosecutor must show that there is *probable cause* to believe that the defendant committed the felony. Probable cause can be proved by showing that a crime has been committed and that it is likely that the defendant committed it. Evidence requirements, however, are less strict than during a trial. If the judicial officer determines that probable cause is present, the defendant is bound over to the grand jury. If not, the defendant is released and the charges dismissed.

The preliminary hearing is limited primarily to felony cases. Not all states require a preliminary hearing, and some limit its use to very serious crimes like murder for which the death penalty may be imposed. Where preliminary hearings are held, however, few cases are dismissed for lack of probable cause.

Defense Attorneys.   The Sixth Amendment specifies: "In all criminal prosecutions, the accused shall enjoy the right . . . to have the Assistance of Counsel for his defence." The U.S. Supreme Court has ruled that the right to counsel includes the obligation of the state to provide an attorney for those too poor to hire one of their own. The Court reasoned that the assistance of counsel constituted a vital protection because few nonlawyers are well versed enough in the law to conduct an adequate defense. The right to counsel applies not only to the trial itself but also to all other critical stages in the proceedings.

Most defendants—approximately 60 percent (and up to 80 percent in some large cities)—cannot afford to hire a lawyer. These indigent defendants are represented in one of two ways: assigned counsel or public defender. Under an assigned counsel system, a judge appoints a member of the local bar, sometimes without pay, to represent the defendant. But, increasingly, indigent defendants are represented by public defenders (paid government attorneys responsible for representing all indigent defendants). In small communities the public defender may be a part-time lawyer, but in larger communities, the staff consists of a dozen or more attorneys. Public defenders handle as many as 200 felony defendants per year, a caseload higher than the average prosecutor's (Kamisar, LaFave, and Israel:3).

Grand Jury.   Like the preliminary hearing, the grand jury is designed as a check on unwarranted prosecutions. The U.S. Constitution requires a grand jury in federal felonies, but the U.S. Supreme Court has held that a state is not required to have a grand jury. Only about half of the states use the grand jury. Grand juries usually consist of twenty-three members. If the majority of the grand jury believe that probable cause exists, a *true bill* is voted charging the defendant with a crime. A *no bill* (or no true bill) indicates that the grand jury found insufficient evidence to indict.

true
bill

In practice the grand jury does not function as the independent check that legal theory holds for it. By and large grand juries are dominated by the prosecutor. The prosecutor is the legal advisor to the grand jury and also determines which cases will be considered and which witnesses will be summoned. Thus, the grand jury indicts whom the prosecutors want indicted. Even no true bills are often the product of the prosecutor's assessment that the evidence against a particular defendant is weak. In rare cases, however, grand juries exhibit independence, and when they do so they wield a large amount of power.

Arraignment on the Indictment.   At the arraignment on the indictment (which differs from the initial appearance, although the two terms are often used interchangeably), the defendant is given a copy of the indictment, advised of his or her rights (usually more extensively than at the initial appearance), and called upon to enter a plea. This is the first time a felony defendant is called upon to enter a plea. The defendant can plead guilty (which is rare at this stage), not guilty (the usual plea), or *nolo contendere*, which means the defendant will not contest the charge but does not admit it.

Pretrial Motions.   *Motions* are requests for the judge to make a legal ruling. During trial, lawyers will make various types of motions relating to the admissibility of evidence and the like. Similarly, before the trial certain kinds of legal questions require a determination. The process of making formal written motions along with written reasons are termed *pleadings*. A prosecutor may file a motion to require the defendant to produce documents or to give a handwriting sample, for example. Most motions, however, are filed by the defense. The most common ones are motions to suppress evidence (arguing that the police searched illegally) and motions to suppress a confession (contending that the confession was coerced, for example). Because many of these motions involve only questions of law, they can be decided at a hearing where the attorneys argue why the motion should—or should not—be granted.

Plea Bargaining.   Most findings of guilt result not from a trial verdict but from a voluntary plea by the defendant. Roughly 80 to 90 percent of all guilty findings in felony cases (and an even higher percentage in misdemeanor and minor offenses) result from a plea. Even when a case goes to trial, it is likely there were plea discussions.

Plea bargaining is pervasive but hardly uniform; indeed the numerous variations almost defy classification. It is important to bear in mind that plea bargaining is a general term that represents a variety of different practices and court traditions. Participation in plea bargaining varies. Some judges are active participants; others may refuse to take part. The nature of the final plea also varies. In some jurisdictions it is common for the defendant to plead to a less serious charge than the one initially charged (for example, the defendant might plead to simple robbery rather than armed robbery, the original charge). Or the defendant might plead to only some of the counts, and in return the government will dismiss other charges. In still another type, the defendant agrees to admit guilt in return for a specified sentence. And, finally, some pleas are entered without any promises whatsoever—the defendant pleads to all the charges as specified in the indictment or information.

Jury Trials. Along with the right to be presumed innocent until proven guilty, the right to a trial by jury is one of the most fundamental rights granted those accused of violating the criminal law.

A defendant can be tried either by a judge sitting alone (called a bench trial) or by a jury. A jury trial begins with the selection of twelve people (fewer in some cases). The prosecutor and the defense make opening statements, indicating what they think the evidence in the case will show. The prosecutor has the burden of proving the defendant guilty and is the first to call witnesses. Rules guide the type of evidence that may be introduced and how it may be interpreted. Witnesses are subject to cross-examination. When all evidence has been introduced, each side makes a closing argument to the jury, and the judge then instructs the jury about the law. The jurors retire to deliberate in secret. In most states jury verdicts must be unanimous, although a couple of states accept verdicts of ten out of twelve. While the details of the jury procedure vary from state to state, one factor is constant— the defendant's chances for an acquittal are not good.

Sentencing. Most of the twelve stages of the criminal process are concerned almost entirely with determining legal innocence or guilt. As important as the question of the defendant's guilt or innocence is, most of the time of the members of the courtroom work group is spent on deciding what sentence to impose on the guilty. Indeed, defendants are more concerned about the possible prison time they will have to serve than the question of guilt. Judges have wide discretion in imposing sentences. State or federal law specifies a potential penalty. Some states simply employ definite sentences, which means that the judge must sentence the defendant to a fixed number of years. Other states use indeterminate sentences, which allows the judge to specify a sentencing range (say one to ten years.) Alternatively, the judge may place the defendant on probation (the sentence is served in the community under supervision) for a fixed period or suspend the sentence (the jail or prison sentence is not served). In some states probation is specifically disallowed for certain categories of convictions, often armed robbery and first-degree murder. The law also may allow the judge to impose a fine, but this is rarely used in felony cases. The death penalty is allowed in several states. By and large the main decision is whether to place the defendant on probation or to impose a sentence for a certain period of time.

Clearly, the law offers a wide range of sentencing opinions. Furthermore, there is disagreement about the purpose of imposing sentence. At least four competing views on sentencing can be found in American society. Some say the sentence should be punishment, pure and simple. Others argue that sentences should be set to deter other wrongdoers. To others the purpose of sentencing should be to rehabilitate the defendant. Finally, some argue that defendants should be sentenced to protect society. Judges' sentencing decisions reflect these varying sentencing perspectives. Their rationales result in marked sentencing disparities.

Estimates indicate that a quarter of a million people are inmates in state and federal prisons. Although there is no accurate count on how many convicted defendants are on probation, the number is much higher. Indeed, the majority of

sentencing

defendants are placed on probation rather than incarcerated, but the ratio of probation to prison decisions varies from judge to judge and court to court.

Conclusion

The prosecution, conviction, and sentencing of a defendant is a complex, multifac-
eted, and somewhat fragmented process. It is through the criminal law that certain
acts are defined as so threatening to the entire society that special sanctions are
provided. Although the control and prevention of crime is a major goal of the law,
this goal must be accomplished within the framework of the law. In particular, the
law recognizes certain rights for all defendants. The courts are the forum for deciding guilt or innocence and imposing sentence. But in turn the criminal courts are
not a single entity. Under the adversary system, responsibilities are divided among
judge, prosecutor, and defense attorney.

Because of its high commitment to fair treatment under the rule of law, the
Anglo-American legal system specifies a number of steps in the criminal process.
These steps are intentionally designed to be inefficient because inefficiency
through multiple checkpoints is viewed as the best way to ensure that no errors are
made. These multiple checkpoints function as screens, removing some defendants
from the process, diverting others, and forwarding still more to the next stage. To
speak of steps in the criminal process may be misleading because American justice
involves numerous variations in both the structure of these steps, the order in
which they occur, and how these steps operate in practice.

The structure of the courts, the nature of the law, and the steps in the criminal
process provide only the beginning point, however, in understanding how the
criminal courts dispense justice. These elements constitute the law on the books—
the legal and structural components. But as we have argued, one must also understand the law in action. Although the formal model portrays an image of the
individual and separate treatment of all defendants, assembly line justice comes
closer to describing the actual operations of the criminal courts. Similarly, a struc-
tural-legalistic discussion of the criminal courts stresses the conflict at trial, whereas studies have repeatedly shown limited cooperation because of pressures from
the courtroom work group. Finally, whereas the civics book image projects a legal
system that runs almost by itself, in practice discretion is involved in each of the
major steps.

For discussion

1. What are the most important differences between civil law and criminal law?
   What similarities do they share?
2. What are the major differences between the legal outlines of the criminal process (law on the books) and how the process actually operates (law in action)?
3. What are the most important protections given those accused of a crime? In a
   democracy could any of these protections be eliminated without sacrificing individual liberties?

4. How do decisions made during early stages of the criminal court process affect decisions made later? How might anticipation of the last steps of the criminal process—jury trial and sentencing—affect earlier stages?

5. What are some of the beneficial uses of discretion? What are some of the misuses of discretion? What are some ways that discretion could be used to inhibit the misuse of discretion? Would beneficial uses of discretion suffer?

References

American Bar Association. *Standards Relating to the Prosecution Function and the Defense Function*. Chicago: American Bar Association, 1970.

Kamisar, Yale, Wayne LaFave, and Jerold Israel. *Basic Criminal Procedure*. St. Paul, Minn.: West Publishing, 1974.

National Center for State Courts, National Court Statistics Project. *State Court Caseload Statistics: Annual Reports 1977 and 1978*. Washington, D.C.: U.S. Government Printing Office, 1980.

President's Commission on Law Enforcement and the Administration of Justice. *Task Force Report: The Courts*. Washington, D.C.: Government Printing Office, 1967.

Skolnick, Jerome H. *Justice Without Trial—Law Enforcement in a Democratic Society*. New York: John Wiley, 1966.

U.S. Department of Justice. Bureau of Justice Statistics. *Profile of Jail Inmates*. Washington, D.C.: Government Printing Office, 1980.

Wheeler, Russell, and Howard Whitcomb, "The Literature of Court Administration: A Bibliographical Essay." *Arizona State Law Journal* (1974): 689.

For further reading

Glick, Henry. *Courts, Politics and Justice*. New York: McGraw-Hill, 1983.

Israel, Jerold, and Wayne LaFave. *Criminal Procedure: Constitutional Limitations*. St. Paul, Minn.: West Publishing, 1975.

Jacob, Herbert. *Justice in America: Courts, Lawyers and the Judicial Process*, 3rd ed. Boston: Little, Brown, 1978.

———. *Crime and Justice in Urban America*. Englewood Cliffs, N.J.: Prentice-Hall, 1980.

Karlen, Delmar. *Anglo-American Criminal Justice*. New York: Oxford University Press, 1967.

McLauchlan, William. *American Legal Process*. New York: John Wiley, 1977.

CHAPTER 3

Finding the Courthouse: The Confusing Structure of American Courts

American courts represent a bewildering variety of names, structures, functions, and types. Mayor's court, city court, justice of the peace, county court, superior court, district court, chancery court, and common pleas are just a few of the over two dozen names of courts found in America. If the varying names of the courts were the only problem, there would be no great difficulty—we could learn the names much as we learn classifications in biology. The drawback is that the names are seldom cues to either what the courts do or how they function. For example, if your case is in the supreme court, what level of court would you be in? If you thought the highest appellate court, you are probably right, except if you are in the state of New York. In New York the supreme court is the major trial court, and the highest appellate court is called the court of appeals. Not only do courts with similar names sometimes have different functions, the opposite is also true. Courts with different names may have roughly identical functions. Moreover, every state court system is somewhat different and even within a state, the names, functions, and jurisdictions may vary and even overlap.

The purpose of this chapter is to provide some clarity in the sea of confusion over the structure and functions of the American courts. We will begin with a discussion of the development of American courts and then move on to a consideration of some basic concepts underlying the structure and function of American courts. Next, using these basic concepts, we will examine the federal judicial system and then state court systems. Finally, we will examine the consequences of the court organization for the operations of the criminal justice system.

How courts grew

Just as the American law borrowed heavily from English common law, the organization of American courts reflects their English heritage. These ancient common law traditions are important factors shaping current court systems. For example, Ohio and Pennsylvania call their major trial courts Courts of Common Pleas, a title taken directly from England. However, while certain traditions persist, court structures have also changed over time. Increases in population, the concentration of people in cities, and the shift from an agricultural to an industrial economy all necessitated changes in court organization. Such alterations, though, were far from automatic since basic political issues were often at stake. The clash of opposing economic interests, the debate over state versus national power, and outright partisan political considerations are some political conflicts that account for the current structure of American courts.

Colonial courts

During the colonial period, political power was concentrated in the hands of the governor, an appointee of the English king. Governors performed executive, legislative, and judicial functions. The courts in the early colonial period were rather simple institutions. The structure of these early American courts followed the form, but not the substance, of courts in England. The complex, numerous, and highly specialized courts of the mother country were ill-suited to the needs of a small group of colonists trying to survive on the edge of the wilds, so the colonists greatly simplified the English procedures. The county courts stood at the heart of the American colonial government. Besides adjudicating cases they also performed important administrative functions (Friedman:32). Appeals from all courts were taken to the governor and the colonial council.

As population increased and towns and villages became larger, new courts were created so that people would not have to travel long distances to have their cases heard. Through the years each colony modified its own court system according to variations in local demands, local customs, differing religious practices, and the nature of commercial trade. These early variations in legal rulings and court structures have persisted and contribute to the great variety of U.S. court systems today (Glick and Vines:19).

Early American courts

After the American Revolution, a major dispute developed over whether there should be a federal court system separate from the state systems. When the U.S.

Anti-
Federalists

Constitution was being drafted, the *Anti-Federalists*, who feared a strong national government and thought the new national government threatened both individual liberties and states' rights, wanted only a limited federal system. The Federalists, on the other hand, fearing the parochial prejudices of states, believed that lawsuits tried exclusively in state courts would put out-of-state litigants—those involved in the suit—at a distinct disadvantage. Although the Federalists were successful in creating federal district courts (first in the Judiciary Act of 1789 and later in the Reorganization Act of 1801), the system adopted was a compromise that allayed some of the fears of the Anti-Federalists. These courts, empowered to enforce national law, were structured along state lines; they did not cut across state boundaries, and the selection process adopted ensured that judges would be residents of that state. Overall, the national courts were organized along local lines with each district court responsible for its own work under minimal supervision (Richardson and Vines:20–21).

Similar political disputes affected the state courts. After the Revolution the powers of the government were drastically reduced and taken over by the legislative bodies. But the structure of the state judiciaries remained largely unchanged. The former colonists, who viewed judicial action as coercive and arbitrary and distrusted lawyers and the common law, were not anxious to see the development of a large independent judiciary. Judicial decisions were scrutinized by state legislatures, which removed some judges from office or abolished a specific court in response to unpopular court decisions.

The distrust of the judiciary increased as courts declared legislative actions unconstitutional. Such actions were a major source of political conflict between legislatures and courts. The conflict often stemmed from opposing interest. Legislators were more responsive to policies that favored debtors (usually small farmers). Courts, on the other hand, reflected the views of creditors (merchants). In several instances state courts declared legislative acts favoring free money as unconstitutional. Out of this conflict over legislative and judicial power, though, the courts gradually emerged as an independent political institution.

Courts in a modernizing society

After the Civil War the structure of American courts changed in many important ways. Rapid industrialization produced fundamental changes in all aspects of American life, the law included. Increases in population, the growth of cities, and the rise of industrialization greatly expanded the volume of litigation. Moreover, the types of disputes coming to the courts changed as well. Not only did the growth of industry and commerce result in disputes over this new wealth, but the concentration of people in the cities (many of whom were immigrants), coupled with the pressures of industrial employment, meant the courts were faced with a new set of problems. The American courts, still reflecting the rural agrarian society of the early nineteenth century, were inadequate in the face of rising demands for services (Jacob:161–163).

States and localities responded to the increased volume of litigation in a number of ways. City courts were created to deal with new types of cases in the urban areas; specialized courts were formed to handle one specific class of case (small claims courts, juvenile courts, and family relations courts are examples); and more courts were added, often by specifying the court's jurisdiction in terms of a geographic boundary within the city. The result was sporadic and unplanned growth. Each court was a separate entity; each had a judge and a staff. Such an organizational structure meant there was no way to shift cases from an overloaded court to one with little to do. In addition, each court produced political patronage jobs for the city political machines.

Chicago illustrates the confusion, complexity, and administrative problems that resulted from this sporadic and unplanned growth of American courts. In 1931 Chicago had 556 independent courts; the large majority were justice of the peace courts, which handled only minor offenses (Glick and Vines:505).

Other state and local courts included municipal, circuit, superior, county, probate, juvenile, and criminal courts. Sometimes other courts, such as the rackets court, were added to deal with special problems. The jurisdiction of these courts was not exclusive; that is, a case could be brought before a variety of courts depending on the legal and political advantages that each one offered. Factors such as court costs, the reputation of the judge, court delay, and the complexity of the court procedures were considered in determining which court to use. For example, a prosecuting attorney in a criminal case could chose a court likely to produce either a harsh or lenient judgment. Other attorneys sought to have their cases entered in courts with procedures so complex that they would entangle and confuse the opposition in legal technicalities. Partisan political considerations were also involved. The numerous justices of the peace competed for fees and therefore were often eager to trade favorable decisions for court business (Glick and Vines:25).

A complex court structure

The sporadic and unplanned expansion of the American court system has resulted in an often-confusing structure. In many states there are several courts in one county: several lower courts and one or perhaps two major trial courts. To add further confusion, some major trial courts have overlapping jurisdiction with the lower courts. Moreover, there may be major variations in court jurisdiction from one county to the next within one state. An example is Maryland: "There are no less than 16 different types of courts, with little uniformity from one community to another. A lawyer venturing into another is likely to feel almost as bewildered as if he had gone into another state with an entirely different system of courts" (Institute of Judicial Administration:11–12).

> In short, despite experiments in diversity, colonial conditions shaped court organization in all, or almost all, colonies along similar lines in the 17th century. Court structures moved from the simple to the more complex, from the undifferentiated to the hierarchical. English models, English terms, and English customs were a more or less powerful influence everywhere. Executive, legislative, and judicial power were not clearly fenced off from each other. But as time went on, differentiation became more marked. Legislatures still heard appeals, but they conducted few or no trials.
>
> The colonies had another trait in common. For all their geographic and political isolation, they owed some sort of allegiance to the crown. Their charters spoke

explicitly of the duty to conform their laws to English laws. The distant king held at least some nominal authority, particularly in chartered colonies. Many colonies actively resisted English influence.

Lawrence Friedman, *A History of American Law* (New York: Simon and Schuster, 1973), p. 40.

Basic principles of American courts

Although American courts appear to resemble a bramblebush of names, functions, and types, there are some basic principles underlying their organization. It is helpful to understand these basic principles of jurisdiction, the dual court system, and the differences between trial and appellate courts before embarking on a detailed discussion of any given court structure.

Jurisdiction

jurisdiction

Court structure is largely determined by the legal limitations on the types of cases a court may hear and decide. The persons over whom a court has power and the subject matter over which a court can make a legally binding decision are referred to as *jurisdiction* (Oran:181). Constitutions, statutes, and court decisions define a court's jurisdiction. The authorization for the federal court system is found in Article III of the Constitution: "The judicial power of the United States shall be vested in one supreme court, and in such inferior courts as the congress may from time to time ordain and establish." This provision was deliberately left vague because the Founding Fathers were deeply divided over whether there should be a separate federal court system. Thus, it was left to Congress to provide the working details of the federal court structure.

Similarly, state and municipal courts derive their power and authority from the respective state constitutions and state statutes. Typically, however, state constitutions are more detailed than the U.S. Constitution. In many states, for example, the names and geographical territory of the courts are individually specified in the constitution. As a result, to create a new court to handle a rising caseload or to restructure the entire state court system requires a statewide constitutional amendment. As in the federal system, though, the legislative bodies flesh out the organizational skeleton provided in the state constitution by specifying the number of judgeships and the like. A court's jurisdiction can be classified according to three subcomponents: geographical jurisdiction, subject matter jurisdiction, and hierarchical jurisdiction.

Geographical Jurisdiction.   Courts are authorized to hear and decide disputes arising within specified political boundaries (a city, a county, a group of counties). For example, a California court has no jurisdiction to try a person accused of committing a crime in Oregon. These geographical limitations on judicial powers present a number of problems for courts and law enforcement agencies. Sometimes it is difficult for a court to obtain personal jurisdiction over a defendant. If a defendant is being held in another part of the state, the court requests the cooperation of the other jurisdiction. But if that jurisdiction does not wish to relinquish control, either because the defendant has strong political ties or it wishes to try the person first, heated exchanges can develop. Similarly, if a defendant has left the state, either unintentionally or intentionally to avoid prosecution, the state may request extradition. Defendants in foreign countries present even more complex problems since the United States has no extradition treaty with some nations (Argentina is one), and some nations will not extradite a person unless the alleged crime also violates their own law.

Subject Matter Jurisdiction.   Another key element of jurisdiction is subject matter. Trial courts of limited jurisdiction are restricted to hearing only a limited number of cases, typically misdemeanors and civil suits involving small sums of money. Trial courts of general jurisdiction are empowered to hear all other types of cases. In addition, certain types of cases are not allowed to be brought to court. The U.S. Supreme Court has ruled, for example, that courts have no jurisdiction to decide church disputes over doctrinal matters. Similarly, the U.S. Supreme Court will hear no cases involving political questions, although some ambiguity exists over what constitutes a political question.

Hierarchical Jurisdiction.   The structure of courts also reflects differences in

original jurisdiction
appellate jurisdiction

functions and responsibilities, referred to as original jurisdiction and appellate jurisdiction. *Original jurisdiction* means that a court has the authority to try a case and decide it. *Appellate jurisdiction* means that a court has the power to take cases on appeal already decided by a trial court. Trial courts are primarily courts of original jurisdiction, but they occasionally have limited appellate jurisdiction (for example, when a trial court hears appeals from lower trial courts like mayor's courts or a justice of the peace court). Appellate courts often have a very limited original jurisdiction. In disputes between states, the U.S. Supreme Court has original jurisdiction, and a number of state supreme courts have original jurisdiction in matters involving disbarment of attorneys.

Dual court system

dual court system

America has a *dual court system:* one national court structure and court structures in each of the fifty states. The end result is fifty-one separate court systems—one for the national government and fifty different ones in the states. The dual court system mirrors the federal system of government. In the federal system of government of the United States, powers are divided between the national government and the state governments, with each legally supreme in its own sphere. The two levels of government, however, share other powers, such as taxation and penalizing violators of their respective laws. Applying the federal principle to the courts, federal courts have exclusive power over violation of federal criminal law, and state courts have the exclusive right to try those accused of breaking state laws. Figure 3-1 shows the ordering of cases in the dual court system. The division of responsibilities is not as clear-cut as it looks because the same judicial powers are shared by the state and federal courts. Civil suits between citizens of different states may be heard by either a state or federal court. The possession of narcotics or the interstate

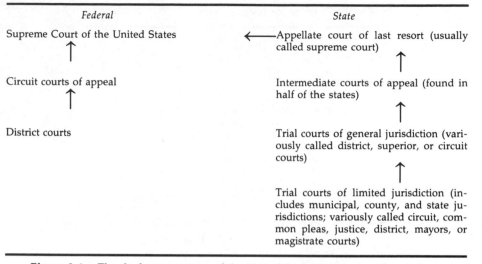

Figure 3-1. The dual court system of the United States and routes of appeal.

transportation of a kidnap victim violates both state and federal laws, which means the accused could be tried twice. In addition, defendants convicted in state court may appeal to the U.S. Supreme Court, a federal court. Defendants convicted in state court may also seek a further review of their case in a U.S. district court by filing a writ of *habeas corpus* (a claim that the person is being held illegally).

Trial and appellate courts

trial courts With only a few exceptions, all cases, civil and criminal, begin with a *trial court*. If the case is a criminal one, the trial court arraigns the defendant, sets bail, conducts a trial (or takes a guilty plea), and imposes sentence if the defendant is found guilty. If the case is a civil one, the trial court operates in much the same fashion, ensuring that each party is properly informed of the complaint, conducting pretrial procedures (such as settling disputes over exchange of information), and conducting a trial or accepting an out-of-court settlement, and awarding damages. Because only trial courts hear disputes over facts, it is only in trial courts that witnesses appear. Trial courts are considered finders of fact, and the decision of the judge (or jury) about factual disputes normally cannot be appealed (in Louisiana and Wisconsin, however, trial court findings of fact in civil cases are appealable). While in theory every trial court decision may be appealed, most cases are settled without a trial; thus there is no appeal.

appellate court **Appeals Courts.** A litigant who believes the trial court decision was wrong has the right to appeal that decision to an *appellate court*. As table 3-1 shows there are far fewer appellate judges than there are trial judges. The primary function of the appellate courts is to ensure that the trial courts correctly interpreted and applied the law. A second function is to devise new rules, reexamine old ones, and interpret unclear language of past court decisions or statutes (Wheeler and Whit-

TABLE 3-1. State court judges

Level of jurisdiction	No. of judges
Highest appellate court	348
Intermediate court of appeals	585
Trial courts	7,127
Trial courts of limited jurisdiction	18,001
Total number of state court judges	26,061

Source: U.S. Department of Justice, Bureau of Justice Statistics, *State Court Organization, 1980* (Washington, D.C.: Government Printing Office).

comb:14). Appellate courts also operate much differently from the trial courts. No witnesses are heard; no trials are conducted. Instead each side makes oral arguments to the court. Unless there is an extremely strong showing that the trial judge abused discretion, the appellate court accepts the trial court's findings of facts.

In deciding issues of law, appellate courts operate as collegial bodies—decisions are made by a group of judges. There may be as few as four or as many as twenty-three (the U.S. Ninth Circuit Court of Appeals). These judges usually provide written reasons justifying their decisions (trial court judges rarely write opinions).

opinion of the court If the case is an easy one, the *opinion of the court* may be very short, perhaps a sentence or two. But if the legal issues are important and/or complex, the court's opinion may run into hundreds of pages. It is through such written opinions that appellate courts shape the law. Some legal issues are so close or involve a number of conflicting legal problems that the judges do not always agree among themselves as to the correct answer. Those who disagree with the majority can write a dissenting opinion to explain their views and why they believe their fellow judges reached the wrong results.

> . . . An upper court can seldom do anything to correct a trial court's mistaken belief about the facts. Where, as happens in most cases, the testimony at the trial was oral, the upper court usually feels obliged to adopt the trial court's determination of the facts. Why? Because in such a case the trial court heard and saw the witnesses as they testified, but the upper court did not. The upper court has only a typewritten or printed record of the testimony. The trial court alone is in a position to interpret the demeanor-clues, this "language without words." An upper court, to use Judge Kennison's phrase, "has to operate in the partial vacuum of the printed record." A "stenographic transcript," wrote Judge Ulman, ". . . fails to reproduce tones of voice and hesitations of speech that often make a sentence mean the reverse of what the mere words signify. The best and most accurate record [of oral testimony] is like a dehydrated peach; it has neither the substance nor the flavor of the peach before it was dried." That is why, when testimony is taken in a trial court, an upper court, on appeal, in most instances accepts the facts as found by the trial court, when those findings can be supported by reasonable inferences from some witnesses' testimony, even if it is flatly contradicted in the testimony of other witnesses.
>
> Jerome Frank, *Courts on Trial: Myth and Reality in American Justice* (New York: Princeton University Press, 1973), p. 23. (Copyright 1949 by Jerome Frank; copyright renewed © 1976 by Princeton University Press.) Reprinted by permission of Princeton University Press.

If the court believes that a legal error was made (for example, illegally seized material was allowed as evidence), the appellate court can order a new trial. The majority of criminal appeals cases are affirmed; that is, the court finds no error of law sufficient to have deprived the defendant of rights. In approximately 20 percent of the cases, the court reverses and remands (sends back) the case, which usually means the defendant will be tried a second time. Since the mid-1960s, the volume of criminal appeals has increased dramatically. In roughly half of the states, there are intermediate courts of appeals that function to relieve the highest court of the burden of hearing a large number of routine appeals.

Federal courts

Only the federal courts operate over the entire territory of the United States. Federal courts are structured along state lines. Thus, although they enforce a uniform body of national criminal laws, local concerns influence the justice dispensed. As a result, there are important variations in the application of law, an indication that American courts are deeply rooted in a local heritage. The federal courts handle far fewer cases than do their state counterparts, although in general the cases they do handle tend to be more serious and complex. Because the federal courts are organized in a clear order of district courts, circuit courts of appeals, and the U.S. Supreme Court (see figure 3-2), it is best to consider them before turning to the more varied structure of state courts.

District courts

In the federal system the district courts are trial courts of original jurisdiction. There is at least one district court in each state. Some states—California, New York, and Texas, for instance—have as many as four. Altogether there are ninety-four district courts—eighty-nine within the fifty states and five for the U.S. territories. The number of judges in each district varies from one in sparsely populated Wyoming to twenty-seven in densely inhabited Manhattan (technically known as the Southern District of New York). Because district courts often encompass large geographical areas (for historical reasons, the western states tend to have only one court for the entire state), they hold court in various locations, termed *divisions*. While some districts hold court in only one division, others have as many as eight. In the five U.S. territories, the district courts may also be responsible for local as well as federal matters.

The district courts are staffed by district court judges who are nominated by the President and confirmed by the Senate; they serve for life. District court judges possess full judicial powers, including conducting trials, accepting guilty pleas, and imposing sentences. In addition, there are 488 U.S. magistrates (only 204 of whom are full-time). Created by Congress in 1969 to replace the former position of U.S. commissioner (who had very limited powers), U.S. magistrates are empowered to hear petty and some minor offenses, as well as to conduct the preliminary stages of felony cases. U.S. magistrates are appointed for an eight-year term by the district court judges and do not have lifetime tenure.

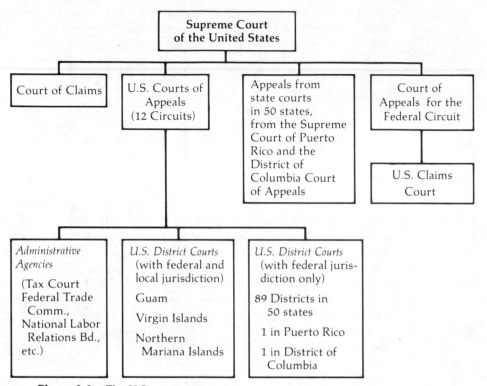

Figure 3-2.   The U.S. court system.

The district courts have original jurisdiction over both civil and criminal cases; thus they are the trial courts for all violations of the federal criminal law. During the early 1970s, the criminal caseload of the U.S. district courts remained fairly constant at about 40,000 cases per year. By 1980, the yearly caseload had declined to only about 29,000. This one-third decline in federal criminal cases reflects changed prosecutorial priorities of the U.S attorney general. During the same period, however, the volume of civil cases doubled to almost 169,000. These figures reflect that civil lawsuits consume more time of the federal courts than criminal ones (see table 3-2). While federal district courts handle far fewer cases than state trial courts, civil cases in federal court often raise more complex legal issues than those in state courts and the amount of money in controversy is also often quite a bit larger.

Circuit court of appeals

Created in 1891 to relieve the U.S. Supreme Court of hearing the growing number of appeals, the circuit courts of appeal are the intermediate appellate courts of the federal system. Eleven of the circuits are identified by number and are organized regionally (see figure 3-3). The twelfth circuit has jurisdiction over the District of Columbia. Like the district courts, the number of circuit court judges varies, de-

TABLE 3-2. Work load of U.S. courts, 1980

	Total cases filed	Minor criminal	Criminal	Civil
U.S. Supreme Court (9 judgeships)	4,781			
U.S. circuit courts of appeal (131 judgeships)	23,200[a]		4,405	14,854
U.S. district courts (516 judgeships)	197,710		28,921	168,789
U.S. magistrates (204 full-time judgeships)[b]	283,217	90,401	105,732[c]	87,083

Source: Administrative Office of the United States Courts, *Annual Report of the Director*, 1980 (Washington, D.C., 1981).
[a] Includes 3,941 appeals from administrative agencies.
[b] There are also 284 part-time U.S. magistrates.
[c] Primarily preliminary matters in felony cases.

pending somewhat on the population and volume of cases. The number of judges authorized for each circuit ranges from four (the First Circuit) to twenty-three (the Ninth Circuit). The chief judge (the most senior judge in terms of service, under seventy years of age) of each circuit has supervisory responsibilities for the district. Like district judges, circuit court of appeals judges are nominated by the President and confirmed by the U.S. Senate.

The circuit courts of appeal have jurisdiction to review the final decisions of the district court, as well as the power to act on certain legal issues that arise while a lawsuit is going on (called *interlocutory appeals*). In addition, the circuit courts hear appeals from a host of quasi-judicial tribunals like the Federal Communications Commission and the Maritime Administration.

In fiscal year 1980, over 23,000 appeals were filed in the circuit courts. Like the district courts, the volume of cases has grown steadily since the mid-1960s. During 1970 to 1980 the number of cases being appealed doubled. In the vast majority of appeals, the circuit courts sustain the original trial court decision; during 1980, only 10 percent of the criminal cases and 19 percent of the civil appeals resulted in appellate court reversal.

The circuit courts normally utilize three-judge panels in deciding cases, which produces some differences in legal interpretation from panel to panel. In controversial cases, though, all the judges may sit together to decide the case. Such *en banc* hearings are rare however; in 1980 only sixty-five were held in the entire nation. A decision by the circuit court exhausts the litigant's right to one appeal. A dissatisfied party may request the U.S. Supreme Court to hear the case, but such requests are rarely granted.

The U.S. Supreme Court

The highest court in the nation is the U.S. Supreme Court. It is composed of nine justices: eight associate justices and one chief justice (who is nominated specifically to that post by the President). Besides presiding over the Court's public sessions,

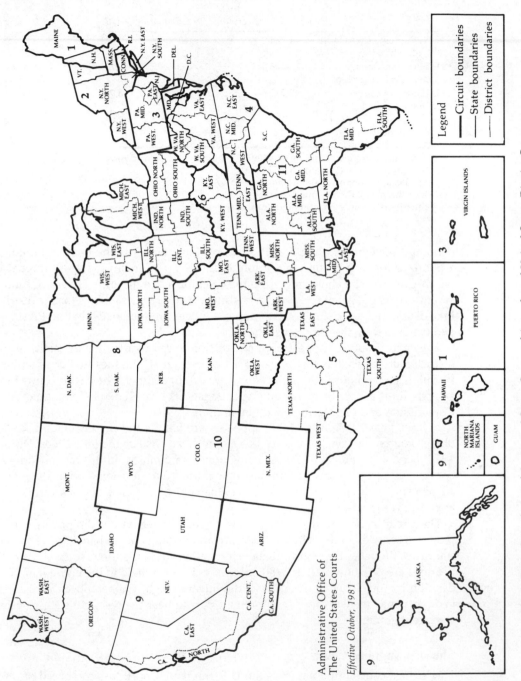

Administrative Office of
The United States Courts

Effective October, 1981

Figure 3-3. Boundaries of the United States Courts of Appeals and United States District Courts.

the Chief Justice conducts the Court's conferences, assigns justices to write opinions (when the Chief Justice votes in the majority), and has supervisory power over the nation's courts. Like other judges appointed under Article III of the Constitution, justices of the Supreme Court are nominated by the President, require confirmation by the U.S. Senate, and serve for life.

writ of
certiorari
    The main way that cases proceed to the U.S. Supreme Court is through the *writ of certiorari*, an order to the lower court whose decision is being disputed to send up the records of the case so that the Supreme Court can determine whether the law has been correctly applied. The Court hears appeals from both U.S. circuit courts of appeals and state appellate courts of last resort. Although the U.S. Supreme Court is the only court in the nation to have authority over all fifty-one separate legal systems, this authority is actually a limited one.

rule of four
    The Court does not have to hear a case unless it wants to. This discretionary power of the Court to decide which cases it will decide allows the Court to regulate its work load. In deciding whether to hear a case the Court employs the *rule of four:* four judges must vote to hear a case before it is placed on the docket. The Court hears only a small percentage of the requests for appeals. By law and custom a set of requirements evolved that must be met before a writ is granted. First, the litigant must have exhausted all other avenues of appeal. Second, the legal issue must involve a "substantial federal question" as defined by the particular Court. This means state supreme courts' interpretations of state law can be appealed to the U.S. Supreme Court only if there is an alleged violation of either federal law or the U.S. Constitution. For example, a suit contending that a state supreme court has misinterpreted the state's divorce law would not be heard because it involves only an interpretation of state law and does not raise a federal question. Therefore, the vast majority of state criminal cases are never reviewed by the U.S. Supreme Court.

    Through its discretionary powers to hear appeals, the U.S. Supreme Court limits itself to deciding between a hundred and two hundred cases a year. It has long been a tradition that the Court should not operate as the court of last resort, trying to correct all possible errors made by other courts, but should marshal its time and energy for the most pressing matters. The necessity for hearing only a small number of the potential cases coming to the Court is underscored by the rapid increase in case filings: 2,321 in 1963 to 4,781 in 1980, an increase of over 100 percent.

State courts

State courts process the vast majority of cases. The courts in a single medium-sized state handle more cases than the entire federal system. The structure of state courts is less clear-cut than the three-tier system found in the federal system. Each state system is different. Although some states have adopted a unified court structure, in many there are still numerous local courts with overlapping jurisdiction. In examining the sometimes bewildering array of state courts, it is useful to divide state courts into four levels: trial courts of limited jurisdiction, trial courts of general jurisdiction, intermediate appellate courts, and courts of last resort.

Trial courts of limited jurisdiction: lower courts

lower courts (inferior courts)

At the first level are trial courts of limited jurisdiction, sometimes referred to as *inferior courts* or more simply *lower courts*. The lower courts are by far the most numerous. They constitute 77 percent of the total number of judicial bodies. Variously called justices of the peace, city court, county court, magistrate, or municipal court, the lower courts handle minor cases: traffic violations, ordinance violations, petty criminal cases, and civil disputes under a set amount (often $500 or less). Generally, lower courts are restricted to imposing a maximum fine of $1,000 and no more than a year in jail. In some states, though, they are authorized to levy fines as high as $5,000 and to sentence defendants to up to five years in prison. In addition, some of these courts are responsible for the preliminary stages of felony cases. Thus, trial courts of limited jurisdiction often hold arraignments, set bail, appoint counsel for indigents, and conduct preliminary examinations. Later the case is transferred to a trial court of general jurisdiction for trial (or plea) and sentencing. The number of trial courts of limited (and sometimes special) jurisdiction varies from none in Idaho, Iowa, South Dakota, and Illinois (where their functions have been absorbed by the trial courts) to over a thousand in New York (1,507) and Texas (1,115).

trial de novo

The lower courts are not typically courts of record; no official verbatim transcript of the proceedings is made. Appeals from lower court decisions are typically heard in a trial court of general jurisdiction, not in a state's appellate courts. Such appeals are termed *trial de novo* because the case must be heard again in its entirety. There are an estimated 15,000 to 20,000 lower court judges, most of whom are not lawyers. Salaries of these justices of the peace, as they are often called, are usually quite low. Most lower courts are created by local governments—cities or counties—and therefore are not part of the state judiciary.

Although the lower courts hear only minor cases, they are nonetheless quite important, for these are the courts where the vast majority of ordinary citizens have contact with their nation's judiciary (table 3-3).

In trial courts of limited jurisdiction, proceedings are typically informal. Cases are processed on a mass basis. Trials are rare, and most are disposed of quickly. Chapter 17 will discuss in greater detail the quality of justice dispensed by the nation's lowest and most neglected courts.

Trial courts of general jurisdiction: major trial courts

major trial courts

The most common names for *major trial courts* are district, circuit, superior, supreme, or common pleas. Table 3-4 gives the exact names used in all states. The major trial courts have unlimited jurisdiction and therefore are the courts that dispose of serious criminal cases. Thus they may hear all matters not specifically delegated to lower courts. In addition, they sometimes have shared jurisdiction (concurrent jurisdiction) with courts of limited jurisdiction; for example, they may also hear misdemeanor cases. The specific division of jurisdiction between the inferior courts and general trial courts is specified by law, either statutory and/or constitutional.

In most states these courts are divided into judicial districts or judicial circuits.

TABLE 3-3. Total state case flow, 1975

Level of court	Beginning: pending	Filings	Dispositions	End: pending
All appellate courts [a]	27,547	111,625	96,720	32,358
Number of states reporting, including D.C.	33	46	46	33
Percent of total U.S. population represented	45.7	90.9	87.7	45.7
Courts of last resort [b]	10,970	42,701	37,615	12,179
Number of states reporting, including D.C.	35	47	46	36
Percent of total U.S. population represented	56.7	93.2	87.7	56.7
Intermediate appellate courts [c]	25,681	70,863	59,623	30,551
Number of states reporting, including D.C.	18 of 24	23 of 24	22 of 24	18 of 24
Percent of population in the 24 states having IACs	68.2	97.0	89.9	68.2
Courts of general jurisdiction [d]	2,426,268	6,699,378	6,272,137	2,637,096
Number of states reporting, including D.C.	35	44	44	35
Percent of total U.S. population represented	69.1	92.4	92.0	69.1
Civil	1,934,642	4,239,154	3,914,665	2,085,882
Number of states reporting, including D.C.	35	44	44	35
Percent of total U.S. population represented	69.1	92.1	92.0	69.1
Criminal [e]	417,633	1,903,483	1,821,447	466,294
Number of states reporting, including D.C.	34	44	44	34
Percent of total U.S. population represented	60.6	92.1	92.0	60.6
Juvenile (handled in general jurisdiction courts)	73,993	556,741	536,025	84,920
Number of states reporting, including D.C.	14 of 32	22 of 32	21 of 32	14 of 32
Percent of population in the 32 states handling juvenile cases	44.9	79.5	78.5	44.9

Source: *Advanced Report, State Court Caseload Statistics: Annual Report, 1975* (Williamsburg, Va.: National Center for State Courts, 1978).

[a] An "appellate case" includes any direct and regular appeal, original proceeding, or request to appeal. Note that totals for all appellate courts are not simply the sum of the totals for courts of last resort and intermediate appellate courts. States that reported partial data (e.g., statistics from courts of last resort but not from intermediate appellate courts, or vice versa) are not included in the totals.

[b] In 1975 there were fifty-three courts of last resort in fifty states and the District of Columbia.

[c] In 1975 there were twenty-eight intermediate appellate courts in twenty-four states.

[d] Note that totals for general jurisdiction cases are not simply the sum of civil, criminal, and juvenile cases. As with appellate data, states which reported partial data (e.g., data for civil cases but not criminal cases, or vice versa) are not included in the totals.

[e] Criminal data do not include minor traffic and minor ordinance cases handled in these general jurisdiction courts.

Note: More recent, but less complete, data on court case flow can be found in National Center for State Courts, *State Court Caseload Statistics: Annual Report,* 1976 (Williamsburg, Va., 1980).

The exact geographical boundaries of the trial courts of general jurisdiction depend somewhat on the volume of the cases but invariably follow existing political boundaries of counties. These districts or circuits in rural areas encompass several adjoining counties, and judges literally ride circuit, holding court in different counties on a fixed schedule. In larger counties where case volumes are larger, the judges are typically divided into specializations. Such specializations may be either formal or informal. New Orleans is an example of a formal specialization. The parish (county) has two district courts: civil district court and criminal district court. The judges are elected to one or the other court, and each court has separate support staff (sheriff, clerk of court, and so on). Chicago is an example of a trial court of general jurisdiction employing informal specializations. The chief judge of the circuit court of Cook County assigns judges to various divisions: criminal,

TABLE 3-4. Major trial courts in different states

Circuit court	Alabama, Arkansas,[a] Florida, Hawaii, Illinois, Indiana,[b] Kentucky, Maryland, Michigan,[c] Mississippi,[a] Missouri,[d] Oregon, South Carolina, South Dakota, Tennessee,[a,f] Virginia, West Virginia, Wisconsin[g]
Court of common pleas	Ohio, Pennsylvania
District court	Colorado, Idaho, Iowa, Kansas, Louisiana, Minnesota, Montana, Nebraska, Nevada, New Mexico, North Dakota, Oklahoma, Texas, Utah, Wyoming
Superior court	Alaska, Arizona, California, Connecticut, Delaware,[a] District of Columbia, Georgia, Indiana,[b] Maine, Massachusetts, New Hampshire, New Jersey,[e] North Carolina, Rhode Island, Vermont, Washington
Supreme court	New York[e]

Source: Law Enforcement Assistance Administration (LEAA), *National Survey of Court Organization* (Washington, D.C.: Government Printing Office, 1973), p. 1; *National Survey of Court Organization, 1975 Supplement to State Judicial Systems* (September 1975); *National Survey of Court Organization, 1977 Supplement to State Judicial Systems* (May 1977).
[a] Arkansas, Delaware, Mississippi, and Tennessee have separate chancery courts with equity jurisdiction.
[b] Concurrent jurisdiction for felonies. In Indianapolis the court is termed criminal court.
[c] In Wayne County felony court is officially called Detroit Recorder's Court.
[d] Also Hannibal Court of Common Pleas.
[e] New Jersey and New York also have county courts.
[f] Tennessee has also the Dyer County Common Law Court and law and equity courts.
[g] Wisconsin also has county courts.

family, juvenile, civil, and so on. Table 3-2 provides some basic work load data on the major trial courts.

Intermediate courts of appeals

intermediate courts of appeals

Twenty-four states have *intermediate courts of appeals* (see table 3-5). Located primarily in the most populous states with the biggest volume of cases, these courts relieve the state's highest court from the necessity of hearing every case appealed. Table 3-2 shows that the work load of these courts, although much lighter than those of the trial courts, is still substantial. Thus, if the lawyer has complied with the court's rules for appealing a case, the court must hear it. The intermediate courts of appeals hear appeals from both civil and criminal cases except in the states of Alabama and Tennessee, where there are separate courts of appeal for civil cases and criminal cases (LEAA:12).

Like their counterparts on the federal level, these courts typically employ three-judge panels for deciding cases.

Supreme court

supreme court (last resort)

The court of last resort is the *state supreme court*. In states without an intermediate court of appeal, the supreme court has no power to choose which cases will be placed on its docket. To complicate the picture further, both Texas and Oklahoma have two courts of last resort, the supreme court (civil) and the court of criminal appeals. The number of supreme court judges varies from a low of three in some

TABLE 3-5. Courts of intermediate appeals (number of judges)

Appeals Court	Massachusetts(10)
Court of Civil Appeals	Alabama(3),[a] Texas(51)[a]
Superior Court	Pennsylvania(7)
Commonwealth Court	Pennsylvania(9)
Court of Criminal Appeals	Alabama(5), Tennessee(9)
Court of Appeals	Alaska(3), Arizona(12), Arkansas(6), California(59), Colorado(10), Georgia(9), Idaho(3), Indiana(12), Iowa(5), Kansas(7), Kentucky(14), Louisiana(33), Michigan(18), Missouri(30), New Mexico(7), North Carolina(12), Ohio(44), Oklahoma(6), Oregon(10), South Carolina(5), Tennessee(12), Washington(16), Wisconsin(12)
Appellate Division of Superior Court	New Jersey(21)
Appellate Courts	Illinois(34)
Court of Special Appeals	Maryland(13)
Appellate Division of Supreme Court	New York(24)
Appellate Terms of Supreme Court	New York(9)
Appellate Sessions of the Superior Court	Connecticut(3)
District Court of Appeal	Florida(39)
Intermediate Court of Appeals	Hawaii(3)

Source: U.S. Department of Justice, Bureau of Justice Statistics, *State Court Organization, 1980* (Washington, D.C.: Government Printing Office, 1982).
[a] Civil only.

states to as many as nine (see table 3-6). Unlike the intermediate appellate courts, these courts do not use panels in making decisions. Rather, the entire court participates in deciding each case. The state supreme courts are the ultimate review board for matters involving interpretation of state law. The only avenue of appeal for a disgruntled litigant is the U.S. Supreme Court, but successful applications are few and must involve an important question of federal law.

oral argument

While state supreme courts vary greatly in the details of internal procedures used in deciding cases, most follow procedures roughly similar to those found in the U.S. Supreme Court. After notice of appeal is filed, *briefs* (written statements of legal arguments) are prepared, *oral argument* is held, and a written opinion produced. State supreme courts, however, tend to have a higher caseload than the U.S. Supreme Court.

Court unification

unified court system

Since the turn of the century, the organization of American courts has been a central concern of court reformers. Groups such as the American Judicature Society and the American Bar Association believe that the multiplicity of courts is inefficient (because judges can not be shifted to meet the growing volume of cases in other courts) and also inequitable (because the administration of justice is not uniform). Court reformers have placed a great emphasis on implementing a *unified court system*. Although court reformers differ about the exact details of a uniform

TABLE 3-6.   Courts of last resort in different states (number of judges)

Supreme Court	Alabama(9), Alaska(5), Arizona(5), Arkansas(7), California(7), Colorado(7), Connecticut(6), Delaware(5), Florida(7), Georgia(7), Hawaii(5), Idaho(5), Illinois(7), Indiana(5), Iowa(5), Kansas(7), Kentucky(7), Louisiana(7), Michigan(7), Minnesota(9), Mississippi(9), Missouri(7), Montana(7), Nebraska(7), Nevada(5), New Hampshire(5), New Jersey(7), New Mexico(5), North Carolina(7), North Dakota(5), Ohio(7), Oklahoma(9),[a] Oregon(7), Pennsylvania(7), Rhode Island(5), South Carolina(5), South Dakota(5), Tennessee(5), Texas(9),[a] Utah(5), Vermont(5), Virginia(7), Washington(9), Wisconsin(7), Wyoming(5)
Court of Appeals	Maryland(7), New York(7)
Supreme Judicial Court	Maine(7), Massachusetts(7)
Court of Criminal Appeals	Oklahoma(3),[a] Texas(9)[a]
Supreme Court of Appeals	West Virginia(5)

Source: U.S. Department of Justice, Bureau of Justice Statistics, *State Court Organization, 1980* (Washington, D.C.: Government Printing Office, 1982).
[a] Two courts of last resort in these states.

court system, their efforts reflect three general principles: simplified court structure, centralized administration, and statewide financing.

Simplified court structure

The first principle of a unified court system is a simple and uniform structure of courts for the entire state. The myriad minor courts (which often have overlapping jurisdictions) would be consolidated in one county-level court. The court reformers envision a three-tier system: a state supreme court at the top; intermediate courts of appeal (where the volume of appeals makes it necessary), and a single trial court. (Chapter 17 discusses the movement to abolish locally controlled lower courts and to place them within the state judicial system.)

Centralized administration

A second basic principle of the unified court system is centralized administration. The state supreme court should have the power to adopt uniform rules to be followed by all courts in the state. Similarly, a central state office would supervise the work of judicial and nonjudicial personnel (clerks of court and so on.). Moreover, centralized administration would include the power to temporarily assign judges to other courts to alleviate the backlog of cases.

Statewide financing

The third basic principle of the unified court concept is a unitary budget system. The state would assume all or a substantial part of the financial responsibility for the state court system. Decisions about allocating funds would be made at the state level and not at the local level, as now occurs in most states.

The politics of court reorganization

The efforts of judicial reformers have achieved considerable success. Many states have substantially unified their court systems. In recent years, the states of Arizona, Illinois, North Carolina, Kentucky, Oklahoma, Washington, Florida, Wisconsin, and Massachusetts have adopted new court structures. Significantly, however, only a very few states have adopted most or all of principles suggested by court reformers. Several states, for example, have adopted a four-tier system (rather than the recommended three) by retaining magistrates or justices of the peace in separate courts. Along these same lines, a number of states have increased the responsibilities of centralized administration yet still allow significant supervisory power at the local level. Finally, the principle of statewide financing has not fared well. In many states county courts are still financed to a significant degree by the county (or equivalent unit). Moreover, not all reform efforts have been successful. Some states (such as Tennessee) have considered and then rejected constitutional amendments to restructure their courts.

To understand why some reform proposals have been rejected while others have been significantly modified from the reformers' recommended principles, we need to examine the political dimensions of court reorganization. Battles over court organization are usually presented as dry technical issues involving case volume and efficiency. But such arguments really mask the underlying political dynamics.

> Historians have generally viewed the creation of the courts of appeals as a response to increased federal litigation brought about by the "great increase in population" and the "general business revival which followed the civil war." The strain "imposed severe and increasing burdens on the overtaxed federal Supreme Court." We might assume from this explanation that the courts of appeals appeared on the American scene as a logical, painless, almost automatic response to postwar conditions. Such an assumption is erroneous. The creation of the courts of appeals was one of the most enduring struggles in American political history. [Richardson and Vines:26]

The authors go on to note that the creation of the U.S. circuit courts of appeal involved a fifty-year struggle between forces who wished to expand federal power and those who wished to increase state authority.

Philosophical and pragmatic differences are also involved. Any attempt to unify a state judicial system invariably brings opposition from local governments that wish to retain control of their local courts. In turn, these issues of local versus state authority also have important financial dimensions. As a result, most proposals to unify state court systems carry the provision that the state will pay all expenses of the local courts (thus relieving cities of millions of dollars in expense) but allow the local municipalities to retain revenues derived from court fines and court fees.

More mundane political considerations are also involved in attempts at judicial reform. A variety of political interests wish to retain current court structures for practical reasons. Nonlawyer judges oppose court reorganization because their jobs would be abolished under plans requiring all judges to be lawyers. This is why many court reform proposals provide clauses allowing nonlawyer judges to remain in office. Similarly, attorneys are familiar with the current system, have learned how to use it, and view court reorganization as an unnecessary alteration in their routine. Political parties often fear that a unified court system would reduce patronage opportunities. For example, a proposal to merge Maryland's chaotic court structure into a unified system drew the opposition of Baltimore's six elected clerks of court, for the new judicial article would have created one appointed office of clerk of court, thus abolishing significant patronage powers (*Baltimore Sun*, January 30, 1975). Finally, many of the problems associated with the existing structure of courts are concentrated in the large cities. Rural politicians and rural lawyers, because they see no problems in their own area, are not sympathetic to major overhauls that would not benefit them but might mean a decreased control of local courts (Glick and Vines:16–17).

Attempts to reorganize state court systems seldom generate much popular interest (Jacob:158). Thus the flow of public discussion favors those who support the status quo.

Despite these political obstacles, court reformers have made great strides in unifying America's court systems. At the same time, however, others have begun to question the assumptions and philosophy of the court reformers. These critics argue that the concept of a unified court system reflects a classical view of public administration, one that stresses a strong central administration rather than active participation by those most affected. Furthermore, the reformers hold a limited view of politics. In the words of Carl Baar, "The persistence of politics has been a failure not of court reformers but of those who have articulated reform arguments in the past." Some of principles of a unified court system, it is believed, would not remove politics from the system but rather allow the governor much greater political control over the state's judiciary. Finally, the standard blueprint of court reorganization does not allow for a desirable diversity: instead, local diversity is considered illegitimate. For these reasons, a new generation of scholars, concerned about improving the quality of justice in American courts, now believes that the old principles of court reorganization hamper creative thinking about new directions for court reform.

Consequences of court organization

How the courts are organized and administered has a profound effect on the way defendants are processed in the criminal courts, as well as the type of justice that results.

Decentralization

Because there are fifty-one legal systems in America, there are significant differences in the law from one state to the next. On the civil side the grounds for divorce vary from rather rigid criteria in some states to rather minimal ones in others (of which Nevada is the most prominent example). On the criminal side differences in how crimes are defined are evident among the states.

Within each legal system there are also notable variations. The enforcement of the criminal law is almost entirely a local enterprise. Courts are structured on a local basis. The officials that staff the courts—judges, prosecutors, and defense attorneys—are often recruited from the community they now serve, and thus reflect the sentiments of that community. Together these factors produce a system of justice with close ties to local communities. The direct result of the enforcement and application of the criminal law by local officials operating in courts reflecting the local community is disparities in matters like release on bail, delay in the courts, plea bargaining practices, and sentencing.

Local control and local corruption

local control

Local control of justice has some obvious advantages. The courts are close to the people, and by and large the public respects the courts in America more than it does in Europe, where judges are viewed as faceless bureaucrats responding to the dictates of the national government, oblivious to local customs and needs. But local control has been the incubator for local corruption, local injustice, and, in some limited instances, local tyranny.

Every state invariably has a town or two where gambling and prostitution flourish because the city fathers agree to look the other way. Not surprisingly, they often receive monetary benefits from being so nearsighted. Increasingly, though, such activities are decreasing as state police or state attorneys general take a more active stand.

The locally administered criminal justice system has also been marked by pockets of injustice. At times the police and the courts have been the handmaidens of the local economic elite. In the South the police and the courts have hindered efforts to exercise civil rights by arresting or harassing those who sought to register

---

IN THE NEWS: PUBLIC OFFICIALS FOR SALE: NOW A CRACKDOWN

From small towns to the nation's capital, prosecutors are zeroing in as never before on public officials accused of lining their own pockets.

Just in recent weeks:

————A federal grand jury in Washington, D.C., began digging into sweeping charges that as many as 50 members of Congress may be involved in accepting payoffs from South Korean interests.

————A Boston school-committee member started serving a two-year jail term for taking kickbacks from the salaries of school employees.

————The speaker of the house in Pennsylvania was indicted on charges of bribery and other illegal acts.

————Former Oklahoma Governor David Hall went to prison for offering a bribe to a State official.

————A State judge in Florida was arrested on charges of attempting to distribute 1,600 pounds of marijuana.

————Four present and former members of the New York State attorney general's staff were indicted on charges of taking bribes.

————A former chairman of the Iowa liquor commission was sentenced to three years in prison for extortion and income-tax violations while in office.

Such cases give only the flavor of what has been happening around the country in recent years.

More than 1,000 key officials from county sheriff to U.S. Vice President have been brought to the bar of justice since 1970 on federal charges growing out of bribery, kickbacks, extortion, and similar schemes. Including people cited for violating State and local laws, the total figure runs even higher. Comments U.S. Acting Deputy Attorney General Richard L. Thornburgh, until recently head of the Justice Department's criminal division: "There's no way to tell whether we have more corruption than we had 100 years ago. But there's no question that the efforts to prosecute those who betray public office are at a higher pitch than ever before."

Reprinted from *U.S. News & World Report*, February 28, 1977, p. 36. Copyright 1977 U.S. News & World Report, Inc.

to vote, eat at the whites-only lunch counter, or simply speak up to protest segregation.

The dual court system has provided a safety valve for checking the most flagrant abuses of local justice. The dual court system allows for alternative tribunals in some situations. Often, prosecution of local officials is conducted by federal officials.

Lack of administrative monitoring

A major peculiarity of America's judiciary is that within each state, the courts enjoy a wide degree of independence. This is partly the result of the strong tradition of judicial independence in America: each judge rightly views himself or herself as supreme within his or her own court.

To be sure, local judges do not have total freedom in applying the law; appellate courts may review their decisions. But appellate court review is largely confined to the substance of the law and pronouncement of rules of procedure. Questions involving the substance of justice—the length of sentence, the amount of bail, and so on—are not reviewed by higher courts unless there has been gross abuse. Also, local prosecutors are essentially immune from supervision by state attorneys general. Local police are also outside of administrative review by the state police.

administra-tive moni-toring
The lack of *administrative monitoring* is most directly seen in the absence of systematic and reliable data on the number of courts, the activities they perform, and the volume of cases they process. Beginning in 1922, the federal courts have operated under minimal administrative supervision. Data on case filings and closings are reported to the Administrative Office of the U.S. Courts, which publishes an annual report. Although most states have now created an administrative office for the state courts somewhat comparable to the Administrative Office of the U.S. Courts, these state bodies do not wield much power. Local courts do not necessarily report accurate data to the state administrator. Many lower courts, because they are run and administered by local governments, are not required to report data on case volume to the state office. As a result, we cannot be sure how many courts there are in the United States or how many cases they process.

Choice of courts

The multiplicity of local courts as well as the dual court system provides limited opportunities for the government to choose where to file charges. The case of Father Daniel Berrigan, a major critic of the Vietnam War, illustrates this point. Father Berrigan was charged by the federal government with planning the bombing of defense installations in Washington, D.C., and plotting to kidnap presidential adviser Henry Kissinger. Although the alleged criminal activities occurred in the Washington, D.C., area, the government selected Harrisburg, Pennsylvania, for the trial. The government felt that this rather small isolated city in a conservative part of Pennsylvania with a low Catholic population and a rather strict judge would maximize its chances for a conviction. (Despite all this planning, the jury acquitted.) In other trials of prominent critics of the Vietnam War, the government exercised similar care in selecting in which court to prosecute their cases.

Similar questions about choice of court for prosecution are present at the state level. In many communities, when the police arrest for a minor criminal violation they have the choice of filing a state charge in a major trial court or a less serious local ordinance violation in a lower court. Often this choice is made on the basis of perceived advantages of which court will take up less of the officer's time (particularly if the officer is not paid for court appearances), the likely speed of the disposition, and the likely penalty the judge will hand out. Thus, in many cities police prefer to file the least serious charges because the local lower court will dispose of the case immediately and will probably hand out a heavier sentence than would a state court for the same offense.

Conclusion

Because the courts are so diverse, finding the right courthouse confuses laymen and lawyers alike. Let a lawyer, now a U.S. magistrate, explain the problem:

> You stand on the courthouse steps trying to explain to your client that he's not going to get any money because his lawyer filed suit in the wrong court. The case involved a few hundred dollars. I filed suit in small claims court, but a few months later it turned out that all of the actions occurred in the next county. So I mailed the papers to the small claims court in the neighboring county. When we got there to try the case I found out that the small claims court in the neighboring county has a different jurisdictional amount and I should have filed in county court. Only the statute of limitations had run out so I couldn't file there. Talk about your clients being mad. [Author's interview]

The exact details of jurisdiction, names, and functions of courts vary greatly among states and often within a state as well. Such variations in court structure not only affect lawyers trying to decide where to file cases, but also have a wide-ranging impact on the entire criminal justice process. The local control of courts, the lack of administrative monitoring, the long history of local corruption, and the ability to choose a court for a criminal prosecution exert a long-term affect on the criminal court process.

Dissatisfaction with this system is legendary. But by and large, the judicial reformers have lacked the political power to make wholesale changes, mainly because there are so many built-in impediments to change. Nonetheless, court reformers have won a number of important victories. Although they have not been able to achieve widespread adoption of a three-tier system, every year at least one state makes significant advances.

For discussion

1. Does your state have a unified system of lower courts? What are the names, functions, and jurisdictions of the lower courts in your state and city? What is the name of the major trial court(s) in your state? Is there an intermediate court of appeals? What is the name and jurisdiction of your state's court of last resort?
2. What U.S. district court governs your community? What circuit court of appeals governs your state?

3. Discuss with lawyers, judges, prosecutors, and police officers any informal rules for deciding in which court a minor criminal case will be filed.
4. Have there been any efforts to reorganize the courts in your state? How successful were these efforts? What factors aided these efforts? What factors tend to prevent court reorganization?
5. Given the difficulties of achieving court reorganization, would the time and effort of judicial reformers be better spent on other issues? Which ones?
6. What advantages would result from greater centralized administration of state courts? What disadvantages?

References

Administrative Office of the United States Courts. *Annual Report of the Director*, 1980. Washington, D.C,: Government Printing Office, 1981.

Baar, Carl, "The Scope and Limits of Court Reform." *Justice System Journal* 5 (Spring 1980): 274–290.

Baltimore Sun, January 30, 1975.

Glick, Henry, and Kenneth Vines. *State Court Systems*. Englewood Cliffs, N.J.: Prentice-Hall, 1973.

Friedman, Lawrence. *A History of American Law*. New York: Simon and Schuster, 1973.

Institute of Judicial Administration. *Survey of the Judicial System of Maryland*. New York: Institute of Judicial Administration, 1967.

Jacob, Herbert. *Justice in America*, 3rd ed. Boston: Little, Brown, 1978.

Law Enforcement Assistance Administration (LEAA). *National Survey of Court Organization*. Washington, D.C.: Government Printing Office, 1973.

Oran, Daniel. *Law Dictionary for Non-Lawyers*. St. Paul, Minn.: West Publishing, 1974.

Richardson, Richard, and Kenneth Vines. *The Politics of the Federal Courts*. Boston: Little, Brown, 1970.

Wheeler, Russell, and Howard Whitcomb, "The Literature of Court Administration: A Bibliographical Essay." *Arizona State Law Journal* (1974):689.

For further reading

Berkson, Larry, and Susan Carbon. *Court Unification: History, Politics and Implementation*. Washington, D.C.: U.S. Department of Justice, Law Enforcement Assistance Administration, National Institute of Law Enforcement and Criminal Justice, August, 1978.

Glick, Henry, and Kenneth Vines. *State Court Systems*. Englewood Cliffs, N.J.: Prentice-Hall, 1973.

Hurst, James Willard. *The Growth of American Law*. Boston: Little, Brown, 1950.

Law Enforcement Assistance Administration (LEAA). *National Survey of Court Organization*. Washington, D.C.: Government Printing Office, 1973.

Richardson, Richard, and Kenneth Vines. *The Politics of the Federal Courts*. Boston: Little, Brown, 1970.

Wheeler, Russell, and Howard Whitcomb. *Judicial Administration: Text and Readings*. Englewood Cliffs, N.J.: Prentice-Hall, 1977.

CHAPTER 4

What Is a Crime?

Crime. Mention the word to a cross section of people and you are likely to uncover a variety of connotations. In popular use the word often means activities we do not like; we expect the law to punish the bad acts of others. The word *crime* often implies not just bad acts but also immoral ones as well. Webster's dictionary, for example, defines crime as "an offense against morality," which makes it synonymous with "bad," "evil," or "sinful." To some, societal punishment of immorality serves both to deter possible wrongdoers and educate the young or unwary. More immediately, though, we often associate the word *crime* with muggings, rapes, and murders that fill the headlines of the morning newspaper or draw our attention on the nightly television news.

These popular views, however, are not necessarily the same as the legal meaning of crime. Legally no activity is a crime unless it has been specified as such by the law. The legal definitions of crime thus can be both broader and narrower than popular usage. Crime in a legal sense, therefore, is not the same as activity we do not like. The popular expression "There oughta be a law" expresses the frustration associated with finding out that some bad conduct we have witnessed or experienced is not a crime.

This chapter focuses on the importance of legal definitions of crime for the operations of the criminal courts. The starting point is how crime is defined. We will examine the general principles underlying activities labeled criminal as well as the technical aspects of criminal definitions. Second, this chapter will explore the common law heritage that guides the development and application of these criminal definitions. Third, this chapter will look at the pattern of the American criminal law and attempts to revise it. Finally, we will discuss the consequences of the criminal law for the criminal courts. The criminal law constitutes the basic source of authority for the criminal courts. Before we can assess the type of justice produced by the courts, we need to know something about the law that is applied in reaching those results.

How crimes are defined

In American society, there can be no crime without *law*. Public wrongs must be defined by the law and punishment specified before antisocial conduct can be considered criminal. These overall requirements differentiate crime from other types of activities. Telling a lie or accidentally hitting another car are examples of activities that are not good but are not criminal. Violations of the first we handle informally through our friends (you can't trust John) or by the civil law (a suit for damages). In outline form, crime involves three components: a public wrong, punishment, and law.

Public wrong

public wrong
Not all violations of the law are crimes. A crime must involve a *public wrong;* the public, not merely a private individual, is harmed. A claim that money is owed under a contract or that the insurance company should pay to repair your damaged car are examples of private wrongs for which civil remedies are available. As a sociologist notes, "the concept of criminal law developed only when the custom of private or community wrongs was replaced by the principle that the state is injured when one of its subjects is harmed" (Quinney:44).

> . . . If two men had walked down Fifth Avenue a year ago—that would have been March, 1933—and one of them had a pint of whiskey in his pocket and the other had a hundred dollars in gold coin, the one with the whiskey would have been called a criminal and the one with the gold an honest citizen. If these two men, like Rip Van Winkle, slept for a year and again walked down Fifth Avenue, the man with the whiskey would be called an honest citizen and the one with the gold coin a criminal.
>
> Samuel Insull, Americal financier, quoted in H. D. Schultz, *Panics and Crashes* (New Rochelle, N.Y.: Arlington House, 1972).

Punishment

punishment
That a *punishment* must be provided is a second distinguishing feature of the criminal law. Punishment is viewed as necessary for protecting the public. It may be a fine, imprisonment, probation, suspended sentence, or death.

In setting penalties, the common law made a distinction between a felony and misdemeanor. But like so many other legal terms, the original rationale for the distinction has been lost. Although *felony* and *misdemeanor* are commonly used terms, there is no general agreement as to what they mean. In some states the distinction is made on the basis of where the guilty will be confined—felons in state prisons and misdemeanants in local jails. In other states, the distinction is based on the length of the sentence; generally a felony is punishable by imprisonment for over a year and misdemeanor by less than a year. In still other states, it is difficult to determine what criteria are used. Because of this confusion the popular assumption that a felony is a more serious offense than a misdemeanor is not entirely accurate. What is a felony in one state may be only a misdemeanor in another. This confusion produces some strange results. In Maryland it is a felony to break open a hogshead of tobacco, but it is a misdemeanor to use a machine gun in committing a crime of violence.

*felony mis-
demeanor*

Law

The third basic principle of the criminal law is that there can be no crime unless that activity has been made illegal. This is best expressed in the ancient Latin maxim, *nullum crimen, nulla poena, sine lege* (no crime, no punishment without law). Thus, before public wrongs can be considered criminal and before a punishment can be imposed for committing these public wrongs, both the public wrong and the punishment must be specifically stated in the *law*. The maxim of "no crime without law" expresses the fundamental concern of the common law that no innocent person should be subjected to the criminal process. The best way to ensure that an innocent person is not wrongly accused of violating the law is to require that criminal violations be known in advance so that law-abiding citizens can conform their behavior to the law. For this reason criminal statutes are always interpreted strictly. Any ambiguities in the meaning of the law are resolved in favor of the accused. Thus courts may hold a criminal statute "void for vagueness" if it does not adequately specify the conduct to be prohibited.

Elements of a crime

The common law insists that criminal definitions be strictly interpreted. This fundamental requirement is expressed in the phrase *corpus delicti*, which means "body of the crime." The requirements for the body of the crime provide the technical (that is, legal) definitions of a crime. No behavior can be called criminal unless a guilty act was committed, with a guilty intent, and the guilty act and the guilty intent are related. In addition, a number of crimes are defined on the basis of attendant circumstances and/or specific results. Each of these basic concepts is called an *element of a crime*. All elements of the offense must be proven before there can be a conviction. An understanding of these basic concepts embodied in statutory definitions of crime is essential for correctly interpreting specific definitions of crime. In turn, these basic concepts produce numerous categories of criminal activities (murder, voluntary manslaughter, and involuntary manslaughter, for example).

*corpus
delicti*

*elements of
a crime*

Guilty act

guilty act
(actus reus)

Before there can be a crime, there must be a *guilty act (actus reus)*. Such behavior can either be acts of commission or acts of omission. The necessity of a guilty act reflects a fundamental principle of American law: no one should be punished for bad thoughts. There are different types of guilty acts, depending on the crime involved. For example, the guilty act in the crime of possession of an illegal drug is the possession. Differences in the nature of the guilty act account for many of the gradations of criminal offenses. To choose one obvious example, stealing property is considered separately from damaging property.

attempts
(inchoate
offenses)

An important subdivision of the guilty act is a class of offenses labeled as *attempts* or *inchoate* (uncompleted) *offenses* (for example, attempted burglary or attempted murder). The law does not want a person to avoid legal liability merely because someone or something prevented the commission of a crime. Typically, though, the penalties for attempt are less severe than if the act had succeeded. One result is that in some states, defendants often plead guilty to attempt to reduce the possible severity of the prison sentence.

Guilty intent

The criminal law also requires proof that the guilty act was intentional. Justice Oliver Wendell Holmes pithily expressed the importance of intent when he commented, "Even a dog distinguishes between being stumbled over and being kicked." Most crimes require that the defendant knew he or she was doing something wrong. The requirement of *guilty intent* is referred to as *mens rea* ("guilty mind").

guilty
intent
(mens rea)

There are some important qualifications, however, in the meaning of a guilty mind. A person cannot avoid legal liability by later saying "I didn't mean to do it." Futhermore, the law assumes that people know the consequences of their acts.

How varying degrees of intent are employed in differentiating categories of criminal offenses is illustrated by statutes involving homicide. Murder requires proof that the defendant intended to kill or cause great bodily harm. In addition, most state statutes include deaths resulting from a felony (like armed robbery) under murder, even though the defendant did not specifically set out to kill the victim. Voluntary manslaughter involves death resulting from a sudden or intense passion. Involuntary manslaughter is involved if death occurred from an act performed recklessly. The following Illinois homicide statute illustrates these differences:

Article 9. Homicide

§9-1. Murder.   (a) A person who kills an individual without lawful justification commits murder if, in performing the acts which cause the death: (1) He either intends to kill or do great bodily harm to that individual or another, or knows that such acts will cause death to that individual or another; or (2) He knows that such acts create a strong probability of death or great bodily harm to that individual or another; or (3) He is attempting or committing a forcible felony other than voluntary manslaughter.

§9-2. Voluntary Manslaughter.   (a) A person who kills an individual without lawful justification commits voluntary manslaughter if at the time of the killing he is acting under a sudden and intense passion resulting from serious provocation by: (1) The individual killed, or (2) Another whom the offender endeavors to kill, but he negligently or accidentally causes the death of the individual killed. Serious provocation is conduct sufficient to excite an intense passion in a reasonable person. . . .

§9-3. Involuntary Manslaughter and Reckless Homicide.   (a) A person who unintentionally kills an individual without lawful justification commits involuntary manslaughter if his acts whether lawful or unlawful which cause the death are such as are likely to cause death or great bodily harm to some individual, and he performs them recklessly, except in cases in which the cause of the death consists of the driving of a motor vehicle, in which case the person commits reckless homicide. . . . [Illinois Revised Statutes: Chapter 38]

Note that if death occurred solely because of negligence, no criminal violation is involved. Here the civil law takes over; wrongful death is considered a private wrong.

One major consequence of how the concept of criminal intent defines different categories of homicide is varying penalties. Under Illinois law, a defendant convicted of murder may be sentenced to death or a minimum of fourteen years in prison. Conviction of voluntary manslaughter carries a maximum sentence of twenty years in prison, involuntary manslaughter ten years, and reckless homicide three years.

Fusion of guilty act and guilty intent

fusion of guilty act and guilty intent

The criminal law requires that the guilty act and the guilty mind occur together. Here is an example that illustrates this concept of *fusion of the guilty act* and *guilty intent*. Suppose a husband planned to kill his wife; he purchased some poison but never got around to putting the poison in her drink. The husband returns home late one night, an argument ensues, and he stabs her. In this situation the intent to kill necessary for a murder conviction did not occur along with the death. Therefore the correct charge would be voluntary manslaughter.

Attendant circumstances

attendant (accompanying) circumstances

Some crimes require the presence, or absence, of *attendant (accompanying) circumstances*. Most states differentiate between classes of theft on the basis of the amount stolen. In Illinois, for example, the law provides that theft of less than $300 is treated as a misdemeanor and over $300 as a felony. The amount stolen is the attendant circumstance. Similarly, the common law crime of burglary was limited to breaking and entering a dwelling house at night. Both the dwelling house and at night were attendant circumstances. Thus a person who broke into a business during the day was not guilty of burglary under the common law (although these actions fall under other criminal offenses).

Results

results

In a limited number of criminal offenses the *results* of the illegal act play a critical part in defining the crime. The difference between homicide and battery, for example, depends on whether the victim lived. A number of states distinguish between degrees of battery depending on how seriously the victim was injured. Note that the concept of result differs from that of intent. In all of the preceding examples, the defendant may have had the same intent. The only difference was how hearty the victim was or perhaps how skillful the defendant was in carrying out his intentions.

Modern advances in medicine present some major legal complications in this regard. For a homicide to occur, there must be a death. The modern complication revolves around the ability to prolong life. In the last few years the courts and the legislatures have been forced to confront the legal meaning of death. Some doctors argue that death occurs when the brain has stopped functioning. This definition is of particular utility when a person has been critically injured and the vital organs can be transplanted to another patient. But the brain theory of death differs from another definition: namely, the ceasing of all bodily functions. The following hypothetical case is much on the lawmakers' minds. During an armed robbery, a victim is shot in the head. At the hospital the surgeons determine that the brain has stopped functioning and wish to transplant the victim's vital organs quickly. But the victim's heart continues to beat. Some defense attorneys argue that if the victim's vital organs are transplanted, the suspect could not be convicted of murder since in some sense the victim was still alive. The appellate courts will consider such modern-day problems for years to come.

Legal defenses

legal defenses

Under the law people who may have performed illegal acts may not be criminals because of a legally recognized justification for their actions or because legally they were not responsible for their actions. These *legal defenses* derive from how crime is defined. For example, guilty acts must be voluntary. A person who strikes another while having an epileptic seizure would not be guilty of assault because the act (hitting) was not voluntary. Similarly the law recognizes circumstances in which a person is forced to commit an illegal act because of threats or force. The requirement of a guilty act before there can be a crime forms the basis for two legal defenses: the acts were involuntary or the acts were committed under duress.

The requirement of intent or a guilty mind produces several legal defenses to criminal offense. The law considers some types of persons incapable of being able to form criminal intent, and therefore they cannot be legally held responsible for their actions. The prime examples are children. States vary, however, in how old children must be before they are presumed responsible for their actions. In most states, no child under seven can be held responsible for criminal actions. For children over seven, states differ in their definitions of *juvenile delinquency*. State juvenile delinquency laws are premised on the idea that those under a certain age have less responsibilty for their actions than adults do.

juvenile delinquency

Insanity is a second legal defense stemming from *mens rea*. Persons suffering from defects of the mind—senility, idiocy, or psychoses—are considered incapable of forming criminal intent. Again, however, states vary greatly in defining insanity. By and large the courts rather than the legislatures have been responsible for determining the test for insanity.

In recent years the insanity defense has sparked controversy. Heated outcries were heard when the jury acquitted would-be presidential assassin, John Hinckley, Jr., on the basis of "not guilty by reason of insanity" (even though Hinckley was then confined to a mental institution). Critics argue that defendants try to avoid punishment by pretending that they are insane. In the aftermath of the Hinckley verdict, the state of Alabama abolished the insanity defense, and other states are considering similar actions.

IN THE NEWS: A NEEDED VERDICT: GUILTY BUT INSANE   BY CHARLES NESSON

To understand the true purpose of the insanity defense, one must first appreciate the broader aims of criminal law. The object of criminal trials is not simply to pass moral judgment on a defendant. Criminal process is an instrument of societal control. One of its most important objectives is to enhance the resolve of all good citizens to be law-abiding.

This is deterrence but not in the simplistic sense of pain versus gain. Law has a moralizing educational function. The idea is that punishment, as a concrete expression of society's disapproval of an act, helps to form and to strengthen the public's moral code and thereby affirm conscious and unconscious inhibitions against committing crime. As the French sociologist Emile Durkheim observed, there is an apparent paradox: "Punishment is above all designed to act upon upright people."

Back in the days of bedlams when psychiatric notions of insanity were extremely crude, criminal law could tolerate a defense for insane killers because they were obviously so different from the rest of us that it made no sense to judge them by human standards. There was no lesson to be learned from punishing them any more than there would be from punishing a wild animal. The advance of psychiatry has now blurred the distinction between normal and crazy people.

John W. Hinckley, Jr. is not obviously insane. It took considerable expertise to convince attentive jurors of his insanity. A friend who attended the trial said to me, "if you had been there, you would understand how crazy this guy is." But to many of those who were not there and who, therefore, were not swept along by the testimony of the psychiatric experts, Mr. Hinckley seems like a kid who had a rough life and who lacked the moral fiber to deal with it.

This is not to deny that Mr. Hinckley is crazy but to recognize that there is a capacity for craziness in all of us. Lots of people have tough lives, many tougher than Mr. Hinckley's, and manage to cope. The Hinckley verdict let those people down. For anyone who experiences life as a struggle to act responsibly in the face of various temptations to let go, the Hinckley verdict is demoralizing, an example of someone who let himself go and who has been exonerated because of it.

We need a new kind of verdict in criminal law— guilty but insane—"guilty" to express the objective truth that intentionally and unjustifiably killing someone is wrong, and that all people must resist temptations to murder, and "insane" to express the subjective truth about the defendant, arrived at with all the help that modern psychiatry can offer, that the defendant is sick and that his sickness contributed to his disposition to kill.

The consequence of the verdict "guilty but insane" should be the commitment of the defendant to the penal system under terms both legal and medical. Within the penal system, the defendant should receive medical treatment. But his ultimate release should be dependent on a judgment by appropriately constituted authority not only that he is no longer dangerous but also that he has served a sufficient term to affirm the rule of law.

Charles Nesson, "Guilty but Insane," *New York Times*, July 1, 1982, p. A19. © 1982 by The New York Times Company. Reprinted by permission. Charles Nesson, professor of law at Harvard Law School, teaches criminal law and evidence.

An illustration of elements of a crime

Criminal statutes must be read clause by clause because each clause constitutes a critical part of the offense. Failure to prove one element bars a conviction for that offense. The common law definition of burglary is useful for demonstrating what we mean by the *elements of a crime*. It will also give us an opportunity to review our discussion thus far.

At common law, the offense of burglary was defined as "breaking and entering the dwelling house of another, in the nighttime, with intent to commit a felony therein." Six elements are present: (1) "breaking" and (2) "entering," both of which involve guilty acts, (3) "dwelling house," (4) "of another," and (5) "in the nighttime." All are examples of attendant circumstances that must be present before the common law crime of burglary exists. The final element—(6) "with the intent to commit a felony therein"—involves *mens rea*. Note that results are not encompassed in common law burglary; there is no requirement that the person actually did take anything, only that he or she intended to commit a felony.

The common law definition seems to square with our image of the burglar: the stealthy nighttime prowler who breaks the back window and takes our color television set. But a closer examination reveals some peculiarities. Why was burglary limited to nighttime? Why was it restricted to a dwelling house? We normally think of a burglary of not only a house but also a car, business, trailer, and so on. In both instances the answer is that the common law judges, in formulating this definition, were responding to specific problems of earlier centuries. Obviously, in examining how crimes are defined, we need to examine the common law heritage from which these definitions were developed.

The common law heritage

The American legal system is based on English common law. (Louisiana is the only exception; its civil legal system is based on the Napoleonic Code and the Continental legal heritage). Common law originated sometime after the Norman conquest of England in 1066 and is derived from the practices of the itinerant judges. Traveling from shire to shire (our word *sheriff* comes from this ancient English phrase), the judges settled disputes on the basis of the customs of the individual community; hence the name common law. Because the system of justice was locally based, the law varied from one community to another. Gradually the twin forces of an increasingly commercial economy and the drive of the English kings to solidify their political control over the local noblemen produced a more uniform legal system for England. What is critically important is that in the development of the common law legal system, a distinctive way of doing business gradually emerged. There are three key characteristics of this common law heritage: the law was *judge-made* rather than legislatively enacted; the law was based on *precedent* (rulings in past cases guide decision making); and finally, it was *uncodified* (it could not be found in any one place).

Judge-made law

judge-made law

A key characteristic of the common law is that it is predominantly *judge-made law*. Initially the common law recognized a few basic rights. As English society, and later American society, became more complex, the judges adapted the old rights to new problems. Hence the law dealing with property, contracts, and torts (a wrong done to a person) developed from the English law courts. Even today the law in these areas remains predominantly made by judges.

By the 1600s, the English judges had defined such felonies as murder, suicide, manslaughter, arson, robbery, larceny, rape, and mayhem. The common law defenses of insanity, infancy, self-defense, and coercion had also entered the law. These English criminal law concepts, often with some adaptations, were transplanted to America by the colonists. After the Revolution those common law crimes considered applicable to local conditions were retained. The process of the courts' creating and defining new crime continued in America during the nineteenth century. During this period offenses involving conspiracy and attempt were developed. Although today legislative bodies—not the courts—define crime, these statutory definitions often reflect their common law heritage.

Precedent

precedent (stare decisis)

A second key characteristic of the common law is the doctrine of *precedent*, often referred to as *stare decisis* ("let the decision stand"). The doctrine of precedent requires a judge to decide a case by applying the rule of law found in previous cases provided the facts in the current case are similar to the facts in the previous cases. Figure 4-1 illustrates the citation system used in American law. Through following previous court decisions, the legal system promotes the twin goals of fairness and consistency.

The reliance of the common law on precedents reflects the law's approach to problem solving. Rather than issue a court opinion attempting to solve the entire range of a given legal problem, common law courts decide only as much of the case as they must to resolve the individual dispute. Broad rules and policy directives emerge only through the accumulation of court decisions through time. Unfortunately, many Americans make the mistake of translating common law heritage, particularly the doctrine of precedent, into a static view of the courts. Some critics of the Warren Court, for example, were fond of saying that it is no business of the courts to create new law, a position that conveniently ignores the entire history of Anglo-American law. Stated another way, common law courts have always been called on to shape the old law to new demands. The common law, though, is committed to stability by gradual change (hence the typical comment that the law and the courts are conservative institutions). One way courts achieve flexibility is in adapting old rights to new problems. For example, some prosecutors are attempting to adapt the old common law offense of nuisance and apply it to houses of prostitution and pornographic movie theaters. A second dimension of flexibility is the ability of courts to distinguish precedents. Recall that we said the doctrine of precedent affects previous cases based on a similar set of facts. Courts

Figure 4–1.   How to read legal citations.

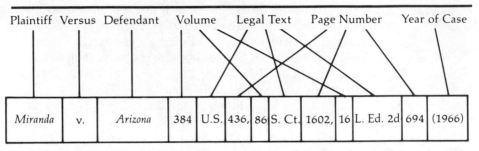

Plaintiff	Versus	Defendant	Volume	Legal Text	Page Number	Year of Case
Miranda	v.	*Arizona*	384	U.S. 436, 86 S. Ct. 1602, 16 L. Ed. 2d 694		(1966)

Students first confronted with legal citations are often bewildered by the array of numbers. But with a few basics in mind, these citations need not be confusing; they are very efficient aids in finding court decisions.

The full citation for *Miranda* is as follows: *Miranda* v. *Arizona* 384 U.S. 436, 86 S.Ct. 1602, 16 L.Ed.2d 694 (1966). The lead name in the case usually refers to the party who lost in the lower court and is seeking to overturn that decision. That party is called the *appellant*. The second name refers to the other party (or parties) who won at the lower level—in this instance the state of Arizona. The second party is called the *appellee* or, more simply, the *respondent*. Miranda is the appellant who is seeking to overturn his conviction. The state of Arizona is named as the respondent because criminal prosecutions are brought in the name of the state.

After the names of the parties come three sets of references. All decisions of the U.S. Supreme Court are reported in the *Supreme Court Reports*, which is published by the U.S. Government Printing Office. It is the official reporting system, and is abbreviated U.S. In addition, decisions of the Supreme Court are reported in two private reporting systems: the *Supreme Court Reporter*, which is abbreviated S.Ct., and in *Lawyers Supreme Court Reports, Lawyers Edition*, which is abbreviated L.Ed.2d.

The numbers preceding the abbreviation for the volume refer to the volume number. Thus *Miranda* can be found in volume number 384 of the United States *Supreme Court Reports*. The numbers after the abbreviation refer to the page number. Thus the *Miranda* decision in volume 384 begins on page 436, as well as volume 86 of the *Supreme Court Reporter* page 1602, and so on. Typically a library will carry only one of the reporting systems. Therefore the multiple references make it easy to locate the given case no matter to which of the three reporting systems one has access.

Decisions of other appellate courts at both the federal and state level are reported in a similar manner in other volumes.

---

sometimes simply state that this set of facts differs from the previous decisions and make another ruling. Finally, a court will occasionally (but very reluctantly) overturn a previous decision by acknowledging that the previous court opinion was wrong.

Uncodified

uncodified   The third key characteristic of the common law is that it is *uncodified*; the law is not written in any one place. In deciding the legal meaning of a given crime (murder or burglary, for example), it is not sufficient to look just at the legislative act. One must also know how the courts have interpreted the statute. Further, in interpreting and applying the statute, one must be aware of possible legal defenses (insanity or age) that are not specifically mentioned in the law but exist nonetheless. To aid lawyers and others in determining the legal meaning of crimes, there are a variety of annotated works, books that contain the law plus commentary (history, explanations, and major court cases discussing the law). Although these books are helpful, they are intended only as guides. Annotated works are not official; they are not accepted by courts as definitive statements of the law.

Common law criminal definitions

Recall that earlier we provided the following common law definition of burglary: "breaking and entering the dwelling house of another in the nighttime with intent to commit a felony therein." Now that we have discussed some of the most salient characteristics of the common law heritage, we can consider some of the peculiarities of this definition of burglary. What is even more important, we can also analyze the effects such a definition has on modern criminal law.

The common law definition of burglary was very limited. Key elements involved the attendant circumstances of nighttime and a dwelling house (which is different from a place of business or a car). Most of the common law definitions were defined very narrowly because conviction carried severe punishment—typically the death penalty. In this way, the courts sought to ease the severity of punishment by carefully restricting criminal definitions. But such constricted definitions of crime require reexamination as changes in society occur. English judges were called upon to interpret the meaning of each of the six elements of the crime of burglary, and through the years the words took on different meanings.

> It is revolting to have no better reason for a rule of law than that it was so laid down in the times of Henry IV. It is still more revolting if the grounds upon which it was laid down have vanished long since, and the rule simply persists from blind imitation of the past.
>
> Justice Oliver Wendell Holmes, in an 1897 address, reprinted in *Collected Legal Papers* (Boston: A. Harcourt, 1920), p. 187.

Consider the meaning of *breaking*. Obviously a door splintered by a hammer constitutes breaking, but does breaking always necessitate physical force? Eventually the courts expanded the legal meaning of breaking beyond the seemingly common-sense requirement of physical force. Thus most courts ruled that pushing open a door already slightly ajar constituted breaking. The word *entering* presented similar problems. Again the law seems to envision a person walking into the house through the splintered door. But how much of the person must enter? The whole person or just an arm? The courts decided that even the slightest entry was sufficient. The courts eventually moved the legal definition further beyond our commonsensical notions by holding that the accused need not enter at all. Pushing a pole through a window also constituted entry, and if the accused employed an assistant (child, trained dog, or what have you) to do the actual entering, the accused was still deemed to have entered.

We could consider the other four elements of the common law crime of burglary, but by now the major points should be clear: the legal meanings of the words are not necessarily as clear as they first appear. New problems require rethinking old legal concepts. Sometimes these applications extend the meaning of the words far beyond what might have initially been envisioned. It is important to study the historical background because in many states laws on burglary (and most other crimes as well) are based on attempts to solve some of the problems raised by the common law definitions.

Although initially the common law courts defined criminal offenses, this power to create and define criminal conduct gradually shifted from the courts to the legislature. Early in the nineteenth century legislators began to enact criminal statutes to cover gaps in court definitions of specific crimes rather than wait for the courts to cure the problem. By the beginning of the twentieth century, this shift was completed; most state legislators had enacted comprehensive criminal codes to replace the uncodified definitions produced by the courts. Although a majority of states still allow courts to define common law crimes in the absence of a state statute, this power is a very restricted one and seldom used. Yet these statutory criminal offenses have been greatly influenced by the original common law definitions. Not only do the legislatively enacted criminal codes reflect the basic principles found in the common law definitions (*mens rea*, *actus reus*, and so on), but they often adopted the same words and phrases initially developed by the judges.

The Michigan burglary statute provides a convenient illustration of a legislatively enacted statute derived from judge-created criminal definitions:

750.110 Breaking and Entering

Sec. 110. Any person who shall break and enter with intent to commit any felony, or any larceny therein, any tent, hotel, office, store, shop, warehouse, barn, granary, factory or other building, structure, boat or ship, railroad car or any private apartment in any of such buildings or any unoccupied dwelling house, shall be guilty of a felony punishable by imprisonment in the state prison for not more than 10 years. Any person who breaks and enters any occupied dwelling house, with intent to commit any felony or larceny therein, shall be guilty of a felony punishable by imprisonment in the state prison for not more than 15 years. For the purpose of this section "any occupied dwelling house" includes one that does not require the physical presence of an occupant at the time of the breaking and entering but one which is habitually used as a place of abode.

A quick scanning of this definition of breaking and entering highlights many of the elements of burglary at the common law—breaking, entering, dwelling house, for example, have been retained. But there are some important differences. Note, for example, that nighttime is no longer included in the definition. Further, it is immediately obvious that the original common law definition—which took only a line and a half—has now been expanded into eleven lines. The added phrases are attempts to adapt the law to modern conditions and at the same time avoid some of the tortuous definitions the courts had been forced to provide.

That the Michigan law describes in great detail the meaning of an occupied dwelling clearly indicates that the legislature was trying to adapt the law to problems not present in medieval England. But even though the courts no longer create and define criminal conduct, they still play a role. It is still the responsibility of the appellate courts to clarify the meaning of the legislative words. Similarly, as new problems appear, the courts are often forced to interpret the old law in light of the new problems.

The sometimes crazy quilt pattern of criminal laws

crazy quilt pattern

Under California law, breaking into the glove compartment of a car is punishable by a maximum sentence of fifteen years of imprisonment; stealing the entire car is punishable by a maximum sentence of ten years. In Colorado, a defendant convicted of stealing a dog faces a maximum sentence of ten years; if the same defendant killed the dog, the maximum punishment is six months. These are just two examples cited by Marvin Frankel (a former U.S. district court judge particularly interested in sentencing disparities) of what he called the sometimes *crazy quilt pattern* of state criminal statutes. Not all criminal statutes are as obsolete or as inconsistent as these examples might suggest, but they do draw our attention to the fact that many states lack a consistent set of criminal definitions and penalties.

Since each state last revised its criminal code, changes have occurred piecemeal. As specific deficiencies in the law became apparent or new events intruded that could not be easily accommodated under existing provisions, individual changes designed to cure isolated problems were voted into law. Most changes in the criminal code involve alterations in statutory definitions, shifts in the classification of crimes from misdemeanor to felony (or vice versa), or adjustments in allowable punishments (Jacob:18). Because such changes are usually perceived as technical ones, they are of interest only to the professionals involved with law enforcement—judges, lawyers, district attorneys, and so on.

Changes in the criminal law are also prompted by public concern over crime. Increases in crime invariably produce calls in the legislature for corresponding increases in prison penalties. A rash of one type of crime—armed robberies or rapes are typical examples—results in legislative activity. The emergence of new forms of deviance—for example, glue sniffing and LSD use—is a prime illustration of events that attract legislative attention in the form of new prohibitions.

Another stimulus for legislative alterations in the criminal code is court decisions. Conflicting court interpretations often prompt legislative attempts to clarify conflicting court standards. Similarly, when a court declares a law unconstitutional, the legislature may pass a new law during the next session trying to remedy the deficiencies. After the U.S. Supreme Court's decision in *Gregg v. Georgia* (1976) upholding the Georgia death penalty law but striking down other state laws, a number of states drafted new laws attempting to reimpose capital punishment within the dictates of the Court's ruling. Court decisions invalidating laws, however, may draw no response; legislatures might not try to resurrect a law struck down by the courts (Wasby). Some laws struck down by the courts still remain technically on the books—unrepealed—a reminder that in a common law country the law is uncodified.

Whatever the source or cause of the piecemeal changes, the end product is a set of criminal laws with obsolete prohibitions and inconsistent penalties. Until recently, marijuana smoking was legally a more serious offense than using LSD (despite medical evidence clearly establishing LSD as a greater danger to health). The point is that no one set out to create such inconsistencies; they just happened. That changes in one section of the law may be inconsistent with another section of the law is not always immediately obvious. Recent legislative responses to armed robbery bring into focus the inconsistencies resulting from the historical accumulation of criminal prohibitions. As armed robberies increased, legislatures responded by increasing the penalty. Sometimes the unintentional result was that armed robbery was punished more severely than even murder. In practice, of course, judges and prosecutors treat murder as more serious than armed robbery.

Revising the criminal law

Why in a nation that prides itself on providing equal protection under the law is the criminal law so inconsistent and perhaps even unequal? The answer lies in the legislative process. Contemporary definitions of crime are provided by the legislatures, not the courts. How and why legislatures define criminal activity and specify a punishment has major implications for the criminal courts.

Criminal codes are historical accumulations of legislative prohibitions. The base point is the last comprehensive criminal code revision. Although a few states have enacted a comprehensive revised criminal statute fairly recently—Illinois (1962), for example—in most states there has been no systematic reexamination of the criminal law for decades. Louisiana's last comprehensive revision was 1940. In some states the basic criminal provisions date to the nineteenth century.

One impediment to modernizing the criminal code is that the patchwork of criminal law is occasionally useful. After all, the criminal law really amounts to an arsenal of weapons that can be marshaled against those viewed as deviants (Arnold:27). Sometimes ancient criminal prohibitions can be resurrected to prosecute notorious lawbreakers. This method has been aptly termed the "Al Capone theory of law making" (Newman:65). Al Capone, the notorious Chicago gangster leader, was never successfully prosecuted for his bootlegging, gambling, or prostitution activities. Instead he was convicted of income tax violation.

A more serious impediment to criminal code revision is the very nature of the legislative process. Legislative bodies approach problem solving as virtually all other organizations do—incrementally. Organizations do not review all possible options each year. Instead they adopt the outlines of what has occurred in the past (budgets, structures, and the like) and devote themselves to the most pressing problems. In addition to this built-in inertia against taking a comprehensive look at a problem, there is an additional consideration: few political benefits accrue to politician-legislators who devote their time to technical matters such as code revisions. Politically, then, legislative revision of the criminal code is one of those technical, mundane issues that represents few political advantages. Indeed, revising it can present major political liabilities. To be effective, the revision must be comprehensive—not only to accomplish its intended task but also to offer enough compromise to the clashing views so the law can be passed. On the other hand, in being comprehensive such bills often offend many political interests. Piecemeal changes in the criminal law narrow controversy since only individual items are presented for debate. Comprehensive change guarantees a divisive controversy encompassing all the controversial issues.

Consequences for the criminal court

The substantive criminal code constitutes the basic source of authority for law enforcement agencies. As a result, the nature of the criminal code has a profound effect on how law enforcement agencies function (but obviously does not account for all such activity). Sir Robert Peel, called the Father of the English Police, recognized this early in the nineteenth century (Skolnick:2). Before introducing a new police system, he first reformed the criminal law. Prior to Peel's reforms, even minor offenses carried the death penalty. In the latter part of the twentieth century, the National Advisory Commission on Criminal Justice Standards and Goals reached the same conclusion, arguing that substantive criminal law revision "is a necessary concomitant to modernization of the criminal justice system" (Task Force on the Administration of Justice:173). What constitutes a crime (as well as what does not) has major consequences for how the criminal courts dispense justice.

Law and plea bargaining

plea bargaining

The way crimes are defined has an important bearing on the entire administration of criminal justice. The next chapter will consider some of the specific ways that the criminal law produces discretion. At this point, though, we need to examine one specific aspect of discretion: *plea bargaining*. For how crimes are defined, particularly the numerous differences in degrees of seriousness, makes the criminal courts ripe for plea bargaining. Negotiating pleas is bound to emerge when the legislatively specified penalties are viewed by the law appliers—the judges, prosecutors, and defense attorneys—as not applicable to the defendants they see before them. Furthermore, the categories provide the vehicle for plea bargaining aimed at reducing the possible severity for a given offense. In at least one state, assault and battery involves five degrees (categories). Although the law must attempt to differentiate between, say, a fist thrown in anger from a deliberate gunshot wound that leaves its victim permanently paralyzed, too many different degrees of seriousness invite pleas to less serious offenses.

Another form of plea bargaining is count bargaining, in which the defendant pleads guilty to only some of the counts (charges) in the indictment, and the others are dismissed. Realistically, defendants often face the same penalty whether they plead to just one or all counts. Such bargaining is particularly common in federal district courts because the federal criminal law is ideally suited for multicount indictments. In short, such multicount possibilities are the facilitators of count bargaining.

It should be obvious that the courts must apply the law as they find it. The corollary is that the courts often must rectify inconsistencies in that law. Disparities in possible sentences as provided in state statutes require the judges, prosecutors, and defense attorneys to arrive at a workable penalty structure. Otherwise society would be outraged if serious crimes were punished the same as minor ones, even though the law technically allowed both categories of offenses to be treated the same.

Language of the law

Americans pride themselves on living in a law-abiding nation. Our system takes seriously the notion that we are a society of laws, not of men. At the same time, though, Americans remain somewhat mystified by the law. While in general the law is regarded with great respect, in particular applications of the law Americans are often less satisfied. The most common complaint is that the law is too technical. The image of the "Philadelphia lawyer" (a reference to slyness and trickery) symbolizes to many people a legal system in which the technicalities of the law stand in the way of proper conclusions. The public perceives that the criminal law is unduly technical. When a judge suppresses evidence (drugs, for example), the newspapers often report that the refusal to admit the drugs was based on a "technicality."

It is important to realize that the law must be technical; it must communicate precisely. In our everyday lives, we are able to communicate with our friends by using ambiguous terms because the people we communicate with have a similar reference point; we know what they mean. But we have all experienced situations in which disagreement with our friends, colleagues, spouses, or lovers—and even our college professors—arose because of verbal misunderstandings. Only too late did we realize that we either did not say exactly what we meant, or we used an ambiguous term; we meant one thing but they thought we meant another. The law seeks to avoid such ambiguities. Recall that the simple definition of burglary provided by the common law judges required amplification and clarification as situations changed. The meanings of *breaking, entering,* and *at night* required greater precision than we normally need in our ordinary conversations. Viewed from this vantage point, the law is technical because it must attempt to be unambiguous.

language of the law

Yet another reason that laymen are mystified by the *language of the law* relates not to the attempt of the law to be precise but to a corollary problem: the law not being precise. We often turn to the law for answers to problems. In a number of situations the law is able to provide answers (for example, a competent lawyer is able to draft a will to meet the needs of the ordinary citizen). In developing areas of the law, however, the law is not settled. Not only does it lack precision when trying to grapple with emerging problems, at times statutes are drafted and court opinions written that contain ambiguities. The people who staff the legal system are only human. State legislators, pushed by the impending end of the session, pass hastily drafted legislation. The ambiguities appear only later. At other times legislators deliberately author ambiguous statements in order to compromise and appear to give each side half a loaf. This deliberate use of ambiguous language is often done with a conscious effort of letting the courts resolve the problem later. Thus, while laymen view the law as providing precision, legal professionals are likely to stress its ambiguity (Edelman:39).

> To a considerable degree, the legislature becomes an agency of harshness and the courts become agencies for protecting citizens from this harshness. The net effect between the legislature and the courthouse is a rather steady increase in statutory severity for certain crimes. Such legislative action follows an established pattern:

Step I. Laws calling for severe punishments are passed by legislatures on the assumption that fear of great pain will terrorize the citizenry into conformity.

Step II. Criminal justice personnel soften these severe penalties for most offenders (a) in the interests of justice, (b) in the interests of bureaucracy, and (c) in the interests of gaining acquiescence.

Step III. The few defendants who then insist on a trial and are found guilty, or who in other ways refuse to cooperate, are punished more severely than those who acquiesce.

Step IV. Legislatures, noting that most criminals by acquiescing avoid "the punishment prescribed by law," (a) increase the prescribed punishments and (b) try to limit the range of discretionary decision making used to soften the harsh penalties.

Step V. The more severe punishments introduced in the preceding step are again softened for most offenders, as in Step II, with the result that the defendants not acquiescing are punished even more severely than they were at Step III.

Step VI. The severity-softening-severity process is repeated. Several social trends suggest that it is legislators rather than court personnel who are out of step with the times.

From pages 95, 157, and 161 of *Justice by Consent: Plea Bargains in the American Courthouse*, by Arthur Rosett and Donald R. Cressey. Copyright © 1976 by J. B. Lippincott Company. By permission of Harper & Row, Publishers, Inc.

Conclusion

There is a wide range of actions that we as individuals or as a society disapprove of, yet only some of these actions have been labeled criminal. Actions declared to constitute public wrongs (as distinct from personal wrongs) and labeled by a law, along with a penalty for violation, are legally criminal offenses. Although murder, robbery, and rape are defined as criminal in virtually every society, beyond these basics, official definitions of criminal conduct vary. Gambling, for example, is illegal in most states but not in Nevada. What activity should be labeled criminal is the source of constant political discussion. Actions viewed as bad in the past may no longer be considered such. As society changes, so do public perceptions of public wrongs, and pressures develop to add more activities to the list of officially proscribed ones. Through all of this change, we must not lose sight of the essential fact that law is an integral part of society. Law is not imposed upon society; rather it reflects the sociology, economy, history, and politics of society. Law was created to help society, not the other way around.

For discussion

1. How does the burglary statute of your state differ from the statutes reprinted in this chapter? Does your statute resemble the common law statute or the revised statute?

2. State statutes typically give the date on which they were enacted. Compare these dates for a number of crimes and think about the following questions. Has your state criminal code been significantly rewritten in the last ten years? Are there any patterns of particular crimes (theft, for example) that periodically have been rewritten (perhaps to adjust for inflation)? Are any statutes out of date? Do you think the state statutes need to be rewritten?

3. State legislatures usually meet every other year (although some meet yearly). Look at the record of the last full legislative session to see what changes in the criminal code were proposed, by what groups, and which ones were enacted. Did any other proposed changes generate much public debate? Did any of these proposed changes appear to be merely symbolic efforts by legislators unlikely to change anything?

4. Each year the Federal Bureau of Investigation publishes the *Uniform Crime Reports*, available in most libraries. The most serious crimes are referred to as type I offenses and include murder and nonnegligent manslaughter, aggravated assault, forcible rape, robbery, burglary, larceny, and auto theft. Compare your state's definition of these offenses with the definitions used in the *Uniform Crime Reports*. What serious crime under the *Uniform Crime Reports* fails to meet statutory requirements in your state?

   You may also wish to talk to the official in the police department who regularly prepares their annual crime report about the problems of contrasting definitions of offenses such as burglary. Does the local police department keep two sets of figures? (They probably should.)

   A discussion with a local prosecutor about these contrasting definitions might produce some interesting insights into problems of police departments enforcing the FBI definitions, not the state criminal code.

5. Divide the members of the class into teams. Assign each team to interview a key member of the criminal justice community—judge, prosecutor, defense attorney, police official, or beat cop—on problems they may see in the state's current criminal code. Do these officials perceive any major gaps in the criminal code— that is, acts that cannot now be punished but should be? Are there any major inconsistencies in the code? Do they think the state needs a comprehensive revision of the state penal code along the lines suggested by the National Advisory Commission? (If you go to school in a state that has revised its criminal code in the last few years, you can ask these people how the new code has worked out in practice.) Do not be surprised if the people interviewed do not agree. You may also consider interviewing some representatives in the community that are interested in the criminal law—American Civil Liberties Union, Catholic church, good-government groups such as the League of Women Voters.

References

Arnold, Thurman, "Law Enforcement." In George Cole, ed., *Criminal Justice: Law and Politics*. North Scituate, Mass.: Duxbury Press, 1972.

Edelman, Murray. *Symbolic Uses of Politics*. Chicago: University of Illinois Press, 1964.

Gardner, Thomas, and Victor Manian. *Criminal Law: Principles, Cases and Readings*, 4th ed. St. Paul, Minn.: West Publishing, 1980.

Illinois Revised Statutes, 1981.

Jacob, Herbert. *Urban Justice: Law and Order in American Cities.* Englewood Cliffs, N.J.: Prentice-Hall, 1973.

National Advisory Commission on Criminal Justice Standards and Goals. *Courts.* Washington, D.C.: Government Printing Office, 1973.

Newman, Donald J. *Introduction to Criminal Justice.* Philadelphia: J. B. Lippincott, 1975.

Quinney, Richard. *Criminology: Analysis and Critique of Crime in America.* Boston: Little, Brown, 1975.

Skolnick, Jerome H. *Justice Without Trial.* New York: John Wiley, 1966.

Task Force on the Administration of Justice. *Task Force Reports: the Courts.* President's Commission on Law Enforcement and the Administration of Justice. Washington, D.C.: Government Printing Office, 1967.

Wasby, Stephen L. *The Impact of the United States Supreme Court.* Homewood, Ill.: Dorsey Press, 1970.

For further reading

Abraham, Henry. *The Judicial Process,* 4th ed. New York: Oxford University Press, 1980.

Gusfield, Joseph. *Symbolic Crusade: Status Politics and the American Temperance Movement.* Urbana: University of Illinois Press, 1963.

LaFave, Wayne, and Austin Scott. *Criminal Law.* St. Paul, Minn.: West Publishing, 1972.

Statsky, William. *Legal Research Writing and Analysis: Some Starting Points.* St. Paul, Minn.: West Publishing, 1974.

2

The Legal Actors

The law is not self-executing. Prosecutors, judges, and defense attorneys must exercise discretion. What types of people are recruited to these positions, the nature of the work they perform, and the pressures they must deal with are the core issues of the four chapters of part 2.

Chapter 5 analyzes the dynamics of courthouse justice with particular emphasis on how these separate actors work together as a group.

Chapter 6 discusses why the prosecutor is the most important member of the courtroom work group, for the discretionary powers of the office structure virtually all of the decisions of the criminal courthouse.

Chapter 7 considers the role of the judge. Of prime concern is how the judge shapes and in turn is shaped by the courtroom work group.

The subject of chapter 8 is the defense attorney. The nature of the attorney's clientele, the lack of monetary rewards, and the other members of the courtroom work group are three of the primary factors that explain why most defense attorneys act nothing like the famous television figure of Perry Mason.

CHAPTER 5

The Dynamics of Courthouse Justice

For the last decade or so, a number of social scientists and a handful of lawyers and law professors have been exploring the dynamics of the criminal courts. They have documented that the administration of justice bears only a slight relationship to the popular picture of American criminal justice: that the guilt or innocence of a defendant is determined at trial after a hard-fought contest. A more realistic assessment portrays a system in which guilt is largely assumed, and most defendants plead guilty after a series of mostly cooperative negotiations.

Realizing that law on the books is not the same as law in action is only the beginning. The crucial step is trying to understand and explain why the law as practiced differs from the seeming intent of the formal rules.

This chapter analyzes three major explanations for why the work of the courts differs so greatly from the textbook image of court combat and trials. "Too many cases" is the most commonly advanced reason, and it contains certain kernels of truth. On the other hand, this justification masks important considerations, not the least of which is the fact that most criminal cases are routine. The second explanation, discretion, begins to grapple with the day-to-day realities of courthouse dynamics. The third is the courtroom work group, the complex network of interaction between the courthouse regulars.

Assembly line justice and excessive caseloads

excessive caseloads

The most commonly advanced reason for why the criminal courts do not administer justice according to the textbook image is *excessive caseloads*. This orthodox explanation is advanced by the President's Commission on Law Enforcement and Administration of Justice:

> The crux of the problem is that there is a great disparity between the number of cases and the number of judges.
>
> It is not only judges who are in short supply. There are not enough prosecutors, defense counsel, and probation officers even in those courts where some of them are available. The deluge of cases is reflected in every aspect of the courts' work, from overcrowded corridors and courtrooms to the long calendars that do not allow more than cursory consideration of individual cases. [p. 31]

Strengths of the explanation

The caseload explanation has the advantage of bringing out some important dimensions of these judicial bodies. No one disputes that the volume of cases is large and that within most courts, particularly in large urban areas, there are pressures to move cases quickly. In direct and indirect ways, officials view one of their tasks as keeping the docket current; thus they seldom have much time to spend on any one case.

specialization

This explanation also focuses attention on *specialization*. In devising procedures for handling these large caseloads, court officials have usually opted for the technique of mass society: specialization. Just as cars are built in a number of steps with each worker responsible for a small part of the overall product, workers in the criminal court specialize. This is most readily seen in the operations of big city public defenders. One assistant will conduct the initial interview with defendants, another will

---

IN THE NEWS: PLEA BARGAINING CALLED NECESSARY EVIL

. . . Plea bargaining has been criticized for shortchanging society. Critics argue it is lenient. Prosecutors say it is justice. Almost everybody admits that at this time it is a necessary evil that society would be hard put to do without.

Prosecutors say that because of the volume of cases, there is no way every defendant could have a trial unless there were 50 criminal courts. There are six in Shelby County.

If defendants formed a union, went on strike against plea bargaining, and demanded a trial in every case, the system would collapse, one prosecutor said.

"We've got to have plea bargaining—it's a matter of necessity," said Criminal Court Judge William H.

Williams. He had just finished disposing of about 60 cases in one week.

The average trial takes 2½ days, court records show. If Williams had been in trial, he would have disposed of 2 cases instead of 60.

The system, then, fosters few trials in comparison to the number of cases handled . . .

But U.S. Supreme Court Chief Justice Warren Burger has called plea bargaining "an essential component of the administration of justice. Properly administered, it is to be encouraged."

John Triplett, (Memphis, Tenn.) *Commercial Appeal*, January 27, 1975.

represent them at the initial appearance, still another will argue pretrial motions, and yet another assistant will conduct the plea negotiations and/or the trial. Prosecutors' offices are similarly divided into such specializations, which means that no single attorney follows a case from start to finish. The problem is that specific cases and defendants may not receive the individual attention they deserve.

group processing

The final strength of the case overload explanation is that it underscores the fact that defendants accused of different and unrelated crimes are often processed in groups rather than individually. During initial appearances, defendants are often advised of their rights in one large group. This *group processing* at times even extends to the final plea. Defendants are also questioned in groups of various sizes about their desire to plead guilty. Moreover, court officials categorize defendants into easily identifiable classes on the basis of the nature of the crime and the background of the defendant. Thus, around courthouses, one often hears phrases like "he's just a harmless drunk" or "here's another peeping Tom." In turn, sentences are fixed on the basis of the defendant's membership in a given class rather than detailed individual attention.

Weakness of the explanation

The excessive caseload explanation draws our attention to some important aspects of the criminal courts, but it also obscures as many aspects of the courts as it highlights. First of all, the stress is usually placed on the fact that these excessive caseloads are a modern problem; there are repeated references to the "rise" of plea bargaining, the "decline" of the trial, and the "twilight" of the adversary system. In fact, however, this position distorts history; for decades the courts have been characterized by too many cases. Even more important, plea bargaining predates any of the modern problems of the courts. Recent historical research reveals that plea bargaining "began to appear during the early or mid-nineteenth century, and became institutionalized as a standard feature of American urban criminal courts in the last of the nineteenth century" (Haller:273). The explanation of too many cases stemming from the growth of big cities and big city problems ignores the historical evidence.

routine adminis- tration

The excess caseload explanation detracts attention from an important consideration: most criminal cases are routine. They represent no disputed questions of law or fact. This observation has been documented in a study of litigation in two California counties from 1890 to 1970 (Friedman and Percival). The authors argued that dispute settlement is the function most clearly associated with the courts. Yet in most civil cases the courts were not called on to resolve any actual dispute; they merely provided a legal and formal authorization to a private settlement. The authors concluded that the courts engaged in *routine administration*: "A matter is *routine* when a court has no disputed question of law or fact to decide. Routine administration means the processing or approving of undisputed matters" (p. 267). Civil cases are negotiated in a manner very similar to plea bargaining in criminal cases, for essentially the same reason. The courts are confronted with a steady stream of routine cases in which the only major question is the sentence to be imposed.

Excess caseloads reconsidered

The effect of heavy caseloads is part of the conventional wisdom surrounding the operations of criminal courts. Unfortunately, while it is often stated and restated, very little effort has been devoted to investigating its effects. Malcolm Feeley's study of two Connecticut courts is particularly important; it is the first research to concentrate on this problem.

Feeley compared two Connecticut courts, one with a heavy caseload, one with a light one. Although he expected that there would be major differences in how cases were processed and in the substance of justice handed out, the results indicated that the courts were remarkably similar. Neither court had many trials. In neither did the defense attorneys engage in pitched battle. Both courts set bail in roughly the same amounts and imposed roughly similar sentences. Each court spent the same amount of time per case, moving through its business "rapidly and mechanically." The only major difference was that the busier court was in session longer than the court with fewer cases.

Another study, this time of Chicago, concluded that "variations in caseloads did not affect the guilty plea decision, the sentence in guilty plea cases, or the decision to pursue a case to trial" (Nardulli). Thus, recent research indicates that trying to understand the criminal courts on the basis of excessive caseloads is inadequate because such an explanation omits too many important considerations.

Discretion

discretion

Discretion lies at the heart of the criminal justice process. Indeed, from the time a crime is committed until after sentence is imposed on the guilty, *discretion* is part of all the key decisions. Often the victim decides not to report the crime to the police. Even if the crime is known to the police, they may decide not to seek out the offender; or, if the offender is known, they may decide not to make an arrest. After arrest the prosecutor may decide not to prosecute. Once charges have been filed, a magistrate must make a decision about the amount of bail, and whether there is sufficient probable cause to hold the defendant for the grand jury. In turn, grand juries have discretion over indictments, trial juries over conviction, and the judge over sentencing. Even after sentencing, prison officials exercise discretion in awarding "good time" (reducing the sentence for good behavior), and pardon and parole boards must decide whether to release on parole and/or grant a pardon.

Clearly, discretion pervades the criminal justice process. Opinion is divided over whether such discretion is proper in a system premised on the equal application of the law. To some it can lead to tyranny and injustice. To others it is not only necessary but desirable in preventing injustices. In turn, many reform efforts are directed at reducing or at least structuring discretion.

Low visibility

The existence and pervasiveness of discretion does not differentiate the courts from other organizations (for example, insurance executives must decide what types of claims are valid and establish procedures for processing them). What is distinctive

---

CLOSE-UP: STRUCTURING DISCRETION

One thread common to many of the standards is an attempt to utilize and improve the informal, essentially administrative, processes that affect the flow of most criminal cases through the court system. The thrust of the standards and recommendations is the regularization of these processes and the recognition of them as appropriate aspects of the criminal justice system.

Only a small percentage of cases that go through all or part of the court process involves the full litigation to which much of the formal law addresses itself and which is embodied in the traditional image of the criminal trial. . . .

It is the view of the Commission that limited use of the full trial procedure is not only inevitable but desirable. Not all cases present issues best solved by traditional full-scale litigation, and such litigation often involves costs to the public and the defendant—both in terms of financial outlay and emotional strain—that are best avoided if possible. The Commission also recognizes, however, that extensive use of informal processes creates a dual danger.

National Advisory Commission on Criminal Justice Standards and Goals, *Report on Courts* (Washington, D.C.: Government Printing Office, 1973), pp. 2–3.

---

about the criminal court process is not the existence of discretion but where that discretion is located.

In most organizations discretion increases as one moves up the administrative ladder; the lowest-ranking members perform routine tasks under fairly close supervision, which provides a relatively high degree of quality control. In the criminal justice system, however, discretion is exercised most frequently by the lowest members of the administrative hierarchy. Police officers, for example, have a great deal of discretion in deciding whether to arrest. Similarly, assistant district attorneys who decide whether prosecution is in order are typically the newest, least experienced members of the office.

low visibility

This aspect of the criminal court process is of special concern because it is discretion marked by *low visibility*. Since many of the key decisions are not directly observable, it is often difficult to determine what decisions are being made and on what basis they are made. In short, there is relatively little administrative monitoring, which can lead to inconsistencies. For example, one assistant district attorney might routinely refuse to prosecute for a given offense (say possession of small amounts of marijuana), while another will always file such charges. Such differences are also found in sentences judges impose. As a result of such policy inconsistencies, it is common for police officers to shop around for a prosecutor favorable to their view or for a defense attorney to "judge shop" in hopes of getting a lenient sentence for the client.

The basis of discretion

Discretion flows from the substantive and procedural law, and it is also the product of court officials' attempts to achieve the important goal of seeing that justice is done.

Discretion stems in part from the lack of a clear and coherent criminal law. This point is made by Wayne LaFave and Austin Scott in their widely used law school textbook, *Criminal Law*.

> It is important to note that in large measure such discretion is exercised because of the scope and state of the substantive criminal law. Because no legislature has succeeded in formulating a substantive criminal code which clearly encompasses all conduct intended to be made criminal and which clearly excludes all other conduct, the exercise of discretion in interpreting the legislative mandate is necessary. In part the problem is the result of poor draftmanship and a failure to revise the criminal law to eliminate obsolete provisions. [pp. 18–19]

Because the criminal codes of the various states often contain contradictory prohibitions, judges, prosecutors, defense attorneys, and police officers must exercise discretion to rectify these problems. Moreover, the criminal law must be broad and general. Even carefully drafted statutes cannot anticipate every situation that might arise. For example, a law might be broadly written to ensure that some offenders that the legislature wishes to punish cannot escape through a loophole. But it is left to the criminal court community to remove those who fall under the law's broad mandate but the legislature meant to exclude (LaFave and Scott:19).

Similarly, in determining what penalties should be applied to a given criminal offense, legislators invariably set a penalty for the most heinous offender imaginable (Newman:62). Yet the vast majority of violators fall far short of being that bad. In context, events are less serious than the abstractions of the criminal law envision (Feeley). As a consequence courts must shape the penalties to the violators before them, not to the theoretical villains imagined when the penalty was enacted.

Some discretion, therefore, is the product of either ambiguous laws, laws that are broad and general, or laws that create so many prohibitions that priorities have to be assigned. In this sense the law provides too many guidelines. At other times discretion is the product of the failure of the law to provide any workable guidelines at all. On many important matters—most notably criteria for setting bail, standards for sentencing, and yardsticks for filing criminal charges—the appellate courts and legislative bodies are largely silent. In these areas local court officials have been left to develop their own guidelines.

Finally, discretion results from attempts by court officials to fulfill some very important, but at the same time ill-defined, goals of individualizing justice and seeing that justice is done. This is most graphically apparent during sentencing.

Legislative definitions of serious offenses are sometimes at odds with the court's definition of serious and threatening violations. For example, in attempting to combat the perceived increase in drug usage and crime related to drug usage, several states have increased the penalties upon conviction by specifying mandatory life imprisonment for a drug sale or mandating no parole. Criminal District Court Judge Jerome Winsberg of Orleans Parish (New Orleans) labels his state laws as having "no relationship to reality" (*Times-Picayune*, February 26, 1976). The drug sellers he sees in court are seldom the profiteering illegal businessmen envisioned by elected state legislators but usually junkies making small sales to maintain their habit. To compound the problem, the structure of current drug laws in Louisiana allows a defendant to plead guilty to a greater offense than charged and receive a lesser penalty.

The many faces of discretion

Although the pervasiveness of discretion is well accepted, what is not well accepted is any common meaning of the term. Political scientist George Cole provides a broad definition: "the authority to make decisions without reference to specific rules or facts, using instead one's own judgment" (Cole:477). In context this seems to be the way the term is most often used, for it implies decisions made on the basis of an actor's personal values. But at other times discretion takes on an even more inclusive meaning. Sociologist Donald Newman, for example, writes that discretion is "the authority to choose among alternative actions or of not acting at all" (Newman:479). This makes discretion synonymous with decision making. Some authors seem to adopt this definition when speaking of discretion, but such a view is not particularly helpful because it maintains that all decisions are discretionary. The danger is that discretion becomes merely a residual category for lumping together everything an author cannot otherwise explain. It is important, therefore, to recognize that there are three major subcomponents of discretion: legal judgment, policy priorities, and personal philosophies.

> Engraved in stone on the Department of Justice Building in Washington, on the Pennsylvania Avenue side where swarms of bureaucrats and others pass by, are these five words: "Where law ends tyranny begins" (William Pitt).
>
> I think that in our system of government, where the law ends tyranny need not begin. Where law ends, discretion begins, and the exercise of discretion may mean either beneficence or tyranny, either justice or injustice, either reasonableness or arbitrariness.
>
> Kenneth Culp Davis, *Discretionary Justice: A Preliminary Inquiry* (Urbana: University of Illinois Press, 1971), p. 3.

legal judgments

Legal Judgment.   Many discretionary decisions in the criminal courts process are made on the basis of *legal judgments*. A typical example would be a prosecutor who refuses to file a criminal charge (even though the police have made an arrest) because of her legal judgment that there is insufficient evidence to prove all the elements of the offense. Whether this would be considered discretion by everyone is not clear, but it is clear that decisions made by lawyers and nonlawyers alike about the law are a key element in decision making.

In turn, some legal judgments stem from a prediction about the likely outcome of a case at a later stage in the proceedings. Consider another example involving a prosecutor's decision not to charge a defendant. The prosecutor may believe that the defendant did violate the law but that no jury would convict. In a barroom brawl, there might be no legal question that the defendant struck the victim but the prosecutor may believe that a jury would decide that the victim had provoked the assault and therefore acquit.

Policy Priorities.   Because criminal laws are so broad and general, there is a need for selective enforcement. We have all violated some law at some time. Essentially the supply of criminal illegality is almost infinite. Yet the resources devot-

policy priorities

ed to detecting wrongdoers and processing them through the courts (and later incarcerating them) are limited. Policy decisions must be made about priorities for enforcing the law. As a result, court officials employ a set of informal *policy priorities* in applying the law. Some prosecutors' offices, for example, have a house policy for prosecutions in minor theft or embezzlements. U.S. attorneys will not normally file embezzlement charges when the suspect is a young employee of the bank who stole small amounts and was fired when discovered. Prosecutors' policies on possession of small amounts of marijuana present similar issues. Overall, court officials devote more resources to prosecuting serious crimes like murder, rape, and armed robbery than more minor offenses.

personal philoso- phies

Personal Philosophies.   Some discretionary decisions obviously are a reflection of the decision makers' personal values and attitudes—their *personal philosophies.* Judges and prosecutors vary in what offenses they view as serious and deserving of a high priority. Burglaries are typically perceived as more threatening in small rural towns than they are in larger cities where burglary is a daily occurrence. Not only do judges, prosecutors, and others differ according to their ranking of serious crimes, they also vary according to their views on the purpose of the criminal law. Those who believe that the courts can deter crime (through heavy sentences, for example) will behave differently from those who discount the general role the courts can play in deterrence.

Occasionally commentators charge that court officials decide what actions to take on a whim (Cole:126). No doubt in a small proportion of cases whim does affect the ultimate decision, but to argue that the decisions in the court system are systematically influenced by such whims is clearly misplaced (Neubauer:119–123).

The courtroom work group

courtroom work group

courthouse regulars

A defendant approaching the bench is literally surrounded by a dozen official and unofficial court personnel. In addition to the three legal actors embodied in the adversary model—judge, prosecutor, and defense attorney—those in attendance also include a host of support personnel without whom the court could not operate: a clerk, a court reporter, a bailiff, a police officer, a family court liaison official, a matron, and an interpreter. (A bail bondsman may also be in attendance.) This is the *courtroom work group*—the officials who on a day-to-day basis decide which cases will be carried forward, which defendant will be released on bail, what guilty pleas will be accepted and, finally and most importantly, what sentence will be imposed on the guilty.

To even the most casual observer these courthouse regulars occupy a special status. They freely issue instructions (don't smoke, don't talk, don't read the newspaper) to the temporary visitors to the courthouse, though they smoke, talk, and read the newspaper themselves. The ordinary citizens—defendants, friends of defendants, victims, witnesses, and disinterested observers—sit on hard benches in the rear of the courtroom and may approach the bench through a gate dividing the courtroom only when specifically requested. The courthouse officials, on the other hand, enjoy easy access to the front part of the courtroom, freely passing the railing into the area near the judge's bench. The final indicator of the special status of the courthouse regulars is the nature of their casual conversations. Courtrooms are subject to numerous and unpredictable periods of inactivity; during these times, the courthouse regulars engage in casual conversations that clearly indicate that they know each other well. Observers expecting to view an adversarial battle are struck by the cordiality of the opponents engaging in casual conversations. Indeed, defense attorneys are much more likely to talk to their nominal adversary, the prosecutor, than to pass the time of day with their clients.

Since about the mid-1960s, a number of studies have attempted to assess the activities of these officials (Blumberg; Neubauer; Eisenstein and Jacob). They found a complex network of ongoing social relationships among judges, prosecutors, and defense attorneys who work together on a daily basis. The result is a level of cooperation not envisioned by the formal adversary model. Not all studies, however, are agreed upon the effects this cooperation has on the administration of justice. Some contend that the actors are so concerned with maintaining good relationships with the other courthouse regulars that they are not particularly interested in the justice meted out in individual cases. Nonetheless, these relationships are as important as they are complex. Given the complexity of this network we need some intellectual tools to guide our analysis. Toward this end James Eisenstein and Herbert Jacob have proposed that the best way to analyze the network of ongoing relationships among the courthouse regulars is to view the courts as work groups.

Work group formation

One of the major factors that differentiates modern societies from traditional ones is large formal organizations marked by numerous actors, whose duties are specialized, and where specific rules of conduct govern the behavior of these workers in their joint activity in pursuit of common interests. Certainly courts fall under this broad definition. But in certain ways the courts are also unique. The criminal courts are not a single organization but rather a collection of several separate institutions that gather in a common workplace: the courtroom. Whereas most large organizations—General Motors for example—consist of distinct divisions operating under a central leadership, the criminal courts consist of separate institutions but with no hierarchical system of control. There is no central authority. A judge cannot reward a clerk, a prosecutor, or a public defender who performs well. The courts are not a central organization. Each of the courthouse regulars is a representative of a sponsoring institution, which in various ways monitors their activities, hires them, fires them, and rewards them. In turn, these sponsoring institutions have many clients with whom they interact and on whom they are dependent for support.

Interaction. Every day the same group of courthouse regulars assembles in the same courtroom, sits or stands in the same places, and performs the same tasks that they performed the day before. The types of defendants and the types of crimes they are accused of committing remain constant too. Only the names of the victims, witnesses, and defendants are different. Thus, while defendants come and go, the judges, prosecutors, defense attorneys, clerks, bailiffs, and so on remain.

These representatives from separate and independent sponsoring institutions are drawn together by a common task: each must do something about a given case.

None of these actors can perform their tasks independently; they must work together. These interactions are critical because none of the courthouse regulars can make decisions independently; each must consider the reactions of others. This is most readily seen in the work of the defense attorney. In representing the client, the defense attorney must consider the type of plea agreement the prosecutor may offer, the sentencing tendencies of the judge, the likelihood of a jury verdict of guilty, as well as the possibility that the probation officer will recommend probation. Prosecutors and judges fall into a similar pattern.

Through working together on a daily basis, a limited set of personal ties develop. The word *limited* is used because some researchers have suggested that these ties are strong ones (judges play golf on the weekends with prosecutors or defense attorneys). Although in a few situations these ties are strong, they are hardly the major consideration. However, personal acquaintance does allow the participants to joke among themselves, particularly about difficult cases. More important, these personal interactions convey to each participant the pressures and problems faced by the other organizations.

mutual interdependence

Mutual Interdependence. Each member of the work group can achieve individual goals and accomplish separate tasks only through work group participation. The actors come to share common interests in disposing of cases. Hence cooperation—*mutual interdependence*—within the work group produces mutual benefits.

A judge who allows a backlog of cases to develop can expect to feel pressure from other judges or the chief judge to dispose of more cases. Assistant prosecutors are judged by their superiors not so much on how many cases they win but on how many they lose; the emphasis is on not losing by securing convictions. Defense attorneys face a more complicated set of incentives. Public defender organizations prefer to dispose of cases quickly because they have a limited number of attorneys to represent a large number of indigents. Private attorneys also need to move cases. Since most defendants are poor and can afford only a modest fee, private attorneys make an economic livelihood through representing a large number of clients. The fee in each case is insufficient to allow the expenditure of much time on any given case. There is a need for a high turnover. In short all participants receive benefits from disposing of cases with minimal effort.

The impact of courtroom work groups

The key to understanding the criminal court process lies in understanding how the representatives of separate sponsoring institutions, each with their own needs and pressures, end up cooperating on a range of matters. Toward this end, the impact of courtroom work groups can be divided into five categories: shared decision making, shared norms, socialization, sticks and carrots, and goal modification (Clynch and Neubauer).

informal
authority

Shared Decision Making.   In courtroom work groups, there are *informal patterns of authority* underlying the formal ones. For example, judges retain the legal authority to make the major decisions such as setting bail, adjudicating guilt (except if there is a jury trial), and imposing sentence, but they often rely on others: they may routinely follow the bail recommendations of the prosecutor, accept guilty plea agreements reached by defense and prosecution, or follow the recommendations of the probation officer. This does not mean that the judge is without power. These actors in turn are sensitive to what the judge might do. Bail recommendations and sentence recommendations are the product of a two-way communication process. Prosecutors (and defense attorneys) know that in past situations the judge set bail in X amount, so that is what they recommend in the current case.

These modifications of formal authority patterns are partially the result of control over information. Knowledge is power, and whoever controls the knowledge has a great deal of power. Overall, prosecutors know the most about a case, defense attorneys less, and judges even less. As a result the nominal subordinates of judges can influence their decisions by selective information flow.

These informal patterns of authority result in a shared decision-making process that apportions power and responsibility. Judges, prosecutors, defense attorneys, bail officials, and the like are aware that the decisions they must make can turn out to be wrong. A defendant who is released on bail may kill a police officer the next day. Since such dire results cannot be predicted ahead of time, the members of the courtroom work group share a sense that when one of their members looks bad, they all look bad. In our example, all the sponsoring institutions would face a great deal of public displeasure. Therefore it is highly functional for the members of the courtroom work group to diffuse power and responsibility. Decisions are made on a joint basis and if something later goes wrong, they have protected themselves by saying that everyone thought it was a good idea at the time.

shared
norms

Shared Norms.   The hallmark of work groups is regularity of behavior. This regularity is the product of *shared norms* about how each member should behave and the types of decisions that are desirable. The courthouse workers can make their common worksite a fractious and unpredictable place for carrying out their assigned tasks. Or, through cooperation, they can make it a predictable place to work. The greater the certainty, the less time and resources they must spend on each case. The shared norms that provide a structure and framework to what otherwise first appears to be an unstructured, almost chaotic process fall into three categories.

outsiders

The first shared norm involves shielding the work group from *outsiders.* The greatest uncertainty comes from outside forces that the members of the work group cannot control. For example, during a trial all participants are at the mercy of what witnesses will say. Since their testimony at times produces surprises, the work group finds that their participation produces uncertainty. Similarly jurors are an unknown quantity. The courthouse regulars as much as possible seek to avoid such sources of uncertainty by making decisions among themselves on the basis of factors they can control. Plea bargaining provides the clearest example of such an effort.

A second set of shared norms centers on standards of personal and professional conduct. Attorneys are expected to stick by their word and never deliberately mislead. They are also expected to minimize surprises (Eisenstein and Jacob:28). Although in the television show Perry Mason often called in an unknown witness to win his case dramatically, members of the work group view such activities as a violation of social norms because surprise adds uncertainty to their work environment. Members who violate these rules of personal and professional conduct can expect sanctions from the other members of the work group.

The third set of shared norms relates to policy standards. As we noted, most of the matters before the courts are routine. And although each case is unique in that no two events are exactly similar, most cases fall in a limited number of categories. Just as a child learns to sort various four-legged animals into distinct categories of dog, cat, cow, and so on, the members of the work group develop concepts about types of crime and types of criminals. One study of public defenders has aptly

normal
crime

labeled this phenomenon as the concept of the *normal crime* (Sudnow). The legal actors categorize crimes on the basis of the typical manner in which they are committed, the typical social characteristics of the defendants, the settings of the crimes, and the types of victims. Once a case has been placed into one of these categories, it is typically disposed of on the basis of a set pattern. Routinely in the community that Sudnow studied, child molesting cases were reduced to loitering charges, drunkenness to disturbing the peace, and burglary to petty theft. The existence of such agreed-upon categorizations allows the members of the work group to dispose fairly rapidly of the large number of routine cases that require their attention. These policy norms are one solution to the problems facing the courtroom work group. They form a common orientation consisting of rules, understandings, and customs that accommodate the differing demands of the sponsoring institutions. A group sense of justice is the result.

Though the interests of the courthouse regulars are formally at odds, in operation they come to share common interests. The shared norms channel and limit conflict, but by no means do they eliminate it. Members of the work group still disagree, for example, over whether a defendant fits into the normal crime category or over whether a proposed sentence is too light. Their shared norms establish boundaries for what behavior is expected and which issues are debatable.

There is a large universe of practices which, for lack of a better word, I shall call "pre-plea discussions" regarding the outcome of a case. A subset of these practices are the actual "plea bargains." But pre-plea discussions encompass a much larger range than plea bargaining, and are actually a more appropriate way of talking about what goes on in court these days. . . . On a three count forgery case, the defense attorney asks the D.A., "Can I have one count?" The D.A. says, "Yes, which one?" The defense attorney says "Count 2." And that's it. No bargain has been made. No promise made that counts 1 and 3 will be dismissed in exchange for the plea to count 2. *It's simply that everyone knows what the standard practice is.* Or here's another example. The defense attorney comes into court and asks the D.A., "What does Judge Hall give on bookmaking cases?" The D.A. asks if there are any priors [prior offenses]. The attorney says "no," and the D.A. says, "He usually gives $150 fine on the first offense." The attorney says, "Fine. We'll enter a plea to count one." Again no promise was made by anybody. *It's just that everybody knows what customarily will happen.* This is what I mean by the larger arena of pre-plea discussion.

> Quoted in Lynn Mather, ''Some Determinants of the Method of Case Disposition: Decision-Making by Public Defenders in Los Angeles,'' *Law and Society Review* 8 (Winter 1974):199.

Socialization.   Court work groups have needs quite apart from the legal mandate of adjudicating cases: they must preserve the ongoing system. A problem common to all organizations is the need to break in new members, a process *socialization* referred to as *socialization*. Through the socialization by a variety of persons, newcomers are taught not only the formal requirements of the job (how motions are filed and so on) but also the informal rules of behavior.

Newcomers learn not only from their peers but from other members of the social network. One veteran court aide put it this way:

> Most of the judges are pretty good—they rely on us. Sometimes you get a new judge who wants to do things his way. We have to break them in, train them. This court is very different. We have to break new judges in. It takes some of them some time to get adjusted to the way we do things. [Wiseman:99]

Given the rotation of judges through the various assignments, often the only official with some permanency is the clerk of court, the court official who keeps court records and files. In fact, in many jurisdictions the clerk serves as an informal adviser to the judge.

Sticks and Carrots.   To be effective, social norms must be enforceable. Efficient routines are threatened not only by new members but also at times by current members of the work group. A variety of rewards (carrots) are available as benefits *sanctions* to those who follow the rules. In turn, some *sanctions* (sticks) may be applied to those who do not. By far the more effective is the carrot, because it operates indirectly and is less disruptive. The impositions of sanctions can result in counter-sanctions being applied, with the result that the network is disrupted even further.

In discussing sticks and carrots, let us again concentrate on the defense attorneys. Defense attorneys who do not unnecessarily disrupt routines are eligible for several types of rewards. First, they receive greater information from prosecutors, who more often have the resources to conduct an independent investigation. Prosecutors may show the police reports to cooperative defense attorneys or may be more willing to negotiate a slightly lower-than-normal sentence. In return, defense attorneys are expected to avoid filing unnecessary motions, to be reasonably accommodating when the state needs more time to prepare, and to resist pushing too hard for sentence bargains.

As for sticks, a variety of sanctions are available for use against uncooperative defense attorneys. They may be allowed less access to case information, or the judge can keep them waiting. But mainly the clients of these attorneys are punished: they receive longer-than-normal penalties (Mileski:489). Ultimately, however, uncooperative members of the team are punished in some way. When asked what would happen if a prosecutor out of zeal or inexperience charged defendants with potential charges severe enough to discourage pleas of guilty, a judge replied as follows:

I would talk to him and try to teach him how I wanted him to conduct himself in my court. [And if that didn't work?] I often have occasion to see the district attorney—that is—on social occasions. If I am running the criminal department, he might ask me how things are going, and I'd suggest to him that the deputy he has in there isn't doing a very good job, and that I think he ought to be replaced. Usually, when I make such a judgment, the district attorney will go along with me. [Skolnick:57]

Goal Modification   It is impossible to assess court work groups properly without considering the overall *goal of justice* that they are expected to achieve. A wide variety of studies have shown that organizations—General Motors, the police, the Social Security Administration, the courts, and so forth—are greatly affected by the ultimate goals they are expected to produce. In some cases these overall goals are fairly precise: General Motors is expected to make a profit, which is a fairly well-understood yardstick of achieving a goal. But public bodies usually do not have such clear goals. Rather they have multiple, often conflicting, and typically hard-to-measure ones. This is the case with the criminal courts. The public, the press, the defendants, the legal community, and the courthouse regulars all expect the courts to "*do justice.*"

goal of justice

doing justice

This overall goal of doing justice produces a maze of difficulties for court officials. First, there is no agreement as to the meaning of justice. The courts are expected to do numerous things—respect individual liberties, protect the public, deter wrongdoers, punish the guilty, rehabilitate the transgressors. Indeed we often expect the courts to do all of these simultaneously, which is obviously impossible. Obvious disagreement exists over which of these is the most important goal. Embedded in the overall goals of the court is a built-in conflict over what the end product should be. Just as important, there is no ready way to evaluate whether justice is actually being done. Courthouse statistics—the number of cases processed, the number of convictions, the number of trials—are substituted as measures for doing justice. At the end of the month a supervisor need not ponder whether a subordinate achieved justice, she need only count how many cases were disposed of. The result is that the vague goals and complex needs of the organizations become hopelessly intermixed.

CLOSE-UP: JUSTICE BY CONSENT

In metropolitan courthouses, there is simply not enough time to give each defendant all of the attention he wants, and probably needs. Most urban public services suffer from this overload problem—schools, hospitals, welfare offices and building inspectors.

In practice, most cases are disposed of in cooperative agreements reaching a consensus on facts and, therefore, on appropriate punishment. The watchwords are accommodation and compromise, not adversary combat. Incidents of genuine adversariness are rare in most courthouses, principally because the courthouse subculture itself represents a negotiated compromise position. Courthouse controversy is softened by a system that quietly balances conflicting community interest which, if pushed too blatantly, would lead to combat. Then it becomes a breech of etiquette for a lawyer to take a stance so adversary that it disturbs the conditions of peaceful coexistence.

The overload, weak case and poker attitudes about plea bargaining all imply that the prosecutor's role is totally adversary and that calendar problems, backlog, caseload, time pressures and similar indices of the burden of overwork are the evil roots of the problem. But it is simply not true that in an ideal criminal justice system every guilty offender would receive the full statutory penalty for the gravest crime that could be charged against him, and that only the burden of overwork forestalls this idyllic state. The idea that overwork forces the prosecutor to grant concessions to defendants in exchange for a bluffed out guilty plea all but ignores the prosecutor's concern for adjusting penalties to individual crimes and criminals in the interest of justice. It portrays the prosecutor both as a weakling and as an inhuman and unjust automaton who has been programmed to obtain the severest possible punishment for as many criminals as possible. Sadly enough, this damning but highly distorted portrait of the prosecutor is often painted by prosecutors themselves. . . .

. . . In the real world, prosecutors are looking for justice rather than just for penitentiary time. They routinely grant so-called concessions to many of the lawyer's clients. They do so knowing full well that the attorney will not take up their time with a trial if they do not. "A defendant shouldn't be punished severely or treated unfairly just because he has a poor lawyer," one prosecutor said. "So we ignore the fact that this guy won't go to trial. We treat his clients just like those with good attorneys who might go to trial. Everybody might go to trial. That's not the problem. The problem is, is it worth it?" . . .

Attributing negotiated pleas to overwork is a political explanation of court practice. Voicing this explanation neutralizes important and powerful interest groups who say they want adversary procedures that would maximize the amount of punishment meted out to criminals. If the explanation is accepted, prosecutors can go about their plea-arranging way of doing justice without encountering too much damning criticism from community leaders who want them to be tough on criminals. They avoid losing elections or being fired. . . .

Interest groups pressing for strict law enforcement can understand the idea that tactical considerations, such as overload or a weak case, reduce penalties. On the other hand, a prosecutor who publicly admits that he is in sympathy with some defendants, or reduces charges because he believes the law too harsh, must do some fast talking. Similarly, proponents of adversariness on the part of defense lawyers can understand and accept tactical explanations for not fighting to the finish, but they are not likely to support an attorney who admits that his main job is to find some reasonable disposition of defendants he knows are guilty. It is therefore convenient, safe and reasonable for prosecutors and defense lawyers alike to attribute plea bargaining to mere defect in the warrior's armament—too much work and too many weak cases.

But the danger of such explanations of the guilty plea system is that they distort everyone's perceptions of what the courthouse is for. They create a reality which community leaders act upon but which is a misconception of what actually occurs. By decorating the courthouse to look like a slowed-down factory assembly line, they make people forget that it still bears some resemblance to a place of justice.

The overwork explanation implies that the function of the courthouse is to sentence guilty men to the punishments long ago stipulated by a legislature. If taxpayers would just pour enough financial support into the system, the idea goes, the county could hire the number of prosecutors and judges it would take to apply the rules rigidly in each case, and discretionary decision making would disappear.

From pages 105–108, and 111–112 of *Justice by Consent: Plea Bargains in the American Courthouse*, by Arthur Rosett and Donald R. Cressey. Copyright © 1976 by J. B. Lippincott Company. By permission of Harper & Row, Publishers, Inc.

Variability in court work groups

Virtually all of the criminal courts studied to date exemplify these patterns of how court work groups operate, but there are important variations that need to be considered.

- The stability of the work groups can vary. Eisenstein and Jacob reported that work groups were much more stable in Chicago than in Baltimore, where the key officials rotated jobs more often than in Chicago, thus producing numerous disruptions of the ongoing network of relationships.

- Rules of behavior that guide the key actors vary from courtroom to courtroom. There is room for mavericks. Some defense attorneys march to a different drummer. They maintain hostile relations with prosecutors and exhibit many "Perry Mason" attributes of adversarial behavior. They do so at a price, however. They are seldom able to negotiate effectively for good deals. But at the same time, they tend to represent clients whom the court network is predisposed to treat harshly. In short, the normal range of sanctions and rewards does not apply to them.
- There are important variations in how judges control their courtrooms. Although the formal authority of the judge is shared with the informal network, judges respond in different ways. Some prefer to parcel out decisions to others and are therefore receptive to recommendations from prosecutors, probation officers, and perhaps even defense attorneys. Other judges play a much more dominant role. Most federal judges, for example, will not even allow the prosecutor or defense attorney to suggest a possible sentence.
- The content of the policy norms varies from community to community and from courtroom to courtroom. Property crimes are viewed as more threatening in rural areas than in urban ones; therefore the appropriate penalty applied to a defendant convicted of burglary in a rural area carries a more severe penalty than to one convicted in a big city.

Conclusion

The actual operations of the criminal courts differ greatly from official expectations. The three concepts of excessive caseloads, discretion, and the courtroom work group attempt to offer explanations for this gap between law in action and law on the books. Although courts have too many cases, excessive caseload volume is at best only a partial explanation for why the criminal courts behave the way they do. More fundamentally, discretion is an important component of the court system. There is a need to shape the dictates of the formal law to the actual cases and defendants that come to the criminal courts. The courtroom work group concept emphasizes the interactions among these key actors. In the next three chapters, we will examine in greater depth how and why prosecutors, judges, and defense attorneys work within the courtroom work group.

For discussion

1. Throughout this book, we will discuss varying proposals for reducing the caseload of the courts. What problems might be helped by a reduction in caseload? What problems might remain largely the same? Why?
2. To many defendants, victims, and witnesses, a case in criminal court is a unique experience. Yet to the courthouse regulars most of these matters are quite routine. What effects might this situation have on the attitudes and expectations of the defendants, victims, witnesses, and others? On the courthouse regulars? Medical personnel adopt a professional, nonemotional response to sickness and accidents. Do the same factors apply to the courthouse regulars? What steps might be taken to alter this attitude of routine justice?

3. How does the court work group affect the exercise of discretion?
4. Make a list of situations that you think are appropriate for discretion. Also list situations that are not appropriate for discretion or where discretion has been abused. What do your lists reveal about your own views of the goals of the criminal court process? Are your lists similar to or different from those of your classmates?
5. Observe a court work group in your own community and talk to its members. How long have the same people worked together? Do they share common perceptions of normal crimes and appropriate penalties? What matters do they disagree over? What rewards and sanctions are used? Obtaining answers to these questions will not be easy. Why might the courthouse regulars be reluctant to discuss such matters?
6. In what ways might defendants receive a break depending on how closely their defense attorneys work with the court work group? Some defendants receive a stiffer-than-normal penalty because the work group wishes to penalize the attorney? What might be done about correcting this problem?

References

Blumberg, Abraham S. *Criminal Justice.* New York: Quadrangle Books, 1970.
Clynch, Edward, and David Neubauer. "Trial Courts as Organizations: A Critique and Synthesis." *Law and Policy Quarterly* 3 (January 1981):69–94.
Cole, George F. "The Decision to Prosecute." *Law and Society Review* 4 (1970):331.
Eisenstein, James, and Herbert Jacob. *Felony Justice: An Organizational Analysis of Criminal Courts.* Boston: Little, Brown, 1977.
Feeley, Malcolm. *The Process is the Punishment: Handling Cases in a Lower Criminal Court.* New York: Russell Sage Foundation, 1979.
Friedman, Lawrence, and Robert Percival. "A Tale of Two Courts: Litigation in Alameda and San Benito Counties." *Law and Society Review* 10 (1976):267.
Haller, Mark. "Plea Bargaining: The Nineteenth-Century Context." *Law and Society Review* 13 (Winter 1979):273.
LaFave, Wayne, and Austin W. Scott, Jr. *Criminal Law.* St. Paul, Minn.: West Publishing, 1972.
Mileski, Mauren. "Courtroom Encounters: An Observation Study of a Lower Criminal Court." *Law and Society Review* 5 (1971):473.
Nardulli, Peter. "The Caseload Controversy and the Study of Criminal Courts." *Journal of Criminal Law and Criminology* 70 (1979):101.
Neubauer, David W. *Criminal Justice in Middle America.* Morristown, N.J.: General Learning Press, 1974.
Newman, Donald. "Pleading Guilty for Considerations: A Study of Bargain Justice." *Journal of Criminal Law* 37 (1970):665.
President's Commission on Law Enforcement and Administration of Justice. *Task Force Report: The Courts.* Washington, D.C.: U.S. Government Printing Office, 1967.
Skolnick, Jerome H. *Justice Without Trial.* New York: John Wiley, 1966.
Sudnow, David. "Normal Crimes: Sociological Features of the Penal Code in a Public Defender Office." *Social Problems* 12 (1965):254.
Times-Picayune, February 26, 1976.
Wiseman, Jacqueline. *Stations of the Lost: The Treatment of Skid Row Alcoholics.* Englewood Cliffs, N.J.: Prentice-Hall, 1970.

For further reading

Burstein, Carolyn. "Criminal Case Processing from an Organizational Perspective: Current Research Trends." *Justice System Journal* 5 (Spring 1980):258–273.

Davis, Kenneth C. *Discretionary Justice: A Preliminary Inquiry.* Urbana: University of Illinois Press, 1971.

Eisenstein, James, and Herbert Jacob. *Felony Justice: An Organizational Analysis of Criminal Courts.* Boston: Little, Brown, 1977.

Nardulli, Peter. *The Courtroom Elite: An Organizational Perspective on Criminal Justice.* Cambridge, Mass.: Ballinger, 1978.

Neubauer, David W. *Criminal Justice in Middle America.* Morristown, N.J.: General Learning Press, 1974.

Rosett, Arthur, and Donald P. Cressey. *Justice by Consent: Plea Bargaining in the American Courthouse.* Philadelphia: J. B. Lippincott, 1976.

CHAPTER 6

The Prosecutor

The prosecutor is the most powerful official in the criminal courts. From the time of arrest to the final disposition, how the prosecutor chooses to exercise discretion determines to a large extent which defendants are prosecuted, the type of bargains that will be struck, and the severity of the sentence.

These wide-ranging discretionary powers illustrate that the prosecutor occupies a central position in the criminal justice system. While police, defense attorneys, judges, and probation officers specialize in a specific phase of the criminal justice process, the duties of the prosecutor bridge all of these phases. This means that the prosecutor is the only official who must on a daily basis work with all the various actors of the criminal justice system. In turn, these various actors have conflicting views about how prosecutorial discretion should be used—the police push for harsher penalties, the defense attorneys for giving their client a break, and judges to clear the docket. As a result, the prosecutor stands center stage in an extremely complex and conflictive environment. With the possible exception of big city mayors, prosecutors (also called district attorneys or DAs) occupy a highly visible and uniquely powerful position.

103

This chapter examines a number of factors that affect how prosecutors exercise their wide-ranging discretionary powers. We will begin with a discussion of the decentralized organization of the prosecutor's office and then examine the key work requirements of the job. We will then turn our attention to the social forces that shape how these powers are actually applied. In particular we will look at the fact that most of the work of the office is carried out by young assistant attorneys, whose activities are greatly affected by their membership and acceptance in the courtroom work group. Finally, the chapter will focus on the conflicting goals that underlie the tasks of the American prosecutor.

Structure and organization

prosecutor The prosecutor, known as the district attorney in some jurisdictions and state's attorney in most others, is the chief law enforcement official of the community. The prosecutor works in the courthouse but is part of the executive branch of government. This independence from the judiciary is vital for the proper functioning of the adversary system, for prosecutors at times challenge judicial decisions.

Decentralization

decentral-
ized organ-
ization
Decentralized organization is the key characteristic of the office of prosecutor. In most states the district attorney has countywide responsibility, although some rural counties are grouped into prosecutorial districts (see table 6-1). The actual division of responsibility follows local, state, and federal jurisdictional boundaries. In large counties, like those of Los Angeles and Chicago, the prosecutor has a staff of over one hundred full-time assistants. The great majority of the nation's 2,700 prosecutor's offices however, serve in small offices with no more than one or two assistants (U.S. Department of Justice). Frequently, rural prosecutors are part-time officials who also maintain a private law practice.

attorney
general
The activities of the prosecutor's office typically are not monitored by state officials. Although the *attorney general* is the state's chief law enforcement official, the authority over local criminal procedures is quite limited. In a handful of states the attorney general has no legal authority to intervene in or initiate local prosecutions. In other states this authority is limited to extreme conditions. Thus, the state attorney general exercises virtually no control or supervision over district attorneys. This lack of supervisory power, coupled with the decentralization of offices, means that local prosecutors enjoy almost total autonomy. Only the local voters have the power to evaluate the prosecutor's performance and vote the current officeholder out of office.

The decentralization of America's prosecutor authority results in divided responsibility. In a single city there are often three separate prosecutors—city, county, and federal. Competition between such separate agencies over which office will prosecute which defendants does occur. In addition, coordination on common problems is often lacking. Most major metropolitan areas encompass numerous counties and cities and gaps in jurisdiction allow sophisticated and organized criminal conspiracies to operate across several boundaries. In response to such activi-

special pros-
ecutor's
offices

ties, some areas have created *special prosecutor's offices* to focus on organized crime in designated substantive areas.

Prosecutors as public officials

Most prosecutors are locally elected officials. The primary exceptions are U.S. attorneys who are nominated by the president and confirmed by the Senate. In addition, in two eastern states (New Jersey and Connecticut) the local prosecutor is appointed, while in three states (Alaska, Delaware, and Rhode Island) the state attorney general also serves as the local prosecutor (see table 6-1).

TABLE 6-1.   Characteristics of local prosecutors

	Title	Area	Number of units	How selected	Term (years)
Alabama	District attorney	Judicial district	37	Elected	4
Alaska	(No local prosecutor)				
Arizona	County attorney	County	14	Elected	4
Arkansas	District prosecuting attorney	Judicial district	19	Elected	2
California	District attorney	County	58	Elected	4
Colorado	District attorney	Judicial district	22	Elected	4
Connecticut	State's attorney	Judicial district	9	Superior Court	
Delaware	(No local prosecutor)				
Florida	State attorney	Judicial district	20	Elected	4
Georgia	District attorney	Judicial district	43	Elected	4
Hawaii	County or city prosecutor	County	4	Elected or appointed	4
Idaho	Prosecuting attorney	County	44	Elected	2
Illinois	State's attorney	County	102	Elected	4
Indiana	Prosecuting attorney	Judicial district	87	Elected	4
Iowa	County attorney	County	99	Elected	4
Kansas	County attorney	County	105	Elected	2
Kentucky	County attorney	County	120	Elected	4
	Commonwealth attorney	District	51	Elected	6
Louisiana	District attorney	Judicial district	34	Elected	6
Maine	County attorney	County	16	Elected	2
Maryland	State's attorney	County or city	24	Elected	4
Massachusetts	District attorney	Judicial district	9	Elected	4
Michigan	Prosecuting attorney	County	81	Elected	4
Minnesota	County attorney	County	87	Elected	2
Mississippi	District attorney	Judicial district	20	Elected	4
	County prosecuting attorney	County	60	Elected	4
Missouri	Prosecuting attorney	County	115	Elected	2
Montana	County attorney	County	54	Elected	4
Nebraska	County attorney	County	93	Elected	4
Nevada	District attorney	County	17	Elected	4
New Hampshire	County attorney	County	10	Elected	2
New Jersey	County prosecutor	County	21	Governor with consent of Senate	5
New Mexico	District attorney	Judicial district	13	Elected	4
New York	District attorney	County	62	Elected	4

(continued)

TABLE 6-1.   Characteristics of local prosecutors (*continued*)

	Title	Area	Number of units	How selected	Term (years)
North Carolina	Solicitors	Solicitorial district	30	Elected	4
North Dakota	State's attorney	County	53	Elected	2
Ohio	Prosecuting attorney	County	88	Elected	4
Oklahoma	District attorney	District	27	Elected	4
Oregon	District attorney	County	36	Elected	4
Pennsylvania	District attorney	County	67	Elected	4
Rhode Island	(No local prosecutor)				
South Carolina	Solicitor	Judicial district	16	Elected	4
South Dakota	State's attorney	County	67	Elected	2
Tennessee	District attorney general	Judicial district	26	Elected	8
Texas	State's attorney	County	222	Elected	4
	District attorney	District	91	Elected	4
Utah	County attorney	County	29	Elected	4
	District attorney	District	7	Elected	4
Vermont	State's attorney	County	14	Elected	2
Virginia	Commonwealth attorney	County or city	122	Elected	4
Washington	Prosecuting attorney	County	39	Elected	4
West Virginia	Prosecuting attorney	County	55	Elected	4
Wisconsin	District attorney	County	72	Elected	2
Wyoming	County and prosecuting attorney	County	23	Elected	4
Total counties:			2,127		
Total districts:			552		
Total units:			2,679		

Source: National Association of Attorneys General, Committee on the Office of Attorney General. *Survey of Local Prosecutors: Data Concerning 1000 Local Prosecutors* (1973), pp. 2, 3.

The elected term is typically four years, although in some states it is only two. These elections indicate that the work of the American prosecutor is deeply set within the larger political process. For a lawyer interested in a political career, the prosecutor's office provides a built-in launching pad. Numerous government officials—governors, judges, and legislators—began their careers as crusading prosecutors (Schlesinger). Not all prosecutors, though, plan to enter politics. Studies in Wisconsin and Kentucky, for example, indicated that more than half of the prosecutors had no further political ambitions. They viewed the office as useful for gaining visibility before establishing a private law practice (Jacob; Engstrom). Overall, most prosecutors are young. One survey indicated that about one-half were serving their first term of office (Morgan and Alexander:43).

The tremendous power of the prosecutor's office means that political parties are very interested in controlling it. The county district attorney provides numerous opportunities for patronage. But even more fundamentally, political parties want one of their own supporters serving as district attorney to guarantee that their affairs will not be closely scrutinized and to act as a vehicle for harassing the opposition. This power is most aptly shown in Chicago. The Republican U.S. attorney, James Thompson (1971–1975) secured indictments and convictions against numerous Democratic officials and then used his record as U.S. attorney as the basis for winning the governorship of Illinois (1977–).

The prosecutor at work

The word *lawyer* usually evokes the image of someone arguing before a jury, and until the twentieth century, this was a good description. The most famous lawyers of the past—Daniel Webster and Clarence Darrow, for example—were skilled trial orators. But times have changed. The vast majority of American lawyers never try a case. The prosecutor's office, though, is one place where trials are still an important part of what lawyers do. The activities of American lawyers—and particularly the prosecutors—can be conveniently divided into five categories: fighting, negotiating, drafting, counseling, and administering (Mayer:39).

Fighting

fighting
A trial lawyer must be a *fighter* who likes to question witnesses, object to other lawyers' questions, and appeal to juries.

A criminal case does not arrive in the prosecutor's office neatly packaged and awaiting the summoning of a jury. One of the most vital skills of an attorney is taking a disorganized case and preparing it for trial. Such case preparation and eventual trial involve numerous tactical decisions. Will this person make a good witness? How can we show the jury the strongest points of the case while minimizing the weaknesses? What type of defense is the opposition likely to mount, and how can it be countered? How can we introduce a vital piece of evidence on the borderline of admissibility? Obviously a working knowledge of the rules of evidence is the starting point. But perhaps equally as important is an insight into the psychological and sociological dynamics of juries, judges, defendants, and witnesses. What looks like an unbeatable case to a law professor may appear as a case with major difficulties to a seasoned trial prosecutor.

Negotiating

negotiating
Only a handful of cases are ever tied; the rest are plead out or dismissed. One of the most important tasks of the prosecutor is to *negotiate* with the opposition. Reputation as a trial attorney is an important factor in negotiations. An advocate will exploit a weakness; poor trial attorneys therefore make poor negotiators as well. Like trial work, negotiating requires numerous tactical decisions. Does this type of case and type of defense attorney suggest that it is best to divulge all the prosecutor's case in hopes of inducing a guilty plea? Or would it be better to play it close to the vest and tell the opposition nothing? During negotiations, attorneys must constantly reevaluate the weaknesses of their own case and the strengths of the opposition. For example, a victim's reluctance to testify may necessitate a lesser sentence than normal.

Drafting

drafting

briefs

Courts are paper bureaucracies. Like many other governmental bodies, no decisions can be made, no case advanced from one step to the next, without the proper paperwork. While the clerk of the court is primarily responsible for keeping these papers in order, the prosecutor is the one charged with *drafting*—preparing—these vital documents. Search warrants, for example, are often prepared by the prosecutor's office. When charges are filed, the prosecutor must specify the section of the criminal code that the defendant allegedly violated. The prosecutor must also prepare motions involving defense allegations that evidence was improperly seized or that a confession was coerced. Most of the prosecutor's legal research involves preparing such motions and *briefs* (the technical term for the form that written arguments are presented to the court). At the close of the trial the prosecutor is involved in the preparation of the final charge to the jury. And after conviction, the prosecutor must prepare and argue before the appellate court. If the documents are not properly prepared, the case may be either irretrievably lost or much extra effort must later be expended to remedy the initial mistake.

Counseling

counseling

A critical aspect of a lawyer's responsibility is advising and *counseling* clients. Just as patients judge doctors by their bedside manner, lawyers are often measured by their friendly, courteous, and understanding relationship with their clients. In the prosecutor's case, the counseling dimension is complicated because the prosecutor's client is the state. Nonetheless, prosecutors spend part of their time talking to victims, witnesses, and police officers. Before trial a lawyer must prepare witnesses by going over the questions to be asked, advising them how to testify, and telling them matters to be avoided. A poorly coached witness can easily cause an acquittal or a hung jury. Prosecutors counsel victims of crimes about why a plea bargain was entered into or why the charges were dropped. It is not unusual for a victim to want to prosecute to the fullest but for the lawyer to believe that no crime was committed. Prosecutors must also advise police about why a case is weak, what additional evidence is needed, and so on.

Administering

administering

Like the other members of the courtroom team, prosecutors handle a large volume of cases. A typical big city prosecutor, for example, has a yearly work load of one hundred cases (Jacoby). A major concern of prosecutors is *administration*—keeping the cases moving. In doing so they execute a number of important administrative responsibilities. In a number of jurisdictions, prosecutors are responsible for setting dates for trial; as the case approaches trial, they must make sure that subpoenas are issued for all the witnesses they plan to call. Faced with numerous cases, district attorneys and their top aides must decide how to allocate resources. Should some attorneys be shifted from an existing section to make room for a new division in white-collar crime, for example? Indeed, in the largest offices, keeping the bureaucracy running—hiring new assistants, promoting deserving old assistants, preparing and fighting for the budget—consume major amounts of time.

Assistant district attorneys

On a day-to-day basis the work of the prosecutor's office is executed by the assistants. Recruiting, training, socializing, and supervising these assistant district attorneys have a major bearing on how prosecutorial power and discretion are exercised.

assistant district attorneys

Most *assistant district attorneys* (sometimes called deputy district attorneys) are hired directly after graduation from law school or after a short time in private practice. Typically, they have attended local law schools rather than the nation's most prestigious law schools, whose graduates prefer higher-status, better paying jobs in civil practice. Traditionally, big city prosecutors hired assistants on the basis of party affiliation and the recommendations of ward leaders and elected officials. Increasingly, however, greater stress is being placed on merit selection, a trend exemplified by the Los Angeles prosecutor's office—the nation's largest and probably most professional—where hiring is on a civil service basis.

turnover

The *turnover* rate among assistant district attorneys is quite high. Most serve only an average of two to four years before entering private practice. Low salaries are one reason for the high turnover rate. Although starting salaries are generally competitive with those in private law offices, after a few years the salary levels are markedly less. The high rate of turnover is also a product of the nature of the office. Prosecutors' offices present numerous openings for braves, but only a few chiefs are needed. After two years on the job, the young assistants have learned about all they will learn—there are only a few ways to prosecute a burglary case and only a few possible defenses that must be countered. Young assistants looking for new challenges turn either to promotion to an elite, specialized unit within the office—armed robbery or murder, for example—where trials are more numerous and more demanding, or they turn to private practice. Finally, some assistants grow tired of the job. The criminal courthouse—with its constant, never-ending stream of society's losers—can become a depressing place to work. And constant trial work creates numerous physical and psychological pressures. Being a trial attorney is only for the young. Most assistants view their job as a brief way station toward a more lucrative and more varied private practice.

Learning the job

Most assistant DAs have been admitted to the practice of law only recently and therefore are unfamiliar with the day-to-day realities of their profession. Although law schools provide an overview of major areas of the law—criminal law, tax, torts, and contracts, to name just a few—they give their students very little exposure to how law is actually practiced.

> For the first week or two, I went to court with guys who had been here. Just sat there and watched. What struck me was the amount of things he [the prosecutor] has to do in the courtroom. The prosecutor runs the courtroom. Although the judge is theoretically in charge, we're standing there plea bargaining and calling the cases at the same time and chewing gum and telling the people to quiet down and setting bonds, and that's what amazed me. I never thought I would learn all the terms. What bothered me also was the paperwork. Not the Supreme Court decisions, not the *mens rea* or any

of this other stuff, but the amount of junk that's in those files that you have to know. We never heard about this crap in law school.

Quoted in Milton Heumann, *Plea Bargaining* (Chicago: University of Chicago Press, 1978).

training

For decades the position of assistant district attorney has provided young attorneys with the opportunity to serve an apprenticeship in legal practice primarily on the job. It was not unusual in the past for new employees—with no experience—to be sent into court their first day on the job. More recently large prosecutor offices have begun to provide new employees with a systematic introduction to the work to *train* them. New assistants are given a week of general orientation to the various divisions of the office, are allowed to watch various proceedings, and often observe veteran trial attorneys at work. Such formalized indoctrination is still relatively rare, however.

promotion

Young assistants quickly learn to ask questions of more experienced prosecutors, court clerks, and veteran police officers, who are willing to share their knowledge about courtroom procedures. Through this socialization process, new assistants learn the important unwritten rules about legal practice. The courthouse environment has developed shared conceptions of what types of violations should be punished and the appropriate penalties to be applied to such violations. Assistants learn that their performance (and chances for promotion) are measured by how promptly and efficiently they dispose of cases. They become sensitive to "hints"— for example, a judge complaining that prosecutors are bringing too many minor cases and a backlog is developing usually conveys the message to the new assistant that she is pressing too hard. *Promotions* are also tied to reputations as a trial attorney. Assistants are invariably judged by the number of convictions they obtain. In the courthouse environment, though, not losing a case has a higher value than winning. Thus, young assistants learn that if the guilt of the defendant is doubtful or the offender is not dangerous, it is better to negotiate a plea rather than disrupt the courtroom routine by attempting to gain a jury conviction.

Too often, the criminal court system appears to be operated in an aimless, unfocused, and arbitrary fashion, ingesting and disposing of its workload without any sense of direction. . . .

The court in many respects is an arbitrator, and essentially plays a passive role. It can only consider matters brought to its attention. . . .

By contrast, the prosecutor is an advocate and essentially plays an active role. Unlike the court, the prosecutor is not constrained to accept passively as his workload every matter that is presented to him. He can screen out matters referred to him by police agencies that fail to meet his standards and priorities. He can initiate and channel investigations into types of matters that he views as having prosecutive priority. . . .

By properly exercising his role, the prosecutor performs a vitally important function for the court which the court is prevented from performing for itself: he precludes random access to limited adjudicative resources, and preserves these resources for the timely judgment of the matters to which the public attaches priority. It is in this sense that the prosecutor serves as the guardian, protector, and custodian of the community's scarce resources for adjudication.

William A. Hamilton and Charles R. Work, "The Prosecutor's Role in the Urban Court System: The Case for Management Consciousness," *Journal of Criminal Law and Criminology* 64

(1973): 183–184. Reprinted by special permission of *The Journal of Criminal Law and Criminology*, © 1973 by Northwestern University School of Law.

Promotions and office structure

As assistants gain experience and settle into the courthouse routine, they are promoted to more demanding and also more interesting tasks. Promotions are tied to office structure. In small prosecutors' offices, assistants are given a case at the time charges are filed to follow through arraignment, preliminary hearing, pretrial motions, trial, sentencing, and, if necessary, appeal. In these offices assistants are promoted by being given more serious cases. While such an assignment system reflects the lawyer–client relationship, it is administratively burdensome in large courthouses; assistants would spend much of their time moving from one courtroom to another and wasting time while waiting for their one or two cases to be called. Therefore most big city prosecutors assign personnel on a zone basis: screening, misdemeanor, arraignment, preliminary hearing, trial, and so on. Most commonly, prosecutors have specialized bureaus for major offenses (drug, homicide, armed robbery, and white-collar crime), which are staffed by most experienced trial attorneys. (Figure 6-1 provides a typical example.) These specialized units are the most prestigious mainly because trial work is plentiful and challenging. This means that on a regular basis one or two attorneys are regularly assigned to one courtroom with a given judge. The consequence is that through time prosecutors come to know the judge's views on sentencing and so on.

Supervision

supervision   Assistant district attorneys are *supervised* by a bureau chief who is supposed to ensure that they follow policies of the office. Most prosecutors' offices have general policies, but these are often somewhat vague and in small offices are seldom even reduced to writing. They are simply part of what the young assistant learns informally.

For several reasons, however, assistant district attorneys enjoy fairly wide freedom. Supervisors can exert only limited control over individual cases or individual assistants. They spend most of their time out of the office in the courtroom and therefore have difficulty being physically present to observe and possibly monitor the young DA's activities. Indeed, in crowded courthouses the trial assistants may have offices adjoining the judge's chambers and only rarely appear in the prosecutor's office at all. This lack of physical proximity is underscored by the types of decisions that must be made and how they are made. Each assistant has dozens of cases that require individual decisions on the basis of specific facts, unique witness problems, and so on. A supervisor has no way to monitor such situations except on the basis of what the assistant relates or writes in the file. Here as elsewhere, information is power. Assistants can control their supervisors by selectively telling them what they think they should know (Neubauer, 1974:49).

Perhaps most importantly, assistant district attorneys are professionals licensed by society with special and unique powers, most of which center on their ability to exercise judgment. Moreover, assistants view their brief tenure in office as an ap-

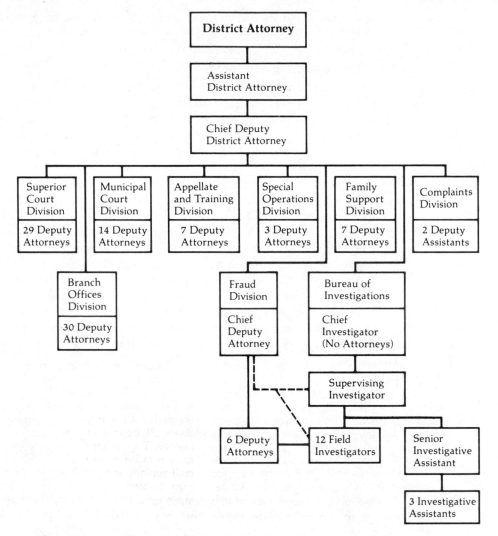

Figure 6-1. Office of the San Diego District Attorney: Organization and Distribution of Attorneys.

Source: Peter Finn and Alan Hoffman, *Exemplary Project: Prosecution of Economic Crime* (Washington, D.C.: Government Printing Office, 1976), p. 31.

prenticeship for learning the practice of law. Attempts by supervisors to control the work of the assistants invariably seriously erode the morale of the office. Assistants argue that their professional status has been reduced to that of a clerk.

Attempts at greater supervision

The typical autonomy of the individual assistant district attorney has resulted in what Joan Jacoby has called the unit style. Each assistant makes his or her own decisions. In the last decade a number of big city prosecutors have become concerned that this unit style allows too much unchecked discretion. In cities such as Detroit and New Orleans the prosecutors have imposed bureaucratic controls. Decisions on charging and plea bargaining are scrutinized by supervisors. A trial assistant, for example, is not allowed to offer a plea less than the original charge filed unless prior permission is granted. Moreover, these offices now carefully compile statistics on all aspects of the unit to allow supervisors to more effectively manage the work of the office and to spot any changes or potential problems. Head prosecutors believe that these management systems monitor prosecutorial discretion, minimize differences between individual assistants, and concentrate scarce crime-fighting resources (Jacoby).

CLOSE UP: JOE CARBO, ASSISTANT DISTRICT ATTORNEY

. . . The majority of prosecutors' offices give only on-the-job training to a new staff. Thus Joe spent his first week on the job familiarizing himself with the courthouse operations and personnel. He dogged a senior prosecutor on his rounds. He learned all of the judges' names, the names of most of the prosecutors, and the names of a few public defenders. He watched preliminary hearings, arraignments and sentence hearings. He saw only one trial.

The following week, Joe was assigned four cases. He was delighted. By the end of the week, the four cases had grown to a dozen, and by the end of the month he was carrying a workload of about fifty files, most of them misdemeanor complaints and relatively petty charges. After another month, the fifty cases had multiplied and changed character. By then many of the misdemeanor complaints were handled by a new assistant district attorney. Joe was involved in screening and prosecutorial decisions, was dealing with the police on search and arrest warrants and was handling mostly felony cases.

Those early weeks were hectic. Despite his law firm experience, Joe was forced to learn a lot on the run. He often had to find out what he was supposed to do by asking an experienced police officer, a court clerk, or one of the secretaries in the office. Mostly he relied on his colleagues, all of whom had been in similar circumstances not long before. They encouraged him and seemed to expect that as a new man he would come to them for help. They also kidded him a lot, but tried to keep him out of serious trouble. "We're like doctors except that we don't have to bury our mistakes, they just go out and steal again," the man in the next office said. Several times during this period, Joe had to

jump up in the middle of a phone call or an interview and hurry into the office next door to ask a more experienced man what to do. Gradually he became aware of the gap between "the way things are done around here" and the law as stated in the books. Without thinking much about it, Joe soon accepted the unwritten laws imparted to him by his colleagues as his guiding principles for handling cases.

It was imperative that Joe learn these unwritten laws well, because acceptance by the other members of the courthouse community was and is central to his whole reason for being in this job. He wants very much to succeed, to get promoted to greater responsibility and to be rewarded with a high salary and position. But above all, he wants to earn a reputation as a trial lawyer. That is an asset, a commodity he can market in his pursuit of a career. Joe Carbo is a civil servant and a public administrator, but he regards himself primarily as a trial lawyer. Involvement with the criminal law is his job, but the job is merely a means to an end.

This professional viewpoint characterizes Joe's approach to his work with the police, whom he considers clients. Like any private attorney, Joe sits in his office waiting for clients who have legal burdens, in this instance arrest reports. His duty, he knows, is to prosecute these cases for the police just as a private lawyer works for his clients. But there is a difference. Much more frequently than a private lawyer, Joe must tell a client that he does not have a chance of winning—the evidence is no good, the witnesses are weak, the arrest was wrong.

This duty makes Joe an administrator of senior rank. Even police captains with twenty years' experience must come to him for decisions, and he usually has the last word. Joe's

(continued)

lawyer status makes him an expert who advises and counsels policemen in addition to serving them. Further, he sees the same policemen over and over. He comes to know and understand them, and they him. Like a corporation lawyer paid an annual salary to do legal work for a company, Joe is retained to do legal work for the police.

From pages 87–88 of *Justice by Consent: Plea Bargains in the American Courthouse*, by Arthur Rosett and Donald R. Cressey. Copyright © 1976 by J. B. Lippincott Company. By permission of Harper and Row, Publishers, Inc.

Prosecutors and courtroom work groups

Much of the prosecutor's time is spent working directly with other members of the courtroom work group. Even when interviewing witnesses, conducting legal research, or reviewing a file, the prosecutor is anticipating the reactions of judges and defendants. Thus the activties of prosecutors and assistant prosecutors can be understood only within the setting of the courtroom work group.

Generally the prosecutor is the most important member of the courtroom work group. How the prosecutor exercises the discretionary powers of the office sets the agenda for judges and defense attorneys—the types of cases being prosecuted, the nature of plea agreements, and the sentences to be handed out. In addition, the prosecutor has more information about the case than anyone else: police reports, records of previous arrests and convictions, physical evidence, and laboratory tests.

A prosecutor's actions are in turn influenced by other members of the courtroom work group. Through the socialization process the assistant prosecutor's evaluation of a case is influenced by the courthouse environment. The types of pleas normally agreed to and the typical sentences imposed upon the guilty reflect the shared norms of the courtroom.

Prosecutors who stray too far from accepted ways of doing things can expect sanctions. The judge may informally indicate that the state is pushing too hard for a harsh sentence. Or the judge may verbally chastise a district attorney in open court, thus threatening the attorney's status among peers. The defense attorney might not agree to a prosecutor's request for a continuance, might use delaying tactics to impair the state's efforts to schedule cases, or might even call for a jury trial, thus further disrupting the prosecutor's and the court's efforts to move the cases. (The prosecutor is not without countersanctions. These will be discussed in the following two chapters.)

The actions of the prosecutor, then, are constrained by other members of the courtroom work group. Within these constraints, effective assistant DAs are the ones who make tactical decisions that maximize their objectives. Prosecutors, for example, learn which defense attorneys have reputations for persuasiveness at trial. Attorneys with such reputations are more likely to obtain dismissals or reduced charges from the prosecutor. Assistants also learn which defense attorneys can be trusted and grant these people greater access to the prosecutor's information about the case. They are also more likely to be listened to when they present an argument that the case involves unusual circumstances. Prosecutors quickly learn the tendencies of the judge. No experienced prosecutor can afford to ignore how the judge wishes the courtroom to be run. On the other hand, the prosecutor can attempt to maneuver the case before a favorable judge and can also stress or withhold information to influence the judge's decision.

> I get so damned pissed off and tired of these guys who come in and cry, "My guy's got a job" or "My guy's about to join the army," when he's got a rap sheet as long as your arm. His guy's a loser, and he's wailing on my desk about what a fine man he is. What really wins me is the guy who comes in and says, "O.K., what are we going to do with my criminal today? I know he has no redeeming social value. He's been a bad son of a bitch all his life, so just let me know your position. But frankly, you know, my feeling is that this is just not the case to nail him on. We all know if he does something serious, he's going." And before long the guy who approaches it this way has you wrapped around his little finger.

> Quoted in Lief Carter, *The Limits of Order* (Lexington, Mass.: D. C. Heath, 1974), p. 87.

Contrasting work groups

The work of the prosecutor reflects two important considerations about America's criminal court process. First, prosecutors possess an immense amount of discretion. Second, they exercise this discretion in the context of other courtroom actors (the courtroom work group). In combination, these factors produce marked diversity. William McDonald cautions, therefore, that we must consider the domains of the prosecutor not as fixed by law and tradition but rather as blurred, shared, evolving, and open to negotiation. A recent study by Pamela Utz highlights this marked diversity. She examined two prosecutors' offices in the state of California—San Diego and Oakland. Despite the fact that both were operating within the same legal environment, Utz discovered contrasting operating styles.

The prosecutor in San Diego reflects an adversarial model. Assistant district attorneys presume that cases are serious, routinely overcharge, and set plea bargaining terms so high that many cases are forced to trial. Because there is a pronounced distrust of defense attorneys, plea bargaining involves a gamelike atmosphere. In general, the San Diego office is dedicated to the "full enforcement" of the law.

The operating style in Oakland, on the other hand, reflects a magisterial model. There are office policies about which types of cases involve serious violations of the law, and there are also strict standards in terms of charging. The office philosophy is that if the case is not "prison material," then there should be no trial. Plea bargaining proceeds on the basis that defense attorneys are fellow professionals. Overall, there appears to be more of a search for the truth in Oakland than in San Diego.

The contrasts in operating style between San Diego and Oakland reflect what James Eisenstein has labeled the competing perspectives of the law enforcement approach and the officer of the court approach. These competing perspectives are the subject of the next section.

Conflicting goals

At first the goals of the prosecutor's office seem to be the model of simplicity: their job is to convict the guilty. But a closer examination shows that the goals are not as clear-cut as they first appear.

Prosecutors may define their main job in different ways. Some may serve primarily as trial counsel to the police department, and thus they reflect the views of the police. Others act as "house counsel" to the police; they give legal advice to the department on enforcement practices that will withstand challenge in court. Still others consider themselves mainly representatives of the court; they enforce rules designed to control police practices and act in other similar ways for the benefit of the accused. Finally, some prosecutors, as elected officials, try to reflect the opinion of the community in making their decisions (LaFave:515). The uncertainties about which of these tasks should come first create many of the dynamic issues facing American prosecutors.

On the one hand, prosecutors are law enforcement officials, which implies that the primary duty is to protect society. In the adversary system the prosecutor is expected to advocate the guilt of the defendant vigorously. But at the same time, *officer of the court* the prosecutor is a lawyer and is therefore an *officer of the court*, that is, has a duty to see that justice is done. Violations of the law must be prosecuted, but in a way that guarantees that the defendant's rights are respected and protected. In a 1935 Supreme Court decision, Justice Sutherland spelled out the limitations that the officer of the court obligation imposes on prosecutors: "He may prosecute with earnestness and vigor—indeed, he should do so. But while he may strike hard blows, he is not at liberty to strike foul ones. It is as much his duty to refrain from improper methods calculated to produce a wrongful conviction as it is to use every legitimate means to bring about a just one" (*Berger* v. *U.S.*, 295 U.S. 78, 1935).

Recently the Supreme Court has held that because prosecutors are officers of the court, they have an obligation to provide the defense with information that may show innocence. Defense attorneys, though, are under no obligation to provide the prosecution with incriminating evidence. If prosecutors conceal or misrepresent evidence, such misbehavior can be sanctioned by a reversal of the conviction.

James Eisenstein has aptly labeled the two competing perspectives as the *law enforcement approach* and the *officer of the court approach*. Because of the varied *law enforcement approach* environment in which prosecutors operate—pressures from judges, defense attorneys, police officers, and so on—it should not be surprising to discover that different prosecutors come to emphasize differing orientations. A survey of prosecutors in Kentucky found that almost half stated they viewed their job in terms of being a law enforcement official while the remainder came closer to the officer of the court orientation (Engstrom).

The differing orientations of American prosecutors appear to be related to varying goals. Prosecutors with a law enforcement orientation are more likely to stress punishing the guilty. And those with an officer of the court approach are more likely to define major goals as securing convictions.

> The classic (or Jim Garrison) image of the fighting D.A. is today an intolerable anachronism. If our system of criminal law is to be even minimally fair, the D.A.'s office must become, county by county, a ministry of justice. . . .

Everybody starts in the complaint bureau [New York City, Borough of Manhattan], where Melvin D. Glass, the youngest of the bureau chiefs (nine years out of Pennsylvania Law School) offers "a seminar in advanced criminal procedure." In the first week the neophyte learns how to fill out a complaint card, "what to say on the phone and what not to say on the phone," how to tell people that even if what they say is true they have a civil lawsuit rather than a criminal charge against the storekeeper or the landlord or the neighbor or the bigamous husband (bigamy is a crime in New York if the second marriage was performed in the state). Then there are two weeks of following in great detail a hypothetical robbery case, from the policeman at the scene to the decision on appeal. "We introduce them," Glass says, "to police forms, court forms, our forms. They hear lectures from experts on gypsies and con games, burglary, homicide, larceny; visit the prison; observe the summons procedure; watch a full trial; do a moot court on a gambling case."

New York Times, July 23, 1967. © 1967 by The New York Times Company. Reprinted by permission.

Police and prosecutors

The police and prosecutor are commonly viewed as members of the same crime-fighting team. Newspapers often refer to police–prosecutor spokesmen, particularly when they are reporting on negative reactions to Supreme Court decisions. Television shows project the image of the prosecutor working with the police to fight crime. Such a linkage appears to be a natural one. Not only are police and prosecutor dedicated to the same overall goal—the sanctioning of criminal behavior—but they also work together on a day-to-day basis. Each is dependent upon the other. The prosecutor must rely on the police to provide the evidence necessary for a conviction. Similarly, the police are not satisfied merely with arresting an offender; they also want sanctions applied and therefore look to the prosecutor to ensure that the guilty are convicted and sentenced.

But embedded in this relationship are potentials for conflict. Police spokesmen, for example, are often publicly critical of the local district attorney for dismissing too many cases or bargaining too many out. In turn, prosecutors are often privately critical of the police for conducting inadequate investigations. In *Helter Skelter* Vincent Bugliosi describes how he was able to secure a conviction against Charles Manson for the bloody ritualistic murders of several Hollywood celebrities, including the movie actress Sharon Tate. One of the minor themes of the book is how the prosecutor's office had to overcome slipshod investigation by the Los Angeles Police Department. Studies in California, Wisconsin, and Illinois have also shown varying degrees of tension between the prosecutor's office and the police departments (Carter:76–78; Milner:88; Neubauer, 1974:58–62).

The prosecutor as police legal adviser

Prosecutors are dependent upon the police for their raw materials: arrests and investigations. How the police conduct investigations and the legality of the searches they make affect how the prosecutor processes cases and the likelihood of obtaining a conviction. If the police do not prepare complete and accurate reports—they may fail to provide full names and addresses of victims and witnesses, leave out details on how the crime was committed, or neglect to include vital laboratory reports—the prosecutor may be forced to drop charges. District attorneys also depend on police officers to testify before grand juries, during pretrial hearings, and at trials. If police officers forget court appearances or are not subpoenaed, cases can be delayed or lost altogether. The police often believe that an arrest closes the case, but the prosecutors believe they need additional information to win in court.

Inadequate police reports present a classic illustration of noncoordination within the criminal justice system. Most police officers have only a limited knowledge of the criminal law and the evidence required to sustain a conviction in court. Prosecutors, however, have done little to bridge this gap. Few try to provide legal counsel to the police (President's Commission:50). By and large, the contacts between police and prosecutor are routine and formalized: the police file reports that the prosecutors process. Individual police officers, usually detectives, through time, often develop a working relationship with specific prosecutors. Rarely, however, do the top officials of the organizations confer on mutual problems. For example, when the Prairie City (Illinois) prosecutor's office was faced with a question of how to handle domestic disturbances, it made a policy decision that the police would be responsible for determining whether criminal charges should be filed. Although this policy had a major impact on the police, the police chief and his staff were not contacted. Moreover, most prosecutors' offices do not require that the assistants spend time at the police station or on patrol seeing the process through the eyes of the policemen. When assistants do spend time riding with the police, it is usually without encouragement from their superiors.

STANDARD 12.9

The prosecutor should be aware of the importance of the function of his office for other agencies of the criminal justice system and for the public at large. He should maintain relationships that encourage interchange of views and information and that maximize coordination of the various agencies of the criminal justice system.

The prosecutor should maintain regular liaison with the police department in order to provide legal advice to the police, to identify mutual problems and to develop solutions to those problems. He should participate in police training programs and keep the police informed about current developments in law enforcement, such as significant court decisions. He should develop and maintain a liaison with the police legal adviser in those areas relating to police–prosecutor relationships.

The prosecutor should develop for the use of the police a basic police report form that includes all relevant information about the offense and the offender necessary for charging, plea negotiations, and trial. The completed form should be routinely forwarded to the prosecutor's office after the offender has been processed by the police. Police officers should be informed by the prosecutor of the disposition of any case with which they were involved and the reason for the disposition.

National Advisory Commission on Criminal Justice Standards and Goals, *Courts* (Washington, D.C.: Government Printing Office, 1973), p. 247.

Police view the prosecutor

Police often voice a number of complaints about prosecutors. One is that prosecutors superficially review cases and do not prosecute when they should. The police also generally dislike plea bargaining practices, believing that DAs allow too many defendants to escape with light penalties. They are also frustrated by the absence of legal advice for police and complain that prosecutors display condescending attitudes toward them.

Varying perspectives on the law

The tensions between police and prosecutor are partially the result of inadequate communications between the two separate organizations. But conflict between the two is also the product of varying perspectives on the law. The police and prosecutor see the law in very different terms.

Police and prosecutors usually come from different social backgrounds (Skolnick; McNamara; Reiss and Bordua; Niederhoffer). Most policemen are recruited from the working class; prosecutors are likely to have middle-class backgrounds. These differences in social background are magnified by differences in education. Most police seldom have worked beyond a high school diploma, but all prosecutors are college graduates with a professional degree. The police and prosecutors also approach their law enforcement jobs from decidedly different vantage points. For police officers, particularly detectives, their job is a permanent career; for prosecutors, law enforcement is a way station on the road to private legal practice.

These differences in social background, education, and career commitments produce markedly different perspectives on the law. An in-depth study of police reactions to the law showed how the police are hostile to the formal law, especially to the procedural restrictions on their activities. For example, police officers view themselves as experts in criminal investigation, but the courts refuse to recognize such expertise, a refusal the police regard as unjustified (Skolnick:196–199). Thus, standards conflict about what the police should do—one set of standards is based on norms of the police organization and another set is based on the law. As Reiss and Bordua comment, the courts often find fault with an officer's conduct which may have been "well within the reasonable limits of departmental policy or regulation" (Reiss and Bordua:39). Police often view the procedural restrictions of the law as unreasonable. Prosecutors, however, view the law from a different perspective. To be sure, prosecutors may be critical of some restrictions on the police. Nevertheless prosecutors have been trained in the law and the law's dedication to protecting individual rights. They are more likely to understand the reasons for such restrictions and are not as critical of procedural restrictions on the police.

Two types of prosecutorial decisions illustrate these differing perspectives. During the charging decision, the police and prosecutor often have divergent expectations. The police think that a valid arrest should be followed by prosecution. To the district attorney, however, a reasonable and valid arrest might not produce sufficient evidence for conviction. The same differences arise during the drafting of search warrants. Typically the police come to the district attorney's office, state their problem, and ask how to search (or perform similar tasks) in conformity with the law. They want answers. But the prosecutors are unable to provide the certainty that the police desire. Where the police see simple problems, the prosecutors see complex issues and respond, "It's six of this and half a dozen of the other."

Reformers often assume that increased contact between the prosecutor and police will lead to a higher level of legal sophistication on the part of the latter. What they fail to realize is that fundamentally different views of the law are involved. Indeed, increased contacts may only produce increased friction. I spent six months observing the activities of a prosecutor's office in central Illinois and witnessed several police–prosecutor meetings that led to abrasive interactions, not educational dialogue. Both sides became more annoyed without attempting to understand the other's position (Neubauer, 1974:185).

The work environment

The work environments of the police and the prosecutor produce different perspectives, too. The primary task of police officers is to locate and arrest suspects; prosecutors are primarily interested in convicting. For the police the most relevant area is the scene of the crime; for the prosecutor the arena is the courtroom. Prosecutors spend most of their time in court or talking with defense attorneys and judges outside of court. In short, they find themselves in the middle. The police view the prosecutor as their spokesman in court; however, the prosecutor must work with the judges and defense attorneys and is subject to their pressures. One major pressure is the need to dispose of cases. Prosecutors have many more cases than they can try. As a result, most cases are disposed of by bargaining with the defendant and reaching a compromise. Not surprisingly, the police may view such compromises as selling them out.

> Police get conditioned to the idea that we are the only people with our finger in the criminal dike in this country. They feel that everyone else "lets him go." Police differ from the D.A. The D.A. is satisfied with the conviction, finding him guilty. But police want him punished. They become outraged when the result of their work is ignored. "What if they let him off, I get him tomorrow: those bastards kiss him on the cheek and let 'em go," is their attitude of how the D.A. and the judge handle their cases. [Reiss and Bordua:37]

It is apparent that the police and prosecutor want different results from the ultimate court process. The police want vindication: a conviction for the crime charged is positive reinforcement that the police officer is doing his or her job. Prosecutors, however, pursue goals other than convictions.

Conclusion

The prosecutor is the most important official in the criminal courts system. By law and custom, prosecutors possess wide-ranging discretionary powers. The exercise of this discretion provides the dynamics of the courthouse. In effect, all others involved in the criminal courts—judges, defense attorneys, probation officers, juries, witnesses, and so on—must react to the decisions made by the prosecutor. But as we have seen, the law imposes few formal restrictions on the use of these discretionary powers. Not only are prosecutors' offices decentralized, they are also headed by locally elected officials. Moreover, the young assistants who make most of the key decisions are generally attorneys fresh out of law school with little background in how the law is actually administered. Most will serve only a short time before entering the private practice of law.

This does not mean that prosecutorial discretion is uncontrolled; rather it is influenced by other members of the courtroom work group. Through the socialization process and the occasional application of sanctions, young prosecutors are educated in the norms of the courtroom work groups.

For discussion

1. How important do you think local autonomy is in the operations of the prosecutor? What benefits and drawbacks would act to control prosecutors at the state level?
2. Given that prosecutors are generally elected officials, what effect does this have? Is it desirable to have the chief law enforcement official responsive to public opinion?
3. Interview a prosecutor. Of the five major tasks—fighting, negotiating, counseling, drafting, and administering—what are the most important? Why? Which tasks take the most time?
4. What kinds of controls should be placed on an assistant prosecutor's discretion?
5. Discuss the ways that prosecutorial discretion is influenced by courtroom work groups. If possible, discuss with a prosecutor his or her relationships with judges and defense attorneys.
6. Check local newspapers to see how much is written about the local prosecutor. What do these news items indicate about the goals of the local prosecutor?
7. If you were a prosecutor, what goals would you stress: the law enforcement or the officer of the court approach? Why?

References

Bugliosi, Vincent, with Curt Gentry. *Helter Skelter.* New York: Bantam Books, 1974.

Carter, Lief H. *The Limits of Order.* Lexington, Mass: D. C. Heath, 1974.

Eisenstein, James. "The Federal Prosecutor and His Environment." Paper delivered at the annual meeting of the American Political Science Association, Washington, D.C., September 2–7, 1968.

Engstrom, Richard. "Political Ambitions and the Prosecutorial Office." *Journal of Politics* 33 (1971):190.

Jacob, Herbert. "Judicial Insulation—Elections, Direct Participation, and Public Attention to the Courts in Wisconsin." *Wisconsin Law Review* (Summer 1966): 812.

Jacoby, Joan. *The American Prosecutor: A Search For Identity.* Lexington, Mass.: D. C. Heath, 1980.

LaFave, Wayne. *Arrest: The Decision to Take A Suspect Into Custody.* Boston: Little, Brown, 1965.

McDonald, William. "The Prosecutor's Domain," in William McDonald, (ed.), *The Prosecutor.* Beverly Hills, Calif: Sage Publications, 1979.

McNamara, John. "Uncertainties in Police Work," in David Bordua, ed., *The Police: Six Sociological Essays,* pp. 163–252. New York: John Wiley, 1967.

Mayer, Martin. *The Lawyers.* New York: Dell Publishing, 1968.

Milner, Neal. *The Court and Local Law Enforcement.* Beverly Hills, Calif: Sage Publications, 1971.

Morgan, Robert, and C. E. Alexander. "A Survey of Local Prosecutors." *State Government* 47 (1972):42.

Neubauer, David. *Criminal Justice in Middle America.* Morristown, N.J.: General Learning Press, 1974.

Niederhoffer, Arthur. *Behind the Shield.* Garden City, N.Y.: Doubleday, 1969.

The President's Commission on Law Enforcement and Administration of Justice. *Task Force Report: The Police.* Washington, D.C.: Government Printing Office, 1967.

Reiss, Albert J., and David Bordua. "Environment and Organization: A Perspective on the Police." In David Bordua, ed., *The Police: Six Sociological Essays.* New York: John Wiley, 1967.

Schlesinger, Joseph. *Ambition and Politics: Political Careers in the United States.* Chicago: Rand McNally, 1966.

Skolnick, Jerome. *Justice Without Trial.* New York: John Wiley, 1967.

U.S. Department of Justice. Law Enforcement Assistance Administration. *State and Local Prosecution and Civil Attorney Systems.* Washington, D.C.: Government Printing Office, 1978.

Utz, Pamela. "Two Models of Prosecutorial Professionalism." In William McDonald, ed., *The Prosecutor.* Beverly Hills, Calif.: Sage Publications, 1979.

For further reading

Carter, Lief H. *The Limits of Order.* Lexington, Mass.: D.C. Heath, 1974.

Dewey, Thomas. *Twenty Against the Underworld.* Garden City, N.Y.: Doubleday, 1974.

Eisenstein, James. *Counsel for the United States: U.S. Attorneys in the Political and Legal System.* Baltimore: Johns Hopkins University Press, 1978.

Jacoby, Joan. *The American Prosecutor: A Search for Identity.* Lexington, Mass.: D. C. Heath, 1980.

McDonald, William, ed. *The Prosecutor.* Beverly Hills, Calif.: Sage Publications, 1979.

Miller, Frank. *Prosecution: The Decision to Charge a Suspect with a Crime.* Boston: Little, Brown, 1969.

Neubauer, David. *Criminal Justice in Middle America.* Morristown, N.J.: General Learning Press, 1974.

Weimer, David. *Improving Prosecution? The Inducement and Implementation of Innovations for Prosecution Management.* Westport, Conn.: Greenwood Press, 1980.

CHAPTER 7

Judges

The judge is the symbol of justice for most Americans. Of all the actors in the criminal justice process, the public holds the judge responsible for ensuring that the system operates fairly and impartially. Thus we commonly equate the quality of justice with the quality of the judge. The judge and the symbol of justice is reinforced by the mystique surrounding the position—the flowing black robes, the gavel, and the honorific "all rise" when the judge enters the courtroom.

As important as these symbols are, though, they sometimes raise obstacles to understanding what judges actually do and how they influence the criminal justice process. The symbols of the bench coupled with its vast array of legal powers often cause us to overestimate the actual powers of the judge and ignore the importance of the other actors in the courtroom work group. At the same time, the mystique of the office often results in an underestimation of the role of the judge. Judges are not merely impartial black-robed umpires who hand down decisions according to clear and unwavering rules. "This view of the judge as an invisible interpreter of the law, as a part of the courtroom with no more individual personality than a witness chair or a jury box, is a fiction that judges themselves have done much to perpetuate" (Jackson:vii).

The purpose of this chapter is to untangle the conflicting notions about what judges do and how they do it. We will begin by examining the powers and responsibilities of the judge and how various pressures (the large number of cases, for example) have eroded the ideal image of a judge's power. Next we will consider the judge as a member of the courtroom community. A judge's actions are shaped and influenced by actions of prosecutors, other judges, defense attorneys, among others. Yet at the same time, the type of justice handed out varies from one judge to another. A persistent concern is whether judges are as qualified as they should be. Therefore, we will examine three suggestions for improving the quality of the judiciary: the adoption of merit selection, increased training, and mechanisms for removing unfit judges.

Judges at work

The formal powers of judges extend throughout the criminal court process. From arrest to final disposition, the accused face judges whenever decisions affecting their futures are made. Judges set bail and revoke it; they determine whether there is sufficient probable cause to hold the defendant; they rule on pretrial motions to exclude evidence; they accept pleas of guilty; if there is a trial, they preside; and after conviction they set the punishment. Throughout the process judges are expected to discharge these powers and responsibilities judiciously and without the appearance of impropriety.

Although we tend to think of judges primarily in terms of presiding at trials, their work is much more varied. Much of their work day is spent conducting hearings, accepting guilty pleas, imposing sentence, or working in their office (called *chambers*). In carrying out the responsibilities of the office, judges mainly react to the work of prosecutors and defense attorneys.

A recent study asked more than 5,000 judges in courts of general jurisdiction to report on the types of tasks they perform in a typical work day. Table 7-1 summarizes the variety of tasks judges engage in, using the same categories employed in chapter 6: fighting, negotiating, drafting, counseling, and administering (Ryan et al.).

> This is the dilemma of a judge and of many officials in the legal system. Following the rule of law may result in hardship and essential unfairness. Ignoring the law is a violation of one's oath of office, an illegal act, and a destruction of the system. Some choose to ignore the law in the interests of "justice." Others mechanically follow precedent. Neither course is satisfactory. The judge who frees a defendant knows that in most instances the state cannot appeal. Unless there is an election in the offing and the prosecutor chooses to use this case as a political issue, there will be no repercussions. But it is his duty, as it is that of the accused, to obey the law. If the judge is not restrained by the law, who will be? On the other hand, it is unrealistic to say, "Let the defendant appeal." In the long period between the trial judge's ruling and that of the higher court, if it hears the appeal, a human being will be in jail. One does not easily deprive a person of his liberty without very compelling reasons. Almost every day, the guardians of the law are torn between these conflicting pulls.

> Judge Lois Forer, *The Death of the Law* (New York: David McKay, 1975), pp. 85–86. © 1975 by Lois G. Forer.

TABLE 7-1.   Trial judges' common work day

Tasks	Percent of Judges Engaging in Task Daily
Fighting	
Reading case files	70%
Civil or criminal calendar	52
Presiding at non-jury trial	45
Presiding at jury trial	44
Waiting time	42
Negotiating	
Case related discussions with attorneys	48
Socializing with attorneys and others	39
Settlement discussions	32
Plea negotiation discussions	19
Drafting	
Keeping up with the law	68
Preparing/writing decisions, judgments, orders	56
Counseling	
Attending bar association meetings	0
Talking to civic groups	0
Teaching	0
Administering	
General administrative work	71

Source: Adapted from *American Trial Judges* by J. P. Ryan, A. Ashman, B. Sales, and S. Shane-DuBow. Copyright © 1980 by The American Judicature Society. Reprinted by permission of the publisher, The Free Press.

Fighting

fighting

Serving as an umpire during trial is a primary task of judges. Indeed, seven out of ten judges with a criminal assignment report that on a typical day they preside over a trial (Ryan et al.). While presiding at trial judges are expected to be neutral and not intervene to the undue advantage of either side. Because no legal code can furnish clear, unambiguous rules for every case, judges must use discretion in determining how the law applies to the particular facts of the case. They are the final arbiter of the law for the number of legal questions that may arise during trials: what questions may be asked potential jurors, what evidence is admissible, what instructions of law should be given the jury. Incorrect rulings on matters like these may result in an appellate court ruling that judicial error was committed and a new trial required.

Negotiating

negotiating

Most criminal convictions result not from a finding of guilt but from the defendant's plea of guilty. As table 7-1 documents, negotiating activities form a common part of the judge's work day. Judges vary greatly in the extent to which they participate in such plea bargaining negotiations. Some are active participants; along with prosecutors and defense attorneys, they discuss the evidence in the case, the type of charge the defendant will plead, and the sentence to be imposed. Others, however, refuse to participate. In these cases, the defense and prosecution take into consideration the judge's past practices.

Drafting

drafting

Only on rare occasions do trial judges draft legal opinions setting forth reasons for their decisions. But they do rule on numerous legal motions drafted by the prosecutor or defense. They are required by law to sign search warrants. They must rely on defense motions to exclude evidence because of improper police conduct or to change the site of the trial because of prejudicial pretrial publicity. Most of these matters are fairly routine and receive only brief examination by the judge. Thus contrary to popular perceptions, trial judges in criminal cases seldom decide complex legal issues. The Ryan study (see table 7-1) indicates, however, that drafting documents and keeping up with the law are tasks judges commonly engage in.

Counseling

counseling

Although prosecutors and defense attorneys must deal with clients, trial judges have no direct counseling role. Indeed, canons of judicial ethics generally prohibit judges from dealing directly with victims, witnesses, defendants, or police officers. Occasionally, however, judges will offer advice to police officers on how to draft a warrant properly. Similarly, some judges try to ensure that jurors and witnesses are treated fairly and courteously. Table 7-1 indicates, however, that counseling activities are not part of the trial judge's common work day.

Administering

docket

administering

chief judge

Judges must also be administrators. Judges try to keep their *dockets* (the calendar of cases scheduled to be heard) current. One major management task is the scheduling of cases. Dates for hearing pretrial motions and dates for trial must be established. How generously judges grant an attorney's requests for continuances (additional time) greatly affects how speedily or slowly cases are disposed of. Another major management problem is keeping track of the cases and all the papers involved in a specific case. Lost cases or lost paper can have serious consequences. Assisting judges in these administrative tasks are bailiffs, clerks, and/or law clerks. In large courts the administrative tasks are so time-consuming that one or more judges are designated *chief judges* and devote almost full time to administering the court. In a growing number of courts, particularly in large ones, court administrators may also be present.

Benefits of the job

In discharging their duties, judges enjoy some distinct benefits of office. Traditionally they have been surrounded with a high level of prestige and respect. Lawyers address the judge as "your honor," and all rise when the judge enters or leaves the courtroom. For many lawyers, a judgeship is the capstone to a successful career. Judges also enjoy other trappings of office. Federal judges enjoy life terms, as do judges in a handful of states. More commonly, terms of office range from six to ten years, considerably longer than those of other public office holders—a reflection of the independence of the American judiciary.

Judicial salaries are not the highest incomes of the legal profession, but they are higher than the average of other criminal justice personnel. Salaries of general jurisdiction trial judges range from a low of $34,000 in Alabama to a high of

---

CLOSE-UP: A TYPICAL DAY OF A JUDGE IN CRIMINAL COURT

A typical day for the judge of criminal assignment began around 9:00 A.M., when the judge arrived in chambers, read his mail, and skimmed the day's case files. The call of criminal cases generally started soon after but might be delayed if the judge were in conference with lawyers, or if lawyers were in conference with each other. More times than not, the judge and the court were forced to wait while lawyers concluded bargains, talked with clients, or hurried from an appearance in another courtroom. In many courts the call itself tended to be a rather chaotic process, with attorneys coming in and out of court, whispered plea negotiations continuing throughout the room (and sometimes back in chambers), and a variety of people approaching the clerk's desk (usually immediately adjacent to the bench) for one reason or another. In most instances, the criminal call not only served an attendance-taking function but afforded a review of the status of each case. The call could also assume some legal importance as defense lawyers jockeyed for advantageous (i.e., later) trial dates, while the judge used the threat of immediate trial as his own form of bargaining leverage. Often, short hearings, arraignments, the taking of guilty pleas, sentencings, and probation violations were disposed of in the criminal call.

After the completion of the call (or the first round), the judge might attend to some minor administrative matters, socialize with attorneys or court personnel, take a coffee break, or participate in case-related discussions with attorneys. Then, the judge might begin formal court proceedings—a motions hearing, a bench trial, or (most likely), a jury trial. These proceedings would continue for the rest of the morning, with adjournment around noon for a lunch break. While some judges gulped sandwiches at their desks and worked through lunch, most criminal judges lunched with court or law enforcement personnel, lawyer acquaintances, former political associates, or other judges. Occasionally judges attended bar luncheons, spoke at civic meetings, or participated in more specialized meetings such as judicial seminars, advisory board meetings of a halfway house, and the like. Frequently lunch conversations included mention of past and current cases, and from time to time some judicial business of a minor nature was transacted (usually pertaining to scheduling). However, politics, financial affairs, and travel plans were also common topics of conversation.

Returning to chambers somewhere between one hour and ninety minutes later, the judge might meet with some lawyers, catch up on correspondence, sign orders, or glance through the "advance sheets" (early publication of recent appellate cases) before the afternoon court session. After the court was reconvened, unfinished matters of the morning might again be taken up, whether continuation of the call or of a bench or jury trial. Jury proceedings were planned to begin and end for juror convenience; but while there might be a half-hour comfort break during the afternoon, many judges preferred to finish as much of the scheduled proceedings as possible before leaving for the day. Departure ranged anywhere from 3:00 to 6:00 P.M. or later, though the majority probably left sometime around 4:30 or so. The judge might attend to some minor matters after adjourning court or go to a meeting of the judiciary before leaving the building, but such activities were generally infrequent and not very lengthy. Most of the criminal judges whom we observed did not take case files or journals home, though some may have read the latter at home.

Source: From *American Trial Judges*, by J. P. Ryan, A. Ashman, B. Sales, and S. Shane-DuBow. Copyright © 1980 by The American Judicature Society. Reprinted by permission of the publisher, The Free Press.

$58,000 in New York (1980). For some lawyers a judicial salary represents an increase over that received in private practice and certainly a more secure one. For others, however, a judgeship represents a significant decrease in earning power. For almost a decade, Congress refused to raise the $40,000 pay of federal judges, (since increased to $70,300), which led to the resignation of a number of young competent judges, as well as difficulties in attracting good lawyers to fill the resulting vacancies.

Many judgeships carry with them considerable patronage powers. Court posts of bailiff, clerks, commissioners, reporters, probation officers, and secretaries must be filled. Since many of these positions are usually not covered by civil service, judges can award such positions to friends, relatives, campaign workers, and party leaders. In some cities judicial staff positions are a significant reservoir for party patronage.

Frustrations of the job

The pressures of today's criminal justice system often mean that the ideals surrounding the judge are not what they appear to be. Trial court judges in the nation's largest cities face sometimes staggering caseloads. Instead of having time to reflect on challenging legal questions or to consider the proper sentence for a convicted felon, trial judges must move cases, acting more like an administrator in a bureaucracy than a judicial sage. As a New York judge put it:

> It is clear that the "grand tradition" judge, the aloof, brooding, charismatic figure in the Old Testament tradition, is hardly a real figure. The reality is the working judge who must be politician, administrator, bureaucrat, and lawyer in order to cope with a crushing calendar of cases. A Metropolitan Court judge might well ask, "Did John Marshall or Oliver Wendell Holmes ever have to clear a calendar like mine?" [Blumberg:120]

Moreover the judge's actions are limited by the system—lawyers who are late, court documents that get lost, jails that are crowded. Added to these general constraints is the overall low prestige of criminal court judges, who occupy the lowest rung within the judicial system. Like the other actors in the criminal justice system, the judge becomes tainted by close association with defendants who are perceived as societal outcasts.

Thus the frustrations of the criminal trial court judge are many. Some judges prefer the relative peace of civil court where dockets are less crowded, courtrooms quieter, legal issues more intriguing, and witnesses more honest than the criminal court atmosphere of too many cases, too much noise, too many routine (and often dull) cases, and too many fabricated stories. Other judges, however, like the camaraderie of the criminal court and the easier legal issues.

Judges within the courtroom work group

The public believes judges are the principal decision makers in courts. Often they are not. Instead they defer to the judgments of the other members of the courtroom work group—prosecutors, witnesses, defense attorneys, psychiatrists, clerks, jail wardens, sheriff's deputies—who may have a greater knowledge about particular cases. Thus judges often accept bail recommendations offered by prosecutors, plea agreements struck by defense and prosecution, and sentences recommended by the probation officer. In short, while judges still retain the formal legal powers of their office, they often informally share these powers with other members of the courtroom work group.

Sanctions can be applied against judges who deviate from the consensus of the courtroom work groups. Defense attorneys and prosecutors can foul up judges' scheduling of cases by requesting continuances, being unprepared, or failing to have witnesses present when required. Particularly in big city courts, judges who fall too far behind on disposing of the docket feel pressures from other judges, especially the chief judge. Judges who fall behind may be transferred to less desirable duties.

Differences among judges

By no means are judges totally controlled by the courtroom work group. As the most prestigious members of the group, they have numerous types of pressures they can bring to bear on prosecutors, defense attorneys, probation officers, and so on. A verbal rebuke to a defense attorney in open court, a comment to the head prosecutor that the assistant is not performing satisfactorily, or a suggestion to the attorneys that they should get together on a specific case are types of judicial actions that can go a long way in shaping how the courtroom work group disposes of cases.

The amount of actual influence that a judge exerts upon the other members of the courtroom workgroup depends on several factors. Judges themselves are one factor. Some judges are active leaders of the courtroom work group. One study found that of a group of Colorado judges, some ran a "tight ship" (Beaney). They pressured attorneys to be in court on time, for example. These judges fully participated in the dynamics of courthouse judges. On the other hand, some judges ran a "loose ship," allowing, for example, the attorneys to have as many continuances as they requested. Such judges have in essence abdicated responsibility to prosecutors, defense attorneys, and others.

A second factor affecting the role of the judge within the courtroom work group is the stability of the work group. In this case stability refers to the length of time a judge works with the same set of basic actors. Greater familiarity among work group members means smoother negotiations, more common use of informal arrangements (rather than formalities), and a better knowledge about sentences a certain judge is likely to mete out (Eisenstein and Jacob:35–36).

Yet a third factor is the size of the court, that is, the number of judges on the court. In small courts judges rarely specialize, rather each one handles all stages of a case. Sixty percent of American judges serve on courts with nine or fewer judges. In large courts, with twenty-six or more judges, the work environment is strikingly *judge* *shopping* different. Judges are assigned to specific stages of cases. As a result, *judge shopping* is a common practice in some big city criminal courts. By the strategic use of motions for continuances and motions for a change of venue (a request for another judge), defense attorneys attempt to maneuver their clients before the judge they perceive to be most favorable. Such judge shopping is the most direct evidence of variations between judges. Although organizational pressures work to provide a certain degree of consistency among judges, any examination of a multijudge court immediately shows that judges differ in terms of sentences handed out, how they run their courtroom, and the number of cases pending. A mastery of these judicial differences is often as necessary for the practicing attorney as knowledge about the law and rules of procedure.

Quality and qualifications of judges

In large measure the quality of justice depends on the quality of the judges who dispense it. As the noted American jurist Benjamin Cardozo once put it: "In the long run, there is no guarantee of justice except the personality of the judge" (Cardozo:149). Unfortunately there is no agreed-upon set of criteria about what personality good judges should have—to say nothing about their legal talent and insight into human affairs.

"Scratch the average person's idea of what a judge should be and it's basically Solomon," says Yale law professor Geoffrey Hazard (Jackson:7). We expect judges to be honest, patient, wise, tolerant, compassionate, strong, decisive, articulate, courageous—a list of virtues similar to those in Boy Scout handbooks (Jackson:7).

The difficulties of establishing the qualities of what makes a good judge, to say nothing of determining what constitutes a poor judge, are summarized by the President's commission: "Although it is possible to identify such factors as professional incompetence, laziness, or intemperance which should disqualify a lawyer from becoming a judge, it is much more difficult to choose confidently the potentially superior judge from among a number of aspirants who appear generally qualified" (p. 66).

Gauging the correct type of judicial personality is particularly perplexing because of the wide array of both formal and informal tasks judges must perform. Moreover, a number of these tasks—keeping the docket moving comes to mind—are not directly related to legal wisdom or other seemingly obvious qualifications. Thus, while there is a strong reform movement to recruit better-quality men and women to the bench (which often means more learned), many of those who become judges have more modest credentials that are probably better suited to the actual functions that trial judges perform (Jacob, 1973:69).

Despite the lack of clarity in what attributes a good judge should possess, one central conclusion stands out: some judges do not fulfill the high minimal standards; they are senile, prejudiced, vindictive, tyrannical, lazy, and sometimes corrupt.

Although many factors have a bearing on the quality of judicial personnel—salary, length of term, prestige, independence, and personal satisfaction with the job—the factor considered most important by legal reformers is judicial selection. (President's Commission:66; National Advisory Commission:145). The training of judges and removal of poor judges are additional methods prominently mentioned for upgrading the quality of judges.

Varying roads to a judgeship

A variety of methods are used for selecting judges: partisan elections, nonpartisan elections, executive appointment, legislative election, or merit selection (usually referred to as the Missouri Bar Plan). Moreover in some states, different procedures are used for varying levels of the judiciary. Table 7-2 shows that there is a definite regional pattern in what states use which methods. Partisan elections are concentrated in the South, nonpartisan elections in the West and upper Midwest, legislative elections and executive appointments in the East, and merit selection west of the Mississippi River.

Formal selection methods are not always a guide to how judges are actually selected, however. When a judicial vacancy occurs, there is need for interim selection methods. Gubernatorial appointment and merit selection predominate in fill-

TABLE 7-2.   Initial (and interim) selection methods of trial judges in the states

Partisan Election		*Nonpartisan Election*		*Gubernatorial Appointment*	
Alabama	(G or M)	California	(G)	Connecticut	(G)
Arkansas	(G)	Florida	(M)	Delaware	(G-M)
Georgia	(G-M)	Idaho	(M)	Hawaii	(G)
Illinois	(SC)	Kentucky	(M)	Maine	(G)
Louisiana	(SC)	Maryland	(G-M)	Massachusetts	(G-M)
Mississippi	(G)	Michigan	(G)	New Hampshire	(G)
New Mexico	(G)	Minnesota	(G)	New Jersey	(G)
New York	(G-M)	Montana	(M)	Rhode Island	(G)
North Carolina	(G-M)	Nevada	(M)		
Pennsylvania	(G-M)	North Dakota	(M)		
Tennessee	(G)	Ohio	(G)		
Texas	(G)	Oklahoma	(G-M)		
West Virginia	(G)	Oregon	(G)		
		South Dakota	(G-M)		
		Washington	(G)		
		Wisconsin	(G)		

Merit		*Legislative Selection*		*Hybrids*	
Alaska	(M)	South Carolina	(G or LS)	Partisan or merit, depending on locale:	
Colorado	(M)	Virginia	(G)		
D.C.	(M)			Indiana	(G)
Iowa	(M)			Kansas	(G)
Nebraska	(M)			Missouri	(G or M)
Utah	(M)			Nonpartisan or merit, depending on locale:	
Vermont	(M)				
Wyoming	(M)			Arizona	(G)

Note: Codes for interim appointments: G = gubernatorial appointment; M = merit appointment; G-M = gubernatorial apointment, but merit system currently in effect by executive order; G or M = gubernatorial appointment or merit depending upon locale; SC = state supreme court appointment; LS = legislative selection.

Source: Adapted from *American Trial Judges*, by J. P. Ryan, A. Ashman, B. Sales, and S. Shane-DuBow, Copyright © 1980 by The American Judicature Society. Reprinted by permission of the publisher, The Free Press.

ing temporary vacancies. In the populous state of California, for example, 88 percent of the trial judges initially were appointed by the governor to fill a temporary vacancy. Indeed, a recent study estimated that half of all trial judges initially received their position through some form of interim selection (Ryan et al.:122). It is the combination, therefore, of formal selection and initial selection methods that accounts for how trial judges first arrive on the bench.

Election of judges

elections

Over half the states select judges through popular *election*, either partisan or nonpartisan. Election of judges was the product of Jacksonian democracy and the populist movement between 1840 and World War I. According to the Jacksonian philosophy, there should be no special qualifications for any public position; the popular vote should be the arbiter. Not incidentally, this philosophy helped to divide up the spoils by ensuring that the party elected could distribute patronage among their supporters.

At the turn of the century, however, a countertrend began. Spurred by widespread corruption in city governments resulting from dominance of political parties, the progressive movement sought to weaken the influence of the parties. One major technique was the nonpartisan ballot: officials would run for office not on the basis of party affiliation but on personal qualifications. Nevertheless, where nonpartisan elections are employed, partisan influences are often present. A fair estimate is that in half of the state using nonpartisan judicial ballots, the political parties play some role (Jacob, 1978:112–113). For example, both Minnesota and Michigan use nonpartisan ballots, but judicial candidates are endorsed or nominated by parties, receive party support during campaigns, and are readily identified with party labels (Glick and Vines:42).

Campaigns for American judgeships are generally low-keyed, low-visibility affairs marked by the absence of controversy. Voter turnout is low. Judges are seldom voted out of office. Studies in various states indicate that less than 5 percent of the judges were ever defeated for reelection (Jacob, 1978:113). The electoral sway of the incumbent judge is so powerful (indeed the title *judge* is typically listed on the ballot) that sitting judges are seldom even opposed for reelection. Although many judges are never opposed for reelection and fewer still are turned out of office, the possibilities still exist. Elected judges do spend part of their time maintaining contact with the local voters. Maintaining visibility and close ties to lawyers is perhaps the best insurance a judge can buy against having to wage a potentially costly campaign for reelection.

Executive appointments

executive appointment

Eight states plus the federal government select judges through *executive appointment*. The political dynamics involved in the executive appointment process have been most extensively studied in the selection of federal judges (Grossman).

The U.S. Constitution specifies that the president has the power to nominate judges with the advice and consent of two-thirds of the Senate. Based on this constitutional authorization, both the president and Senate have a voice in the selection process. When a judgeship becomes vacant, the deputy attorney general of the U.S. Department of Justice (the executive official authorized by the president to handle judicial nominees) searches for qualified lawyers by consulting party leaders of the state where the vacancy occurred, campaign supporters, U.S. senators, and prominent members of the bar. This initial and private screening has been known to take a year or longer when there are conflicts within the president's party over whom should be selected.

After the president has submitted his nomination for the vacant judicial post, the process shifts to the U.S. Senate. Most nominations are routine. After a hearing by the Senate Judiciary Committee, the full Senate usually confirms. But if the nomination is controversial, the committee hearings and Senate vote become the focus of great political activity. When President Johnson nominated his friend Justice Abraham Fortas to be chief justice of the Supreme Court, the Judiciary Committee delayed its formal vote; eventually the president withdrew the nomination, and Justice Fortas resigned from the Court due to charges of impropriety. Similarly, President Nixon's nomination of justices on two separate occasions were defeated in the Senate after bitter and divisive debates. Senators also influence federal judicial selections through the informal power of senatorial courtesy. Senators expect to be consulted before the president nominates a person for a judicial vacancy from their state if the president belongs to the same party as the senator. A senator who is not consulted may declare the nominee personally unacceptable, and senators from other states—finding strength in numbers—will follow their colleagues' preferences and not approve the presidential nominations. Through this process, senators can make specific recommendations as to who they think is qualified (former campaign managers come to mind) or exercise a direct veto over persons they find unacceptable (political enemies, for example). Procedural changes in the Senate Judiciary Committee, however, have recently lessened the influence of senatorial courtesy (Slotnick).

American Bar Association   Although the *American Bar Association* (ABA), the national lawyers' association, enjoys no formal role in the screening of nominees for the federal bench, through its Committee on Judicial Selection, it plays an increasingly influential role. The committee investigates potential nominees by consulting with members of the legal profession and law professors. It then ranks the candidates as "unqualified," "qualified," "well qualified," or "exceptionally well qualified." Although the president—not the American Bar Association— has the sole power to nominate, most presidents do not wish to name someone who will later be declared unqualified. Therefore the deputy attorney general usually seeks the ABA's recommendations prior to nomination, which often eliminates some potential nominees. This process produces federal judges with two defining attributes: judges who belong to the president's party, and who have often been active in politics.

State appointive systems resemble the presidential system for selecting federal judges, except at the state level there is no equivalent of senatorial courtesy. Like federal appointees, governors tend to nominate those who have been active in their campaigns. At times governors have been known to make appointments to strengthen their position within a geographical area or with a specific group of voters (Crow).

In recent years some governors informally have allowed bar associations to examine the qualifications of potential nominees. Much like the ABA influence on federal judicial appointees, state bar associations are gaining an increasing role. But unlike the federal process, governors have greater independence to ignore the bar association advice.

Missouri Bar Plan

"Remove the courts from politics" has been the long-standing rallying cry of judicial reformers. The National Advisory Commission on Criminal Justice and Goals (146) diagnosed three adverse effects of the popular election of judges. First, popular election has failed to encourage the ablest lawyers to seek judicial posts and works to discourage qualified persons from considering running because they wish to avoid the ordeal of an election. Second, popular election may suggest the appearance of impropriety because it provides an incentive for judges to decide cases in a popular manner. Thus, "an elective system does little to dissuade minority groups from believing that an elected judge must pander to the popular viewpoint in order to remain in judicial office" (National Advisory Commission:146). Third, the elective system is set in a context in which the electorate is least likely to be informed about the merits of the candidates. Implicit in these and other arguments of judicial reformers is the identification of poor judges with political hacks subservient to the party that initially slated them for a judgeship.

Missouri Bar Plan (merit selection)

To cure these ills, legal reformers advocate the *merit selection* system. Also known as the *Missouri Bar Plan* because that state was the first to adopt it in 1940, merit selection has won increasing acceptance. Eight states now utilize the plan for selecting all major judges, and three other states select appellate court judges under this method. In addition, a number of other states have considered implementing merit selection. The growing importance of this system is demonstrated by the fact that all states that have altered judicial selection techniques have adopted the Missouri Bar Plan.

Merit selection is actually a hybrid system incorporating elements from all the other selection methods: gubernatorial appointment, popular election, citizen involvement, and, most important, a formalized role for the legal profession. The merit selection system works as follows, although the details vary slightly from state to state. The governor appoints the judge from a list of names (typically there are three) submitted by a judicial nominating committee. Of the seven members of the judicial nominating commission, three are elected from the bar association, three are nonlawyers appointed by the governor to represent citizens' interests, and the final commission member is a judge. After appointment, the judge serves for one year and then goes before the voters in a plebiscite. The sole question on the ballot is "Should Judge X be retained?" The judge thus runs unopposed and if elected serves for life, or for a very long term. Most judges are returned by a healthy margin. However, some thirty-three have been removed to date. During the 1970s for example, 1.6% of the judges running on retention ballots were removed (Carbon and Berkson: 65–66).

Although backers of the Missouri Bar Plan contend that it will significantly improve the type of judges selected and remove the courts from politics, studies of the merit selection system in operation have reached different conclusions. While the politics of judicial selection has been altered, it has not been removed; in fact, removing politics does not seem possible. What the reformers presumably mean is the removal of "partisan" politics. In operation, the Missouri Bar Plan has reduced the influence of political parties while at the same time greatly increasing the power of the legal profession (Watson and Downing). Merit selection procedures were also used by President Carter for affirmative action purposes. During his term of office a higher proportion of women and racial minorities were appointed to the federal bench than were appointed by previous presidents.

Which system is best?

There is an extensive debate over which method of judicial selection is best. On the one hand the very nature of the judiciary is premised on the ability of judges to apply the law in a fair and impartial manner to ensure equal justice under the law. Obviously this rule of law requires judges to exercise professional judgment without regard to popular sentiments or pressures (Ducat and Flango). On the other hand, democracies are suspicious of governmental leaders with an independent base of power, fearing that they may become too distant from the people and at the same time arbitrary, if not abusive. Less philosophically, these competing perspectives find expression in tension between the legal profession and political parties over influencing judicial selections. The different methods of judicial selection heighten or diminish the influence of the bar or the influence of political parties.

In evaluating which selection system is "best," a key criterion is whether one system produces better judges than another. That is, do the judges in one system differ from those in others? Certainly it is part of judicial folklore that they do. Conversations with appointed judges indicate that some believe they would never have attained their position if they had to run for election. On the other hand, discussions with elected judges show that many believe that they would never have been selected under an appointment system. The only attribute these judges share in common is that they appear to fellow judges, members of the bar, and outside observers to be good judges. Several studies have systematically analyzed the folklore of the judges and supporters of one system over another and concluded that different selection systems are associated with different backgrounds of judges.

Where legislators appoint judges, it is quite clear that former legislators are more likely to be selected than in other systems. Similarly, elected systems elevate to the bench a higher proportion of persons who have held local political office. By contrast, where the governor appoints, the system benefits those who have held state office (such as legislators). We can perhaps best evaluate these differences by asking what systems appear to favor candidates with local political office, which typically means the elected local district attorney. Under the Missouri Bar Plan and elective systems, former DAs are more often selected as judges. Where the executive or legislature makes the selection, though, fewer DAs become judges.

Varying backgrounds of judges are related to differing selection systems, but by and large the differences are rather small. When judges' prior political experience, local ties, party affiliation, and quality of legal education have been analyzed, the systems of judicial selection do not appear to be very different. Pulling together the findings of many diverse studies, Nagel concluded that elected and appointed systems do not differ "as much in their results or in the behavior of voters and appointers as the debate in literature would have us believe" (Nagel: 36). Canon reached a similar conclusion in studying state supreme court judges: "Institutional mechanisms surrounding recruitment do not have the impact on personal characteristics which advocates of competing selection systems often imply they have" (Canon: 588).

Similarities in judges' backgrounds

Although America uses a wide variety of methods for selecting judges, it is important to note that overall judges share some important similarities, similarities that may be of even greater importance than the differences (table 7-3). In general, judges are males from the upper middle class, and their backgrounds reflect the attributes of that class: they are more often white, Protestant, and better educated than the average American.

Another similarity is that most judges were born in the community in which they serve. Trial court judges are usually appointed from particular districts. This local selection results in elevating persons who were born in that area and often attended local or state colleges before going on to a law school within the state. (The only major exception is in New England, where the schools have a strong regional orientation.) These patterns are revealed in a study of Louisiana judges. Over 90 percent of Louisiana judges were born in the state, 75 percent attended college within the state, and most of the rest attended a southern school (Vines).

Finally, judges are seldom newcomers to political life. As table 7-3 shows, almost three out of four state supreme court judges surveyed held a prior nonjudicial political office. Trial court judges also have held prior office, with the model category being district attorney or state legislator. Eighty percent of federal judges had

TABLE 7-3.   Selected background characteristics of state supreme court judges, 1969

Characteristics	Percent of judges (N = 306)
Spent childhood in same state as court	89.0
Spent childhood in same region but not state as court	6.1
Attended law school in same state as court	60.4
Attended law school in same region but not state as court	20.5
Had law degree	92.4
Held previous state or local judgeship	31.2
Held at least one nonjudicial political office	72.5

Source: From *State Court Systems*, by H. R. Glick and K. N. Vines. Copyright © 1973, p. 48. Reprinted by permission of Prentice-Hall, Inc.

prior governmental experience. Before becoming judges, they had some familiarity with the range of public issues that governments as well as courts must solve. These factors mean that few political mavericks survive the series of screens that precede becoming a judge. The process tends to eliminate those who hold views and exhibit behavior widely different from those of the mainstream of local community sentiment.

How selection systems recruit judges with attitudes reflecting those of the local community is shown in a study of Pittsburgh and Minneapolis. These two cities were chosen because of major differences in their political systems and their methods of judicial selection. In Pittsburgh judicial selections reflect a highly politicized environment dominated by the Democratic machine. Lawyers wanting to be judges patiently "wait in line" because of the party's need to maintain ethnic and religious balance on the judicial ticket (Levin: 332). As a result, almost all Pittsburgh judges held government positions prior to coming to the bench, and some still remain active in party affairs. Because of the dominance of partisan politics in the city, it is widely accepted that courts should be staffed with party workers. Bar associations play only a very limited role in judicial selection, and there is little support for efforts to reform the judiciary.

The political culture of Minneapolis is strikingly different. It is a "good government or reformed city" with a weak political machine. Political parties have only a limited role in judicial selection; instead the bar association is quite influential. Before a judicial election the Minneapolis Bar Association polls its members, and the winner in the lawyers' poll almost always wins in the general election. If a vacancy occurs, the governor appoints judges according to the preferences of the bar association. As a result of this selection process, Minneapolis judges are seldom drawn from party activists; they tend to be lawyers in large, business-oriented law firms.

The vastly different political cultures and judical selection processes in Pittsburgh and Minneapolis produce judges with contrasting judicial philosophies. Minneapolis judges are more oriented to the needs of "society" than toward the defendant. Typically they are more concerned with universal legal requirements and adopt a formalistic approach; that is, they see the purpose of sentencing in terms of punishment and deterrence, and they make few efforts to individualize justice.

Pittsburgh judges, on the other hand, stress common sense and practical day-to-day experiences in making decisions. In place of abstract and universal legal principles, they attempt to reach "just" solutions. Courtrooms are run informally. In short, Pittsburgh judges place a high premium on individualizing justice and little on deterrence or punishment.

Women in the Judiciary . . .

Until this century, the number of women judges in America was so small that one could literally count them all on one hand. The first woman on the bench in this country, Esther Morris (who, incidentally, was not a lawyer), was appointed to serve as a justice of the peace in the Territory of Wyoming in 1870. At the end of the nineteenth century, no other state had selected any women judges, nor had any women been appointed to serve in the federal judiciary.

The twentieth century began witnessing changes, though not very quickly. By 1950, women had achieved at least token representation on the bench. It was not until 1979, however, that every state could report that its bench had included at least one woman judge. [As of 1982, there were 549 female judges serving on state courts. As part of his affirmative action program, President Carter appointed 40 women to the federal bench.]

Susan Carbon, "Women in the Judiciary" *Judicature*—(December–January 1982): p. 285.

These opposing judicial philosophies produce contrasting sentences. Pittsburgh judges are more lenient than those in Minneapolis. A higher percentage of defendants are placed on probation, and when a prison sentence is imposed, it is shorter. Overall, black defendants are treated more favorably in Pittsburgh than in Minneapolis (Levin).

Learning to be a judge

Unlike most other countries, the United States does not rely on a group of career judges who undergo special training beyond a law degree. Our various methods of judicial selection all recruit essentially judicial amateurs to the bench who have no practical experience or systematic exposure to the judicial world. Many new judges find that being a judge varies greatly from what they had expected. Robert Carp and Russell Wheeler studied the experiences of newly appointed federal judges. In an appropriately titled article, "Sink or Swim: The Socialization of a Federal District Judge," they found that new federal judges experience three general kinds of problems. First is mastering new areas of substantive and procedural law. In sharp contrast to private lawyers who specialize in a few areas of the law, judges must be generalists; they must rule on a diverse range of legal matters, some of which they were exposed to in law school but some of which are entirely new. Many federal judges (but fewer state judges) therefore come to the bench with no background in criminal law and procedure. The President's Commission highlighted the deficiencies of judicial preparation: ". . . it is still possible for a judge who the day before had made his living drafting corporate indentures to be called upon to rule on the validity of a search or to charge a jury on the law of entrapment" (p. 68).

A second set of problems facing new judges is administrative in nature. Supervising the court staff, efficiently and wisely using their time, and managing the hundreds of cases on the court's docket are types of problems many judges from private practice have never previously faced.

Finally, new judges experience psychological discomfort in adjusting to their new job. The bench can be a lonely place. Another difficult psychological problem is sentencing. Most judges find sentencing the hardest part of being a judge. A federal judge in Louisiana summarized this difficulty: "You see so many pathetic people and you're never sure of what is a right or a fair sentence" (Carp and Wheeler:373). Some judges have difficulty in abandoning the adversary role that marked their legal career. One judge indicated "the major problem along these lines is that a judge has got to look at both sides of the case whereas an attorney need only look at one" (Carp and Wheeler:373).

. . . After you become a federal judge some people tend to avoid you. For instance, you lose all your lawyer friends and generally you have to begin to make new friends. I guess the lawyers are afraid that they will some day have a case before you and it would be awkward for them if they were on too close terms with you. I guess other people think a judge is sort of aloof and they don't feel so much at ease with you as they did before.

Quoted in Robert Carp and Russell Wheeler, "Sink or Swim: The Socialization of a Federal District Judge," *Journal of Public Law* 21 (1972):372–373. Reprinted by permission of the *Emory Law Journal* of the Emory University School of Law.

Mastering new areas of the law, administering the court, and psychologically adjusting to the new role are all problems that confront new judges. But judges are assisted by a variety of other people in learning how to deal with the problems facing them. Fellow trial judges are the first and foremost training agents. Through formal meetings, but mainly through more informal exchanges, judges discuss common problems and possible techniques. Lawyers who appear in court are another source that judges can mine to learn what the law says in an area new to them. Local court staff—clerks, bailiffs, secretaries, probation officers, and law clerks—often provide new judges with advice on administrative or procedural matters (Blumberg:124). But in the end judges must rely on themselves. Through reading in the law library and seeking out knowledgeable persons, judges engage in self-education.

Judicial education

judicial education

A major development in the last few years has been judicial training schools and seminars to ease the adjustment problems of new judges. Such programs are by no means limited to new judges. Even veterans of the bench may benefit from a systematic exposure to types of administrative techniques for keeping the docket current or from seminars on rapidly changing areas of the law.

Judicial education in America caught on during the 1960s. Until then the idea that judges should go back to school was not widely accepted, mainly because it might appear to downgrade the judiciary, which was supposed to know the law. Under the prodding of the American Bar Association and Supreme Court Justice Tom Clark, judicial education programs were developed (Jackson:29). In 1956 the Institute for Judicial Administration initiated seminars for state appeals court judges. The National College of the State Judiciary conducts two- and four-week summer courses for trial judges. The Federal Judicial Center conducts seminars for newly appointed federal judges as well as continuing education seminars for veteran judges. Other such national programs have sprung up (National Advisory Committee:157).

At the state level, however, institutionalization of training programs for new judges or yearly educational conferences for all judges has been slower. Five states (Maine, Montana, Vermont, West Virginia, and Wyoming) have no training programs. And of the states with programs, only slightly more than half are mandatory. In short, judicial education is just in the beginning stages.

Judging the judges

Although judicial selection techniques attempt to recruit Solomon-like figures to the bench and although judicial education programs can fill in a new judge's deficiencies and keep sitting judges abreast of changes in the law, the troublesome problem still remains of what to do with unfit judges. At issue is how to devise a system for removing unfit judges while at the same time guaranteeing an independent judiciary.

The need for such protections is illustrated by attempts of the ultraconservative John Birch Society to impeach Chief Justice Warren in the 1960s. The Impeach Earl Warren campaign charged the Supreme Court with making "unconstitutional . . . pro-Communist racial integration policies." These critics of Earl Warren were attempting to remove him not because of a lack of ability as a judge but because they disagreed with the Court's decisions on racial integration, freedom of religion, and criminal procedure. Protections against unpopular court rulings constitute the hallmark of an independent judiciary. Yet judicial independence is not an end in itself. As University of Chicago law professor Philip Kurland has put it, "the provisions for securing the independence of the judiciary were not created for the benefit of the judges, but for the benefit of the judged" (quoted in Byrd:267).

Proper judicial conduct is indispensable to the confidence of the people in their judiciary, a confidence that itself is an indispensable ingredient in the rule of law (Greenberg:460). In recent years such public confidence has been eroded by scandals surrounding the courts. Two judges of the Illinois Supreme Court were forced to resign in 1969. In California, New Mexico, New York, Florida, and Oklahoma—to name just a few other states—judicial conduct has been called into question, resulting in investigations, indictments, and resignations of some judges.

recall elections

impeachment

judicial conduct commission

The fundamental problem is that judges—whether elected or appointed—exercise more power with less accountability than any other official in our society. Moreover, formal methods for removing unfit judges—*recall elections* and *impeachment*—are generally so cumbersome that they have seldom been used.

A more workable method for dealing with unfit judges is the *judicial conduct commission*. The most well-known example is California's. Created by a constitutional amendment in 1960, the commission consists of two appeals court judges, two superior court judges, and one municipal judge, all appointed by the state supreme court. In addition, the commission includes two lawyers selected by the state bar association and two citizens nominated by the governor. The California commission receives, investigates, and screens complaints by any person against any judge in the state. If it finds that the complaint is justified, the commission may recommend to the supreme court that the judge be retired for any permanent disability that interferes with performance. In addition the commission may recommend either censure or removal for willful misconduct, persistent failure to perform duties, and habitual intemperance or conduct that is prejudicial to the administration of justice (National Advisory Commission:154).

The state supreme court retains final power to remove errant judges. Although the commission is thus armed with the potent weapon of a public recommendation, it prefers to act more informally. When it finds misconduct, it conducts a

IN THE NEWS: CALLED TOO HARSH AND TOO EASY, A PANEL JUDGING JUDGES IS FACING JUDGMENT
BY SELWYN RAAB

Six years after it was established to uproot corrupt and abusive judges, the New York State Commission on Judicial Conduct is being criticized for its tactics, its record and its plans for the future.

A variety of critics take virtually opposite positions. One group says that the commission has been too harsh and that possible overzealousness in trying to find misconduct has intimidated judges and weakened judicial independence.

Others say that the commission has been dominated by judges and lawyers and is too sympathetic and secretive in its overall dealings with judges. They also contend that the agency has made little effort to uncover irregularities committed by any of the state's 3,500 full-time and part-time judges.

According to the commission, out of 1,599 investigations—sometimes involving the same judge more than once—it has found 191 judges guilty of some type of ethical misbehavior. Thus, the vast majority of cases led to exoneration without disclosure of the inquiries. . . .

Defending the commission, Mrs. Gene Robb, the chairman of the agency, said investigations and hearings, like grand jury proceedings, were confidential to protect the reputations of judges who are unjustly accused.

The commission, she said, had "served as a deterrent" against improprieties by judges in and out of courtrooms, adding: "The record will show how extremely fair and effective we have been."

The commission, which has the authority to investigate, hold hearings and recommend punishment—including removal from the bench—is the chief watchdog over the state's judges. Its findings and punitive recommendations can be overruled only by the Court of Appeals, the state's highest court, but this has rarely happened.

New York Times, September 16, 1981. © 1981 by The New York Times Company. Reprinted by permission.

confidential conference and discusses the matter with the judge, who has an opportunity to rebut the charges. The commission may try to correct the matter. But most importantly, it usually seeks to force the voluntary retirement of the judge. The informal pressures and the threat of bringing public proceedings are apparently enough to force the judge in question off the bench. The complaints and investigations remain confidential unless the commission finds it necessary to seek a reprimand or removal before the California Supreme Court. This confidentiality is essential lest a judge's reputation be tarnished by a crank complaint. Many complaints are issued against judges by disgruntled litigants whose charge is no more serious than that the judge did not rule in their favor.

Since 1960, all states have created commissions on judicial conduct. The precise names of these bodies, as well as their structures, powers, and procedures vary among the states (Tesitor). In 1980 the U.S. Congress passed the Judicial Councils Reform and Judicial Conduct and Disability Act, which created new procedures for investigating complaints about federal judges.

Conclusion

The workaday world of the trial judge bears little resemblance to the high expectations we have about the role of the judge. The trial judge is expected to dispose of a large caseload but is often frustrated by the lack of preparation of the attorneys, missing defendants, misplaced files, little time to reflect, and, probably most importantly, insufficient control over many vital aspects of the case. For these and other reasons, judges depend on other members of the courtroom work group.

Some depend heavily on the prosecutors and defense attorneys and probation officers, feeling content to let them make the difficult decisions. Others, however, are much more active participants and are truly leaders of the courtroom work group.

To a large extent the public's impression of justice is shaped by the trial judge's demeanor and the dignity the judge imparts to the proceedings. Given the very high ideals society holds for judges, however, not all measure up. To a certain extent, this is because we expect too much of judges. It is as if we think that merely placing a black robe on a lawyer will cure all the shortcomings that the person had as a lawyer. Ultimately, the quality of judges ranges from some who are highly competent and extremely dedicated, to many who are average, and to a few who fall below minimal standards.

For discussion

1. What are the most important tasks that a judge performs? How do these tasks differ from popular images citizens hold about judges? Why?
2. What system of judicial selection do you think is best? What dangers do you perceive in letting bar associations select judges? What dangers do you perceive in letting the voting public choose?
3. Discuss with a judge his or her first year on the bench. Did the judge consider herself or himself prepared? What unexpected problems did he or she encounter?
4. Examine local news coverage of judges. What issues do the media bring up? Do you think these stories show the full range of tasks and difficulties that judges must deal with?
5. Are judges and lawyers too protective of judges who do not live up to our expectations? What procedures would you recommend for removing unfit judges?

References

Beaney, William. "Relationships, Role Conceptions, and Discretion among the District Court Judges of Colorado." Paper presented to the annual meeting of the American Political Science Association, Washington, D.C., 1970.

Blumberg, Abraham. *Criminal Justice.* Chicago: Quadrangle Books, 1967.

Byrd, Harry. "Has Life Tenure Outlived Its Time?" *Judicature* 59 (January 1976):266.

Canon, Bradley. "The Impact of Formal Selection Processes on the Characteristics of Judges—Reconsidered." *Law & Society Review* 6 (May 1972):579–594.

Carbon, Susan, and Larry Berkson. *Judicial Retention Elections in the United States.* Chicago: American Judicature Society, 1980.

Cardozo, Benjamin. *The Nature of the Judicial Process.* New Haven, Conn.: Yale University Press, 1921.

Carp, Robert, and Russell Wheeler. "Sink or Swim: The Socialization of a Federal District Judge." *Journal of Public Law* 21 (1972):359–394.

Crow, John. "Subterranean Politics: A Judge is Chosen." *Journal of Public Law* 12 (1963):275–289.

Ducat, Craig, and Victor Flango. "In Search of Qualified Judges: An Inquiry into the Relevance of Judicial Selection Research." DeKalb, Ill.: Center for Developmental Studies, Northern Illinois University, 1975.

Eisenstein, James, and Herbert Jacob. *Felony Justice: An Organizational Analysis of Criminal Courts.* Boston: Little, Brown, 1977.

Glick, Henry Robert, and Kenneth N. Vines. *State Court Systems.* Englewood Cliffs, N.J.: Prentice-Hall, 1973.

Greenberg, Frank. "The Task of Judging the Judges." *Judicature* 59 (May 1976):458–467.

Grossman, Joel. *Lawyers and Judges: The ABA and the Politics of Judicial Selection.* New York: John Wiley, 1965.

Jackson, Donald Dale. *Judges.* New York: Atheneum, 1974.

Jacob, Herbert. *Urban Justice: Law and Order in American Cities.* Englewood Cliffs, N.J.: Prentice-Hall, 1973.

————. *Justice in America: Courts, Lawyers, and the Judicial Process,* 3rd ed. Boston: Little, Brown, 1978.

Levin, Martin A. "Urban Politics and Policy Outcomes: The Criminal Courts." In George F. Cole, ed. *Criminal Justice: Law and Politics,* 2nd ed. North Scituate, Mass.: Duxbury Press, 1976.

Nagel, Stuart. *Comparing Elected and Appointed Judicial Systems.* Beverly Hills, Calif.: Sage Publications, 1973.

National Advisory Commission on Criminal Justice Standards and Goals. *Courts.* Washington, D.C.: Government Printing Office, 1973.

President's Commission on Law Enforcement and Administration of Justice. *Task Force Report: The Courts.* Washington, D.C: Government Printing Office, 1967.

Ryan, John Paul, Allan Ashman, Bruce Sales, and Sandra Shane-DuBow. *American Trial Judges.* New York: The Free Press, 1980.

Slotnick, Elliot. "The Changing Role of the Senate Judiciary Committee." *Judicature* 62 (May 1979):502–510.

Tesitor, Irene. *Judicial Conduct Organizations.* Chicago: American Judicature Society, 1978.

Vines, Kenneth. "The Selection of Judges in Louisiana." *Tulane Studies in Political Science* 8 (1962):99–119.

Watson, Richard, and Rondal Downing. *The Politics of the Bench and Bar: Judicial Selection under the Missouri Nonpartisan Court Plan.* New York: John Wiley, 1969.

For further reading

Dubois, Philip. *From Ballot to Bench: Judicial Elections and the Quest for Accountability.* Austin: University of Texas Press, 1980.

Goulden, Joseph. *The Benchwarmers.* New York: Ballantine Books, 1974.

Grossman, Joel. *Lawyers and Judges: The ABA and the Politics of Judicial Selection.* New York: John Wiley, 1965.

Harris, Richard. *Decisions.* New York: Ballantine Books, 1970.

Jackson, Donald Dale. *Judges.* New York: Atheneum, 1974.

Watson, Richard, and Rondal Downing. *The Politics of the Bench and Bar: Judicial Selection under the Missouri Nonpartisan Court Plan.* New York: John Wiley, 1969.

CHAPTER 8

Defense Attorneys

In America when you say *defense attorney*, most people think of Perry Mason. As rerun on late-night television, the fictionalized character of Perry Mason embodies our image of the defense attorney fighting to free his falsely accused client. He always succeeded. The public often contrasts this favorable image with a less complimentary one of real attorneys. Concerned about rising crime rates, many Americans also view the defense attorney as a conniver who uses legal technicalities to free the guilty. In the eyes of other members of the legal profession, the defense attorney is viewed as a virtual outcast who knows little law and who may engage in unethical behavior. To a client, the one whose future is literally in the lawyer's hands, the defense attorney is often perceived as just another member of the courthouse gang who does not fight hard enough.

This chapter assesses these conflicting images against the daily realities of the small proportion of the legal profession that represents defendants accused of violating the criminal law. The picture is a complicated one. Some defense attorneys suffer from all the shortcomings mentioned by their critics. Others do not. But all face day-to-day problems and challenges not usually encountered by the bulk of

American lawyers who represent higher-status clients. The key topics of this chapter are the factors influencing the type of legal assistance available to those who appear in criminal courts: the legal right to counsel, the tasks defense attorneys must perform, the relationship they have with courtroom work groups, the nature of the criminal bar, the relationship between lawyer and client, and, finally, differing systems for providing legal assistance to the poor.

The right to counsel

right to counsel

Like most other provisions of the U.S. Constitution, the Sixth Amendment has a different meaning today than it did when it was first inserted into the Constitution. Under the ancient common law, defendants could be tried without a lawyer, even if they wanted to hire their own. The Sixth Amendment was meant to correct this situation by providing the right to counsel. But until the early 1960s, this provision did not extend to many felony defendants too poor to hire their own lawyer. A significant minority had to face the legal maze of the courts by themselves. To many this meant that the quality of justice a defendant received depended on the quantity of money she or he possessed.

Gideon v. *Wainwright*

In *Gideon* v. *Wainwright* (372 U.S. 335, 1963), the Supreme Court reversed earlier interpretations of the Sixth Amendment. In *Gideon* the Court held that indigent (poor) defendants charged with a felony were entitled to the services of a lawyer paid by the government. Justice Hugo Black's opinion for the Court is worth quoting at length because it aptly summarizes the importance of counsel in the adversary system:

> . . . in our adversary system of criminal justice, any person hailed into court, who is too poor to hire a lawyer, cannot be assured a fair trial unless counsel is provided for him. This seems to us to be an obvious truth . . . there are few defendants charged with crime, few indeed, who fail to hire the best lawyers they can get to prepare and present their defenses.
>
> That government hires lawyers to prosecute and defendants who have the money hire lawyers to defend are the strongest indications of the widespread belief that lawyers in criminal courts are necessities, not luxuries.

Argersinger v. *Hamlin*

But as so often happens, answering one question raises several new ones. Thus in the wake of *Gideon*, the Court wrestled with the question of extending the right to counsel to include not only felony defendants but also those accused of minor violations (misdemeanor or ordinance violations) as well. In *Argersinger* v. *Hamlin* (407 U.S. 25, 1972), the Court ruled that "absent a knowing and intelligent waiver, no person may be imprisoned for any offense, whether classified as petty, misdemeanor, or felony unless he was represented by counsel." This decision requires trial judges to decide before sentencing if a jail sentence is likely; if it is not, there is no need to appoint counsel. Few of the nation's lower courts, however, have taken steps to implement the Court's *Argersinger* decision (Krantz et al.).

The *Gideon* decision spawned another important question: where in the criminal process does the right to counsel begin (and end)? Some argued that the right to legal representation is applicable only after a defendant is officially charged with a crime and brought into court, but the Supreme Court adopted a more expansive view. Note that the Sixth Amendment protects the right to counsel in "all criminal prosecutions," not just the criminal trial. Thus a defendant is entitled to legal representation at "critical stages" of prosecutions, that is every stage "where substantial rights of the accused may be affected," that require the "guiding hand of counsel" (*Mempa* v. *Rhay*, 389 U.S. 128, 1967). These critical stages include arraignment and the preliminary hearing but not the initial appearance.

Some extensions of *Gideon* proved more controversial than the initial decision itself. For in *Miranda* and companion cases, the right to counsel was extended to the police station to include police interrogations and police lineups. Not only did the Warren Court steadily extend the right to counsel at trial and prior to trial, they also applied the right to posttrial proceedings. Working on the assumption that a person's right to one appeal can be effective only if counsel is available, the Court held that indigents have the right to court-appointed counsel for the appeal as well as free transcripts of the trial. To quote the Court, "There can be no equal justice where the kind of trial a man gets depends on the money he has" (*Griffin* v. *Illinois*, 351 U.S. 12, 1956).

Defense attorneys at work

advocate

To a large extent, the adversary system is dependent upon defense attorneys. Lawyers are expected to be *advocates* for their client's case, arguing for legal innocence. As one defense counsel phrased it, "If the attorney does not appear to be taking the side of the defendant, then no one will" (Neubauer:73). The adversary system also charges defense attorneys with ensuring that defendants' constitutional rights are respected. Thus, irrespective of guilt or innocence, the defense attorney is a *challenger* who must seek out possible violations of these rights. Attorneys must also be *counselors* and advise their clients. Finally, defense attorneys must fulfill these responsibilities within the framework established by legal ethics. The zealous advocacy of a client's case is not the same thing as winning at all costs. As a member of the legal profession, a lawyer's advocacy of a client's case is limited by professional obligations. Attorneys are officers of the court and must follow court rules. They cannot deliberately mislead the court by providing false information. Nor can they knowingly allow the use of perjured testimony.

challenger

counselor

We can best dissect the multiple (and sometimes conflicting) responsibilities of defense attorneys by examining their work in fighting, negotiating, drafting, counseling, and administering.

Fighting

fighting

The objectives of defense attorneys are diametrically opposed to those of the prosecutor. Whereas the state seeks to prove the defendant guilty, defense attorneys seek to disprove the criminal charges. Under the adversary system, they are charged with zealously advocating their clients' cases to ensure that the defendants receive justice. The defense attorney as *fighter* is most visible during trial. Through cross-examination, for example, they search for weaknesses in the state's case. In most trials attorneys seek to convince the jury that the defendant is not guilty beyond a reasonable doubt by presenting a case of their own. Throughout the trial the defense attorney manages the case and must make important tactical and strategic decisions. (Chapter 14 will discuss some of the factors guiding such decisions.)

> The duty of a lawyer, both to his client and to the legal system, is to represent his client zealously within the bounds of the law, which includes Disciplinary Rules and enforceable professional regulations. The professional responsibility of a lawyer derives from his membership in a profession which has the duty of assisting members of the public to secure and protect available legal rights and benefits. In our government of laws and not of men, each member of our society is entitled to have his conduct judged and regulated in accordance with the law, to seek any lawful objective through legally permissible means, and to present for adjudication any lawful claim, issue, or defense.
>
> A lawyer as adviser furthers the interest of his client by giving his professional opinion as to what he believes would likely be the ultimate decision of the courts on the matter at hand and by informing his client of the practical effect of such decision. He may continue in the representation of his client even though his client has elected to pursue a course of conduct contrary to the advice of the lawyer so long as he does not thereby knowingly assist the client to engage in illegal conduct or to take a frivolous legal position. A lawyer should never encourage or aid his client to commit criminal acts or counsel his client on how to violate the law and avoid punishment therefor.

American Bar Association, *Code of Professional Responsibility and Code of Judicial Conduct* (Chicago, 1977). p. 32.

Negotiating

The defense attorney's role as advocate is not confined solely to trial. The lawyer's multiple roles as advocate and counselor produce conflicting yardsticks for assessing the work performed. Simply put, how do we define winning? For Perry Mason, winning meant an acquittal. And most defendants define winning in this way. A study of over 2,000 writs of habeas corpus filed by Florida prisoners demonstrated that defendants believed it was their lawyer's job to "get them off" no matter how guilty they were (Kerper:442). Such expectations are unrealistic. As the ABA Standards on the Administration of Justice spell out, lawyers who define success as gaining an acquittal are doomed to disappointment (Nelson:192). An experienced Los Angeles public defender explains: "What is our job as a criminal lawyer in most instances? Number one is . . . no kidding, we know the man's done it, or we feel he's done it, he may deny it, but the question is: *Can they prove it?* The next thing is: *Can we mitigate it?* Of course you can always find something good to say about the guy—to mitigate it. Those are the two things that are important, and that's what you do" (Mather:278). Thus many defense attorneys define winning in terms of securing probation, attempting to avoid a felony conviction by accepting a plea to a misdemeanor, or seeking to avoid long prison sentences. Such alternative goals to gaining an outright acquittal focus on sentencing, whereas the prescribed role of advocate centers on contesting guilt or innocence.

negotiating   One attorney put it this way: "Given the situation, what is the best that can be done for my client" (Neubauer:74). Often the best that can be done for the client is to *negotiate* the best possible deal.

Drafting

drafting

Under the adversary system, defense attorneys are also charged with protecting the defendant's constitutional rights. The defense attorney is thus built into the adversary system as a challenger whose role is to keep the system honest. Defense attorneys are catalysts who question whether the police or prosecutor have acted properly. Most of these activities occur when attorneys file motions they have *drafted* to suppress confessions or evidence because the police acted improperly. Or defense attorneys may file a motion for a change of venue because of prejudicial pretrial publicity. In many instances, defense attorneys file pretrial motions in an effort to gain a tactical advantage over the prosecutor.

Counseling

counseling

One of the most important tasks of defense attorneys is *counseling*. As advocates, they are expected to champion their client's cases. But as counselors, they must advise their clients about the possible legal consequences involved. Thus lawyers must fully and dispassionately evaluate the strengths and the weaknesses of the prosecutor's case, assess the probable success of various legal defenses, and—most importantly—weigh the likelihood of a jury conviction or acquittal. In appraising the risks and outlining the options, lawyers interpret the law to their clients, clients who are often unversed in what the law considers important, what the law demands, and what the law views as irrelevant. (Later in this chapter we will examine why the counseling role is a difficult one for the defense attorney.)

Administering

Like judges and prosecutors, defense attorneys represent numerous clients at the same time. Typically, though, the caseload of defense attorneys is heavier than that of prosecutors. Moreover these cases are all at different stages of the criminal court process. Defense attorneys must keep numerous balls in the air by trying to meet various scheduled court appearances: initial appearances, bail hearings, arraignments, pretrial motions, plea bargaining sessions, trial settings, and sentencing hearings. On a typical day defense attorneys must appear in several different courts and thus spend part of their day waiting for everyone else to assemble.

administer-ing

Besides scheduling personal court appearances, defense attorneys are also responsible for other *administrative* duties: making sure that necessary witnesses are subpoenaed to be in court, filing motions on time, and so on.

The fact that a lawyer represents numerous defendants typically means that there is often insufficient time to investigate each case thoroughly. Like judges and prosecutors, defense attorneys must be able to process many cases. Consider the assessment by a public defender of a former colleague: "She wasn't a good PD [public defender] in the sense that she couldn't handle cases on a volume basis. She wanted to act like a private lawyer and the Office couldn't afford to give her that much time. She was eased out of the office" (Platt and Pollock:254).

Defense attorneys and courtroom work groups

How defense attorneys perform their multiple tasks as fighters, negotiators, counselors, drafters, and administrators is directly tied to their relationship with other members of the courtroom work group.

Although the names and faces of defendants change daily, the defense attorneys who represent them are a regular fixture of the criminal court. Typically assistant public defenders are permanently assigned to a single courtroom and work every day with the same judge, the same prosecutor(s), the same court reporter, and the same clerk of court. Similarly, private defense attorneys—although they practice before several judges—are a permanent fixture in the criminal courts, for in any city only a handful of lawyers dominate the representation of fee-paying criminal defendants. This daily interaction of the criminal bar with the court community shapes the type and quality of legal representation received by those accused of violating the law. Whereas the adversary system stresses the combative role of the defense attorney, the day-to-day activities of the courtroom work group stress cooperation.

Rewards and sanctions

rewards

Defense attorneys who maintain a cooperative stance toward judges, prosecutors, and clerks can expect to reap some *rewards*. Defense attorneys have limited (and in some instances nonexistent) investigative resources. Prosecutors can provide cooperative defense attorneys with information about the cases by letting them examine the police reports, revealing the names of witnesses, and so on. Private defense attorneys may need the court's cooperation in collecting fees from the defendant. Thus judges will grant continuances to cooperative defense attorneys who need more time and leverage to obtain their fee.

sanctions

The court community can also *sanction* defense attorneys who violate the norms. For example, the clerk can refuse to provide beneficial scheduling of cases, or the judge can drag out a trial by continuously interrupting it for other business. These actions indirectly reduce a lawyer's income-generating ability. Other sanctions are more direct. A judge can criticize a lawyer in front of his or her client (thus scaring away potential clients in the courtroom) or can refuse to appoint certain attorneys to represent indigents, a significant source of income for some lawyers (Nardulli:157). A final category of sanctions involves the prosecutor's adopting a tougher stance during bargaining by not reducing charges or by recommending a higher-than-normal prison sentence.

Sanctions against defense attorneys are not often invoked, but when they are, they can have far-reaching effects. Every court community can point to an attorney who was sanctioned, with the result that the attorney either no longer practices criminal law in the area or has mended his or her ways.

Variations in cooperation

Defense attorneys are the least powerful members of the courtroom work group. Because of the numerous sanctions that can be applied to defense attorneys, they are forced into a reactive posture. Moreover, the lack of a central organization against the unified prosecutor's office further decreases their ability to exert a systematic influence on how criminal cases are processed.

Members of the defense bar respond to pressures of the courtroom work groups in various ways. Prosecutors assess defense attorneys in terms of their "reasonableness," that is, their ability to "discern a generous offer of settlement and to be willing to encourage his client to accept such an offer" (Skolnick:58). Based on Skolnick's criterion, attorneys fell into three categories. One category consisted of defense attorneys who handled few criminal cases. One might suppose that the prosecutor preferred dealing with such inexperienced attorneys, but they did not. Because these attorneys did not know the ropes, they were too unpredictable and often caused administrative problems. In another category were attorneys who had an active criminal practice and maintained a hostile relationship with the prosecutor's office. Known as "gamblers," these attorneys exemplified the aggressive, fighting advocate, but because they either won big or lost big, they also served to show the other attorneys the disadvantage of this type of posture. The final category of attorneys consisted of both public defenders and private attorneys who represented the large number of defendants. These attorneys worked within the system.

An assessment

Given the defense attorneys' regular interaction with the criminal court community, do defendants receive the type of legal representation they should or do the defense attorneys' ties to the courthouse conflict with the adversary ideal? Some studies argue that the defense attorneys' ties to the court community mean that the defendants' best interests are not represented (Sudnow; Blumberg, 1967). Others, however, have concluded that defendants' best interests are not eroded when their attorneys adopt a cooperative posture (Skolnick; Neubauer).

A sociologist studied a public defender's office and concluded that the public defender and prosecutor had adopted a common orientation to cases. He found that public defenders were more interested that a given case fit under one of several categories of offenses than in determining if the event met the proper penal code provisions. As a result, the public defenders seldom geared their work to securing acquittals for their clients. They took it for granted that those before the courts were guilty and were to be treated accordingly (Sudnow:269). Thus, from the beginning, the presumption of guilt permeated the public defenders' assessment of cases.

A study of a large New York court likened the practice of law to a confidence game in which both sides—defendant and attorney—must have larceny at heart (Blumberg, 1967b). The lawyer regulars of metropolitan court sought to preserve their relations with the court at all cost. The judges and prosecutors depended upon the defense attorneys to suggest that defendants plead guilty. The author placed great stress on the fact that it is the defense attorney who first suggested a guilty plea to the defendant—a suggestion that a number of defendants initially respond to in a negative way because they expect their attorney to be their champion.

Still another study concluded that the defendant's best interests are not eroded by the defense attorney's ties to the courtroom community; in fact the clients do better as a result of a cooperative posture (Skolnick). Working within the system will benefit the client because the prosecutor will be more amenable to disclosing information helpful to the defense, the bargains struck will be more favorable, and the defendant will not be penalized for the hostility of the defense attorney. Furthermore, attorneys identified as agitators may harm their clients' causes because prosecutors and judges will hand out longer sentences (Skolnick:61). Similarly, it appears that attorneys who maintain friendly relationships with the court community are better able to act as counselors to defendants because they are better able to predict what the reactions of the court community will be to individual cases (Neubauer).

CLOSE-UP: CRIMINAL DEFENDERS: LAW'S OUTCASTS

The criminal lawyer's work goes far afield from what happens in court. It is the "getting around" which [is important].

And getting around Richard Daly does.

By 8:30 A.M., on any given court day, his 1973 Thunderbird is parked on Market Street in front of the courthouse and he's soon into the flow.

A prostitute who had once been helped by Daly gladeyes him in the corridor, tapping her lavender thick-soled shoes in a tattoo on the bare floor. "Stay cool, Mr. Richard," she said. Daly gives her his Jimmy Cagney smile; lots of teeth, briefly.

A clerk with a sheaf of traffic violations whispers something and Daly says thanks, which seems to please the clerk.

One after another, a variety of people moved toward him like pieces of metal attracted to a magnet.

By 9 A.M., he is in the office of George Solomon, clerk of the Circuit Court of Criminal Causes. Solomon is a cousin of Sarkis Webbe, who shares Daly's office.

In Solomon's office, there is the special coterie gathered for morning coffee. The talk is easy. It's about cases. Solomon is there. And Daly. And Sidney Faber, the associate prosecuting attorney for the city of St. Louis, and Robert Wendt, an associate of Daly, and Norman London, and another lawyer, Gordian S. Benes.

Staying "tight" with Solomon's office is important to Daly because much of the processing flows through the clerk's hands. The better the relationship, the fewer the snarls and hassles.

He also is "tight" with Sidney Faber, the prosecutor. It is a mutual feeling. From Daly's point of view, he can pretty well talk out a case with Faber and get something favorable for his client. From Faber's point of view, it is profitable because by reaching an accord he doesn't have to fight Daly in court.

At 10 A.M., court opens and Daly is working the courthouse. This does not necessarily mean that he may be arguing a case. Mostly, it is filing of motions, seeing that certain things get done, seeing that he stays "tight" with the right people. James Lavin, for example. Lavin is clerk for two judges.

"Say I need a copy of all search warrants in cases I'm involved in," explains Daly. "It is proper that I get them, but getting them can be achieved efficiently and cooperatively, or can be full of hassles and delays. Of course, I want to get along with Lavin."

Which also means getting along reasonably well with the 20 or so others in the clerk's office.

At noon, the Daly coterie assembles near the chambers of Judge David Fitzgibbon. Lunch time. Cold cuts, coffee and Coke and conversation.

The talk got around to fame and what it does to the lawyer and to his client ultimately, how it affects the performance of the criminal justice system.

"Frankly," Daly said, "Becoming as well known as Morris Shenker or F. Lee Bailey or Percy Foreman could hurt my professional activity. I'd have to do something altogether different."

"Now, you might say that I have the courthouse wired. That is, I know how it works to the Nth degree. I have things functioning very smoothly. I'm not a big star, I don't draw outside attention. I'm able to accomplish a very good job as a defense lawyer."

Bernard Gayzer, © *The Washington Post*, February 18, 1973, p. F2.

We need to place this discussion of the interaction of the defense attorney with the criminal court community in perspective lest we leave the impression that the adversary ideal has no meaning whatsoever. The legal system, civil and criminal, is based on controversy. Norms of cooperation work to channel such controversy into constructive avenues. All too often advocacy is falsely equated with antagonism. Although defense attorneys exchange pleasantries with judges and prosecutors, their personal contacts with these officials outside of the courtroom are much more limited than some other studies suggested (Mather).

Another qualification to bear in mind is that cooperative attorneys do not bargain out every case. They also take cases to trial. If the defense attorney thinks the prosecutor is driving too hard of a bargain or that the state cannot prove its case to the jury, a trial will be recommended. Furthermore there is no evidence that during a trial cooperative attorneys do not argue the case to the best of their ability.

The criminal bar

solo practitioners
Law offices of *solo practitioners* are a permanent feature of urban architecture. They can be found huddled around the stone edifice of the criminal courts and interspersed between the neon lights garishly proclaiming "Harry's 24 Hour Bail Bonds." In Detroit they are called the Clinton Street Bar, in Washington, D.C., the "Fifth Streeters," titles that are not meant to be complimentary. These lawyers spend little time in their offices; they are most often at the courthouse socializing with other members of the courtroom work group. Often dressed in bright colors, they can be observed soliciting new clients in the corridors in violation of the legal profession's canons of ethics. Their proximity to the criminal courts and the bail bondsmen and the sparseness of the law books in their offices are good indicators that the type of law practiced from these offices bears little resemblance to our Perry Mason notions of the defense attorney. A number of factors account for the low economic and professional status of the criminal bar.

Stratification of the bar

stratification of the bar
A diverse array of lawyers appears in criminal court, reflecting the *stratification of the bar*. The availability of lawyers and the type of law they practice has been influenced by two major forces: urbanization and specialization. Although the law has always been an urban profession, the small-town lawyers who handled a wide variety of cases were once more typical than they are today. As wealth and population became increasingly concentrated in large cities, so too did lawyers. The growing complexity of society has meant that lawyers can no longer be generalists; they must concentrate on mastering a few areas of the law. Most lawyers specialize (drafting wills, contracts, and so on). Increasingly the practice of criminal law is also highly specialized. The increase in appellate court decisions involving criminal law and criminal procedure requires a large investment of a lawyer's time and energy to keep abreast of changes in the law. But most lawyers never handle criminal cases, largely because other areas of the law are much more lucrative. Studies of private attorneys in such differing cities as Denver, Washington, D.C.,

and Prairie City, Illinois, reached the same conclusion: the bulk of nonindigent defendants are represented by a handful of attorneys (Taylor et al.:12; LEAA:9; Neubauer:69).

Legal practice in the urban bar can be divided into three parts. First there is an inner circle, which handles the work of banks, utilities, and large corporations. The law firms of the inner circle are quite large (up to two hundred partners in New York, Chicago, and Los Angeles). These lawyers are recruited from the nation's most prestigious law schools, earn large salaries, and almost never appear in criminal court. Another circle includes lawyers representing interests opposed to those of the inner circle—the injured party in personal injury cases, small- to medium-sized businesses, and so on. Most practicing attorneys fall into this category. They earn a comfortable living. They also rarely handle criminal cases. The major exception is that in most communities there is at least one attorney known for being a good trial advocate. This person will occasionally represent criminal clients who can afford a substantial fee.

The bulk of the attorneys who appear in criminal court are drawn from the third or outer circle. They are often referred to as solo practitioners because they practice alone or share an office with another attorney. In sharp contrast to the elitist backgrounds of the big corporation attorneys, solo practitioners have often worked their way up from working-class backgrounds. Many are members of a racial or ethnic minority and in past years were often immigrants' children. They typically graduated from the least prestigious law schools (often night programs at city colleges).

Solo practitioners are the least prestigious members of the legal profession. They are viewed by other lawyers as having little legal ability. Economically, they barely eke out an existence. In essence this outer ring handles all the legal business that other lawyers find either too messy or too financially unrewarding. Divorce, small personal injury cases, and criminal cases are the major types of cases.

The stratification of the legal profession affects the criminal courts in two major ways. First, a few attorneys handle most of the criminal cases. For this group of courtroom regulars, criminal cases constitute a dominant part of their economic livelihood. Second, because few lawyers practice criminal law, bar associations have little interest in the work of criminal courts. Most of the time of the bar associations is spent considering matters of the better paying and more socially acceptable business and middle-class clients. Short of a major scandal that forces the attention of the organized bar, the criminal courts are treated with a healthy dose of "out of sight and out of mind."

Not all private defense attorneys, however, fall into the pattern of essentially unethical, poorly trained wholesalers. This pattern appears to predominate in America's older central cities. Newer cities have a different type of defense bar, who are younger, more skilled, and more committed to providing quality representation (Stover). The old-time solo practitioner appears to be a vanishing breed. A study of private defense bars in nine U.S. cities reported that as the older attorneys of this type die or retire, they are not being replaced (Wice). Part of the reason is economic pressure. Public defenders are now available to provide legal services.

IN THE NEWS: STUDY ASSAILS SOME LAWYERS PAID BY U.S. TO DEFEND POOR

One man spent two weeks in jail because his attorney failed to tell him his bail had been lowered. Another was indicted on two felony counts because he couldn't reach his lawyer to find out if he should plead guilty to lesser charges.

These and other cases were cited in a District of Columbia Bar report as examples of "substandard performance" by attorneys paid with federal Criminal Justice Act funds to represent indigent defendants in D.C. Superior Court.

"Unfortunately, a disproportionate share of CJA cases has in the past been assigned to a small group of regular CJA practitioners who are chronically unprofessional," the report said.

"We believe that steps should be taken to remove such attorneys from the list of those eligible for CJA appointments," it continued.

This would remove these lawyers who do little else but handle cases paid by CJA funds, from their major source of income. Known informally as the "Fifth Street Bar" because of the court's location, these lawyers often have no offices, law library or telephones. They spend their time in the courthouse, which is often the only place where clients can reach them.

While the problem of inferior representation by some of the Superior Court's regular lawyers has been well recognized in legal circles here, this is the first time the bar has taken such a strong step toward reform.

The report said there are 11 Superior Court regulars "frequently mentioned by judges and attorneys as being either incompetent, uninterested, overloaded with cases or all three.". . .

"We believe that the problem of substandard performance by court appointed attorneys is one which has been created in substantial part by the tolerance of such conduct for more than a decade," the report said.

The committee was headed by Peter H. Wolf, a former member of the "Fifth Street Bar."

The committee acknowledged that it is hard to second guess a lawyer's strategy on cross-examination, but "there is no difficulty in stating that an attorney who permits his client to remain in prison for two months merely because he or she lacks the initiative to confirm the client's address and employment has not performed at the level of professional service required by the court.". . .

Stuart Auerbach, © *The Washington Post*, July 7, 1977.

Younger attorneys are more professionally and ethically committed to providing higher-quality legal services to criminal indigents. They prefer working for public defenders' offices than eking out an economic existence as a solo practitioner.

Environment of practice

It is no accident that in many large cities, there is a distinct criminal bar of low legal ability and at times questionable ethics. Low status, low fees, and the difficulty in securing clients are three factors that shape the availability of lawyers to represent those accused of violating the law. These factors are also a reflection of the problems associated with trying to dispense justice in America's courthouses.

Low Status.   Most lawyers view criminal cases as unsavory. Criminal clients are not noted for being honest with their attorneys. Representing criminal defendants also produces few chances for victory; most defendants either plead guilty or are found guilty by a judge or jury. Moreover, many lawyers who represent middle-class clients do not want accused drug peddlers brushing shoulders in the waiting room with their regular clients. And despite the legal assumption of innocent until proven guilty, once defendants are arrested, the public assumes they are guilty. As a result, the general public perceives attorneys as freeing known robbers and rapists to return to the streets. Law professor Murray Schwartz succinctly notes: "Realistically, the lawyer who defends notoriously unpopular clients runs a risk of identification in the public mind (and not infrequently in the mind of his own profession) with his client" (Kaplan).

Securing Cases.   To earn a living, lawyers first need clients. For lawyers who handle criminal cases, securing clients often presents greater problems than for those who practice strictly civil law. Unlike the attorneys in large or even medium-sized law firms who represent regular clients over long periods of time, defense attorneys seldom have such regular clientele. Accordingly, a part of their time is spent *securing future cases.*

securing cases

The criminal lawyer's most important commodity in securing clients is his or her reputation. This reputation often develops on the basis of the lawyer's handling of a specific case. A lawyer's reputation is important in several ways. First, defendants want a specific attorney to represent them, not a firm of lawyers. Such preferences may result from recommendations from satisfied past clients. Second, attorneys who do not practice criminal law often refer clients to a specific lawyer who does. Third, a repeat offender may seek out the previous attorney, if he or she felt the lawyer had provided good representation in the past. Finally, judges may formally or informally assign a case to a lawyer (Wice: 104–106).

In securing clients, defense attorneys often rely on policemen, bail bondsmen, and court clerks to give their names to defendants who need counsel. In return, the attorney compensates the referee. Such practices, of course, may violate legal ethics. To secure cases, solo practitioners are known as "joiners" because they spread their name by belonging to as many groups as possible. The need to secure cases is also a reason why solo practitioners are often active in local politics. Not only does their name become familiar, but it also holds out the promise of a future appointment, perhaps as a judge.

fees

Fees.   Obtaining clients is only half the problem facing private attorneys who represent criminal clients. The second half is collecting the fee. There has been a myth that criminal lawyers receive fabulous salaries. While a few have become quite wealthy, most earn a modest middle-class living. After interviewing 180 criminal attorneys from all over the nation, Wice reports that most earned between $15,000 and $35,000 in annual salaries (1978). This is less than most attorneys make practicing civil law.

The three most important considerations in setting the fee are the seriousness of the offense, the amount of time it will take the lawyer to deal with the case, and the client's ability to pay. It is hazardous to estimate specific fees, but one study provides the following ranges: $500–$1,000 for misdemeanor (drunk driving included): $1,000–$2,500 for a nontrial felony; and $2,000+ for a felony trial (Wice). Well-known criminal lawyers may charge their well-heeled clients considerably more, however. In New Orleans, for example, an indicted state official paid $5,000 per day of trial (and $250 per hour for out-of-court work) in an unsuccessful effort to avoid conviction on bribery charges.

How does the lawyer determine the amount of the fee? One San Francisco lawyer speaking at Nate Cohn's criminal law seminar answered this question with the vague answer of "what is reasonable," and when pressed as to what he considered a reasonable fee, he only half jokingly replied, "It is as much as you can get. . . ."

Most of the lawyers interviewed did not exhibit such a blatant disregard for their clients' welfare and were very thoughtful about how to set a proper and just fee. Most complained that this was by far the lousiest aspect of their job and felt very uncomfortable during any financial deliberations.

The most critical factor shaping the legal representation of defendants is economics. From these fees lawyers must pay for an office, perhaps a secretary, their out-of-pocket expenses, and, of course, themselves. Because of the small fees involved in any single case, private attorneys must handle a large number of cases and thus cannot afford to devote much time to any single case. In purely economic terms, it is more profitable to bargain the case out (a few minutes in the prosecutor's office) than to engage in a lengthy trial because the fee is set on the basis of representation of the case rather than on a per-hour basis.

For private attorneys, collecting fees is an important but difficult task. A defendant found guilty is not likely to want to pay for losing and might not be able to pay. Even in the unlikely event the client is acquitted, collecting fees is just as difficult, for the lawyer no longer has any leverage. Defendants quickly become forgetful of, if not ungrateful for, the services performed by counsel. As a result, attorneys demand their fees in advance and sometimes work out a time payment plan with the payments coinciding with scheduled court appearances. A commonly retold story involves defense attorneys requesting a continuance because "Mr. Green" has not yet arrived. This code for the lack of payment of the fee is typically honored by court officials (Mayer:160). Other techniques for obtaining a fee from clients may involve solicitation of the defendant's family to pressure them to contribute. At other times, attorneys will take whatever the defendant has in his or her pocket. Judge Charles Halleck of the superior court in Washington, D.C., observed, "Sometimes the attorney asks a jailed defendant 'You got $15 or $25? Here let me hold it for you.'" Later that becomes part of the fee (Downie:176). Despite all these efforts, however, the majority of fees go partially unpaid.

Reprinted from Paul Wice, *Criminal Lawyers: An Endangered Species*, p. 111. © 1978 Sage Publications, Inc., with permission.

Providing indigents with attorneys

Most defendants cannot afford to hire a lawyer. A survey conducted by the National Legal Aid and Defender Association estimated that nationwide 65 percent of felony defendants were legally indigent (too poor to pay a private attorney). The percentage is slightly higher in urban areas than in rural ones (Benner et al.:83). Obviously the Supreme Court's decision in *Gideon* that the state must provide attorneys for the poor applies to a substantial number of criminal defendants.

Jurisdictions vary for the stage of the criminal proceedings when counsel is provided. In some areas the court appoints an attorney to represent the indigent as early as the initial appearance. In other areas, however, appointment may be delayed until later in the case (see table 8-1), a practice that can undermine the effectiveness of court-appointed counsel.

indigency standards

Who qualifies for court-appointed counsel also varies. Some judges apply stringent *indigency standards* before appointing counsel. For example, in a number of counties, defendants are disqualified from receiving court-appointed lawyers if a monetary bond has been posted, even though that might exhaust all their money. In other areas, however, eligibility standards are less stringent.

How best to provide legal representation for the poor has been a vital issue of long standing to the courts and the legal profession. In the United States, there are two primary methods: the assigned counsel system (attorneys are appointed by the judge on a case-by-case basis) and the public defender system (a salaried public official represents all indigent defendants). Each system has its supporters and critics. The debate over the advantages and disadvantages of the assigned counsel versus the public defender highlight some important issues involving the quality of legal representation provided the poor.

Assigned counsel

assigned counsel

The *assigned counsel* system is the oldest and most widely used (over 2,700 of the 3,100 counties in the United States employ this method). It predominates in rural areas. The assigned counsel system reflects the traditional way that professions like the law have responded to charity cases: lawyers represent indigent defendants on a case-by-case basis. Appointments are made by the judge from a list which may consist of all practicing attorneys in the jurisdiction or only those who have volunteered to defend indigents.

Critics contend that the result of the system is that the least qualified lawyers are appointed to defend indigents. In most counties the only attorneys who volunteer are either young attorneys who desire courtroom experience or those who seek numerous appointments to make a living. Even where appointments are rotated among all members of the practicing bar (as in New Jersey or Houston), there is no

TABLE 8-1. Stage of criminal proceedings when counsel is appointed for indigents in felony cases

Stage of Criminal Proceedings	Public defender		Assigned counsel	
	No.	%	No.	%
Immediately after arrest	10	5	12	2
After arrest but before defendant's first appearance before a judge or magistrate	27	13	62	11
At first appearance before judge or magistrate	130	61	385	67
Preliminary hearing	20	9	17	3
Arraignment	15	7	65	11
After first appearance but before trial	3	1	9	11
Trial	0	0	1	0
Other	8	4	22	4
Number of defenders reporting	213	100	573	99

Source: Laurence A. Benner, Beth Lynch Neary, and Richard M. Gutman, *The Other Face of Justice: A Report of the National Defender Survey* (Chicago: National Legal Aid and Defender Association, 1973), p. 24.

guarantee that the lawyer selected is qualified to handle the increasing complexity of the criminal law (the appointee may be a skilled real estate or a good probate attorney, but these skills are not readily transferable to the dynamics of a criminal trial).

This overall pattern that assigned counsel are recent law school graduates or old "has beens," to quote a Seattle judge, is confirmed by a study of lawyers in Oregon showing that court-appointed attorneys were younger, less experienced, and rated by other members of the bar as less competent than retained counsel (Moore).

Many jurisdictions do not pay attorneys for representing indigents nor do they reimburse the attorney for out-of-pocket expenses; the attorneys do the work as part of their professional responsibilities. Assigned counsel systems seldom provide funds to hire investigators or secure services of expert witnesses, further weakening the ability to provide a thorough defense. Even where court-appointed attorneys are paid, compensation is minimal, adding another obstacle to qualified attorneys who might serve (Silverstein). Inadequate compensation pressures attorneys to dispose of the case quickly in order to devote time to fee-paying clients. An Oregon district attorney made the following observation: "Counsel for indigents very often display an attitude of 'let's get it over with.' The same lawyer, whom I know to be a veritable tiger for a paying client, is in many cases a pussy cat when representing the indigent client. Such are the economic facts of life" (Moore:283).

To its backers, a major benefit of the assigned counsel system is that it disperses the responsibility for defending the poor among the practicing lawyers.

> Many problems in the administration of criminal justice, both at the federal and state levels, result from absence of involvement of most lawyers in the practice of criminal law. An almost indispensable condition to fundamental improvement of American criminal justice is the active and knowledgeable support of the bar as a whole. There is no better way to develop such interest and awareness than to provide wider opportunities for lawyers to participate in criminal litigation at reasonable rates of compensation. [Attorney General's Committee on Poverty and the Administration of Federal Criminal Justice:40]

To many the overall lack of organization and coordination make the assigned counsel system unsuited for modern criminal courts, particularly in large or medium-sized jurisdictions. According to the President's Commission on Law Enforcement, a central administration program is necessary for an assigned criminal system to function properly. A prime benefit of central administration is that it can provide for investigative staff and securing the services of expert witnesses. The lack of overall supervision and coordination also means that the quality of appointed attorneys is not monitored. By contrast, in Los Angeles the federal judges conduct a yearly review of the panel of attorneys, weeding out those not providing adequate or vigorous defense.

Public defender

public defender

The *public defender* is a twentieth-century response to the problem of providing legal representation for the indigent. Under a defender system a salaried lawyer (working full-time or part-time for the jurisdiction) represents criminal indigents in the jurisdiction. Los Angeles was the first city to create a public defender office in 1914. In subsequent decades the program spread slowly; by 1965, the National Legal Aid and Defender Association—the national organization that promotes better legal representation for civil as well as criminal indigents—reported programs in only 117 counties (out of 2,750). Since 1965 public defender programs have spread rapidly because of Supreme Court decisions (*Gideon* and later *Argersinger*) as well as increased concern for the need for more adequate representation of indigents.

Today the public defender system is used in most big cities and is being adopted in small and medium-sized jurisdictions. Alaska, New Jersey, and Colorado have established statewide, state-funded programs. Illinois employs a state appellate defender who handles all indigent appeals.

Proponents of the public defender cite several arguments in favor of its adoption. One is that a lawyer paid to represent indigents on a continuous basis will devote more attention to cases than a court-appointed attorney who is not compensated (or only minimally so). And many members of the practicing bar like the idea that they no longer have to take time away from fee-paying cases to meet their professional obligations.

A second advantage often claimed for the public defender system is that it provides more experienced, competent counsel. Because public defenders concentrate on criminal cases, they can keep abreast of changes in the law, and the day-to-day courtroom work keeps their trial skills sharp. By contrast, assigned counsel often are neither knowledgeable in criminal law nor specialists in trial work. The public defender is also likely to be more knowledgeable about informal norms and is therefore in a better position to counsel defendants and negotiate the best possible deal.

Finally, a defender system "assures continuity and consistency in the defense of the poor" (Silverstein:47). Issues that transcend individual cases—criteria for pretrial release, police practices, and so forth—are more likely to be considered by a permanent, ongoing organization than under appointment systems.

But critics contend that public defenders—as paid employees of the state—will not provide a vigorous defense because they are tied too closely to the courtroom work group. Edward Bennett Williams, a nationally known defense attorney, has even suggested that the prosecutor and public defender are like two professional wrestlers; they fight each other in a different town every night, making sure that they do not hurt each other. In a similar vein, David Sudnow, a sociologist, writes:

> He [the public defender] will not cause any serious trouble for the routine motion of the court conviction process. Laws will not be challenged, cases will not be tried to test the constitutionality of procedures and statutes, judges will not be personally degraded, police will be free from scrutiny to decide the legitimacy of their operations, and the community will not be condemned for its segregative practices against Negroes. The PD's defense is completely proper, in accord with correct legal procedure, and specifically amoral in its import, manner of delivery, and perceived implications for the propriety of the prosecution enterprise. [p. 273]

More recent studies, however, have concluded that this problem is not unique to public defenders; it pertains to all lawyers who maintain close ties with courtroom work groups.

Lawyers and clients

privileged communi-cation

The adversary system is premised on a good working relationship between lawyer and client. The American legal system surrounds the lawyer–client relationship with special protections. In order to be an effective advocate and counselor, the lawyer must know all the facts of a case. Thus any information communicated by the client is treated as *privileged communication;* it cannot be disclosed without the client's consent. (There are certain exceptions, however. For example, if a client tells her lawyer that a crime is about to be committed, the lawyer as an officer of the court is required to bring such knowledge to the attention of the proper authorities.) Based on this trust and a full exchange of information, the attorney assumes the difficult task of advocating a client's case. In civil litigation the relationship between lawyer and client is often (but not always) characterized by such trust and full disclosure. In criminal cases, however, the relationship may be marked by distrust and hostility.

Lawyers view their clients

A study in Oakland, California, revealed that getting along with clients was one of the most difficult tasks of public defenders. Many eventually left the office because of the difficulty of dealing with their clients, who were often sullen, distrustful, ungrateful, and dishonest in dealing with them (Platt and Pollock). At times defendants tell their attorneys implausible stories, invent alibis, and/or withhold key information. The defendant's lack of candor greatly complicates the job of the attorney in representing the defendant. The following example illustrates: "A legal secretary indicted for forgery and embezzlement, told her public defender that she had no prior record. But during the sentencing hearing it emerged that she had several previous East Coast convictions for similar offenses. Knowledge of these previous convictions would have greatly altered the public defender's approach to the case" (Mather:282). The lack of trust in the lawyer–client relationship may be determined by the necessity of the lawyer to prepare the client for a less than total victory.

To return to the counselor role, the defense attorney must at some point inform the defendant that given the crime, the prior record, facts of the case, and so forth, it is likely that the person will be imprisoned. Since defendants involved in the criminal process typically live a day-to-day existence postponing bad news, such statements are not to their liking. Preparing the client for less than total victory obviously clashes with traditional notions that the attorney should always win.

It may often be a lawyer's duty to emphasize in harsh terms the force of the prosecution's evidence: "What about this fact? Is it going to go away? How the hell would you vote if you were a juror in your case?" It may sometimes be a lawyer's duty to say bluntly, "I cannot possibly beat this case. You are going to spend a long time in jail, and the only question is how long." It may even be a lawyer's duty to use the kind of language illustrated by a recent Massachusetts case: "The jury will fry your ass." "You're going to die if you take the stand." "You will burn if you do not change your plea." "The jury wants your blood."

Albert Alschuler, "The Defense Attorney's Role in Plea Bargaining." Reprinted by permission of The Yale Law Journal Company and Fred B. Rothman & Company from *The Yale Law Journal*, Vol. 84, p. 1307.

Ultimately it is the defendant's choice whether to accept the attorney's advice to plead guilty or to go to trial. The importance of the defendant having the final decision is underscored by a Los Angeles public defender: "You know, the DAs can holler all they want about what fools we are sometimes to turn down their deals. But you gotta remember that we've got our clients to answer to. We're not free agents in this thing like the DAs are" (Mather:281).

Lawyers differ in their ability to influence their clients. Private attorneys find their advice accepted more readily than court-appointed lawyers do, a difference partially accounted for by the type of commitments the defendant has made. Whereas the indigent defendant has no choice in receiving the services of a public defender or assigned counsel, defendants with private attorneys have a choice because they have selected their counsel themselves.

Defendants view their lawyers

Often defendants view their lawyers (either public or private) with suspicion, if not bitterness. This is particularly the case with court-appointed attorneys, whom the defendants consider just another government-paid attorney. Some defendants think public defenders will not work hard on their case because they will get paid whether they win or not. To others, the defense attorney is ambitious to become a judge or prosecutor and therefore does not want to antagonize the court system by fighting too hard. Overall, then, many defendants view the public defender as no different from the prosecutor. In prison, "PD" stands not for "public defender" but for "prison deliverer." In what has become an almost classic statement, a Connecticut prisoner responded to Jonathan Casper's question as to whether he had a lawyer when he went to court with the barbed comment, "No, I had a public defender."

A partial explanation for a breakdown of trust between the client and public defender involves the absence of one-to-one contact. Most public defender offices are organized on a functional basis. Attorneys are assigned to various courtrooms and/or responsibilities—arraignment court, preliminary hearing, trial sections, and so on. Each defendant sees several public defenders, all of whom are supposed to be "his" lawyer. This segmented approach to representation for indigents—which a number of progressive public defender programs are trying to counter—decreases the likelihood that a bond of trust will develop between attorney and client.

This form of representation also increases the probability that some defendants will be overlooked and no attorney will work on the case or talk to the defendant. One can certainly understand the frustration of this thirty-three-year-old accused murderer with no previous criminal record:

> "I figured that with he being my defense attorney, that as soon as that grand jury was over—because he's not allowed in the hearing—that he would call me and then want to find out what went on. After that grand jury I never saw him for two months." "You stayed in jail?" "Yeah." [Casper:8]

Nor do such experiences appear to be atypical. The same interviewer reported that the bulk of defendants he interviewed spent little time with their attorney; public defenders spent only five to ten minutes with the defendants, usually hurried conversations in the bullpen (room where jailed prisoners are temporarily held awaiting court appearance) or corridors (Casper:106).

Quite clearly not all of defendants' criticisms of their lawyers are valid. But valid or not, defendants' lack of trust and confidence in their lawyers is a major force in shaping the dynamics of courthouse justice. Defendants try to con their lawyers, and the lawyers respond by exhibiting a strong dose of disbelief when defendants state unrealistic expectations or invent implausible alibis.

Conclusion

Perhaps nowhere else is there a greater contrast between the images and realities of the criminal court process than in the activities of the defense attorney. Unlike Perry Mason who always successfully defended innocent clients, most defense attorneys plea bargain out the steady stream of factually guilty defendants. Defense attorneys in representing clients must serve as advocate, counselor, and challenger, all within the canons of legal ethics. These conflicting duties account for some, but certainly not all, of the criticism surrounding them. Mainly because of economic forces, only a handful of lawyers represent criminal defendants, and for decades these lawyers have been the less-qualified members of the bar. Today, however, most defendants are represented by court-appointed attorneys. Opinion is divided over which is the better method for providing court-appointed counsel.

For discussion

1. Does your community use assigned counsel or public defenders? Interview a judge, prosecutor, and/or defense attorney to get their views on which system is best and why. Which system do you think is best?
2. Examine local newspapers. Are references to defense attorneys favorable or unfavorable?
3. Interview a public defender and/or a private defense attorney. What are the major types of problems they face in representing clients?
4. If you needed to hire a lawyer for a criminal case, what type of lawyer is available? How would you go about finding a good defense attorney?
5. Why do many defense attorneys maintain a cooperative stance with prosecutors? In what ways does such cooperation enable the defense attorney to represent the client better? In what ways does such cooperation jeopardize the rights of the defendant?
6. You are the defense attorney. Your client denies guilt. What are your responsibilities? If the defendant admits guilt, would these responsibilities be similar or different? Why?
7. Discuss with a prosecutor his or her relationship with defense attorneys. How does the DA evaluate the effectiveness of defense attorneys as advocates for their clients?

References

Attorney General's Committee on Poverty and the Administration of Federal Criminal Justice. *Report*. Washington, D.C.: Government Printing Office, 1963.

Benner, Laurence A., Beth Lynch Neary, and Richard M. Gutman. *The Other Face of Justice: A Report of the National Defender Survey*. Chicago: National Legal Aid and Defender Association, 1973.

Blumberg, Abraham. *Criminal Justice*. Chicago: Quadrangle Books, 1967a.

———. "The Practice of Law as a Confidence Game." *Law and Society Review* 1 (June 1967b):15–39.

Casper, Jonathan. *American Criminal Justice: The Defendant's Perspective*. Englewood Cliffs, N.J.: Prentice-Hall, 1972.

Downie, Leonard, Jr. *Justice Denied: The Case for Reform of the Courts*. New York: Praeger, 1971.

Kaplan, John. *Criminal Justice: Introductory Cases and Materials*. Mineola, N.Y.: Foundation Press, 1973.

Kerper, Hazel B. *Introduction to the Criminal Justice System*. St. Paul, Minn.: West Publishing, 1972.

Krantz, Sheldon, Charles Smith, David Rossman, Paul Froyd, and Janis Hoffman. *Right to Counsel in Criminal Cases: The Mandate of Argersinger v. Hamlin*. Cambridge, Mass.: Ballinger, 1976.

Law Enforcement Assistance Administration (LEAA). *The D.C. Public Defender Service*. Vol. 1: *Policies and Procedures*. Washington, D.C.: Government Printing Office, 1974.

Mather, Lynn. "The Outsider in the Courtroom: An Alternative Role for the Defense." In Herbert Jacob, ed., *The Potential for Reform of Criminal Justice*. Beverly Hills, Calif.: Sage Publications, 1974.

Mayer, Martin. *The Lawyers*. New York: Dell, 1968.

Moore, Michael. "The Right to Counsel for Indigents in Oregon." *Oregon Law Review* 44 (1965):255–300.

Nardulli, Peter. *The Courtroom Elite: An Organizational Perspective on Criminal Justice*. Cambridge, Mass.: Ballinger, 1978.

Nelson, Dorothy W. *Cases and Materials on Judicial Administration and the Administration of Justice*. St. Paul, Minn.: West Publishing, 1974.

Neubauer, David. *Criminal Justice in Middle America*. Morristown, N.J.: General Learning Press, 1974.

Platt, Anthony, and Randi Pollock. "Channeling Lawyers: The Careers of Public Defenders." In Herbert Jacob, ed., *The Potential for Reform of Criminal Justice*. Beverly Hills, Calif.: Sage Publications, 1974.

The President's Commission on Law Enforcement and Administration of Justice. *Task Force Report: The Courts*. Washington, D.C.: Government Printing Office, 1967.

Silverstein, Lee. *Defense of the Poor*. Chicago: American Bar Foundation, 1965.

Skolnick, Jerome. "Social Control in the Adversary System." *The Journal of Conflict Resolution* 11 (March 1967):52–70.

Stover, Robert V. "The Indigent's Right to Counsel: How Much Does It Help?" Paper presented at the annual meeting of the Midwest Political Science Association, Chicago, Illinois, May 3–5, 1973.

Sudnow, David. "Normal Crimes: Sociological Features of the Penal Code in a Public Defender Office." *Social Problems* 12 (1965):209–215.

Taylor, Jean, Thomas Stanley, Barbara deFlorio, and Lyne Seekamp. "An Analysis of Defense Counsel in the Processing of Felony Defendants in Denver, Colorado." *Denver Law Journal* 50 (1973):9–44.

Wice, Paul. *Criminal Lawyers: An Endangered Species*. Beverly Hills, Calif.: Sage Publications, 1978.

For further reading

Blumberg, Abraham. *Criminal Justice.* Chicago: Quadrangle Books, 1967.

Law Enforcement Assistance Administration (LEAA). *The D.C. Public Defender Service: An Exemplary Project.* Washington, D.C.: Government Printing Office, 1974.

Silverstein, Lee. *Defense of the Poor.* Chicago: American Bar Foundation, 1965.

Skolnick, Jerome. "Social Control in the Adversary System." *Journal of Conflict Resolution* 11 (March 1967):52–70.

Wice, Paul. *Criminal Lawyers: An Endangered Species.* Beverly Hills, Calif.: Sage Publications, 1978.

PART 3

Is the Defendant Guilty?

The six chapters of part 3 follow the steps of criminal prosecution from arrest to the determination of guilt or innocence. The central concerns are why many cases are eliminated from the process early and why most cases end not with a trial but a plea of guilty.

Chapter 9 examines the types of cases that come to the criminal courts. It considers the volume of police arrests, the characteristics of those arrested, and the nature of victims and witnesses.

Chapter 10 looks at case screening. Well before trial, many cases are eliminated by actions of prosecutors, grand juries, and/or preliminary hearings.

Chapter 11 focuses on the American bail system.

Chapter 12 considers the preparation of cases for trial. The primary topics are discovery and the suppression of evidence.

Plea bargaining is a much publicized but little understood part of the criminal court process. Why cases are plead out and whether plea bargaining is fair are the central topics in chapter 13.

Chapter 14 examines the trial process: selection of a jury, presentation of evidence, and the eventual jury verdict. Even though only a handful of cases go to trial, jury verdicts nonetheless have a major impact on how the courts exercise discretion.

CHAPTER 9

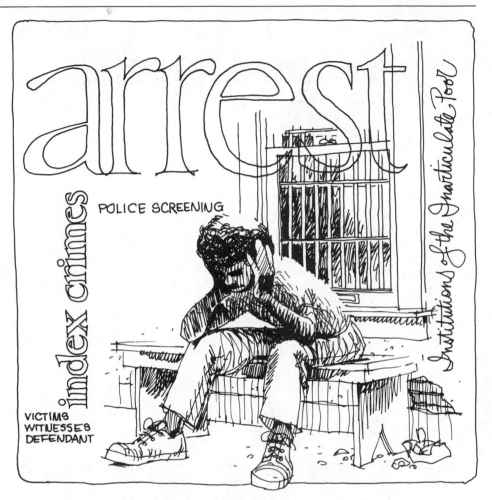

The Case Begins: Arrests, Victims, Witnesses, and Defendants

clientele

A variety of studies have indicated that the behavior of organizations is affected by the types of persons (often termed *clientele*) they must deal with. The nature of an organization's clientele is related to public assessments of the organization, influences how the clientele are processed and handled, and is associated with conflicts between the organization and those they must deal with. The criminal courts are no exception. Therefore we need to consider the nature of the raw material the courts must process and how the characteristics of that raw material influence the type of justice dispensed in the criminal courts. The specific topics to be discussed include the volume of arrests, the quality of police investigations, the types of crimes involved, victim and witness perceptions of the court process, and the characteristics of defendants.

Arrests

arrest

Every year the police *arrest* almost 11 million persons for nontraffic offenses; 2.4 million of these arrests are for the serious crimes of homicide, rape, arson, aggravated assault, robbery, burglary, auto theft, and larceny over fifty dollars. These

171

type I
offenses
index
crimes

eight crimes, considered in the FBI's *Uniform Crime Report* as *type I offenses* and generally referred to as *index crimes*, are the ones that make headlines about rising crime rates. Note, though, that some other serious crimes (possession of drugs for one) are not included. Also many types of crimes committed primarily by the upper classes—fraud and stock manipulations, for instance—are also excluded, even though their economic costs are equally as great as those committed by the poor. The remaining 7 million arrests are for less serious crimes like assault, public drunkenness, possession of marijuana, and so on.

Although the volume of arrests for type I crimes is heavy, they represent only a fraction of crimes committed. The *Uniform Crime Reports* are based only on crimes known to the police. Surveys of crime victims estimate that only half of all crimes are reported to the police (Ennis). Moreover, of the crimes brought to the attention of the police, only about 19 percent result in an arrest (FBI). Even after arrest, the police may determine that some crime reports are unfounded or that there is insufficient evidence to hold the suspect. As a result, the vast majority of crimes never reach the courts.

Hidden beneath these national arrest figures are important variations in types and volumes of crimes among communities. Large urban areas not only have more crime than rural areas or medium-sized cities, but the types of offenses are more serious. Serious street crimes like murder, rape, armed robbery, and drugs constitute a larger proportion of the work load of big city courts. In rural and suburban areas most crimes involve property—burglaries and thefts, for example. Such differences are relative, however. Contrary to public perceptions, most felony arrests are for nonviolent offenses involving burglary and larceny. Only 19 percent of police arrests for major offenses involved homicide, rape, robbery, or aggravated assault. (See figure 9-1).

Increasing crime

During the last decade, the increase in crime has strained the capacity of courts to process the ever-rising volume of cases. Figure 9-2 graphically illustrates this upsurge in official reported crime, an upsurge that far outstrips growth in the population. Although not all of these 10 million arrests ended up in court, there is every indication that court cases increased as well. Many believe that this increasing volume of cases has undermined the ability of the courts to keep up with the volume and at the same time process defendants with dignity.

The very visible rise in the amount of crime has tended to obscure other changes that have also added extra burdens to the work of the courts. One has been the shift in the types of cases being prosecuted. In efforts to fight the alarming increase in drug addiction, law enforcement officials have increasingly sought to prosecute major drug dealers rather than street-level pushers, who are easier to apprehend and prosecute. Public pressures have resulted in more prosecutions of major white-collar crimes. What is significant is that such cases, because they are more complex, require more time of the court officials than more run-of-the-mill possession of drugs charge or felony theft. In addition, during the 1960s and 1970s, appellate

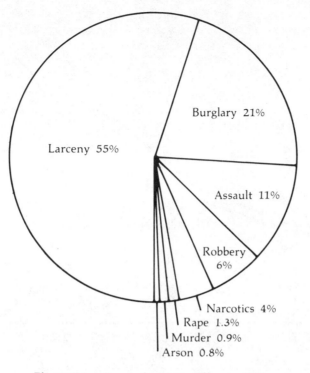

Figure 9-1.   Arrests for Major Offenses, 1981.

   Note: Although drug offenses are not considered type I offenses, they are included here because they are a major category of felony arrests. Marijuana arrests, however, have been excluded.
   Source: FBI, *Uniform Crime Reports—1981* (Washington, D.C.: Government Printing Office, 1982).

courts, led by the U.S. Supreme Court, have imposed more procedural require-ments (*Miranda*, for example) on the criminal courts. Taken together, these factors have increased the relative amount of time required per case.

   Figure 9-3 shows how the more than $25.8 billion spent in 1979 on the criminal justice system was distributed. The vast majority went to the police, who catch criminals. The second largest amount was spent on corrections. The courts (includ-ing judicial, prosecution, and indigent defense) came in third, with 28 percent. Funding under the Law Enforcement Assistance Administration (LEAA—the con-gressional and executive response to the crime problem) initially invested most of its funds in improving the police, then shifted to the corrections system. Only belatedly was it recognized that it does no good to implement a program geared to increasing arrests substantially if there are no corresponding efforts to alleviate crowded court dockets and overburdened prosecutors.

   The amount of money devoted to court activities has been increasing steadily over the last decade. While conventional wisdom holds that court resources did not increase as rapidly as the crime rate, a recent study reaches a different conclusion.

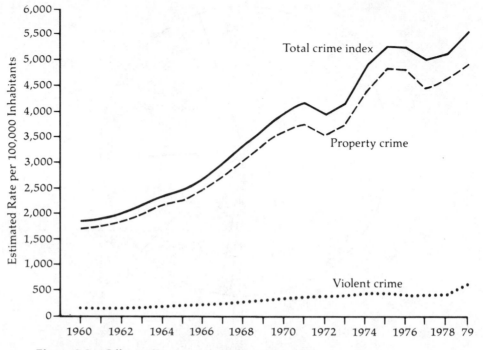

Figure 9-2. Offenses Known to the Police, 1960–1979.

Source: Timothy Flanagan, David J. Van Alstyne, and Michael Gottfredson, eds., *Sourcebook of Criminal Justice Statistics—1981* (U.S. Department of Justice, Bureau of Justice Statistics, 1982).

After conducting an in-depth examination of ten major American cities in the post–World War II era, Jacob and his colleagues concluded that "everywhere except in Boston (where reported crime rose the most), some of the court resources increased more than arrests; indeed, in most cities, all the indicators showed a greater increase than the number of arrests" (p. 78). That resources devoted to the court process have increased more swiftly than the arrest rate is also indicated in figure 9-3.

Police screening

police screening

The courts are able to exert only minimal control over the volume of cases sent to them. Most police departments forward those arrested to the prosecutor without conducting a review of the strength of the case. In general the police prefer to leave assessments of legal matters to others. In Chicago, for example, "In deciding to invoke the criminal process the police are guided by the strong belief that analysis of the evidence both in regard to its admissibility and its weight are matters that should be decided by higher authority" (McIntyre:469). This lack of *police screening* is particularly important because in some communities, police control the decision to prosecute. It is common practice in most cities for misdemeanor or ordi-

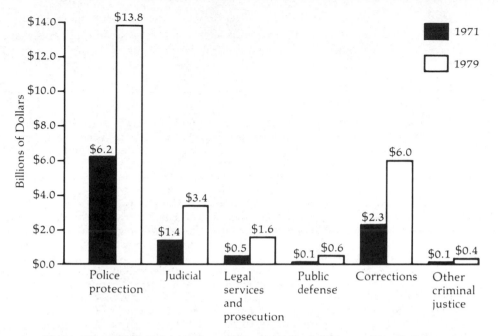

Figure 9-3. Criminal Justice Expenditures of Federal, State, and Local Governments, by Type of Activity, Fiscal Years 1971 and 1979.

Source: Timothy Flanagan, David J. Van Alstyne, and Michael Gottfredson, eds., *Sourcebook of Criminal Justice Statistics—1981* (U.S. Department of Justice, Bureau of Justice Statistics, 1982).

nance violations arrests to result in charges being filed without further review. In some cities (Chicago, Brooklyn, and Baltimore) the police file criminal charges.

After an arrest, however, the police may not hold the defendant without going to court. The Supreme Court has ruled that an arrested person is entitled to a judicial determination of probable cause promptly after arrest. This preliminary examination, though, does not have to involve an adversary hearing. (*Gerstein* v. *Pugh*, 420 U.S. 103, 1975)

Quality of the investigation

The volume of police arrests is one way that police departments affect the operations of the court. Another is the quality of the investigation. In general, police officers define their jobs as investigating crimes and making arrests. They are less interested in writing police reports, which they regard as time-consuming paperwork that has little relationship to their principal tasks. As a result, police officers and police departments vary greatly in the quality, thoroughness, and readability of police reports.

Studies old and new have called for improvement in the investigative and evidence-gathering functions of the police. One report noted that prosecutors complained that police tend to be sloppy in their investigations, often missing important evidence and improperly seizing, marking, or storing items that are gathered. Police officers complained in turn that prosecutors did not provide adequate guid-

---

CLOSE-UP: DALLAS REDUCES POLICE ERROR

Failure to provide full names and addresses of victims and witnesses, to perform necessary laboratory tests or give complete data on tests, to give a grand jury a defendant's prior arrest and conviction records, or to properly cross-reference companion charges—all of these mistakes in a police prosecution report can mean waste of law enforcement manpower when a grand jury returns a "no bill" or the court dismisses the case.

Dallas, Texas, tackled the problem of poor police reports by hiring two full-time attorneys with LEAA funds for the police department. Another LEAA grant in 1973 allowed expansion to the staff to further reduce police error through training and to review case documents. In 1975 the Dallas city council voted to assume the total cost for the project which was about $125,000 for that year. According to Dallas City Manager George R. Schrader: "The record of achievement of the Dallas Legal Liaison Division not only prompted the council to pick up the tab, but it also persuaded LEAA to name it an 'Exemplary Project,' the first one in Texas."

The unit is now composed of five attorneys. The director is also a sworn police officer, and the other four are assistant city attorneys on temporary assignment to the police department. While the director is responsible for overall administration, the assistant city attorneys are each responsible for advising one or two patrol divisions and at least one nonpatrol bureau (one attorney to every 500 officers). Each also specializes in legal matters corresponding to the needs of the assigned unit.

Services include:

—round-the-clock consulting (at least one attorney is on call at all times to provide quick advice to patrol and investigative personnel);

—legal review of every case prepared for prosecution;

—assistance in warrant or affidavit preparation;

—training in all relevant aspects of the law

for both new recruits and veterans;

—help in advising the department on how changes in statutory and case law affect day-to-day operations;

—general in-house legal support to police administrators and line officers.

The Dallas model functions much like a law firm within the police department. The attorneys work together to provide back-up assistance and to avoid inconsistent legal advice. The assignment of each attorney to specific units promotes good officer/attorney rapport and mutual trust. Top level city management contacts with the director of the legal unit are kept to a minimum so that line officers will not feel that information given the attorneys may later be used against them in such proceedings as labor negotiations.

The Dallas Legal Liaison Unit is organized differently from most other legal advisor systems in that the director is completely under police department authority. The other attorneys are supervised daily by the unit director, but their personnel matters are handled by the city attorney's office. This structure is not generally consistent, however, with the recommendation of the American Bar Association or the International Association of Chiefs of Police, which call for administrative subordination only to the commissioner or chief of police. But the Dallas attorneys and the city manager's office have not seen administrative problems developing from this arrangement.

The Legal Liaison Unit reviews about 2,000 prosecution and supplemental reports each month, and the unit has been credited with helping successfully prosecute more than 1,000 cases per year and reducing the number of cases dismissed by grand juries due to police error by 0.6 percent a month.

"Dallas Reduces Police Error," *Target* 5 (October 1976):2. Reprinted by permission of the International City Management Association.

ance but expected them to file perfect cases (Battelle Law and Justice Study Center). A study conducted in Washington, D.C., pointed out that the police who respond to calls of victims and other witnesses may not be fully aware of the crucial importance to the success of the case in court of recovering physical evidence. They found that arrests unsuccessfully prosecuted tend to have less evidence at the time the case is presented to the prosecutor than those that end in conviction. When tangible evidence was recovered by the police, the number of convictions per 100 arrests was 60 percent higher in robberies, 33 percent greater in other violent crimes, and 36 percent higher in nonviolent property offenses (Institute for Law and Social Research). It is common in major cities where prosecutors must deal with numerous police departments to find major differences; some have a much better record of forwarding to the courts the information necessary for prosecution. In Salt Lake City, for example, 85 percent of sheriff's felony arrests are accepted by the prosecutor compared with 67 percent for the police department. The same pattern appears in Los Angeles: 86 percent acceptance for the sheriff arrests compared with 60 percent for the police (Brosi). An earlier study indicated that an important factor was the prosecutorial perception that some police agencies conduct more thorough investigations than others (Neubauer:127). In recent years some important steps have begun to improve the quality of police investigations. Close-up features one of these programs.

Victims and witnesses

victims
witnesses
Victims and *witnesses* are the forgotten people in the criminal justice system. For decades reformers have urged that they be accorded better treatment. In 1931, the National Commission on Law Observance and Enforcement concluded that the economic losses caused by service as witnesses in criminal cases have a special significance: "They come definitely home to the individual citizen, and may affect in some cases his whole attitude toward the administration of public justice. Effective administration of criminal law requires . . . willing witnesses. If . . . [testifying] in court [imposes] unreasonable burdens on the citizen, the administration of justice is bound to suffer" (418–419). A decade later nothing had changed. The American Bar Association in 1938 reported that witness fees were deplorably low; courthouse accommodations were inadequate and uncomfortable; witnesses were being intimidated; and frequently witnesses were summoned to court numerous times only to wait around all day and eventually be informed that the case was continued again or dismissed (8–11). The ABA argued that "the state owes it to the witness to make the circumstances of his sacrifice as comfortable as possible."

In the view of many, the courts have ignored the interests of victims and witnesses while they were busy protecting the interests of the defendant. Not only the courts but the entire criminal justice community (including legal scholars) have largely ignored victims. There is an enormous literature on offenders; much less is known about victims. This is particularly the case with the relationships of victims and witnesses to the courts. A couple of studies, however, have yielded some valuable insights into this area.

Through the eyes of victims and witnesses

Richard Knudten and three associates surveyed crime victims who actively partici-pated in the criminal justice process in Milwaukee, Wisconsin. Some minor incon-veniences voiced by victims were getting to the courthouse itself, finding the court-house, or finding a parking place.

> Judges, prosecutors, defendants, defense counsel—they all know how to make their voices heard to some extent . . . but victims? They're a changing constituency. No one is really listening to them and their particular problems. Railroads for some time have not done much to please the customer. But airlines . . . compete in their services. Look at Dulles Airport. You walk in there and you're taken care of in a very few steps. There is someone to tell you what to do, to take your bags, to be polite. Our system has been behaving like a railroad, because maybe it figures the victim can't just choose another court system. We've got to look at the victim like he's a customer who requires service.

This excerpt is reprinted from a quote by David Epstein, Trial Attorney, in *Criminal Justice and the Victim*, vol. 6, Sage Criminal Justice System Annuals, William F. McDonald, ed., © 1976, p. 17 by permission of the Publisher, Sage Publications, Inc. (Beverly Hills/London).

More serious problems related to the administrative runaround once the court-house was located. Cases often required numerous court appearances, some of which were continued with no reason given. Some defense attorneys, for example, use delaying tactics to wear down the victim in hopes that they will eventually not appear for a critical hearing, thus producing a dismissal. The economic cost of losing a day or more of work is also significant.

The victim as witness

Victims also face major problems in testifying in court. Because few people are accustomed to testifying, lawyers must coach their witnesses ahead of time to answer only the question asked, to speak forcibly (but not belligerently), and not to become rattled by cross-examination. Even after such preparation, however, many witnesses become uncomfortable during cross-examination as the defense attorney attempts to tie their story into knots and discredit them.

Most of what we know about the ordeal of testifying in court comes from studies of rape victims. That the victim, not the defendant, is on trial is the conclusion of a study by Holmstrom and Burgess, both of whom counsel rape victims in Boston City Hospital. They followed the cases of fourteen women who testified in court during a rape trial. Often the trauma is significant; the victims must publicly repeat in specific detail how the rape occurred. Moreover the legal definition of rape (in Massachusetts and most other states as well) adds to the humiliation. A major element of rape is sexual penetration against the woman's will. The defense often seeks to blame the victim by suggesting she consented, did not struggle, was pro-vocatively dressed, and so on. Further, a woman's past sexual conduct is generally deemed relevant. It can take little to discredit the victim.

Support for the system

A few studies have begun to examine systematically the problems that victims and witnesses face in court. What is most surprising about these studies is not so much the documentation that problems exist but the fact that victims still express overall favorable support for the criminal courts. In the Milwaukee study, for instance, many said, that they were satisfied or very satisfied with the handling of their case by the police (81 percent), district attorney (75 percent), and judge (66 percent). Overall less than 15 percent said they were dissatisfied (Knudten et al.:118). This study and another one in Minnesota also suggest that favorable support exists independently of whether the victim was satisfied with the eventual outcome of the case (Stookey and Oman:22).

Through the eyes of the court

Despite the fact that victims and witnesses have been treated as the forgotten people in the criminal courts, their actions and inactions have an important influence on the outcome of cases. In large measure, victims and witnesses, along with the police, provide the raw materials for the court process. The types of complaints they bring to the court and how they are viewed by the courtroom work group are relevant factors.

Lack of Cooperation. A number of victims and witnesses are reluctant to become involved in the criminal justice process. Half of all major crimes are never reported to the police; even when they are, not all victims wish to prosecute. They fear reprisals by the suspect, prefer not to go through the ordeal of the court process (delays, loss of income, and testifying in court), especially if it is likely to result in sending a person to prison. These factors are particularly pronounced in assault cases in which typically the victim and defendant know one another. In domestic disturbance cases, for example, many women call the police in order to stop the violence but later refuse to sign a complaint, thus effectively ending the case.

Some specific witness-related problems include refusal to sign a complaint, failure to show up in court, giving the police incorrect addresses and testimony that is confused, garbled, or contradicted by other facts. These witness-related problems result in a significant number of cases in which the prosecutor refuses to file charges or the case is later dismissed (chapter 10 will discuss these topics in greater depth). In Indianapolis, for example, 40 percent of cases dropped from the system before trial stemmed from witness problems. Comparable figures for other cities are Golden, Colorado (20 percent), New Orleans (40 percent), and Los Angeles (70 percent) (Boland et al.).

The following case is a good example of witness-related problems.

> An auxiliary police officer watched a woman approach a man as he emerged from a liquor store. It was dark. The officer thought he saw a knife flash in her hand, and the man seemed to hand her some money. She fled, and the officer went to the aid of the victim, taking him to the hospital for treatment.
>
> The officer saw the woman on the street a few days later and arrested her for first degree robbery on the victim's sworn complaint. It was presumably a "high quality" arrest—identification of the perpetrator by an eye-witness, not from mugshots or a line-up, but in a crowd. Yet, shortly thereafter, this apparently airtight case was dismissed on the prosecutor's motion.
>
> What the victim had not explained to the police was that the defendant, an alcoholic, had been his girlfriend for the past five years; that they had been drinking together the

night of the incident; that she had taken some money from him and got angry when he took it back; that she had flown into a fury when he then gave her only a dollar outside the liquor store; and that she had slashed at him with a pen knife in anger and run off. He had been sufficiently annoyed to have her charged with robbery, but, as the judge who dismissed the case said, "He wasn't really injured. Before it got into court they had kissed and made up." In fact, the victim actually approached the defense attorney before the hearing and asked him to prevail upon the judge and the Assistant District Attorney (ADA) to dismiss the charges against his girlfriend. [Vera Institute of Justice: xii]

This case is one of many cited by the Vera Institute (a nonprofit group devoted to criminal justice reform) in its in-depth analysis of felony case dispositions in New York City. It found that in half of all felony arrests, the victim had a prior relationship with the defendant. Prior relationships were frequent in cases of homicide and assault, where they were expected, but they were also frequent in cases of robbery, where they were not. Criminal court officials, therefore, regard these crimes as not very serious.

Court-Caused Problems.   Not all of the uncooperative behavior of victims and witnesses can be blamed on them. The court system can be equally at fault. A study in Washington, D.C., focused on what it called "noncooperative" witnesses and reported that 41 percent were never told they should contact the prosecutor, 62 percent said they were never told when to appear in court, and 43 percent stated neither police, prosecutor, nor judge explained their rights and duties as witnesses. Besides a lack of communication, the report also concluded that "prosecutors misinterpreted the witnesses' intentions and therefore regarded them as uncooperative, when indeed such a decision was premature at best and incorrect at worst" (Meyer:1).

Aiding the victims and witnesses

Chapter 1 argued that it is important to adopt a consumer's perspective in viewing the criminal courts. In the last few years a limited number of court projects have taken this view seriously and have created programs to aid victims and witnesses. For example, the Brooklyn Criminal Court received a million-dollar federal grant to construct a larger complaint room staffed by a bilingual staff, to provide better notifications to police and civilian witnesses about scheduled court appearances, to provide vans to pick up elderly and disabled witnesses, and to transport night witnesses to and from court ("New York City Aids Crime Witnesses": 452). Other programs are run by the prosecutor's office. Their principal aim is to provide more coordination of victims and witnesses so that fewer cases will be lost because of communications failures.

Such programs are important first steps in providing better services to citizens who are thrust into the criminal court process. But not all agree. Sociologist William McDonald charges that "some projects that are billed as 'assisting victims' are more accurately described as assisting the criminal justice system and extending government control over victims. Whether the victims so controlled would regard the project as 'assisting' them is problematic" (35). Some victims do not wish to become involved or have government officials verifying their address. More fundamentally, though, such programs do not involve the victim in the decision-making process. Law professor Norval Morris for one believes that victims should have the opportunity to be present during plea bargaining. They would not have veto power, however:

> If the criminal process is the taking over by the state of the vengeful instincts of the injured person—buttressed by the recognition that the harm to the victim is also harm to the state—then it would seem, at first blush, that the victim at least has a right to be informed of, and where appropriate involved in, the processes that have led to whatever is the state settlement of the harm that has been done to him. In that respect, one would hardly need to make an affirmative argument; it is a matter of courtesy and respect to the dignity of the individual victim. [p. 56]

Rosett and Cressey argue that additional efforts must be made to bring the criminal courts back to the people, to break down the barriers between courts and citizens. While there are numerous problems with such proposals—important details require specification—these ideas incorporate a true consumer perspective on the citizens', not the court officials', terms.

The defendant

defendant   The *defendant* is supposed to stand at the center of the criminal court drama. Yet like victims and witnesses, defendants are often the forgotten participants, more objects to be acted upon than the key to what happens. The typical felony defendant is powerless.

The Watergate scandal dramatically showed that violators of the criminal law belong to all social and economic groups. The convictions of the attorney general, assorted cabinet and subcabinet officials, to say nothing of a host of lawyers and big businessmen, demonstrate that defendants come from all social strata. Nothing generates headlines more than when a famous actor or other well-known public personality is indicted. But although these highly publicized cases illustrate the range of defendants appearing before the criminal courts, they hardly constitute the norm. The vast majority of violators form a distinct profile.

One profile shows that defendants differ in important ways from the average citizen. They are younger, predominantly male, disproportionately black (or other racial minority), less educated, seldom fully employed, and typically unmarried (Gertz). By the time the sorting process has ended, those sent to prison will consist of an even higher proportion of young, illiterate, black males (see table 9–1). They are society's losers.

As a result, criminal courts are a depressing place to work. Judges, prosecutors, and defense attorneys seldom come away from their day's activities with a sense of accomplishment, for many of the criminal cases involve social problems like drug addiction, marital problems, lack of education, and mental illness, over which the court personnel have no control. A Vera Institute study in New York City summed it up this way:

> . . . the incidents that give rise to arrest are frequently not the kind that the court system is able to deal with satisfactorily. At the root of much of the crime brought to court is

TABLE 9-1. Characteristics of state inmates

Age (median)	27 years
Sex (male)	96%
Race:	
White	49.6%
Black	47.8%
Other	2.5%
Education (mean years)	11.2 years
Prior incarceration record	64%
Current offense:	
Violent	58%
Property	31%
Drug	7%
Prearrest employment status:	
Full-time	60%
Part-time	10%
Not employed	30%
Prearrest annual income:	
Less than $3,000	19%
$3,000–$9,000	30%
$10,000+	25%

Source: *Bureau of Justice Statistics*, U.S. Department of Justice. "Prisons and Prisoners," *1982* (Washington, D.C.: 1982).

anger—simple or complicated anger between two or more people who know each other. Expression of anger results in the commission of technical felonies, yet defense attorneys, judges and prosecutors recognize that in many cases conviction and prison sentences are inappropriate responses. High rates of dismissal or charge reduction appear to be a reflection of the system's effort to carry out the *intent* of the law—as judges and other participants perceive it—though not necessarily the letter of the law. [p. xv]

Contrary to public perceptions, most defendants are not dangerous. Most felony charges involve property offenses or disputes between people who knew one another.

Court personnel have little empathy with or understanding of the types of defendants whose fate they must decide. Judges, prosecutors, defense attorneys, and probation officers are essentially middle class. Little in their background or training has equipped them to deal with the poor.

Nor are the poor or uneducated equipped to deal with the technical abstractions of the criminal court process. Many are incapable of understanding even the simplest instructions about the right to bail or the presumption of innocence. Many are too inarticulate to aid their attorney in preparing a defense. Many hold unfavorable attitudes toward the law and the criminal justice system and thus regard the judge and all other court personnel, including their defense attorneys, with hostility and distrust.

As a result, the huge majority of defendants . . . submit to the painful consequences of conviction but do not know for certain whether they committed any of the crimes of which they are accused. Such defendants are so unschooled in law that they form no firm opinion about their technical innocence or guilt. Neither do they actually agree or disagree that it is just to punish them. They do not know enough about themselves to tell the lawyers what to do. [Rosett and Cressey: 146]

Simply put, the criminal courts are poor peoples' institutions. They share many of the same characteristics of other institutions like welfare bureaucracies and charity hospitals that deal almost exclusively with the poor. Unlike the middle class, the poor are accustomed to accepting the conditions they find themselves in. They do not protest long waits before government officials can see them nor do they demand that buildings they wait in be improved. In cities with separate civil and criminal courts, the former are typically newer and cleaner. Such contrasts emphasize the differing clientele of civil and criminal courts.

Conclusion

The volume of cases, the quality of police investigations, the cooperation of victim and witnesses, and the characteristics of the defendant are all factors that shape how the criminal courts dispense justice. There is a striking contrast between how these matters are portrayed on television and the reality of American courts. Television detectives investigate a crime, gather evidence, and eventually make an arrest. Invariably the defendant is white, middle-aged, and somewhat sophisticated.

This chapter portrays a very different pattern. Given the large volume of cases, no one in the courtroom work group has time to devote to a single case. Most arrests are made on the spot or after only a brief investigation. Seldom is much physical evidence (fingerprints, for example) gathered. Most of the crimes are never solved, and when an arrest is made, it is typically for a crime like burglary or theft (not murder as shown on television). Most defendants are young, illiterate, impoverished, and members of minority groups. To complicate matters further, some witnesses and victims are reluctant to become involved. On television, the case ends with an arrest. For the courts, however, an arrest is only the beginning of a long and sometimes drawn-out process.

For discussion

1. In the most recent volume of the FBI's *Uniform Crime Reports*, look up your local community. How many crimes were reported? How many arrests? Is your community similar to or different from the national average? What proportion of arrests involve crimes of violence?
2. Interview a local police official about police standards for arrest and procedures for booking a suspect. Do they make any efforts to screen cases before forwarding the case to the prosecutor? Also inquire about their perceptions of prosecutorial charging standards. Are these too stringent?
3. Interview several people who have been witnesses in criminal court. What

problems do they mention? Did they find their experience satisfying or frustrating?

4. What types of programs would you recommend for improving court treatment of victims and witnesses?
5. While you are in court, observe the facial expressions and body motions of the defendants. What might they indicate? For a representative day in court, prepare a tally of the age, race, sex, poverty level, and so on of both witnesses and defendants. How does this profile compare to table 9–1?
6. How do the characteristics of defendants in criminal courts shape the process? Why do judges, prosecutors, defense attorneys, and probation officers often believe that because of the nature of the court's clientele, cases are really less serious than they legally appear to be?

References

American Bar Association. "Recommendations of the Committee on Improvements in the Administration of Justice of the Section of Judicial Administration (As approved by the Assembly and House of Delegates, July 27, 1938)." Chicago, 1938.

Battelle Law and Justice Study Center. *Forcible Rape: A National Survey of Responses by Prosecutors.* Washington, D.C.: Government Printing Office, 1977.

Boland, Barbara, Elizabeth Brady, Herbert Tyson, and John Bassler. *The Prosecution of Felony Arrests.* Washington, D.C.: Institute for Law and Social Research, 1982.

Brosi, Kathleen. *A Cross-City Comparison of Felony Case Processing.* Washington, D.C.: Institute for Law and Social Research, 1979.

Ennis, Philip. "Criminal Victimization in the United States: A Report of a National Survey." *Field Surveys II. President's Commission on Law Enforcement and Administration of Justice.* Washington, D.C.: Government Printing Office, 1967.

Federal Bureau of Investigation (FBI). *Uniform Crime Reports—1981.* Washington, D.C.: Government Printing Office, 1982.

Gertz, Mark. "Comparative Justice: A Study of Five Connecticut Courts." Paper presented at the annual meeting of the New England Political Science Association, Durham, New Hampshire, April 9–11, 1976.

Holmstrom, Lynda, and Ann Burgess. "Rape: The Victim Goes on Trial." In Israel Drapkin and Emilio Viano, eds., *Victimology: A New Focus,* pp. 31–48. Lexington, Mass.: D.C. Heath, 1975.

Institute for Law and Social Research. *What Happens After Arrest? A Court Perspective of Police Operations in the District of Columbia.* Washington, D.C.: Institute for Law and Social Research, 1977.

Jacob, Herbert, with Duane Swank, Janice Beecher, and Michael Rich. "Keeping Pace: Court Resources and Crime in Ten U.S. Cities." *Judicature* 66 (1982): 73–83.

Knudten, Richard, Anthony Meader, Mary Knudten, and William Doerner. "The Victim in the Administration of Criminal Justice: Problems and Perceptions." In William McDonald, ed., *Criminal Justice and the Victim,* pp. 115–146. Beverly Hills, Calif.: Sage Publications, 1976.

McDonald, William F., ed. *Criminal Justice and the Victim.* Beverly Hills, Calif.: Sage Publications, 1976.

McIntyre, Donald. "A Study of Judicial Dominance of the Charging Decision." *Journal of Criminal Law, Criminology and Police Science* 59 (1968):463–490.

Meyer, Eugene. "Witnesses' Feelings Misread." *Washington Post,* December 14, 1975.

Morris, Norval. *The Future of Imprisonment.* Chicago: University of Chicago Press, 1974.

National Commission on Law Observance and Enforcement. *Report on the Cost of Crime,* no. 12. Washington, D.C.: Government Printing Office, 1931.

Neubauer, David. *Criminal Justice in Middle America*. Morristown, N.J.: General Learning Press, 1974.

"New York City Aids Crime Witnesses." *Judicature 58* (April 1975):452.

Rosett, Arthur, and Donald Cressey. *Justice by Consent*. Philadelphia: J. B. Lippincott, 1976.

Stookey, John, and Colleen Oman. "The Victim's Perspective on American Criminal Justice." Paper presented at the annual meeting of the Midwest Political Science Association, Chicago, Illinois, April 29–May 1, 1976.

Vera Institute of Justice. *Felony Arrests: Their Prosecution and Disposition in New York City's Courts*. New York: Vera Institute of Justice, 1977.

For further reading

Cannavalle, F. J. *Witness Cooperation with a Handbook of Witness Management*. Lexington, Mass.: D. C. Heath, 1975.

Greenwood, Peter, Sorrel Wildhorn, Eugene Poggio, Michael Strumwasser, and Peter De-Leon, *Prosecution of Adult Felony Defendants in Los Angeles County: A Policy Perspective*. Lexington, Mass.: D. C. Heath, 1976.

Institute for Law and Social Research. *What Happens After Arrest? A Court Perspective of Police Operations in the District of Columbia*. Washington, D.C.: Institute for Law and Social Research, August 1977.

McDonald, William, ed. *Criminal Justice and the Victim*. Beverly Hills, Calif.: Sage Publications, 1976.

Wood, P. L. "The Victim in a Forcible Rape Case: A Feminist View." *American Criminal Law Review* 11 (1973):335–354.

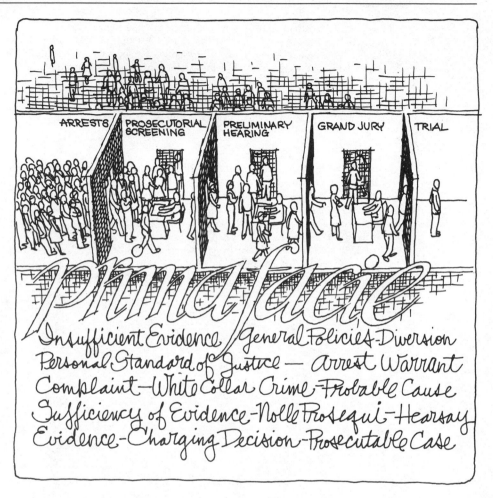

After the Arrest: Case Attrition

After the arrest, what next? At first glance this rather simple question seems to suggest an equally simple answer: the arrested person will be formally charged with a crime. Being booked in the police station, however, is not the same as being charged in court with a criminal violation.

Cases do not automatically move through the criminal justice process. At numerous stages in the proceedings, prosecutors, police officers, victims, and judges have the option of advancing a case to the next step, seeking an alternative (noncriminal) disposition, or eliminating the case altogether. Much as a set of sieves may be used to sort gravel, the steps of the criminal court process screen cases. A nonconviction disposition is referred to generally as *attrition* or screening or simply case drop-out.

attrition

This chapter looks at three stages where attrition occurs: prosecutorial screening, the preliminary hearing, and the grand jury. The decisions made at these points set the tone, tenor, quality, and quantity of cases moving through the criminal court process (Jacoby:2). Clearly, the volume of cases is directly tied to screening decisions. It is common in many areas for roughly half of the defendants to have their cases dismissed during these early stages. As a result, the bulk of the decisions about innocence is made not during a trial but during the earlier stages. The nearer a case moves to trial, the less latitude court officials have and the greater the likelihood that the defendant will be found guilty. Once a case has cleared the initial hurdles, the system operates on the assumption that the defendant is guilty. How these cases are eventually disposed of reflects how cases were initially screened. For instance, it is a practice of long standing in many communities for prosecutors to overcharge a defendant (that is, file a charge more serious than the evidence indicates) in order to provide themselves leverage for later allowing a defendant to plead guilty to a less serious charge.

The attrition process also has important consequences for the defendant. A decision by the state to label one of its citizens a defendant in a criminal case should be undertaken only with the full seriousness of the action understood. Once a suspect is converted to a defendant, the full power of the criminal justice process comes into effect. A defendant accused of a crime may have to raise money to hire a lawyer or pay a bail bondsman. And unless bond can be posted, the defendant must await trial in jail. An accused also faces other penalties. The person's reputation may be damaged, for example. Even for defendants who are later acquitted or have their cases dismissed, the criminal court process has imposed significant penalties on the accused.

Case attrition: an overview

Case attrition occurs both before and after charges are filed. Figure 10-1 provides a tree diagram illustrating this point. These data come from 1977 and 1979. Note that in 20 percent of the cases no formal charges are filed. This is referred to as *prosecutorial screening*. Moreover, after charges are filed, some cases are dismissed (30 percent in the fourteen cities studied). A dismissal is often referred to as a *nolle prosequi* or *nolle* for short.

prosecutorial screening
nolle prosequi

Figure 10-2 provides a visual overview of the statistical impact of case attrition, this time for three cities. In the case of Washington, D.C., while only 17 percent were rejected during prosecutorial screening, 34 percent were later dropped by the prosecutor's office. Half of the cases did not survive to the trial stage. Observe also that this high mortality rate of felony cases contrasts sharply with the very small percentage of cases (2 percent) in which the defendant was acquitted by a judge or jury. Viewed from a different perspective, the activity of prosecutors is much more important in terminating cases than are the later activities of judges and juries. Similar patterns emerge in other cities.

Case attrition is the product of a complex set of factors, among them the relationships between the major components of the criminal justice system, patterns of informal authority within the courthouse, perceived standards of the community, the backlog of cases on the court's docket, and so on. For example, a case may be screened out because of the unpopularity of the law in a particular type of case or because the court's docket is crowded with more serious matters.

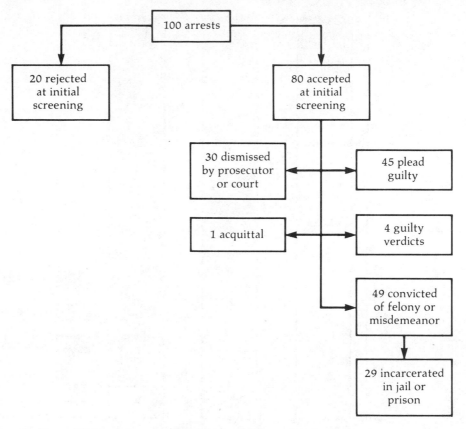

Figure 10-1.   Outcome of 100 "Typical" Felony Arrests.

Source: Barbara Boland, Elizabeth Brady, Herbert Tyson and John Bassler. *The Prosecution of Felony Arrests.* Washington, D.C.: Institute for Law and Social Research, 1982.

One of the key considerations in analyzing case attrition is that the stage at which cases drop out varies from city to city. In looking at figure 10-2, notice that in New Orleans, where prosecutorial screening is high, later case dismissals are relatively low. Conversely, in Washington, D.C., high rates of case dismissals reflect low levels of prosecutorial screening. Another study concluded that in Los Angeles and Detroit the prosecutor made the important screening decisions, meaning that the preliminary hearing was relatively unimportant. In contrast, in Chicago, Brooklyn, and Houston, the preliminary hearing emerged as the most important stage at which case attrition occurred (McIntyre and Lippman).

These differences are partially the result of state law, the structure of state courts, and local tradition. For example, case review by prosecutors varies with the structure of state courts and the nature of state criminal procedures. In states with two levels of trial courts and two levels of prosecutors, prosecutors responsible for felony prosecutions have no control over the screening decisions made by local

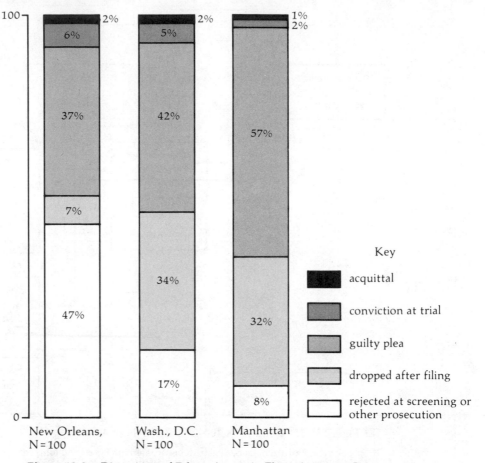

Figure 10-2. Disposition of Felony Arrests in Three American Cities.

Note: Derived from statistics presented in Barbara Boland, Elizabeth Brady, Herbert Tyson and John Bassler. *The Prosecution of Felony Arrests.* Washington, D.C.: Institute for Law and Social Research, 1982.

prosecutors in the lower courts. Similarly, some states allow police officers to file charges on arrest warrants without the necessity of prosecutorial review (Jacoby:13–14).

More importantly, however, variations in where the screening decisions are made are the product of differing attitudes of the major courtroom actors. State statutes provide no guidelines on how the charging decisions should be handled or who is responsible. As a result each community may adopt different procedures, procedures that allow certain actors more influence than others. Four actors may exert influence over who will be charged with a criminal offense: the policeman, the prosecutor, the judge, and the complainant. Which actor, or which combination of them, is allowed to make the charging decision has a great influence on the results. For example, if the police dominate, they are likely to employ different standards than a prosecutor or judge would. If the complainant is allowed a major role, it is possible that the criminal courts might be used as a forum for personal vendettas or family fights. Viewed from this perspective, asking who controls the screening process requires asking who is the gatekeeper to the powers of the criminal courts: who regulates the flow of cases to the courts (Goldman and Jahnige:114).

Filing of charges

complaint
information
arrest
warrant
charging
document

The prosecutor controls the doors to the courthouse. He or she can decide which arrests will result in criminal charges and which will not. The formal criminal court process begins with the filing of either a *complaint*, an *information*, or an *arrest warrant* (all are also referred to as *charging documents*). A complaint must be verified by oath or affirmation by either the victim or the arresting officer. Complaints are commonly used for violation of city ordinance offenses or of misdemeanor offenses. In a few states, however, they are used for felony cases prior to the holding of the preliminary hearing. An information is virtually identical in form to the complaint except it is signed by the prosecutor. A bill of information is required in most states where a grand jury indictment is not a requirement, but it is also often used for initiating felony charges prior to grand jury action. Arrest warrants are issued by a judicial officer—typically a lower court judge or magistrate. In a very small percentage of cases, the warrant is issued prior to arrest. But the vast majority of street crimes begin with an arrest without a warrant. In such an instance many states require that an arrest warrant be issued only if the prosecutor approves the request in writing (McIntyre, 1967:967).

Whether an information, complaint, or arrest warrant is used depends on the severity of the offense, the applicable state or federal law, and local customs. All are similar in that they must set forth the essential facts of the case and the specific section(s) of the criminal law violated. A typical charging document states that on or about a given date in the county, city, or district, the defendant violated a stated section of the law. The exact wording of the charging document contains all the essential elements (*corpus delicti*) of the crime. The purpose of the charging document is to satisfy the Sixth Amendment provision that a defendant be given information upon which to prepare a defense. Technical aspects of the law of the jurisdiction deal with matters like the precise drafting of the document, procedures for later making minor amendments, and so on.

Prosecutorial control of the charging decision

charging
decision

Although legislative mandates normally command prosecution for "all known criminal conduct," the courts have traditionally granted prosecutors wide discretion in deciding whether to prosecute (Baker). There are, for example, no legislative or judicial standards governing which cases merit prosecution and which should be dismissed. Moreover, if a prosecutor declines to file charges, there is no possible review of this decision; courts have refused to order a prosecutor to proceed with a case.

prosecutorial
dominance
of charging

Although the prosecutor has the legal authority to *dominate the charging process*, some choose to share this power with the police. The American Bar Foundation study of Milwaukee concluded that some prosecutors defer to police assessment

---

IN THE NEWS: CONNICK'S OFFICE DISMISSES NEARLY HALF OF PENDING CASES

Nearly half the cases brought to the Orleans Parish district attorney's office since April have reportedly been dismissed.

Sources said 46 percent of all cases brought since Dist. Atty. Harry Connick took office have been refused, although some of these have been transferred to Municipal Court for action. Exact figures are unavailable.

Refusal to bring charges in nearly half the cases has demoralized the police force, said one officer.

"You cannot convince me the police are wrong almost 50 percent of the time when they make arrests," he said. "After police have gone to the trouble of making an arrest, going through the booking procedure and writing up an extensive report, they're very demoralized when they're told they're wrong nearly 50 percent of the time."

This trend, he said, could lead to a breakdown of trust between the policemen and Connick's office, he said, and in that case policemen "are not going to function in their best capacity."

During DA Jim Garrison's tenure, one or two people manned the desk, but Connick has boosted the number to seven.

"We felt a lot of bad cases went by and wanted to make a better determination of what cases should be accepted or rejected," said Connick. "If we spend more time in the beginning, we'll spend more time with the victims and witnesses, bring more cases to court and move cases more quickly."

New Orleans States-Item, September 14, 1974.

(Miller:338). In these communities the police file criminal charges with minimal supervision by the prosecutor. In essence, these prosecutors have transferred their decision-making power to the police (Mellon et al.:59). In others, the prosecutor retains the formal authority to file charges, but the police influence the prosecutor's decision. Studies of Oakland (Skolnick:199–202), of Seattle (Cole:334–337), and of assistant U.S. attorneys (Eisenstein:8–9) indicate that the police and prosecutor jointly discuss cases before charges are filed. The influence of the police in such an interchange is revealed by Skolnick's finding that police pressure resulted in suspects being charged on the basis of weak evidence or being initially overcharged.

In communities where prosecutors choose to control the filing of criminal charges, a substantial percentage (a third to a half) of persons arrested are released without the filing of criminal charges. I analyzed all nontraffic arrests for a month in a medium-sized Illinois community and found that a third of police arrests resulted in no criminal charges being filed (Neubauer, 1974a:124). Another study (summarized in figure 10-1) likewise concluded that in court systems with strong prosecutorial screening, up to half of all felony arrests do not result in criminal charges (Boland et al.).

One of the major recommendations of the National Advisory Commission on Criminal Justice Standards and Goals was that prosecutors should exercise the dominant role in the charging decision. The primary justification is efficiency. Removing weak cases and cases that do not warrant prosecution eliminates the need for judges and other court personnel to devote time to them. Moreover, civilian witnesses and police officers are not required to appear, which translates into additional savings on witnesses and police overtime, and allows civilians and police alike to use their time in more productive ways (Rossman and Hoffman).

Arguments in favor of prosecutorial control of the charging decision that are anchored in a view that such actions will increase "efficiency" neglect something vital:

Those who have studied the pretrial screening process have failed to see it as part of either the prosecutorial system or the criminal justice system. The result is, in part, a failure to see pretrial screening as part of a continuum rather than as an isolated act and as a means to an end, the disposition of a case, rather than as a goal in itself. Screening cannot be separated from the larger system of which it is part if it is to be evaluated. It is an implicit part of that system, and must be treated as such. [Jacoby:12]

A major dimension of this failure to see the screening process as part of the entire criminal justice process is a disregard of the relationship between police and prosecutor. The police often view a prosecutor's failure to file charges as a rebuke of their actions. Other studies have also indicated that prosecutors who choose to control the charging process generate a great resentment with local police departments (Neubauer, 1974a). As a result, some prosecutors choose to maintain good relationships with their police departments and demonstrate a posture of being part of the law enforcement team by granting police a major voice in the charging decision.

Screening criteria

screening Despite the importance of the *screening* process, the standards governing these decisions are imperfectly understood. Appellate courts and legislative bodies have generally failed to provide a set of legal criteria to guide decision making, preferring instead to leave it to prosecutorial discretion. Most studies of the criminal courts have focused on the latter and on the more dramatic stages of plea bargaining, trial, and sentencing. Although the statistical data suggest the importance of the screening process in shaping the flow of cases, we tend to know relatively little about how these decisions are made. In turn, one of the major concerns of the National Advisory Commission was that the screening criteria are too informal. They therefore recommended that prosecutors develop explicit criteria.

> Among the types of cases in which thoughtful prosecutors commonly appear disinclined to seek criminal penalties are domestic disturbances; assaults and petty thefts in which victim and offender are in a family or social relationship; statutory rape when both boy and girl are young; first offense car thefts that involve teenagers taking a car for a short joyride; checks that are drawn upon insufficient funds; shoplifting by first offenders, particularly when restitution is made; and criminal acts that involve offenders suffering from emotional disorders short of legal insanity.
>
> President's Commission on Law Enforcement and Administration of Justice. *Task Force Report: The Courts* (Washington, D.C.: Government Printing Office, 1967), p. 50.

A handful of studies suggests that cases are dropped or reduced because of insufficient evidence, general policies, or personal standards of justice. Note that these categories parallel the threefold categorization of discretion (developed in chapter 5) of legal judgments, priorities, and personal standards of justice. And like any other attempt to categorize discretion, the reader must always bear in mind that these are not mutually exclusive—some decisions reflect more than one criterion.

sufficiency
of evidence

Sufficiency of Evidence.   Is there a case? Is there *sufficient evidence* to prove the elements of the offense? These are important questions in the decision to file charges. Here is how one assistant state's attorney in Illinois phrased this point: "When I examine the police report I have to feel that I could go to trial with the case tomorrow. All the elements of prosecution must be present before I file charges" (Neubauer, 1974a:118).

A large proportion of arrests rejected during prosecutorial screening stems from insufficient evidence. Looking at table 10-1, we find that evidence problems are a major reason for rejection of cases ranging from 6 percent in Los Angeles to 33 percent in New Orleans. Witness problems (discussed in chapter 9) are another evidence-related reason for charges not being filed.

prosecutable
case
probable
cause

The common emphasis on conviction produces an important change in the nature of the case from a *prosecutable case* to one that satisfies *probable cause*. At the preliminary hearing the judge determines whether there is probable cause: that a crime has been committed and there are grounds to believe that the suspect probably committed it. From the prosecutor's perspective, however, probable cause is too gross a yardstick; even though it is present, a case may still be legally weak. Thus, a prosecutable case is not one merely satisfying probable cause—a standard required of police in making an arrest and used by the judge in the administration of the preliminary hearing. Rather, it is a case that meets the standards of proof necessary to convict. Skolnick distinguishes between factual and legal guilt. Prosecutors who emphasize factual guilt focus on whether the suspect committed the crime. In contrast, those who decide on the basis of legal guilt look at what can be proved about the suspect's activities.

Various studies of prosecutors' offices in Seattle (Cole:334), central Illinois (Neubauer, 1974b:117–119), and Los Angeles ("Prosecutorial Discretion in the Initiation of Criminal Complaints") all report that screening on the basis of the sufficiency of evidence is an important factor. There appear to be some variations, however, in how prosecutors employ this yardstick. For instance, when deputy prosecutors in Los Angeles were interviewed, 20 percent felt prosecutors should file charges even if the case "will probably not get past the preliminary hearing stage." Thirty percent stated charges should be filed if the case would survive the preliminary hearing but probably lose at trial. Only half agreed with the Prairie City practice

TABLE 10-1. Reasons for case drop-out (prosecutorial screening and dismissals)

	New Orleans	Cobb County (Atlanta)	Los Angeles	District of Columbia
Evidence problems	33%	19%	6%	17%
Witness problems	15%	58%	26%	81%
Policy reasons	19%	12%	22%	0%
Other	33%	8%	37%	2%
Total cases	552	1,356	5,514	2,781

Source: Barbara Boland, Elizabeth Brady, Herbert Tyson, and John Bassler. *The Prosecution of Felony Arrests*. Washington, D.C. Institute for Law and Social Research, 1982.

(Neubauer, 1974a) of filing charges only "if the case will probably win at trial" ("Prosecutorial Discretion":526).

general policies

General Policies. | Decisions about whether to file criminal charges are also made on the basis of *general policies* | Just as police departments have informal norms governing arrests (they will not arrest for gambling among friends in private homes, for example) criminal courts have similar yardsticks, For example, a number of U.S. attorneys will not prosecute bank tellers who embezzle small amounts of money (generally under $100 to $300), get caught, and lose their job. The stigmatization of being caught and losing the job is viewed as punishment enough. Similarly in the last few years, numerous local and state prosecutors have virtually decriminalized possession of small amounts of marijuana by refusing to file charges. The study of the Los Angeles County district attorney's office found that informal office policies controlled the charging decision. The office was reluctant to prosecute interfamily assaults, neighborhood squabbles, and noncommercial gambling ("Prosecutorial Discretion").

personal standards of justice

Personal Standards of Justice. The judicial process is expected to individualize justice. *Personal standards of justice*—attitudes of members of the courtroom work group about what actions should not be punished—constitute the third category of criteria guiding screening. In chapter 5, we argued that this constitutes the third subcomponent of discretion. When McIntyre studied screening in Chicago, he found that "many cases are dropped or reduced for reasons other than failure to establish guilt" (1968:485). And even if the evidence was strong, a defendant might not be prosecuted if his conduct and background indicated that he was not a genuine threat to society (1968:481). In Detroit, among other places, a different term is used—prosecution would serve no useful purpose—but the thought is the same (McIntyre, 1967). In table 10-1, these reasons for rejection are included under the category of policy reasons

An important dimension of personal standards of justice involves a subjective decision on the part of the prosecutor that the case is not as serious as the legal charge suggests. In most courthouses, officials refer to some cases as "cheap" or "garbage" cases. Rosett and Cressey provide the following example: An old man stumbled drunkenly into a liquor store waving a cap pistol and demanding a bottle of whiskey. While all the elements of the offense of armed robbery were clearly present, the judge, complaining witness, and prosecutor did not take the case seriously. It was viewed as a "cheap" robbery. Decisions not to file charges in cheap cases reflected the effort of court officials to produce substantive justice.

A noisy party attracted the attention of three police officers patrolling in an unmarked car in the early hours of the morning. The only officer in uniform was in the back seat, out of view from the house. There was heavy drinking going on, and people were going in and out of the party, stopping in groups on the steps outside. As they drove off down the street, the officers heard a shot and, when looking back, saw a man holding a gun that seemed pointed in their direction. They returned the fire. (The arresting officer explained that two police officers had been shot and killed recently.) The three people on the steps ran inside, locking themselves in an upstairs room with others from the party. Police reinforcements were called, and the house was stormed, but the door was finally opened from the inside. Nine persons were charged with resisting arrest, and the three who had been seen on the steps when the shot was fired (including our two co-defendants) were charged with attempted murder. Neither of the two had been seen holding the gun, and neither knew why or in which direction the gun had been fired. . . .

The police officer thought it might have been an overcharge. He said: "Most times if there is a problem [on charging] we will get an ADA to come to the station. An ADA came down in this case and advised charging all three with attempted murder, as the gun may have changed hands after the shot was fired." The ADA who handled the cases in court was critical of the charging decision. "At least," he said, "these two cases shouldn't have got past the Complaint Room because the police officers were in there and said only the other man had the gun." When that testimony was repeated at the preliminary hearing the cases were dismissed. (The man who had actually fired the gun pled guilty to reckless endangerment.)

Vera Institute of Justice, *Felony Arrests: Their Prosecution and Disposition in New York City's Courts* (New York: Longman, 1981) pp. 59–60.

CLOSE-UP: ONE MAN IN THE MAZE OF JUSTICE

The complaint room on the fourth floor of the Criminal Court Building in Manhattan is a drab place with institutional yellow cinder-block walls and 88 green, molded-plastic chairs.

As on every morning of the week, the seats are all filled, mostly with drowsy policemen. In the second row is Patrolman Stanley Cagney. Like all the others, he is there because he arrested a suspect within the previous 12 hours.

It is 9 A.M., and Patrolman Cagney has already brought his prisoner to the massive court building at 100 Centre Street and turned him over to the Correction Department. The prisoner is being fingerprinted, photographed and interviewed by probation officers. Ultimately, he will be put into a cell with 20 other men to wait for his arraignment.

Meanwhile, Patrolman Cagney is in the complaint room waiting to see an assistant district attorney to describe the arrest for him. The complaint room procedure is a preliminary step that accompanies practically every arrest in Manhattan. It is the prime intake valve for the system of criminal justice.

In the room, separated from the waiting area by a glass partition, are six cubicles, each with a typist. There are four young assistant district attorneys on duty, and they hop from one cubicle to another, listening to the accounts of policemen and civilian complainants. Then the prosecutors dictate formal charges to the typist who fills out court papers on each case.

One of the assistant district attorneys is William Purcell, who is two years out of law school. He joined Frank S. Hogan's office nine months ago after clerking for a Federal judge.

In the two hours before he got around to Patrolman Cagney, Mr. Purcell handled five other cases. They involved the theft of a $45 wristwatch; an alleged kidnapping and theft of $52; a robbery at gunpoint; a forged driver's license; and the illegal possession of a gun.

"We try to determine how strong a case we have," Mr. Purcell explained to a visitor. "In cases where there is a complainant, we try to determine whether he will cooperate and be available. In cases where there is physical evidence, like a gun or drugs, we have to determine whether these could withstand defense motions for suppression on illegal search and seizure."

After listening to the accounts of the policeman and complainant in each case, Mr. Purcell weighed the factors and then dictated notes and a summary of the crime, both to be routed to Arraignment Court. Such notes form the basis of moves made at the arraignment by another assistant district attorney, who usually does not have a chance to speak to the arresting officer.

In the wristwatch case, for example, where the suspect had an arrest record and was caught red-handed, Mr. Purcell indicated in his notes a willingness to forego felony charges and accept a plea of guilty to a lesser misdemeanor charge, with a maximum sentence of one year. The complainant, Mr. Purcell noted, lived out of town and there was little chance of getting him back to the city for hearings.

It took about 10 minutes to clear the paperwork on the wristwatch case before the typist summoned another policeman to the cubicle to tell his story.

In the case involving illegal possession of a gun, Mr. Purcell recommended dismissal of the charges. After the arresting officer left, the prosecutor [said] this was "a garbage charge" because the confiscation of the gun resulted from an obviously illegal search.

Then the typist again shouted "Next!" and it was Patrolman Cagney's turn. The red-haired officer, who works in northern Harlem, entered the cubicle with Ralph Carnillo, the complainant.

Patrolman Cagney outlined the case. At 10:50 the night before, he and his partner were cruising in a patrol car. As they turned the corner on 165th Street and Edgecombe Avenue, they saw Mr. Carnillo standing beside a car with two men who were holding knives to him. Mr. Carnillo, a gypsy cab driver, screamed, and the knife-wielders fled in opposite directions.

"Yellow Sheet" Checked   "I ran my guy down," said the patrolman, who bears a resemblance to his uncle, the actor James Cagney. "The other perpetrator escaped, although my partner re-covered a dropped knife. I was also able to recover a knife from the suspect's person."

The cab driver, who speaks no English, filled in the story with the aid of a bilingual friend. He said he had picked up the two men, taking them to the 165th Street address. They drew knives, took $50 and were about to take his car when the police arrived.

"Did the suspect say anything to you?" Mr. Purcell asked Patrolman Cagney. "He just said he had been a junkie for 20 years and had 20-bag $75 a day habit. But I'll tell you, he didn't look like a junkie, and I've arrested a lot of them. . . ."

The lack of an arrest record, Mr. Purcell said, made it an unusual case. The offense was serious, and with both the complainant and the policeman as witnesses, the prosecution, he added, had a strong case.

Two-Court System   Furthermore, he went on explaining his thoughts for a visitor, as an addict the man would make a very bad bail risk. After deliberating these variables, Mr. Purcell wrote up the case, recommended bail of $3,500 and observed, in writing, that notice should be served on the defense during arraignment that the prosecution intended to present the case to a grand jury.

Michael Kaufman, *New York Times*, December 3, 1972. © 1972 by The New York Times Company. Reprinted by permission.

Preliminary hearing

preliminary hearing
The *preliminary hearing*, or *preliminary examination* as it is called in some states, is held before a lower court judge (magistrate, justice of the peace, or so on). It represents the first time that a case is reviewed by someone other than a law enforcement official. The purpose of the preliminary hearing is to protect an innocent defendant from being held on a baseless charge: "to prevent hasty, malicious, improvident, and oppressive prosecutions, to protect the person charged from open and public accusations of crime, to avoid both for the defendant and the public the expense of a public trial, and to save the defendant from the humiliation and anxiety involved in public prosecution, and to discover whether or not there are substantial grounds upon which a prosecution may be based" (*Thies* v. *State*, 178 Wis. 98, 103, 189 N.W. 539, 541 [1922]).

prima facie case
During a preliminary hearing the state does not have to prove the guilt of the defendant. All that is necessary is that the government establish a *prima facie case*.

Prima facie is a Latin term meaning "at first sight" or "on the face of it." Thus the prosecutor must establish probable cause that a crime has been committed and the defendant committed the crime. Since the defense seldom introduces evidence during the hearing, it is not difficult for the state to establish probable cause.

In states that do not require a grand jury indictment for felony prosecutions, the preliminary hearing serves as the sole basis for determining if sufficient probable cause exists for prosecution. On the other hand, in states that employ grand juries, *bind over* — the preliminary hearing serves only to *bind over* (hold) a defendant for the grand jury action. As a result, a magistrate's ruling that probable cause does not exist does not necessarily end the case. The prosecutor can take the case to the grand jury.

The legal requirements concerning the conduct of the preliminary hearing vary from state to state. In some jurisdictions, the preliminary hearing is an adversary proceeding. The defendant, represented by counsel may challenge the prosecution's evidence and present his or her own witnesses. But in other states, the preliminary hearing need not be a formal proceeding.

hearsay evidence — *Hearsay* (secondhand) *evidence*, for example, is admissible. Similarly there is no requirement that the court appoint counsel to represent indigent defendants. Nor is there generally a right of cross-examination, although some states and some magistrates will permit attorneys to ask witnesses questions.

Waiving the preliminary hearing

For a variety of reasons, many defendants and/or their attorneys choose to waive the preliminary hearing. An American Bar Foundation study found that in 28 percent of the cases in Detroit and 34 percent in Wichita, Kansas, the preliminary hearing was waived (Miller). This pattern holds in other communities as well. A limited number of waivers are the result of an unrepresented defendant not realizing that a preliminary hearing may be useful. Normally, however, waiving of the preliminary hearing requires a positive step. Thus if the defendant is confused, the judge will typically conduct the preliminary hearing. Waivers of hearings may also be the product of defense counsel perceptions that the holding of a preliminary hearing might work to the defendant's disadvantage. For example, in a rape case, the defense attorney may prefer to reduce potential prejudicial pretrial publicity and at the same time hope that if the defense waits long enough, the victim's testimony will change. Such a waiver involves a tactical decision that the information to be gained from holding a preliminary is less than the potential damage to the defendant's case. At other times, though, waivers result from defense attorneys' adopting a cooperative stance toward judge and prosecutor by not forcing them to waste time. Many Detroit defense attorneys waive the preliminary hearing for this reason (Eisenstein and Jacob:221).

The preliminary hearing in practice

Although the legal purpose of the preliminary hearing is simple, the actual conduct of these hearings is quite complex. In some jurisdictions they resemble minitrials and last an hour or more. More typically, though, they last less than a minute. In some jurisdictions they are an important stage in the proceedings because cases are screened; in others they are a perfunctory step in which probable cause is found to exist in virtually every case. To complicate matters further, preliminary hearings are rare in some courts. Given this widespread variability, it is virtually impossible to make any blanket statement about the importance and significance of the preliminary hearing. Various studies, though, indicate four major patterns.

Preliminary Hearings Seldom Held.   In some jurisdictions preliminary hearings are almost never held. The prime example is the federal courts. The majority of federal criminal cases begin not with an arrest but with a grand jury indictment, which means that there is no need for a preliminary hearing. But even when there is a street arrest, it is common practice in federal courts to seek a grand jury indictment before the ten-day period required for conducting the preliminary hearing. As a consequence, probable cause hearings are held in a very small proportion of cases in the federal courts. Similar practices are found at the state level.

Short and Routine Preliminary Hearings.   Probably the most common practice is for preliminary hearings to be short and routine. In these jurisdictions, a typical case would involve a police detective testifying from a police report he probably had not written to the effect that a Mrs. Jones had reported a crime was committed. Then a minimal amount of information would be given as to why the police arrested Mr. Smith. The total time consumed is generally no more than a minute or two.

Such short and routine preliminary hearings seldom result in a finding that probable cause does not exist. My own study of Prairie City, Illinois, for example, documented that only 2 percent of the defendants had their cases terminated at the preliminary hearing (1974b:132–134). Often defense attorneys view such judicial proceedings as useless and are inclined to waive them. Thus in jurisdictions where preliminary hearings are short and routine, they are generally held only when a defendant is not yet represented by an attorney.

Preliminary Hearing as a Minitrial.   For decades Los Angeles has used the preliminary hearing in a unique fashion; it is actually a minitrial where the prosecution calls all of its principal witnesses, and the defense is allowed to call witnesses and cross-examine the state's witnesses. (Not insignificantly, Los Angeles was the setting for the books and television series on Perry Mason.) But despite the time-consuming process of conducting a full-fledged minitrial, the rate of no probable cause findings is small. Only about 10 percent of cases are dismissed or reduced to a misdemeanor at this stage (Greenwood et al.). This low rate results from extensive prosecutorial screening before the preliminary hearing. Although few cases are screened out of the system, the preliminary hearing in Los Angeles has a major impact on the court process, for a transcript of the proceedings is made. Many cases are disposed of not by a guilty plea or a trial but by the opposing parties submitting the transcript to a judge (termed *submission on the transcript*). After reading the transcript the judge typically finds the defendant guilty after a brief bench trial (Mather:195).

submission on the transcript

Preliminary Hearing as a Screening Device.   Although in most areas the preliminary hearing is largely ceremonial, resulting in few cases being screened out of the criminal process, in a few courts it is quite significant. In Chicago and Brooklyn, for example, the preliminary hearing is a major stage of the proceedings. Because the prosecutor has not previously reviewed the case, it is left to the judge to separate the strong cases from the weak ones. As a result, the preliminary hearing is a major stage in Chicago, where 80 percent of the cases are disposed of by dismissal or reduction to a less serious misdemeanor. Similarly, in Brooklyn 65 percent of felony cases receive a final disposition during the preliminary hearing (McIntyre and Lippman).

McIntyre explored what he called the "judicial dominance of charging process." His research provides a good insight into the Chicago process, as well as a useful overview of some of the major factors shaping the screening process. After a routine felony arrest, the Chicago police alone decide whether to file a complaint. They seldom drop a case. Thus the state's attorney neither reviews a case prior to filing nor has any contact with it until the preliminary hearing. Therefore it is the judge's responsibility to screen cases. As a result only 20 percent of the approximately sixteen thousand preliminary hearing cases yearly in Chicago are bound over to the grand jury. Of the remainder, a large number are dismissed either because there was insufficient evidence, the victim did not appear (thus indicating a reluctance to prosecute), or the court determined that key evidence (often illicit narcotics) was suppressed because of illegal search and seizure. In addition, a number of felony cases were reduced to misdemeanor charges either because the evidence was not sufficient to sustain a felony or because the judge believed the defendant was not a threat to society. In short, the screening and charging decisions that in most communities are made by the prosecutor or the police and prosecutor together are in Chicago dominated by the judiciary. This practice is a long-standing one dating at least to the 1920s and has survived numerous changes in court personnel and legal procedure.

McIntyre argues that the system is unique to Chicago because of important political reasons, mainly that the Chicago judges "are less susceptible to criticisms for showing leniency" than the police or prosecutor are. The preliminary hearing allows the police to build an impressive record of "crime clearance rates" unhampered by a lack of prosecution. At the same time, these procedures allow the prosecutor to point to a high conviction rate (after the preliminary hearing) without the necessity of making the type of decision that could be viewed as unduly lenient.

Grand juries

grand jury
indictment

A *grand jury* differs from a trial jury. Whereas the grand jury determines probable cause and returns an accusation (an *indictment*), the trial jury determines guilt or innocence. Similar institutions existed in ancient Greece, Rome, Scandinavia, and Normandy. It emerged in English law in 1176 during a political struggle among King Henry II, the church, and noblemen. At first criminal accusations originated with members of the grand jury themselves, but gradually this body came to consider accusations from outsiders as well. The jurors heard witnesses and, if con-

true bill
no true bill

vinced there were grounds for trial, returned an indictment. Grand juries also considered accusations brought before them by prosecutors, returning a *true bill* (an indictment) if they found the accusation true and a *no true bill* if they found it false. Historically, therefore, the grand jury has two functions: to serve as an investigatory body and to act as a buffer between the state and its citizens to prevent the government from using the criminal process against its enemies.

After the American Revolution, the grand jury was incorporated into the Fifth Amendment to the Constitution, which provides that "no person shall be held to answer for a capital, or otherwise infamous crime, unless on a presentment or indictment of a grand jury." The archaic phrase "otherwise infamous crime" has been interpreted to mean felonies. This provision, however, applies only to federal prosecutions. In *Hurtado* v. *California* [1884], the Supreme Court held that states had the option of using either an indictment or information. Slightly under half of the states require that prosecution for all felonies be initiated by indictment (see table 10-2). All states, however, provide for grand juries as investigative bodies.

Grand juries are typically composed of twenty-three members, although a handful of states allow as few as six (Indiana), twelve (Colorado), or sixteen (numerous other states). These members are normally selected by lot in a manner similar to the selection of trial jurors. However, in Arkansas, Colorado, Illinois, Nevada, Maine, Texas, and Virginia, judges or county boards are allowed to select grand jurors.

The grand jury in operation

Grand juries are empaneled (formally created) for a set period of time (typically three months). During this time they meet periodically to consider the cases brought to them by the prosecutor and to conduct other investigations. If a grand jury is conducting a major and complex investigation its time may be extended by the court.

The work of the grand jury is shaped by a number of legal dimensions that differ

TABLE 10-2.   Grand jury requirements

Requirement	State
Required in all felony cases (unless waived by the defendant)	Alabama, Alaska, Arkansas, Delaware, Georgia, Illinois, Iowa, Kentucky, Maine, Massachusetts, New Hampshire, New Jersey, New York, North Carolina, Ohio, South Carolina, Texas, Virginia, Washington, D.C., West Virginia, United States
Required only for offenses punishable by life imprisonment or death	Connecticut, Florida, Louisiana, Rhode Island, Vermont
Not required, but may be required for crimes involving offenses by public officials	Arizona, California, Colorado, Hawaii, Idaho, Indiana, Kansas, Maryland, Michigan, Minnesota, Mississippi, Missouri, Montana, Nebraska, Nevada, New Mexico, North Dakota, Oklahoma, Oregon, Pennsylvania, South Dakota, Tennessee, Utah, Washington, Wisconsin, Wyoming

Source: Conference of State Court Administrators and National Center for State Courts. *State Court Organization, 1980.* Washington, D.C., 1982.

greatly from the legal protections embodied elsewhere in the criminal court process. One of these is secrecy. Since the grand jury may find insufficient evidence to indict, it works in secret (the rest of the process is required to be public) to shield those merely under investigation. Another unique aspect is that indictments are returned by majority vote (unanimity is required in most trial juries). In most states twelve out of twenty-three votes are sufficient to hand up an indictment. By contrast, trial jurors can convict only if the jurors are unanimous or near unanimous in a very few states. Finally, witnesses before the grand jury have no right to representation by an attorney. Although defendants may have a lawyer at all vital stages of a criminal prosecution, none is allowed at this stage. Nor do suspects have the right to go before the grand jury to protest their innocence or even to present their version of the facts.

The work of the grand jury is shaped by its unique relationship with the prosecutor. In the vast majority of states, grand juries are considered part of the judicial branch of government. In theory at least, the prosecutor functions only as a legal adviser to the grand jury. But in practice, the prosecutor dominates. Grand jurors hear only the witnesses summoned by the prosecutor. And as laypeople, they are heavily influenced by the legal advice of the prosecutor.

The net result is that grand juries often function as rubber stamp for the prosecutor. A study of the Harris County (Houston), Texas, grand jury found that the average time spent per case was only five minutes, in 80 percent of the cases there was no discussion by members of the grand jury, rarely did members voice a dissent, and finally, the grand jury approved virtually all of the prosecutor's recommendations (Carp). In short, grand juries indict whom the prosecutor wants indicted.

Nor are no true bills necessarily an indication that grand juries fulfill a significant screening function. A prosecutor who believes a case is weak, subtly conveys this feeling. One assistant prosecutor I interviewed says that grand jurors "get the feeling when we're not pressing a case real hard" (Neubauer, 1974b:134). In turn, the secrecy of the grand jury proceedings may lead prosecutors to use it as a "safety valve." That is, if a case involves a prominent citizen and/or has received extensive publicity, the prosecutor may hesitate to dismiss the case even though a conviction appears unlikely.

Abolish or reform the grand jury

The theory that the grand jury serves as a watchdog of prosecutors has been transformed into an institution that serves as a rubber stamp for the official it is supposed to oversee. Earlier in this century judicial reformers strove to abolish the grand jury and succeeded in a number of states. More recently, the National Advisory Commission has also urged abolition. But such efforts require a major political effort—a constitutional amendment.

The grand jury as an instrument of political abuse?

Throughout this book we have discussed the evolutionary nature of law. As new events intrude, legal principles and legal institutions adapt to these changes. One of the most interesting evolutionary changes is in the role of the grand jury. Initially it was created to stand between government and the citizen as a protection against unfounded charges and unwarranted prosecutions. But in the words of Sam Pizzigati, director of the Coalition to End Grand Jury Abuse, "It has become an instrument of the very prosecutorial misconduct it was supposed to buffer the citizen against."

Critics contend that grand juries have been misused to serve partisan political ends by harassing and punishing those who criticize the government. Some of the most prominent cases involve prominent opponents of the Vietnam War. But concern over misuse of the grand jury extends beyond liberal groups to include prosecutors as well. Assistant Watergate Special Prosecutor Charles Ruff and former prosecutor Seymour Glanzer told a conference that "judges and attorneys should become increasingly concerned about the virtually unlimited power of grand juries and consider adopting rules to govern procedures used by the investigating bodies" (Robinson). Two of the major concerns about the powers of the grand jury center on immunity and contempt.

immunity

transactional immunity

use immunity

Immunity.   A common complaint about the abuse of the grand jury involves *immunity*. The Fifth Amendment protects a person against self-incrimination. Traditionally the government could compel a witness to testify and still protect a person's privilege against self-incrimination by providing *transactional immunity;* the witness was granted immunity against prosecution in return for testifying. But in 1970 the U.S. Congress adopted a new form, *use immunity:* a witness is promised protection against prosecution on the basis of evidence provided the grand jury. Thus witnesses could still be indicted on the basis of evidence gathered apart from their testimony. There was no way for a witness to refuse the government's offer of immunity. (If the government offers immunity, the witness must accept. Failure to testify results in a contempt charge and a jail term.) As a result critics contend that there is no way for witnesses to know that what they said will not be used by the government. Moreover, courts currently automatically approve prosecutor's request to grant immunity.

contempt power

Contempt Power.   Grand juries possess *contempt power* so that they can compel witnesses to provide testimony needed for a criminal investigation. Critics contend that some prosecutors call political dissidents to testify to find out information unrelated to criminal activity. The contempt power can also be used for punishment. A prosecutor may call a witness knowing that she or he will refuse to testify and then have the witness jailed. A witness who refuses to testify can be confined for an indefinite period of time until they "purge" themselves of contempt by providing the requested information. In this way a person can be imprisoned without a trial. This has happened mainly to newspaper reporters. In *Branzburg* v. *Hayes* (408 U.S. 665, 1972), the Supreme Court ruled that journalists must testify before a grand jury. As a result, some journalists have gone to jail rather than reveal their confidential sources because they believe that to do so would erode the freedom of the press, protected by the First Amendment.

Are the right people being prosecuted?

Do white-collar crimes go unprosecuted because they are committed by more "respectable" people? Does the criminal justice system prosecute defendants who would be best handled in a noncriminal manner? By raising questions like these, scholars have forced the criminal justice process to begin rethinking the entire screening process. Through research, studies have provided tentative answers to these questions—answers that suggest a qualified yes. As a consequence major programs have been instituted in the last few years to focus on white-collar crime and deferred prosecution (diversion).

White-collar crime

white-collar crime

Society feels most threatened by violent street crimes—murder, robbery, rape, and so on. But increasingly the public is aware that *white-collar crime* (embezzlement, consumer fraud, and corrupt public officials) also exacts a high toll. One estimate places the yearly dollar loss at $42 billion, considerably higher than the economic loss from burglary, auto theft, and other such street crimes. Since the Watergate scandal the public has been concerned that those with power or prestige escape criminal prosecutions. In addition, white-collar offenses victimize all classes of citizens, with the consequence that many citizens believe that their government is not providing sufficient protection.

economic crime

Actually, the term *white-collar crime* is misleading and limited, for it implies that only the relatively well-to-do are involved. A better term is *economic crime*, for it is not related to social class, and this term highlights the key element: the method used to commit the crime. Economic crimes involve deception, guile, and trickery and the purpose is economic gain (Finn and Hoffman:2). These crimes present the criminal courts with a vastly different problem from those involved in more ordinary crimes. One official who works in the area pinpoints the problem:

> Much of the difficulty in preparing such cases stems from the particular complexity of the offense involved. . . . The question at trial is not whether the defendant committed a certain act, such as is the case when prosecuting street crime. Rather, the state must prove that a certain constellation of facts constitute a crime in that the defendant *intended* to commit a fraudulent act. [Finn and Hoffman:4]

In addition, major consumer frauds involve systematic practices and therefore require systematic investigations. Yet police and prosecutors swamped by numerous street crimes often believe they cannot spare the resources to investigate a few crimes of a different variety.

In response to these problems and with the financial backing of LEAA, a number of prosecutors' offices have created specialized units to deal with major commercial and consumer frauds. Such specialization is viewed as necessary for both the attorneys and investigations (often an integral part of the unit) to develop the needed expertise. Politically, local prosecutors can reap important benefits from such specialized units. But we do not yet know the long-term political implications of these white-collar units; powerful local economic interests may oppose white-collar prosecutions. As federal money dries up and with local or state funds increasingly scarce, such units may be in jeopardy. This undermining process may be accelerated if prosecutors also begin to investigate substantial citizens of the community.

Diversion

diversion

Diversion is premised on the idea that there are more appropriate ways to deal with particular types of defendants than through criminal prosecution. It refers to a discretionary decision by a court official to suspend criminal prosecutions on the condition that the defendant does something in return. Diversion thus uses the threat of a criminal conviction to encourage a defendant to participate in a rehabilitation program or to make restitution to the victim. For example, a judge can offer a young defendant the option of proceeding with the case or joining the marines. Similarly, prosecutors have informally used diversion, calling it "deferred prosecution." One of the earliest such programs was operated by the U.S. attorney for the Eastern District of New York and is therefore commonly referred to as the Brooklyn Plan. What is distinctive about the current interest in diversion is the emphasis on institutionalizing formal programs. This thinking is summarized by the National Advisory Commission:

> In appropriate cases offenders should be diverted into noncriminal programs before formal trial or conviction.
> Such diversion is appropriate where there is a substantial likelihood that conviction could be obtained and the benefits to society from channeling an offender into an available noncriminal diversion program outweigh any harm done to society by abandoning criminal prosecution. Among the factors that should be considered favorable to diversion are: (1) the relative youth of the offender; (2) the willingness of the victim to have no conviction sought; (3) any likelihood that the offender suffers from a mental illness or psychological abnormality which was related to his crime and for which treatment is available; and (4) any likelihood that the crime was significantly related to any other condition or situation such as unemployment or family problems that would be subject to change by participation in a diversion program. [p. 32]

This standard advocates diversion as a legitimate and appropriate part of the criminal justice process for minimal-risk defendants.

In outline form a diversion program works as follows. As part of the charging process, the prosecutor decides whether a case has a sufficient legal merit for prosecution. If so, defendants who fit the criterion of minimal risk—are viewed as not likely to commit another offense and have been charged with a nonviolent

---

IN THE NEWS: PROSECUTOR PROPOSES OPTION TO PROSECUTION

Whitney North Seymour Jr., outgoing U.S. attorney for the Southern District of New York, told an American Bar Association committee yesterday that prosecutors need more options if suspects are to be treated as human beings than just deciding whether to prosecute.

"If I feel a particular man can be salvaged as a human being, what can I do?" he asked. "If I decide not to prosecute and let him go, it's sometimes like throwing fat in the fire. If I decide to prosecute, the prosecutorial process by itself can do tremendous damage."

Among the options he suggested are deferring prosecution, and extending to all under 25 years of age the so-called Brooklyn plan which gives special protection to juveniles.

Cathe Wolhowe, © *The Washington Post*, August 8, 1973. Reprinted by permission.

crime—are given the option of accepting diversion. The exact requirement of the diversion alternative depends on the needs of the defendant and the nature of the crime but often includes taking part in a drug treatment plan, participating in an alcoholic treatment project, accepting a rehabilitation program, performing voluntary public service, receiving mental health treatment, or making restitution to the victim. At the end of a set period (typically twelve months), the case is formally dismissed unless the offender has failed to participate as agreed; in that case, the offender could still be prosecuted.

Proponents of diversion cite a number of potential advantages. The major benefit is that it broadens the resources available to deal with offenders. Clearly diversion is viewed as a better way for providing defendants with the help they need for drug, alcohol, or psychological problems. Another benefit is that defendants who participate avoid being labeled with criminal conviction, which can stigmatize them and negatively affect their future employment opportunities. Diversion, like screening in general, also allows an adjustment for the fact that the law treats a number of minor violations as crimes. Finally, diversion is advocated as more economical because it reduces the costs and resources necessary for formal court proceedings. In short, diversion "offers the promise of the best of all worlds: cost savings, rehabilitation, and more humane treatment" (Vorenberg and Vorenberg:152).

But as compelling as the rationale for diversion may be, we need to scrutinize carefully how such programs work. Although initial reports have claimed major success, more recent independent evaluations have begun to raise some important questions about how such programs actually operate. One of the most important issues centers on the type of defendant selected for diversion. Generally they are defendants with the lowest risk—for example, white, suburban, middle-class youths accused of smoking marijuana or committing a theft. This practice of *creaming*—selecting those least in need of rehabilitation programs—means that diversion programs have been able to demonstrate impressive success rates because their clients were least in need of treatment in the first place. Thus it is unclear that diversion programs have actually resulted in major changes in the criminal justice process.

creaming

A second major question involves the selection criteria of diversion projects. Although in theory defendants are supposed to be chosen only after the prosecutor has decided a strong case exists, in practice there is the strong likelihood that prosecutors faced with a somewhat weak case may recommend diversion. In short, diversion may increase the number of court cases and not result in a reduction as proponents claim. Thus skeptics are concerned that these programs disguise coercion. Again theory says the defendant has the option of participating. But in fact, diversion may be "a new arena for plea bargaining which is fundamentally coercive. . . . In plea bargaining the defendant pleads guilty to a lesser charge, and of course his plea is duly recorded in all the appropriate places. But the person who agrees to deferred prosecution never formally pleads guilty and does not acquire a criminal record. There is an added incentive to submit. . . . The potential for abuse is therefore immense. Persons could be arrested on relatively weak grounds and then threatened with vigorous prosecution if they insist on their right to a trial" (Balch:47).

Conclusion

American courts reflect a very different philosophy than their European counterparts do. The American system looks to the trial as the ultimate forum for clearing a falsely accused defendant; it places few restrictions on the initiation of criminal charges and imposes relatively few procedures prior to trial. In Europe, on the other hand, an elaborate series of checks is built in before a criminal case can be initiated. In short, the philosophy of American courts is to clear the innocent at trial, while European courts seek to clear the innocent before formal court proceedings begin.

Despite these conflicting philosophical traditions, in operation American courts and European courts share an important similarity: many of the key decisions are made early in the process. In the United States, of those arrested for a serious crime, many are never prosecuted, and of those charged with a crime, many never see the inside of a trial courtroom before their case ends.

As we have seen, roughly half of all felony arrests are either rejected by the prosecutor or later dismissed. It is during the screening process, therefore, that the bulk of the decisions about innocence is made. The closer a case moves toward trial, the greater the likelihood of a guilty finding being entered.

The screening process must be analyzed not in isolation but by how it relates to the entire criminal justice process. As the last two chapters have demonstrated, there are major differences among communities in whether police arrests, prosecutorial charging, the preliminary hearing, or the grand jury is the key stage for screening decisions. Such varying arrangements reflect important differences in the dynamics of courthouse justice, differences that must be considered in any effort to alter the process.

Conversely one cannot properly evaluate the screening process without considering its impact on the entire court process. The types of defendants tried and sentenced are the product of earlier screening decisions. To choose but one example, how cases are plea bargained is directly dependent on whether cases are carefully screened, not screened at all, or screened so that defendants are deliberately overcharged.

Important substantive issues are involved. All too often the emphasis is solely on procedural and administrative considerations. To quote the district attorney of New Orleans, "We've been accepting too much junk" (*Times-Picayune*, May 5, 1973). He promised to institute a screening process modeled after the one proposed by the National Advisory Commission to eliminate weak cases and thereby reduce the large number of cases clogging the courts. But this emphasis should not be allowed to obscure the substantive issues involved. What cases should be prosecuted? As we have seen, cases are dismissed for a variety of reasons—weak evidence, informal guidelines on what offenses are serious enough to warrant prosecution, and individual standards of justice. In turn, diversion and white-collar programs are institutional responses to a question increasingly being raised: are court resources being directed toward the right targets? We cannot allow important substantive issues about the nature of criminal justice, and toward what ends, to remain hidden behind a barren emphasis on efficiency.

For discussion

1. If you were a prosecutor, what standards would you employ in deciding which cases to file? What types of cases do you think should not be prosecuted? Prosecuted more vigorously? Why?

2. Interview the prosecutor(s) in your community who handle the charging decision. What procedures and criteria do they use? How do they evaluate the quality and thoroughness of police investigations? Ask for specific examples. Also interview a trial prosecutor. Ask if they have too many minor cases.

3. Observe a preliminary hearing. How long does it take? What witnesses were called? Does the preliminary hearing function as a major stage in the criminal process?

4. Does your state use a grand jury? If so, for what cases? Since grand jury proceedings are secret, you cannot observe them in operation. You can, however, interview a prosecutor and ask what cases are sent to the grand jury and why, what procedures are followed, and whether grand juries ever refuse to indict and why.

5. Do you think the grand jury should be abolished? Do you think it currently fulfills its historical purpose of protecting citizens from governmental persecution?

6. If you were a prosecutor with only enough money in the budget to establish one program, would you chose a white-collar prosecution unit or a diversion program? Why? What does your choice reveal about your priorities?

7. Where does screening occur in your community?

References

Baker, Newman. "The Prosecutor—Initiation of Prosecution." *Journal of Criminal Law, Criminology and Police Science* 23 (January–February 1933):770–796.

Balch, Robert. "Deferred Prosecution: The Juvenilization of the Criminal Justice System." *Federal Probation* (June 1974).

Boland, Barbara, Elizabeth Brady, Herbert Tyson and John Bassler. *The Prosecution of Felony Arrests.* Washington, D.C. Institute for Law and Social Research, 1982.

Carp, Robert. "The Behavior of Grand Juries: Acquiescence or Justice?" *Social Science Quarterly* (March 1975):853–870.

Cole, George. "The Decision to Prosecute." *Law and Society Review* 4 (February 1970):313–343.

Eisenstein, James. "The Federal Prosecutor and His Environment." Paper presented at the annual meeting of the American Political Science Association, Washington, D.C., 1968.

———, and Herbert Jacob. *Felony Justice: An Organizational Analysis of Criminal Courts.* Boston: Little, Brown, 1977.

Finn, Peter, and Alan Hoffman. *Prosecution of Economic Crimes.* Washington, D.C.: LEAA, National Institute of Law Enforcement and Criminal Justice, 1976.

Goldman, Sheldon, and Thomas Jahnige. *The Federal Courts as a Political System.* New York: Harper & Row, 1971.

Greenwood, Peter, Sorrel Wildhorn, Eugene Poggio, Michael Strumwasser, and Peter De-Leon. *Prosecution of Adult Felony Defendants in Los Angeles County: A Policy Perspective.* Lexington, Mass.: D. C. Heath, 1976.

Jacoby, Joan. *The Prosecutor's Charging Decision: A Policy Perspective.* Washington, D.C.: Government Printing Office, 1977.

Mather, Lynn M. "Some Determinants of the Method of Case Disposition: Decision-Making by Public Defenders in Los Angeles," *Law and Society Review* 8 (1974):187.

McIntyre, Donald. "A Study of Judicial Dominance of the Charging Decision." *Journal of Criminal Law, Criminology and Police Science* 59 (1968):463–490.

———, ed. *Law Enforcement in the Metropolis.* Chicago: American Bar Foundation, 1967.

———, and David Lippman. "Prosecutors and Disposition of Felony Cases." *American Bar Association Journal* 56 (1970):1156.

Mellon, Leonard, Joan Jacoby, and Marion Brewer. "The Prosecutor Constrained by his Environment: A New Look at Discretionary Justice in the United States." *Journal of Criminal Law and Criminology* 72 (1981):52.

Miller, Frank. *Prosecution: The Decision to Charge a Suspect with a Crime.* Boston: Little Brown, 1969.

National Advisory Commission on Criminal Justice Standards and Goals. *Report on Courts.* Washington, D.C.: Government Printing Office, 1973.

Neubauer, David. "After the Arrest: The Charging Decision in Prairie City." *Law and Society Review* 8 (Spring 1974a):495-517.

———. *Criminal Justice in Middle America.* Morristown, N.J.: General Learning Press, 1974b.

Pizzigati, Sam. Personal interview, March 18, 1977.

"Prosecutorial Discretion in the Initiation of Criminal Complaints." *Southern California Law Review* 42 (1969):519–545.

Robinson, Timothy. "Two Prosecutors Eye Rules to Curb Grand Jury Power." *Washington Post*, June 3, 1975.

Rossman, David, and Jan Hoffman. *Intake Screening: A Proposal for Massachusetts District Attorneys.* Boston: Center for Criminal Justice, Boston University, 1975.

Skolnick, Jerome. *Justice Without Trial.* New York: John Wiley, 1966.

Times-Picayune, May 5, 1973.

Vorenberg, Elizabeth, and James Vorenberg. "Early Diversion from the Criminal Justice System: Practice in Search of a Theory." In Lloyd E. Oblin, ed., *Prisoners in America.* Englewood Cliffs, N.J.: Prentice-Hall, 1973.

For further reading

Clark, Leroy. *The Grand Jury: The Use and Abuse of Political Power.* New York: Quadrangle Books, 1972.

Finn, Peter, and Alan Hoffman. *Prosecution of Economic Crimes.* Law Enforcement Assistance Administration, National Institute of Law Enforcement and Criminal Justice. Washington, D.C.: 1976.

Frankel, Marvin, and Gary Naftalis. *The Grand Jury: An Institution on Trial.* New York: Hill & Wang, 1977.

Greenwood, Peter, Sorrel Wildhorn, Eugene Poggio, Michael Strumwasser, and Peter DeLeon. *Prosecution of Adult Felony Defendants in Los Angeles County: A Policy Perspective.* Lexington, Mass.: D. C. Heath, 1976.

Miller, Frank. *Prosecution: The Decision to Charge a Suspect with a Crime.* Boston: Little, Brown, 1969.

Mullen, Joan. *The Dilemma of Diversion: Resource Materials on Adult Pre-Trial Intervention Programs.* Law Enforcement Assistance Administration, National Institute of Law Enforcement and Criminal Justice. Washington, D.C.: Government Printing Office, 1974.

Neubauer, David. *Criminal Justice in Middle America.* Morristown, N.J.: General Learning Press, 1974.

Nimmer, Raymond. *Diversion: The Search for Alternative Forms of Prosecution.* Chicago: American Bar Foundation, 1974.

CHAPTER 11

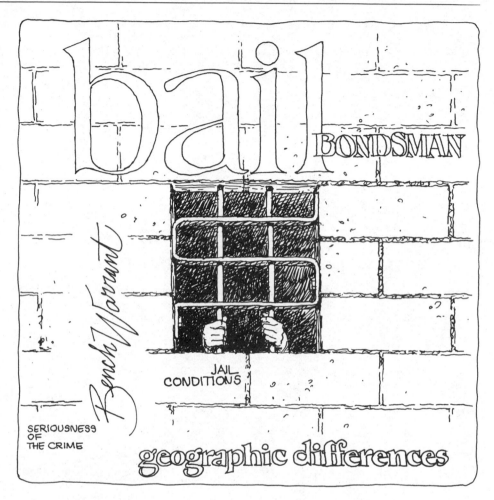

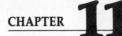

Freedom for Sale

Bail represents a defendant's first major encounter with the courts. For the price of the bondsman's fee the accused can purchase freedom and return to home, family, the streets, or whatever. Bail also represents the arresting officer's first major encounter with the courts, but for the police it means that the defendant may have the opportunity to commit more crimes while awaiting trial. These competing perspectives fuel the often-heated debate over how effectively America's system of monetary bail operates.

This chapter examines how America's system of pretrial release works, the factors that shape its operation, and the consequences of these decisions. Some of the key areas discussed include whether bail discriminates against the poor, whether it unfairly exposes the general public to risks of being victimized, whether the system works and defendants appear for trial, and what alternatives have been suggested.

The monetary bail system

bail   *Bail* is a guarantee. In return for being released from jail, the accused guarantee their future appearance for trial by posting a security with the court. When defendants appear in court as required, the security is returned. If they fail to appear, the security is forfeited.

The colonists brought the concept of bail with them across the Atlantic where it eventually became embedded in the Eighth Amendment, which provides that "excessive bail shall not be required." Although this wording is somewhat ambiguous, most believe that it creates a *right to bail*. Federal law and the constitutions in most states directly guarantee the right to bail for all crimes except capital offenses.

right to bail

> A bail system like the one in use in the United States today developed during the first thousand years A.D. in England. Judges traveled on circuits, and their visits to an area might be several years apart. Until the judges arrived, prisoners were held in the custody of the local sheriffs. Prison conditions, however, were atrocious. Prisons were also insecure, and inmates frequently escaped. Maintaining the prisons was a financial burden. Thus, the sheriffs were happy to have someone else assume the responsibility of maintaining custody of defendants. They frequently relinquished defendants into the custody of sureties, usually friends or relatives of the accused. [Originally, if the accused did not appear for trial, his sureties, who had promised his return, would themselves be tried. As time passed if] . . . the defendant failed to appear for his trial, the custodian was no longer seized bodily, but was required to pay over a sum of money. This liability of the surety for the appearance of the defendant, and the ability to discharge the liability by the payment of a sum of money remain the basis of our present system of bail.

> *Law and Order Reconsidered,* report of the Task Force on Law and Law Enforcement to the National Commission on the Causes and Prevention of Violence (Washington, D.C.: Government Printing Office, 1968), pp. 427–430.

Bail procedures

The law not only guarantees the right to bail but also requires that it be set within a "reasonable" time. How long an arrested person must remain in custody, however, varies according to the seriousness of the crime and the city involved. Those arrested for minor misdemeanors can be released fairly quickly by posting bail at the police station. In most communities the lower court judges have adopted a fixed bail schedule (also known as an *emergency bail schedule*), which specifies an exact amount for each offense. Table 11-1 provides some additional details on bail setting in a few of the nation's largest cities.

Bail procedures for felony or serious misdemeanor cases are considerably more complex. The arrestee must appear before the central court for the setting of bail. As a result, those accused of serious crimes must remain in police custody a number of hours (and sometimes over the weekend) before they have the opportunity to make bail. Some police departments attempt to circumvent judicial rules requiring a bail hearing "without unnecessary delay" in order to question suspects (Wice:21).

Forms of bail

Once bail has been set, there are four basic ways that a defendant can gain pretrial release. First, the accused may post the full amount of the bond in *cash* with the court. All of this money will be returned when all court appearances are satisfied.

cash bail

TABLE 11-1.   The initial bail-setting stage

City	Who sets the bail		Where it is done		How it is done	
	Misdemeanor	Felony	Misdemeanor	Felony	Misdemeanor	Felony
Washington	Desk sergeant	Judge	Stationhouse	Court of general session	Schedule	Discretion
San Francisco	Clerk of criminal court	Judge	Hall of justice	Hall of justice	Schedule	Discretion
Los Angeles	Police captain	Judge	Stationhouse	Regional	Schedule	Discretion
Oakland	Police captain	Judge	Stationhouse	Courthouse	Schedule	Discretion
Detroit	Desk sergeant or arresting magistrate	Arresting magistrate	Police station	Hall of justice	Schedule	Discretion
Chicago	Desk sergeant	Judge of bond court	Police station	Bond court or electronically	Schedule	Discretion
St. Louis	Desk sergeant	Judge	Police station	Police station or courthouse	Schedule	Flexible schedule
Baltimore	Desk sergeant	Judge	Police station	Police court	Schedule	Schedule
Indianapolis	Turnkey	Turnkey	City jail	City jail	Schedule	Schedule
Atlanta	Police	Police	Police headquarters	Police headquarters	Discretion schedule	Discretion schedule
Philadelphia	Desk sergeant	Magistrate and district attorney	Stationhouse	Police headquarters	Schedule	Schedule

Source: Reprinted by permission of the publisher, from *Freedom for Sale* by Paul B. Wice (Lexington, Mass.: D. C. Heath and Company, p. 26.

Note: Wice personally visited the eleven cities and, in addition, contacted a total of seventy-two by mailed questionnaires. This is the only study to date of bail practices and procedures in the United States.

property bond

personal recognizance

bail bondsman

Because it requires a large amount of cash, this form of bail is seldom used. The typical bail amount for a minor felony is $1,000, for example, and most persons—particularly felony defendants—cannot easily and quickly raise that amount of money. The second method for securing pretrial release is a *property bond.* Most states allow a defendant (or friends and relatives) to use a piece of property as collateral. If the defendant fails to appear in court, the property is forfeited. Property bonds are also rarely used because courts generally require that the equity in the property must be double the amount of the bond. Thus a $1,000 bond requires equity of at least $2,000. A third alternative for making bail is *personal recognizance.* Judges are allowed to release defendants from jail without monetary bail if they believe the person is not likely to flee. Personal bonds are used most often for defendants accused of minor crimes and for prominent members of the community.

Because most of those arrested lack ready cash, do not own property, or lack social clout to qualify, the first three options for making bail are only abstractions. The majority of those released prior to trial use the fourth method; they hire a *bail bondsman,* a middleman, to post bail. The bondsmen post the amount required and charge a fee for their services, typically 10 percent of the amount of the bond. Thus a bondsman normally would collect $100 for writing a $1,000 bond. None of that money is refundable.

America's system of monetary bail means that those who are rich enough or have rich friends can buy their freedom and await trial on the streets. But the poor await trial in jail. Thus what began in medieval England as a humane innovation has evolved into a regressive practice. At any given time, there are approximately 160,000 adults held in jail; nearly 67,000 of whom have not been convicted of any crime (U.S. Department of Justice, 1980:38). Moreover, a number of defendants who are released on bail spend several days in jail while friends or relatives try to obtain the necessary funds to meet the bondsman's fee.

Conflicting theories of bail

Administration of bail has been greatly influenced by a long-standing division over the purposes of bail. The basic question is whether society should release a defendant who is probably guilty before trial. Pretrial release, for example, is very limited in the Continental legal system. American law, however, deeply suspicious of the possibility of a misuse of official power, refuses to allow officials to detain anyone merely accused of a crime (except under very limited circumstances). And this is the source of the conflict.

To Ensure Appearance at Trial.   In theory the only purpose of bail is to ensure that the defendant appears in court for trial. Under this theory, a judge is supposed to fix bail in the amount calculated to guarantee the accused's availability for court hearing. This view of bail flows from the adversarial premise that a person is innocent until proven guilty and therefore should not suffer any hardships—such as a stay in jail—while awaiting trial.

To Protect Society.   The assumption that bail should be set solely to ensure the defendant's appearance, however, does not do away with the central problems raised by the Continental legal system: what to do with potentially dangerous defendants who might commit additional crimes while awaiting trial. Informally, therefore, some judges deliberately set bail so high that dangerous defendants or those likely to intimidate witnesses will be jailed while awaiting trial. A survey of seventy-two major U.S. cities indicates that the use of bail as a form of preventive detention is extensive; over half of those questioned stated that bail in their community was used as a form of pretrial detention (Wice:3).

> Punishment before trial, then, shares the same features as sentencing following conviction. Defendants lose their liberty, spend time in jail, and incur financial penalties. What distinguishes them, of course, is the finding of guilt through legal process that forges the link between crime and punishment. At the time bail conditions are imposed or reconsidered, this link is missing. As a matter of public policy and legal principle, therefore, if the presumption of innocence is to have substantive meaning, the scope and cost of pretrial sanctioning should be minimized for the maximum number of defendants.

> Source: Roy Flemming, *Punishment Before Trial: An Organizational Perspective on Felony Bail Process* (New York: Longman, 1982), p. 2. Reprinted by permission of Longman Inc., New York.

In practice, therefore, America's bail system represents a compromise between the legally recognized purpose of setting bail to ensure reappearance for trial and the belief that some defendants are too dangerous to be let out on the streets.

Throughout this chapter we will see how these competing views affect the daily realities of bail setting and how these unresolved conflicting purposes lead various officials to manipulate the process.

The context of bail setting

Deciding whom to release prior to trial and whom to detain pending trial poses critical problems for American courts. At the heart of the problem are the efforts to balance the conflicting theories of bail—the right to bail as guaranteed by the Constitution and the need to protect society. As Roy Flemming argues, one can imagine two improbable extremes. On the one hand, the courts could release all defendants prior to trial. On the other, they could hold every suspect. But neither of these extremes is possible. Freeing all those accused of murder, robbery, and rape is politically unfeasible, no matter what the chances are of the accused later appearing in court. Similarly, jailing all is not possible because prisons are simply not large enough. Nevertheless, court officials must make decisions every day that fashion a balance between these competing demands (Flemming:13).

Legal protections like the right to bail are meaningful only in the context of the policies that execute those protections. Only rarely do judges directly decide that a defendant should remain in jail pending trial. Rather this important decision is made indirectly—when the amount of bail is fixed. The higher the amount of bail the less likely the accused will be able to secure pretrial release. A study in New York City found that half of the defendants for whom a bail was set could not make that amount of money and therefore remained in jail pending trial (Zeisel:775). Figure 11-1 demonstrates that as the amount of bail increases, fewer defendants are able to secure pretrial release.

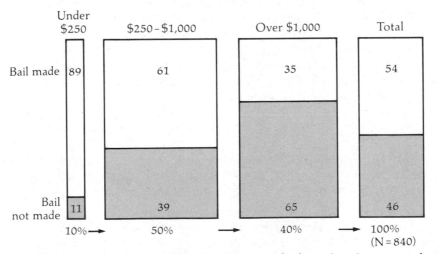

Figure 11-1.   Amount of bail related to pretrial release, based on a sample of felony arrests in New York City.

Source: Hans Zeisel, "Bail Revisited," *American Bar Foundation Research Journal* (1979):774.

Trial court judges have a great deal of discretion in fixing bail. Statutory law, for example, provides few specifics of how much money should be required. Appellate courts have spent even less time deciding what criteria should be used. While the Eighth Amendment protects against excessive bail, appellate courts will reduce a trial judge's bail amount only in the rare event that flagrant abuse can be proven. In practice, trial court judges have virtually unlimited legal discretion in determining the amount of bail.

The political and institutional factors that shape pretrial release policy in a court involve the context of bail setting, by determining the range of choices available to court officials. Uncertainty, risk, and jail resources are primary factors that influence bail setting.

Uncertainty

Uncertainty is a major problem facing court officials in making bail decisions. The defendant appears in court for bail setting within a few short hours after arrest. Because the time span is short, only a limited amount of information is available. In all likelihood the defendants are total strangers to the court officials. Moreover, the details of the alleged crime—the who, what, when, where, and especially why—are troublingly vague. Compounding the information void is the lack of adequate facts about the defendant's past criminal history. While in some courts police "rap sheets" (lists of prior arrests) are available, in others they are not. Moreover, rap sheets typically contain only information on prior arrests, and not on how the case was eventually disposed of (dismissal, plea, or prison, for example). Defendants may, of course, volunteer information on their background, prior experience with the court and so on, but understandably court officials may view this information as very unreliable.

Faced with limited information, some of which may prove to be either incomplete or inaccurate, court officials must make a number of decisions. Is this specific defendant likely to appear in court? Is he or she dangerous to the community? What kind of bail is most appropriate? In the context of the crime and the defendant what is considered "reasonable" or "nonexcessive" bail? The scarcity of knowledge means that defendants may be classified incorrectly as good or bad candidates for release and the wrong bail decisions made.

Risk

The uncertainty forced on court officials during bail setting is aggravated by the risks involved. Potentially any defendant released on bail may commit another crime. This is how one judge expressed this risk factor:

> If you let [the defendant] out on personal recognizance, with the understanding that he would reappear again for trial, and then the victim was badly injured, or killed, you have the problem of the newspapers coming [out] in a very critical vein. You have to have some security for the particular judge. [Suffet]

Police groups, newspapers, district attorneys and the general public may severely criticize a judge for granting pretrial release to defendants. In 1974, for example, a New York judge was nicknamed "Turn 'Em Loose Bruce" by the Patrolman's Benevolent Association. The judge was later reassigned to civil court after a series of public controversies about his setting low bail for defendants accused of violent crimes.

It is important to recognize that in bail setting judges and other court officials may make two types of mistakes. Type 1 errors involve releasing a defendant who later commits another crime or fails to appear in court. Type 2 involves detaining a suspect who should have been released. These two types of errors are inversely related; that is, the more type 2 errors, the fewer type 1. Type 2 errors, however, are hidden. They appear only if a major tragedy occurs—a suicide while in jail for example. Type 1 errors, on the other hand, form the stuff of which newspaper headlines are made. In short, judges face public criticism mainly for type 1 errors. Thus, in assessing the risk factors, court officials tend to err on the conservative side, preferring to make type 2, not type 1 errors.

Jail conditions

The context of bail setting involves not only uncertainty and risk, but also available resources. In this situation the jail is the principal limiting factor. In most big cities jails regularly hold more than their capacity. As a result, court officials are forced to make uncomfortable decisions: they may believe that the defendant should be held in jail awaiting trial, but realize that arrestees who have committed more serious offenses have already filled the jail. Several studies have found that as jails become overcrowded, or threaten to exceed their capacity, bail-setting practices become more lenient (Roth and Wice; Flemming).

The process of bail setting

The principal way that court officials respond to the context of bail setting (uncertainty, risk, and limited jail capacity) is through the application of bail tariffs. Bail tariffs are "rules of thumb," general guidelines concerning the proper bail amount. Judges do not ponder each case as a totally isolated event; rather based on past experience the bail tariff provides cues and guidelines for evaluating specific cases. It "involves a search by officials to establish whether or not they should follow custom" (Flemming: 29). In some communities bail tariffs can be found in written guidelines, in others they exist informally but have a major impact nonetheless.

Two factors are particularly important in shaping bail tariffs: the seriousness of the crime and the prior criminal record of the defendant.

Seriousness of the crime

seriousness of the crime

By far the most important consideration in setting bail is the *seriousness of the crime*. The amount of bail almost always is related to this criterion. For example, a study of bail practices in seventy-two cities reported that 86 percent of the judges believed that the seriousness of the charge was the most important pretrial release criterion in their city. The assumption underlying this belief is that the more serious the crime, the greater the urge to forfeit bail and therefore the greater the financial costs should be for such flight (Wice:28). It is a common practice for judges to use a bail schedule, which they determine themselves. For each offense a normal amount of bail is specified, with the judge or magistrate responsible for setting bail having the discretion to require more or less.

Prior criminal record

prior crimi-
nal record
A second criterion used in setting the amount of bond is the defendant's *prior criminal record.* Typically defendants with prior criminal records have bond set higher than normal for the offense charged. Eighty-five percent of the judges in one survey reported using the defendant's prior criminal record and found it important (Wice).

> After 18 months on the bench, a judge vividly recalled a time when he had been "jolted." At their arraignment before a different judge on rape charges, two defendants received cash bails of $50,000 and $70,000. The judge thought the amounts were excessive and, although he felt the charges were serious, agreed to a defense motion to reduce them. The reductions, he decided, would be symbolic so that while the bails were lower the defendants still would not be able to make them. He accordingly reduced the bails to $15,000 each. A short time later he discovered through the newspapers that one of the defendants posted bail and had been rearrested on a murder charge. "It was a real jolt," he said. "I'm sure that it affected me emotionally" and it probably influenced his later decisions, but "you try to keep it within certain bounds; you try to limit it."
>
> Source: Roy Flemming, *Punishment Before Trial: An Organizational Perspective on Felony Bail Process* (New York: Longman, 1982), p. 50. Reprinted by permission of Longman Inc., New York.

Situational justice

The usage of bail tariffs allows the courts to set bail rather rapidly for most defendants. After a consideration of the charge and the prior record, the judge typically announces the bail amount or may agree to grant a recognizance bond. This does not mean that all bail settings are automatic. Judges often seek to produce situational justice, in which they weigh the individual facets of the case and the defendant. Judges also employ hunches. In the face of so little knowledge, judges may construct honesty tests like the following.

> "Have you ever been arrested anywhere in the world since the day you were born to this day?" The defendant replied that he was arrested two or three years ago. "What for?" "I forget," the defendant answers.
> "Weren't you arrested this year. In April? Weren't you in the Wayne County Jail for a day or so? On the 26th?" The judge asks the questions without giving the defendant a chance to reply.
> After pausing a moment, the judge informed the defendant he had a "pretty bad memory" and added, "Have to have a bondsman for people with bad memories." He set surety bail at $1,000.
> The defendant then spoke up and told the judge that he hadn't thought it was very important to remember the charge in the earlier case. The judge smiles. "You didn't think it was very important? Well, bond isn't either." [Flemming:57]

Bail setting and the courtroom work group

In the majority of cases, bail setting involves a unilateral decision-making process—the judge reviews the case and sets a bond amount (Flemming). There are two important ways, however, for members of the courtroom work group to influence this decision. One is direct: the actors seek to provide information, and therefore, influence the decision.

The police can influence a judge's bail decision in their selection of charges. They can deliberately overcharge—for example, arrest for a felony rather than a more appropriate misdemeanor—in order to increase the amount of bail or to punish defendants (Wice:6). In Des Moines, Iowa, for example, the police arrested men for drunk driving even when they knew they lacked evidence to obtain a conviction: "The boys figured the defendant would at least be rapped for the bond [defendants pay a bail bondsman $25 to write a $300 bond . . .] and also spend a night in jail" is how one police captain justified such practice (James:114). Such police practices can often be traced to the view that bail allows defendants to "beat the system." Frustrated and angered by what they see as undue leniency, the police seek to manipulate the court process for their own ends (Wice:6).

Next to the judge, the prosecutor is the most important actor in setting bail. The prosecutor is often present during the initial appearance when bail is set, and through time the judges come to know and respect the prosecutor's assessments. An excellent study of bail setting in the New York criminal court explores the interaction among judges, prosecutor, and defense attorney (Suffet). The author observed 1,473 bail settings. In 49 percent the judge made the decision without discussing the matter with the attorneys. Thirty-eight percent of the time the judge set bail in the amount suggested by either the prosecutor or defense. One point of interest, therefore, is that in a large proportion of cases, the judge, prosecutor, and defense attorney apparently agreed on how much bond should be required. Such lack of disagreement is the result of widely accepted standards.

Of equal interest are the cases in which there was disagreement. When the participants disagreed, the prosecutor was more influential than the defense attorney. One reason is that prosecutors have more prestige; they are more likely to make the initial suggestion. Moreover when prosecutors thought the judge's initial bail suggestion was too low, they were successful 80 percent of the time in getting the amount increased. When the situation was reversed, however, the defense attorney was less successful. The author concluded that the prosecutor's ability to influence bail setting derived from the fact that the judge and prosecutor held similar views about the proper amount of bail, and these views were reciprocally supportive (Suffet).

Besides these direct attempts of members of the courtroom work group to influence bail setting, important indirect factors are at work as well. Note that in Suffet's study agreement was relatively high about proper amounts of bail. This shared point of view has an important consequence: it diffuses responsibility. In releasing defendants on bail, there is no way to avoid making mistakes. If a number of people thought release for a particular defendant was acceptable, it is much more difficult later to single out the judge for blame if a crime is committed.

Geographic differences

geographic
differences

Pretrial release policies and practices vary widely in America's criminal courts. Table 11-2 illustrates these important variations for two cities: Detroit and Baltimore. In use of release on recognizance (ROR), for example, Detroit grants ROR for almost half the cases compared with only 12 percent in Baltimore. Other studies have documented similar disparities in other cities as well (Thomas). Likewise, the amount of cash bail required varies between courts. The typical cash bail in Baltimore is more than double the amount required in the Motor City. An earlier study found the same disparities (Silverstein:621). Finally, and most importantly, the actual rate of pretrial release of felony defendants exhibits marked differences. To cite the sharpest contrast, Thomas reports that in Kansas City 63 percent of the defendants await trial in jail compared with only 13 percent in Minneapolis (41).

The National Jail Census (U.S. Department of Justice, 1980: 37) found that half of the jailed inmates were in just six states: California, New York, Texas, Florida, Pennsylvania, and Georgia. Since these states include only one-fourth of the nation's population and some of the most populous states (with high crime rates, such as Illinois, Ohio, and Michigan) are not included while some smaller ones are, the only conclusion is that defendants' chances of pretrial release are heavily dependent on the community where they are arrested.

These differences in the scope and cost of pretrial punishment are not the result of differences in crime severity. When studies include controls for the seriousness of the crime, they have found that variations in ROR use, cash bail amounts, and overall pretrial release rates persist. Rather these variations reflect important differences in the political dynamics surrounding pretrial release policies and procedures. Thus the influence of the courtroom work group varies. In one court the prosecutor may play a dominant role, usually urging high bail amounts. In yet another the prosecutor may play no role at all; the judge sets bail quite independently.

The Flemming study uncovers another important dimension of these political dynamics. His analysis explains the markedly different bail policies found in table 11-2. Both cities faced a jail crisis—overcrowding, riots, unsanitary conditions, and so forth. In Detroit, however, the federal court imposed a maximum capacity on the jail population. This court order forced the judges of Detroit Recorder's Court

TABLE 11-2. Bail setting policies for felony defendants in Detroit and Baltimore

Bail decision	Percent of defendants	
	Detroit	Baltimore
Recognizance release	48.8	11.8
Cash Bails	48.2	75.3
Remands (no bail allowed)	3.0	12.9
Total	100.0	100.0
Median Cash Bail	$2,000	$4,650
Number	1536	1676

Source: Roy Flemming. *Punishment Before Trial.* (New York: Longman, 1982), p. 9. Reprinted by permission of Longman Inc., New York.

IN THE NEWS: A TALE OF TWO CITIES: TWO BRANDS OF JUSTICE

This is a tale of two cities . . . two brands of justice . . . in the same state.

Jacksonville Leon Louis Bell, 42, black, jobless and broke because of a longshoremen's strike, got drunk, got in a fight, pulled his gun and shot a man in the shoulder. He was charged with assault with intent to kill, use of a firearm in a felony, and drunkenness. He went to jail.

At 2 P.M. the next day, in what is now a routine procedure here, Bell went before Criminal Court Judge Everett Richardson. The judge scanned a brief background report prepared by the Florida Parole Commission and released Bell without bail to report for trial a month later.

"If you are black on the streets of Jacksonville and you are 42 and you don't have a record, you have come up clean," Richardson explained.

Bell showed up for trial, as he had promised, pleaded guilty of aggravated assault and was given probation. He had not spent the month learning crime in the county jail.

Tallahassee Mary, 27, a divorcee with a 6-year-old child, mistook the identity of a plainclothes deputy who had walked in her home seeking a friend on bad-check charges. She ordered him out and before the shouting was over was charged with resisting arrest with violence, a felony, and interfering with the law.

She says the deputies hauled her off to jail without making any provisions for her boy, whom her mother-in-law found wandering on the street three hours later.

It was a Friday night. Not until Tuesday did Mary—not her real name—manage to scrape up the $100 that it would take to hire a bondsman to guarantee her $1,000 bail. She was not told until Saturday afternoon what her bail would be.

"They throw you in there, and they just forget about you," she said of the law. "You're just dirt, and that's it."

Sometime later, she told a Tallahassee radio talk show what she thought of local justice.

And not long after, she says her bondsman threw her back in jail—keeping what she paid him—with the curt explanation, "You're going to learn to keep your mouth shut, or I'll see you sit in jail."

Mary, a long-time resident who works for a state agency and had no criminal record, had to pay another bondsman another $50 to go free pending her sentence on a guilty plea to a reduced charge of resisting arrest without violence.

Leon County—like most Florida jurisdictions—depends almost exclusively on bail bondsmen to decide who goes free pending trial and who does not.

Mary should have lived in Jacksonville.

St. Petersburg Times, January 31, 1972.

to alter their bail policies and practices. In Baltimore, on the other hand, the federal court ordered some improvements in the local jail but did not impose a cap on jail population. The state courts, therefore, were not under the same pressure as their counterparts in Detroit to make changes.

The disparities between the two cities, though, run deeper than a federal court order. In Detroit, pro-defendant groups are politically active. Their activities forced the judges to respond. By contrast in Baltimore the dominant political culture is conservative. Pro-defendant groups in particular and black political activity in general are not very influential. Moreover, in Baltimore bail is determined not by judges but by commissioners. These low-status court officials are more vulnerable to negative sanctions. Thus within the context of bail setting—uncertainty, risk, and limited jail resources—the political environment of Detroit supported bail reform, while the dynamics of Baltimore supported more punitive policies.

Bail bondsmen

Clustered around urban courthouses are the bright neon lights of the bail bondsmen. Boldly proclaiming: "Bail Bonds, 24 Hour Service," they are a constant reminder that freedom is available—for a price. Bail bondsmen are as important to

America's monetary bail system as they are controversial. Reformers believe that the bondsman is a cardinal flaw in the system, a parasite who preys on human misery. For over a decade, reformers have been bringing to light the sometimes flagrant abuses of the bondsmen, contending that they are a constant source of corruption and collusion in the criminal courts. For these reasons abolition of the bail bondsmen is a key objective of many reformers. In a handful of states the bondsmen have, in effect, been driven out of business by bail reform.

What little is known about bail bondsmen has been strongly biased by the reform-oriented literature. Grand jury investigations, legislative studies, journalistic exposés, and, perhaps most importantly, the reports of two national commissions have portrayed bondsmen as fixers of cases and corruptors of the system. In short, bail bondsmen have been viewed as essential links in the chain of official corruption. Forrest Dill, however, spent several months studying bail bondsmen in two California cities. He concluded that past studies leave the simplistic and incorrect impression that the bondsman is an isolated sore. Commenting on the linkage of bondsmen to official corruption, Dill argues that "such findings contain an element of truth, of course, but it is hardly surprising that bail bondsmen in corrupt jurisdictions participate in corrupting practices" (643). He persuasively argues that to understand the role of bondsmen in the criminal justice system, one must examine two aspects of their existence: the business setting and the court setting.

The business setting

Bondsmen are small businessmen. But the business they are in is a unique one. By allowing commercial middlemen to post bond, the state has created a business operation within the criminal courts. The bondsman is a private government subcontractor. In essence, the key decisions on pretrial release have been transferred from public officials to a private party who represents neither the interests of the courts nor the interests of the defendant.

Bail bondsmen make money by providing a specialized form of insurance. For a nonrefundable fee, they post a surety bond with the court. If the defendant does not appear for trial, the bondsman is responsible for the full amount of the bond. For assuming this risk, the bondsman is permitted to charge a fee, usually 10 percent.

Bail bondsmen almost never directly post a cash surety with the court. Rather they purchase a surety bond from a major insurance company, which charges 30 percent of the bondsman's fee. Thus if the total amount of the bail is $1,000, the bondsman receives $100 from the client and keeps $70 of it. The profit margin in each case is seldom large, so bondsmen need to find enough clients willing to purchase their services while simultaneously accepting only those who present a minimal risk of fleeing.

Securing Clients.   Competition among local bondsmen to gain "good" clients is stiff. Since the only legitimate business techniques bondsmen may use are quite limited and engaged in by all—advertising and a reputation for prompt, courteous, twenty-four-hour service—bondsmen must rely on other techniques—sometimes legal, sometimes not—to ensure a steady supply of clients.

There are four major sources of clients. In descending order of importance, first are family and friends. After the defendant is taken into custody and is allowed to make one or two telephone calls, the family or friend often seeks out a bondsman. A second way the clients come to the bondsman is more direct. Defendants with prior court experience know how to contact bondsmen who have provided good service in the past. Defense attorneys are a third source of referrals. Lawyers may legitimately refer a client to a bondsman, but at times bondsmen and lawyers exchange favors. For example, bondsmen can help lawyers by providing knowledge about the defendant's financial situation, by referring clients to a specific lawyer (which is illegal), or by giving kickbacks (which are also illegal). In turn, defense attorneys may reciprocate with information, or fees for referrals (also illegal). Police officers, court clerks, or bailiffs are the fourth source of clients. Again it may be a subtle suggestion—"I hear Al's Bail Bonding Service is good"—or it may be more direct—pointing to a particular bondsman's number in the phone book and pushing a dime in the defendant's hands. Sometimes such referrals stem from an attempt to be helpful, but more often there is an expectation that the person making the referral will be compensated in some way.

Reducing Risks.   Once bondsmen have made contact with a particular defendant, they must decide if they are willing to take the person as a client. In general, bondsmen consider the following types of defendants bad risks: first offenders (because they are likely to panic); recidivists whose new crime is more serious than previous ones; and violent defendants (they may harm the bondsman). In assessing which defendants are financially reliable, bondsmen use the very criteria ignored by the court: employment history, family situation, and roots in the community. If a defendant is marginal, bondsmen may require the posting of collateral in addition to the fee. Bail bondsmen may also revoke the bond of any client they fear might be contemplating flight (but are under no obligation to rebate the fee).

Contrary to popular belief, bondsmen do not accept just anyone as a client. They prefer to write bonds when the bail is low because their risks are also low. Thus many bondsmen make a living by posting collateral for the numerous defendants accused of minor crimes and an occasional large bond when repayment is assured.

Bond Jumping.   After a bondsman has decided to accept a defendant as a client, a key factor determining whether there will be a *bond forfeiture* is the degree of supervision the bondsman exercises over the client. Although some bondsmen work long and hard to maintain contact with their clients, most are quite lax (Wice:58). Once a defendant skips, however, bondsmen attempt to find the person.

bond forfeiture

Bail bondsmen have extraordinary legal powers over bailed defendants who *jump bond* and flee. When the bondsman makes bail, the clients are required to sign a contract waiving the right to extradition and allowing the bondsman to retrieve them from wherever they have fled. These powers exceed any possessed by law enforcement officials. The bondsmen need not even secure a warrant. Some law enforcement officials contend that the bondsman renders an important service to the state by retrieving bond jumpers (National Conference on Bail and Criminal Justice:237). However, chasing bond jumpers is often too expensive since the

bond jumping

bondsman must hire a "trace skipper" to locate the person and then pay for the travel expenses. As a result, bondsmen often find it unprofitable to chase defendants. Abuses of these bond-jumping powers—including murder and kidnapping—have long been noted.

Bail bondsmen and the courtroom work group

Experienced bail bondsmen are on a first-name basis with court personnel—bailiffs, clerks, prosecutors, and so on—who represent a vital part of their business. Bondsmen are often financial contributors to judges' reelection campaigns. Each of these officials can help (or hinder). As one bondsman noted: "The court clerk is probably one of the most important people I have to deal with. He moves cases, he can get information to the judge, and he has control over various calendar matters. When he's not willing to help you out, he can make life very difficult. He knows he's important, and he acts like it" (Dill:658). The relationships between bail bondsmen and the courts are reciprocal.

Bondsmen Aid the Courts.   One way that bondsmen help the courts is by managing the population of arrested persons. This insight is as obvious as it is basic. Without an organization like the bail bondsmen, the courts would be faced with an intolerably large jail population or would be forced to make major alterations in their own procedures. For decades the bail bondsmen have been the course of least resistance. At the same time, bondsmen may also cooperate in preventing some defendants from being released. When court officials desire that a particular defendant not be released, the bondsmen often cooperate by failing to post surety.

Bondsmen also help the courts by directing defendants through the bureaucratic maze of the court system. Defendants come to the court with varying backgrounds and differing expectations and thus have the potential for disrupting the smooth operations of the court system. Bondsmen know the local routines and help educate their clients to accept these routines. They urge unrepresented clients to hire a lawyer if the case is a major one. They may ease the defendant's anxiety. And in some cases, they encourage defendants to plead guilty:

> Shortly after lunch on another afternoon, a young man who had been charged with littering and possessing open containers of beer in his car stopped by to see Al [a bondsman] about his case. He was apprehensive about the outcome because the girl who had been arrested with him had already "copped out as charged." He asked: "What will happen if I change my earlier plea to guilty?"
>
> Al answered: "It won't make any difference. They got the girl and all they want are guilty pleas. The judge will fine you $25, and that will be the end of it."
>
> Al was correct. Later that afternoon the client returned and jubilantly told Al, "It's all over. I got out for $29." [Dill:655–656]

Like defense attorneys and probation officers, therefore, bail bondsmen are "agent mediators." They help defendants adapt to and accept their newly acquired role of defendant.

*failure to
appear*

The Court Aids the Bondsmen.   The major financial risk facing bondsmen is that clients will jump bond and *fail to appear* in court, and the entire amount of the bond will have to be made good. Yet in many cities, forfeited bonds regularly go uncollected. During one year, 318 bonds were forfeited in St. Louis, but 304 were set aside by the court (Wice:61). To encourage bondsmen to seek out and find those who have fled, states allow a grace period before bonds can be forfeited (ranging from a short 14 days in Detroit to a rather lengthy 180 days in California). But the key reason that many bonds go uncollected is the discretionary power of judges to exonerate bondsmen from outstanding bonds. In many cities, bondsmen will not have to pay a bond forfeiture if they can convince the judge that they made every effort to find the missing client (Wice). But these considerations cannot explain all of the uncollected bonds. One newspaper estimated that $2 million in bond forfeitures went uncollected in Dallas. In New Orleans the figure was almost a million dollars. Such large amounts of uncollected bond forfeitures often stem from judges deliberately not trying to collect. Given the reciprocal relationships between the bondsmen and the court, and the help the bondsmen offer the courts, the major way the courts can help the bondsmen is by not trying to collect bond forfeitures.

Effects of bail

Pretrial detention affects not only those detained but also has an important impact on the criminal court process as well. Despite the fact that detained defendants are presumed innocent until proven guilty, they suffer the same disadvantages as those incarcerated after conviction. Economically they may lose jobs. Socially they are stigmatized by the jail label. Psychologically they are subjected to stress, anxiety, and isolation. Physically they are held in a violence-prone atmosphere. The President's Commission on Law Enforcement and Criminal Justice chose the following examples to dramatize the human toll that pretrial detention may exact.

> —A man was jailed on a serious charge brought last Christmas Eve. He could not afford bail and spent 101 days in jail until a hearing. Then the complainant admitted the charge was false.
> —A man could not raise $300 bail. He spent 54 days in jail waiting trial for a traffic offense, for which he could have been sentenced to no more than five days.
> —A man spent two months in jail before being acquitted. In that period he lost his job, and his car, and his family was split up. He did not find another job for four months. [p.30]

But the effects of pretrial detention are not limited to those detained. The decision on bail—made within the first hours of contact with the court—reverberates through all subsequent stages of the court proceedings. In a variety of ways detained defendants are at a disadvantage during pretrial, plea bargaining, trial, and sentencing.

Jail conditions

Jail conditions are often poor. Many big city jails and some county ones are chronically overcrowded. Many regularly hold twice their intended capacity; four inmates may be housed in a six-by-nine-foot cell, confined to their cells, or in a narrow adjoining corridor (Goldfarb:7). Idleness is the norm. Rehabilitative services are notably lacking. Prisoners are let out of their cells only for meals or an occasional but short period of recreation. Food may be of low quality and nutritionally poor. Medical care may be lacking. Physically jails are often ugly, ancient, almost medieval structures. Jail is a brutal environment. The threat of attack—including homosexual rape—is always present. And because jails are so overcrowded, it is often impossible to separate young defendants from old, novices from career criminals, the especially vulnerable from the likely aggressors.

> Viewed from the perspective of maintaining the plea-bargaining system, pretrial detention and demoralizing conditions in jails are highly functional. They discourage the defendant from bargaining too hard; they place a high price upon filing motions or demanding a trial; they encourage him to rat out his friends in order to end his own ordeal. This is not to argue that those in authority consciously plan rotten jails; clearly most are concerned about jail conditions. But it is to suggest that such conditions are functional, do serve the needs of the production ethic that dominates our criminal justice system.

> Jonathan Casper, *American Criminal Justice: The Defendant's Perspective,* © 1972, p. 67. Reprinted by permission of Prentice-Hall, Inc., Englewood Cliffs, New Jersey.

It is into this undesirable atmosphere that all who cannot pay the bondsman's fee are thrust. One author has likened the American jail to the twentieth-century poorhouse (Goldfarb). The inmates are disproportionately poor and disproportionately members of minority groups. Perhaps because jails hold society's outcasts, relatively little is known about them. Until the National Jail Census, there were no statistics on how many jails there were in the country; the census found 4,037 adult jails holding 153,063 adults, over half of whom were awaiting trial. By all accounts the conditions in jails (which hold those awaiting trial) are significantly worse than in prison. Indeed because pretrial detainees have not been convicted, they have fewer rights and privileges than those in the same jail who have been convicted. They are not eligible to participate in rehabilitation programs, for example.

Jails are also expensive. Estimates are that it costs at least thirty dollars per day to house one inmate in an average city. Bail reformers argue that pretrial release programs can greatly reduce this economic burden on the taxpayers.

Legal consequences

Pretrial detention has a large impact on the legal processing of defendants. Detained defendants exist in a state of limbo. While sitting and waiting, their primary concern is what is going to happen with their case. But jail isolates them from any control over their fate. At times it is difficult for them to communicate with their attorneys. Months may pass between contacts with their lawyer. And because they are detained, defendants cannot help their lawyer in preparing a defense. Most defense attorneys, for example, lack the resources of an investigator to search out witnesses favorable to the defendant.

Pretrial detention places great pressure on defendants. They are anxious and uncertain over their case, and this anxiety and uncertainty significantly affect tactical decisions. In some instances, delay may be to the defendant's advantage. Even so, waiting is much easier spent out of jail. Moreover, the time spent awaiting trial may be "dead time," time not counted in the final sentence. Thus pressures build on defendants to get the process over with. Some prefer to plead guilty and be done with it. At least after sentencing, defendants know how much time they will have to serve, when they will be eligible for parole, and that the time served will be in the state prison.

A predominant concern of bail research centers on the discriminatory impact of bail practices. Simply put, do defendants in jail have higher rates of conviction and prison sentence? Table 11-3 presents data from the Manhattan bail project, the first systematic investigation of the effects of bail on the criminal court process. Conducted by the Vera Institute of Justice in 1963, the data clearly show that detained defendants are more likely to be convicted. Almost three out of five persons charged with assault and detained before trial were convicted; but only one of five (23 percent) of those charged with the same offense but not detained were convicted. Another study of preventive detention found that defendants' chances of being convicted increased by at least 20 percent when they were detained before trial (Ervin:29–30).

The effects of pretrial detention continue after conviction and sentencing. Detained defendants have a greater likelihood of being sentenced to prison and for longer terms than those who posted bond. Often pretrial detention has stripped defendants of attributes that might contribute to a lighter sentence. If they had a job, they have lost it, and their family lives have been disrupted, therefore making them poorer probation risks. Those who have been detained present a very different physical appearance in court. Dressed in jail garb, with a pallid complexion caused by confinement, detained defendants are less able to project a favorable image. Finally, the special status of detained defendants is underscored by the fact

TABLE 11-3. Case dispositions, by jail status and charge

Charge	At liberty before trial		Detained before trial	
	Percent convicted	Total cases	Percent convicted	Total cases
Assault	23	126	59	128
Grand larceny	43	96	72	156
Robbery	51	35	58	100
Dangerous weapons	43	23	57	21
Narcotics	52	33	38	42
Sex crimes	10	49	14	28
Others	30	47	78	23

Source: Ares, Rankin, and Sturz, "The Manhattan Bail Project: An Interim Report on the Use of Pre-Trial Parole," 38 *N.Y.U.L. Rev.* 67, 84 (1963).

that they are brought to court in handcuffs by sheriff deputies who maintain a watchful vigilance, another cue that society has already labeled these people as dangerous.

These findings, that jailed defendants are more likely to be convicted and also more likely to be sentenced to prison, have been disputed by more recent research. After analyzing over 8,000 criminal cases from 1975 in Philadelphia, John Goldkamp found that jailed defendants did not differ from their bailed counterparts in terms of findings of guilt. At all the significant stages—dismissal, diversion, and trial—jailed defendants were as likely as bailed ones to receive a favorable disposition. When it came to sentencing, however, jailed defendants were more likely to be sentenced to prison, but interestingly the length of the sentence was not related to bail status (Goldkamp). Similarly, the three-city study of Chicago, Baltimore, and Detroit revealed that there was no uniform impact of bail status on either findings of guilt or sentencing (although in some cities in some situations there was an impact) (Eisenstein and Jacob). The emerging literature in the field is not easily summarized. Perhaps the best response is provided by Goldkamp. Does bail status negatively affect the defendant's case? His verdict is "it depends."

Failure to appear

bench
warrant

Not all defendants on pretrial release appear in court when required. Skipping bail entails several consequences. First, bail is forfeited. Second, a warrant is issued for the suspect's arrest. This warrant is termed a *bench warrant* or a *capias* and commands the sheriff or police to take a person into custody. The person must be delivered to the judge issuing the warrant and cannot make bail. Finally, failure to appear often subjects the defendant to a separate criminal charge of bond jumping.

Nationally the nonappearance rate varies from 3 to 7 percent (table 11-4). But as with so many other areas of the criminal court system, reliable figures are extremely hard to come by. Typically a failure to appear involves several separate court agencies—judges, clerks, police, and prosecutor—whose activities are not well co-

TABLE 11-4. Forfeiture rates

	Rate	Source of statistics and clarification
Chicago	8.7%	Clerk of circuit court of Cook County (1969)
Philadelphia	4.0%	Estimate by court administrator (1970)
Indianapolis	5.4%	Survey by Indianapolis Bail Project (1969) surety bonds
Detroit	24.0%	Recorders court annual report (1969): 8% for surety bonds, 40% for personal bonds
Baltimore	5.0%	Estimate by public officials and bondsmen
Atlanta	7.0%	Exact figure from district attorney's office
St. Louis	5.0%	Exact figure from clerk of circuit court, criminal division
Washington	3.7%	Exact figure from the report of the D.C. judicial court, Report on the Operation of Bail (1969)

Source: Reprinted by permission of the publisher, from *Freedom for Sale* by Paul B. Wice (Lexington Mass.: Lexington Books, D. C. Heath and Company, Copyright 1974, D. C. Heath and Company), p. 67.

ordinated. In addition, many courts do not keep such records, or if they do, usually in a careless and unreliable manner. Moreover data on failure to appear can easily be manipulated either to show the success of pretrial release or to discredit it. Note in Table 11-4 that Detroit seems to have an extremely high forfeiture rate. During the time the statistics were gathered, the court was under pressure to keep pretrial release to a minimum and used two forms of statistical manipulation to make it seem as if release did not work. First, a strict definition was used. A defendant who was even a minute late was counted as skipping. (Most of the nonappearing defendants actually showed up within two days.) Second, when a defendant fled, the Detroit court counted each missed court appearance as a separate count. Discounting these statistical manipulations, the failure-to-appear rate in Detroit came close to the national average.

Defendants who fail to appear do not always intend to do so. Failure-to-appear rates are closely tied to practices within the court itself. A number of defendants do not show up because they were not given clear notice of the next appearance date. The noise of the courtroom or language barriers often mean that defendants are confused about when to appear next. Similarly, most courts still keep records by hand. Simple clerical errors as to the defendant's correct name or current address often mean that notices are never delivered. Perhaps above all, many courts are simply unwilling to try to communicate with defendants while they are on pretrial release. The lack of proper administrative procedures continues after defendants have failed to appear. In many communities, the sheriff or police are lax in serving bench warrants.

Another way that courts themselves contribute to nonappearances is by lengthy delay in disposing of the case. As the time from arrest to trial increases, the rate of nonappearances rises even faster. (And crimes committed while out on bail are also tied to delay in court disposition time.) A study in Charlotte, North Carolina, for example, estimated that every additional two-week delay increased by 5 percent the chances a defendant either would not appear or would commit another crime (Clarke et al.:240).

A basic question in evaluating the effectiveness of bail is how well judges (in their bail-setting decisions) are able to predict the likelihood of a defendant's appearance. The study in Charlotte provides some tentative answers. The authors found that numerous variables thought to be important were not: age, race, sex, income, and seriousness of the crime *were not* related to nonappearance. Thus the factor most used by the courts in setting bail—severity of the crime—is, at least in this one community, not related to the final outcome (Clarke et al.:21-23). More recent research underscores this point. Separate studies in Washington, D.C. (Roth and Wice) and New York City (Zeisel) concluded that the most dangerous defendants jumped bail the least. By contrast those accused of more minor offenses had higher rates of failure to appear. The Charlotte study had found that the only other major factor related to failure to appear was the criminal history of the defendant. At least this one factor used in setting bail has some relationship to the intended results.

Toward bail reform

In response to the inadequacies of the monetary bail system, reformers have moved to develop alternatives to traditional methods of pretrial release. The shift in thinking about monetary bail is exemplified by the Bail Reform Act of 1966 passed by the U.S. Congress. This act creates a presumption favoring pretrial release. Unless the judge is convinced that pretrial release "will not reasonably assure the appearance of the person as required" (18 U.S.C.A. §3146) the defendant is to be released. More specific reforms include use of citations in lieu of arrest, a 10 percent bail deposit system, and bail reform projects. All seek to decrease discrimination against the poor by developing better ways of ensuring that defendants will appear in court. These programs offer new ways to accomplish the historical goal of bail: guaranteeing appearance at trial. Although a number of cities and states have adopted bail reform measures, substantial political obstacles still remain.

Citation in lieu of arrest

Every year the police arrest over 10 million people, most of them for minor offenses. But even though the violations are minor, they are often treated the same as felonies; the person is arrested, booked at the police station, and must pay a bondsman to secure release.

citation in lieu of arrest
An alternative to requiring those arrested for minor offenses to post bond is a *citation in lieu of arrest.* A citation works much like an ordinary traffic ticket. Suspects are given a summons directing them to appear in court at a given time and place. These are commonly used for a specified list of misdemeanors.

Citation programs have proven quite successful. In California, for example, defendants given a citation in lieu of arrest failed to appear only 4.5 percent of the time (Kalmanoff:191). Yet only a handful of cities have adopted such programs. One of the reasons is that programs like these are strongly opposed by bail bondsmen, who have sufficient political muscle to block enactment of the necessary legislation. Just as importantly, adoption of a citation-in-lieu-of-arrest program requires the coordinated efforts of several independent agencies—local police departments, lower court judges, clerks of court, and so on—each of which dislikes any change in their routines. Moreover bail reform has no built-in political constituency because it is viewed by the public as helping criminals. Programs like these are a low-priority item. And even when formally adopted, citation programs may prove ineffective. Police officers are naturally suspicious and therefore reluctant to issue citations. Thus without strong backing from police administrators, citation in lieu of arrest can remain empty legislation.

10 percent bail deposit

10 percent bail deposit
Bail bondsmen charge a nonrefundable 10 percent fee for posting bond. Given that bondsmen seem to perform few services for their fee and have often been the sources of corruption, bail reformers have attempted to legislate an economic end run around the bondsmen. In a handful of states (Illinois, Pennsylvania, and Kentucky) plus the U.S. courts, defendants may gain pretrial release by posting 10

percent of the bond amount with the court. At this point there is no difference between what the bondsman charges and the court requires. But when the defendant makes all scheduled court appearances, the court will refund 90 percent of the amount posted with the court. (It uses the extra 10 percent to cover the costs of administering the program.) Defendants who fail to appear, however, are still liable for the full face amount of the bond.

The 10 percent bail deposit program directly threatens the bail bond industry. Indeed, in Illinois, the first state to adopt this program, the bondsmen have virtually disappeared. In other states, however, bondsmen have been successful in defeating such programs in the legislature.

Bail reform projects

bail reform projects

release on recognizance (ROR)

Bail reformers have been critical of traditional methods of bail setting because the bail amount is fixed not on the basis of whether the defendant will likely appear in court but on the basis of the crime charged. Moreover, the court makes no attempt to determine which defendants are good risks. *Bail reform projects* seek to remedy these deficiencies by investigating the background of arrested persons and then recommending *release on recognizance* (release without bail) for those who are reliable.

First developed and tested by the Vera Institute of Justice in New York City, the program works as follows. A program worker (either a paid staff member or a volunteer law student) interviews the defendant shortly after arrest about family, job, prior criminal record, and length of time lived in the community. Persons who are deemed good risks are recommended for release on recognizance. Not all defendants are eligible for the program, however. Those arrested for serious charges like murder, armed robbery, or sale of drugs are excluded in most communities. After a person has been released on recognizance, the bail reform project makes follow-up contacts to ensure that the defendant knows when the court appearance is scheduled and will show up.

The guiding assumption of the Vera Project is that defendants with ties to the community are not likely to flee. And by providing information about these ties (which normally is not available when bail is set), the program provides a more workable way for making sure that the wrong persons are not detained prior to trial. Research has confirmed the operating assumption. Where bail reform projects have been tried, the rate of nonappearances for those released on recognizance has been lower than for those released through bail bondsmen (Wice:67). Supporters also argue that bail reform projects save money. Because more defendants are being released, costs for holding these persons in jail are significantly reduced.

There are often major gaps between an idea in theory and its actual implementation, and this is so with bail reform projects. Although a number of cities have implemented bail reform programs, there are often important differences in how these programs are administered.

Bail reform projects must operate in a very restricted political atmosphere. Thus, programs aimed at helping those accused of crime face an uphill battle. Moreover there are often conflicts among judges, court administrators, prosecutors, defense attorneys, and the police about who will control and administer the program. In several cities Wice visited such disputes have seriously weakened the effectiveness of the program.

In an effort to head off possible negative public relations, bail reform projects have maintained a conservative stance by selecting only the most reliable persons for pretrial release. As a result, bail reform projects, like all too many other criminal justice reforms, end in concentrating government resources among those least in need. The initial concern was with truly poor defendants, many from the inner cities and minority members, but in practice bail reform has been least able to help this group. A study of the pretrial release program in Charlotte found that most of the defendants released by the program would have been released on recognizance anyway or would have been able to hire a bondsman. Thus the pretrial release program produced only a slight dent in the proportion of defendants released prior to trial (Clarke et al.:23). A study in an unnamed eastern city concluded:

> Thus, to the degree that recognizance standards emphasize employment history, length of residence, and social ties (which is the case in Metro City and other cities), they tend to screen out precisely those defendants who are most likely to have difficulty making financial bail in the first place. [Flemming et al.:969]

The net result is that bail reform programs seem to release those who would have posted cash bail anyway; the overall pretrial release rate is more dependent on jail capacity than on the reform efforts (Mahoney:19).

IN THE NEWS: BAIL PANEL TOLD MAN FREED FIVE TIMES

In the last eight months, a Washington man has been arrested on five occasions for crimes ranging from murder to attempted petty larceny. But he is still on the streets while awaiting trial.

The defendant, who was not identified by name, because his case is still pending in court, was used as an example yesterday by Chief Maurice Cullinane of the metropolitan police department to describe to a House District subcommittee the problems he sees in the criminal justice system here.

It was one of three examples he gave the subcommittee, and Cullinane said there were "literally hundreds" of such cases in the police department's files. . . .

Cullinane again reiterated his concern that a proportionally small number of criminals commit a large number of crimes in the city, pointing out that one of every four persons arrested in 1975 for serious offenses was already on some type of conditional pretrial or post-conviction release. . . .

The example cited earlier by Cullinane began on October 15 of last year when the defendant was arrested for homicide. He was released on personal recognizance, indicted for murder and trial was set for June 14 of this year.

Seven days after his initial arrest, the defendant was arrested for carrying a dangerous weapon. He was again released on personal recognizance.

On November 28, the same defendant was arrested for unlawful entry, Cullinane continued. He was again released on personal recognizance.

On Dec. 3—while released on three personal recognizances—the same defendant was arrested for grand larceny. He again was released on personal recognizance.

The last arrest came on Feb. 17, when the defendant was arrested for attempted petit larceny. This time, a $1,000 bond was set and the defendant was allowed to post $100 of it and was released. All his trials were set for June 14, but have now been continued until Sept. 27.

Cullinane said that a criminal justice system that allows such incidents to occur causes "many criminals in this city to regard it with scorn and derision."

He said he had few specific suggestions to make to the subcommittee in the form of comments on their pending bills, but said it is clear that the present law "is not adequately coping with the problem."

Timothy S. Robinson, © *The Washington Post*, June 22, 1976. Reprinted by permission.

Conclusion

Bail serves several purposes in the American court system, some legally sanctioned, others definitely extralegal. Bail is used to guarantee a defendant's appearance at trial, to protect society by holding those perceived to be dangerous, to punish those accused (but not yet convicted) of violating the law, and to lubricate the system by softening defendants up to enter a plea of guilty. These varying purposes are partially the result of the tension between conflicting principles. Although the law recognizes that the only legal purpose of bail is to guarantee a suspect's future appearance at trial, in practice court officials perceive a need to protect society. Out of these conflicting principles arise compromises. Bail setting is also influenced by the conditions under which it must be executed. Shortly after arrest, based on at best sketchy information, a decision must be made.

Few are happy with how the system actually operates. Some defendants are held in jail who clearly should not be. Others are released who threaten society. Until recently such problems attracted little attention. The course of least resistance was to delegate the responsibility to private businessmen—bail bondsmen. Now a great deal of rethinking is focused on improving the system.

For discussion

1. Under the Constitution, what is the purpose of bail? What additional purposes does bail fulfill in practice? Why?
2. Do you think that for certain defendants, bail should not be allowed? What kinds of cases?
3. You are the judge. In setting bail, how may the nature of the crime, the characteristics of the defendant, the conditions in the local jail, and local community pressures influence your decision?
4. Examine the local newspapers. Have there been reports of defendants committing crimes while out on bail? Have there been reports on poor conditions in the local jail? How might these reports affect bail setting?
5. Attend a court session where bail is set. Do prosecutors make bail recommendations? The defense attorney? Does the judge appear to be influenced by these recommendations? What information is available in setting bail?
6. Using court records and other sources if necessary, determine the amount of bond set in various types of cases. Also try to determine what forms of bail predominate—recognizance, bondsmen, and so on. Try to estimate the proportion of defendants who are released on bail.
7. Interview a judge, prosecutor, defense attorney, and bail bondsman. Determine bail-setting criteria in your community. Also ask about problems these officials perceive in the bail process.
8. Check your telephone directory. How many bondsmen are listed?

References

Clarke, Stevens, Jean Freeman, and Gary Koch. *The Effectiveness of Bail Systems: An Analysis of Failure to Appear in Court and Rearrest While on Bail.* Institute of Government, University of North Carolina, Chapel Hill: 1976.

Dill, Forest. "Discretion, Exchange and Social Control: Bail Bondsmen in Criminal Courts." *Law and Society Review 9* (Summer 1975):639–674.

Eisenstein, James, and Herbert Jacob. *Felony Justice: An Organizational Analysis of Criminal Courts.* Boston: Little, Brown, 1977.

Ervin, S. J. *Preventive Detention.* Chicago: Urban Research Corp., 1971.

Flemming, Roy. *Punishment Before Trial: An Organizational Perspective on Felony Bail Process.* New York: Longman, 1982.

————, C. Kohfeld, and Thomas Uhlman. "The Limits of Bail Reform: A Quasi-Experimental Analysis." *Law and Society Review 14* (Summer 1980):947–976.

Goldfarb, Ronald. *Ransom: A Critique of the American Bail System.* New York: Harper & Row, 1965.

Goldkamp, John. "The Effects of Detention of Judicial Decisions: A Closer Look." *Justice System Journal 5* (Spring 1980):234–257.

James, Howard. *Crisis in the Courts.* New York: David McKay, 1971.

Kalmanoff, Alan. *Criminal Justice: Enforcement and Administration.* Boston: Little, Brown, 1976.

Mahoney, Barry. "Evaluating Pretrial Release Program." Paper presented at the annual meeting of the American Political Science Association, Chicago, Illinois, 1976.

National Conference on Bail and Criminal Justice. *Proceedings and Interim Report.* Washington, D.C.: Government Printing Office, 1965.

President's Commission on Law Enforcement and Administration of Justice. *Task Force Report: The Courts.* Washington, D.C.: Government Printing Office, 1967.

Roth, Jeffrey, and Paul Wice. *Pretrial Release and Misconduct in the District of Columbia.* Washington, D.C.: Institute for Law and Social Research, 1980.

Silverstein, Lee. "Bail in the State Courts—A Field Study and Report." *Minnesota Law Review 50* (1966):621.

Suffet, Frederick. "Bail Setting: A Study of Courtroom Interaction." *Crime and Delinquency 12* (October 1966):318.

Thomas, Wayne. *The Current State of Bail Reform: Bail Projects.* Davis, Calif.: Center on the Administration of Justice, 1970.

U.S. Department of Justice. Bureau of Justice Statistics. *Profile of Jail Inmates: Sociodemographic Findings from the 1978 Survey of Inmates of Local Jails.* Washington, D.C.: Government Printing Office, 1980.

U.S. Department of Justice. Law Enforcement Assistance Administration. *1970 Jail Census.* Washington, D.C.: Government Printing Office, 1971.

Wice, Paul. *Freedom for Sale.* Lexington, Mass.: D. C. Heath, Lexington Books, 1974.

Zeisel, Hans. "Bail Revisited." *American Bar Foundation Research Journal* (1976):769.

For further reading

Ervin, S. J. *Preventive Detention.* Chicago: Urban Research Corp., 1971.

Flemming, Roy. *Punishment Before Trial: An Organizational Perspective on Felony Bail Process.* New York: Longman, 1982.

Freed, Daniel, and Patricia Wald. *Bail in the United States.* Washington, D.C.: National Conference on Bail and Criminal Justice, 1964.

Goldfarb, Ronald. *Ransom: A Critique of the American Bail System.* New York: Harper & Row, 1965.

Wice, Paul. *Freedom for Sale.* Lexington, Mass.: D. C. Heath, Lexington Books, 1974.

CHAPTER 12

Preparing for Trial

Miranda card

"You have the right to remain silent. You have the right to a lawyer. If you cannot afford a lawyer, one will be provided for you. Anything you say can be used against you." This police ritual can be witnessed almost every night on prime-time television. Invariably the information is delivered in a perfunctory manner, the detective reading from the *Miranda card* in a monotone. These *Miranda* warnings are the most controversial part of the Supreme Court's revolution in criminal justice. Responding to criticisms that police procedures were unfair and that the police were not adhering to the procedural requirements of the law, the Supreme Court imposed additional restrictions on police investigative techniques, such as searches, interrogations, and line-ups. In turn the Court's decisions produced extensive national controversy. Based on *Miranda* and similar cases, trial judges sometimes rule that otherwise valid evidence cannot be admitted at trial.

This chapter examines some of the diverse activities that may occur between arraignment and the final disposition (either a guilty plea or a trial). We will begin with the gathering of evidence, termed *discovery*. Next we will discuss how and why some evidence is excluded from trial.

Discovery

discovery
The informal and formal exchange of information between prosecution and defense is referred to as *discovery*. Results of laboratory analysis, medical examinations, fingerprint results, ballistics tests, written statements of witnesses, defendants' confessions, lists of potential witnesses, police reports, and so on are some prominent examples of information that prosecutors often gather and defense attorneys want to know prior to trial. Does the notion of a fair trial require the prosecutor to disclose such information to the defense? What of the defense attorney? Should there be an obligation for the defense to disclose aspects of its case, or would this erode the basic protection that a defendant is innocent until proven guilty? These questions echo current debate over the extent of pretrial discovery.

The guiding assumption of the adversary system is that truth will emerge after a struggle at trial. In an influential article, though, Supreme Court Justice William Brennan questioned whether criminal trials were a sporting event or a quest for the truth. Historically civil trials were largely sporting events, with decisions heavily dependent upon the technical skills of the lawyers. In an effort to eliminate the worst aspects of such contests, the Federal Rules of Civil Procedure were adopted for U.S. courts in 1938, and most states have since followed the federal example. These rules reflect the philosophy that prior to trial, every party in a civil action is entitled to the disclosure of all relevant information in the possession of any person (unless that information is privileged) (Wright:354). These discovery rules are intended to "make a trial less a game of blind man's bluff and more a fair contest with the basic issues and facts disclosed to the fullest practicable matter" (*U.S. v. Procter and Gamble Co.*, 356 U.S. 677, 683, 1958).

Justice Brennan believes that the liberal discovery rules of civil procedure should apply to criminal cases as well; he based his argument on the fact that defense attorneys seldom have the investigative resources that the state does. Most defense attorneys have difficulty preparing criminal cases. Typically defendants are unable to aid the attorney either because they are too inarticulate and/or because they are held in jail prior to trial, thus preventing them from searching for witnesses. Thus defense attorneys may go to trial not knowing what evidence they must defend their clients against. This position would make it mandatory for prosecutors to inform the defense of virtually all evidence in their possession.

Only a handful of states, however, have adopted Justice Brennan's position. In most states mandatory prosecutorial disclosure is much more limited. This countertheory was expressed by the New Jersey Supreme Court in *State* v. *Tune* (13 N.J. 203, 1953): "Liberal procedures for discovery in preparation for trial are essential to any modern judicial system in which the search for truth in the aid of justice is paramount and in which concealment and surprise are not to be tolerated. However, such liberal fact-finding procedures are not to be used to defeat the ends of justice." The court went on to cite examples in which prosecutorial disclosure might result in the defendant's taking undue advantage. For example, the defendant, knowing of the state's case, might procure perjured testimony or might harass and intimidate witnesses who are likely to testify.

These competing philosophies have resulted in considerable variation among jurisdictions over the type of information that is discoverable. Some jurisdictions allow only limited discovery. The trial court has the discretion to order the prosecutor to disclose the defendant's confession and/or other physical documents, but that is all. Other jurisdictions take a middle ground. Discovery of confessions and physical evidence is a matter of right, but discovery of the other items (witnesses' statements, for example) is more difficult. Finally, a few states have adopted Justice Brennan's position of liberal discovery. There is a presumption strongly in favor of prosecutorial disclosure with only certain narrow exceptions (Kamisar, et al.: 1216–1217).

Prosecutorial disclosure

A few jurisdictions have an office policy prohibiting assistant prosecutors from disclosing any information not required by law. More typically, however, assistant DAs voluntarily disclose to defense attorneys certain aspects of the state's case. Such informal discovery operates within the norms of cooperation of courtroom work groups. Defense attorneys who maintain good relationships with prosecutors and are viewed as trustworthy (they will not use information for nefarious purposes) receive selected information about the case. Conversely defense attorneys who maintain hostile relationships with the prosecutor and/or represent clients who are viewed as troublemakers (the two frequently go together) find the prosecutors holding the cards as tightly to the vest as the law allows.

informal prosecutorial disclosure   *Informal prosecutorial disclosure* does not stem from a basic sympathy for the defendant. Rather it flows from a long-held courthouse theory that an advance glimpse at the prosecutor's case often encourages a guilty plea.

> In criminal law there is significant variation from state to state and sometimes, on an informal basis, from community to community, as to how open the discovery procedures are in allowing the defense to examine the strength of the state's case. . . .
>
> Whether a court system utilizes open or closed discovery is of crucial importance to the defense attorney. It can greatly affect the lawyer's relationship with his client. In an open system, the lawyer can go straight to the prosecutor's files and obtain an official set of the facts of the case, which usually amount to the essentials of the state's case against the defendant. By learning the facts of the prosecutor's case, the defense attorney need not face the difficult task of trying to force his client to voluntarily disclose this information. Nearly all lawyers interviewed felt that clients' veracity is questionable and in need of thorough verification. This forces the attorney to devote extra hours, frequently wasted, verifying a client's version of the facts, which also puts a strain on their relationship—especially when the attorney is forced to confront the defendant with his prevarications.
>
> A lack of adequate discovery may also impede an early or at least an intelligent plea negotiation, which may eventually result in a jury trial and severe sentence or a premature settlement of the case without an aggressive defense. In the cities which tended toward closed discovery, there was often a failure to plea bargain, and a large number went to trial, frequently without a jury. Philadelphia is probably the best example of a city whose district attorney has taken a hard stance toward giving information to the defense attorney, and where, as a result, an extremely large percentage of cases go to trial—albeit nonjury trials, which are frequently described as

"slow pleas." At the other extreme, Los Angeles and Denver with very open discovery policies, probably try only one-third of the percentage of cases tried in Philadelphia. They are also able to initiate their plea bargaining at an earlier time and are therefore blessed with significantly smaller backlog than is found in most cities with closed discovery.

Paul Wice, *Criminal Lawyers: An Endangered Species* (Beverly Hills, Calif.: Sage Publications, 1978), pp. 45–46.

According to prosecutors, defendants often tell their lawyers only part of what happened. Therefore the defense attorney who learns what evidence the prosecutor possesses can use it to show the defendant that contesting the matter may be hopeless. The following case involving a liquor store burglary is a good illustration. The client told his attorney that the police had stopped him several blocks from the alleged break-in and that he had nothing to do with it. The prosecutor relayed a different version. According to the police reports, the squad car was on routine patrol checking stores. When the squad car pulled into the parking lot, its headlights illuminated someone inside the store. The officers went to the back of the store and observed a suspect leaving the store and entering a car. They chased the car, stopped it several blocks away, discovered the car "loaded with goodies," and arrested the defendant. After such disclosures, the prosecutors contend that the lawyer goes back to his client and says, "You lied to me, you bastard. Tell me the truth or I'll pull out of the case" (Neubauer:200). Prosecutors, however, are not prone to revealing weaknesses in their case, just the strengths.

Mandatory disclosure

Brady v.
Maryland

Jencks v.
U.S.

Growing discontent with the discovery system has prompted American courts to expand mandatory disclosure by the prosecutor cautiously. In *Brady* v. *Maryland* (373 U.S. 83, 1963) the Supreme Court held that due process of law is violated when prosecutors hide evidence in their possession that might be favorable to the defense. Similarly in *Jencks* v. *U.S.* (353 U.S. 651, 1957), the Court ruled that prior inconsistent statements of a witness must be made available to the defense. Read together, these decisions stand for the proposition that as officers of the court, prosecutors can no more suppress evidence than they can knowingly use perjured testimony. These decisions, however, were technically limited to trial; the prosecution must disclose such information to the defense after the witness has testified at trial so it can be used for cross-examination. Some courts, however, have broadened the ruling to require disclosure prior to trial.

Defense and disclosure

As noted earlier, defense attorneys often encounter major stumbling blocks in obtaining information that can be valuable for constructing a defense at trial. In addition to relying on informal prosecutorial disclosure, resourceful defense attorneys may utilize a variety of proceedings not directly designed for discovery purposes. Filing a pretrial motion to suppress evidence may disclose facts related to the defense because key government witnesses will testify. And the preliminary hearing, intended to test the sufficiency of the evidence for holding the defendant, affords an opportunity for the defense to hear at least part of the story of some critical witnesses (Uviller:80).

Defense attorneys understandably press for broader discovery laws. A major issue in broadening discovery involves the extent to which the defense should also be required to disclose relevant materials in their files. A few states, for example, require that the defense file a notice of *alibi defense* (the crime was committed while the defendant was somewhere else), complete with a list of witnesses to be called to support the alibi. Such notice prior to trial allows the prosecutor to investigate the backgrounds of these witnesses and thus be prepared to undermine the defendant's contention that he or she was somewhere else when the crime was committed. Some proposals go even further. Under recently amended rule 16 of the Federal Rules of Criminal Procedure, the defense can require the prosecutor to divulge certain types of information only by agreeing to reciprocal discovery by the prosecutor.

alibi defense

Suppressing evidence

exclusionary rule

The *exclusionary rule* is a judge-made rule of evidence prohibiting the use of evidence obtained by law enforcement officials by means forbidden by the Constitution, statute, or court rule. It applies primarily to physical evidence gathered during an illegal search and seizure or to a confession obtained through improper methods. The exclusionary rule is the Supreme Court's sole technique for enforcing several vital protections of the Bill of Rights. Two types of justifications have been offered for the exclusionary rule: a court of law should not participate in illegal conduct and excluding evidence will deter law enforcement officials from illegal behavior (Oaks:665).

Mapp v. Ohio

Miranda v. Arizona

Early in the twentieth century, the Supreme Court applied the exclusionary rule to federal officials. But it was not until the early 1960s that these same restrictions were applied to state (and local) officials. The Court's decisions in *Mapp* v. *Ohio* (367 U.S. 643, 1962) and *Miranda* v. *Arizona* (384 U.S. 436, 1966) aroused a storm of controversy. The Court was accused of hampering law enforcement because otherwise valid and trustworthy evidence was excluded from trial.

Numerous studies investigating the extent to which the police have complied with the Court's rulings report a pattern of evasion (Wasby). Many have called for eliminating the exclusionary rule because it has not functioned as an effective deterrent of illegal law enforcement conduct (Oaks). But although these decisions are ultimately directed at the police, enforcement is in the hands of the trial courts. To understand how the trial courts have responded, we need to begin with a brief overview of procedural restrictions on how confessions and evidence may be obtained.

Confessions

free and voluntary confession

In *Miranda*, the Court added to earlier decisions on confessions. The traditional rule was that only confessions that were *"free and voluntary"* would be admitted at trial. Confessions obtained by *physical coercion* (beatings or torture, for example)

physical coercion

psychologi-cal coercion

were not allowed into evidence because they were not trustworthy; someone in fear of a beating is likely to say what his or her antagonists want to hear. In the 1930s the Court rejected confessions based on physical coercion, and subsequently such practices largely ceased. The Court then was confronted with the slightly different issue of confessions obtained as a result of lengthy interrogations, psycho-logical ploys, and the like. The Court reasoned that confessions based on *psycho-logical coercion* should be rejected just as if they were based on physical coercion because such statements were not likely to be free and voluntary. But it is not easy to define what constitutes psychological coercion, and in over twenty cases the Court sought to spell out what factors the trial court should use in making this determination.

The Court standards, however, were far from precise, so in an attempt to pro-vide more precision, the Court, in *Miranda*, wrote some new requirements. The requirements did not relate to psychological coercion but dealt instead with the procedures the police were to follow before and during questioning. The police were required to tell the suspects of their right to remain silent, to have a lawyer present, to provide a court-appointed attorney for the indigent, and to end ques-tioning when requested (see figure 12-1). In addition, *Miranda* shifted the burden of proof from the defense, who had to prove that the confessions were not "free and voluntary," to the police and prosecutor, who must prove that they had ad-hered to the requirements.

Searches

search with-out proba-ble cause

unreason-able search and seizure

Until *Mapp* v. *Ohio*, the United States had operated largely under the common law rule that "if the constable blunders, the crook should not go free." This meant that if the police made an illegal search (*search without probable cause*), the evi-dence obtained still could be used in court. The issue of improper police search was a separate issue. Evidence was admitted in court on the basis of its truthfulness, not on the basis of how it was obtained. Thus there were no effective controls on police conduct during a search. Policemen who searched illegally faced no sanctions. The *Mapp* decision changed this by imposing the *exclusionary rule*.

The Fourth Amendment prohibits *unreasonable search and seizure:* "The right of the people to be secure in their persons, houses, papers and effects against unrea-sonable search and seizure, shall not be violated." Police officers may lawfully conduct a search in one of three ways: if the search is related to a lawful arrest, if the evidence is in plain view, or if there is a valid search warrant. The precise grounds for a lawful search, however, are complex and often highly technical. For example, if an officer seizes illegal contraband (narcotics, for example) on the basis of a search warrant, the court may later declare the search illegal and suppress the evidence if the warrant was improperly drafted. The police must often make on-the-spot decisions about these technical and complex requirements.

Pretrial motions

Defense attorneys who believe that defendants have been victims of an illegal search or an improperly obtained confession can file a motion to suppress the

Metropolitan Police Department Warning as to Your Rights

You are under arrest. Before we ask you any questions, you must understand what your rights are.

You have the right to remain silent. You are not required to say anything to us at any time or to answer any questions. Anything you say can be used against you in court.

You have the right to talk to a lawyer for advice before we question you and to have him with you during questioning.

If you cannot afford a lawyer and want one, a lawyer will be provided for you.

If you want to answer questions now without a lawyer present you will still have the right to stop answering at any time. You also have the right to stop answering at any time until you talk to a lawyer.

Waiver

1. Have you read or had read to you the warning as to your rights? _____

2. Do you understand these rights? _____

3. Do you wish to answer any questions? _____

4. Are you willing to answer questions without having an attorney

present? _____

5. Signature of defendant on line below.

_____

6. Time _____ Date _____

7. Signature of officer _____

8. Signature of witness _____

Figure 12-1.   This is a typical form required for all interrogations. Similar forms are used throughout the United States.

Source: U.S. Department of Justice, Legal Enforcement Assistance Administration, *The D.C. Public Defender Service, Vol.II, Training Materials* (Washington, D.C.: Government Printing Office, 1975), p. 58.

evidence. Most states require that objections be made prior to trial. But several states continue to treat suppression of evidence as subject to the "usual principle that the admissibility of evidence is determined when it is tendered [presented] and not in advance of trial" (Kamisar et al.:729). There are also important variations in *pretrial motions* when such *pretrial motions* must be filed. In some jurisdictions, they may be filed at any time prior to trial, which means that the defense attorneys can wait until the day of trial to raise an objection, with the result that the trial is usually delayed. Other jurisdictions specify that the trial judge can require that pretrial motions be filed in advance of trial to prevent the defense from dragging out the proceedings.

A hearing is held on the motion, and the defense attorney has the burden of proving that the search was illegal or that the confession was coerced. The only exception involves an allegation that the *Miranda* warnings were not given, in which case the state has the burden of proof. The judge's ruling in the pretrial hearing is binding on the later trial.

A basic question in assessing the impact of *Mapp* and *Miranda* is how many pretrial motions are filed and how many are sustained. The answer depends on which jurisdiction is being studied. In Los Angeles, there were pretrial motions in 20 percent of the cases (Mather:265). In Prairie City, Illinois, there were far fewer (Neubauer). Some of the disparity is clearly tied to local police practices. The type of case being processed also has an effect. Pretrial motions to suppress evidence are concentrated in weapons, gambling, and narcotics cases. But even within these high-incident crimes there are variations among cities: 81 percent of the gambling cases in Chicago but only 12 percent in Washington, D.C., involved suppression motions (Oaks).

There are also variations in the percentage of motions granted. In Chicago, for example, 24 percent of the motions in weapons cases were granted, but only 1 percent in Washington, D.C. If the motion to suppress is granted, the case is usually dismissed. Without the physical evidence, the prosecution cannot sustain a conviction.

Despite the controversy over the Supreme Court decisions in *Mapp* and *Miranda*, studies show that only a handful of cases are lost for due process reasons. Table 12-1 summarizes data from four cities. In Atlanta and Washington, D.C., less than 1 percent of the cases are lost due to a prosecutorial or judicial determination that a defendant's rights had been violated. In Los Angeles and New Orleans the figures are a little higher, but still due process fails to emerge as a major reason for case attrition (Brosi). Another study in New York reached a similar conclusion (Vera Institute of Justice). While the Supreme Court decisions may affect police operations in other ways, they are not a major reason that defendants once brought to court are not convicted.

Pretrial hearings on a motion to suppress evidence are best characterized as "swearing matches." As one defense attorney phrased it, "The real question in Supreme Court cases is what's going on at the police station" (Neubauer:167). Seldom is there unbiased, independent evidence of what happened. The only witnesses are the participants—police and defendant—and not surprisingly they have different versions of what happened. As James Vorenberg, who was executive director of the President's Commission on Law Enforcement and Administration

CLOSE-UP: A FAKED ROBBERY?

Call him Danny. He was 17, white, and a high school dropout. To support himself and his pregnant wife, Danny worked at a gas station. According to his original report to the police, a man walked into the station, pointed a gun in his face, and took the large denomination bills from the cash register. The police investigated but could find no corroboration for his story. Other people who had been in the area did not remember seeing a big black man leaving the gas station. Other discrepancies in Danny's story led the police to believe that he had reported a false armed robbery to cover up his theft. They interviewed him, and after signing the custodial interview form, Danny signed a confession, admitting he had stolen the money. The defense attorney challenged the confession, contending that the *Miranda* warnings were not properly given, and that the confession had been psychologically coerced. At the hearing the testimony of the detectives and the defendant agreed on only two points: the custodial interview form had been signed and a confession given. Beyond these basics, however, the testimony clashed sharply on five key points.

Two detectives testified separately, but they told the same story. They went to Danny's house and asked him to come to the police station—a request with which he willingly complied. Once at the police station, the custodial interview form was signed and the detectives then told Danny their theory: the armed robbery report was a cover up for his theft of the money. At this point Danny confessed, saying he had needed the money to pay his bills. After making a written statement the defendant asked if he could go home, saying he had never spent the night away from his wife and felt that he should be with her since she was pregnant. The detectives indicated that in the normal felony arrest the suspect must first post bail, but since Danny had been cooperative they would ask their supervisor if he could be released on his own recognizance. The sergeant reluctantly agreed. At the end of the interrogation, Danny asked about his chances for probation. The detectives replied that the court normally gave first offenders in theft cases probation, especially if they had been cooperative.

Danny told a different story. He had not wanted to go to the police station, but the detectives had insisted. Once at the station he was questioned for a long time and not until midway through the interrogation was he asked to sign the custodial interview form. The defendant claimed that he had repeatedly denied his guilt and asked to go home, at which point the detective replied that the defendant could not go home until he confessed. Further, if he did confess he could go home right away. In addition, Danny said the police told him that if he confessed he would get probation so there was nothing to worry about. Because he just wanted to go home and be with his wife, Danny signed the confession, although he did not commit the theft.

It is obvious that Danny's and the detectives' testimony clash on a number of major points. This is significant because the contrasting versions lead to different decisions. For instance, the defense attorney, in his summation at the end of the hearing, argued that the evidence showed a psychologically coerced confession. The defendant almost had been forced to go to the station house; the interrogation had lasted a long time; promises of pretrial release and mention of probation were illicit inducements. These factors taken together meant the confession was not "free and voluntary." He further argued that the *Miranda* warnings had not been properly given since the defendant's testimony indicated that the custodial interview form was not signed until midway in the questioning.

By contrast the state's attorney pictured the facts as showing a routine police interrogation. The defendant had gone willingly to the police station, the interrogation had been a short one, and probation had not been used as an inducement since the defendant had first raised the issue. Releasing the suspect on ROR was portrayed as a product of the detectives' humanity. As for the *Miranda* warnings, the prosecution concluded that the detectives' testimony showed that the custodial interview form had been presented before questioning and that the time on the form supported the police version.

* * *

As for Danny—he lost the battle but won the war. The judge accepted the detectives' testimony and ruled that the confession could be introduced as evidence during the trial. During the trial, however, the defense attorney hit hard at the circumstances surrounding the confession. Evidently the jury was more sympathetic to Danny than the judge because he was acquitted. The police had a cynical reaction to the verdict. They thought the jurors were influenced by the visibility of Danny's pregnant wife during the trial.

David Neubauer, *Criminal Justice in Middle America* (Morristown, N.J.: General Learning Press, 1974).

TABLE 12-1.   Minimal case attrition due to U.S. Supreme Court decisions in four cities

	New Orleans	Cobb County (Atlanta)	Los Angeles	District of Columbia
Cases not filed or dismissed for due process reasons	186 (5.9%)	4 (0.6%)	709 (3.7%)	27 (0.8%)
Total arrests	3,167	632	19,418	3,141

Source: Kathleen Brosi, *A Cross-city Comparison of Felony Case Processing*. Washington, D.C.: Institute for Law and Social Research, 1979, pp. 16, 20.

notes that *Miranda* "just moves the battleground from the voluntariness of the confession back to the voluntariness of the waiver . . . the police have done pretty well with these swearing contests over the years" (quoted in Cipes: 55).

The exclusionary rule and the courtroom work group

In cases in which the defense questions the nature of the search or a confession, the dominant issue involves the facts of the case. The dispute over the facts structures and apportions the roles that the police, defense attorneys, judges, and prosecutors play. Defense attorneys are forced into a catalytic role since they must search out the issues. Judges, by virtue of their power as fact finder at the hearing, become the supreme umpire that legal theory indicated they should be. Prosecutors are forced into a passive role. Although pretrial motions place the prosecutor in a defensive posture, they are not at a major disadvantage because the police typically are able to provide information indicating compliance.

Defense attorney as prime mover

Defense attorneys charged with protecting the constitutional rights of the defendant, are the prime movers in suppression matters. Unless they object, it is assumed that law enforcement officials behaved properly.

For the defense a number of benefits flow from filing pretrial motions to suppress. If the motion is granted, the case will be won because the prosecutor will dismiss the case for lack of evidence. Even if the motion is denied, the defense may be able to discover information that may later prove valuable at trial. Moreover, filing a pretrial motion keeps options open. The defense may later decide to plea bargain the case, for example.

IN THE NEWS: SLAY CONFESSION IS RULED ILLEGAL

Criminal Dist. Court Judge Jerome W. Winsberg ruled a confession given police by a co-defendant in the aftermath of the shooting of Gov. Edwin Edwards' blind 73-year old uncle is inadmissible.

The district attorney's office acknowledged that without the confession as evidence, the case against 20-year-old Lawrence Williams is in jeopardy.

Winsberg ruled this week that Williams was arrested without "probable cause" and his statement was not given to arresting officers in conformity with due process of law.

Asst. Dist. Atty. Lawrence Centola of the Career Criminal Bureau, urged by Winsberg himself, announced he would take an appeal to the Louisiana Supreme Court on the judge's ruling.

Williams will remain in Parish Prison while the case is before the high court.

Williams, 901 St. Mary, apt. D, was arrested May 22, 1975, with Ronald Williams (no relation) and David Adams, the day after Bernard Segura was shot to death in the presence of his blind wife in front of their St. Thomas Street apartment.

Adams has been convicted of first degree murder and will soon be sentenced by Winsberg to a mandatory death sentence.

Lawrence Williams, in his confession to the police, admitted, " . . . we attempted the robbery but not to kill him." After being shot several times, Segura was robbed of $3. His wife, Mabel, was also shot. She recovered.

* * *

Essentially, "you just can't arrest a man illegally and profit from his confession," argued Williams' court-appointed attorney, Clyde D. Merritt of the Orleans Indigent Defender Program.

Merritt said "an anonymous telephone call" precipitated his client's arrest . . .

* * *

The jury room in Judge Frank Shea's court darkened and the confiscated film was shown before the judge, attorneys and sheriff's deputies.

The mid-morning showing of two movies seized from the Midtown News bookshop, 4059 Tulane Ave., attracted more than the usual number interested in "the legal technicalities" which comprise an obscenity case, as one deputy put it.

The lights wouldn't go out in the courtroom so Shea, wanting to get the show on the road, moved the troupe into the jury room. "Only people directly connected with the case," announced Shea's minute clerk, "will be allowed in." The room quickly filled up.

The two 10-minute peep shows were, obviously, a welcome diversion to the happenings which occur daily at Criminal District Court.

Except, as defense attorney, Joe Marcal pointed out, the screening was no bachelor's party but rather a serious moment. His client, Donald Plessala, 25, had been charged with two counts of obscenity for allegedly showing the "explicit" films at the bookstore.

"It's amazing," Marcal noted for the record following the screening, "but it's a crime to see these movies in a bookstore, but we can all sit here and watch them and not break the law."

The films, "Hot Teenager" and "The Swimming Party," were seized by vice squad officers Dec. 10.

Shea took the case under advisement (the defense waived a jury trial) for almost one month and rendered his verdict this week. Plessala was found guilty and faces a maximum jail term of one year and a $1,000 fine. Sentencing is set for April 5.

* * *

In an unrelated obscenity case Thursday, Municipal Court Judge Eddie L. Sapir viewed five minutes of "The Massage is the Message," a movie confiscated from the Carrollton theater, and rendered his verdict: "It's obscene—boring, but obscene."

Pierre DeGruy, *New Orleans Times Picayune*, March 26, 1976.

Despite the advantages, defense attorneys face major barriers in raising objections. According to many defense attorneys, the police follow proper procedures most of the time. The task of the lawyer is to separate the out-of-the-ordinary situation from the more numerous ones in which the police have not violated Supreme Court rulings. It is not an easy task. As one lawyer commented: "Illegal searches are hard to get at. . . . The defendant doesn't know if the police had probable cause. Sometimes the police get an anonymous phone call that a burglary is in progress. . . . Or the police get a tip that guns are in a car. Well, the prosecutor doesn't tell you that. You have to root around to find out if probable cause existed. You have to ask, "How did the police get to it in the first place?" A search without probable cause is hard to find out about (Neubauer:173).

Possible violations of *Mapp* or *Miranda* do not come into the lawyer's office prepackaged just awaiting a court hearing. On the contrary the lawyer must frame the issue and determine if enough facts exist to support her contention. Often the attorney is unaided by her client. As the lawyer just quoted went on to say, "For the defendant the case starts when he's arrested. Search and seizure and probable cause, however, start before that."

Not only is it difficult for a defense attorney to develop evidence to support a motion to suppress, it also requires a thorough knowledge of changing appellate court decisions on these matters. As with most other areas in a complex society, only a specialist possesses the necessary knowledge and skill to effectively handle a given problem. The impact of the Supreme Court decisions is tied to the existence of lawyers who keep up on the changes in the law. A study of four Wisconsin cities found that lawyers varied in their knowledge and use of *Miranda* (Milner). In some cities, such as Green Bay, lawyers had only limited knowledge of the Court's decision. In several communities, however, there was at least one lawyer who was particularly knowledgeable about the decision, and it was only in those towns that challenges were raised in court (Milner:111–113).

Defense attorneys' activities in filing pretrial motions are also influenced by the informal norms of the courtroom work group. Pretrial motions require extra work not only for the defense attorney but also for the judge and prosecutor as well. Moreover they often contribute to delay. Defense attorneys who file too many frivolous motions or use them to harass the judge and/or prosecutor can be sanctioned in a variety of ways. One prosecutor told me about a defense attorney who had filed numerous motions in a case, apparently just to make the DA work harder, and after winning the motion (which was unexpected), he gloated over the victory. The DA replied simply that he may have won the battle but not the war. In a subsequent case the defense attorney's client received a harsher-than-normal sentence. The defense attorney is now much more selective in filing pretrial motions. In a similar manner, judges can make uncooperative defense attorneys wait for their cases to be called or refuse to appoint them for indigent defendants.

The courtroom work group has another side, however. For cooperative defense attorneys, it can provide informal avenues of protest. A defense attorney I interviewed believed that one police officer consistently violated procedural rules. But rather than challenge him through formal means, the attorney chose a different route:

> Very few officers use improper means to get a statement. I know because I hear about it when it does occur. But one particular officer I have heard complaints about from all

types of defendants—all races, creeds, crimes, situations, etc. In all of these cases invalid promises are being made to defendants. Invalid promises to get him probation, to keep the case out of the paper, or that no charges will be filed. Of course the officer later denies making any promises. By way of contrast, I have never heard a complaint about some officers.

I have recently informed the court and the state's attorney about this particular officer. If he is not stopped, then I will make a vendetta out of this. I will take case after case until there is enough evidence that they will have to believe that this officer is not telling the truth.

We had the same situation with the sheriff's department. I went to the boss and laid it on the line and it was stopped.

This may sound horrible, but it is the most effective means to stop this sort of thing. Motions to suppress in court don't get anywhere so it is better to try and get to the source. [Neubauer:178]

There was every indication that his informal approach proved effective.

The defensive posture of the prosecutor

A pretrial motion to suppress evidence represents only liabilities for prosecutors. At a minimum, they must do extra work. At a maximum, they may lose the case entirely. Even if they win the suppression motion, they may have to expend extra effort defending that decision on appeal, where they may again lose.

Despite these drawbacks, however, prosecutors maintain the upper hand. For once they need only defend, because in reality the defense attorney bears the burden of proof. Because the police control the information involved, prosecutors are generally in a favorable position to argue against excluding evidence. For example, in most instances the police are able to obtain the defendant's signature on the *Miranda* warning form, which indicates compliance with *Miranda*. Similarly, in a search and seizure case the officers know enough law to know how to testify in order to avoid suppression of evidence. Finally, if the DA finds a case with potential problems, it can be dropped.

Trial judges as decision makers

The decision to suppress evidence rests with the trial judge. After hearing the witness and viewing the physical evidence (if any), the judge makes a legal ruling based on appellate court decisions. Thus trial court judges are key policymakers in applying and implementing Supreme Court decisions concerning confessions and search and seizure.

A pretrial motion is essentially a clash over the facts. Returning to the example of the pretrial motion concerning the armed robbery that may have been faked, recall that the judge accepted the police version of the facts, thus upholding the confession. Such findings are seldom reviewed by appellate courts. On appeal, upper courts examine whether the law was correctly applied by the trial judge. They will rarely scrutinize the facts to which the law was applied. Such deference toward trial judges is based on their proximity to the event. Only trial judges have the opportunity to observe directly how witnesses testify—their responsiveness to questions, their attempts at concealment. Such nuances are not reflected in the trial court transcript. A prosecutor pointed to an additional reason why appellate courts do not scrutinize the trial judge's finding of fact:

> If a defense attorney appeals on an unsuccessful pretrial motion, the appellate court would have to find that the trial judge abused his discretion. When an appeals court reverses in one of these cases they are saying that another judge abused his discretion. They are understandably reluctant to do so. Normally appellate courts accept the trial judge finding of fact because he is closer to the action. [Neubauer:175]

The trial court judge possesses virtually unfettered discretion in making findings of fact. This discretionary power can be used to buttress the judge's opinion on how a matter should be decided. As one attorney put it, "A judge who knows what he is doing can keep making findings of fact so that no appellate court can ever rule he didn't apply the law properly" (Neubauer:175). Thus a judge out of sympathy with Supreme Court decisions, by making findings of facts, can distinguish the given case from the decision that in theory should govern.

> Yes, I've started lying! What the hell, I'd hardly ever convict any of these crooks if I didn't lie at least a little bit. You know what the search and seizure and arrest rules are like nowadays.
>
> Officer Bumper Morgan in Joseph Wambaugh, *The Blue Knight* (New York: Dell Publishing, 1972), p. 215.

How judges view the truthfulness of police officers' testimony is an important consideration. A study of eight newly appointed judges to the city of Detroit's Recorder's Court highlights variations in how judges assess the truthfulness of police testimony (Luskin:35–36). The author analyzed weapons charges of carrying a concealed weapon (CCW) on one's person without a permit to do so and carrying a pistol in a motor vehicle without a permit. CCWs are police-initiated and usually occur in the course of writing a ticket for a traffic violation when the police officer sees the weapon "on view." Since the police officers cannot search a car or person in the course of issuing a ticket, they must have seen the weapon or a portion of it without a search. Whether this is what happened—the defense often claims it is not—the arresting officer will testify that the gun "slid out from under the seat when the car stopped" or "the gun butt was protruding from under some papers on the car seat."

Four judges believed that the police officers frequently lied or at least colored their stories. For a period, one judge kept a list of police officers he thought often gave less than truthful testimony. If these judges found the police officer's story was "too incredible" about the weapons search, they would dismiss the case without a suppression motion. What is particularly interesting is that this group of four judges included one strong advocate of gun control, two former prosecutors, and one former defense attorney. Hence their attitudes reflect their experience on the bench more than their personal ideas formed prior to donning the black robe.

Three other judges, however, held different views. One rated the police as lying only infrequently about the circumstances of arrests and searches. (The views of the eighth judge could not be determined.)

Conclusion

This chapter has examined several important aspects of what occurs while cases are being prepared for trial. One is discovery, the formal or informal exchange of information. What information is subject to discovery varies greatly. Typically, though, defense attorneys who are cooperative members of the courtroom work group receive more information than others. Another important aspect of preparing for trial centers on suppression of evidence. Confessions and physical evidence that have been illegally obtained cannot be used at trial. If the defense believes this has occurred, it files a pretrial motion to suppress the evidence. Prosecutors are usually in a favorable position to show that the evidence was obtained legally.

When an accused pleads not guilty at arraignment, a date for trial is set and bail continued. Typically by this time the defendant is represented by counsel. The plea entered at arraignment may be made with the intention of going to trial or to gain a tactical advantage. The defendant may plan to plead guilty later but may be delaying in order to await assignment of the case to a different judge. The not-guilty plea also allows time for the defense to learn more about the case.

Preparation for trial may be very brief. The day of trial the defense and prosecution may quickly scan their individual files. Or it may be extensive. In a big murder trial, for example, both sides devote considerable time to interviewing witnesses, examining physical evidence, and arguing legal motions.

For discussion

1. What type of discovery law does your state have? Do you think that the defense should have the right to discover the entire case of the state? Do you think there should be a reciprocal requirement for the defense?
2. Discuss with a defense attorney and prosecutor how they prepare for trial. Also ask about their views of the state's discovery law and informal discovery practices.
3. By examining court files and talking to court officials, try to determine how many motions to suppress are filed and how many are granted.
4. Observe a pretrial hearing to suppress evidence. To what extent does the judge's decision depend on what version of the facts he or she accepts?
5. Examine the local newspapers to see how often the press reports that evidence is suppressed. What types of reactions do these stories report—favorable or unfavorable?

References

Brennan, Justice William. "The Criminal Prosecution: Sporting Event or Quest for Truth?" *Washington University Law Quarterly* (1963):279–294.

Brosi, Kathleen. *A Cross-City Comparison of Felony Case Processing.* Washington, D.C.: Institute for Law and Social Research, 1979.

Cipes, Robert. "Crime, Confessions and the Court." *Atlantic Monthly* (September 1966):55.

Kasimar, Yale, Wayne LaFave, and Jerold Israel. *Modern Criminal Procedure,* 4th ed. St. Paul, Minn.: West Publishing, 1974.

Luskin, Mary Lee. "Determinants of Change in Judges' Decisions to Bind Over Defendants for Trial." Paper presented at meeting of American Political Science Association, September 2–5, 1976.

Mather, Lynn. "The Outsider in the Courtroom: An Alternative Role for the Defense." In Herbert Jacob, ed., *The Potential for Reform of Criminal Justice*. Beverly Hills, Calif.: Sage Publications, 1974.

Milner, Neal. *The Court and Local Law Enforcement*. Beverly Hills, Calif.: Sage Publications, 1971.

Neubauer, David. *Criminal Justice in Middle America*. Morristown, N.J.: General Learning Press, 1974.

Oaks, Dallin. "Studying the Exclusionary Rule in Search and Seizure." *University of Chicago Law Review* 37 (1970):665–753.

Uviller, H. Richard. *The Process of Criminal Justice: Adjudication*. St. Paul, Minn.: West Publishing, 1975.

Vera Institute of Justice. *Felony Arrests: Their Prosecution and Disposition in New York City's Courts*. New York: Longman, 1981.

Wasby, Stephen. *The Impact of the United States Supreme Court: Some Perspectives*. Homewood, Ill.: Dorsey Press, 1970.

Wright, Charles. *Handbook of the Law of Federal Courts*, 2d ed. St. Paul, Minn.: West Publishing, 1970.

For further reading

Canon, Bradley. "The Exclusionary Rule: Have Critics Proven That It Doesn't Deter Police?" *Judicature* 62 (March 1979):398–403.

Kamisar, Yale. "Is the Exclusionary Rule an 'Illogical' or 'Unnatural' Interpretation of the Fourth Amendment?" *Judicature 62* (August 1978):66–84

Milner, Neal. *The Court and Local Law Enforcement*. Beverly Hills, Calif.: Sage Publications, 1971.

Schlesinger, Steven. *Exclusionary Injustice: The Problem of Illegally Obtained Evidence*. New York: Marcel Dekker, 1977.

"The Exclusionary Rule: Have Proponents Proven That it is a Deterrent to Police?" *Judicature* 62 (March 1979):404–409.

Wasby, Stephen. *The Impact of the United States Supreme Court: Some Perspectives*. Homewood, Ill.: Dorsey Press, 1970.

Wilkey, Malcolm. "The Exclusionary Rule: Why Suppress Valid Evidence?" *Judicature 62* (November 1978):214–232.

CHAPTER 13

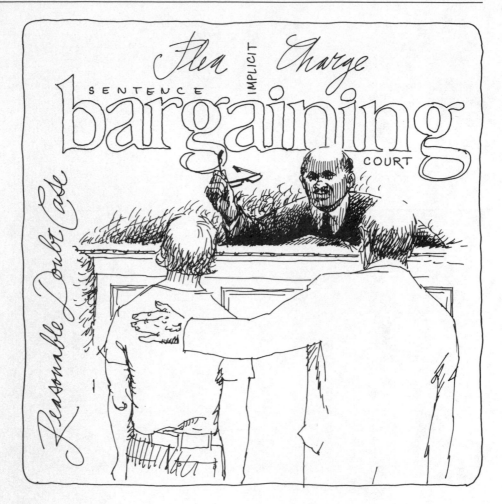

Negotiated Justice and the Plea of Guilty

Although criminal justice is popularly equated with trials, only a handful of defendants are ever tried. Most plead guilty. To some, plea bargaining erodes the very idea of a legal system based on the presumption of innocence and the right to trial. To others, it is a modern-day necessity if the courts are to dispose of their large caseload. All agree, however, that it is the most important stage of the entire criminal court process.

What is plea bargaining? What forms does it take? Why would prosecutors accept a plea of guilty to a lesser charge when there is the possibility of convicting the defendant on a more serious charge? Why would defendants waive their right to be presumed innocent at trial and instead plead guilty to charges as serious as armed robbery or second-degree murder? Are the judge's routine questions of a defendant entering a guilty plea really important? Is plea bargaining a fair and equitable procedure? Why is it that in a system of justice premised on a trial, the vast majority of cases are never tried? These are some of the questions this chapter seeks to answer.

The many faces of plea bargaining

Guilty pleas are the bread and butter of the American criminal courts. Somewhere between 80 and 90 percent of felony convictions are the result not of a guilty verdict after a contested trial but of a voluntary plea by the defendant. The data in table 13-1 demonstrate the pervasiveness of guilty pleas. The possibility of trial shapes all considerations that enter into the decision to enter a plea.

*plea bar-
gaining*

A substantial proportion of guilty pleas are the result of plea bargaining. Through *plea bargaining*—which is also termed negotiating a settlement, copping a plea, or striking a deal—prosecutor, defense attorney, defendant, and sometimes the judge reach an accommodation on the disposition of the case. We can best define plea bargaining as the process through which a defendant pleads guilty to a criminal charge with the expectation of receiving some consideration from the state.

Plea bargaining is a very general term that encompasses a wide range of practices. There is, for example, no agreement among court officials about what is meant (or at least what they mean) by plea bargaining. A major study of twenty-three cities reported that some prosecutors refuse to admit that they engage in bargaining—they simply called it something else (Miller et al.). Any discussion of negotiated justice, therefore, must recognize that there are important variations both in the types of plea agreements and the process by which such agreements are reached.

TABLE 13-1.   Mean guilty plea rate of convictions by population of the jurisdiction in selected states

| States | Jurisdictions by population | | | |
	Up to–100,000	100,000–250,000	250,000–500,000	500,000 & over
Idaho	87.8	94.5	—	—
Illinois	91.4	86.5	82.6	84.0
Kansas	71.0	69.3	69.8	—
Louisiana	72.0	92.8	86.4	85.1
Michigan	86.4	88.8	90.4	93.5
Minnesota	83.6	89.3	85.5	85.4
Missouri	73.8	79.6	—	87.6
New Jersey	96.2	92.3	88.1	88.2
New York	92.1	89.9	94.5	92.7
North Dakota	89.7	—	—	—
Ohio	68.9	80.4	88.8	78.5
Oklahoma	67.3	89.0	90.7	80.9
Pennsylvania	82.3	86.6	85.5	65.6
South Carolina	95.8	97.3	—	—
South Dakota	91.5	—	—	—
Texas	90.9	89.6	92.7	91.6
Utah	71.5	78.8	80.4	—
Vermont	95.2	100.0	—	—
Wyoming	55.4	—	—	—

Source: U.S., Department of Justice, Herbert S. Miller, William F. McDonald, and James A. Cramer, *Plea Bargaining in the United States* (Washington, D.C.: Government Printing Office, 1978), p. 19 (adapted).

Types of plea agreements

explicit bargaining

There are important differences in the types of plea agreements that result from negotiations. Some plea agreements are *explicit:* the defendant pleads guilty with a specific understanding. Others are *implicit:* the defendant pleads guilty in general

implicit bargaining

anticipation of receiving a lenient sentence. Typically plea agreements take one of three forms.

Charge Bargaining.   One inducement a prosecutor can offer in return for a plea

charge bargaining

of guilty is a reduction of charges *(charge bargaining).* A defendant may be allowed to plead guilty to robbery rather than the original charge of armed robbery, for example. Or a defendant enters a plea to misdemeanor theft rather than the initial accusation of felony theft. The principal effect of a plea to a less serious charge is to reduce the potential sentence. Some offenses carry a very stiff maximum sentence. A plea to a lesser charge therefore greatly reduces the possible prison term the defendant will have to serve. Bargains for reduced charges are most commonly found in jurisdictions where the state's criminal code is rigid and/or where prosecutors routinely overcharge to begin with. Thus some charge reductions reflect the probability that the prosecutor would not be able to prove the original charge in a trial.

Count Bargaining.   Another common type of plea agreement is called *count*

count bargaining

bargaining. In return for a defendant's plea of guilty to one (or more) criminal charges, the prosecutor dismisses all other pending charges. For instance, a defendant accused of three burglaries would plead guilty to only one burglary charge, with the two remaining accusations being dismissed. Count bargaining is also typically used in situations in which the defendant engages in what is in essence a single criminal act, but the law specifies several separate and often technical criminal violations. For example, in a forgery case the defendant may be charged not only with forgery but also with uttering (circulating) a forged document, as well as obtaining property by false pretenses (Alschuler, 1968:87).

Like charge reduction agreements, a count bargain reduces the potential sentence but in a very different manner. A defendant charged with many counts theoretically could receive a maximum sentence of something like 135 years, a figure arrived at by multiplying the number of charges by the maximum jail term for each charge and assuming that the judge will sentence the defendant to serve the sentences consecutively (one after another). Such figures are totally unrealistic for consecutive sentences are very rare. In practice, the defendant will often receive the same penalty no matter how few (or how many) charges are involved.

> Discussions of plea bargaining often conjure up images of a Middle Eastern bazaar, in which each transaction appears as a new and distinct encounter, unencumbered by precedent or past association. Every interchange involves higgling and haggling anew, in an effort to obtain the best possible deal. The reality of American lower courts is different. They are more akin to modern supermarkets, in which prices for various commodities have been clearly established and labeled in advance. Arriving at an exchange in this context is not an explicit bargaining process—"You do this for me and I'll do that for you"—designed to reach a mutually acceptable agreement. To the extent

that there is any negotiation at all, it usually focuses on the nature of the case, and the establishment of relevant "facts"—facts that flow from various interpretations of what is and is not said in the police report, rap sheet, and the like. . . . The term plea bargaining has come to refer to almost any type of negotiation, even one in which the defense successfully convinced the prosecutor to drop all charges, which is clearly not a *plea* bargain in the conventional sense of the term.

Malcolm Feeley, "Pleading Guilty in Lower Courts," *Law and Society Review* 13 (1979):462.

sentence bargaining

Sentence Bargaining.   The third common form of plea agreements is called *sentence bargaining.* A plea of guilty is entered in exchange for a promise of leniency in sentencing. There may be a promise that the defendant will be placed on probation or that the prison term will be no more than a given figure, say five years. Typically, in a sentence bargain, the defendant pleads to the original charge (often termed a *plea on the nose*), although in some areas sentence bargaining operates in conjunction with either count bargaining or charge reduction bargaining.

Invariably in sentence bargaining, the defendant receives less than the maximum penalty. To some this is an indication that defendants get off too easily. Realistically, though, only defendants with long criminal records who have committed particularly heinous crimes will receive the maximum. In practice, courts impose sentence on the basis of normal penalties for specific crimes involving typical types of defendants. Thus in sentence bargaining the sentence agreed to is the one that is typically imposed in cases like this one.

The bargaining process

The process by which a plea agreement is reached varies greatly from court to court and often from judge to judge in a given jurisdiction. Some judges are major participants in the bargaining process. They will, for example, agree ahead of time that if the defendant enters a plea of guilty, a specific sentence (sentence bargaining) will be imposed. Other judges refuse to participate in bargaining at all. Here prosecutors dominate the bargaining process.

How negotiations are conducted varies. At times negotiations are rather casual:

The elevator doors opened into a smoky, crowded corridor at the Hall of Justice. Stepping out, a deputy public defender encounters a deputy district attorney.
   "Hey," said the defender hurriedly, "How about Alvarado? We plead and you recommend 45 days."
   "No way," replied the D.A.'s man. "Gotta have at least 90."
   "Oh," said the defender, moving on down the corridor, "We'll think about 60."
[Hager]

Contrast this example with the institutionalization of plea bargaining in Detroit's Recorder's Court, where for every four judges there is only one assistant prosecutor authorized to negotiate guilty pleas. After the state has made an offer, the defense attorney must sign a form indicating the nature of the plea bargain offered. To complicate matters still further, a handful of courts (Baltimore, Pittsburgh, and Los Angeles are prime examples) employ a procedure termed a *slow plea* (part plea, part trial). A slow plea involves a short (usually fifteen-minute) bench trial in which the defense does not contest the issue of guilt but rather presents favorable evidence about the defendant in hopes that the judge will impose a light sentence (Levin:80; Mather:190; Eisenstein and Jacob:250).

The context of plea bargaining

These varying practices illustrate that the process of negotiated justice does not operate in isolation from the other stages of the criminal court process. What has gone before—the setting of bail, the return of a grand jury indictment, the prosecutor's evaluation of the strengths of a case are prime examples—is intimately intertwined with how courts dispose of cases on a plea. The opposite is equally true. Throughout the life history of a case, decisions on bail, indictment, or screening have been premised on the assumption that the vast majority of defendants will end up pleading guilty. The place to begin in analyzing the diversity of negotiated justice is with the context of plea bargaining.

The common explanation for plea bargaining is that the courts have too many cases. Plea bargaining is usually portrayed as a regrettable but necessary expedient for disposing of cases. Chapter 5 argued that although this explanation contains some truth, it obscures too many important facets of what the courts do and why. Certainly the press of cases and lack of adequate resources shape the criminal court process—plea bargaining included. Certainly because prosecutors need to move cases, they agree to a more lenient plea than they might prefer. But the excess caseload hypothesis cannot explain why plea bargaining is as prevalent in courts with heavy caseloads as it is in courts with relatively few cases (Eisenstein and Jacob:238).

The principal weakness of the excess caseload hypothesis is that it assumes a purely mechanical process, while ignoring the underlying dynamics of the process. It seems to suggest that if there were only more judges, prosecutors, defense attorneys, and courtrooms, there would be many more trials, and the penalties imposed on the guilty would also increase. Such a view ignores the context of plea bargaining. Plea bargaining is a response to some fundamental issues, the first of which centers on the question of guilt.

Presumption of factual guilt

It is important to recall from chapters 9 and 10 that the bulk of the legally innocent defendants are removed from the criminal court process during the screening process through the preliminary hearing, grand jury, and/or the prosecutor's charging decision. By the time a case reaches the trial stage, the courtroom work group presumes that the defendant is probably guilty. Survival through the prior processing means that prosecutors, defense attorneys, and judges alike perceive that trial defendants are in serious trouble (Eisenstein and Jacob:231).

dead bang case   The following case illustrates what some court officials term a *dead bang case,* a case with very strong evidence against the defendant and with no credible explanation by the defendant for innocence (Mather:198):

A neighbor saw a young black man entering the rear door of the house. The police were called and arrested the defendant, Ronald Phillips (not his actual name but the case is a real one nonetheless) within a block of the house in possession of a color TV set. According to Phillips the TV came from his "Aunt's" house. [Winsberg]

One Illinois state's attorney summarized the strong evidence of guilt in cases like this one: "The pervasiveness of the facts should indicate to any competent attorney that the element of prosecution is present and a successful prosecution is forthcoming" (Neubauer:200).

> Prosecutors and state's attorneys learn that their roles primarily entail the processing of factually guilty defendants. Contrary to their expectations that problems of establishing factual guilt would be central to their job, they find that in most cases the evidence in the file is sufficient to conclude (and prove) that the defendant is factually guilty. . . . Of the cases that remain after the initial screening, the prosecutor believes the majority of defendants to be factually guilty.
>
> Furthermore, he finds that defense attorneys only infrequently contest the prosecutor's own conclusion that the defendant is guilty. In their initial approach to the prosecutor they may raise the possibility that the defendant is factually innocent, but in most subsequent discussions their advances focus on disposition and not on the problem of factual guilt. Thus, from the prosecutor's own reading of the file (after screening) and from the comments of his "adversary," he learns that he begins with the upper hand; more often than not, the factual guilt of the defendant is not really disputable.
>
> Milton Heumann, *Plea Bargaining* (Chicago: University of Chicago Press, 1978), p. 100.

No two cases are ever the same, of course. Many discussions of plea bargains leave the false impression that the attorneys haggle only over the sentence. This is not true. Courtroom work groups spend a lot of time discussing and analyzing how the crime was committed, the nature of the victims and witnesses, and the background of the defendant. In most cases, however, there is little likelihood of the defendant's receiving an outright acquittal, only that he or she might be convicted of a less serious offense. The question of what charge the facts will support is an important part of plea bargaining.

Costs and risks of trial

Trials are a costly and time-consuming means for establishing guilt. Consider our earlier example. To try Ronald Phillip's case would probably take two days and require the presence of the judge, bailiff, clerk, defense attorney, prosecutor, and court reporter. During this period, none could devote much time to the numerous other cases requiring disposition. Moreover each would be forced to spend time preparing for this trial. A trial would also require the presence of numerous non-court personnel: police officers, witnesses, victims, the defendant, and twelve jurors. For each of these persons, a trial represents an intrusion into their daily lives.

Based on these considerations, all members of the courtroom work group have a common interest in disposing of cases and avoiding unnecessary trials. Their reasons diverge: judges and prosecutors want high disposition rates in order to prevent case backlogs and to present a public impression that the process is running well. Public defenders prefer quick dispositions because they lack enough people to handle the caseload. Because most clients of private defense attorneys can afford only a modest fee, these attorneys are dependant on a high turnover of cases to earn enough money. All members of the courtroom work group, then, have more cases to try than time (or resources) to try them (Eisenstein and Jacob:26).

To a large extent, then, a trial is a mutual penalty that all parties seek to avoid through plea bargaining. To be sure not all trials are avoided. But through plea bargaining the scarce resources of trial can be applied to the types of cases that should be tried.

What to do with the guilty

The adversary proceedings of trial are designed to resolve conflict over guilt or innocence. In practice, however, it is not the issue of legal guilt that is disputed but what sentence to impose. Decisions on sentencing do not involve the simple alternative of the yes or no issue of guilt present at trial. Rather they incorporate difficult judgment issues about the type of the crime and the nature of the defendant. Moreover, because of the standards of evidence, the type of information relevant to sentencing is not easily introduced at trial (Mather: 188). Unlike a trial, plea bargaining does focus on what to do with an offender—particularly how much leniency is appropriate. The case of Ronald Phillips illustrates these factors. Whether the stolen color television came from Phillip's aunt's house is not relevant to the issue of legal guilt. It may, however, be highly important when it comes to sentencing. For if the victim was really the aunt, this might suggest that the crime was not one of economic motive, but stemmed from a family dispute. (In this case, however, it turned out the victim was not truly Phillip's aunt.)

Criminal statutes are broad and encompassing. The courtroom work group is called upon to apply these broad prohibitions to very specific and variable cases. They are concerned with adjusting the penalties to the specifics of the crime and the defendant. In the interest of fairness, they seek to individualize justice. Consider a case with two co-defendants with unequal culpability—for example, an armed robbery involving an experienced robber who employed a youthful accomplice as a driver. Technically both are equally guilty, but in the interest of fairness and justice, the prosecutor may legitimately decide to make a concession to the young accomplice but none to the prime mover. How members of the courtroom work group individualize justice is greatly shaped by the criminal code under which they work.

The criminal code

The dynamics and goals of plea bargaining are a reflection of how crimes are legally defined and the penalty structure provided for these violations. The close relationship between plea bargaining practices and the state's sentencing structure are illustrated by Donald Newman's study of plea bargaining in three states, Wisconsin, Michigan, and Kansas. Newman uses the following common type of burglary to illustrate the point:

A defendant was arrested by a policeman in the act of stealing electrical appliances from a warehouse at 3:00 A.M. He had gained entry to the building by forcing a rear door with a crowbar. [Newman:55]

In Wisconsin, the defendant would probably be charged with burglary and plead on the nose to that offense. In Michigan, by contrast, the defendant would likely be charged with breaking and entering in the nighttime and later would plead to the reduced charge of breaking and entering in the daytime. In Kansas, on the other hand, the initial charge would be first-degree burglary with a later plea to the lesser offense of third-degree burglary. These differences in customary ways of dealing with cases are largely the result of differences in sentencing structure in the states. In Wisconsin sentencing laws are very flexible, leaving great discretion to the judge. As a result guilty pleas involve little explicit bargaining. In Michigan and Kansas, legislative statutes have fixed sentencing to allow for little judicial discre-

---

CLOSE-UP: NAME OF THE GAME IS PLEA BARGAINING

The public defender stuck a patent-leather loafer on the lowest rung of the holding cell and wedged an elbow in between the gray steel bars. "Cedric," he said quietly, "Cedric, listen to me, please."

Cedric looked back at him without an emotion crossing the flat, black expanse of his face.

"Cedric, how are we going to explain the coats in the back of the car?" the defender asked. "Somebody's going to want to know how they got there."

The pale sunlight came into the cell in neat squares through the wire mesh windows. On the floor behind Cedric, bundled heaps of men tried to escape into unconsciousness. Every now and then one would mumble in his half-sleep or lash out with a savage elbow to protect his floorspace.

"Uh, look," Cedric said, the barest of smiles on his lips. "We just say somebody threw them there, you know, was running by and threw them in."

Kent Brody, the defender, took his foot off the cross-bar and looked directly at Cedric. They were both young, each almost with a baby face, but more than just jail bars separated them.

"Cedric, there comes a time to face facts," Brody said. "The facts of the case are against you. We both know it. They offered a better deal than I thought. They offered flat time on the armed robbery and that would cover the arson and the probation violation. I assumed they'd give a spread, but they are offering you flat time, Cedric."

Cedric was not impressed. He gripped the bars, but casually, his slim body leaning gently against the steel, he said nothing.

"OK," said Brody, "Four years is a long time, but armed robbery carries a minimum of four to life, Cedric. You don't want it. OK. But if you get convicted, it won't be the minimum."

There was a pause and Cedric spoke softly. "Fight it," he said.

"Sure," Brody said. "Fine. OK now, so what's our defense? How'd the stuff get in the car, Cedric?"

Cedric Malthia may not know much about the law, but he knows what he likes. And he doesn't like the idea of going to prison for four years in exchange for saying he held up a clothing store at gunpoint. No, for a four-year sentence he was not going to say it.

Now if Brody had gotten him the deal he asked for, it might have been different. If that gun had been made to magically disappear and he had been offered two on a simple robbery, now that he might go along with. He might save the state the trouble of proving him guilty for that. He might take the plea bargain if they would agree to two. . . .

But Cedric was not co-operating. Not yet, anyway. For while the system may be in a hurry, Cedric had nothing but time.

Excerpted from a *Chicago Sun-Times* article by Roger Simon. Copyright © Chicago Sun-Times, 1975. Reprinted with permission.

tion in sentencing. As a result, these states are marked by a widespread use of explicit bargaining, especially charge reduction bargaining (Newman:56). Often members of the courtroom work group enter into plea agreements because they perceive the penalties to be inappropriately harsh.

Sentencing provisions in many states are very severe because those who draft the laws have in mind the worst offenders: professional, hardened, and violent criminals. Courtroom work groups rarely, however, encounter such stereotyped bad guys. Most defendants are less threatening and less dangerous than the formal law envisions. Where legislative definitions of serious offenses are at odds with the courts' definition of serious and threatening violations, plea bargaining provides flexibility in making adjustments.

Bargaining and courtroom work groups

Plea bargaining is a contest involving the prosecutor, defendant, defense counsel, and, at times, the judge. Each party has its own objectives. Each attempts to structure the situation to its own advantage by employing tactics to improve its bargaining position. Each views success in reaching their objectives from its own perspective. Within these conflicting objectives accommodations are possible because each side can achieve its objectives only by making concessions on other matters. Plea bargaining is typical of "most bargaining situations which ultimately involve some range of possible outcomes within which each party would rather make a concession than fail to reach agreement at all" (Schelling:70). Bargaining is also possible because each of the legal actors understands the context of plea bargaining: the presumption of guilt, the costs and uncertainties of trial, the concern with arriving at an appropriate sentence, and the nature of the criminal code. All of these factors influence bargaining positions.

Prosecutors

To the prosecutor, a plea bargain represents the certainty of conviction without the risks of trial. Recall that prosecutors emphasize convictions. Because they value the deterrent objectives of law enforcement, they prefer that those guilty of a crime be convicted of some charge rather than escape with no conviction at all. Not incidentally a conviction by a plea also allows prosecutors to project to the public an image that criminals are being convicted.

The certainty and finality of the defendant's pleading guilty contrasts sharply with the potential risks at trial. During trial a number of unexpected things can occur, most of them to the detriment of the prosecutor. The victim may refuse to cooperate. Witnesses' testimony may differ significantly from earlier statements made in investigative reports. A witness may make an unfavorable impression on the jury. Moreover, there is always the possibility that a mistrial (the judge ends the trial without a verdict because of a major defect in the proceedings) will be declared and even after a jury verdict of guilty the appellate courts may reverse, thus necessitating that the whole process be repeated.

Plea bargains can also benefit prosecutors. Police reward informants with promises of reduced charges or leniency, promises they expect prosecutors to honor. Through plea bargaining the prosecutor can accommodate such requests. Similarly prosecutors use plea bargains to reward cooperative defendants. A typical example would be a crime involving a major figure and a secondary one. In exchange for providing evidence against the major figure, the secondary one may be allowed to enter a plea to a less serious charge, greatly increasing the likelihood of conviction of the major figure.

In seeking a conviction through a guilty plea, the prosecutor is in a unique position to control the negotiating process. To begin with, the prosecutor proceeds from a position of strength: in most cases the state has sufficient evidence for conviction. A survey of chief prosecutors in various states showed that the strength of the state's case was the most important (85 percent) motivation in this bargaining decision (Vetri:901). If, however, the case is weak, the prosecutor can avoid the embarrassment of losing a case at trial by either dismissing it all together or offering such a good deal that the defendant cannot refuse.

To improve their bargaining position, it is common practice for some prosecutors to overcharge deliberately:

> "Sure, it's a lever," says one San Francisco prosecutor, referring to his office's practice of charging every non-automobile homicide as murder. With unusual candor he adds, "And we charge theft, burglary, and the possession of burglar's tools, because we know that if we charged only burglary there would be a trial." [Alschuler, 1968:90]

This is not a universal practice, however. The chief assistant prosecutor of Minneapolis described attempts to reduce charges as follows:

> It's the attitude of my boss, and it was the attitude of his predecessor, that we stick with the charge on the "information" unless some new evidence comes up. When we move to reduce a charge our boss asks us if the evidence was good when the "information" was issued. Then he wants to know what we have learned since to justify a reduction. . . . We also don't reduce charges as much as the East because we're not yet in that position of tremendous caseload pressure. [Levin:70–71]

Prosecutors, of course, control several of the forms of plea bargaining, including the ability to offer a charge reduction or a count bargain. In general, they can threaten to throw the book at a defendant who does not plead. Or they may refuse to bargain at all. If the crime is a serious one and the defendant is viewed as very dangerous, the prosecutor may force the defendant either to plead on the nose with no sentencing concessions or run the additional risk of trial.

Defendant

But if a plea gives the prosecutor a much sought after conviction, why do defendants plead guilty? To understand plea bargaining it is important to recognize that it is often in the defendant's best interest to give up the right to be presumed innocent at a trial. The primary benefit of a plea is the possibility of a lenient sentence.

Around the courthouse, it is a common perception that defendants who refuse to plead guilty receive harsher sentences. Sometimes the penalty for going to trial works indirectly. For example, a judge may impose a higher sentence because the defendant compounded the crime by lying on the witness stand or getting some friends to perjure themselves. Or during a trial the full details of the crime will emerge—often to the detriment of the defendant. On a plea, though, the judge will be shielded from such details. Finally, a prosecutor may agree not to invoke the state career criminal provisions that impose higher penalties for those with a prior felony conviction.

Pleading guilty may also benefit defendants in ways not directly tied to sentencing. For poor defendants unable to post bail, a guilty plea can mean an immediate release either on probation or for time served or a transfer to better prison facilities and the beginning of serving the sentence. A plea can also mean the opportunity to avoid a conviction for a crime with an undesirable label—rapist or homosexual—by pleading to an offense with a less pejorative title, and it can avoid the possibility of embarrassing publicity of a trial.

Ultimately defendants must decide whether to go along with the plea bargain or take their chances at trial. Few defendants are in a position to make a reasoned choice between the advantages of a plea and the disadvantages of a trial; most are poor, inarticulate, and have little formal education. For these defendants the experience in the courts is like their life on the streets: one goes along. Often softened up by the experience in jail awaiting trial, many defendants find that entering a plea is the best way to go along and avoid the possibility of even harsher penalties.

Defense counsel

If the prosecutor enters negotiations from a position of strength, the opposite is true of the defense attorneys, who have few bargaining chips. They may, however, attempt to gain some tactical advantages through several maneuvers. For one, they can seek to drag out the case in hopes that witnesses and victims lose interest or otherwise become unavailable. For another, they may file pretrial motions either to suppress the confession or the evidence that was seized. Finally they can threaten to go to trial. But if the chances of winning are not high, and they rarely are, they must also consider the strong possibility that after a trial conviction, the defendant may be penalized with a higher prison sentence.

In recognition of the fact that the defense starts from a position of weakness, it is generally up to the defense attorney to initiate plea discussions. These discussions may occur at any time in the case—shortly after arrest, at the arraignment on the indictment, or, most likely, shortly before the trial date. The lawyers' main resource is their knowledge of the courtroom work group—the types of pleas the prosecutor usually enters, the type of sentence the judge normally imposes in cases like this, and so on.

Defense attorneys act as classic negotiators, trying to get both the best deal possible for their clients while at the same time explaining to the clients the realistic alternatives. As we noted in chapter 8, there can be conflict in these two roles. A defense attorney, for example may negotiate what she considers the best deal given the circumstances, only to have her client refuse to go along.

In this relationship there is an understandable concern that a few defense attorneys manipulate clients. For example, defense attorneys might tell a client that the prosecutor is pushing a hard deal in this case and is insisting on a seven-year jail term. The defendant says he will not do more than four. Yet the defense attorney and prosecutor have not yet talked. When later they do, the prosecutor suggests a five-year sentence, the defense attorney says his client wants probation but he might agree. When the defendant is informed that the state will go with five, the impression is left that the defense attorney is really a great bargainer (Winsberg). The judge who provided this example concluded by saying that if he has any indication that the defense attorney is manipulating his client in such a fashion, he will monitor the attorney closely.

> There are some attorneys with whom we never bargain, because we can't. We don't like to penalize a defendant because he has an ass for an attorney, but when an attorney cannot be trusted, we have no alternative.
>
> Prosecutor quoted in Albert Alschuler, "The Prosecutor's Role in Plea Bargaining," *University of Chicago Law Review* 36 (1968):87

Judges

Several factors limit a judge's ability to control, supervise, or participate in plea bargaining. Given the divisions of powers of the adversary system, judges are reluctant to intrude on prosecutorial discretion. Prosecutors control many of the key bargaining mechanisms—specifically the charges filed and the charges to allow the defendant to plead to. Thus, when a prosecutor, defense attorney, and defendant have agreed either to a count bargaining or a charge reduction bargaining, the judge has no legal authority to refuse to accept the plea.

Even more fundamentally, however, the judge knows relatively little about each case. Only the prosecutor, defendant, and defense attorney know the evidence for and against the defendant. Without a knowledge of why the parties agreed to a plea bargain, it is obviously difficult for a judge to reject a plea agreement. In short, the judge is dependent on the prosecutor and, to a lesser extent, the defense attorney.

Within these restraints, though, judges have a limited ability to shape the plea bargaining process. The extent to which they are involved in the process varies greatly. A survey of state trial court judges revealed four basic patterns. Some judges are actively involved in plea negotiations. They make recommendations about the disposition of cases. Seven percent of the judges fall into this category. A second set of judges is indirectly involved. They review the recommendations made by defense and prosecutor. Twenty percent of the judges reported such participation. Next, a small percentage of judges (4 percent) attend plea discussions but do not participate. By far the largest category involves judges who do not attend plea negotiating sessions. Rather, their role is limited to ratifying agreements reached by others. Fully 69 percent of the judges fall into this category (Ryan and Alfini:486). Even judges who only ratify plea negotiations can have an important impact on the process. Regular members of the courtroom work group know the sentence the judge is likely to impose. They, therefore, negotiate case dispositions incorporating these sentencing expectations. On rare occasions judges may reject a plea agreement. Such rejections serve to set a baseline for future negotiations.

The extent to which a judge is actively involved in the plea bargaining negotiations is influenced by a number of factors. One is the judge's perceptions of his or her negotiating skills. Judges who view themselves as having good negotiating skills are more likely to be active participants. Judges in large cities are also more likely to be active participants. More stable courtroom work groups tend to encourage judicial involvement. In addition, a judge's expectation that a trial will be lengthy encourages his or her active participation. Acting to discourage judicial involvement are state rules and state court decisions. Some states have adopted clear statements prohibiting judges from participating in plea negotiations. In these states, naturally, judicial participation is rare (Ryan and Alfini, 1979). It appears that judicial participation is shaped by forces involving the judge's individual talents as well as the type of court over which he or she presides.

Dynamics of bargaining

Negotiations are a group activity. Through working together on a daily basis, the members of the courtroom work group come to understand the problems and demands of the others. They develop shared conceptions of how given types of cases and given types of defendants should be disposed of. Everyone except the outsider or the novice knows these customs of the courthouse.

These shared norms provide structure to plea negotiations. In each courtroom work group there is a well-understood set of allowable reductions. Based on the typical manner in which the crime is committed and the typical background of the defendant, nighttime burglary will be reduced to daytime burglary, drunkenness to disturbing the peace, and so on. Writing about a misdemeanor court, Malcolm Feeley offers an economic analogy of shared norms.

> It is the salesman's stock-in-trade to represent a "going rate" as if it were a special sale price offered only once. The gap between theoretical exposure and the standard rate allows defense attorneys and prosecutors to function much the same way, making the defendant think he is getting a special "deal" when in fact he is getting the standard rate. Together prosecutors and defense attorneys operate like discount stores, pointing to a never-used high list price and then marketing the product at a supposedly "special" sale price, thereby appearing to provide substantial savings to those who act quickly. [p. 191]

Contrary to many popular fears, defendants are not allowed to plead to just any charge. If a defendant has been charged with armed robbery, the defense attorney knows that the credibility of her bargaining position will be destroyed if she suggests a plea to disturbing the peace. Such a plea would be out of line with how things are normally done. Courtroom work groups have similar shared norms about sentencing.

On the basis of these shared norms, all parties know what is open for bargaining and what is not. The following example is a good one:

On a three count forgery case, the defense attorney asks the D.A., "Can I have one count?" The D.A. says, "Yes, which one?" The defense attorney says "Count 2." And that's it. No bargain has been made. No promise made that counts 1 and 3 will be dismissed in exchange for the plea to count 2. *It's simply that everyone knows what the standard practice is.* [Mather:199]

These shared norms provide a baseline around which specific cases are disposed of. Around this baseline sentence, there will be upward or downward adjustments, depending on the circumstances of the individual case.

Why cases go to trial

Although most cases are disposed of by a guilty plea, an important percentage (10 to 20 percent) of defendants are tried. Cases go to trial when the parties cannot settle a case through negotiation. Thus in large measure the factors that shape plea bargaining—the strength of the prosecutor's case and the severity of the penalty— are the same ones that enter into the decision to go to trial. Defense attorneys recommend a trial when the risks of trial are low and the possible gains are high.

reasonable doubt case
This broad calculation leads to two very different types of trial cases. In one, the possible gains for the defendant are high because there is a chance of an acquittal. There may be *reasonable doubt* that the defendant committed any crime, or two sets of witnesses may tell conflicting versions of what happened (Neubauer:232). A second category of cases going to trial involves situations in which the prison sentence will be high. Even though a judge or jury is not likely to return a not guilty verdict, the defendant may still decide that the slim probability of an acquittal is worth the risks of the trial penalty.

Not all trial cases, however, are the result of such rational calculations. Some defendants want a trial no matter what. Judges, prosecutors, and defense attorneys label as irrational defendants who refuse to recognize the realities of the criminal justice system and insist on a trial even when the state has a strong case (Neubauer:233–234).

The net effect of these plea versus trial considerations is that some types of cases are more likely to go to trial than others. Table 13-2 presents data from a study in a large metropolitan court, Los Angeles. Property offenses (burglary, theft, forgery) are unlikely to go to trial because the state is apt to have a strong case (usually buttressed by the presence of indisputable physical evidence) and the prison sentence will not be long. Serious crimes like murder, rape, and robbery are much more likely to be tried. In these crimes of violence, there may be reasonable doubt because the victim may have provoked the attack. Moreover, a convicted defendant is likely to serve a long prison term and therefore more disposed to take the chances on an outright acquittal.

There are widespread variations in the decision to go to trial. Southern states have an average of seventy trials per 100,000 population compared to the national average of thirty-four (Kalven and Zeisel:502–503). In some rural areas, trials occur only once a decade, but in other rural places, trials are more common.

TABLE 13-2. Rank ordering of trial disposition of felony defendants in Los Angeles Superior Court, 1970

Offense	Total defendants	Percentage of defendants disposed of by full court or jury
Homicide	398	36.1%
Kidnapping	189	28.0
Rape, forcible	391	27.1
Other sex offenses	769	22.9
Robbery	1,875	22.2
Assault	1,640	21.5
Opiates	1,250	16.8
Hit and run	109	13.7
Theft, except auto	2,092	11.1
Deadly weapons	377	10.6
Burglary	4,670	10.4
Manslaughter, vehicular	69	10.1
Theft, auto	1,582	9.4
Drunk driving	371	8.6
Marijuana	5,529	8.2
Dangerous drugs	6,851	8.2
Other drug violation	194	7.2
Forgery and checks	2,107	6.2
Bookmaking	701	5.0
Escape	146	2.7
Other	261	16.8
Total	31,571	11.6%

Source: Bureau of Criminal Statistics, State of California, n.d. Cited in Lynn Mather, "Some Determinants of the Method of Case Disposition: Decision-Making by Public Defenders in Los Angeles," *Law and Society Review* 8 (Winter 1974):248.

Jury trial penalty

jury trial penalty

Although most defendants plead guilty, a significant minority of cases do go to trial. As previously indicated, it is a common assumption in courthouses around the nation that defendants who do not enter a plea of guilty can expect to receive harsher sentences. Typically called the *jury trial penalty*, the notion reflects a philosophy of "He takes some of my time; I take some of his." Here *time* refers to the hours spent hearing evidence presented to a jury (Uhlman and Walker). This is how one judge expressed his philosophy:

If someone has a trial and it's apparent that there is some question of a good defense . . . then the sentence is probably no harsher than it would have been if he'd entered a plea. It's a delight to have a good trial, handled by a good attorney. He knows what he is doing and comes up with sharp things during the trial. . . . But I think there are times when you see a completely frivolous trial which . . . is a waste of everyone's time. Take the guy who is caught with his hand in the till, and there's no question but that he's guilty. And the case is still tried, and his hands are still in the till, and he hasn't been able to get them out, and you wonder why he's wasted everyone's time. . . . [Heumann:142]

Several recent studies have provided empirical documentation for these court-house perceptions. One study of a major eastern city concluded that "the cost of a jury trial for convicted defendants in Metro City is high: sentences are substantially more severe than for other defendants" (Uhlmann and Walker:337). The same conclusions emerged in a study of three California counties (Brereton and Casper). Such findings, however, have not gone unchallenged. Research conducted on some other courts was unable to document the existence of a jury trial penalty. In their three-city study, Eisenstein and Jacob concluded that "the effect of disposi-tional mode was insignificant in accounting for the variance in sentence length" (270). Their conclusion was supported by a study in Washington, D.C. (Rhodes). Read together these various studies suggest that it is very difficult to make conclu-sions about nationwide practices, because of the tremendous amount of discrepan-cies among jurisdictions. Moreover, it appears that the jury trial penalty may be applied more selectively than earlier research indicated.

Despite the uncertainty over the extent of the jury trial penalty, the U.S. Su-preme Court has clearly sanctioned the practice. A Kentucky defendant accused of forging an $88.30 check was offered a five-year prison sentence if he entered a plea of guilty. But the prosecutor indicated that if the defendant rejected the offer, the state would seek to impose a life imprisonment because of the defendant's previ-ous two felony convictions. Such enhanced sentences for habitual criminals were allowed at that time by Kentucky law. The defendant rejected the plea, went to trial, was convicted, and was eventually sentenced to life imprisonment. In *Borden-kircher* v. *Hayes* (434 U.S. 357, 1978), the high court held that "The course of conduct engaged in by the prosecutor in this case, which no more than openly presented the defendant with the unpleasant alternative of forgoing trial or facing charges on which he was plainly subject to prosecution" did not violate constitu-tional protections. In dissent, however, Justice Powell noted that the offer of five years in prison "hardly could be characterized as a generous offer." He was clearly troubled that "persons convicted of rape and murder often are not punished so severely" as this check forger.

Copping a plea

"Your honor, my client wishes at this time to withdraw his previous plea of not guilty and wishes at this time to enter a plea of guilty." In phrases very similar to this one, defense attorneys indicate that the case is about to end; the defendant is ready to plead. A plea of guilty is more than an admission of conduct; it is a conviction that also involves a defendant's waiver of the most vital rights of the court process: presumption of innocence, jury trial, and confrontation of witnesses (*Boykin* v. *Alabama*, 395 U.S. 238 1969).

For defendants in a crowded urban court, the entry of the plea may be nothing more than a hurried, confused period of standing before a judge and mumbling the expected words. For others, it represents a careful and dignified proceeding. Until fairly recently, the taking of a guilty plea operated in an informal manner and was largely dependent on what local court officials believed should be done. Because the courts and the legal process as a whole were reluctant to recognize the existence of plea bargaining, little statutory or case law guided the process. Under the leadership of Chief Justice Warren Burger, however, the U.S. Supreme Court has sought to set standards for the plea bargaining process.

Questioning the defendant

Boykin v. *Alabama*

Before a defendant's plea of guilty can be accepted, the judge must question the defendant. This was not always the case. Judges merely accepted the attorney's statement that the defendant wanted to plead guilty. But in *Boykin* v. *Alabama* in 1969, the Supreme Court ruled: "It was error, for the trial judge to accept petitioner's guilty plea without an affirmative showing that it was intelligent and voluntary."

In questioning the defendant, the judge inquires whether the defendant understands the nature of the charge, the possible penalty upon conviction, whether any threats were made, if the defendant is satisfied with the services of defense counsel, and whether the defendant realizes that a plea waives right to a jury trial (see figure 13-1). In theory, such questioning serves to ensure that the guilty plea reflects the defendant's own choice, is made with a general understanding of the charges and consequences of conviction, and was not improperly influenced by prosecution, law enforcement officials, or the defendant's own attorney. Such questioning also provides an official court record designed to prevent defendants from later contending they were forced to plead guilty.

Some courts go a step further by also requiring that a brief summary of the case be entered in the record. Either a law enforcement officer or the prosecutor states that if a trial were held, the evidence would show the defendant is guilty and then proceeds to summarize the evidence sufficient to prove each of the elements of the offense. The defendant then has the opportunity to offer any corrections or additions.

Accepting a plea

Alford v. *North Carolina*

Judges have discretion in deciding whether to accept the defendant's plea of guilty. Some judges refuse to do so unless the defendant fully admits guilt. If the defendant wishes to plead guilty but refuses to admit any wrongdoing, the judge may reject the plea and order the case to be tried. Other judges insist on a less stringent admission of wrongdoing. This issue arose in a case where the defendant was indicted for first-degree murder, a capital offense. The defendant protested his innocence but entered a plea anyway, saying: "I pleaded guilty on second-degree murder because they said there is too much evidence, but I ain't shot no man. . . . I just pleaded guilty because they said if I didn't they would gas me for it. . . . I'm not guilty but I pleaded guilty." The Court held that given the defendant's desire to avoid the death penalty and the existence of substantial evidence of guilt, the plea of guilty was valid (*Alford* v. *North Carolina* 400 U.S. 25, 1971).

Placing the plea agreement on the record

Until the mid-1960s, plea negotiations were still officially denied (President's Commission on Law Enforcement and Administration of Justice: 135–136). As a result, the taking of a plea was often a sham. The defendant was expected to lie by denying that a deal had been made. This is how one defendant described the experience:

> Did your lawyer tell you how to answer them beforehand? No, but you know how to answer them. He [the judge] asked me, you know, like had you ever been—you haven't been offered any kind of deal or nothing. He didn't put in that word, but it was meant the same thing. You have to say "No." If anybody's in the courtroom, you gotta make a little show for them. [Casper:84]

To prevent the possibility of covering up plea bargaining, some courts now require that a plea agreement be placed on the record. This public disclosure allows defendants and attorneys to correct any misunderstandings.

To ensure fairness in negotiations between defense and prosecution, the law now provides defendants with a limited right to withdraw a guilty plea. In the case *Santobello v.* of *Santobello* v. *New York,* (404 U.S. 257, 1971), the prosecutor agreed to permit the *New York* defendant to plead to a less serious offense and to make no recommendations as to sentencing. Months later at the sentencing hearing, however, a new prosecutor, apparently ignorant of his colleague's commitment, recommended the maximum sentence, which the judge imposed. The defendant was not allowed to withdraw the plea. Chief Justice Burger's opinion ordered that the defendant be allowed to withdraw the plea, arguing, "When a plea rests in any significant degree on a promise or agreement of the prosecutor, so that it can be said to be a part of the inducement or consideration, such promise must be fulfilled."

Figure 13-1.   Institutionalizing plea bargaining—a sample *Boykin* form.

CRIMINAL DISTRICT COURT
PARISH OF ORLEANS
STATE OF LOUISIANA
SECTION "C"

JUDGE JEROME M. WINSBERG

STATE OF LOUISIANA   CASE NO. _____

VERSUS   VIO. _____

_____

**WAIVER OF CONSTITUTIONAL RIGHTS
PLEA OF GUILTY**

I, _____, before my Plea of Guilty to the crime of _____, have been informed and understand the charge to which I'm pleading guilty.

_____

I understand that I have a right to trial by Judge or Jury, and if convicted, a right to appeal. And by entering a plea of guilty in this case, I am waiving my rights to trial and appeal. _____

The acts constituting the offense to which I am pleading guilty have been explained to me as well as the fact that for this crime I could possibly receive a sentence of _____.

I understand that by pleading guilty that I am waiving my rights to confront and cross examine the witnesses who accuse me of the crime charged, and to compulsory process of the Court to require witnesses to appear and testify for me. _____

I am entering a plea of guilty to this crime because I am, in fact, guilty of this crime. _____

I have not been forced, threatened or intimidated into making this plea. _____

I am fully satisfied with the handling of my case by my attorney and the way in which he has represented me. _____

I further understand that I am waiving my right against self-incrimination, that at my trial I would not have to testify, and if I did not testify, neither the Judge nor the Jury could hold that against me. I also give up the right not to say anything against myself, or against my interest, such as I am doing by pleading guilty. _____

I understand that if I elected to have a trial, I have a right to have competent counsel to represent me at trial. And if I was unable to pay for counsel, the Court would appoint competent counsel to represent me, but by entering the plea of guilty, I am waiving these rights. _____

If a plea bargain agreement has been made, I understand that no other promises which may have been made to me other than as set out hereinabove in this plea bargain are enforceable or binding. _____

The Judge has addressed me personally as to all of these matters and he has given me the opportunity to make any statement I desire. _____

| _____ | _____ |
| DATE | DEFENDANT |

| _____ | _____ |
| JUDGE | ATTORNEY FOR THE DEFENDANT |

But is this justice?

Plea bargaining is a hotly debated topic that people either strongly favor or strongly oppose. In recent years it has come under intense scrutiny. What is particularly interesting is that opposition comes from persons with contrasting ideological positions. Civil libertarians as well as law and order spokesmen see it as a danger, but often for different reasons. But not all opposition to plea bargaining can be categorized along a continuum from individual rights to societal protection. Many legal professionals are also concerned that plea bargaining reduces the courthouse to a position in which guilt or innocence, prison or probation are negotiated just as one might haggle over the price of copper jugs at a Turkish bazaar (Rubin). They see it as justice on the cheap and therefore inherently destructive of the concept that the rule of law exists to protect society. What unites these otherwise contrasting perspectives is the concern that plea bargaining works to make the jobs of the judge, prosecutor, and defense attorney much easier but sacrifices the legitimate interests of the police, victim, witnesses, defendant, and the public in general.

An evaluation of the type of justice resulting from plea bargaining must recognize the overriding fact stressed earlier in this chapter: plea bargaining encompasses a wide variety of very different practices. The debate over the merits and demerits of bargaining reflects contrasting perceptions of realities. For instance, defenders of plea bargaining tend to see guilty pleas occurring when the state has a very strong case, while opponents tend to see it occurring most frequently where the evidence is weak. Proponents see plea bargaining as a reflection of an experienced defense counsel's perception of the likely result of trial. Opponents, on the other hand, are more inclined to see a bargained agreement as the product of tactical considerations and inherent biases in the system (Nardulli:50).

Does plea bargaining sacrifice the rights of the defendant?

Supporters of the values of the due process model are concerned that plea bargaining undercuts the protections afforded individuals. This view is aptly expressed by the leading academic critic of plea bargaining—law professor Albert Alschuler:

> . . . the plea bargaining system is an inherently irrational method of administering justice. . . . [It] subjects defense attorneys to serious temptations to disregard their clients' interests. . . . Today's guilty-plea system leads even able, conscientious, and highly motivated attorneys to make decisions that are not really in their clients' interests. [1975:1180]

A prime concern of due process adherents is that a criminal court process geared to produce guilty pleas negates the fundamental protection of the adversary system—a public trial where the defendant is presumed innocent—for plea bargaining discourages trials by imposing a penalty on those who lose at trial. They therefore advocate abolishing bargaining in favor of a vast increase in the number of trials. Such a position, however, ignores the reality of criminal courts: in most cases there is no substantial disagreement over the facts. Moreover, civil libertarian critics look to the jury as the proper forum for sifting guilt from innocence. Yet experienced trial attorneys often have grave doubts about such an approach. In the words of a Los Angeles public defender:

If you've got an exceptional case—one which is weak and there's a good chance that the defendant may be innocent—then you don't want to take it before a jury because you never know what they'll do. And besides you don't want to try it because it's such a bad case. So you chamberize with the judge. [Mather:202]

Some are concerned that plea bargaining works to shield police misconduct from scrutiny. Questions about police adherence to constitutional protections against illegal search and seizure, for example, are compromised away in the bargaining process.

A final concern is that in a criminal court process geared to guilty pleas, an innocent defendant might be forced to enter a plea of guilty. Consider the statement of a minor Louisiana politician who contended he was forced into pleading guilty to charges of vote fraud despite his innocence: "I was faced with six felonies and 41 years. . . . I didn't have the time or money to clear my name" (Degruy and Simon:1). It is difficult to evaluate such a statement, for any protestations of innocence after entering a plea of guilty are obviously self-serving. Given that courts are human institutions, it is unlikely that an innocent defendant has never been pressured to plead, but there is no evidence that this is a systemic problem. Questions of doubtful validity are screened throughout the court process. And, the vast majority of defense attorneys will not let their clients enter a plea unless they are convinced that there is enough evidence for a guilty verdict. Even when the guilty enter a plea, due process advocates suspect that the defendant receives few advantages.

Do the guilty benefit?

If holders of due process values are uneasy that plea bargaining jeopardizes the rights of the individual, the backers of the crime control model express the opposite concern. They believe plea bargaining allows defendants to avoid a guilty label for crimes they actually committed, results in lenient sentences, and in general gives criminal wrongdoers the impression that the courts and the law are easily manipulated.

The police in particular much prefer a conviction on the crime charged rather than a plea to a lesser one. In the words of one detective in downstate Illinois: "When we arrest them, they should be found guilty on that charge, not some lesser charge. I don't believe in reduced charges, they should be made to answer" (Neubauer:61). Law enforcement officials often equate plea bargaining with excessive leniency.

It is not a difficult task to single out individual cases in which these law enforcement criticisms of plea bargaining have merit. But the argument obscures too much. In particular, it confuses cause with effect. A bargained agreement on reduced charges, for example, may be the product of initial overcharging and/or of evidence problems that surface later. Moreover such criticisms suggest that in plea bargaining anything goes—the prosecutor and judge will make any deal to dispose of a case. Yet each court employs a more or less consistent approach to what charge or count reductions are customary, plus a set of sentencing rules of thumb. Many of the law enforcement criticisms of plea bargaining may be reduced to an

IN THE NEWS: MEIGS SAYS CLAIMS "OVERSIMPLIFIED"

Plea bargaining, the practice of permitting a defendant to plead guilty to a lesser charge to secure a conviction, became a central issue in last week's Democratic primary for Franklin commonwealth's attorney.

In often shrill terms, primary winner Ray Corns and incumbent Commonwealth's Attorney William Brooks lashed at each other over whether criminals are running loose in Franklin County because they were able to bargain their ways out of jail. The public, as so often happens in hotly contested elections, is left not really knowing what the truth may be.

Two-term Franklin Circuit Judge Henry Meigs called the plea bargaining charges and counter-charges in the commonwealth's attorney's primary an "oversimplification" of a perfectly acceptable judicial procedure for securing criminal convictions.

"The impression was given that there has been plea bargaining for ridiculously low penalties. I can think of only one or two instances when I refused a plea because of the inadequacy of the penalty recommended," Meigs said this week. . . .

Todd Duvall, (Frankfort, KY) *State Journal*, June 1, 1975.

overall displeasure with the leniency of the courts. Whether sentences are too harsh or too lenient should be a separate issue from the vehicle—plea bargaining—for reaching these sentencing dispositions.

Abolishing/reforming plea bargaining

In recent years, some court systems have attempted to either abolish or reform plea bargaining. Such efforts conform to one of the most controversial recommendations of the 1973 National Advisory Commission on Criminal Justice Standards and Goals:

> As soon as possible, but in no event later than 1978, negotiations between prosecutors and defendants—either personally or through their attorneys—concerning concessions to be made in return for guilty pleas should be prohibited. In the event that the prosecution makes a recommendation as to sentence, it should not be affected by the willingness of the defendant to plead guilty to some or all of the offenses with which he is charged. A plea of guilty should not be considered by the court in determining the sentence to be imposed. [p. 46]

This recommendation was prompted primarily by the commission's view that plea bargaining produces undue leniency.

The main weakness of the commission's recommendation to abolish plea bargaining is that it refuses to recognize the context of plea bargaining. Rosett and Cressey forcefully make this point:

> These proposals ignore the underlying conflicts to which negotiation is a response.
> They assume that justice can be administered without confronting these differences.
> They seek an idealized criminal law that is clear and precise, and that does not have to accommodate messy disagreements and accidents. Such proposed cures are futile. [p. 95]

Many efforts to abolish plea bargaining are really surface changes that are unresponsive to the dynamics of the courthouse.

Faced with mounting public criticisms and professional concern, prosecutors and judges in a number of American communities have tried to alter traditional plea bargaining practices. The state of Alaska along with the cities of New Orleans and

El Paso are commonly identified with efforts to abolish plea bargaining altogether. Other communities, such as Detroit and Denver, have sought to reform the process by regularizing it.

Drawing conclusions from these efforts, however, is somewhat difficult. The reason traces back to the original theme of this chapter—plea bargaining practices are quite varied. In some instances attempts of a given jurisdiction to abolish plea bargaining often mean that they simply abolished one form of plea bargaining—typically sentence bargaining—but continued other practices. Moreover, while the changes instituted in a given court may represent a major departure from past practice in that jurisdiction, they might be commonplace elsewhere. Claims that plea bargaining has been abolished or that major reforms have been instituted require critical analysis. Based on a growing number of studies of such efforts, we can point to some important areas of interest.

In analyzing the impact of changes in plea bargaining practices, a basic question asks whether the changes were indeed implemented. Written policy changes do not always alter the behavior of the court actors. Efforts in Denver to adopt mandatory pretrial conferences, for example, met with resistance from defense attorneys and others. As a result the programs did not have their intended impact and were later dropped (Nimmer and Krauthaus). A similar finding was reported by Lief Carter, who studied a county in northern California where the grand jury had publicly criticized plea bargaining for bestowing undue leniency. In response, the prosecutor tried to eliminate plea bargaining. The defense attorneys, however, began to take more cases to trial. After the state lost twelve out of sixteen jury verdicts, the prosecutor quietly returned to the old policies (Carter:109–111). Not all efforts at reform, however, are short lived. Separate efforts in Detroit to use pretrial conferences (Nimmer and Krauthaus) and to abolish plea bargaining in cases involving the Michigan Felony Firearm Statute (Heumann and Loftin) were successfully implemented.

Even when programs are successfully implemented, they may not have the impact intended. Typically, efforts to abolish or reform plea bargaining aim to eliminate or reduce discretion. Several studies indicate, however, that eliminating discretion at one stage often serves to foster it in other parts of the process. Alaska provides the clearest example. In that state, the attorney general forbade assistant prosecutors from engaging in plea bargaining or from making sentencing recommendations to the judge.

> Judges complain now that, although their responsibilities have increased dramatically, they have very little opportunity to give sentencing thorough consideration, partly because of insufficient time to review the defendant's files, partly because of other calendar pressures which shorten the time available for sentencing hearings, and partly because the law itself offers so little guidance. [Rubenstein and White:277]

An excellent in-depth study of a Michigan county revealed a similar pattern (Church). After a "law and order" antidrug campaign, the newly elected prosecuting attorney instituted a strict policy forbidding charge reduction plea bargaining in drug sale cases. One result was an increased demand for trials, although it was not as great as some judges feared. But at the same time, outright dismissals increased because of insufficient evidence. Moreover, much higher proportions of defendants were sentenced as juveniles not as adults, thus avoiding a felony record for them. Most importantly, plea bargaining (involving defense attorney and judge) in drug cases continued. Hence the assistant prosecutor's ability to control the disposition of the case weakened. In short, an attempt to abolish plea bargaining produced a number of offsetting changes because the overall policy failed to consider the reasons for negotiations.

Should the Government Agree to Plea Bargain?

In determining whether it would be appropriate to enter into a plea agreement, the attorney for the government should weigh all relevant considerations, including:

(a) the defendant's willingness to cooperate in the investigation or prosecution of others;

(b) the defendant's history with respect to criminal activity;

(c) the nature and seriousness of the offense or offenses charged;

(d) the defendant's remorse or contrition and his willingness to assume responsibility for his conduct;

(e) the desirability of prompt and certain disposition of the case;

(f) the likelihood of obtaining a conviction at trial;

(g) the probable effect on witnesses;

(h) the probable sentence or other consequences if the defendant is convicted;

(i) the public interest in having the case tried rather than disposed of by a guilty plea;

(j) the expense of trial and appeal; and

(k) the need to avoid delay in the disposition of other pending cases.

Source: U.S., Department of Justice, *Principles of Federal Prosecution* (Washington, D.C.: Government Printing Office, 1980), p. 23.

Conclusion

Plea bargaining vividly illustrates the difference between the law on the books and the law in action. The rules of criminal procedure, appellate court decisions, and theories of the adversary system suggest that the trial is the principal activity of the criminal courts. Instead plea bargaining is the predominant activity. Bargaining is best understood not as a response to the press of cases but as an adaptation to some realities of the types of cases requiring court disposition. In most cases, there is little question about the defendant's legal guilt. A trial is a costly and sometimes risky method of establishing that guilt. A trial cannot wrestle with the most pressing issue of what sentence to impose upon the guilt. Finally, through plea bargaining courthouse officials are able to individualize justice. In short, it is neither necessary nor desirable that every defendant have a trial.

It is important to bear in mind, however, that plea bargaining is not one single easily definable practice. All of the complexities and differences of America's legal system are reflected in the wide variety of practices that are collectively referred to by some as plea bargaining. We defined bargaining as the process through which a defendant pleads guilty to a criminal charge with the expectation of receiving some consideration from the state. Some bargains are explicit; others are implicit. Some defendants plead guilty on the nose, others after a charge reduction, still others after count bargaining, and finally some after sentence negotiations. Equally varied are the processes through which such bargains are reached. Based on divergent concerns, different persons have observed roughly similar plea bargaining practices and procedures but have reached very different conclusions about the type of justice dispensed and what improvements need to be made.

For discussion

1. What form of plea bargaining—sentencing, charge reduction, or count pleading—predominates in your community? Why?
2. Observe the taking of a plea in a local court. Do you think the procedures follow the legal standards? What improvements might be made? What are your impressions of the dignity of justice? What are the most important characteristics of the cases where guilty pleas are entered?
3. Should a defendant be allowed to plead guilty without fully admitting guilt? Would you limit the *Alford* guidelines solely to situations in which the death penalty was involved? Why?
4. What do you consider the major disadvantages of plea bargaining? Why?
5. What would you recommend be done to standardize plea bargaining?
6. Discuss plea bargaining with criminal justice officials. Do they believe it is necessary? If so, why? Compare and contrast their views on the problems associated with negotiating justice.

References

Alschuler, Albert W. "The Prosecutor's Role in Plea Bargaining." *University of Chicago Law Review* 36 (1968):61.

———. "The Defense Attorney's Role in Plea Bargaining." *Yale Law Journal* 84 (1975):1179–1314.

Brereton, David, and Jonathan Casper. "Does It Pay to Plead Guilty? Differential Sentencing and the Functioning of Criminal Courts." *Law and Society Review* 16 (1981–1982):45–70.

Carter, Lief. *The Limits of Order*. Lexington, Mass.: D. C. Heath, 1974.

Casper, Jonathan D. *American Criminal Justice: The Defendant's Perspective*. Englewood Cliffs, N.J.: Prentice-Hall, 1972.

Church, Thomas W., Jr. "Plea Bargains, Concessions and the Courts: Analysis of a Quasi-Experiment." *Law and Society Review* 10 (1976):377.

Degruy, Pierre V., and John Alan Simon. "Poll Official 'Forced' into Guilty Plea." *New Orleans Times-Picayune*, April 14, 1977.

Eisenstein, James, and Herbert Jacob. *Felony Justice*. Boston: Little, Brown, 1977.

Feeley, Malcolm M. *The Process is the Punishment: Handling Cases in a Lower Criminal Court*. New York: Russell Sage Foundation, 1979.

Hager, Philip. "Plea Bargaining—Is Justice Well Served?" *Los Angeles Times*, February 25, 1975.

Heumann, Milton. *Plea Bargaining: The Experience of Prosecutors, Judges and Defense Attorneys*. Chicago: University of Chicago Press, 1978.

———, and Colin Loftin. "Mandatory Sentencing and the Abolition of Plea Bargaining: The Michigan Felony Firearm Statute." *Law and Society Review* 13 (1979):393–430.

Kalven, Harry, and Hans Zeisel. *The American Jury*. Chicago: University of Chicago Press, 1966.

Levin, Martin. *Urban Politics and the Criminal Courts*. Chicago: University of Chicago Press, 1977.

Mather, Lynn M. "Some Determinants of the Method of Case Disposition: Decision-Making by Public Defenders in Los Angeles." *Law and Society Review 8* (1974):187–216.

Miller, Herbert, William McDonald, and James Cramer. *Plea Bargaining in the United States.* Washington, D.C.: National Institute of Law Enforcement and Criminal Justice, 1978.

Nardulli, Peter. *The Courtroom Elite: An Organizational Perspective on Criminal Justice.* Cambridge, Mass.: Ballinger Publishing Co., 1978.

National Advisory Commission on Criminal Justice Standards and Goals. *Courts Report.* Washington, D.C.: Government Printing Office, 1973.

Neubauer, David W. *Criminal Justice in Middle America.* Morristown, N.J.: General Learning Press, 1974.

Newman, Donald. *Conviction: The Determination of Guilt or Innocence Without Trial.* Boston: Little, Brown 1966.

Nimmer, Raymond, and Patricia Ann Krauthaus. "Plea Bargaining Reform in Two Cities." *Justice System Journal* 3 (1977):6–21.

President's Commission on Law Enforcement and Administration of Justice. *Task Force Report: The Courts.* Washington, D.C.: Government Printing Office, 1967.

Rhodes, William. *Plea Bargaining: Who Gains? Who Loses?* Washington, D.C.: Institute for Law and Social Research, 1978.

Rosett, Arthur, and Donald R. Cressey. *Justice by Consent.* Philadelphia: J. B. Lippincott, 1976.

Rubenstein, Michael, and Teresa White. "Plea Bargaining: Can Alaska Live without It?" *Judicature* 62 (1979):266.

Rubin, Alvin B. "How We Can Improve Judicial Treatment of Individual Cases Without Sacrificing Individual Rights: The Problems of the Criminal Law." *Federal Rules of Decisions* 70 (1976):176.

Ryan, John Paul, and James Alfini. "Trial Judges' Participation in Plea Bargaining: An Empirical Perspective." *Law and Society Review* 13 (1979):479–507.

Schelling, Thomas. *The Strategy of Conflict.* Cambridge: Harvard University Press, 1960.

Uhlman, Thomas, and Darlene Walker. "'He Takes Some of My Time: I Take Some of His': An Analysis of Judicial Sentencing Patterns in Jury Cases." *Law and Society Review* 14 (Winter 1980):323–342.

Vetri, Dominick R. "Plea Bargaining: Compromises by Prosecutors to Secure Guilty Pleas." *University of Pennsylvania Law Review* 112 (1964):901.

Winsberg, Jerome. Telephone interview. July 1977.

For further reading

Heumann, Milton. *Plea Bargaining: The Experiences of Prosecutors, Judges and Defense Attorneys.* Chicago: University of Chicago Press, 1978.

Klein, John. *Let's Make a Deal.* Lexington, Mass.: D. C. Heath, Lexington Books, 1976.

McDonald, William, and James Cramer, eds. *Plea Bargaining.* Lexington, Mass.: Lexington Books, 1978.

Newman, Donald. *Conviction: The Determination of Guilt or Innocence Without Trial.* Boston: Little, Brown, 1966.

CHAPTER 14

Trial

Of all the steps of the criminal process, the trial attracts the most public attention. Every year books, movies, and television dramas use courtroom encounters to entertain. Trials of well-known people receive extensive national press coverage. Some of these—the Watergate trials come quickly to mind—become the center of a ritual drama of good and evil. Even a local murder trial is the subject of many newspaper stories and the topic of local conversation.

This public interest is partially a reflection of the key role the trial plays in American criminal law. Almost half of the Bill of Rights guarantees dealing with criminal procedure specifically refer to the trial stage. To Anglo-American criminal jurists, the trial serves as the ultimate forum for vindicating the innocence of the accused.

This public interest combined with the centrality of the trial to American law would seemingly make the trial the prime ingredient in the criminal courts. Yet as we saw in chapter 13, roughly 90 percent of the felony cases (and a much higher percentage of misdemeanor offenses) are disposed of by a guilty plea. Thus in a very fundamental sense, a trial represents a deviant case. But at the same time, the few cases that are disposed of at trial have a major impact on the operations of the whole criminal justice system. Trials are the balance wheel of the process.

Although states vary, a trial generally follows these steps: selection of a jury; opening statements by prosecution and defense; presentation of the state's evidence and witnesses; presentation of defense's evidence and witnesses; rebuttal witnesses; arguments by both sides to the jury; instructions to the jury by the judge; and decision by the jury. This chapter concentrates on the most important aspects of the trial. We will examine the history and function of trials, selection of juries, prosecutor's approach to trial, defense strategies during trial, and how juries reach a decision. The end of the chapter discusses the important impact trials have on cases not brought to trial as well as a major and current problem area: prejudicial pretrial publicity.

History and function

The primary purpose of the jury is to provide the accused a safeguard against governmental oppression arising from the activities of a corrupt or overzealous prosecutor and/or a biased, eccentric judge. Ideally juries are a group of fair-minded laymen who are representative of a cross section of the local population where the defendant is tried (Simon and Marshall:214). Once selected, the jury becomes the sole judge of the weight of the evidence and the credibility to be given to the testimony of the witnesses. While judges rule on matters of law, the jury is the sole judge of the facts of the case. Thus the use of juries represents a deep commitment to the use of laymen in the administration of justice. The views and actions of judges and lawyers are constrained by a group of average citizens who are amateurs in the ways of the law (Kalven and Zeisel:3–4).

The modern heritage of a trial by jury traces its roots deeply into Western history. Used in Athens five or six centuries before the birth of Christ, juries were later employed by the Romans. They reappeared in France during the ninth century and were transferred to England from there. These early bodies, however, served purposes vastly different from the modern institution. For example, in England prior to 1066, settling disputes by a trial took one of two forms. Trial by compurgation was based on a community approach. If the defendant could recruit thirty men to certify that he was an honorable person, then he was considered truthful. Trial by ordeal involved subjecting the accused to torture by fire or water. Those who survived were considered truthful because God had directed it. Trial by ordeal was used by the American Puritans who tested the truthfulness of witnesses by dunking them in a pond; those who did not float were lying.

The concept of the jury functioning as an impartial fact-finding body was first formalized in the Magna Carta of 1215 when English noblemen forced the king to recognize limits on the power of the Crown:

> No Freeman shall be taken or imprisoned, or be disseized of his Freehold, or Liberties, or free Customs, or be outlawed, or exiled or otherwise destroyed, nor will we pass upon him nor condemn him but by lawful Judgment of his peers or by Law of the Land. We will sell to no man, we will not deny or defer to any man, either Justice or right.

This protection applied only to noblemen (freemen). Its extension to the average citizen occurred several centuries later. As with much of English law, this early trial system was clearly oriented to protecting property rights.

In the centuries after the Magna Carta, the legal status of the jury continued to evolve. Early English juries did not determine guilt or innocence. They were composed of witnesses to a crime and served to compel testimony, thus they functioned much like the modern-day grand jury. Only later did they become impartial bodies selected from citizens who knew nothing of the alleged event.

By the time the U.S. Constitution was written, jury trials in criminal cases had been in existence in England for several centuries. It was this legal principle that was transferred to the American colonies and later written into the Constitution.

The pivotal role that the right to trial by jury plays in American law is underscored by the number of times it is mentioned. Article III, Section 2 provides that "the trial of all crimes, except cases of impeachment shall be by jury and such trial shall be held in the state where the said crimes shall have been committed." This section not only guarantees the right to a trial by jury to persons accused by the national government of a crime but also specifies that such trials shall be held near the place of the offense. This prevents the government from harassing defendants by trying them far from home.

The Sixth Amendment guarantees that "in all criminal prosecutions, the accused shall enjoy the right to a speedy and public trial, by an impartial jury." The requirement of a public trial prohibits secret trials, a device commonly used by dictators to silence their opponents.

The Seventh Amendment provides: "In suits at common law . . . the right to trial by jury shall be preserved." This provision is a historical testament to the fact that the framers of the Constitution greatly distrusted the judges of the day.

In the last few years the courts have been forced to grapple with the problem of determining the precise application of these constitutional protections of the right to a trial by jury to some twentieth-century developments. The scope of the right to a jury trial, the size of the jury, and unanimous versus nonunamimous verdicts are three modern-day problem areas.

Scope of the right to a trial by jury

petty offense

While trial by jury may be "fundamental to the American scheme of justice" (*Duncan* v. *Louisiana*, 391 U.S. 145, 149, 1968), it is wrong to conclude that all persons accused of crime enjoy a right to a trial by jury. Youths who are prosecuted as juveniles are frequently denied a jury trial, as are adult offenders charged with a *petty* (minor) *offense*.

right to trial by jury

Although the laws of every state guarantee a *right to a jury trial* in serious cases, the definition of a serious versus a petty case varied greatly. It was not until *Duncan* that the Sixth Amendment right to a jury trial applied to the states as well. (Technically the Sixth Amendment was incorporated into the due process clause of the Fourteenth Amendment, which restricts state power.)

The *Duncan* decision, however, did not define serious offense. Two years later, the Court held that "no offense can be deemed 'petty' for purposes of the right to trial by jury where imprisonment for more than six months is authorized" (*Baldwin* v. *New York*, 399 U.S. 66). Adult defendants are now entitled to a trial by jury in a prosecution in either state or federal court involving an offense for which the punishment exceeds six months. States and localities may extend the right to a jury trial to petty offenses.

Jury size

petit juries

Historically trial juries (also termed *petit juries* to differentiate them from grand juries) consisted of twelve persons. In some courts it is common practice to select several alternate jurors who will serve if one of the regular jurors must withdraw during the trial. Recent efforts to modernize court procedures, relieve congestion of court calendars, and reduce court expenditures have included recommendations to adopt six-person juries. The National Advisory Commission on Criminal Justice Standards and Goals, for instance, argued that *twelve-person juries* were an accident of history and suggested that fewer than twelve can provide a reliable and competent fact-finding body (101). It therefore recommends that "juries in criminal prosecutions for offenses not punishable by life imprisonment should be composed of less than 12 but at least six persons."

twelve-person jury

The road to adopting juries of less than twelve in the states was paved by the decision of the Supreme Court in *Williams* v. *Florida* (399 U.S. 78 1970), which upheld the constitutionality of a Florida law allowing six-person juries in all except capital cases. Since that landmark decision, thirty-three states have specifically authorized juries of fewer than twelve in some courts (see figure 14-1). In federal courts, though, defendants are entitled to a twelve-person jury unless the parties stipulate in writing to a jury of less than twelve. *Six-member juries* in federal civil cases are quite common, however.

six-member jury

Twelve-Member Juries Required
Alabama, Hawaii, Illinois, Maine, Maryland, New Jersey, North Carolina, North Dakota, Rhode Island, Vermont, West Virginia, Wisconsin.

Juries of Fewer than Twelve Specifically Authorized
Alaska, Arizona, Colorado, Connecticut, Florida, Georgia, Idaho, Indiana, Iowa, Kansas, Kentucky, Louisiana, Massachusetts, Michigan, Minnesota, Mississippi, Missouri, Montana, Nebraska, New Hampshire, New Mexico, New York, Ohio, Oklahoma, Oregon, South Carolina, South Dakota, Tennessee, Texas, Utah, Virginia, Washington, Wyoming.

Juries of Fewer than Twelve Permitted by Agreement
Arkansas, California, Delaware, Nevada, Pennsylvania.

Figure 14-1. State provisions on size of criminal juries.

Source: Based on data from National Center for State Courts, *Facets of the Jury System: A Survey* (1976), pp. 41–44.

There has been a good deal of debate over whether or not small juries provide the defendant a fair trial. Critics contend that six-member juries will be more likely to ignore conflicting points of view and will be too hasty in reaching a verdict. Social science evidence suggests there are few differences between six- and twelve-person juries. Both small and large juries, for example, spend about equal time deciding similar cases (Pabst). Research also indicates that small juries do not exclude important points of view in reaching a verdict (Roper). In terms of the types of verdicts reached, however, the evidence is mixed. A few studies suggest that case outcomes are about the same regardless of jury size. But other studies indicate that twelve-member juries were more likely to vote for the plaintiff in civil cases and were more generous in their financial awards (Zeisel and Diamond; Beiser, 1975).

Unanimity

Traditionally a jury verdict in a criminal case had to be unanimous. (Nonunanimous civil verdicts have been allowed.) In a pair of 1972 decisions, however, the unanimity rule was shaken. The Supreme Court allowed a 9-to-3 verdict (*Johnson* v. *Louisiana*, 406 U.S. 356) and a 10-to-2 guilty finding (*Apodaca* v. *Oregon*, 406 U.S. 404). Despite the Court's ruling, however, only four states (Oklahoma, Texas, Louisiana, and Oregon) permit *nonunanimous* criminal verdicts. Many state constitutions specify unanimity and therefore are not subject to the Court's ruling on this matter. In all federal criminal cases, however, the rule of unanimity still applies.

nonunanimous jury

The purpose of allowing a nonunanimous verdict is a hedge against a juror who does not agree with the finding of the others. Not only would it reduce the expensive and time-consuming process of conducting a second trial, but it is also likely to reduce deliberation time. Opponents of nonunanimous verdicts argue that the conservative majority on the Burger Court misread the history of the jury, with the result that a basic constitutional right is being sacrificed. They point out that proof beyond a reasonable doubt has not been shown if only some of the jurors vote to convict. So far the Court has given no indication what size majority is constitutionally mandated.

Jury selection

Even before the first word of testimony, trials pass through a critical stage: jury selection. Many lawyers believe that trials are won or lost on the basis of which jurors are selected. Juries are chosen in a three-stage process that combines random selection with deliberate choice. The first step is the compilation of a master jury list. Next, the venire, the citizens available for jury duty on a particular date, is randomly drawn from the master jury list. Finally, some members of this jury pool are questioned (called *voir dire*) about possible bias in a specific case. If juries are to function as a fair and impartial body that carefully weighs the facts of the case, it is important that fair and impartial jurors be initially selected. Whether the three stages of jury selection actually produce fair and impartial juries has been the subject of much concern.

Master jury list

cross section of the community

Juries are supposed to be a group of fair-minded laymen, representatives of the community in which the defendant allegedly committed the crime. Therefore the first step in jury selection is the development of procedures that will produce a representative *cross section of the community* (Simon and Marshall:214). These sentiments are well reflected in the Federal Jury Selection and Service Act of 1968, designed to ensure that juries are "selected at random from a fair cross section of the communities in the district or division wherein the court convenes [and that] no citizen shall be excluded from service as a grand or petit juror in the district courts of the United States on account of race, color, religion, sex, national origin, or economic status." This act was prompted by evidence that selection of federal juries was systematically biased. Similar concerns have been expressed about jury selection at the state level.

Jury panels have been challenged because of their failure to include blacks, women, Chicanos, Native Americans, and many others. For example, until 1968 women in Mississippi could automatically be excluded from jury service. A Louisiana law excluded women from the master jury list unless they requested jury duty. The Supreme Court held that these practices, which eliminated women from jury duty, were unconstitutional (*Taylor* v. *Louisiana*, 19 U.S. 522 1975). Increasingly, therefore, the appellate courts are holding that master jury lists must reflect a true cross section of the community.

master jury list

The most frequent source for assembling the names for the *master wheel* or *master jury list* (sometimes called *jury wheel*) are voter registration lists. These lists have major advantages: they are usually readily available, frequently updated, and collected in districts within judicial boundaries. Basing the master jury list on voter registration, however, tends to exclude the poor, the young, racial minorities, and the less well educated. A recent study found that in one jurisdiction blacks constituted 30 percent of the population but only 17 percent of the jury list. In another jurisdiction, about 20 percent of the population were between the ages of twenty-one and forty-nine, but only 3 percent were on the jury list. In the same jurisdiction 53 percent of the population consisted of women, yet only 17 percent of the jury list did (Kairys et al.). In addition, blacks and Mexican Americans have been prevented from registering to vote in the South, which meant that these minorities never served on juries.

Because of these limitations, twenty states plus the federal government either require or allow the use of other sources—city or telephone directories, utility customer lists, or driver's license lists—in drawing up the master list. The use of multiple sources achieves a better representation of a cross section of the community on jury panels.

Venire

venire

The jury pool (or *venire*) is a list or group of people from among whom a trial jury will be selected. Periodically the clerk of court, judge, or jury commissioner determines how many jurors are needed for a given time. A sufficient number of names are then randomly selected from the master jury list, and the sheriff issues a summons for these citizens to appear at the courthouse for jury duty.

Not all those summoned, however, will actually serve on the venire. Virtually all states have laws that require jurors to be citizens of the United States, residents of the locality, of a certain minimum age, and be able to understand English. Most states disqualify convicted felons and insane persons. A majority also specify that jurors be of "good character" and/or be "well informed." Persons who fail to meet these requirements are eliminated from the venire. Others will be excused because of *statutory exemptions.* Variations in those exempted from jury duty by statute are great but commonly include judicial and government officials, medical personnel, ministers, educators, and lawyers. Those not exempt by law may still be excused if they can convince the judge that jury duty would work an undue hardship.

statutory
exemptions

> . . . What I don't want is some little old lady who has three locks on her door and who thinks that just because the defendant was arrested and is sitting in court means he is guilty.
>
> Maurice Hattier, *New Orleans Times-Picayune,* March 19, 1975.

Once summoned, citizens spend from a day to several months on the venire. In some states, jurors are called for a particular trial. If they are excused from that trial, their service is completed for the year. If they are selected for trial, they serve until the trial is over. In smaller courts, prospective jurors are called only on the days when jurors are chosen. Those not selected for a particular jury remain on call for the next trial day.

An increasing number of large court systems make use of a more efficient jury pool system. Potential jurors are summoned for a specified period of time ranging from a day to several weeks. During this time they wait in the jury assembly room until they are called. If they are not selected for jury service, they return to the assembly room. These systems are more efficient because they call a fewer number of citizens for jury duty and therefore citizens are spared showing up at the courthouse, often leaving work, but never being used.

Voir dire

voir dire

Voir dire (meaning "look-speak" in French) refers to the examination of a possible juror to decide whether he or she is acceptable to decide a specific case. The venire people are questioned by the attorneys and/or judge about their background, familiarity with the case, friendship or acquaintance with persons involved in the case (defendant, witness, lawyer), attitudes about certain facts that may arise during trial, and any other matters that may reflect upon their willingness and ability to judge the case fairly and impartially.

challenge
for cause

peremptory
challenge

If during the interrogation it develops that a juror cannot fairly judge the case, the juror may be *challenged for cause* by either defense or prosecution. The presiding judge rules on the motion and, if sustained, the juror is excused. In practice, few challenges for cause are made, and even fewer are sustained (Simon and Marshall:217). *Peremptory challenge* is the second—and much more important—

technique used by prosecution and defense in influencing who will sit on the jury. Each side has a limited number of peremptory challenges they can use to exclude a juror. Based on hunch, insight, whim, prejudice, or pseudoscience, a lawyer may peremptorily exclude a juror without giving a reason.

In recent years attorneys have employed the assistance of social scientists to aid them in a more intelligent and systematic use of the *voir dire*. By determining the social characteristics and attitudes of the local population that would be beneficial to the accused, lawyers could reject some jurors while retaining others. These techniques have been used primarily in trials involving political radicals—the Harrisburg Seven, Angela Davis, and Wounded Knee, for example. But radicals do not have a monopoly on the use of social science. When former Attorney General John Mitchell and former Secretary of Commerce Maurice Stans were tried, defense attorneys were advised to seek a jury of working-class Catholics of average income and who read the *New York Daily News*. Potential jurors to be avoided were the college educated, Jews, and readers of either the *New York Post* or the *New York Times* (Etzioni:A3). Whether the use of such social science data is helpful has yet to be conclusively shown. In most trials, though, where it has been used, the defendants were acquitted.

In practice, attorneys use the *voir dire* for more than just trying to choose a fair and impartial jury. The primary function is to educate the citizen into the role of juror. Attorneys and judges make frequent requests for the juror's assurance that he or she can set aside past experiences and biases to judge the case fairly and objectively. Some practicing attorneys interpret the answers given by the venire person as promises, and restate them later in their summation. The questioning of jurors develops rapport between the attorneys and the jurors. In turn, the *voir dire* provides the lawyers the opportunity to attempt to influence jurors' attitudes and perhaps their later vote. Defense attorneys in particular view the *voir dire* as necessary for ensuring that potential jurors will presume the defendant innocent until proven guilty. Many lawyers view the *voir dire* as the final safeguard against unstated biases or prejudices by jurors that ensures a fair and dispassionate jury.

In some areas the *voir dire* has become a time-consuming process. Some cases have consumed six weeks or more in jury selection process. For instance, when Black Panthers Bobby Seale and Ericka Huggins were tried in New Haven, Connecticut, on a charge of murdering a fellow Panther, lawyers questioned 1,035 prospective jurors over a four-month period (*New York Times*, March 12, 1971). In other areas, though, jury selection is usually accomplished in under two hours. The delay caused by jury selection is a cause for concern; also some fear that through the selection process attorneys seek to select jurors prejudiced to their side. As the National Advisory Commission has said, "A defendant is entitled to an unbiased jury; he is not entitled to a jury biased in his favor" (99).

Jury duty

Every year thousands of Americans are called to serve as jurors. Jury duty is currently the only time that citizens are directly required to perform a service for their government. Unfortunately many jurors experience great frustration in the process.

They are made to wait endless hours in barren courthouse rooms; minimal compensation often works a hardship because not all employers pay for the time lost

---

CLOSE-UP: LAWYER TRIES TO MOLD A FAVORABLE JURY, BUT COULD CREATE A MONSTER.

... Thousands of Greater Clevelanders will come face to face with it this year as they are called for jury duty. Lawyers will look them over, listen to them answer questions, weigh the possibility of getting worse jurors if they kick them off and make their choices. . . .

Lawyers here have their own methods of jury selection. Some, a survey showed, insist their goal is the proverbial fair and impartial jury while others say they're more interested in finding one likely to vote for their side. "Impartial, but they're on my side," is the way one lawyer put it.

The picking, which is actually deciding who of prospective jurors will not be on the jury, is based, the lawyers said, on instinct, experience, psychology, guesswork.

And some theories which, they said, are seldom automatic.

Women generally make better jurors than men for the defense of rape cases where there is a question of consent, said two criminal defense lawyers. Women tend to be more critical of other women, they said.

Professionals are good for the defense, bad for the prosecution in cases that could result in the electric chair, said a lawyer who has been on both sides of the trial table. Professionals, he said, tend to be against capital punishment. . . .

Divorced men make good jurors for the defense in cases of men accused of killing unfaithful wives, said a defense lawyer.

Ministers and priests are bad for the prosecution, one prosecutor said, because "part of the Lord's work is to be charitable, and I'm not looking for charity."

The type of juror to look for depends largely on the type of case and the client, some lawyers said.

One of them is Gerald S. Gold, a criminal defense lawyer, who said he likes jurors who can identify with the defendant, particularly if the defendant is going to testify, because they are more likely to give him "a full listen."

In a homicide case, where there is no question the defendant killed someone, but there is a question whether it was manslaughter, murder or aggravated murder, Gold said he would look for jurors who are "forgiving, understanding, social-minded, generous, nice people."

"There was a rule that you always keep Jews, Italians, blacks, Irish, all the minority groups because they're more sympathetic and they've been put upon themselves and they understand," Gold said. "But I think that's been overdone. You can't really use those sterotypes."

Gold said his jury selection is based on "feel and experience and knowledge of people."

"What you're doing," he said, "is playing psychologist."

"You're trying to get a jury that's favorable to you," he said. The opposing lawyer, presumably, is trying to get a jury favorable to his side. The result, said Gold, could well be a fair and impartial jury.

James R. Willis, another defense lawyer, said he looks for "a genuine cross section of the community," but tries to avoid government employees as being generally too regimented, "not free thinkers."

In cases that could end in the death penalty, he said he tries to get as many Catholics and Jews on the panel as possible. Catholics, he said, would be opposed to the death penalty and Jews are sympathetic, "an oppressed people."

Willis said he also tries to avoid middle-class black jurors when there is a poor black defendant because middle-class blacks generally "can't identify with the struggle as much as people who are in it or people who are way above."

In cases where there will be a question of a witness' ability to identify the defendant, Willis said he may look for a juror of the same age as the witness, and with glasses, if the witness wears them, the better to assess the witness' ability to identify. He said he also likes jurors who can identify with defendants. . . .

Leslie Kay, *Cleveland Plain Dealer*, June 1, 1975.

from work; and some are apprehensive about criminals in general and criminal courthouses in particular.

In spite of these hardships, however, most citizens express an overall satisfaction with jury duty. Of 3,000 jurors surveyed in one study, almost 90 percent stated they were favorably impressed with jury duty (Pabst:166). The report concluded that they "view their experience as a precious opportunity of citizenship rather than an onerous obligation" (164). Just as importantly there is every indication that jurors take their job seriously.

The prosecution presents its case

opening statement

Once the jury has been selected and sworn, the trial begins. Each side is allowed (but not required) to make a brief *opening statement*. It is not evidence but is intended to provide the jurors a guide to the case. Both lawyers argue what they think the evidence will show and highlight areas they think are particularly important.

After the opening statement, the prosecution presents its main evidence. In preparing for trial, the prosecutor often must wrestle with difficult problems of how to prove each element of the offense. If the burden of proof is not met, the judge will grant the defense motion for an acquittal. How the prosecutor proceeds is affected by two important aspects of the law: presumption of innocence and rules of evidence.

Presumption of innocence

One of the most fundamental protections recognized in the American criminal justice process is the right to be presumed innocent. The state has the burden of proving the defendant guilty of the alleged crime; the defendant is not required to prove himself or herself innocent. This difference is a fundamental one. A moment's reflection will indicate the difficulty in proving that something did not happen or that a person did not do the alleged criminal act, for it is very difficult to rule out all possibilities. Therefore a defendant is cloaked with the legal shield of innocence through the criminal justice process.

reasonable doubt

In meeting the obligation to prove the defendant guilty, the prosecution is required to prove the defendant guilty beyond a reasonable doubt. Beyond a *reasonable doubt* is a legal yardstick measuring the sufficiency of the evidence. This burden of proof does not require that the state establish absolute certainty by eliminating all doubt, just a reasonable doubt.

Rules of evidence

evidence

The state proceeds to convince the jury to return a guilty verdict by presenting *evidence*. Evidence can be classified into real evidence, testimony, direct evidence,

*real evi-
dence
testimony
direct
evidence
circumstan-
tial evi-
dence*

and circumstantial evidence. *Real evidence* includes objects of any kind—guns, maps, records and documents, for example. The bulk of the evidence during criminal trial consists of *testimony*—statements by competent witnesses. *Direct evidence* refers to eyewitness evidence. Testimony that a person was seen walking in the rain is direct evidence that a person walked in the rain. Indirect evidence is called *circumstantial evidence.* Circumstantial evidence can be used to prove the truth or falsity of a fact in issue. Testimony that the person was seen indoors with wet shoes is circumstantial evidence that the person had walked in the rain.

*rules of evi-
dence*

The presentation of evidence during trial is governed by principles called *rules of evidence.* A trial is an adversary proceeding in which the rules of evidence resemble the rules of a game with the judge acting as an impartial umpire. These rules of evidence have developed primarily out of appellate court decisions rather than from legislative enactments. Although they may seem to be a fixed set of legal rules, they are not. Like all other legal principles, they are general propositions that courts must apply to specific instances. During such applications judges use a balancing test, carefully weighing whether the trial would be fairer with or without the piece of evidence in question (Rothstein:5).

The purpose of the adversary process is to get at the truth: the primary purpose of rules of evidence is to help achieve this end. For instance, a judge who feels that the jury would give certain evidence undue weight or would be greatly prejudiced would not allow that evidence to be presented. Some rules of evidence, however, have purposes other than truthfulness. Because the law seeks to protect the secrecy of communications (legally called *privileged communications*) between doctor and patient, lawyer and client, and husband and wife, such communications are not normally admissible in open court. Similarly under the exclusionary rule, illegally seized evidence is inadmissible (even if trustworthy) because the laws seek to discourage such activities. Most of the major rules of evidence, however, are directed at achieving the truth. These principles may be briefly summarized under the headings of *trustworthiness* and *relevance.*

*privileged
communi-
cation*

*trustworthi-
ness
relevance*

Trustworthiness.   The basic criterion for admissibility of evidence is trustworthiness. The object of the evidentiary system is to ensure that only the most reliable and credible facts, statements, or testimony are presented to the fact finder. The *best evidence rule* illustrates the point. Ordinarily only the original of a document or object is admissible because a copy or facsimile may have been altered. Similarly a judge may rule that a person of unsound mind or a very young child is not a competent witness because they may not understand what was seen or heard. The mere fact that evidence is legally ruled to be competent does not, of course, mean that the jury must believe it. A wife's alibi for her husband may be competent evidence, but the jury may choose not to believe her.

*best evi-
dence*

*hearsay evi-
dence*

Hearsay evidence is secondhand evidence in which witnesses tell not what they know by their own knowledge but what somebody else told them. An example would be a witness's saying, "I know he was there because my brother told me." The general rule is that hearsay evidence is not admissible because there is no way to test its truthfulness and there is no way to cross-examine as to the truth of the matter. Although the hearsay rule is a staightforward one, its application is complex because there are numerous exceptions. Hearsay evidence is admissible if the defendant is charged with conspiracy or if a witness is unavailable at the time of trial.

Relevance.   To be admissible evidence must also be relevant; there must be a valid reason for introducing the statement, object, or testimony. Evidence not related to an issue at trial is termed *immaterial* or *irrelevant*. If, for example, a defendant is accused of murder, the issue is whether he killed the deceased. Evidence as to motive, intention to commit the offense, and ability to commit the offense are all relevant evidence. But information about the defendant's character—prior convictions or a reputation for dishonesty, for instance—would not normally be admissible because it is not material to the issue of whether the defendant committed this crime. If, however, the defendant testifies, such evidence would be admissible during *rebuttal* for the sole purpose of *impeaching* (casting doubt on) his credibility.

rebuttal

impeach

Traditionally common law allowed a defendant accused of rape to introduce evidence concerning the victim's past sexual activities. The past conduct of defendant is no longer admissible, however. The women's movement views such a dual standard as sexist and argues that it works to discourage a rape victim from testifying at trial. Recently California and Michigan have adopted a new rule that past sexual activity is not generally relevant and therefore is inadmissible at trial. This example illustrates that rules of evidence are involved with important societal issues of interest to others than lawyers.

Objections to the Admission of Evidence.   During trial, attorneys must be continuously alert, ready to make timely objections to the admission of evidence. After a question is asked but before the witness answers, attorneys may object if the evidence is irrelevant, immaterial, or hearsay. The court then rules on the objection and thus permits the evidence to be admitted or not. The judge may rule immediately or may request the lawyers to argue the legal point out of the hearing of the jury (termed a *side-bar conference*). If the objection is to a line of testimony, it may be necessary for the jury to retire to the jury room while the judge hears the testimony and makes a ruling. If the testimony may be admitted, it is then repeated before the jury.

Occasionally inadmissible evidence will inadvertently be heard by the jury. For example, in answering a valid question, a witness may overelaborate. When this occurs and the attorney objects, the judge will instruct the jury to disregard the evidence. But even with such a cautionary warning, jurors may still be influenced by that piece of evidence anyway. If the erroneous evidence is deemed to be so prejudicial that a warning to disregard is not sufficient, the judge may declare a mistrial.

The defense presents its case

Although we generally expect a trial to be a battle between the prosecutor, who asserts that the defendant committed the crime, and the defendant, who maintains innocence, such a view greatly oversimplifies the tactical decisions involved. In deciding upon defense strategy at trial, attorneys must carefully consider the strengths and weaknesses of the state's case, the character of the defendant, how credible the defense witness may be, and how juries are likely to react. In weighing the various factors, defense attorneys invariably start from a position of weakness. They seldom are able to pick cases they wish to try. If the prosecutors consider the case to be weak, they may dismiss it rather than risk an acquittal or offer such a good deal that the defendant cannot turn it down. Defense attorneys are sometimes forced to trial even if they believe the client's story is implausible or dishonest. They must also consider whether the trial should be before a jury or only the judge (a bench trial). Most states allow defendants to waive their right to a jury trial and be tried by a judge. The other states require the prosecution to agree to a bench trial. Although studies indicate that a judge is more likely to find guilt than a jury, in some instances the defendant may wish to avoid a jury trial either because the crime is very inflammatory or because the defendant is using a technical legal defense that a jury is not likely to understand. Most trials, however, are jury trials. Within these constraints, the defense attorney can construct a case along one of three broad lines: reasonable doubt, a denial, or an affirmative defense.

Reasonable doubt

Because the defendant is presumed innocent, the defense does not have to call any witnesses or introduce any evidence. Through cross-examination the attorney can try to undermine the state's case and create in the jury's mind a reasonable doubt as to whether the defendant committed the crime. The key to such a strategy is the skillful use of the right to confront witnesses, one of the criminal court procedures enumerated in the Sixth Amendment: "In all criminal prosecutions, the accused shall enjoy the right . . . to be confronted with witnesses against him." One meaning of this provision is that the defendant must be present during trial—that is, the state cannot try defendants who are absent. (Defendants who disrupt the trial may be removed, however.) The right to be confronted with witnesses guarantees the
cross-ex- right to *cross-examination*. As we have seen, a fundamental tenet of the adversary
amination system is the need to test evidence for truthfulness, and the primary means of testing the truthfulness of witnesses is cross-examination. The following description of a trial illustrates how a defense attorney uses cross-examination to build a reasonable doubt case.

> Xinos [public defender] . . . on cross examination . . . picked skillfully at Parrish's [state's attorney's] case. Playing to his hard hat on the jury, he asked Castelli [victim] whether the stick-up man had one or two hands on the gun. "Only one, sir," said Castelli. "And was that trigger pulled in rapid succession—click-click-click?" Xinos pressed. "Yes, sir," said Castelli, and Xinos had his point: it takes two hands to keep pulling the slide and clicking the trigger. Next came Patrolman Joe Higgins, who remembered, under Xinos's pointed cross-examination, that Castelli had described the gunman as weighing 185 pounds—30 more than Payne [defendant] carries on his spindly 6-foot-1 frame. Payne had nearly botched that point by wearing a billowy, cape-shaped jacket to court, but Xinos persuaded him to fold it up and sit on it so the jurors could see how bony he really was. The 30-pound misunderstanding undercut Castelli's identification of Payne—and suddenly the People and their lawyer, Walter Parrish, were in trouble. [Goldman and Holt:33]

If a defendant has no valid defense but will not plead, the defense attorney's only choice is to force the state to prove its case and hope to create a reasonable doubt in the minds of the jury. But many experienced defense attorneys believe this is the weakest defense. They believe that to gain an acquittal the defense must give the jury something to "hang their hat on." Thus they must consider whether to let the defendant testify.

The defendant as witness

The most important part of defense strategy is the decision whether the defendant will testify. The Fifth Amendment—"No person . . . shall be compelled in any criminal case to be a witness against himself"—protects defendants from being compelled to take the witness stand. If the defendant chooses not to testify, no comment or inference can be drawn from this fact. The prosecutor cannot argue before the jury, "If he is innocent, why doesn't he take the stand and say so?" (*Griffin* v. *California*, 380 U.S. 609, 1965). But this legal protection aside, jurors are curious about the defendant's version of what happened. They expect the defendant to protest innocence and in the secrecy of the jury room can ponder aloud why the defendant refused to testify.

Defendants may, of course, waive the privilege against self-incrimination and take the stand in their own defense. In considering whether to call the defendant to the stand, a major concern of the defense attorney is whether the story is believable. If it is not, the jury will probably dismiss it, thus doing more harm to the defendant's case than if he had not testified at all.

A defendant who takes the stand is subject to cross-examination like any other witness. Because cross-examination is broader than direct examination, the defendant cannot tell merely part of the story and conceal the rest. Once the defendant chooses to testify, the state can bring out all the facts surrounding the event testified to. Just as importantly, once the defendant has taken the stand, the state can impeach the defendant's credibility by introducing into evidence any prior felony convictions. The defense attorney must make the difficult decision whether to

---

IN THE NEWS: HOW JUSTICE WORKS

That they are all nominally innocent under the law is little more than a technicality: public and private defenders learn quickly to presume guilt in most cases and work from there. "I tell 'em I don't have to presume innocence," says one senior hand in the office. "That's a legal principle, but it doesn't have to operate in a lawyer's office." It stops operating when a rookie lawyer discovers that practically all his clients come in insisting that they didn't do it. "You can almost number the stories," says Ronald Himel. " 'I walked into the alley to urinate and I found the TV set.' 'Somebody gave me the tires.' Well, God forbid it should be true and I don't believe you. My first case out of law school, the guy told me he walked around the corner and found the TV set. So I put that on (in court). The judge pushed his glasses down his nose, hunched up and said, 'Fifty-two years I have been walking the streets and alleys of Chicago and I have never, ever found a TV set.' Then he got me in his chambers and said, 'Are you f—ing crazy?' I said, 'That's what he told me.' The judge said, 'And you *believed* that s—? You're goofier than he is!' "

arouse juries' suspicion by not letting the accused testify or letting the defendant testify and be subjected to possibly damaging cross-examination.

Alibi defense

alibi defense

In an *alibi defense*, defendants argue that at the time the crime was committed they were somewhere else. They may independently testify to this and/or call witnesses to testify that during the time in question, the defendant was drinking beer at Mary's or shopping downtown with some friends. Some states require that defendants provide a notice (warning) of alibi defense prior to trial along with a list of witnesses to be called to support this assertion. A notice of alibi defense allows the prosecution the opportunity to investigate the witness's story before trial. Prosecutors who suspect that witnesses have carefully rehearsed the alibi testimony can use clever cross-examination to ask questions out of sequence, hoping to catch each witness in a series of contradictions. Prosecutors can also call rebuttal witnesses to suggest that the witnesses were long-time friends of the defendant who are likely to lie.

Affirmative defense

affirmative defense

An *affirmative defense* goes beyond denying the facts of the prosecutor's case; it sets out new facts and arguments that might win for the defendant. In essence affirmative defenses are legal excuses that should result in a finding of not guilty. They also require the defense to assume the burden of proving these defenses. Although the state has the ultimate duty of proving the defendant guilty beyond a reasonable doubt, under an affirmative defense, the defense has the duty called "the burden of going forward with the evidence." From the defendant's perspective an affirmative defense is tricky, for often it means that the defendant admits the prosecutor's case. Moreover, juries often view such defense strategies as an attempt of the defendant to wiggle out of a guilty verdict. The most common affirmative defenses are self-defense, insanity, duress, and entrapment (someone induced the defendant to commit the crime).

Rebuttal

After the defense rests its case, the prosecution may call rebuttal witnesses, whose purpose is either to discredit the testimony of a previous witness or discredit the witness. The prosecutor may call a rebuttal witness to show that the previous witness could not have observed what she said she did because she was somewhere else at the time. Or the prosecutor may call witnesses (or otherwise present evidence) to show that the previous witnesses have dishonorable reputations. The rules of evidence regarding rebuttal witnesses are complex. In general, evidence may be presented in rebuttal that could not have been used during the prosecution's case in main. For example, the prosecution may legitimately inform the jury of the previous convictions of defendants who take the stand in an attempt to impeach their credibility.

The end of the trial

closing argument

When all the evidence has been presented and both sides have rested (that is, completed the introduction of evidence), each side has the opportunity to make a *closing argument* to the jury. Closing arguments can be very important because they allow each side to sum up the facts in its favor and indicate why they believe a verdict of guilty or not guilty is in order. The prosecutor will carefully sum up the facts of the case, often tying together into a coherent pattern what appeared during the trial to be isolated or unimportant matters. They also typically call upon jurors to do their duty and punish the defendant who has committed the crime. The defense attorney will highlight the evidence favorable to the defendant, criticize the witnesses for the state, and show why they should not be believed. Finally the defense will call upon the jurors to do their sworn duty and return a not guilty verdict. Closing arguments to the jury call for lawyers to muster all the art and skill of their profession. They are also often the most dramatic parts of the trial. There is a fine line, however, between persuasiveness and unnecessary emotionalism. Many jury verdicts have been reversed on appeal because the prosecutor interjected prejudicial statements into the closing argument.

Instructions to the jury

jury instructions

The jury decides the facts of the case, but the judge determines the law. Therefore the court instructs the jury as to the meaning of the law applicable to the facts of the case. These *instructions to the jury* include discussions of general legal principles (innocent until proven guilty, proof beyond a reasonable doubt, and so forth), as well as specific instructions on the elements of the crime in the case and what specific actions the government must prove before there can be a conviction. If the defendant has raised a defense like insanity or duress, the judge instructs the jury as to the meaning of these defenses according to the law in that jurisdiction. In some states judges are also allowed to comment on the evidence. That is, they can express their own views on the credibility of the witnesses, the probabilities of certain acts occurring, and the truth of the matters testified to. Finally the judge instructs the jury on possible verdicts in the case and provides a written form for each verdict of "guilty" and "not guilty." Depending on the state or federal law involved, the jury may also have the option of choosing alternative forms of guilty verdicts. In a murder case, for example, the jury may find the defendant guilty of murder in the first degree, murder in the second degree, or manslaughter. (Or they can acquit on all charges.)

> Now I submit that the jury is the worst possible enemy of this ideal of the "supremacy of law." For "jury-made law" is, par excellence, capricious and arbitrary, yielding the maximum in the way of lack of uniformity, of unknowability. . . . Yet little . . . is done to ensure that these . . . jurymen, "act upon principles and not according to arbitrary will," or to put effective restraints upon their worst prejudices. Indeed, through the general verdict, coupled with the refusal of the courts to inquire into the way the jurors have reached their decisions, everything is done to give the widest outlet to jurors' biases. If only a jury trial is properly conducted according to the procedural rules, the jurors'

decision may be as arbitrary as they please; in such circumstances, their discretion becomes wholly unregulated and unreviewable. . . .

If anywhere we have a "government of men," in the worst sense of the phrase, it is in the operations of the jury system.

Jerome Frank, *Courts on Trial: Myth and Reality in American Justice* (New York: Princeton University Press, 1973) p. 132 (Copyright 1949 by Jerome Frank; copyright renewed © 1976 by Princeton University Press). Reprinted by permission of Princeton University Press.

Instructions to the jury are prepared by the judge and the attorneys during a special charging conference preceding jury deliberations. The prosecution and defense each draft the instructions they think the judge should give to the jury. The judge chooses the instruction that seems most applicable to the case. Each side therefore has an opportunity to enter on the record objections to the judge's instructions, thus preserving the issue for later appeal. Particularly in technical cases like embezzlement or fraud, the judge's instructions to the jury can greatly affect the final verdict. If the judge adopts a very narrow definition of the crime in question, the instructions to the jury virtually mandate an acquittal. The instructions are written out, signed by the judge, and then read to the jury. Some judges allow the jurors to take a copy of the instructions into the jury room as a guide.

The court's instructions to the jury are a formal lecture on the law and are delivered in a formal manner. Because faulty jury instructions are a principal basis for appellate court reversal of the trial verdict, judges are careful in their wordings. Still, the net effect is that instructions to juries contain extensive amounts of legal jargon not readily understood by nonlawyers. There have been some efforts to increase jurors' understanding of these vital matters. An experiment in Florida found that better instructions clarifying the meaning of the judge's charge to the jury did increase understanding. At the same time, juries still did not have an accurate knowledge of the law. For example, the Florida jury instructions stress that a defendant is presumed innocent until proven guilty by the evidence beyond any reasonable doubt. Yet after seeing and hearing the modern instruction on this matter, only 50 percent of the jurors understood that the defendant did not have to present any evidence of innocence; 10 percent were uncertain as to what the presumption of innocence was; and a small but still important 2 percent still believed that the burden of proof of innocence rested with the defendant (Strawn and Buchanan:481).

The jury decides

How juries decide has long fascinated lawyers and laymen alike. Jury deliberations are secret, and therefore there is great curiosity about what goes on behind the locked and guarded jury room door. What factors motivate a decision has always been an intriguing question. Until the deliberations begin, jurors have been passive observers. They are not allowed to ask witnesses direct questions. A juror may pass a question to the judge, who may raise it or ignore it. In most courtrooms jurors are also prohibited from taking notes during the trial. But after the charge to the jury, it

jury delib-
erations

is the lawyers', judge's, and defendants' turn to wait passively, often in tense anticipation, for the jury's decision. During *deliberations* the jury may request further instructions or clarifications from the judge about the applicable law. Juries may also request to have portions of the testimony read in open court.

Because these deliberations are secret, research on this process is indirect. Much of what we know about how juries decide is based either by directly observing mock juries or by indirectly asking jurors to recall what occurred in the jury room. The major studies on jury deliberation were conducted by a team of researchers at the University of Chicago Law School in the 1950s. These studies found that rates of participation varied with social status. Men talked more than women. The better educated also participated more frequently. Persons with high-status occupations were more likely to be chosen as foreman (Strodtbeck et al.; Simon:116). Most of the jury discussions concerned trial procedures, opinions about the trial, and personal reminiscences. There was far less discussion of either the testimony or the judge's instructions to the jury (James:563–570).

hung jury

In most cases juries are able to agree on a verdict with little deliberation. After interviewing jurors in over two hundred criminal cases in Chicago and Brooklyn, the University of Chicago researchers found that almost all juries took a vote as soon as they retired to chambers. In 30 percent of these cases, only one vote was necessary to reach a unanimous verdict. In 90 percent of the rest of these cases, the majority on the first ballot eventually won out (Broeder:746–748). Most importantly, this research found that only very rarely did a lone juror produce a *hung jury*. The psychological pressures associated with small group discussions are so great that a single juror can buck predominant sentiment only if he or she can find at least one ally. Thus Kalven and Zeisel (488) concluded that jury deliberations "do not so much decide the case as bring about a consensus."

double
jeopardy

Once a verdict has been returned, it can be altered only with great difficulty. If the verdict is innocent, the protection against *double jeopardy* prohibits the state from prosecuting the defendant for the same crime (or even crimes that are based on the same evidence), even if later evidence is discovered. If the verdict is guilty, the judge may set the verdict aside only if it is totally contrary to law. Nor can an appellate court second-guess how the jury weighed the evidence. It can only scrutinize possible legal errors made during the trial.

Do juries decide differently than a judge does? To answer this question, the University of Chicago jury project compared the jury's verdict in over thirty-five hundred criminal cases to the one the judge would have given. Judge and jury agreed 75 percent of the time (table 14-1). The relatively high rate of conviction is an indication that most doubtful cases have been eliminated before trial. The table indicates that when judge and jury disagree, the jury is more lenient than the judge.

An analysis of the reasons for the disagreement between judge and jury showed that 54 percent were due to "issues of evidence" (how close the case was); 29 percent because of jurors' "sentiments on the law" (situations in which the jury felt the application of the formal law produced inequitable results); and 11 percent due to "sentiments on the defendant" (these ranged from defendants who evoked sympathy to those who alienated the jury) (Kalven and Zeisel:106–115). According

TABLE 14-1. Agreement between jury and judge (in percent of 3,576 trials)

| | | JURY | | | |
		Acquits	Convicts	Hangs	Total judge
JUDGE	Acquits	13.4	2.2	1.1	16.7
	Convicts	16.9	62.0	4.4	83.3
	Total jury	30.3	64.2	5.5	100%

Source: Harry Kalven Jr. and Hans Zeisel, *The American Jury* (Boston: Little, Brown, 1971), pp. 56, 60.

to these data, the basis of judge–jury disagreements is not random—as some critics of the jury system fear—but is based on rational and justifiable reasons.

Trials as balancing wheels

Trials exert a major influence on the operations of the entire criminal court process. Although only a relative handful of cases go to trial, the possibility of trial operates as a balance wheel on all other cases. The possibility of losing at trial is an important basis for the exercise of prosecutorial discretion during screening. The likelihood of conviction determines the bargaining position of lawyers during plea negotiations. The effects of jury trial must be measured not only by the impact on a specific case but also on the effect on similar cases at a later time.

One important way that trials affect the court process is by introducing popular standards of justice. The University of Chicago jury project found that by far the major reason for disagreement between judge and jury (29 percent) was "jury legislation." Jury legislation is defined as a jury's deliberate modification of the law to make it conform to community views of what the law ought to be (Kalven and Zeisel:111–115). Throughout this book we have referred to possession of small amounts of marijuana as one such area. Another example is where state law requires the suspension of the driver's license upon conviction for drunk driving. Juries often view such a penalty as unduly harsh if no serious accident was involved (Neubauer:231). Jury verdicts thus establish boundaries on what actions the local community believes should (or should not) be punished.

By introducing uncertainty, trials affect the criminal court process in a second important way. During a trial the legal professionals are at the mercy of the witnesses, whose behavior on the witness stand is unpredictable. What witnesses say, and how they say it, often makes the difference between conviction and acquittal

(Eisenstein and Jacob:27). The presence of juries adds another layer of unpredictability. Part of the folklore of any courthouse are stories about the unpredictable jury. Here are two examples. During jury deliberations on a narcotics case, two women announced that "only God can judge" and by refusing to vote hung the jury. In another case, after a not-guilty verdict, a juror put her arm around the defendant and said, "Bob, we were sure happy to find you not guilty, but don't do it again" (Neubauer:228).

Judges and defense attorneys, as legal professionals, resent such intrusion into their otherwise ordered world and seek to reduce such uncertainties. They do so by developing the norms of cooperation we have talked about throughout this book. Viewed in this light, plea bargaining functions to buffer the system against a great deal of the uncertainty resulting from allowing lay citizens to be involved in decisions on important legal matters.

Prejudicial pretrial publicity

For weeks the Cleveland press, through vivid headlines and front-page editorials, pressed for the arrest of Dr. Sam Sheppard. In July 1954, Dr. Sheppard's wife was bludgeoned to death in her bedroom. Sheppard claimed he was asleep on a couch, when his wife's screams awakened him. He went upstairs and grappled with the intruder, who struck him on the back of the head, causing him to lose consciousness. The local press was critical of the handling of the case and implied that Sheppard was guilty but that the police were not pressing hard enough because Sheppard was socially prominent. Later a public inquest was broadcast live with Sheppard being questioned for six hours without benefit of counsel. During the subsequent trial, a radio station broadcast from the room next to the jury room. The courthouse was so packed that newsmen sat right behind the defense table. Moreover the local press carried detailed stories of the trial (including inadmissible evidence), which jurors were permitted to read. Dr. Sheppard was convicted. Years later the Supreme Court reversed (*Sheppard* v. *Maxwell, 384* U.S. *333, 1966*). It likened the trial to a Roman holiday and a carnival atmosphere. In holding that *prejudicial* *prejudicial pretrial publicity* denied Sheppard the right to a fair and impartial trial, *pretrial* the Court set off a long and often heated battle over fair trial versus free press.
publicity   The essential problem underlying the issue of prejudicial pretrial publicity is that two vital protections of the Bill of Rights are on a collision course. The Sixth Amendment guarantees defendants a trial before an impartial jury, a group of citizens who will decide guilt or innocence on the basis of what they hear during the trial—information tested according to accepted rules of evidence—not what they heard or read outside the courtroom. At the same time, the First Amendment protects the freedom of the press; what the reporters print, say on radio, or broadcast on television is not subject to prior censorship. Without the First Amendment, there would be no problem; courts could simply forbid the press from reporting anything but the bare essentials of a crime. This is the practice in England. The *gag order* U.S. Supreme Court, however, has ruled that local courts cannot issue *gag orders* forbidding the press from publishing information about a criminal case. For exam-

ple, when a trial judge in New Orleans issued a gag order forbidding the press from publishing testimony revealed in open court during a pretrial hearing, the Court held that this ruling infringed on freedom of the press (*Times-Picayune* v. *Schulingkamp*, 419 U.S. 301, 1975). Gag orders, though, pose another problem: a journalist who prints information in violation of a court order can be sentenced to jail for contempt of court, even if an appellate body later rules the trial judge's order was illegal.

The great majority of criminal trials do not involve problems of prejudicial pretrial publicity. News coverage usually extends to no more than police blotter coverage. But when there is extensive pretrial publicity, the normal *voir dire* process is greatly strained. Jury selection is geared to ferreting out ordinary instances of bias or prejudice, not correcting the possibility of a systematic pattern of bias. If, for example, one excuses all jurors who have heard something about the case at hand, one runs the risk of selecting a jury solely from the least attentive, least literate members of the general public. If, on the other hand, one accepts jurors on their assertion that they will judge the case solely on the basis of testimony in open court, one is still not certain that psychologically the juror—no matter how well intentioned—can really hear the case with a truly open mind.

Moreover, recent research has demonstrated that pretrial publicity does bias juries. A team of researchers from Columbia University provided one set of "jurors" with "prejudicial" news coverage of a case and a control group with nonprejudicial information. After listening to an identical trial involving a case where the guilt of the defendant was greatly in doubt, the study found that 78 percent of the "prejudiced jurors" voted to convict compared to only 55 percent of the "nonprejudiced jurors" (Padawer-Singer and Barton:131).

In trying to reconcile conflicting principles involved in the First and Sixth amendments, trial courts employ singly or in combination three techniques: limited gag orders, change of venue, and sequestered juries. Each of these methods is a partial one, however, and each suffers from admitted drawbacks.

Limited gag order

The First Amendment forbids the court from censoring what the press writes about a criminal case. It says nothing, however, about restricting the flow of information to the media. Thus in notorious cases in which it seems likely that selecting a jury may be difficult, judges now rather routinely issue an order forbidding those involved in the case—police, prosecutor, defense attorney, and defendant—from talking to the press. Violations are punishable as contempt of court (disobeying a judge's order). Since these are the people who know the most about the case (and often have the most to be gained from pretrial publicity), the net effect is to dry up news leaks. The press, however, consistent with the First Amendment, is free to publish any information it discovers. The greatest difficulty is that sometimes one of the people involved in the case secretly provides information in violation of the judge's order. The judge can then subpoena the reporter and order a disclosure. Reporters believe that disclosing their sources will dry up their sources and therefore refuse to testify. They are cited for contempt and go to jail. The conclusion is obviously far from logical: the court—in the interest of respecting freedom of the press—takes an action, the net effect of which is to send a reporter to jail.

change of venue

change of venue

Venue refers to the local areas where a case may be tried. If the court is convinced that a case has received such extensive local publicity that picking an impartial jury is impossible, the trial may be shifted to another part of the state. Where a case has received statewide coverage, however, a change in venue is of limited use. Generally the prosecution opposes such a move because they believe that the chance of a conviction is greater in the local community and because it is quite expensive to move witnesses, documents, and staff to a distant city for a long trial. Defense attorneys face a difficult tactical decision. They must weigh the effects of prejudicial publicity against a trial in a more rural and conservative area, for example, where citizens are hostile to big city defendants, particularly if they are black.

Sequestering the jury

sequestered jury

A prime defect during the trial of Dr. Sheppard was the failure to shield the jury from press coverage of the ongoing trial. To remedy the defect, it is common in trials involving extensive media coverage to *sequester the jury*. Jurors' activities are tightly regulated: they live in a hotel, take their meals together, and participate in weekend recreation together. Sheriff deputies censor newspapers and mail going to the jury and shut off television news. The possibility of being in virtual quarantine for six weeks or eight weeks, or in some cases even longer, makes many citizens reluctant to serve. When sequestering is probable, the jury selected runs the very obvious risk of representing only those citizens willing to be separated for long periods of time from friends, family, and relatives; who can afford to be off work; are unemployed; or look forward to a spartan existence.

Conclusion

In many ways the trial is the high point of the criminal justice system. Indeed it stands as the symbol of justice. Many of our myths about the court and decisions of the U.S. Supreme Court emphasize the importance of the adversarial procedures at trial. Yet in examining the realities of trial, we are presented with two contradictory perspectives, for as we saw in the last chapter, full-fledged trials are relatively rare. At the same time, trials are a very important dimension of the court process. Every year two million jurors serve in some two hundred thousand civil and criminal cases. Long after trials have declined to minimal importance in other Western nations, the institution of a trial by jury remains a vital part of the American criminal process. Given the availability of counsel, any defendant, no matter how poor and no matter how inflamed the public is about the crime allegedly committed, can require the state to prove its case. Thus, although only a relative smattering of cases are ever tried, the possibility of trial shapes the entire process.

For discussion

1. Talk to some former jurors about their experiences. What did they like? What did they dislike? Do they have any suggestions about improvements in jury service?

2. Observe a *voir dire*. How many jurors are excused? Why do you think the lawyers excused the jurors they did? If possible, talk to the lawyers about the strategies they use in *voir dire*. Overall does *voir dire* take too long? What might speed up the process?

3. What do you think are the major benefits of a jury system? Disadvantages? Would justice be better or worse if America adopted the European model in which professional judges are used and juries have very limited powers?

4. What does the phrase "a jury of one's peers" mean in the context of contemporary society? Are inner-city residents provided equal protection of the laws if they are judged by middle-class, suburban jurors?

5. Follow the newspaper and television coverage of a major crime. Do you think that the defendant's right to an impartial jury is jeopardized? Why or why not?

References

"Six-member Juries in the Federal Courts." *Judicature 58* (April 1975):424.

Broeder, D. W. "The University of Chicago Jury Project." *Nebraska Law Review* 38 (May 1959):744–760.

Eisenstein, James, and Herbert Jacob. *Felony Justice: An Organizational Analysis of Criminal Courts.* Boston: Little, Brown, 1977.

Etzioni, Amitai. "Scientific Jury-Stacking Puts Judicial System on Trial." *Boston Globe,* June 23, 1974.

Goldman, Peter, and Don Holt. "How Justice Works: The People v. Donald Payne." *Newsweek,* March 8, 1971, pp. 20–37.

James, Rita. "Status and Competence of Jurors." *American Journal of Sociology* 69 (May 1958):563–570.

Kairys, David, Joseph Kadane, and John Lehorsky. "Jury Representativeness: A Mandate for Multiple Source Lists." *California Law Review* 65 (July 1977):776–827.

Kalven, Harry, and Hans Zeisel. *The American Jury.* Boston: Little, Brown, 1966.

National Advisory Commission on Criminal Justice Standards and Goals. *Courts.* Washington, D.C.: Government Printing Office, 1973.

Neubauer, David, *Criminal Justice in Middle America.* Morristown, N.J.: General Learning Press, 1974.

New York Times, March 12, 1971.

Pabst, William. "What Do Six-Member Juries Really Save?" *Judicature* 57 (June–July 1973):6.

Padawer-Singer, Alice M., and Allen H. Barton. "The Impact of Pretrial Publicity on Jurors Verdicts." In Rita James Simon, ed., *The Jury System in America: A Critical Overview.* Beverly Hills, Calif.: Sage Publications, 1975.

Roper, Robert. "Jury Size: Impact on Verdict's Correctness." *American Politics Quarterly* 7 (October 1979):438–452.

Rothstein, Paul. *Evidence in a Nutshell.* Minneapolis: West Publications, 1970.

Simon, Rita James. *The Jury and the Defense of Insanity.* Boston: Little, Brown, 1967.

———, and Prentice Marshall. "The Jury System." In Stuart Nagel, ed., *The Rights of the Accused in Law and Action.* Beverly Hills, Calif.: Sage Publications, 1972.

Strawn, David, and Raymond Buchanan. "Jury Confusion: A Threat to Justice." *Judicature* 59 (May 1976):478–483.

Strodtbeck, F. L., R. James, and C. Hawkins. "Social Status in Jury Deliberations." *American Sociological Review* 22 (December 1957):713–719.

Zeisel, Hans, and Shari Diamond. "'Convincing Empirical Evidence on the Six Member Jury.'" *University of Chicago Law Review* 41 (1974):281–295.

For further reading

Heymann, Phillip, and William Kenety. *The Murder Trial of Wilbur Jackson: A Homicide in the Family.* St. Paul, Minn.: West Publishing, 1975.

Kalven, Harry, and Hans Zeisel. *The American Jury.* Boston: Little, Brown, 1966.

National Center for State Courts. *Facets of the Jury System: A Survey.* Denver, 1976.

Simon, Rita James, ed., *The Jury System in America: A Critical Overview.* Beverly Hills, Calif.: Sage Publications, 1975.

Van Dyke, Jon. *Jury Selection Procedures: Our Uncertain Commitment to Representative Panels.* Cambridge, Mass.: Ballinger Publishing Co., 1977.

4

Setting the Penalty

Sentences are the currency of the realm. While reformers, law professors, and appellate courts spend most of their time debating and analyzing how courts determine guilt or innocence, judges, prosecutors, defense attorneys, and defendants focus much of their attention on sentencing. Will the defendant be granted probation, and if not, how many years in prison are the main topics that fuel the dynamics of courthouse justice.

Chapter 15 considers the legal basis for the wide range of discretionary power over sentencing. In addition, the competing theories of sentencing are examined.

Chapter 16 examines how courtroom work groups choose between prison and probation. Of particular interest are the competing criticisms of how these choices are made (too harsh or too lenient) and various proposals to correct these problems.

Sentencing: The Legal Basis of Judicial Discretion

Sentencing is both the beginning and the end of the criminal justice system. It is the beginning because the reasons that society punishes law violators establish the very basis and purpose of the criminal justice system. For the defendant, sentencing is the end of the process, the time when the severity of the punishment is fixed. The courts stand in the middle, wrestling with a host of conflicting and difficult considerations as they try to impose a proper sentence. Few are satisfied that the courts are performing this task fairly or effectively.

Before we can understand the dissatisfaction with how American courts pass sentence, we must examine the legal basis of sentencing. This chapter focuses on conflicting rationales for punishment, the complex and varied sentencing structures found in the United States, and the forms of punishment that can be imposed on those convicted of violating the law.

Why do we sentence?

"An eye for an eye, a tooth for a tooth."
"The punishment should fit the crime."
"Lock 'em up and throw away the key."
"This sentence will be a warning to others."
"The punishment should fit the criminal."
"Sentencing should rehabilitate the offender."
"The public demands a prison sentence."

These statements—variously drawn from the Bible, newspaper headlines, casual conversations, and statements by court officials—aptly demonstrate that there is no consensus on how the courts should go about the task of imposing punishment on the guilty. Retribution, isolation, deterrence, and rehabilitation are the four major reasons advanced for sentencing.

Retribution

retribution

"An eye for an eye, a tooth for a tooth." Since biblical times this phrase has summarized the idea that because the victim has suffered, the criminal should suffer as well. Punishment is a way to satisfy the victim's and presumably also society's desire for revenge. Through the infliction of punishment, the defendant is reconciled to the community by paying a debt to society. This *retribution* rests on the idea that criminals are wicked people who are responsible for their actions and deserve to be punished.

LEVITICUS 25:17–22

When one man strikes another and kills him, he shall be put to death. Whoever strikes a beast and kills it shall make restitution, life for life. When one man injures and disfigures his fellow-countryman, it shall be done to him as he has done; fracture for fracture, eye for eye, tooth for tooth; the injury and disfigurement that he has inflicted upon another shall in turn be inflicted upon him.

Although we cannot deny a human instinct to expect that criminals should pay a price, modern society tends to view a criminal penalty based on revenge as barbaric. Moreover, as a sentencing philosophy, there are several difficulties. Because a democracy seeks to uphold individual rights, there are important limits on how far a society can exact vengeance without denying human rights to individual offenders. For another, retribution can lead to socially undesirable results. Some studies demonstrate that extended periods of custody may actually increase the likelihood that an inmate will commit future criminal acts (Mitford:50). If inmates learn tricks of the criminal trade and become more antisocial while imprisoned, then sentencing for the purpose of retribution is counterproductive to society's attempts to reduce crime. There are few modern-day advocates of the retribution theory of punishment. In outline form, though, this theory is still influential because it ties punishment to the seriousness of the crime irrespective of the characteristics of the defendant.

Isolation

isolation

"Lock them all up and throw away the key." Unlike retribution, *isolation* views the purpose of sentencing as removing dangerous persons from the community. In primitive societies, the severest sanction was banishment from the community. In more modern times, European nations banished criminals to penal colonies, Georgia and Australia among them. In the USSR, dissidents are exiled to cold, barren, and distant Siberia where they are not such a threat to the government.

One problem with the concept of isolation is the severity of the sanction. If the goal is crime prevention, imprisonment may be justified for both trivial and serious offenses. (Note that under retribution, the severity of the punishment is limited to the injury of the victim.) An offender would not be released until it is reasonably certain that he or she will no longer commit a crime. Not only are such predictions impossible to make with any certainty, but the results could be that the offender charged with a trivial offense could be imprisoned for life (Packer:51). Because the isolation position makes simplistic assumptions about the nature of crime and criminals, it cannot provide any standards about how long a sentence should be.

Isolation without efforts at rehabilitation may also produce more severe criminal behavior once the offender is released. As the National Advisory Commission on Criminal Justice Standards and Goals argues, correctional institutions "protect the community but that protection is only temporary. They relieve the community responsibility by removing the offender, but they make successful reintegration of the offender into the community unlikely" (1973a). Finally, of course, isolation would require the building of many more expensive prisons.

As a sentencing philosophy, isolation is somewhat simplistic and has never been well articulated. But as citizens have become increasingly concerned about crime, its popularity has increased accordingly, for it represents the idea of protecting society directly. Moreover, as the utility of deterrence and the workability of rehabilitation are ever more called into question, judges fall back on a more straightforward rationale for prison sentence: isolation.

Deterrence

The most widely held justification for punishment is reducing crime. Neither retribution nor isolation deals with the underlying causes of crime or with the characteristics of criminals. Viewing retribution as pointless and counterproductive, the nineteenth-century British reformer and social theorist Jeremy Bentham articulated the *deterrence* theory. Bentham believed people seek to maximize pleasure and minimize pain. Under this utilitarian theory, the basic objective of punishment is to reduce crime by making it painful. Because they seek to minimize pain, people will refrain from activities (crime in this case) that produce sanctions.

deterrence

Within the general theory of deterrence, there are two, often confused, subconcepts: *general deterrence* and *special deterrence*. By punishing wrongdoers and making a public example of them, general deterrence seeks to discourage those who might be tempted to commit a crime. Special deterrence, on the other hand, seeks to prevent a particular convicted defendant from committing future crimes. Thus

general deterrence, special deterrence

special deterrence is concerned with producing changes in the behavior of the individual defendant. It seeks individualized punishment in the amount and kind necessary so that the criminal will not repeat the crimes. The punishment should therefore fit the criminal. (Note that this is a different concern from the retribution theory that the punishment should fit the crime.)

A difficulty with the deterrence theory is that the goals of general and special deterrence can be incompatible. The severity of the punishment needed to impress the general population about the price of crime may be much higher than that needed to deter the individual defendant from future crimes.

Many question whether court sentences indeed are an effective deterrent. To be sure in a general sense many people refrain from committing illegal acts because they fear the consequences of being convicted. After a party, an intoxicated guest will take a taxi home rather than run the risk of being arrested and disgraced by a drunk driving conviction. In this kind of case, punishment does deter. But beyond such an example, many court officials are cynical about the success of deterrence. To be effective, deterrence requires a rational, consistent, and evenhanded system of imposing sentence. Most observers deny that America has such a system.

Rehabilitation

rehabilitation

The most appealing modern justification for punishment is that crime can be prevented by changing the offender. Like deterrence, the *rehabilitation* model takes into consideration the nature of law breakers and seeks to reduce criminal activity. Rehabilitation, however, goes much further than deterrence in that it assumes that human behavior can be altered. Rehabilitation assumes that criminal behavior is the result of social, psychological, or physical imperfections, and therefore the treatment of such disorders should be the primary goal of corrections. Success is based on the ability to assess the needs of the individual and provide a program to meet these needs. Ultimately, then, offenders are not being punished but are being treated for their own good as well as the general good of society. Under rehabilitation, sentences should fit the offender, not the gravity of the crime.

The goal of rehabilitation shares wide support. Almost three out of four persons surveyed supported the idea that the main emphasis in prisons should be to help the offender become a productive citizen (Harris:67–68).

Until recently the goal of rehabilitation was strongly favored by most court personnel and corrections officials. Within the last decade, however, a number of reservations have been expressed. Some doubt that the causes of crime can be diagnosed or that enough is yet known to engage in major behavior changes. Furthermore, it is not clear that rehabilitation efforts have been successful. California, for example, where the rehabilitative model has been most completely incorporated, is also marked by high rates of recidivism. To some the key weakness is that one cannot coerce a person to change. This is reflected in the fact that some prisoners participate in prison rehabilitation programs like counseling, education, job training, and religious activities out of a desire to gain an early release and not because they wish to change their behavior.

Apart from whether rehabilitation programs have been or can be successful, there is also concern that the humanitarian goal of rehabilitation has served to mask punishment.

Rehabilitation programs are minimal or nonexistent in prison. The rehabilitative ideal has often led to an increasing severity of prison sentences. To critics, then, a sentence based on the hope of rehabilitating an offender may in practice be more punitive than a sentence based on punishment alone.

Competing sentencing philosophies

Throughout the history of the Western world, punishment for violators of the criminal law has been based on philosophical and moral orientations. But of retribution, isolation, deterrence, and rehabilitation, none standing alone is adequate. In reaching a concrete decision, the various goals must be balanced. Thus, elements of each of these four philosophies have been incorporated into society's efforts to control crime. In turn, sentencing decisions reflect ambivalent expectations about the causes of crime, the nature of criminals, and the role of the courts in reducing crime. Sentences also reflect ambivalent expectations about the likely impact of following these philosophies. Pragmatic considerations of overcrowded and sometimes inhumane prisons, public opinion, the absence of rehabilitation programs, and high rates of unemployment are equally as important in assessing whether retribution, isolation, deterrence, and rehabilitation are reachable goals.

Sentencing structures

The competing objectives of retribution, isolation, deterrence, and rehabilitation are reflected in America's complex and varied sentencing structure, which depends both on sources of sentencing authority and limits on sentencing alternatives and lengths. The sentences that can be imposed and the proportion of the sentence that will actually be served are determined by a balance of decision-making power among the three branches of government: legislative, judicial, and executive. The sentences that result can be understood only in terms of the structure in which they exist.

Legislative sentencing responsibility

legislative sentencing responsibility

Recall that under Anglo-American law, there can be no crime and no punishment without law. *Legislative sentencing responsibility* refers to the fact that legislators enact the criminal code. While legislative bodies have done a reasonably good job in defining crimes in a reasonably precise and specific manner, they have generally neglected doing the same for punishment. Instead they have enacted contradictory sentencing provisions and given open-ended powers to judges.

Penal codes have evolved piecemeal, with the result that there are numerous sentencing distinctions. In Wisconsin, for example, there are sixteen separate maximum terms of imprisonment specified for first conviction felonies (Tappan:440). Moreover, as new crimes emerged or more severe punishments provided for existing ones, little effort was devoted to ensuring that a consistent set of penalties existed. The end result is a crazy quilt pattern of sentences. Less serious offenses can be punished more severely than more serious ones. To some, the number and variety of sentencing distinctions is "the main cause of the anarchy in sentencing that is so widely deplored" (Model Penal Code:§601).

A broader concern is that legislators have given judges wide powers to impose sentence but have failed to provide guidance on how those powers should be used. Often the sentencing alternatives range from granting a defendant probation to imposing various terms of imprisonment up to life. In New York, for example, a person convicted of first-degree burglary may be granted probation or sentenced to prison for up to twenty-five years. In other states, the maximum for a burglary conviction is life imprisonment. Such wide-ranging power might be understandable if the legislatures at the same time provided some guidance as to how this sentencing power should be used. They have not. State law requires only that the judge consider the safety of the community or the possibility of the defendant's committing future crimes. Such general statements, of course, provide no guidance at all. In different ways current proposals to restructure sentencing seek to limit this vast judicial discretion.

The problems of a patchwork pattern of sanctions being enacted at the same time that judges are being granted broad sentencing powers has been compounded lately by legislative attempts to make sanctions harsher. In a perceptive analysis of sentencing policy Rosett and Cressey suggest that legislatures are influenced by a severity-softening-severity process. Legislatures pass severe criminal laws on the assumption that fear of pain will terrorize the citizenry into conformity. Court officials, however, soften these penalties because most of the offenders do not fit the criteria that the legislatures initially had in mind. Finding that severe sentences are not being handed out, the legislatures pass laws that are even more severe, thus repeating the process. (1976:159).

Clearly, a systematic relationship exists between the criminal justice system and legislative activity.

Judicial sentencing responsibility

judicial sentencing responsibility

Only judges have the authority to impose sentences. This is referred to as *judicial sentencing responsibility*. Except in a few jurisdictions, the judge's sentence can be appealed only if the penalty did not fall within the legislatively determined penalties.

Under current sentencing laws, state legislatures rarely decide what sentence a "typical" violator of a criminal statute should receive. Instead, they generally determine only what the minimum and maximum sentence for a given offense will be. As a consequence, attention has focused primarily on extremes. What is the most any armed robber should get? What is the *least* any armed robber should get? This tends to encourage unrealistic thinking about criminals. It forces the legislator to concentrate on the unusual cases, such as the mercy killer who "murders" a loved one suffering from a terminal illness, or, at the other extreme, the armed robber who forces his victims to the floor and systematically murders them. Since the imagination is virtually unlimited in coming up with extreme cases that warrant extremely different punishments, legislatures tend to set the minimum and maximum sentences at very great distances from each other.

The resulting legislation tells us what the legislature thinks the appropriate penalty should be for the statistically insignificant number of situations at the extremes of the statute. It does not tell us, however, what the legislature thinks the appropriate sentence should be for the fairly typical case.

The Twentieth Century Fund Task Force on Criminal Sentencing, *Fair and Certain Punishment* (New York: McGraw-Hill, 1976), pp.11–12.

In a few states, though, there are important restrictions on the sentence the judge may impose. Thirteen provide for jury-determined sentences in noncapital cases. Eight of these give sentencing authority to juries in all serious crimes, four restrict the jury's powers to certain types of offenses, and in one (Texas) defendants may request jury sentencing. The National Advisory Commission has recommended that jury sentencing be abolished because it is unprofessional and likely to result in arbitrary and emotional sentences (1973b:110).

The judge's wide discretion reflects the belief that sentences should be individualized, that the punishment should fit the criminal. No two cases are alike, and judges seek to take into account these differences in passing sentence. But there is no agreement on what factors should increase the penalty or what factors should reduce it.

Marvin Frankel, formerly a federal judge in the Southern District of New York, is one of the most forceful critics of this sentencing structure.

The sentencing powers of the judges are, in short, so far unconfined that, except for frequently monstrous maximum limits, they are effectively subject to no law at all. Everyone with the least training in law would be prompt to denounce a statute that merely said the penalty for crimes "shall be any term the judge sees fit to impose." A regime of such arbitrary fiat would be intolerable in a supposedly free society, to say nothing of being invalid under our due-process clause. But the fact is that we have accepted unthinkingly a criminal code creating in effect precisely that degree of unbridled power. [p. 8]

Executive sentencing responsibility

executive sentencing responsibility

Few prisoners serve their maximum terms of imprisonment. During 1979, for example, over 169,000 inmates were released from prison. Fifteen percent of those releases were based on the expiration of prison terms (U.S. Department of Justice, 1982). The vast majority of the remainder of releases occurred before the full term had been served. Typically these inmates were released conditionally, that is, they were subject to supervision. The criteria for release are established and administered by the executive branch of government. The most typical forms of early release involve parole, good time, and executive clemency.

parole

Parole is the conditional release under supervision of an inmate after part of the sentence has been served. When a prisoner is eligible for parole varies among jurisdictions but is generally based on serving one-third of the minimum sentence. Parole boards, which are normally appointed by the governor, make the decisions concerning which prisoners are to be released. Rates of parole vary, ranging from 98 percent to 12 percent. In imposing sentence, judges often take into consideration state laws and parole boards' practices on granting parole.

good time

Through accumulating *good time* (good behavior while in prison), a prisoner may also reduce the length of the sentence. The federal government, forty-six states, and the District of Columbia have statutes providing for good time, but these provisions vary. Only California, Hawaii, and Pennsylvania do not have a statute providing for good time allowances. "Good time" is time subtracted from a sentence of imprisonment by prison authorities as a result of good behavior by the prisoner.

State governors, as well as the president of the United States, have the power to pardon any prisoner in their jurisdiction, reduce the sentence, or make the prisoner eligible for parole. Pardons, however, are not a major method of prisoner release.

executive clemency

Only a small group of inmates are granted this *executive clemency* each year.

How long an offender will be imprisoned depends not only on the length of the sentence imposed by the judge but also on the criteria parole boards use in granting a conditional release and on how correctional officials compute good time. In a fragmented criminal justice system, such executive powers are clearly necessary. Based on experience with the offender and backed up with other information, parole and corrections officials may be in a better position than the sentencing judge to know when the inmate is ready for release. These powers also allow the executive to mute sentencing disparities.

How these powers are utilized is being questioned today. Prisoners and ex-prisoners are strong critics of extensive parole authority because they cannot predict when they will be released. A convict may be denied parole after only a brief hearing. Moreover, because release is tied to rehabilitation, prisoners can con parole and prison officials. Some may attend church on Sunday or enroll in rehabilitation programs not out of any desire to change but to gain an early release.

Forms of punishment

Flogging, the stocks, exile, chopping off a hand, and branding are just a few of the examples of punishments that historically were inflicted upon the guilty. Today such sanctions are viewed as violating the Constitution's prohibition against cruel and unusual punishment. In their place we use imprisonment, probation, fines, and make formal provisions for (but rarely use) capital punishment. In essence these forms of punishment are the tools created under the sentencing structure to advance society's theories of punishment. They are the options from which the judge must choose.

Imprisonment

imprison-ment

Imprisonment of offenders, although employed from time to time throughout history, became the dominant form of punishment only during the last two centuries.

determinate (fixed) sentencing

In the United States there are two different ways that the term of imprisonment is specified. A few states and the federal government use *determinate* (also call *fixed*) *sentencing* under which the judge specifies a given number of years to be served. The defendant would be sentenced to prison for five years or ten. The

*indetermin-
ate sen-
tencing*

majority of states use *indeterminate* (often termed indefinite) *sentencing*, however. The judge specifies a range of years—say, for instance, one to ten. The prisoner is eligible for parole after serving the minimum term but at the discretion of the parole authority may have to serve the entire period. The actual term is set by the parole authority, based on their assessment of the offender's progress toward rehabilitation.

The United States relies on imprisonment more than any other democratic nation in the world. Although during this century the proportion of offenders sentenced to prison has declined, beginning in 1968 the inmate population has steadily increased. By 1982 there were almost 400,000 inmates housed in state or federal correctional facilities. As table 15-1 shows this represents a 55 percent increase since 1975. Prison sentences in the United States are also the longest in the civilized world. In Europe, for example, it is rare for a defendant to be imprisoned for over five years (Frankel:41).

The conditions of America's prisons are increasingly under attack. Although a few prisons in the United States resemble college campuses, many are old and rundown. They are hot in the summer and cold in the winter. Because they are often crowded, they cannot provide security for inmates; the result is that assaults upon inmates and homosexual rapes are a constant part of prison life. In several states conditions are so bad that the courts have declared that they constitute cruel and unusual punishment and have ordered vast upgradings in physical conditions and correctional supervisory personnel. Ameliorating these conditions would prove costly. Construction of a single cell for a prisoner costs at least $30,000. More and better-paid guards would significantly add to the cost of keeping an inmate, costs that are currently estimated at about $12,000 per year.

Knowing of these conditions, judges are often reluctant to send any but the worst offenders to prison. As Martha Kwitny, a former prosecutor and defense attorney put it:

> Judges simply won't impose lengthy sentences to institutions that are overcrowded or that lack minimal standards. . . . Chief Justice Richard Hughes [of New Jersey] instructed the trial courts to postpone all sentences to prison and reformatories for several weeks because these institutions could not accommodate any more inmates.
>
> Even if the courts refuse to order a blanket prohibition on prison sentences, the criminal trial judges will adjust their individual sentences in the light of their knowledge of the conditions in the institutions. Judges now rarely send an urban resident to state prison unless he has committed murder, or is over 25 and has committed rape, armed robbery, or atrocious assault.

Probation

probation

Probation is designed to maintain control over the offenders while permitting them to live in the community under supervision. The practice of probation evolved from efforts of judges to lessen the harshness of the common law penalties by suspending sentences. Over time, probation expanded from the use of volunteers to the employment of probation officers paid by the state (Sutherland and Cres-

TABLE 15-1.   Prisoners in custody in 1975 and 1982

	1975 Dec. 31	1982 June 30	% Change	Number of sentenced prisoners per 100,000 population 6/31/82
United States, total	253,816	394,380	55.3	163
Federal Institution, total	24,131	29,033	20.3	10
State Institution, total	229,685	365,347	59.1	153
Northeast	36,806	57,465	56.1	110
Maine	643	941	46.3	72
New Hampshire	252	418	65.9	44
Vermont	394	631	60.2	88
Massachusetts	2,443	4,164	70.4	72
Rhode Island	594	1,034	74.1	79
Connecticut	3,079	5,351	73.8	104
New York	16,074	27,117	68.7	154
New Jersey	16,164	7,698	24.9	100
Pennsylvania	7,163	10,111	41.2	85
North Central	49,894	74,891	50.1	124
Ohio	11,421	16,319	42.9	151
Indiana	4,547	8,464	86.1	147
Illinois	8,501	13,361	57.2	106
Michigan	10,852	14,935	37.6	163
Wisconsin	2,992	4,544	51.9	96
Minnesota	1,675	2,031	21.3	50
Iowa	1,868	2,774	48.5	91
Missouri	4,371	6,639	51.9	134
North Dakota	209	370	77.0	44
South Dakota	403	742	84.1	105
Nebraska	1,301	1,707	31.2	96
Kansas	1,754	3,005	71.3	126
South	107,392	172,025	60.2	215
Delaware	897	1,937	116.0	229
Maryland	6,965	10,377	49.0	229
District of Columbia	3,327	3,790	13.9	496
Virginia	6,092	9,648	58.4	171
West Virginia	1,176	1,433	21.9	71
North Carolina	12,374	16,562	33.8	258
South Carolina	6,100	9,011	47.7	266
Georgia	10,746	14,053	30.8	245
Florida	15,315	26,466	72.8	248
Kentucky	3,393	4,358	28.4	119
Tennessee	4,575	8,156	78.3	176
Alabama	4,420	8,168	84.8	203
Mississippi	2,422	5,158	113.0	198
Arkansas	2,254	3,607	60.0	156
Louisiana	4,835	10,084	108.6	232
Oklahoma	3,448	5,924	71.9	189
Texas	19,053	33,293	74.8	222
West	38,664	60,966	57.7	132
Montana	485	875	81.4	110
Idaho	695	1,026	47.6	106
Wyoming	340	654	92.4	131
Colorado	2,249	3,026	34.5	101

New Mexico	1,353	1,717	26.9	121
Arizona	2,850	5,641	97.9	199
Utah	810	1,189	46.8	76
Nevada	951	2,552	168.3	295
Washington	3,887	5,896	51.7	139
Oregon	2,859	3,593	25.7	135
California	21,088	32,182	52.6	126
Alaska	528	1,297	145.6	200
Hawaii	569	1,318	131.6	86

Sources: Law Enforcement Assistance Administration. *Prisoners in State and Federal Institutions on December 31, 1975.* Washington, D.C.: Government Printing Office, 1977.

U.S. Department of Justice, Bureau of Justice Statistics. *Bureau of Justice Statistics Bulletin: Prisoners at Midyear 1982.* Washington, D.C.: Government Printing Office, 1982.

sey:463). Today probation provides the major alternative to imprisonment. The major justification for probation is that prisons are inappropriate places for some defendants, and limited supervision is a better way to rehabilitate criminals. It is also significantly less expensive than imprisonment.

State laws provide judges wide discretion in deciding whether to grant probation. According to Illinois law, for example, a defendant "may be admitted to probation when it appears that: (1) The defendant is not likely to commit another offense; (2) The public interest does not require that the defendant receive the penalty provided for the offense; and (3) The rehabilitation of the defendant does not require that he receive the penalty provided for the offense" (Illinois Revised Statute, chap. 38 §117–1). The only legislative restriction to granting probation is that defendants convicted of certain offenses—typically capital offenses and rape—may not be given probation.

When probation is granted, the defendant is commonly required to meet a number of conditions: keep a job, support the family, avoid places where alcoholic beverages are sold, report periodically to the probation officer, and not violate any law. Because probation is a judicial act, the judge may revoke probation and send the defendant to prison if these conditions of probation are violated. Whether this supervision leads to rehabilitation is unclear. In practice, probation officers, faced with large caseloads, are unable to provide anything but limited supervision. Various studies place the success rate of probation between 60 and 90 percent (Cole:364).

Fines

fines

Fines are commonly imposed in misdemeanor cases and city ordinance violations. For local governments, fines, particularly from traffic cases, provide an important source of revenue. With the exception of white-collar crimes like embezzlement, income tax evasion, or corporate fraud, however, fines are rarely levied in felony cases.

Capital punishment

*capital pun-
ishment*

Capital punishment was once the almost exclusive penalty applied to convicted felons. By the time of the American Revolution, the English courts had defined over two hundred felonies, all of which were capital offenses. Through the decades, however, the courts and legislatures began to recognize other forms of punishment, such as imprisonment and later probation. By 1970 all but nine jurisdictions provided for the death penalty, but it was usually limited to murder, treason, and (largely in the South) rape. Through the years the number of executions has steadily fallen. Since 1930, when statistics first began to be collected, executions declined from an annual average of 167 to 21 per year between 1960 and 1970. From 1967 to 1976 an unofficial moratorium on executions existed. Table 15-2 shows executions between 1930 and 1967.

A sentence of death is the ultimate penalty society can impose upon the guilty. Opponents contend that it is morally wrong for the state to take a life, it has no deterrent value, and it is inherently discriminatory. These arguments have lead all Western democracies, except the United States, to abolish capital punishment. Opponents' efforts to declare the death penalty unconstitutional culminated in the case of *Furman* v. *Georgia* (408 U.S. 238, 1972). In this case the Supreme Court decided that existing death penalty laws were unconstitutional. A divided Court held that the Eighth Amendment's prohibition against cruel and unusual punishment was violated because the death penalty was arbitrarily and capriciously imposed. In a 1976 decision, however, the Court by a 7-to-2-vote upheld the constitutionality of several capital punishment laws: "The concerns expressed in *Furman* that the penalty of death not be imposed in an arbitrary or capricious manner can be met by a carefully drafted statute that ensures that the sentencing authority is given adequate information and guidance" (*Gregg* v. *Georgia* 428 U.S. 153). At the same time, though, laws providing for the mandatory imposition of the death penalty were held unconstitutional. In a later case the high court also declared that the rape of an adult woman was not grave enough to warrant the death penalty.

Based on the *Gregg* decision, thirty-seven states have reenacted death penalty statutes, authorizing capital punishment for certain crimes (usually murder). These laws provide for a bifurcated trial. During the first phase the jury considers only the issue of guilt or innocence. If a verdict of murder in the first degree is returned,

TABLE 15-2.   Executions in the United States, 1930–1967

Region	All offenses	Murder	Rape	Other
United States	3,859	3,334	455	70
Northeast	608	606	0	2
North Central	403	393	10	0
South	2,306	1,824	443	39
West	509	496	0	13

Source: Bureau of Prisons "Executions 1930–1967," *National Prisoner Statistics*, no. 42 (Washington, D.C.: Government Printing Office, 1968), pp. 10–11.

then the jury reconvenes. During this second phase, the jury considers aggravating and mitigating circumstances, then decides whether to impose the death penalty. If they decline, the defendant is typically sentenced to life imprisonment. State laws define aggravating and mitigating circumstances. The factors specified are designed to meet the Supreme Court mandate for guided discretion in determining the sentence.

Based on post-*Gregg* statutes, 1050 prisoners were under a sentence of death as of December 31, 1982. Table 15-3 shows that the preponderance of those awaiting execution were in the South. Death-row inmates are also predominantly male (only eleven females are under a sentence of death) and disproportionately black (41 percent).

Despite the swelling population of death-row inmates, there have been few executions. Between 1967 and 1983 six persons were executed. The small number of executions is related to extended appeal processes in death penalty cases. In seeking to avoid the death penalty, defense lawyers file numerous postconviction appeals in a variety of courts including the original trial court, the state appeals courts, and all three levels of federal courts. At times these efforts are successful. During 1981, for example, the courts removed seventy-four prisoners from the threat of the death penalty. These efforts have become largely delaying actions, however. By late 1983, many prisoners appeared to have exhausted their appeals, meaning that the nation might soon experience an execution rate that could match the high rate of three executions per week in the mid-1930s.

Developing sentencing alternatives

Upon conviction judges are faced with the decision of placing defendants on probation or sending them to prison. Lately some imaginative judges have sought to reach beyond these two alternatives to impose sentences that individualize punishment and at the same time serve broader goals for society. For example, in place of a fine or in conjunction with probation, the judge may require the offender to make
restitution *restitution* (to make good for the loss or damage) to the victim. Note that while the oldest theory of punishment—retribution—was hinged on the victim, most modern sentencing alternatives omit a consideration of offsetting the loss the victim has

TABLE 15-3. Prisoners under sentence of death by region (December 31, 1982)

Region	Number of prisoners
Northeast	25
North Central	100
South	711
West	214
U.S. (Total)	1050

Source: U.S. Department of Justice, Bureau of Justice Statistics, *Capital Punishment 1982* (July, 1983).

suffered. Some judges, rather than imprison a defendant in jail, require that the defendant perform public service work. A minor drug offender may be sentenced to work weekends for the local public hospital, or a doctor convicted of income tax evasion may be required to treat patients free several hours a week at a public hospital. At present these sentencing alternatives are not recognized by statute. But numerous proposals have been offered to make these programs more available and more widely utilized.

CLOSE-UP: TWO JUDGES' VIEWS OF SENTENCING

Just as there is no consensus in America about the purposes of criminal sentences, judges hold differing views about the relative merits of retribution, isolation, deterrence, and rehabilitation. Below are the views of two judges. Judge Seagraves is a Superior Court Judge near San Francisco who deals with felonies and serious misdemeanors. He rejects stiff prison sentences as the answer to the crime problem and likewise sees little deterrent effect of the law. Judge Pearce presides over the municipal court of Bismarck, North Dakota, and hears misdemeanor and ordinance violations. He stresses punishment and not rehabilitation in sentencing and believes in the deterrent value of the law. Note that in expressing their views on sentencing both judges discuss how the sentencing structure affects their choices.

PRISON IS NOT THE ANSWER

The "hanging judge" who hands down the stiffest possible sentences is not the answer to America's ever-increasing crime rate, says a California judge who had studied the problem for nine years.

"If we [judges] jailed everyone we could, we would bankrupt the country to pay for their imprisonment," said Judge Roy W. Seagraves of Redwood City, Calif.

"But the popular concept that punishment is a deterrent in crime is a fallacy," he said. "A criminal doesn't consider the punishment at all because he doesn't think he is going to get caught."

The hard-line philosophy that heavy penalties and jail sentences will cut crime is wrong, but it is a popular concept built up by politicians who like to seize on it as a simple solution to a highly emotional problem, he said. . . .

Judges, aware that putting a person behind bars with other criminals leaves little chance for his rehabilitation, are seeking alternatives to imprisonment, Judge Seagraves said.

But he said those convicted of the most serious crimes—murder, kidnap, rape, grand theft—are now regularly jailed and this means "the wishes of the conservatives are being carried out today."

He admitted that some criminals convicted of major crimes are paroled within relatively short periods when "jailhouse lawyers" teach inmates how to fool parole boards into thinking they are going to "go straight."

These too-early paroles sometimes do occur, the judge said, but they are misjudgments on the part of parole authorities and are not based on faulty parole policies.

There is no public "clamor for toughness" in handling persons convicted of the many lesser crimes that make up the bulk of the cases in our courts, Judge Seagraves said.

In one "major minor crime category," drunken driving, many people are not pushing stiff sentences because they are silently reminding themselves: "There but for the grace of God go I."

The only real solution to our frightening increases in the crime rate is education of the nation's youth to make them respect the law, the jurist said. . . .

Neil Swan, *Atlanta* (Ga.) *Journal*, November 18, 1975.

CITY JUDGE SAYS "RIGHT SENTENCE" IS TOP PROBLEM

"Trying to find the right sentence, that's the biggest problem," says Judge Henry J. Pearce of his duties in Bismarck Municipal Court. . . .

"I view sentencing as a punishment rather than as a rehabilitative measure," Judge Pearce said. "I try to see sentencing as setting an example while protecting society."

But while opting for a tougher stand with violators, Judge Pearce, who may hear cases ranging from an illegal turn, to driving while intoxicated, to shoplifting, added, "The problem is what the sentence should be."   *(continued)*

"Take driving while intoxicated, for instance. It doesn't do any good to 'throw the book' at the guy and give him a $500 fine and 30-day jail sentence.

"He may wind up losing his job, his wife may get down on him and he could have five kids at home. You could wind up driving him to drink again.

"On the other hand, if you give him only a fine, he may forget the whole process and you'll see him again in another month."

What Judge Pearce, and other jurists favor, are flexible alternatives in the type of sentences that they may hand down. For that reason Judge Pearce scoffed at an increasing trend by politicians and prosecutors to recommend a "flat" sentence for a law-breaker where a judge is required to hand out a mandatory minimum sentence.

"There is just no flexibility to that type of sentencing," he said. "You have to take each case individually. What are the circumstances involved? What was the person's mental condition at the time of the accident?

"There are times when you can tell that there may be some mental aberration affecting that person. Then he should be sent to Jamestown for tests, and some sentence other than a penalty should be given.

"Or there may be something more to the case. Maybe someone was hurt or killed. Or the arresting officer may have smelled alcohol although the driver was in control of the vehicle. . . ."

Mark Kinders, *Bismarck* (N.D.) *Tribune*, October 31, 1975.

Conclusion

After conviction the defendant is brought before the court for a sentencing hearing and the imposition of sentence. How the law structures sentencing has major implications for how judges carry out this responsibility. Most immediately the judge must choose a sentence prescribed by law, which in a typical felony case means deciding between probation or imprisonment. The decision reached often reflects the judge's views on whether sentences should be for the purpose of retribution, isolation, deterrence, or rehabilitation. In weighing these competing and often contradictory philosophies, the judge must also consider how the options of prison or probation work. Does the prison have a rehabilitation program? Are prisons too crowded and too inhumane for this type of offender? Does the probation department in this court provide effective service? The judge must also consider how state practices on good time and parole release will affect the length of the sentence that will be actually served. As we have seen, legislatures have granted the judiciary authority to make these decisions but have not provided any guidance on what they think the sentence for a typical offender should be.

For discussion

1. Should the punishment fit the crime or the criminal? In what ways do the four justifications for punishment provide different answers to this question?
2. Which of the four justifications for sentencing comes closest to matching your own? How does this view influence your thinking about how the courts sentence?
3. What is the mix of legislative, judicial, and sentencing responsibility in your state?

4. What views of the purposes of sentencing are most often expressed in the local and national newspapers?
5. Interview a judge. What are his or her views of judicial discretion over sentencing? Too much, too little, or just right? Why?
6. Consider the views of Judges Seagraves and Pearce. How are they similar? In what ways do they differ? Even if they differ, do you think they might sentence in similar ways?

References

Cole, George. *The American System of Criminal Justice*, 3rd ed. Monterey, Calif.: Brooks/Cole Publishing Company, 1983.

Frankel, Marvin. *Criminal Sentences: Law Without Order*. New York: Hill & Wang, 1972.

Harris, Louis. *The Harris Survey Textbook of Public Opinion, 1970*. New York: Louis Harris and Associates, 1971.

Kwitny, Martha. "Our Overcrowded Prisons." *Wall Street Journal*, October 1, 1975. Extract reprinted by permission of *The Wall Street Journal*, © Dow Jones & Company, Inc., 1975. All rights reserved.

Mitford, Jessica. *Kind and Usual Punishment*. New York: Vintage Books, 1971.

Model Penal Code, Comment 1 (Tentative Draft No. 2, American Law Institute, 1954).

National Advisory Commission on Criminal Justice Standards and Goals. *Corrections*. Washington, D.C.: Government Printing Office, 1973a.

———. *Courts*. Washington, D.C.: Government Printing Office, 1973b.

Packer, Herbert. *The Limits of the Criminal Sanction*. Palo Alto., Calif.: Stanford University Press, 1968.

Rosett, Arthur, and Donald Cressey. *Justice by Consent: Plea Bargains in the American Courthouse*. Philadelphia: J. B. Lippincott, 1976.

Sutherland, Edwin H., and Donald R. Cressey. *Criminology*. Philadelphia: J. B. Lippincott, 1970.

Tappan, Paul. *Crime, Justice and Correction*. New York: McGraw-Hill, 1960.

U.S. Department of Justice. Bureau of Justice Statistics. *Prisoners in State and Federal Institutions on December 31, 1980*. Washington, D.C.: Government Printing Office, 1982.

For further reading

Frankel, Marvin. *Criminal Sentences: Law Without Order*. New York: Hill & Wang, 1972.

Morris, Norval. *The Future of Imprisonment*. Chicago: University of Chicago Press, 1974.

Packer, Herbert. *The Limits of the Criminal Sanction*. Palo Alto, Calif.: Stanford University Press, 1968.

Van Den Haag, Ernest. *Punishing Criminals*. New York: Basic Books, 1975.

Wilson, James Q. *Thinking About Crime*. New York: Basic Books, 1975.

Wright, Erik Olin. *The Politics of Punishment*. New York: Harper & Row, 1973.

Choosing between Prison and Probation

What sentence would you give the following defendant? He was convicted by a jury in federal district court of theft and possession of goods stolen from an interstate shipment. He is a white male over twenty-six years of age. In imposing sentence what weight would you give the fact that the defendant, although currently unemployed, formerly worked as a cab driver? Would your sentence be influenced by knowing that although the defendant has no prior criminal convictions, several other felony charges are currently pending against him for offenses committed after this one? Should you even consider these factors? Would you want any other additional information before making a decision?

Every day judges all over the nation face questions like these as they impose sentences upon thousands of defendants. As stressed in the last chapter, American judges have been given wide discretionary power in making these decisions. In this case federal law allows the judge to grant probation, and/or fine the defendant up to $5,000 and/or impose a prison sentence of up to ten years.

In reaching these decisions judges do not work alone. They often rely heavily on the sentencing recommendations of other members of the courtroom work group—prosecutors, probation officers, and perhaps even the defense attorney. In turn, many of these sentencing recommendations are based on how long the prison sentence will actually be. Thus they would consider the rules of the federal parole board: a person is eligible for parole after serving one-third of the sentence, which probably means that a three-year sentence would result in one year in prison, assuming the defendant's good behavior in prison. How would this factor affect your sentence?

There is no uniformity in how these decisions are made or the results of these decisions. When a group of fifty federal judges was presented with our hypothetical defendant (drawn from an actual case), they differed greatly in the sentence they would hand down. A few said they would grant probation, most said they would give a prison sentence of a few years, and still a few others said they would impose a rather lengthy prison sentence (Partridge and Eldridge). Such variation prompts one of two major criticisms of sentencing: sentences are disparate. The other is that judges hand out sentences that are too lenient.

This chapter examines how judges determine sentences, the criteria they use, and how various members of the work group influence these sentences. It also analyzes numerous problems associated with sentencing in America and types of proposals designed to alleviate them.

The sentencing process and courtroom work groups

In seeking to understand the sentencing process, we must look not to the formal rules of law found in legislative statutes or appellate court opinions but to the informal rules and practices of the courtroom work groups. Sentencing involves a collective decision-making process. For example, in jurisdictions where sentence bargaining predominates, the judge almost invariably imposes the sentence that the prosecutor and the defense attorney have already agreed upon. Rosett and Cressey (33) relate a pattern in which the prosecutor talks to the probation officer about the sentencing agreement that has already been reached. This conversation indicates that information should be stressed to justify the sentence that will be imposed. The probation report then provides a rationale for the sentence already agreed upon. Although only the judge possesses the legal authority to impose sentence, probation officers, prosecutors, and defense attorneys are also influential.

Presentence investigation

presentence investiga-tion

The *presentence investigation* is designed to aid the court in arriving at a fair and appropriate sentence by providing information about the defendant. Presentence reports include such information as the offender's previous arrest and conviction record, sociological background, employment history, psychological evaluation (if needed), and the circumstances of the offense. These reports are compiled by probation officers from official records and documents, interviews with persons who know the defendant, and an interview with the defendant. Depending on the law of the jurisdiction and the work load of the probation department, a judge may request a presentence investigation in all cases, in only certain categories of offenders, or only when probation is a likely sentence (Katkin:16–17). The National Advisory Commission has recommended that presentence investigations should be conducted in all felony cases, as well as serious misdemeanor offenses for which a prison term might be imposed.

Probation reports also typically include a recommendation whether the defendant is a good candidate for rehabilitation by probation. Although sentencing judges are not obliged to follow such recommendations, they usually do. After studying sentencing decisions in California, the authors concluded that the court followed the presentence investigation report's recommendation in favor of probation 96 percent of the time (Carter and Wilkins:507). When the probation report recommended incarceration, however, the court was slightly less likely to follow the advice of the probation officer, an indication that probation officers tend to be more punitive than judges. This overall high rate of agreement shows that judges often use probation officers as sentencing advisers, relying on them for information about sentencing alternatives and candid evaluations of the defendant.

One marked advantage of the judge's using the probation officer as sentencing adviser and following the recommendations is that sentencing disparities among judges on the same court are reduced. Yet some question whether probation officers are as independent of the judges as they should be. Although probation departments are supposed to be independent of the other parts of the judicial system, a number of factors combine to tie the probation department to the judges of the court. In many areas, the probation department is part of the judiciary. The courts control the department's budget, supervise recruitment practices, and monitor their supervisory practices over defendants on probation. And as with other dimensions of the courtroom community, the probation officers come to work closely with the judges. This practice obviously increases the trust the judge has in the probation officer's recommendation, but it can also mean that these recommendations are not independent and impartial. Rather they can be the product of second-guessing the sentence that the judge is likely to impose. On the other hand, there is equal concern that given the pressures of disposing of cases, the judge may come to rely on the probation officer's recommendations totally. If the sentence is the mere ratification of the presentence investigation, then the judicial control of sentencing has been improperly delegated to a nonjudge.

I have sentenced hundreds of criminal offenders and the difficult responsibilities that attach to sentencing haven't become any easier for me the longer I have done it. From my own experience, about ten percent of the time involves a case in which I can't readily determine what I want to do. I've got to think about it for a while, may confer with some of my colleagues. Figuratively speaking, it's a coin flip sometimes and that is rather drastic when you are talking about somebody's personal liberty.

Judge Critelli, Des Moines, Iowa, in Leslie Wilkins et al., *Sentencing Guidelines: Structuring Judicial Discretion* (Washington, D.C.: Government Printing Office, 1976), p. vii.

Prosecutor

Prosecutors can influence the sentencing decision in several important ways. By agreeing to a count or charge bargain, prosecutors limit the maximum penalties that the judge may impose. During the sentencing hearing, prosecutors can bring to the court's attention factors that are likely to increase the penalty—for example, that the victim was particularly vulnerable or that the defendant inflicted great harm on the victim. Alternatively, though, prosecutors can bring out factors that would lessen the penalty—for example, the defendant's cooperation with the police. Finally, prosecutors may make a specific sentencing recommendation. If, for example, there has been a sentence bargain, the prosecutor will indicate the penalty agreed on, with the usual result that the judge will adopt that recommendation as the sentence. When such prosecutorial recommendations are based on officewide policy, they can have the positive effect of muting sentencing disparities among the different judges. In some courts, however, prosecutors are not allowed to make sentencing recommendations because sentencing is viewed solely as a judicial responsibility.

Defense attorney

The defense attorney's role in sentencing begins early in the history of a case. The decision of whether to go to trial or enter a guilty plea is partially based on the attorney's realistic assessment of the likely sentence to be imposed. Based on the knowledge of what sentences have been handed out to other defendants accused of similar crimes and with similar backgrounds, the attorney must advise (and at times prepare) the client as to the probable sentence. At the same time, the defense attorney seeks to obtain the best sentence possible. One way to accomplish this goal is by trying to maneuver the case before a judge with a lenient sentencing record. Another way is to discuss the case with the prosecutor in hopes that he or she will agree to (or at least not oppose) a recommendation of probation in the presentence investigation. Defense attorneys also try to show certain circumstances to make the defendant look better in the eyes of the judge, prosecutor, and probation officer. They may try to downplay the severity of the offense by stressing the defendant's minor role in the crime or the fact that the victim was not without blame, or they may have friends or employers testify about the defendant's general good character and regular employment.

Overall, though, defense attorneys are less influential than prosecutors in obtaining a less severe punishment than is typical. At times judges and prosecutors view the defense attorney's arguments for leniency as an effort to impress their clients that they tried as hard as they could.

The judge

Courtroom work groups impose informal limits on how judges exercise their formal legal authority to impose sentences. Judges are well aware that the disposition of cases is tied to plea bargaining and that in turn plea bargaining depends on being able to anticipate the sentencing tendencies of judges.

No matter how aloof a judge may think he is and no matter how eccentric others may think he is, he shares in a framework of understandings, expectations and agreements that are relied upon to dispose of most criminal cases. As does a prosecutor or a defense attorney, he can deviate from this consensus only slightly; otherwise he threatens the whole working structure of the courthouse. When he strays too far from expectations by imposing a sentence either substantially more lenient or more severe than the one agreed on by defendant, defense lawyer and prosecutor, it becomes more difficult for the prosecutor and defense counsel to negotiate future agreements. [Rosett and Cressey:81]

In working within the limits established by the consensus of the courtroom work groups, judges are also constrained because the other members of the work group possess a more thorough knowledge of the details of the defendant and the nature of the crime. This does not mean that judges are without influence. Judges are the most experienced members of the courtroom team, and therefore their views carry more weight than the relatively inexperienced prosecutors or defense attorneys. Thus differing judicial attitudes on sentencing are reflected in the courtroom work groups' common understanding of what sentences are appropriate.

Factors in sentencing

Sentencing is not an easy task. The vast majority of judges say it is the most difficult part of their job. Part of the reason is that sentencing requires weighing the possibility of rehabilitation, the need for protecting the public, popular demands for retribution, and any potential deterrent value in the sentence. But courtroom work groups do not consider these competing perspectives in the abstract. They must sentence real defendants. Each defendant and crime is somewhat different. Sentences are expected to be individualized—to fit the penalty to the crime and the defendant. The seriousness of the crime, prior criminal record, aggravating or mitigating circumstances of the crime, and the social stability of the defendant are just a few of the general factors that must be considered in seeking to individualize sentences. Recall also from the discussion in chapter 13 that defendants who go to trial rather than plead guilty may also receive higher-than-normal sentences.

Normal penalties

normal
penalties

In seeking to produce individualized sentences, courtroom work groups employ what have been labeled *normal penalties* (Sudnow). Based on the usual manner in which crimes are committed and the typical backgrounds of the defendants who commit them, courtroom work groups develop typical sentences of what sentences are appropriate for given categories. It is within these normal penalties that individualization occurs. Upward and downward adjustments are made. Typical sentences are not used mechanically; rather they guide sentencing.

Sentencing involves a two-stage decision-making process. After conviction, a decision is made whether to incarcerate the defendant or grant probation. The second one is how long the sentence should be. This process can be used to illustrate that different courtroom work groups employ varying concepts of normal penalties. From one courtroom to the next, there are important differences in the threshold for granting probation. And once it has been decided that a defendant should be imprisoned, there are important differences in the factors used to determine the length of that sentence. Stated another way, courtroom work groups tend to look at the same set of general factors in passing sentence. But there is no uniformity in the relative weights that are assigned these general or individual factors.

Seriousness of the offense

seriousness of the offense The most important factor in setting normal penalties is the *seriousness of the offense*. The more serious the offense, the less likely the defendant will be granted probation. And as table 16-1 illustrates, the more serious the offense, the longer the prison sentence. These conclusions are hardly surprising. Society expects that convicted murderers will be punished more severely than those found guilty of theft. What is important is how courtroom work groups go about the task of deciding what offenses are serious.

When weighing the seriousness of the offense, courtroom work groups examine the harm or loss suffered by the crime victim in what they perceive to be the "real offense" (what really happened, not the official charge). This information is provided either in the official version of the offense part of the presentence report or by the police arrest report (Wilkins et al.:88). By focusing on the "real offense" judges can counteract charge bargaining. In Detroit, for example, presentence reports in simple robbery reports will include the type of weapon used. Thus the defendant who has been found guilty only for unarmed robbery may often be sentenced on the basis that he really committed an armed robbery. The opposite also happens. By examining the prior relationship between the defendant and the victim, courtroom work groups often perceive that the underlying crime is a squab-

TABLE 16-1. Average prison sentences in Baltimore, Chicago, and Detroit

Offense originally charged	Months					
	Baltimore		Chicago		Detroit	
	Mean	N	Mean	N	Mean	N
Murder	155.8	22	129.0	20	95.3	23
Armed robbery	105.1	121	57.4	98	46.1	73
Assault	77.6	25	25.0	25	23.6	22
Heroin dealer	79.7	52	32.1	17	11.4	8
Heroin user	33.1	12	25.5	4	6.4	17
Burglary-theft	52.6	70	16.1	57	15.6	83
Rape	83.7	11	56.0	15	91.2	5
Robbery	74.8	41	27.5	26	33.9	10
Weapons			21.1	20	9.3	26
Other	30.3	25	19.3	24	16.7	94

Source: From James Eisenstein and Herbert Jacob, *Felony Justice: An Organizational Analysis of Criminal Courts*, p. 280. Copyright © 1977 by Herbert Jacob and James Eisenstein. Reprinted by permission of the publisher, Little, Brown and Company.

Note: Life sentences excluded from calculations.

ble among friends and therefore less serious than the official charge indicates (Vera Institute of Justice).

Court work groups vary in what offenses they view as serious and the severity of the penalties to be applied. Courts differ over the threshold of seriousness of the offense in granting probation. I found that in one downstate Illinois county, defendants convicted of aggravated assault with a weapon were never granted probation because this crime was viewed as very serious. But in Los Angeles, some defendants convicted of assault with a weapon would be considered for probation (Mather).

Sentencing on the basis of seriousness is one of the major ways courts attempt to arrive at consistent sentences. Most courts employ a rank ordering that incorporates the full range of offenses from the most serious crimes of armed robbery and rape, through middle-level crimes of domestic homicide to the lowest level of forgery, theft, and burglary. One reason that sentences appear to critics to be lenient is that most cases are distributed on the lowest level of this ranking. Many critics also fail to consider that judges do not wish to punish minor violators more harshly than serious ones. When a sentence is criticized for being too lenient, the usual response is that to give this defendant a longer prison term would necessitate an upward adjustment in all penalties.

Prior record

prior record

After the seriousness of the offense, the next most important factor considered in sentencing is the defendant's *prior record*. Defendants with prior criminal convictions are sentenced more harshly than first offenders. Table 16-2 shows data from a study of sentencing for four federal crimes. Overall those with prior convictions received longer sentences than those with none or only one prior offense. The study noted, though, that prior record had its greatest impact on less serious offenses: "When the crime is perceived as being less serious, individual factors such as prior record seem to be given relatively more weight than when the crime is more serious—there uniformity 'let the punishment fit the crime' seems to be more important" (Tiffany et al.:379).

TABLE 16-2.   Effects of prior record on sentencing in federal courts

Crime	Sentences [a]			
	None	Some prior record	High	All records
Bank robbery	26.7	30.2	35.8	30.9
Auto theft	7.1	6.5	9.2	7.6
Securities	9.3	9.6	13.9	10.9
Forgery	3.3	4.2	10.6	6.0
All crimes	11.6	12.6	17.4	13.9

[a] Sentence is computed from a sentencing index that ranges from 0 (probation) to 50 (over 120 months in prison).

Source: Lawrence Tiffany, Yakov Avichai, and Geoffrey Peters, "A Statistical Analysis of Sentencing in Federal Courts: Defendants Convicted After Trial, 1967–1968," *Journal of Legal Studies* 4 (June, 1975), p. 378.

Such a rule is not necessarily applied automatically. Courtroom work groups often consider the length of time between the current offense and the last one. If there is a significant gap, they will sentence more leniently. Again, though, courts apply this factor in different ways. In Prairie City, Illinois, a single previous conviction was sufficient to deny probation. But in Kansas, Milwaukee, and Michigan, the courts were more flexible (Dawson:81). Some defendants with prior records were granted probation. The federal sentencing data show the same pattern. Courts also differ in whether they consider only previous convictions or also include prior arrests without conviction.

Aggravating or mitigating circumstances

In passing sentence judges and other members of the courtroom work group consider not only the formal charge but also how the crime was committed.

> We found that prosecutors and defense counsel engage in a very fine calculation of moral turpitude. Compared with the layperson's, the experienced criminal justice actor's analysis of moral turpitude is like the difference between measuring things in terms of pounds and ounces and measuring them in the finer units of grams, milligrams, and micrograms. There are subtle shades of differences and nuances which experienced attorneys appreciate but which are lost on the layperson.
>
> For instance, in pretesting our hypothetical robbery with a knife case, prosecutors wanted to know such things as: Was the slashing completely unprovoked by the victim? Had the victim said anything at all or resisted in any way? Was the slashing necessary to accomplish the crime? Was it done out of nervousness? When the robber presented the knife, how did he present it? Was there actual contact of the knife with the victim? . . . Prosecutors wanted to know not just whether there had been a slashing but how deep it was, whether there would be permanent injury or ugly scars in visible areas such as on the face. This kind of information was used by prosecutors to assess not only how serious the crime had been but also how "mean" or "bad" the defendant was. There was no question that a robbery with a slashing was a serious matter and had to be punished, but there was a question about the precise degree of punishment that this particular robbery deserved. [McDonald et al.:157]

aggravating circum-stances

mitigating factors

Some of the *aggravating circumstances* that lead to higher penalty often include the use of a weapon, and personal injury to the victim. For example, an offender who pistol whipped an elderly woman during a mugging would receive a higher penalty than one who merely threatened the victim with a weapon. *Mitigating factors* include youth of the defendant, lack of mental capacity, and role (principal or secondary actor) in the crime. There is no uniformity in what factors should be considered in weighing aggravating and mitigating circumstances, however.

Social stability

social sta-bility

The perceived *social stability* of the defendant is particularly important when probation is under consideration. Whether the defendant is married, the relationship with the family, length of employment, and prior alcohol or drug abuse represent some indicators of social stability. In an exhaustive study of factors in sentencing, Wilkins and his associates investigated over two hundred sentencing variables in the Denver and Vermont courts. They found that presentence reports often contained significant missing data about social stability but concluded that judges have enough other data available to form a judgment. In both areas social stability turned out to be an important predictor of judges' sentencing.

Uncertainty and public opinion

uncertainty

Sentencing is more art than science. Judges, prosecutors, probation officers, and defense attorneys are well aware that in considering the seriousness of the offense, prior record of the defendant, aggravating or mitigating circumstances, and stability of the defendant, they will make mistakes. *Uncertainty* is deep-seated in the process. They may send someone to prison who should not be there or impose a

---

CLOSE-UP: JUDGE EXPLAINS SENTENCING RULES

Although the public apparently feels judges are too lenient in criminal cases, an experiment conducted by a Jefferson Parish judge indicates a better understanding of the law and problems of sentencing would change some minds.

Judge Thomas C. Wicker of 24th Judicial District Court, speaking before the Rotary Club of the West Bank at the Gretna United Methodist Church, presented a hypothetical case involving a negligent homicide [in which four persons were killed by a car driven by an intoxicated driver], first, through information from an initial newspaper report, secondly through a probationary report on the defendant's background and thirdly with Judge Wicker explaining some of the problems involved in sentencing.

After each presentation, Judge Wicker asked his listeners to indicate on a form what type of sentence they would give the defendant.

The speaker said previous presentations of the same case showed much harsher sentences were given by the listeners before they were aware of the "defendant's" background and of the problems of sentencing.

For example, of 64 members of the Metairie Rotary Club, 38 would have sentenced the defendant to Angola [state prison], nine to Parish Prison [local jail], and 17 suspended sentences, based on the initial newspaper report.

Following a report on the defendant's background and an explanation by Judge Wicker of the legalities and problems involved, eight sentenced to Angola, four to Parish Prison, and 53 gave a suspended sentence.

Of those same 64 persons, 58 had indicated they felt the public believed judges were either "much too lenient" or a "little bit lenient."

"In presenting this to you," the judge told the Rotarians, "I am trying to demonstrate the process which judges must go through in weighing the considerations in each individual case."

He said there are three principles of sentencing which must be kept in mind:

—Deterrence. Would the sentencing deter others from committing the same crime? Would it deter the defendant from committing the same or another crime? Or would it make him a hardened criminal apt to commit violent crimes?

—Rehabilitation. Judge Wicker said that, unfortunately, rehabilitative facilities are limited at both the Jefferson Parish Prison and at the state penitentiary at Angola.

—Retribution. "The consideration here is that if a person violates the law, he should pay the penalty," Judge Wicker said.

As for the victim, the judge said that "unfortunately, at this time, the law is barren of a means of aiding the victim except through civil remedies."

Judge Wicker also explained such practical limitations as federal court orders specifying the maximum number of prisoners which may be housed at Angola (2,600) or in the Parish Prison (162).

The judge said recent statistics show that while crime rates are up and arrest rates are down, the U.S. still has more individuals in jail per capita than any other country in the "free world."

New Orleans Times-Picayune, April 27, 1977.

prison sentence longer than necessary. Or they may err in the opposite direction. A defendant recently granted probation may commit a serious and well-publicized crime. Note, though, that only the second type of error will reach public attention. Mistakes of the first kind appear only later.

The uncertainties inherent in sentencing are particularly important at a time when public opinion is increasingly critical of the courts and sentencing. The majority of Americans feel that sentences are too lenient. In response, courts are sentencing a higher proportion of defendants to prison. Yet at the same time prisons are overcrowded, adding another complexity to the difficult task of arriving at a fair and appropriate sentence.

Sentencing disparities

Federal trial judges in New York, Connecticut, and Vermont were surveyed to see what sentences they would give twenty hypothetical defendants. One of those cases we summarized at the beginning of this chapter. As table 16-3 shows, the judges varied in their responses. Even if the most extreme sentences are eliminated, the data clearly indicate that substantial disagreement exists among the judges about what constitutes a fair and appropriate sentence.

These results based on similar but still hypothetical cases conform to the results of numerous previous studies using a different approach. A number of studies have statistically analyzed sentences imposed by judges in comparable (but not identical) groups of cases. Table 16-4 reports a statistical study that clearly shows major differences in sentences handed out.

Sentencing represents the conflict between two important goals: equality and

TABLE 16-3.   Sentences of federal trial judges for defendants convicted of theft and possession of stolen goods

Imprisonment (in months)	Probation (in months)	Number of judges
90		1
72		1
60		6
48		10
36		18
24		6
12		1
6	30	1
	48	1
		45

Source: Anthony Partridge and William Eldridge, "The Second Circuit Sentencing Study: A Report to the Judges of the Second Circuit," Federal Judicial Center (August 1974). Constructed from case 4, pp. A-12, A-13.

TABLE 16-4.   Average sentences, in months, by selected offense and judicial circuit, of federal prisoners (fiscal year ended june 30, 1972)

Judicial circuit	Narcotics laws	Forgery	Robbery	All offenses
1st (Me., Mass., N.H., R.I., P.R.)	68.0	19.7	133.5	52.5
2d (Conn., N.Y.)	58.8	30.4	114.7	44.3
3d (Del., N.J., Penna., V.I.)	77.4	27.3	128.3	67.7
4th (Md., N.C., S.C., Va., W.Va.)	77.0	36.4	158.8	57.3
5th (Ala., Fla., Ga., La., Miss., Tex.)	74.8	36.7	144.0	41.3
6th (Kent., Mich., Ohio, Tenn.)	54.0	39.3	134.4	52.8
7th (Ill., Ind., Wisc.)	75.6	38.2	114.4	50.4
8th (Ark., Iowa, Minn., Mo., Neb., N.D., S.D.)	103.3	36.6	155.8	52.4
9th (Alaska, Ariz., Calif., Hawaii, Idaho, Mont., Nev., Ore., Wash., Guam)	70.8	42.9	131.1	40.5
10th (Colo., Kansas, N.M., Okla., Utah, Wyo.)	85.7	56.5	134.9	54.3
Totals	69.7	37.3	134.6	46.8

Source: U.S. Department of Justice, Federal Bureau of Prisons, *Statistical Report, Fiscal Years 1971 and 1972* (Washington, D.C.: Government Printing Office, 1973), pp. 96–101.

individualization (D'Esposito:182). The ideal of equal justice under the law means that all persons convicted of the same offense would receive identical sentences. But not all deviations from equality are unwarranted. The law also strives for individualized dispositions based on the character of the offender. Thus some differences in sentences reflect degree of seriousness of the offense, others the varying characteristics of the offender. What may be disparity to one person may be justifiable variation to another. By combining these two conflicting goals, we can produce a useful definition. *Sentence disparity* means the lack of similar sentences for similar offenders committing similar offenses. Geography and judicial attitudes are commonly mentioned factors associated with sentencing disparities.

sentence disparity

The geography of justice

geography of justice

What counts against defendants is not only what they do but also where they do it; this is referred to as the *geography of justice*. The frequency of fines, probation, or prison varies from county to county. Turning back to table 16-4, note that while the average sentence for forgery in the First Circuit Court of Appeals is 19.7 months, in the Tenth, it is 56.5, a difference of almost three to one. There are similar differences among the states in prisoners imprisoned per 100,000 (figure 16-1). Such differences are the product of a number of factors: the amount of crime, the effectiveness of the police in apprehending offenders, density of population, and types of screening employed by the court, for example. They also result from the fact that some courts deal with more serious offenses, as well as with a higher proportion of defendants with prior record. But even after controlling for factors like these, it is apparent that important geographical differences remain.

Overall it appears that the South imposes harsher sentences than other states. Table 15-2, for example, showed that executions are concentrated in this region. Urban courts are marked by a greater use of probation and shorter prison terms than are their rural counterparts. Such geographical patterns demonstrate that

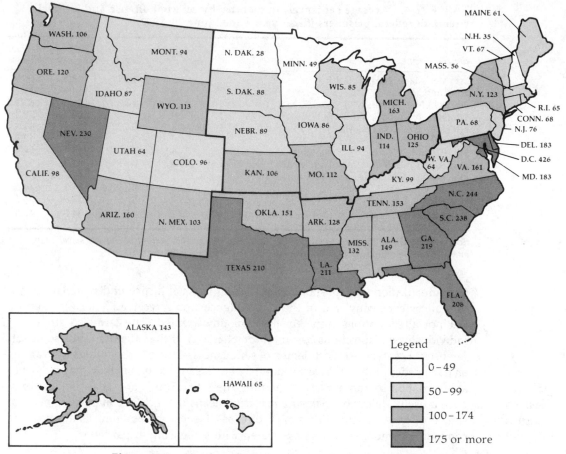

Figure 16-1. Number of prisoners in state institutions per 100,000 civilian population, December 31, 1980.

Source: U.S. Department of Justice, Bureau of Justice Statistics, *Prisoners in State and Federal Institutions on December 31, 1980* (Washington, D.C.: Government Printing Office, 1982), p. 4.

court officials, drawn as they are from the local communities, vary in what offenses are viewed as the most serious as well as what penalty is appropriate.

Judicial attitudes and backgrounds

judicial attitudes and backgrounds   For decades individual differences in judges' sentencing tendencies have fascinated social scientists. A study of women's court in Chicago is typical. It found that the proportion of shoplifting defendants placed on probation ranged from a low of 10 percent to a high of 62 percent (Cameron). An examination of sentences handed out in any multijudge court is very likely to reveal similar differences in the proportion of defendants granted probation and the length of the prison sentence, if one is imposed. Such sentencing disparities are partially the product of differences

IN THE NEWS: UNEQUAL JUSTICE?

Two men occupy the same cell. Both are young, from low-income families. Neither has a previous felony record. Both were indicted for murder, sentenced for first degree manslaughter, the most serious charge for taking a human life, short of murder.

One man is in for a maximum of three years, the other for 25—which may be as long as he lived before the prison doors closed. Is the 25-year man the victim of a tough judge? Did the other face a soft judge?

Most judges in felony courts insist such seeming disparities are not judicial whimsies, but a result of the fact that "every case is different," as Justice Thomas P. Farley, Nassau Supreme Court adminis-

trative justice, puts it. He cites this case:

"Two men rob banks, each carrying a bag, telling the teller they have a gun in the bag. Each gets $5,000. The first man is out of work, with six kids, no job. He had no gun in the bag. The second man had a gun. His record shows three or four run-ins with the law."

"Both are guilty of first degree robbery, with a maximum sentence of 25 years under state law. Do we send them both away for 25 years? Of course not! The disparity here is a disparity of persons. Different sentences are true justice."

Seymour Marks, *Long Island Press*, January 20, 1975.

among judges in their backgrounds, perceptions of what crimes are serious, weights assigned to conflicting goals of sentencing, and the influence of community values.

Because judges come to the bench from a variety of *backgrounds*, we might reasonably expect that those of different backgrounds will behave differently on the bench. An analysis of decisions of appellate court judges found that those who were Democratic, Catholic, and not former prosecutors were more likely to vote for the defendant (Nagel:230–231). Other studies have also shown that background characteristics like these are related to judges' votes in criminal justice cases. Overall, though, the effect is only slight. Judges' backgrounds account for only about 10 percent of the differences in appellate court votes (Bowen; Goldman).

One of the few studies to examine judges' *attitudes* on sentencing and the sentences they impose was conducted by John Hogarth, who investigated magistrates in Ontario. Canadian magistrates handle 94 percent of indictable offenses. Hogarth reported that judges who stress deterrence values are more likely to favor prison sentences over other forms of sentencing. Conversely, judges who are more treatment-oriented use suspended sentences, fewer fines, and relatively few short jail sentences (150).

Hogarth concluded that there were marked inconsistencies in the principles of sentencing held by the magistrates. But most importantly, differences among magistrates were not random: "While magistrates were inconsistent with each other, they were consistent within themselves" (360). A study of sentences imposed by the Philadelphia Court of Quarter Sessions concluded that judges did not sentence by whim (Green). The author found that the degree of disparity among judges was most pronounced in cases at the intermediate level of gravity, tapering off gradually as the cases approached the extremes of mildness or seriousness (99). Thus for serious offenses, there was a high degree of consistency among the judges in the length of the prison sentence imposed.

Relatively little research has been conducted on the relationship between judges' attitudes and backgrounds and the sentences they hand out. In particular, relatively little is known about how judges' sentencing attitudes interact with those of the work group. The studies to date indicate that there is no single set of judges' sentencing attitudes. Although the public generally views judges as harsh or lenient sentencers, detailed studies indicate that the pattern is far more complex. The survey of federal judges in the Second Circuit survey found that of the twenty-nine judges whose general sentences were in the middle range in most cases nonetheless varied in individual instances. A sentence ranked among the ten most severe in at least one case and a sentence ranked among the ten least severe in an additional one (Partridge and Eldridge:37).

Discrimination in sentencing?

No more powerful image of justice exists in American life than the statue of the blindfolded woman holding high the scales of justice in one hand and a sword low in the other. It symbolizes that all who come before her will receive fair and equal justice no matter what their race, color, religion, or social status. In recent years, though, many have questioned whether the administration of justice lives up to the symbol.

Numerous studies have probed the extent to which age, race, sex, and economic status pierce the blindfold when sentences are imposed. These studies have produced mixed results. Some find patterns of discrimination. Most do not. These mixed results partially result from studying varying courts and employing differing statistical techniques, but basically, the divergent conclusions reflect two different theories: functional and conflict.

Functional or traditional theorists believe that the court process is basically impartial. Their studies find that apparent sentencing disparities result from valid legal factors, such as seriousness of the offense and prior record. When these factors are considered (actually controlled in a statistical sense) the sentences handed out do not discriminate against the poor or racial minorities. Stated another way, the reason that poor defendants (or minorities) receive longer sentences is because they have been convicted of more serious crimes, are more likely to have prior convictions, and employ more violence in committing these offenses.

Conflict theorists, on the other hand, view the court process as fundamentally discriminatory.

> Obviously judicial decisions are not made uniformly. Decisions are made according to a host of extra-legal factors, including the age of the offender, his race, and social class.
>
> Perhaps the most obvious example of judicial discretion occurs in the handling of cases of persons from minority groups. Negroes, in comparison to whites, are convicted with lesser evidence and sentenced to more severe punishments. [Quinney:142]

These views reflect a neo-Marxist perspective: because dominant interests in society manipulate the criminal law to keep the poor and the minorities politically powerless, the sentencing process is discriminatory. Social characteristics of the defendant play a major role in sentencing. Moreover, because the process is fundamentally discriminatory, conflict theorists are skeptical about viewing seriousness of the offense and prior record as unbiased factors.

The contrasting theories—functional and conflict—indicate that sentencing discrimination involves complex issues. The courts, of course, deal primarily with poor, uneducated, and disproportionately minority members of society (see chapter 9). In assessing discrimination in sentencing, we need to consider two distinct areas: whether a group receives harsher (or more lenient) sentences and whether these results are the results of discrimination or other factors.

Economic status

economic status

The courts are a sorting process. At several stages, it is obvious that *economic status* makes a difference. The poor receive differential or negative outcomes. We know, for example, that the poor are less likely to receive pretrial release and have little likelihood of hiring a private attorney. These differences are reflected in sentencing. Defendants not released on bail and/or represented by a court-appointed attorney are granted probation less often and are given longer prison sentences. Moreover it appears that only the poorest and least-educated offenders are sentenced to death. Middle- or upper-income defendants are almost never executed. Do these patterns indicate that in sentencing, courts discriminate against the poor, or are they the product of other, legally permissible, factors? A number of studies yield conflicting answers but generally support the latter conclusion.

An analysis of California jury decisions in 238 first-degree murder cases between 1958 and 1966 showed that 42.1 percent of the blue collar defendants but only 4.8 percent of the white-collar defendants received the death sentence. The authors concluded that "the simplest hypothesis to explain this powerful association is that juries are lenient toward white-collar defendants on the basis of their occupational status alone" (Judson et al.: 1379). Hagan reviewed the Judson study plus five others, several of which reported that poor defendants received harsher sentences. He argues that all except Judson's failed to consider legally relevant variables, such as the seriousness of the offense and the prior record of the defendant and also employed inadequate statistical techniques. Because of these weaknesses, he concluded that the evidence does not support a finding of economic discrimination in sentencing.

Several recent studies analyzing a large number of sentences employing commonly accepted statistical techniques point in the same direction. An examination of prison sentences of 10,488 inmates in three southeastern states found that socioeconomic status had no effect on sentencing (Chiricos and Waldo:760). Studies by conflict theorists, however, report that economic factors do influence sentencing (Jacobs; Lizotte). Most other recent studies find no empirical evidence for economic discrimination. In short, the conclusions drawn often appear to reflect the theory employed by the authors.

Race

race

In studies of discrimination in sentencing, the most frequently considered characteristic of the defendant is *race*. Over twenty statistical studies (using varying degrees of statistical sophistication) have investigated whether race makes a difference. The results are not clear.

The most obvious evidence of racial discrimination in sentencing is found in studies of capital crimes in the South. Of 2,306 prisoners executed in the South after 1930, 72 percent were blacks. This proportion is dramatically higher than the proportion of blacks in the population or the proportion of crimes committed by the blacks.

The differential impact is most pronounced in executions for rape. In the South, 90 percent of those executed after conviction of rape were black. A study of rape convictions in eleven southern states from 1945 to 1965 showed that 13 percent of convicted blacks received the death penalty compared with 2 percent of convicted whites. The death penalty rate was even higher (36 percent) for blacks whose victims were white. Controls for other factors like prior record and age failed to account for racial differences (Wolfgang and Riedel).

Hindelang reviewed the studies that found that racial minorities received harsher sentences than whites. He noted that most of these were conducted in the South, focused on capital offenses, were done before the 1960s, and used poor or inadequate statistical measures.

More recent studies have failed to find a link between race and sentencing. Studies in Charlotte, North Carolina (Clarke and Koch), three southeastern states (Chiricos and Waldo), a study in Indianapolis (Burke and Turk), and an analysis of federal offenders (Tiffany et al.) all independently concluded that race had no predictive value on sentencing.

To complicate matters, two other studies found limited patterns of subtle racial differences in sentencing. Analyzing a number of cases from "Metro City" (a large eastern city) Spohn and colleagues found that race did not influence the severity of the prison sentence. They did find, however, that blacks were slightly more likely to be sentenced to prison (rather than granted parole) but once sentenced to prison received shorter sentences than whites. Along similar lines, a study of Atlanta, Georgia, found that overall black defendants received the same sentences as whites after taking into account the effects of seriousness of the crime, prior record, and so on. However, in analyzing sentences handed down by specific judges a more complex pattern emerged. Some judges were clearly antiblack, others problack, and some nondiscriminatory (Gibson, 1978).

Just as in the area of economic discrimination, we are presented with inconclusive findings, which reflect to a certain degree the contrasting perspectives of the functional versus conflict theories.

Age

age
Another variable that might affect the sentence imposed is the *age* of the offender. Young defendants (variously defined as under twenty-one or under twenty-five depending on the study) are often viewed as more likely to be granted probation or, if sentenced to prison, receive a shorter term. This might indicate that court personnel adopt a more protective attitude toward young offenders because they are viewed as better candidates for rehabilitation. Prisons may also be viewed as inappropriate places for the young because they are dangerous.

A number of studies reject this interpretation, arguing that differential sentencing of the young results from other factors. Youthful offenders have fewer prior brushes with the law and commit less serious, less violent crimes than older defendants. When legally relevant factors like these are controlled, age has no independent effect on sentencing (Green; Landes; Burke and Turk; Clarke and Koch).

White-collar defendants

white-collar defendants

John Swainson, once governor of Michigan and later a state supreme court judge, was convicted in 1975 of three counts of perjury. Although he could have gone to prison for up to fifteen years, the sentence was sixty days. Each year about a thousand persons are convicted of cheating on their income taxes. Only one-third go to prison, and then usually for less than a year. Bank robbers, on the other hand, go to prison in almost all cases, typically for five years or longer. These contrasts are the subject of rising debate over the fairness of a criminal court process that seemingly allows *white-collar defendants*—well-tailored, college-educated crooks—to escape with probation while it sends impoverished and poorly educated defendants to prison for years. Underlying this debate is a growing concern that white-collar crime is multiplying rapidly (see chapter 10).

Although the white-collar criminal is not as immediately dangerous as the night-time burglar or a rapist, the nation economically loses more every year from embezzlement, fraud, and the like than it does from well-publicized crimes like burglary or robbery. White-collar crimes take on an extra dimension when they are committed by a government official who has betrayed the public trust.

White-collar defendants contrast sharply with those whom judges usually sentence. They are seldom repeaters. They are nonviolent. They often have a spouse and family. They are often highly educated and have good jobs. In short, judges have great empathy for this type of defendant, who is like their neighbors.

A prison sentence in these cases means something very different from that for the typical street criminal. A conviction and prison sentence stigmatizes the defendant. Often these defendants have already lost their job and will face great difficulty in finding another one at anywhere near a comparable salary or responsibility. These defendants will also have great difficulty adjusting to the environment of prison, where they are likely to be in physical danger.

The trend, though, is toward imposing a prison term, usually a short one, on white-collar defendants, as a deterrent.

Reforming the sentencing process

Not all disparate sentences are unjustified. Based on the goal of individualizing justice, a conviction for the same offense may draw different sentences depending both on how the crime was committed and the nature of the defendant. Dissimilarities in regional norms concerning the seriousness of violations often result in variations in sentences given similar offenders. Sentencing disparities, however, become a major problem when unequal sentences are imposed for the same offense without a reasonable basis. Concern is rising that unchecked judicial discretion has undermined the goal of fair and equal sentencing.

Sentencing disparities also create problems for correctional officials. When prisoners compare sentences, some discover that they were treated leniently and may conclude that because they were smart or lucky, they do not need rehabilitation. Others discover they they received a long sentence and direct their embitterment toward prison programs. Correctional officials worry that disparate sentences work to defeat correctional objectives of rehabilitation (Newman:230).

Reforms have been suggested for rationalizing the sentencing process: sentencing institutes, sentencing councils, appellate review of sentences, and sentencing guidelines. A key consideration is the degree to which each attempts to place restraints on a trial judge's traditional independence in passing sentences.

Sentencing institutes

sentencing institutes

In 1958, Congress provided for *sentencing institutes* for federal judges. New York, California, and Pennsylvania have since inaugurated programs of their own. The institutes are attended not only by judges but also prosecutors, probation and parole officials, and sentencing experts. Some of the topics covered are informational—parole eligibility criteria and changes in the law, for example. Others are instructional; experts conduct seminars. In addition, judges discuss particular cases. Presentence reports are duplicated and distributed, with each judge individually studying them and then presenting views on what sentence should be imposed.

> To nobody's surprise, the judges exhibit huge divergencies in their dispositions of the same case. Everybody tends to gasp a little upon the rehearing of this same old story. Sometimes but not regularly, a judge seems to be persuaded toward some view different from his initial one. But there is no binding "decision" on anything. . . . They leave about as miscellaneous and unpredictable as they were when they arrived. [Frankel:64]

Sentencing institutes serve an important purpose: they provide a forum for airing competing views on sentencing. But because judicial independence in sentencing remains unaltered, they are more a first step than a solution.

Sentencing councils

sentencing councils

Often the severity of the sentence depends on luck in drawing a particular judge. One institutional arrangement used in a few courts to alleviate sentencing disparity is the *sentencing council* composed of other judges from the same jurisdiction. Each participating judge receives a copy of the presentence report and all record their sentence recommendations. The members of the council then meet (usually with the probation officer in attendance), compare their preliminary estimates, and discuss the case. The sentencing judge presides at the hearing, imposing the sentence he or she feels is justified. The sentencing council is purely advisory; the sentencing judge retains complete discretion.

Sentencing councils reduce but do not eliminate sentencing disparities. This conclusion emerges from an analysis of two federal courts that have employed sentencing councils: the Eastern District of New York (Brooklyn) and the Northern District of Illinois (Chicago). In each court the judges disagreed about 30 percent of the time whether the defendant should be imprisoned or be placed on probation.

Even when there was agreement that a custody sentence should be imposed, the judges disagreed on the duration 88 percent of the time in Chicago and 90 percent of the time in New York. One principal effect of the sentencing council was that judges in both courts changed their sentence in about one-third of the cases (Diamond and Zeisel:125). It was more likely for sentences to be reduced than increased. Taken together, the judges participating in sentencing councils are more prone to grant probation and give shorter prison terms. Like sentencing institutes, these councils use peer pressure. The overall effect is that judges are more likely to impose the average sentence of the judges on the court.

Appellate review of sentencing

Unlike most other Western nations, American appellate courts do not generally have the right to review the sentence imposed by the judge. While appellate courts annually write volumes about the guilt adjudication process—pretrial procedure, arrests, searches, and rulings on evidence, for instance—the most important aspect of the majority of criminal cases—sentencing—is unreviewable.

appellate review of sentences

In recent years several important groups and individuals—most notably the American Bar Association Standards Relating to the Administration of Criminal Justice and the National Advisory Commission—have called for *appellate review of sentencing.* One important goal of the review would be to mute gross sentencing disparities found in individual cases. But more fundamentally, advocates contend that appellate review can be an important vehicle for developing legal principles of sentencing.

> The contention that sentencing is not regulated by rules of "law" subject to appellate review is an argument for, not against, a system of appeals. The "common law" is, after all, a body of rules evolved through the process of reasoned decision of concrete cases, mainly by appellate courts. English appellate courts and some of our states have been evolving general, legal "principles of sentencing" in the course of reviewing particular sentences claimed to be excessive. One way to begin to temper the capricious unruliness of sentencing is to institute the right of appeal, so that appellate courts may proceed in their accustomed fashion to make law for this grave subject. [Frankel:84]

Several states allow an appellate body either to affirm or deny the sentence handed out by the sentencing judge. Usually, though, these appellate bodies have more limited powers than reformers would like. Appeals courts have been reluctant to review sentencing because they believe that the sentencing judge, who presided at the trial and possessed all the relevant information, was best qualified for making the decision. A more practical concern is that appeals courts—already overburdened—would be flooded with even more cases.

Sentencing guidelines

sentencing guidelines

The ultimate goal of sentencing institutes, sentencing councils, and appellate review of sentences is to limit or at least minimize sentencing disparities by providing a way to develop sentencing principles and standards. Advocates of *sentencing guidelines* seek to work more directly by providing a set of usable sentencing guidelines or benchmarks. A judge in Des Moines, Iowa, underscores the problem:

A lot of people say sentencing is disparate. That is to say, I'm giving a writer of bad checks a probation and my colleague in Sioux City is giving another check-writer a ten year sentence. These two defendants, it is then claimed, are being treated unequally and therefore unfairly. Now, a lot of this criticism is misdirected because my check-writer may be the first timer with a good chance for rehabilitation while the Sioux City check-writer may be a hardened recidivist.

But, on the other hand, some of the criticism may be correct for sometimes the criminal behavior and the criminal's background may be sufficiently similar to warrant similar treatment. But no judge at present can rightly be blamed for treating these similarly situated individuals differently for there is no way today for either of us to know what the other is doing. We *are* sentencing differently, not out of malice, but out of sheer *ignorance*, or to put it another way, without guidelines—without the tool that tells each of us what the other is doing. [Wilkins et al.:vii–viii]

The purpose is to improve the existing sentencing machinery by channeling discretion.

Wilkins and associates report their research on developing sentencing guidelines for Denver judges. By statistically analyzing sentences imposed by judges, they arrived at a set of formulas for measuring the seriousness of the crime against offenders' previous criminal records, their schooling and employment record, and other factors that reflect social stability. The result was a set of model or average penalties that were able to be used about 85 percent of the time.

The use of sentencing guidelines is seriously questioned by some. Norval Morris argues that sentencing guidelines give "a false precision of that which by its nature can never be precise" (13,50). An evaluation by the National Center for State Courts concludes that sentencing guidelines lack empirical validity because the process by which they were created does not satisfy usual procedural standards. Moreover, the report states that sentencing guidelines had no measurable impact on judicial sentencing behavior. Failure to take into account existing plea bargaining practices may be the root cause for the ineffectiveness of sentencing guidelines.

Increasing the severity of the penalty

The majority of the American public believe that prison sentences are too lenient. When confronted with a crime problem, legislators often believe that the answer is to get tough with criminals by increasing the severity of the penalty. Such views reflect the notion that harsher sentences will deter criminals. This ideology is more often supported by moral claims than valid scientific evidence. A number of studies, however, conclude that increasing the severity of the penalty does not result in lower crime rates (Zimring and Hawkins). For instance, separate studies of increased penalty for rape (Schwarz), marijuana possession, and assaults on police officers (California State Assembly, Office of Research) all report that there were no changes in crime rates.

Increasing the severity of the penalty, though, does have a major impact on courtroom work groups. In particular harsher sentencing laws are associated with the exercise of increased discretion and negative side effects.

Nullification by discretion

Sharp increases in formal penalties tend to be sidestepped by those who apply the law. As James Q. Wilson writes, "No one should assume that any judicial outcome can be made truly 'mandatory'—discretion removed from one place in the criminal justice system tends to reappear elsewhere in it" (1975:187). At a variety of points in the application of legal sanctions—police arrest, prosecutorial discretion, judge and jury convictions, and sentencing—discretion may be exercised to offset the severity of the penalty.

When the severity of the penalty is increased, the police may stabilize or reduce the number of arrests for violations subjected to those penalties. A study of Connecticut's crackdown on speeders reported that police arrests for speeding decreased after the severe penalties were announced.

Prosecutors often responded by reducing the number of charges for that category. In 1973, the New York legislature enacted the toughest drug law in the nation. It provided for stiff mandatory sentences (up to life) and sought to prevent plea bargaining. The Association of the Bar of the City of New York Drug Abuse Council evaluated this law and reported that although indictments for drug violations in New York State remained constant through the first year of the law's implementation, the number of indictments fell by 14 percent the next year (2). Because they anticipate that judges and juries will be reluctant to convict, prosecutors may also choose to file charges for an offense that does not carry the most severe penalties.

A number of studies indicate that convictions decrease when the penalties are severe. The most commonly cited example is capital punishment in late eighteenth- and early nineteenth-century England, when most felonies were punishable by death. Judges strained to avoid convicting defendants, often inventing legal technicalities to acquit the defendant (Hall). In New York State, after the tough drug law was passed, the number of convictions dropped.

Finally, after convictions judges are reluctant to actually apply the severe penalty. Thus when Chicago traffic court judges sought to crack down on drunk drivers by voluntarily agreeing to impose the seven-day jail term, a study found that the penalty was rarely applied (Robertson et al.:1973).

There is thus a relationship between punishment policy and the system that administers it. Through the discretionary actions of police, prosecutor, judges, juries, and executive, harsh penalties are nullified. The more severe the penalty, the less likely it will be imposed when its severity exceeds the limits of punishment viewed as appropriate. The final result is that more produces less. Stepping up the severity of the punishment does not increase the threat of punishment; it reduces it.

Negative side effects

One reason that legislators find raising penalties so attractive is that they appear to be fighting crime but do not have to increase appropriations. It is a policy apparently without costs. But a number of studies suggest that increasing the severity of the punishment produces "hidden costs" and "side effects." Harsher laws have

IN THE NEWS: JUDICIAL SYSTEM REVIEW URGED BY POLICE GROUP

The Brotherhood, a Denver police organization, Friday called for a review of the entire judicial system, including methods of sentencing criminals and the possibility of mandatory sentencing of violent criminals.

A spokesman, Detective James Lux, pointed to a number of recent court actions and sentences which he called "appalling and should be frightening to the general public."

Lux directed his remarks toward a number of recent judicial actions which he said were improper and violated the safety of the public. . . .

"We're called upon time after time to re-arrest these dangerous criminals that the courts are always seeing fit to let loose into society without any rehabilitation," Lux said.

Lux said even when a dangerous criminal is convicted of a major crime, the judges too often give him such a lenient sentence he's "right back out on the street."

The example cited was the case of James A. Lang, one of two men involved in a robbery attempt in which Denver Patrolman Ed Smith was shot to death in January.

"Lang, who had fired shots and menaced innocent people during the robbery attempt, pleaded guilty to aggravated robbery and first-degree murder charges," Lux said.

"The opinion of the district attorneys presenting the case before Salida Dist. Judge Howard Purdy was that due to the seriousness of the crime, Lang be sentenced to the state penitentiary for life, the maximum sentence," Lux said.

"However, the action taken by Judge Purdy was sentencing the defendant to the Colorado State Reformatory at Buena Vista. After a period of nine months, the defendant may be eligible for parole."

Lux said it is the contention of the Brotherhood that criminals can't be rehabilitated in a short time.

"It has been proven in the past that the vast majority of ex-convicts return to society to become repeat offenders," Lux said.

"It is the board of trustees of the Brotherhood concern that the general public is being endangered through the premature release of dangerous criminals."

"The Brotherhood feels it is time for local government agencies to review the judicial sentencing systems and are asking that this review be immediately undertaken together with an investigation of the possibilities of mandatory sentencing for crimes of violence."

Denver Rocky Mountain News, September 6, 1975.

effects, but often not the ones intended. One of these hidden costs is the greater time, effort, and money courts must expend.

Faced with severe sanctions, defendants demand more trials, which consumes more court time. This clearly happened in New York State. Before the drug law, 6.5 percent of the drug cases went to trial; after it, 13.5 percent (Association of the Bar:7). As a result, a backlog of cases develops, delay increases, and the certainty and speed of conviction drops. Moreover, the courts were forced to spend $55 million to comply with the law.

A second unintended consequence is that increasing the severity of penalties increases the pressure to plea bargain. To ensure convictions, avoid expensive and cost-consuming trials, and give expression to their views of benevolence, prosecutors and judges will try to get a guilty plea in return for a lesser sentence (Wilson, 1975:179). To cite but one example, Illinois prosecutors allowed first offender drunk-driving offenders to plea to reckless driving, which did not carry a mandatory one-year suspension of the driver's license (Neubauer).

A final unintended consequence of raising the severity of penalties is that sentencing disparities increase. Even though convictions decrease overall and there is a tendency not to apply the law to the fullest, some defendants are still caught in the net. The *New York Times* surveyed convictions in March 1976 under the New

York drug law and found that only thirty-one persons drew the maximum penalty. They found that "suspects sentenced to the severest imprisonment appeared to be low-level dealers—not major traffickers in heroin or cocaine." In short, when severe penalties are applied, they are often applied randomly (*New York Times*, September 5, 1976).

Mandatory minimum sentences

mandatory minimum sentence

"If Every Criminal *Knew* He Would Be Punished If Caught . . ." is how James Q. Wilson, professor of government at Harvard, titles one of his articles. Wilson argues that the way to improve the deterrent effect of the law is to concentrate on increasing the certainty of sanctions. Particularly popular are laws like those in Michigan providing for a prison sentence for anyone convicted of using a firearm during the commission of a felony. Such *mandatory minimum sentence* proposals are obviously aimed at reducing judicial discretion, which by implication is viewed as the major reason that courts are not providing certain punishment.

Such laws suffer from the same limitations discussed under discretion and increasing severity. By being rigid, mechanical, and inflexible, they fail to deal with the conditions that lead to discretion in sentencing. As the Twentieth Century Fund Task Force on Sentencing noted, flat-time sentencing and mandatory minimum sentences go too far in eliminating all flexibility:

> By requiring every single defendant convicted under the same statute to serve the identical sentence, it threatens to create a system so automatic that it may operate in practice like a poorly programmed robot. This is especially true if statutory definitions of crime remain as broad and inclusive as they are today. [p. 17]

Such principles are unfeasible because judges, prosecutors, and defense attorneys will encounter defendants who would suffer an undue hardship by going to prison or whose crime is too minor to justify such a sentence. Advocates of these laws believe that discretion will be reduced, but the actual effect is to shift discretion. This was the conclusion of a study of the Michigan felony firearm statute. The law did decrease judicial sentencing discretion but at the same time stimulated prosecutorial discretion (Heumann and Loftin:394–395). Moreover, because these proposals are limited to a small number of offenses, the problem of sentencing disparity will remain. Two similarly situated defendants could still receive vastly different sentences, one mandatory minimum, the other a much higher maximum penalty.

Determinate sentencing

In recent years some states have adopted determinate or flat-time sentencing (for example, California, Maine, Illinois, and Indiana). These laws reflect a rejection of the "rehabilitative model" that formed the basis of indeterminate sentencing (see chapter 15). Instead they substituted punishment as the reason for incarceration. Advocates also argue that flat-time sentences will be fairer and remove elements of excessive discretion.

These laws are relatively new; full assessment is not yet possible. Research conducted on the early experiences with determinate sentencing laws, however, suggests two important considerations. First, prison sentences will be longer. This was the conclusion reached in California, where the law led to less usage of probation (Brewer et al.), and in Indiana (Clear et al.). The second conclusion is that the law does not eliminate discretion. Rather it simply shifts discretion from judges to prosecutors (Alschuler). In short, one expects that determinate sentencing laws will have the same impact as direct efforts to increase the severity of sentences.

Conclusion

America sends more people to prison that any other Western nation. At the end of 1981, over 352,000 people were in prison. Added to this number were the 223,000 people on parole and the 1,222,000 on probation. And the rate of incarceration is growing steadily, resulting in severe prison overcrowding in numerous states. This chapter has shown that courtroom work groups consider a variety of factors in making sentencing decisions. They weigh the normal penalty for the offense, the seriousness of the offense, prior record, and social stability of the defendant.

Whether the sentences handed out are too harsh, too lenient, or too unpredictable depends on the views of those making the assessment. Some of the major questions being raised about sentencing—increasing the severity, sentencing disparities, and sentencing discrimination—were discussed here. A wide variety of reforms have been suggested, ranging from imposing mandatory minimum sentences to giving appellate courts the authority to set guidelines. But as long as judges are given discretion in sentencing, disparities will exist.

For discussion

1. What sentence would you impose on the former cab driver convicted of theft from an interstate shipment? What objective do you have in mind: retribution, rehabilitation, deterrence, or isolation?
2. Discuss with a judge and a prosecutor local practices concerning presentence investigations. What type of information is collected? How influential are these reports in setting the penalty?
3. Discuss the effects of courtroom work groups on the sentencing process.
4. Interview a judge, prosecutor, and defense attorney about the most important factors in sentencing in your community.
5. What are the arguments opposed to increasing the severity of sentences? What are the arguments in favor?
6. How do the general goals of equality and individualization lead to sentencing disparities? What do you think are the most relevant factors leading to sentencing disparities?
7. What do the studies of sentencing discrimination indicate? Is there evidence of systematic bias based on age, race, sex, or economic status?
8. Do you think white-collar defendants are treated too leniently? Why?
9. What types of press coverage do sentences receive in the local press? (Remember to examine letters to the editor.) What impact do you think such coverage has on judges, prosecutors, defense attorneys, and probation officers?

10. Which reform—sentencing institutes, sentencing councils, sentencing guidelines, or appellate review—do you think would be most effective in reducing sentencing disparities? Why? Which do you think has the greatest chance for adoption? Why?

References

Alschuler, Albert. "Sentencing Reform and Prosecutorial Power: A Critique of Recent Proposals for 'Fixed' and 'Presumptive' Sentencing." *University of Pennsylvania Law Review* 126 (January 1978):550–577.

Association of the Bar of the City of New York Drug Abuse Council. *The Effects of the 1973 Drug Laws on the New York State Courts.* New York, 1976.

Bowen, Donald. *The Explanation of Judicial Voting Behavior From Sociological Characteristics of Judges.* New Haven, Conn.: Yale University Press, 1965.

Brewer, David, Gerald Beckett, and Normal Holt. "Determinate Sentencing in California: The First Year's Experience." *Journal of Research in Crime and Delinquency* 18 (1981):200–231.

Burke, Peter, and Austin Turk. "Factors Affecting Postarrest Dispositions: A Model for Analysis." *Social Problems* 22 (1975):313.

California State Assembly, Office of Research. *Crime and Penalties in California.* 1968.

Cameron, Mary Owen. *The Booster and the Snitch.* Glencoe, Ill.: Free Press, 1964.

Carter, Robert, and Leslie Wilkins. "Some Factors in Sentencing Policy." *Journal of Criminal Law, Criminology and Police Science* 58 (December 1967):503–514.

Chiricos, Theodore G., and Gordon P. Waldo. "Socioeconomic Status and Criminal Sentencing: An Empirical Assessment of a Conflict Proposition." *American Sociological Review* 40 (1975):753.

Clarke, Stevens A., and Gary G. Koch, "The Influence of Income and Other Factors on Whether Criminal Defendants Go to Prison." *Law and Society Review* 11 (1976):57–92.

Clear, Todd, John Hewitt, and Robert Regoli. "Discretion and the Determinate Sentence: Its Distribution, Control and Effect on Time Served." *Crime and Delinquency* 24 (October 1979):444.

Dawson, Robert O. *Sentencing: The Decision as to Type, Length, and Conditions of Sentence.* Boston: Little, Brown, 1969.

D'Esposito, Julian C. "Sentencing Disparity: Causes and Cures." *Journal of Criminal Law, Criminology and Police Science* 60 (1969):182–194.

Diamond, Shari Seidman, and Hans Zeisel. "Sentencing Councils: A Study of Sentencing Disparity and Its Reduction." *University of Chicago Law Review* 43 (Fall 1975):109–149.

Frankel, Marvin. *Criminal Sentences: Law Without Order.* New York: Hill & Wang, 1972.

Gibson, James. "Race as a Determinant of Criminal Sentences: A Methodological Critique and a Case Study." *Law and Society Review* 12 (Spring 1978):455–478.

Goldman, Sheldon. "Voting Behavior on the U.S. Court of Appeals Revisited." *American Political Science Review* 69 (June 1975):491.

Green, Edward. *Judicial Attitudes in Sentencing.* New York: St. Martin's Press, 1961.

Hagan, John. "Extra-Legal Attributes and Criminal Sentencing: An Assessment of a Sociological Viewpoint." *Law and Society Review* 8 (1974):357–381.

Hall, Jerome. *Theft, Law and Society.* Indiana: Bobbs-Merrill Co. 1952.

Heumann, Milton, and Colin Loftin. "Mandatory Sentencing and the Abolition of Plea Bargaining: The Michigan Felony Firearm Statute." *Law and Society Review* 13 (Winter 1979):393–430.

Hindelang, Michael. "Equality Under the Law." In Charles Reasons and Jack Kuykendall, eds., *Race, Crime and Justice*, pp. 312–323. Pacific Palisades, Calif.: Goodyear Publishing Co., 1972.

Hogarth, John. *Sentencing as a Human Process.* Toronto: University of Toronto Press, 1971.

Jacobs, David. "Inequality and the Legal Order: An Ecological Test of the Conflict Model." *Social Problems* 25 (1978):515–525.

Judson, Charles, James Pandell, Jack Owens, James McIntosh, and Dale Matschullat. "A Study of the California Penalty Jury in First Degree Murder Cases." *Stanford Law Review* 21 (1969):1297.

Katkin, Daniel. "Presentence Reports: An Analysis of Uses, Limitations and Civil Liberties Issues." *Minnesota Law Review* 55 (November 1970):15–31.

Landes, William. "Legality and Reality: Some Evidence in Criminal Procedure." *Journal of Legal Studies* 3 (1974):287.

Lizotte, Alan. "Extra-Legal Factors in Chicago's Criminal Courts: Testing the Conflict Model of Criminal Justice." *Social Problems* 25 (June 1978):564–580.

McDonald, William, Henry Rossman, and James Cramer. "The Prosecutorial Function and Its Relation to Determinate Sentencing Structures." In William McDonald, ed. *The Prosecutor.* Beverly Hills, Calif.: Sage Publications, 1979.

Mather, Lynn. "Some Determinants of the Method of Case Disposition: Decision-Making by Public Defenders in Los Angeles."*Law and Society Review* 8 (Winter 1974):187.

Morris, Norval. "The Sentencing Disease: The Judge's Changing Role in the Criminal Justice Process." *The Judges' Journal* 18 (Summer 1979):8–13, 50.

Nagel, Stuart S. *The Legal Process from a Behavioral Perspective.* Chicago: Dorsey Press, 1969.

Neubauer, David W. *Criminal Justice in Middle America.* Morristown, N.J.: General Learning Press. 1974.

New York Times, September 5, 1976.

Newman, Donald. *Conviction: The Determination of Guilt or Innocence Without Trial.* Boston: Little, Brown, 1966.

Partridge, Anthony, and William Eldridge. *The Second Circuit Sentencing Study: A Report to the Judges of the Second Circuit.* Washington, D.C.: Federal Judicial Center, August 1974.

Quinney, Richard. *The Social Reality of Crime.* Boston: Little, Brown, 1970.

Rich, William, L. Paul Sutton, Todd Clear and Michael Saks. *Sentencing by Mathematics: An Evaluation of the Early Attempts to Develop and Implement Sentencing Guidelines.* Williamsburg, VA, 1982.

Robertson, Leon S., Robert F. Rich, and H. Laurence Ross. "Jail Sentences for Driving While Intoxicated in Chicago: A Judicial Action That Failed." *Law and Society Review* 8 (1973):55.

Rosett, Arthur, and Donald R. Cressey. *Justice by Consent.* Philadelphia: J. B. Lippincott, 1976.

Schwartz, Barry. "The Effect in Philadelphia of Pennsylvania's Increased Penalties for Rape and Attempted Rape." *Journal of Criminal Law, Criminology, and Police Science* 59 (1968):509–515.

Spohn, Cassia, John Cruhl, and Susan Welch. "The Effect of Race on Sentencing: A Re-Examination of an Unsettled Question."*Law and Society Review* 16 (1981–82):71–88.

Sudnow, David. "Normal Crimes: Sociological Features of the Penal Codes in a Public Defender Office." *Social Problems* 12 (1965):254.

Tiffany, Lawrence P., Yakov Avichai, and Geoffrey W. Peters. "A Statistical Analysis of Sentencing in Federal Courts: Defendants Convicted After Trial, 1967–1968." *Journal of Legal Studies* 10 (1975):369.

Twentieth Century Fund Task Force on Sentencing. *Fair and Certain Punishment.* New York: McGraw-Hill, 1976.

Vera Institute of Justice. *Felony Arrests: Their Prosecution and Disposition in New York City's Courts.* New York: Vera Institute of Justice, 1977.

Wilkins, Leslie, Jack Kress, Don Gottfredson, Joseph Calpin and Arthur Gelman. *Sentencing Guidelines: Structuring Judicial Discretion, Final Report of the Feasibility Study.* Washington, D.C.: Government Printing Office, 1976.

Wilson, James Q. "If Every Criminal *Knew* He Would Be Punished If Caught . . ." *New York Times Magazine,* January 28, 1973.

———. *Thinking About Crime.* New York: Basic Books, 1975.

Wolfgang, Marvin, and Marc Riedel. "Race, Judicial Discretion, and the Death Penalty." *Annals of the American Academy of Political and Social Science* 407 (1973):119.
Zimring, Frank, and Gordon Hawkins. *Deterrence: The Legal Threat in Crime Control.* Chicago: University of Chicago Press, 1973.

For further reading

Dawson, Robert. *Sentencing: The Decision as to Type, Length, and Conditions of Sentence.* Boston: Little, Brown, 1969.
Hagan, John. "Extra-Legal Attributes and Criminal Sentencing: An Assessment of a Sociological Viewpoint." *Law and Society Review* 8 (1974):357–381.
Hogarth, John. *Sentencing as a Human Process.* Toronto: University of Toronto Press, 1971.
Twentieth Century Fund Task Force on Sentencing. *Fair and Certain Punishment.* New York: McGraw-Hill, 1976.
Zimring, Frank, and Gordon Hawkins. *Deterrence: The Legal Threat in Crime Control.* Chicago: University of Chicago Press, 1973.

PART 5

What Is Wrong Here?

Parts 2, 3, and 4 have examined numerous reform proposals. This last part examines some additional reform proposals and provides a general overview of the topic.

The nation's lower courts operate very differently from the major trial courts. Chapter 17 considers some of the major criticisms of "conveyor belt justice" and various proposals to improve the quality of justice.

Whether the courts are too slow—and if so, why—is the focus of chapter 18, which considers the important issues involved in judicial administration.

The Lower Courts: Rapid, Rough Justice

Ninety percent of the nation's criminal cases heard are in the less prestigious lower courts. These are the courts that process the millions of Americans accused each year of disturbing the peace, shoplifting, being drunk, and driving too fast. Although individually these cases may appear to be minor, almost petty, collectively the work of the lower courts is quite important.

For decades reformers have pointed out the problems of the lower courts. Only a fraction of the adversary model of criminal justice can be found in these courts. Many defendants are not represented by an attorney. Trials are rare. Jail sentences are imposed, sometimes with lightning speed. Informality, rather than the rules of courtroom procedure, predominates. In short, practices that would be condemned if they occurred in higher courts are commonplace in the lower courts. Is this justice, we might ask? The President's Commission on Law Enforcement and Administration of Justice asked the same question and expressed shock over the conclusions it reached: "No findings of this Commission are more disquieting than those relating to the conditions of the lower criminal courts" (1967b:29).

There is little doubt that lower courts do not always administer justice as well as they might, but placing this shortcoming in perspective is difficult. The literature on the lower courts has been impressionistic rather than systematic. As a result, our knowledge of the operational realities of misdemeanor courts is less advanced than for the felony trial courts (Alfini and Passuth:5). Some recent studies have suggested that we need to take a more objective and realistic approach in evaluating the lower courts. These studies maintain that there are two major factors to bear in mind when assessing the work of the lower courts. First, the lower courts are not just felony courts with a higher volume of less serious cases. Fundamental differences exist between how the lower courts and the major trial courts operate. Lower courts demonstrate greater flexibility because the judges and prosecutors more directly focus on trying to produce substantive justice (rather than just adhering to procedures). Second, lower courts exhibit immense variation. The big city drunk court operations are very different from the rural justice of the peace court. Moreover, even lower courts in big cities have vast differences depending on the particular city.

This chapter discusses the rapid, rough justice dispensed by the lower courts. Some specific topics include the conditions of the nation's lower courts, their impact on citizens, their effects on the criminal justice system, their problems, and what might be done to improve them.

Problems of the lower courts

One reason the lower courts are so important is that they interact with so many ordinary citizens. It is in the lower courts that average citizens form opinions about the speed, certainty, fairness, and incorruptibility of justice while they are being processed by the lowest tribunals. Often they come away with a less-than-favorable impression.

nonjudicial atmosphere   The most lasting impression is of the *nonjudicial atmosphere* of the proceedings. One of the most widely quoted passages of the President's Commission aptly summarizes these conditions:

> The commission has been shocked by what it has seen in some lower courts. It has seen cramped and noisy courtrooms, undignified and perfunctory procedures, and badly trained personnel. It has seen dedicated people who are frustrated by huge case loads, by the lack of opportunity to examine cases carefully, and by the impossibility of devising constructive solutions to the problems of offenders. It has seen assembly-line justice. [1967a:128]

There is little in the process that instills in defendants, witnesses, observers, or court officials respect for the criminal justice system. Because these courts occupy the lowest rung on the judicial ladder, they have been treated as a judicial stepchild. The municipal courts in large metropolitan areas, as well as the justice of the peace courts in small towns, suffer from long-term neglect. By general consensus, the lower courts are the principal weakness in the state court system (Ashman:3).

To identify the most pressing problems of the trial courts of limited jurisdiction, the American Judicature Society surveyed six states: Colorado, Illinois, Louisiana, New Hampshire, New Jersey, and Texas. While they found the problems confronting the lower courts as varied as the courts themselves, four are particularly important: inadequate financing, lax procedures, inadequate facilities, and imbalanced caseloads.

> One step inside "drunk court" in Cleveland, Ohio, the stench of stale whisky, urine, sweat, and vomit confronts the visitor. Sitting down and staying put on one of the dusty old wood benches in the small, stifling courtroom, on the second floor of police headquarters, becomes a test of endurance for mind and stomach.
>
> In the dim light, dozens of haggard men in tattered clothing stand in a seemingly endless line that stretches along a peeling green wall on the side of the courtroom, through a door behind the judge, down a hall leading from a hidden cellblock. These men are alcoholics, arrested the night before for public drunkenness. Most are middle-aged, but they look older, their bodies emaciated, their skin pallid. Some cough and retch violently. A few, suffering delirium tremens, shake uncontrollably, as though they were freezing cold in the hot, sticky courtroom.
>
> These diseased men will find no help in this stinking, depressing place. Many are simply released by the judge to go back to the streets. Others may be sent to jail for a few days, weeks, or months. But it is a safe bet that most of them will return sooner or later to Cleveland's drunk court. They are addicted to alcohol, and nothing is done in the court system or the jail to treat their condition.
>
> Leonard Downie, *Justice Denied* (Baltimore: Penguin, 1972), pp. 52–53.

Inadequate financing

inadequate financing

Generally lower courts are funded locally. As a result, sparsely populated counties and small municipalities often lack funds to staff and equip their courts adequately. Even when local funds are available to local governments, there is no guarantee that these funds will be spent on the lower courts. The suspicion is that in many cities these courts are expected to produce revenue for local governments. Even though they may generate a fairly large amount of income from assessing fines and imposing court costs, the local courts have no control over how these funds are spent. A survey found that 150 Texas municipal courts have revenues five times greater than their operating expenses. Yet over half of these courts lacked adequate courtrooms, supplies, office space, and the like (Ashman, 1975:16–17). The remainder of the funds went to pay for city services. In short, such local funding has meant *inadequate financing* for the nation's lowest tribunals.

Court procedures and administration

court procedures and administration

Critics of lower courts often cite lax *court procedures* and lack of uniformity in the day-to-day *administration* of these courts. There is a wide divergence in the way in which cases are handled in the trial courts of limited jurisdiction. Many do not have written rules for the conduct of cases. Conventional bookkeeping methods are often ignored. If records are kept, they are usually of use only to the individual judge. How much fine money was collected and how it was spent is often impossible to determine. The lack of uniformity and absence of records frustrate any attempts to assess the effectiveness of these courts.

Inadequate facilities

inadequate facilities

Courtrooms that are dirty, crowded, or noisy, or makeshift courtrooms hastily created in a store or garage convey a justifiably bad impression. The lack of dignity that such *inadequate facilities* and conditions convey is detrimental to the attributes of the defendant, prosecutor, judge, and all others involved in the justice process (Ashman, 1975:35). As an example of outdated and rundown facilities, the American Judicature Society singled out Atlantic County Juvenile and Domestic Relations Court (New Jersey). The old stone structure, which once was used as a roller skating rink, is now in a deteriorated condition, with high ceilings, soiled walls, and a wooden floor.

Imbalanced caseloads

imbalanced caseloads

Many lower courts are characterized by moderate to heavy caseloads. But others appear to have little to do. Thus there are often wide differences in caseload from court to court. The *imbalanced caseloads* result in some courts being flooded with huge backlogs for which they are unequipped. But because these courts are locally controlled, there is no way to equalize the work load.

Any general statement about the problems of the lower courts must, however, be immediately coupled with a cautionary note, for the nation's lowest tribunals have been the least studied. Moreover they are tremendously varied. From state to state, between one county and its neighboring county, and even within a city, there are wide discrepancies in the quantity and quality of justice rendered. These wide-ranging variations illuminate the fact that these courts are locally controlled and are not generally part of the state judiciary. In short, there is no easy way to determine what is wrong (or even what is right) about these courts (Ashman, 1975:15). Given this wide-ranging disparity, it is best to examine the rurally based justice of the peace courts separately from the urban municipal courts. Although they share many problems, they are also sufficiently different to warrant separate treatment.

Justice of the peace courts

justice of the peace (JP)

In rural areas, the lower courts are collectively called *justice of the peace courts.* The officeholder is usually referred to simply as a JP. This system of local justice traces its origins to fourteenth-century England when towns were small and isolated. The JP system developed as a way to dispense simple and speedy justice for minor civil and criminal cases. The emphasis was decidedly on the ability of local landowners (squires), who served as part-time JPs to decide disputes on the basis of their knowledge of the local community.

The small-town flavor of the JP system persists today. By and large present-day JPs are part-time, nonlawyers who conduct court at their regular place of business—the back of the undertaker's parlor, the front counter of the general store, or next to the grease rack in the garage. Most of the nation's 15,000 to 20,000 JPs are locally elected officials who serve short terms. Some, however, serve ex officio—

that is, many small town mayors also serve as judges in city court. Although a few are able to earn a comfortable income from the job, overall the salaries are low. Moreover support personnel is often limited. In the smaller courts, the JP's spouse may serve as clerk. But many courts have no clerks at all. JPs in Texas, for example, seldom have any clerical help for record keeping.

Critics argue that the JP system has outlived its purpose. While it might have met the needs of small, isolated, and rural towns of a century ago, it is out of step with the modern era. A Maryland trial judge criticized his own state's JPs in the following terms:

> "[They have] treated some good, decent citizens like common criminals."
>
> "The justice of the peace system is completely outmoded. . . . If things keep going like they've been going, some of these people are going to get us into serious trouble. . . ."
>
> Many of the JP's are just plain nasty to people.
>
> "There have been all sorts of instances where they've been rude to people and when the person complains they tell him to 'go to see your congressman.'
>
> "These people aren't controlled by us. They deny they have any connection with the police department. They tell the police to jump—and they tell us the same thing.
>
> "It's time these people were put under us—or the circuit court—or somebody."
> [President's Commission, 1967b:35]

Examples like these abound to show that the justice a defendant receives in JP court reflects the personality of the judge. Or that out-of-town motorists are treated very differently (high fines to keep the city treasury full) from local speeders. While some lower courts administer fair and even-handed justice, all too many do not. Critics doubt whether the current diversified and fragmented JP system can ever deliver fair, impartial, and even-handed justice. Efforts at improving the quality of justice dispensed by the rurally based lower courts focus on three topics: abolition of the JP courts; elimination of the fee system; and upgrading the quality of the personnel.

Abolition of the JP

abolition of JP

The ultimate goal of the judicial reformers is to *abolish the JP.* A major defect of the JP system is that these courts are not part of the state judiciary; instead they are controlled only by the local governmental bodies that create them and fund them. Only recently have judicial conduct commissions (see chapter 7) been granted the authority to discipline or remove local judges who abuse their office.

trial de novo

Nor are the activities of the lower courts subject to appellate scrutiny. Rarely are trial courts of limited jurisdiction courts of record; no stenographic record is kept of the witnesses' testimony or the judges' rulings. Thus when a defendant appeals, the appeal is heard by a trial court of general jurisdiction, which must conduct an entirely new trial, taking the testimony of the same witnesses and hearing the identical arguments of the attorneys as the lower court did. This is called a *trial de novo.* The *trial de novo* system often unnecessarily increases the already heavy caseload of the state trial courts. But by far the major weakness of the *trial de novo* system is that it insulates the lower courtroom from scrutiny. No opportunity exists for higher courts to discover or correct errors in court procedure, taking of evidence, denial of defendant's constitutional rights, or court's interpretation of the criminal law. The absence of appellate court review also hides patterns and practices that while not illegal are nonetheless problems—ineffective management of the courtroom or disparaging remarks by the judge, for example (Bing and Rosenfeld).

Unifying state courts into a three-tier system of a single trial court, an intermediate appellate court, and a supreme court (see chapter 3) would abolish the justice of the peace, require all judges to be lawyers, and eliminate the *trial de novo* system.

Reformers have had only limited success in their efforts to abolish the JP system. One major obstacle is the powerful influence of nonlawyer judges who do not want their jobs abolished. Another significant obstacle is the belief that JPs are easily accessible, whereas more formal courts are miles away. For example, they are readily available to sign arrest warrants for the police or to try a motorist accused of driving too fast. Supporters contend that a knowledge of the local community better prepares JPs to solve minor disputes than does a law degree, mainly because few minor disputes involve any complex legal issues. Thus JP courts are often viewed as people's courts. As one Florida supporter phrased it, "These are the last bastions of the people without much money. It's a place they can go to resolve their problems" without the necessity of having a lawyer (MacFeely:10A).

Elimination of the fee system

fee system

Historically rurally based, part-time justices of the peace were paid for their services from the fees assessed against a convicted defendant. To many, the *fee system* meant that JP stood for "justice for the plaintiff"; since the judge was paid only if the defendant was found guilty, few were acquitted. In 1927 the Supreme Court seemingly abolished the direct fee system by ruling that it denied defendants the right to trial before an impartial judge (*Tumey* v. *Ohio*, 273 U.S. 510). Yet as late as 1965, three states still used the direct fee system (President's Commission, 1967b:34). Many others used an indirect fee system for compensating lower court judges. Indeed, the President's Commission reported that thirty-two of the thirty-five states where JPs had criminal case jurisdiction, pay was still tied to the fees; the state covered court costs if the defendant was acquitted. But even with this refinement, "justice for the plaintiff" continued. Since states were slow in forwarding funds, the JP tended to convict in order to avoid a lengthy wait for the county to pay. Then too, the fee system exerted pressure on each justice to get more business. Police officers—the major source of the JP's business—naturally patronized JPs sympathetic to the police and prone to convict (President's Commission, 1967b:34–35).

Since the President's Commission report, which singled out the fee system as one of the worst features of the JP courts, major changes have occurred. As states have reexamined their lower courts, the first thing to be abolished has been the fee system. In less than a decade the fee system has gone from the primary way of paying local judges to virtual extinction; only a small handful of states now use it.

It has been replaced by paying lower court judges a salary irrespective of how many cases they handle or whether they find the defendant guilty. The major issue involved now is whether the local government or the state will pay the JP's salary. Typically local governments wish to retain the revenues they receive from JP courts but want the state government to bear the operating costs. A major consequence of the abolition of the fee system has been a marked decrease in the number of JPs.

Upgrading the quality of the personnel

The low pay and equally low status of the JP have not attracted highly qualified personnel. One survey found that only 5 percent of the JPs in Virginia were college graduates. Another, conducted in California, showed that between a third and a half of that state's lower court judges were not even high school graduates. Perhaps most shocking of all, the assistant attorney general of Mississippi, in his brief in a state court case, estimated that "33 percent of the justices of the peace are limited in educational background to the extent that they are not capable of learning the necessary elements of law" (Justice Brennan, dissent, *North* v. *Russell*).

The average JP's unfamiliarity with basic legal concepts is shown in the following testimony of a South Carolina magistrate:

Q. Do you presently have an understanding of what your duties as a magistrate are?
A. Well, not really, no.
Q. Tell me what your understanding of the Code of Laws is. What is contained in the Code of Laws, as you understand?
A. Well, I never have done any reading in it.
Q. You never have had occasion to refer to it?
A. No, sir. [Neither had he read any case of an appellate court.]
Q. What would you do if someone were to request a trial by jury?
A. I would come to Mr. George Stuckey [the county attorney] and find out what I had to do.
Q. What is the purpose of bail?
A. It is for violation and a good reminder not to do it again.
Q. Are you familiar with the concept of probable cause, in connection with preliminary hearings?
A. No, sir.
Q. Or in connection with the issuance of search warrants, or arrest warrants?
A. No, sir.
Q. Have you ever refused to issue an arrest or search warrant?
A. No, sir.
Q. Are you familiar with the rules of evidence which govern the admissibility of evidence at trials?
A. No, sir. [Ashman and Chapin:418]

High on the judicial reformers' list of priorities, therefore, is upgrading the quality of lower court judges. Some states have instituted training programs for lay judges, but only a few of the judges have yet received any training in basic legal concepts or the duties and responsibilities of the office.

IN THE NEWS: JUSTICE OF THE PEACE: SAGE OR SUPERFLUITY?

They are either a useless anachronism standing in the way of judicial reform, or a precious source of common sense justice for the little guy.

They sometimes put on airs and call themselves "judge" despite a lack of legal training that can lead them to ride roughshod over people's constitutional rights.

Yet they are the sole protectors of people with grievances that are not worth the attorneys' fees involved in state district court litigation.

The best of them are tireless workers, widely respected for sensitive resolution of disputes.

The worst of them have sometimes been described as arrogant bullies who frequently exceed their authority and interfere with the administration of justice.

They can issue felony and misdemeanor arrest warrants on a citizen's complaint. They preside over small claims courts in cases involving up to $500 in cash or $750 in movables.

And they can charge healthy fees for conducting marriages to augment the small salaries they are paid by the parish councils or police juries.

They are justices of the peace, required by the state Constitution to be elected in every Louisiana parish except Orleans.

Justices of the peace enjoy their highest esteem in suburban regions.

Jefferson Parish District Attorney John M. Mamoulides said justices of the peace have sometimes caused problems by assuming the right to release serious offenders from the Gretna Correctional Center on bond.

They have also, according to Mamoulides, attempted to mediate disputes that properly belong in criminal court.

Such problems have been ironed out in recent years, Mamoulides said, but he still regards justices of the peace as superfluous in Jefferson, the only parish in the metropolitan area to have parish courts as an extra tier in the judiciary below state district courts.

"I want to abolish the office of justice of the peace to streamline the criminal justice system, although I'm not opposed to any of them personally," Mamoulides said.

"We could do away with them tomorrow without hurting the criminal justice system. They don't issue that many arrest warrants, and what there are are mainly misdemeanors. Politically, JPs are unimportant.

"Our JPs are good people, but if we are going to have them at all, I'd like the job to be filled by young lawyers, or people who know what is required before someone can be arrested."

Mamoulides said he never acts on a warrant of a justice of the peace without first sending it to the Jefferson Parish Sheriff's Office, or a municipal department, so the case can be investigated.

East Jefferson has only one justice of the peace, A. J. Christina, pending the election of a replacement for J. A. "Bob" Wilkes, who resigned in December following his conviction in federal court on two counts of making illegal jail threats to collect debts. Wilkes was sentenced to a year in prison.

Christina, who works out of his tire dealership in Kenner, said, "We're the only place where average people—and they make up the vast majority of citizens—can get help that is simple and direct. The point is everyone wants instant justice, and the JPs are the only ones who can deliver.

"And when a husband and wife get at each other's throats, we're the only sounding board most of them have. They can't afford a psychologist or a professional counselor. Why they don't go to a clergyman I don't know."

On Jefferson Parish's West Bank, and particularly in its less accessible parts, justices of the peace are highly valued by law enforcement officials.

Although the broad consensus in rural areas is that the criminal justice system would falter without justices of the peace, some eccentric personalities sometimes get elected.

In St. Charles Parish, for instance, Justice of the Peace Louie "Chookie" Schexnayder, who compares himself with Judge Roy Bean, has a reputation for overstepping the mark, according to District Court Judge Ruche Marino.

Schexnayder boasts of his power to sway voters on election day. "They'll come ask me, 'Who you going with, judge?'" he said.

In St. Bernard, the general practice is that unless a sheriff's deputy has witnessed a crime, or unless a suspect is fleeing the scene of a felony and may escape, a warrant of arrest is needed from a justice of the peace.

William Alford Jr., St. Tammany first assistant district attorney, who served as special prosecutor for the Judiciary Commission in the Wilkes case, said that in a parish like St. Tammany, justices of the peace perform a useful service.

But Alford said he believes every justice of the peace felony warrant should be reviewed by the district attorney's office before being executed.

"Someone can make a charge, even to attempted murder, to a JP and a warrant is issued. The sheriff's office arrests the man and he is booked and mugged. No matter what happens after that, unless the man goes through the lawsuit expense of filing a suit to have his name cleared, that is forever on his record, even if the district attorney's office decides not to prosecute."

James Gill, "Justice of the Peace: Sage or Superfluity," *New Orleans Times-Picayune*, March 7, 1982.

Nonlawyer judges

nonlawyer judges

A long-standing issue confronting the American judiciary is whether lower court judges should be attorneys. A recent study reveals that there are 13,217 nonlawyer judges in the United States (Silberman et al.). A disproportionate number of these part-time, nonlawyer judges are located in the states of New York, Mississippi, and Texas (Alfini and Passuth:102). Judicial reformers argue that only lawyers should be allowed to judge defendants innocent or guilty and to sentence them to a year (or sometimes more) in jail. On the other hand, defenders of the status quo argue that these courts led by nonlawyer judges are people's courts where common sense is as good a guide as lawbooks in settling disputes. The U.S. Supreme Court con-

North v. Russell

sidered this issue in *North* v. *Russell*, a case that features a number of problems in the lower courts.

The Lynch City Police Court meets every Thursday night, Judge C. B. Russell presiding. Like most others born and raised in Lynch, a small town in Kentucky's coal mining region, Russell dropped out of high school and worked in the coal mines. A few years ago he was elected judge. He is not a lawyer nor has he received any training in the duties of a city judge. On July 8, 1974, Judge Russell found Lonnie North guilty of drunk driving and sentenced him to thirty days in jail. But Kentucky law allows only a fine for Lonnie North's charge. The judge, it seems, exceeded his legal power. Nor was this the only legal irregularity in the proceedings that day. Judge Russell refused the defendant's request for a jury trial, did not inform him of his right to a court-appointed lawyer, and failed to advise the defendant of his right to an appeal. Moreover, during the trial, Judge Russell listened only to the arresting officer's story and did not allow the defendant to tell his version (*North* v. *Russell*, 96 S. Ct. 2709, 1976).

Chief Justice Warren Burger's majority opinion argued that nonlawyer judges do not violate the due process clause of the Fourteenth Amendment. He described the JP system as courts of convenience for citizens in small towns and spoke favorably of the fact that "the inferior courts are simple and speedy." Burger argued that any defects in the proceedings (which were numerous in this case) could be corrected by the availability of defense attorneys, the right to a jury trial, and a *trial de novo*. Significantly, though, these were the specific things that Judge Russell failed to inform the defendant about.

In a dissenting opinion, Justice Brennan stated the case for requiring judges to be lawyers. He found it constitutionally intolerable that a nonlawyer judge could send a defendant to jail or to prison. Brennan further noted that a defendant's right to a lawyer in the lower court is eroded if the judge is not capable of understanding a lawyer's argument on the law.

To many, the JP's unfamiliarity with the law erodes the court's traditional role of independence. Nonlawyer judges may be too easily swayed by a lawyer's argument, often place undue reliance on the opinions of the district attorney, and may give unjustifiable weight to police testimony (Ashman and Chapin:418). A study in the state of New York, for example, determined that lay judges were slightly more favorable toward police officers and prosecutors than were legally trained officials (Ryan and Guterman).

States are beginning to eliminate nonlawyer judges. The California supreme court has ruled that the nonlawyer magistrate violates that state's constitution. Moreover when states adopt court reorganization, they invariably abolish the nonlawyer JP (although typically incumbents are retained). The movement to eliminate the nonlawyer JP is a slow one, however. One reason is that such proposals can appear to be full employment manipulations for the advantage of the legal profession. In an era when there is an oversupply of lawyers, the requirement that all lower court judges be lawyers may be partially motivated by a desire to keep the profession working.

Studies have shown that the shift to legally trained judges may alter the decisions reached. Green and associates found that Iowa's new state constitution requiring legally trained lower court judges resulted in more formal proceedings that frightened away the individual civil plaintiffs of the courts. Moreover, decisions in small civil cases increasingly benefited the merchants. A handful of other studies, however, have found few, if any, differences between the behavior of lay versus lawyer judges. (Provine:33).

Municipal courts

municipal courts   *Municipal courts* are the urban counterparts of the justice of the peace courts. Decades ago the increasing volume of cases coupled with the anonymous conditions of the big cities overwhelmed the ability of the rurally conceived JP system to dispense justice. The forerunner of the municipal court was the police magistrate, who was closely tied to another major nineteenth-century innovation—organized police forces in the big cities. In actuality, police magistrates were combination law enforcement officials and judicial officers. Located in the precinct houses, the police magistrate served as a legal adviser to the police and conducted criminal investigations. At times these police functions obviously conflicted with judicial duties of setting bond, conducting preliminary hearings, and the like. Increasingly, there-

police mag- istrates   fore, *police magistrates* evolved into purely judicial officers. Today most municipal courts hold court in a central location rather than a police station house, which reduces the ties to local police stations.

Municipal courts have also been shaped by another important aspect of the urban political landscape: the political machine. Urban political machines viewed the lower courts as opportunities for patronage. Party bosses controlled the election or appointment of judges. Similarly, positions of bailiff and clerks were reserved for the party faithful. Not surprisingly, therefore, municipal courts were often tainted by corruption. Charges would be dropped or files mysteriously disappear in return for political favors or cash. The judicial reformers of the 1920s and 1930s sought to clean up the courts by removing them from politics.

The assembly line

"Sausage Factories" headlined a *Time* article on municipal courts (November 25, 1974). "Hurricanes of Humanity" wrote the American Judicature Society in the first national survey of the lower courts. Both analogies draw our attention to the overriding reality of municipal courts in the nation's big cities: the press of cases (Ashman, 1975). All too often the major concern is moving cases. "Obstacles" to speedy disposition—warning of constitutional rights, presence of counsel, trials— are neutralized. In a process some have labeled an *assembly line*, shortcuts are routinely taken to keep the cases moving. Thus the municipal courts more closely resemble a bureaucracy geared to mass processing of cases (and not necessarily defendants) than an adjudicative body providing consideration for each case.

assembly line

Arraignment.   The handling of cases begins when the defendant is arraigned. Instead of advising defendants individually—a time-consuming process—municipal court judges often open court by generally addressing everyone in court roughly as follows:

> All of you who have charges against you, listen. You have a right to remain silent if you wish. If you speak, what you say can and probably will be held against you. You have a right to an attorney and to have time to get one. You also may have a right, in some cases—if you have no money—to apply for a court-appointed attorney, and under certain conditions one will be assigned to you. And if your offense is bondable you have a right to bond.

Later the judge may individually or in groups advise defendants more specifically. But some defendants are never advised of their rights at all. One study in a large eastern city found that in one-fourth of all cases, the judge did not inform the defendants of their rights (table 17-1). Few efforts are made to determine if defendants understand what is said or even if, in the noise and confusion of the crowded courtroom, the defendant heard at all. Appraisal of rights is treated by the court as a clerical detail to be dispensed with before the taking of guilty pleas can begin.

TABLE 17-1.   Apprising of rights

Apprising of rights	*Offense charged* Misdemeanor minor	*Serious*	*All cases*
None	35%	6%	26%
In courtroom audience	22	11	18
Groups before bench	20	23	23
Groups before bench with individual follow-up	6	28	11
Individual before bench	18	31	22
Total	101	99	100
(N)	(220)	(35)	(292)

Source: Maureen Mileski, "Courtroom Encounters: An Observation Study of a Lower Criminal Court," *Law and Society Review* 5 (May 1971):485.

Absence of Counsel. Other potential obstacles to the speedy disposition of cases are defense attorneys. Defendants have a constitutional right to be represented by an attorney. In practice, however, the presence of an attorney in the lower courts is rare. A study in one eastern city found that only 12 percent of the misdemeanor defendants were represented by a lawyer (Mileski:486). This absence of defense attorneys is partially the product of the minor nature of most municipal court cases; some defendants believe the charge is too minor to justify the expense of hiring a lawyer. The more serious the alleged offense, however, the more likely a defendant will have an attorney. Thus in Boston "two out of three defendants charged with 'real crimes' are represented by a lawyer" (Bing and Rosenfeld:264). The absence of attorneys is also a product of the economics of the legal profession. Since fees are low, few attorneys will take a case in one of these courts. The general absence of defense attorneys reinforces the informality of the lower courts and does nothing to deter the lack of attention to legal rules and procedures (Bing and Rosenfeld:264–265).

Argersinger v. Hamlin
But what of those too poor to hire a lawyer? In *Argersinger* v. *Hamlin* (407 U.S. 25, 1972) the Supreme Court ruled that "absent a knowing and intelligent waiver, no person may be imprisoned for any offense, whether classified as petty, misdemeanor, or felony unless he was represented by counsel." Thus an indigent defendant may be fined without having a lawyer, but if the judge is considering imposing a jail term, he or she must give the impoverished defendant the opportunity to have a court-appointed counsel at state expense. Although legal experts viewed *Argersinger* as a landmark decision potentially commanding wholesale changes in the lower courts, actual changes have been far less dramatic. After a comprehensive survey, the Boston University Center for Criminal Justice concluded: "Compliance has generally been token in nature," reform "has been chaotic and uneven at best," and the legal right to counsel remains "an empty right for many defendants" (Krantz et al.).

Dispositions. In municipal courts the defendant's initial appearance is the final one. Most persons charged with a traffic violation or a minor misdemeanor plead guilty immediately. In one of the few truly systematic studies of the lower courts, Mileski found that 85 percent of the defendants plead guilty at the first appearance. The rate of guilty pleas varied with the severity of the offense, however. For minor offenses (like public drunkenness) the rate was 98 percent; for more serious cases it was 68 percent. The quick plea represents a fatalistic view of most defendants: "I've done it—let's get it over with." Realistically, a defendant charged with crimes like public drunkenness or disorderly conduct cannot raise a valid legal defense.

What has struck all observers of the lower courts is the speed with which the pleas are processed. Typical are the following rough calculations:

> The Court generally disposes of between 50 and 100 cases per day, but on any Monday there are 200 to 250 and on Monday mornings after holiday weekends the Court may handle as many as 350 cases. I would estimate that, on the average, cases take between 45 seconds and one minute to dispose of. [Wiseman:235]

More systematically, Mileski calculated the median time to accept a defendant's plea and impose sentence at less than a minute. More serious cases were given more time, but the average time was still only two minutes.

Absence of Trials.   Few trials are held in the lower courts. A defendant has a right to a jury trial only if the offense can be punished by imprisonment for more than six months (*Baldwin* v. *New York*, 399 U.S. 66, 1970). The general absence of attorneys and the minor nature of the offenses combine to make requests for jury trials rare. If there is a trial it is a bench trial. The informality of the lower court dominates trials (and almost everything else): rules of evidence are not necessarily followed, no trial record is kept, and trials last only a few minutes.

The courtroom work group

It is no accident that the vast majority of defendants waive their rights to counsel, trial, and so on, thus enabling the court to dispose of its day's business rapidly. The courtroom work group tries to encourage such behavior by controlling the flow of defendants, making quick pleas part of the routine. Some courts manipulate bail to pressure defendants into waiving their right to a lawyer. During the arraignment, each defendant is informed of the right to a full hearing with a court-appointed attorney. But the hearing cannot be held for two or three weeks, which the defendant will have to spend in jail (Wice:7). Not surprisingly the vast majority of defendants choose to waive their right to counsel in favor of a speedy disposition. Quick pleas represent a defendant's unwillingness to take a chance; they surrender the possibility of an acquittal because they fear a harsher penalty if they try but are unsuccessful (Mileski:495).

The routines of the lower courts also may be threatened by uncooperative defendants. Defendants who unreasonably take up too much of the court's time can expect sanctions. Judges and prosecutors dislike defendants who "talk too much." Mileski provides an example of a young middle-class white man who made a detailed inquiry into his rights and then gave a relatively lengthy account (roughly two minutes) of his alleged offense of vagrancy. Although the defendant was polite, the judge interrupted him with "That will be all Mr. Jones" and ordered him to jail. Other defendants who "talked too much" received longer-than-normal sentences.

Sentencing

Municipal courts are not really trial courts because few defendants contest their guilt; in actuality they are a sentencing institution. The municipal court's conveyor belt is geared to making a rapid decision whether to impose a fine, grant a suspended sentence, allow probation, or banish to jail. Table 17-2 reports the outcome of this decision-making process in three cities. Note that few defendants were sentenced to jail. Perhaps one policeman's view, "I might as well not arrest him; the court won't do anything anyway," is understandable (Mileski:503–504). Instead the majority receive a fine. A long-standing practice of lower courts was the

TABLE 17-2.   **Frequency of type of sentence in three lower courts (by percent)**

	Austin, Texas	Tacoma, Washington	Mankato, Minnesota
Probation	15.0%	5.0%	4.4%
Jail	6.7	8.2	11.6
Fine	6.8	71.4	68.4
Fine & probation	48.9	5.5	4.4
Fine & jail	22.3	4.1	2.1
Other	.3	5.8	9.1
(N)	(12.15)	(437)	(731)

Source: Anthony Ragona, Malcolm Rich and John Paul Ryan, "Sentencing in the Misdemeanor Courts: The Choice of Sanctions," Paper presented at the Law and Society Association Annual Meeting, Amherst, Massachusetts, June 12-14, 1981, p. 8.

option sentence of five days or twenty-five dollars. To poor defendants this was not an effective option, and jail was the only alternative. The Supreme Court has ruled that convicted defendants cannot be jailed because of the inability to pay a fine (*Tate* v. *Short*, 401 U.S. 395, 1971).

> . . . By and large, the judge's function is to ratify the decisions of the prosecutors and defense attorneys.
>
> But even in those cases in which judges have "freedom" to sentence, they are left feeling frustrated. "What do you do," one judge asked, "in these petty cases? They're not serious enough to put a person in jail; yet you want to do something to show society's disapproval. Normally a fine would be appropriate, but so many of these people don't have any money. So we end up giving meaningless conditional discharges or probation, and it becomes something of a joke. It's frustrating; there's little we can do."
>
> In the main the courtroom judge is not even manager of his own domain; the activity is too diffuse and the pace too quick. It is perhaps more accurate to say that the judge endures rather than presides over his courtroom.
>
> Malcolm Feeley, *The Process Is the Punishment: Handling Cases in a Lower Criminal Court* (New York: Russell Sage Foundation, 1979), p. 69.

In making sentencing choices, the court relies on some readily identifiable characteristics of the defendant—prior criminal record, type of crime, and dress—in sorting defendants into typical or modal categories. Through time virtually every court has evolved a set of penalties deemed appropriate for given types of offenders in combination with the crimes they have committed. Thus the sentencing process in the lower courts is seldom one of searching for a sentence to fit the individual. Rather it is a process of quickly determining group averages. The result is a high degree of uniformity; by and large a defendant gets the same sentence as all others in the same category.

criminal record

Criminal Record.   A key factor in sentencing is the defendant's prior *criminal record* (unless the offense was very serious). First offenders rarely receive a jail term. Indeed given the pettiness of the offenses, first offenders may be released without any penalty whatsoever. Repeaters are sanctioned more severely. The jailing of defendants for public intoxication increases strikingly as the length and recency of prior arrests increase, for example. The importance of a prior record in sentencing partially explains an otherwise unaccountable pattern. One study found that serious misdemeanants were fined while minor misdemeanants were jailed. The explanation is that few of the serious misdemeanor defendants had prior records, while more of the minor misdemeanor defendants did (Mileski).

nature of the event

Nature of the Event. Offenses can be categorized along two dimensions: the official charge and what actually occurred (substance). While the charge is never more serious than the substance, at times the substance is more serious than the charge. For example, a defendant may be charged with breach of the peace when he had engaged in a more serious violation—threatening his wife with a knife. When the substance is more serious than the charge, judges usually sentence on the basis of the *nature of the event*. Even when the charges have been reduced (after plea bargaining, for example), the defendant receives the penalty that is typical for the more serious charge.

The opposite may also be true. What is perceived by the police officer as trouble serious enough to warrant an arrest may not be viewed equally as seriously by the prosecutor or the judge. On the whole, the court has a higher tolerance for trouble than the police (Feeley). An arrestee who is loud and threatening during booking may appear quiet and nonthreatening the next day in court. As a result court officials may treat some cases as minor. Indeed some arrests are regarded as so trivial that prosecutors and judges resent the police for bringing such cases to court. Feeley has argued that situations like the one just mentioned represent situational justice. Criminal charges are abstractions. Courts respond to the actual events from a perspective of hindsight and cooler temperaments. He concluded that prosecutors and judges look beyond the specific charges to assess the real damage in establishing an appropriate sentence.

CLOSE-UP: ROUGH JUSTICE?

BALTIMORE—It is late morning, and Maryland District Judge Alan Resnick is deciding the 19th case he has heard in the past two hours.

There's not much to go on. A young woman has accused Leroy Odom of following her along a sidewalk, grabbing her hand and threatening to "bang" her face. Leroy Odom says the woman propositioned him, upped her price and started yelling when he turned her down. The policeman who arrested him knows only that the woman was screaming and Mr. Odom was running.

Judge Resnick wastes little time in finding guilt. "I don't think she's a hustler," he tells Mr. Odom, "and I think you assaulted her." The sentence: one year in prison for the misdemeanor.

It seems an inexact sort of justice. But that's the way it often is here in Baltimore's eastern judicial district ("eastern station") and in hundreds of other lower criminal courts across the country. The judge hears a dispute, sizes up the witnesses, perhaps asks a few questions and decides whose word to take. Rarely do eloquent argument or scholarly reflection weigh in the balance; dockets are too crowded, lawyers are in a rush and judges are under constant pressure to issue a ruling and move on to another case.

"This is where the action is," says 47-year-old Judge Resnick, a trim, intense man with long gray-black hair. "You have to make decisions right then and there on the law and the facts as to who you believe.". . . Charles Smith, an at-

(continued)

torney at Boston University's center for criminal justice, says the judge in these courts is "the trier of fact and law, the determinator of guilt and the sentencer—the whole ball game."

Bare-Based Justice   Four days in Judge Resnick's small, dingy courtroom show that many of the traditional formalities of jurisprudence are missing. Defendants, mostly poor and poorly educated, sometimes choose to forfeit their right to have an attorney defend them, and they almost always waive their right to a jury trial. Usually, they "just want to get this thing over with," as Alexander Wilson, charged with carrying a dangerous weapon, tells Judge Resnick. Mr. Wilson is found innocent.

Judge Resnick tries to create an atmosphere of fairness. But his courtroom is in the police station, a locale that hardly reeks of fine impartiality. The judge opens each court session by stressing that "this is not a police court," and he promises that "each case will be decided in accordance with the facts and the laws of Maryland." Still police officers are in sight all day, testifying, fetching defendants from the police "lock-up" or just milling around before the bench.

In some lower courts, "a five-minute trial is a long trial," says David Rossman, another attorney at Boston University's criminal justice center. "There is no prosecutor or defense counsel. The judge just says, 'Okay, what happened?' ". . .

The bench trial sounds more like an informal conversation, most of it inaudible to spectators. Opposing attorneys rarely clash in a serious way, and questioning generally seems designed to elicit little more than factual accounts of what took place. Much of the toughest questioning comes from Judge Resnick, and it's often dripping with disbelief. In Leroy Odom's case, he asks why Mr. Odom didn't bother to tell the arresting officer he had been "hustled." "Why didn't you tell him right then and there, 'Man, am I glad you saved me!' " the judge demands.

Later, in another case, Judge Resnick has a few questions for Yoha Walker. A police officer has testified that she admitted him to her motel room and offered to engage in sex for pay. But she says the policeman barged in uninvited and

"whipped out" a badge just as she was waking up, naked. Did she scream? the judge asks. No. Was there a phone? Yes. Did she use it to call the motel manager? No. Judge Resnick puts the woman on "probation before verdict," explaining that if she misbehaves on probation he will find her guilty of the soliciting charge. . . .

For the most part, Judge Resnick is regarded as a fair man. His decisions, of course, aren't universally popular. When he judges Kingar G. Wilson guilty of a handgun violation, a young woman in the courtroom snaps, "He thinks everybody's guilty. He's prejudiced." (Later, the judge amends his decision and imposes probation before a verdict.) On the bench, Judge Resnick is aggressive, and his temper occasionally flares. Like many other judges, he talks a lot. "When you're elevated and sitting higher than the rest of the world, it's irresistible—you simply must make speeches," says David Berman, executive director of Milwaukee's Legal Aid Society. . . .

The judge saves his toughest talk for what he considers the most serious crimes. "I don't like guns," or "I don't like stealing," he will tell defendants. When Leroy Odom asks the judge to reconsider his one-year prison sentence the judge retorts: "That's why you didn't get three years, because you don't have a record and the girl wasn't hurt." (Mr. Odom is appealing his sentence.) To Lamont Reece, sentenced to one year for assault and larceny, the judge says, "I tell you, young man, if you had any kind of record, I'd give you a minimum of two years."

Such commentary is needed, Judge Resnick believes, because many citizens get their impression of justice from the judge, not from the legal system as a whole. "The man in the street doesn't know anything about the Supreme Court," he says. "People just know about Judge Resnick. Their justice is Judge Resnick, of eastern station."

Wayne E. Green, "How the Law Works in a Criminal Court Run by a Busy Judge," *Wall Street Journal*, September 25, 1975. Reprinted by permission of *The Wall Street Journal*, © Dow Jones & Company, Inc. All rights reserved.

Dress and Demeanor.   A defendant's prior record and the nature of the charge *dress and* are both legally relevant variables in imposing sentence. The *dress and demeanor* of *demeanor* the defendant, on the other hand, are an extralegal consideration that judges sometimes consider. A study of drunk court in a Pacific coast city illustrates the influence that a defendant's physical appearance and social position have on sentencing (Wiseman). In drunk court the physical appearance may be the most important factor in determining the sentence. In an extreme case, where the person looks gravely ill and therefore is probably a chronic alcoholic, the judge sends the defendant to the county hospital. If the defendant is shaky and obviously drying out, then it is likely that a ten-to-fifteen-day jail term would be imposed.

Closely related to the physical appearance of a defendant are indicators of social status—dress and age. Someone who looks down and out is more likely to receive a jail sentence than a well-dressed defendant.

The process is the punishment?

Several recent studies have begun to question the image of the lower courts as assembly line operations. Susan Silbey, for example, argues that the standard picture of lower courts as wholesale, mechanical processors of a high volume of cases is only partially correct. In the first place, the operations of the misdemeanor courts are not as chaotic, disordered, or unreasonable as they may first appear. A second consideration is that the lower courts do try to provide justice. They do so, however, by responding to problems rather than crimes, concentrating their efforts to produce substantive justice rather than focusing on purely formal (due process) justice. Separate studies in New Haven, Connecticut (Feeley,) and Columbus, Ohio (Ryan) have assessed the disparate functions served by the lower courts.

Political scientist Malcolm Feeley spent several years studying the lower court in New Haven firsthand. He concluded that the major punishment of defendants occurs during the processing of cases and not after a finding of guilt. He contends that the pretrial process imposes a series of punishments ("price tags") on the accused. These price tags often include staying in jail (briefly), paying a bail bondsman, hiring a private attorney, and losing time and perhaps wages due to repeated court appearances. These costs far outweigh any punishment imposed after the defendant pleads guilty. Moreover, these price tags affect the roughly 40 percent of the defendants eventually found not guilty. In short, the pretrial process itself is the primary punishment, according to Feeley.

Another study, this time of Columbus, Ohio, reaches a different conclusion. Analyzing statistical data on court sentences, John Paul Ryan concludes that the outcome is the punishment. Unlike in New Haven, lower court judges in Columbus routinely impose fines on convicted defendants. Often these fines are substantial, averaging over $100. Further, 35 percent of the guilty in Columbus are sentenced to jail, six times as many as in New Haven. Finally, in traffic cases defendants often have their driver's licenses suspended and/or are ordered to attend drunk-driver schools. In short, Columbus defendants are more likely to be fined, to pay heavier fines, to go to jail, and to be required to participate in some sort of treatment program than their counterparts in New Haven.

These sharp contrasts between New Haven and Columbus accentuate the point made earlier in the chapter—misdemeanor courts are very diverse in their operations and procedures. A principal reason for such diversity relates to important differences in the political and legal culture. Recall from chapter 7 Levin's comparison of Pittsburgh and Minneapolis. We find similar differences in the cities studied by Feeley and Ryan. New Haven is a very ethnic, Democratic, and political town. In contrast Columbus is middle-class, Republican, and "good government" in orientation.

Another reason for such diversity stems from variations in court procedures. In New Haven the prosecutor controls case processing, whereas in Columbus the police are the dominant influence. In short, any assessment of the activities of the lower courts requires an awareness of their diversity.

Reducing the caseload

The overriding problem of the urban courts is the high volume of cases. To judicial reformers, these excessive caseloads are the crux of the problem for they cause the routine, summary, and often-times perfunctory disposition process. Reduction of the caseload is viewed as an essential first step if the nation's lower tribunals are ever going to utilize a true adversary process. One way to accomplish this is to expand the number of judges and support personnel. But more fundamentally, many believe that the key to making lower court caseloads more manageable is by removing certain types of cases from the courthouse. Diverting public drunkenness cases, creating nonjudicial, private-dispute-settling institutions, and shifting traffic violations to an administrative body are three programs that reflect current thinking on how to shrink lower-court caseloads. Although programs like these are usually presented as methods for reducing administrative burdens, the issues actually are much more fundamental and deep-seated. The root issues are whether minor criminal cases should be handled through formalistic court procedure and whether some of these offenses should be criminal.

Diverting public drunks

Yearly the police arrest two million people for public intoxication. After a brief encounter with the lower courts, they are fined or sent to jail for a few days or a few months. Drunk court is simply a revolving door; many of those arrested for public intoxication have been arrested before and will be arrested again. Jail sentences certainly do not seem to deter. There is general agreement that this process of jailing public drunks is ineffective, inefficient, and all too often inhumane as well. Moreover, the revolving door process greatly strains the criminal justice process.

> . . . the present handling of public drunkenness offenders is often demoralizing to the police, judicial, and jail personnel. It is an immense economic drain—in terms of men, time and space—on these agencies. Furthermore, it seriously undermines the professional character of the work of policemen, judges, district attorneys, and others, and often makes a mockery of the American judicial system. In most courts the average time spent by the judge in the "trial" and sentencing of each public drunkenness offender probably is less than three minutes. This system of handling defendants undoubtedly violates the traditional American conception of the "due process of law." [Plaut:110–111]

diverting
public
drunks

In searching for alternatives to the traditional handling of public drunkenness, emphasis has been placed on *diverting public drunks* to programs that provide better social services while at the same time reducing strains on the criminal justice system. The current thinking has been summarized in a model program the Law Enforcement Assistance Administration has found workable: First, because alcoholism is largely a public health problem, better medical assistance should be available. Second, many persons arrested for public drunkenness actually suffer from being homeless. A shelter would not only get the drunks off the street (the public's major demand) but would also provide facilities for medical treatment. Third, intermediate care should be provided for those who may want to break the skid-row cycle. Fourth, after detoxification many alcoholics are not ready to return to autonomous community living. Therefore, a halfway house facility should be available. Finally, aftercare services should be provided (Weis).

Private disputes

The steady diet of the police and the lower courts is private disagreements between friends, neighbors, spouses, or landlord and tenant. Two factory workers argue over Saturday's football game and a fight develops. After work the loser goes to the police station to file an assault and battery charge. An older neighbor, upset over dogs in his front yard, threatens to shoot the next dog in his yard. The irate dog owner calls the police and wants his neighbor arrested. These actual examples from Columbus, Ohio, are typical of the types of situations confronting the courts and the police (Palmer:23).

private
dispute

The role the courts and the legal system can play in resolving such *private disputes* is not clear. In such cases a trial would only obscure the source of the problem because it is either irrelevant or immaterial to the legal issues. Further in such interpersonal disputes, the person who files a complaint is often as guilty as the defendant. Such disputes are essentially civil matters that the agencies of the criminal law are forced to cool off lest a more serious crime—murder, shooting, or what have you—occurs. It is worth noting that other societies place much greater reliance on informal procedures for resolving these essentially private conflicts. Socialist nations, for example, employ neighborhood tribunals that emphasize conciliatory, nonadversarial techniques (Robertson:346).

Columbus, Ohio, has adopted an innovative program to divert such private disputes from the criminal law. Called the "night prosecutor," it is a citizen-dispute-settlement alternative to the criminal courts. The city prosecutor screens all complaints. If the dispute involves private citizens in which there is a continuing relationship between the "victim" and the "assailant" (much like the examples cited earlier) the case is referred to the night prosecutor. An administrative hearing is held at night because it is the most convenient time for most citizens. The hearing officer (a law student) attempts to mediate the dispute and to arrive at a compromise. The night prosecutor can also refer problem cases to helping agencies—churches, Alcoholics Anonymous, and so on. (If mediation is unsuccessful, criminal charges may result.)

Such programs not only relieve the courts of a large volume of cases for which they can do little but hear the tales of woe, but also promise to coordinate the problems of the citizens with some organization that might be helpful. One thing is clear: the traditional manner of the police arrest, brief hearing before the judge, and a small fine is not the answer.

Traffic court

traffic court

Particularly now that the speed limit has been reduced to 55 mph, few of us make it through life without driving too fast and being caught. Yet in many localities a simple traffic violation is treated the same way as a minor criminal violation: the traffic ticket (actually a court summons) requires attendance at *traffic court*. And after a long wait the motorist is allowed to pay the fine. Not only do such traffic cases unnecessarily clog up many lower courts, but they also give the average citizen a negative view of justice. The National Advisory Commission on Criminal Justice Standards and Goals has urged that traffic cases no longer be treated as criminal violations (except serious traffic violations like drunk driving or negligent homicide).

Administrative disposition of minor traffic cases would work as follows. All minor traffic violators would be allowed to enter a plea by mail, except where the violator is a repeater or where the infraction resulted in a traffic accident. No jury trials would be available. If the alleged violator desires a hearing, one would be provided by a legally trained referee. During the hearing the government would be required to prove the case by clear and convincing evidence (a standard less rigorous than the criminal prosecutor's burden in a criminal case of beyond a reasonable doubt). Appeal would be permitted to an appellate division of the administrative agency. The only grounds for appeal to a court would be abuse of discretion by the administrative agency (National Advisory Commission:168).

Conclusion

The lower courts come into contact with more citizens every year than virtually any other governmental institution. All too often, however, the average citizen comes away from such encounters with the impression of a nonjudicial atmosphere. The overriding concern appears to be a hasty disposition before sending the citizen to the cash register to pay the fine.

Several factors have led to this state of affairs. First, most cases are relatively minor. Perhaps citizens' expectations are too high concerning the quality of courts society uses for processing the large volume of cases where there are essentially no disputes over the facts. Second, the lower courts have historically been neglected by citizens, lawyers, and judges alike. In most states the lower courts operate separately from the other trial courts, which handle more serious offenses. Finally, the courts are extremely diverse. The problems faced by a rurally based JP differ entirely from those of a municipal court judge in a large city. All of these factors raise obstacles to efforts to improve the quality of justice. But as noted throughout this chapter, numerous and varied reforms are being recommended and some implemented.

For discussion

1. Discuss with your friends, parents, and neighbors any experiences they have had with the nation's lower courts. What do these experiences suggest about the nonjudicial atmosphere of these courts?
2. Has your state incorporated the lower courts into the state judicial system? If so, what factors do you think led to abolition of the JP? If not, what are the principal obstacles to abolition?
3. Do you think that all judges should be required to be lawyers? Discuss the pros and cons.
4. Observe a local lower court. Are defendants advised of their rights? How many defendants are represented by counsel? How quickly are cases disposed of? Are there any trials? Does the judge typically impose the sentence recommended by the prosecutor? In many communities there is more than one lower court (one for the city, another for the county). Compare these courts on the above measures. In which court would you prefer to have your case heard? Why?
5. Lower courts have been described as sentencing institutions. Discuss how the courtroom work group influences sentencing.
6. Interview a lower court judge and/or a prosecutor. What frustrations do they express about their job? What problems do they perceive? What reforms do they propose?
7. What proposals do you favor for reducing the caseload of municipal courts? What factors inhibit the adoption of such proposals?

References

Alfini, James J. "Introductory Essay: The Misdemeanor Courts," *Justice System Journal* 6 (Spring, 1981) 5-12.

———— ed. *Misdemeanor Courts: Policy Concerns and Research Perspectives.* Washington D.C.: National Institute of Justice, 1980.

————, and Patricia M. Passuth, "Case Processing in State Misdemeanor Courts: The Effect of Defense Attorney Presence." *Justice System Journal* 6 (Spring 1981):100–116.

Ashman, Allan. *Courts of Limited Jurisdiction: A National Survey.* Chicago: American Judicature Society, 1975.

————, and Pat Chapin. "Is the Bell Tolling for Nonlawyer Judges?" *Judicature* 59 (April 1976):417–421.

Bing, Stephen, and S. Stephen Rosenfeld. "The Quality of Justice in the Lower Criminal Courts of Metropolitan Boston." In John Robertson, ed., *Rough Justice: Perspectives on Lower Criminal Courts*, pp. 259–285. Boston: Little, Brown, 1974.

Feeley, Malcolm M. *The Process is the Punishment: Handling Cases in a Lower Criminal Court.* New York: Russell Sage Foundation, 1979.

Green, Justin, Russell, Ross, and John Schmidhauser. "Iowa's Magistrate System: The Aftermath of Reform." *Judicature* 58 (March 1975):380–389.

Krantz, Sheldon, Charles Smith, David Rossman, Paul Froyd, and Janis J. Hoffman. *Right to Counsel in Criminal Cases: The Mandate of Argersinger v. Hamlin.* Cambridge, Mass.: Ballinger, 1976.

MacFeely, F. T. "J. P. Courts Last Hope for 'Little People.'" *Gainesville Sun*, October 9, 1971.

Mileski, Maureen. "Courtroom Encounters: An Observation Study of a Lower Criminal Court." *Law and Society Review* 5 (May 1971):473–538.

National Advisory Commission on Criminal Justice Standards and Goals. *Courts.* Washington, D.C.: Government Printing Office, 1973.

Palmer, John. "The Night Prosecutor: Columbus Finds Extrajudicial Solutions to Interpersonal Disputes." *Judicature* 59 (June–July 1975):23–27.

Plaut, Thomas, ed. *Alcohol Problems: A Report to the Nation.* New York: Oxford University Press, 1967.

President's Commission on Law Enforcement and Administration of Justice. *Challenge of Crime in a Free Society.* Washington, D.C.: Government Printing Office, 1967a.

———. *Task Force Report: The Courts.* Washington, D.C.: Government Printing Office, 1967b.

Provine, Doris Marie. "Persistent Anomaly: The Lay Judge in the American Legal System." *Justice System Journal* 6 (Spring 1981):28–43.

Robertson, John, ed. *Rough Justice: Perspectives on Lower Criminal Courts.* Boston: Little, Brown, 1974.

Ryan, John Paul. "Adjudication and Sentencing in a Misdemeanor Court: The Outcome is the Punishment." *Law and Society Review* 15 (1980–81):79–108.

———, and James H. Guterman. "Lawyer versus Non-Lawyer Town Justices." *Judicature* 60 (January 1977):272–280.

"The Sausage Factories." *Time*, November 25, 1974, p. 91.

Silberman, Linda J. *Non-Attorney Justice in the United States: an Empirical Study.* New York: Institute of Judicial Administration, 1979.

Silbey, Susan S. "Making Sense of the Lower Courts." *Justice System Journal* 6 (Spring 1981):13–27.

Weis, Charles. *Diversion of the Public Inebriate from the Criminal Justice System.* Washington, D.C.: Government Printing Office, 1973.

Wice, Paul. *Freedom for Sale.* Lexington, Mass.: D. C. Heath, Lexington Books, 1974.

Wiseman, Jacqueline. "Drunk Court: The Adult Parallel to Juvenile Court." In William Sanders and Howard Dandistel, eds. *The Criminal Justice Process: A Reader*, pp. 233–252. New York: Praeger Publishers, 1976.

For further reading

Ashman, Allan. *Courts of Limited Jurisdiction: A National Survey.* Chicago: American Judicature Society, 1975.

Feeley, Malcolm M. *The Process is the Punishment: Handling Cases in a Lower Criminal Court.* New York: Russell Sage Foundation, 1979.

McCrea, Tully, and Don Gottfredan. *A Guide to Improved Handling of Misdemeanant Offenders.* Washington, D.C.: Government Printing Office, 1974.

Mileski, Maureen. "Courtroom Encounters: An Observation Study of a Lower Criminal Court." *Law and Society Review* 5 (May 1971):473–538.

National Center for State Courts. *Rural Courts: The Effects of Space and Distance on the Administration of Justice.* Denver: National Center for State Courts, 1977.

Robertson, John, ed. *Rough Justice: Pespectives on Lower Criminal Courts.* Boston: Little, Brown, 1974.

CHAPTER 18

Administering the Courts

"18-Month Jail Stay Questioned"
"Hit-Run Victims' Widows Unnerved by Trial Delay"
"Killer is Released Through Legal Snafu"

Headlines like these heighten the public's concern that the courts are not well run. Over half of those surveyed by the Yankelovich, Skelly and White polling organization (1978) rate the inefficiency of courts as a "serious" or "very serious" social problem. Two specific findings from this poll press home the public's dissatisfaction. First, persons with direct court experience were more likely to rate the inefficiency of courts as a problem than those with no experience. Second, the general public was more likely to perceive delay as a major problem than were judges and lawyers. Court officials, however, are becoming increasingly alarmed that the effectiveness of the criminal justice system is jeopardized by mismanaged and inefficient courts. Others worry about "assembly line" justice that rushes cases through without careful consideration.

Concern that "justice delayed is justice denied" is as old as the common law itself. In the thirteenth century the nobles forced King John to sign the Magna

Carta and promise not to "deny or delay right or justice." In the nineteenth century the novelist Charles Dickens condemned the tortuous process of litigation in English courts. In America in the late 1960s systematic attention finally began to be directed toward court management. And in the last few years, a new field of interest has arisen: judicial administration. The concept embodies a central concern—justice is affected not simply by how the courts decide the legal merits but also by how the courts process cases (Wheeler and Whitcomb:15).

This chapter examines some of the major topics included under the general heading of judicial administration: the problem of court delay and its causes, case scheduling, the role of technology, court managers, and speedy trial acts.

The problem of delay

Case backlog and trial delay are problems that affect many of the nation's courts. The magnitude of the backlog and the length of the delay vary greatly depending on the court involved. In the first systematic and comprehensive survey of how long it takes for cases to proceed from arrest to disposition, researchers for the National Center for State Courts reported widespread variation (see table 18-1). In some courts (such as New Orleans and Wayne County, Michigan) the typical case proceeds rather rapidly—about two months. But in other courts the duration was much more extensive. In the Bronx, New York, the median time was almost a full year—343 days. (Bear in mind that the median represents the case in the middle, which means half took less time and half took longer). These figures caution us that in some areas the "delay problem" may be less pressing than commonly assumed.

A normal passage of time must be distinguished from unnecessary delay. After all, some time is needed for the preparation of the case. There is no accepted definition of how much time is too much time. Various groups have put it between six months and two years (Wheeler and Whitcomb:15). The National Advisory Commission on Criminal Justice Standards and Goals recommended no more than sixty days between arrest and the beginning of a trial of a felony prosecution (thirty days for misdemeanors) (68). Given the inherent difficulty in distinguishing between necessary time for case preparation and unnecessary "delay," researchers now prefer the term *case-processing time* (Luskin).

Consequences of delay

Concern with court delay flows from a set of common assertions about its costs. Cases that take too long to reach disposition are more than a minor inconvenience. Concern with delay in the courts is warranted, not because of slowness or inconvenience, but because the values and guarantees associated with the legal system may be jeopardized. A number of different costs of delay are commonly cited. We can conveniently group these perceived costs under four headings: defendant, society, citizen, and system resources.

Defendant's rights. In the past, court delay was defined as a problem because it jeopardized the defendant's right to a speedy trial. The Sixth Amendment provides

TABLE 18-1. Median criminal disposition time measures for selected cities[a]

City	Number of days
Wayne County, Michigan[b] (3rd Judicial Circuit Court)	64
San Diego, California (San Diego County Superior Court)	71
Atlanta, Georgia (Fulton County Superior Court)	77
New Orleans, Louisiana (Orleans Parish Criminal Court)	67
Portland, Oregon (Multnomah County Circuit Court)	67
Seattle, Washington (King County Superior Court)	82
Pittsburgh, Pennsylvania (Allegheny County Court of Common Pleas)	103
Oakland, California (Alameda County Superior Court)	116
St. Paul, Minnesota (2nd Judicial District Court)	74
Cleveland, Ohio (Cuyahoga County Court of Common Pleas)	103
Pontiac, Michigan (6th Judicial Circuit Court)	122
Miami, Florida (11th Judicial Circuit Court)	106
Phoenix, Arizona (Maricopa County Superior Court)	114
Fort Lauderdale, Florida (7th Judicial Circuit Court)	105
Houston, Texas (Harris County District Courts)	181
Newark, New Jersey (Essex County Superior Court)	209
Dallas, Texas (Dallas County District Courts)	115
Philadelphia, Pennsylvania (Philadelphia County Court of Common Pleas)	168
Bronx County, New York (Bronx County Supreme Court)	343

[a] Median days from date of arrest to date of either guilty plea, trial verdict, dismissal, or formal determination of entry into diversion program.

[b] The criminal jurisdiction of the Third Judicial Circuit Court includes all of Wayne County except the city of Detroit.

Source: Thomas Church, Alan Carlson, Jo-Lynne Lee and Teresa Tan. *Justice Delayed: The Pace of Litigation in Urban Trial Courts.* (Williamsburg, Virginia: National Center for State Courts, 1978), pp. 14-15.

that "in all criminal prosecutions, the accused shall enjoy the right to a speedy and public trial. . . . " Defendants may languish in jail for a number of months before guilt or innocence is determined. Some suggest that lengthy pretrial incarceration pressures defendants into pleading guilty (Casper). A number of states have enacted speedy trial laws premised on the need to protect the defendant's rights.

Societal protection. More recently, delay has been viewed as hampering society's need for a speedy conviction. This view stresses harm done to the prosecution's case. As the case becomes older and memories of the witnesses diminish, the defendant's chance for an acquittal rises. Delay also strengthens a defendant's bargaining position. Prosecutors are quicker to accept a plea of guilty when dockets are crowded and cases are growing older. Also, when delay occurs for defendants out on bond, the potential for additional criminal activity weighs heavily in the public's mind. In short, the state is also viewed as possessing the right to a speedy trial (National Advisory Commission:68).

Citizen confidence and convenience. Despite costs or benefits to either the defense or prosecution, a third perspective emphasizes that delay erodes public confidence in the judicial process. Citizens lose confidence in the swiftness or certainty of punishment. Additionally, victims and witnesses make repeated and, for them, wasted trips to the courthouse. Appearances can cost citizens a day's pay and lost time, and ultimately discourage them from prosecution.

Strain on resources. Delay in disposing of cases strains criminal justice system resources. Pretrial detainees clog jail facilities. Police officers must appear in court on numerous occasions, at public expense. Attorneys are forced to expend unproductive time because of repeated court appearances on the same case, costs ultimately passed to defendants. Moreover, efforts to reduce delay on the criminal docket may exacerbate delay in disposing of civil cases.

Assessing the costs of delay

Assertions about the alleged costs of delay require careful scrutiny. While a general consensus has emerged that delay is a problem facing the courts, there is no agreement about the particulars. The four perspectives just described stress varying, and at times contradictory, reasons for why delay is a problem. Some perceive that lengthy pretrial incarceration forces the defendant to enter into a less-than-advantageous plea bargain. Others, however, portray caseload pressures as forcing the prosecutor into offering unduly lenient negotiated bargains. The four perspectives, of course, are not necessarily mutually exclusive. Concerns about system resources as well as citizen confidence and convenience may be jointly held. The critical point is that assessment of the costs of delay are inherently subjective.

Not only is agreement absent on the specific costs of delay, but documentation of the evils that flow from it is lacking. In a recent review of the literature, the National Center for State Courts noted that "few of the foregoing assertions [about the social costs of delay] have been subjected to empirical examination" (Church et al., 1978b:15). They find some evidence to indicate that jail overcrowding, failure to appear rates, and citizen respect for the judiciary are tied to case delay. But they find no support for the assertions that deterioration of cases, diminished deterrence, decreased possibilities of rehabilitation, or plea bargaining are the products of case delay.

IN THE NEWS: EIGHTEEN-MONTH JAIL STAY QUESTIONED

A federal district court judge Wednesday ordered the attorney for St. Tammany Parish Sheriff George Broom to find out why an inmate at the jail has been held for 18 months waiting for trial.

U.S. District Court Judge Alvin Rubin gave William Faller 10 days to file an affidavit telling why Glenn Scott Passman is still in the overcrowded jail. . . .

Rutledge C. Clement, the court-appointed attorney representing Passman, told the court . . . that his client has been there 18 months awaiting trial.

Rubin asked Faller the reason for the prisoner's confinement for such a period but Faller said he did not know. . . .

Ed Anderson, *New Orleans Times-Picayune*, February 26, 1976.

Conventional wisdom about court delay

*conven-
tional
wisdom*

Different people have identified many causes for court delay. The literature on the subject contains varying and sometimes conflicting diagnoses. Typically, discussions of the causes of delay are linked to proposed remedies. The central difficulty in understanding the causes of delay is that most analyses have not been grounded in an understanding of the dynamics of the judicial process (Church et al., 1978b). Let us proceed by first discussing some of the *conventional wisdom* about court delay and then examining more recent research. Factors commonly asserted to cause delay can be grouped under two headings: (1) resources and work loads, and (2) administrative and procedural factors.

It is an article of faith among many commentators that the problem of delay results from an imbalance between available resources and mounting caseloads (Church et al., 1978b). A common response is to supplement resources—add judges, prosecutors, clerks and so on. Others urge reducing the number of cases going to court.

Traditional understandings of delay have also identified *administrative and procedural factors*, which stress the legal and managerial aspects of criminal court processing. Various stages of criminal court processing have been mentioned as sources of delay—initial appearance, preliminary hearing, grand jury indictment, and pretrial motions, for example. The recommended solutions involve "streamlining" the courts by eliminating these procedural roadblocks (Church et al., 1978b).

A major difficulty with the conventional wisdom about court delay is that it rests on a meager and inadequate knowledge base. A recent review of the literature, for example, concludes that our understanding of the causes and remedies of court delay has progressed little beyond Roscoe Pound's (an early judicial reformer) much-quoted comments on delay in 1908 (Church et al., 1978b:45). Many studies of delay, particularly those purporting to show that delay has been reduced in a particular jurisdiction, are methodologically weak (Luskin, 1978).

Some recent studies call the conventional wisdom into question. In *Justice Delayed*, the National Center for State Courts reports on twenty-one metropolitan courts. The study focused on the linkage between formal aspects of court operations and case-processing time (see table 18-1). These formal aspects constitute the traditional model of court delay, and are the factors most often cited by practitioners as the reasons for delay. The study found that the relationships were weak

IN THE NEWS: HIT-RUN VICTIMS' WIDOWS UNNERVED BY TRIAL DELAYS

For the widows of Gerald and William Harrell, victims of a hit-and-run traffic incident some 14 months ago, the hallways outside Criminal District Court Judge Israel Augustine's courtroom have become an all-too-familiar scene.

At least four times now, they have come to testify and to witness the trial of a St. Bernard man charged with negligent homicide in the deaths of their husbands, and of a third victim Joseph Martin, 30, killed while fishing from the Paris Road Bridge over Bayou Bienvenue, the morning of Sept. 22, 1975.

Subpoenas in hand, they linger in the hall, waiting with more than a dozen relatives, friends of other witnesses, for the proceedings to begin.

And each time they have been greeted, sooner or later, with the same message: The case has been postponed.

It has been postponed, in fact, mostly on defense motion granted by Augustine, on July 14, July 15, July 29, September 17, Nov. 15, and again this week, court records show. Numerous hearings also have been delayed.

In one instance, a motion by defense lawyer Eddie Bopp to recuse the judge first had to be heard. Bopp claimed Augustine was prejudiced since Wilbourn had first pleaded guilty in his court, then withdrew the plea. Augustine allowed the plea withdrawn in accordance with a prior agreement he made with Bopp that if the judge decided after receiving a pre-sentence report he would not suspend the sentence, Bopp could withdraw the plea on behalf of his client, Hugh Wilbourn, 47, of 513 Norton Ave., Arabi.

Another time Bopp had a conflicting trial in another court, and on yet another occasion his associate presented the court a letter saying Bopp was ill. In the latest continuance, two defense witnesses, said by Bopp to be crucial, had not received their subpoenas from court deputies.

Bopp says the case "has seen an accumulation of various problems." For one, he claims the trial should be held in St. Bernard Parish at Wilbourn's request, since the incident occurred on a bridge dividing the two parishes. Prosecutors from both Orleans and St. Bernard disagree.

Bopp also claims prosecutors have not consulted with him before setting the case for trial, and maintains the delays are not deliberate. . . .

Walt Philbin, *New Orleans States-Item*, December 10, 1976.

(Church et al., 1978a). The size of court was unrelated to delay. Court caseload and trial utilization (as opposed to plea bargaining) also bore little relationship to case-processing time. The type of charging system was the only external variable related to delay (grand jury systems consumed more time).

These findings suggest considerable need to revise conventional wisdom about court delay. The rationale for reassessment is set forth by the National Center for State Courts.

> Consideration of the "state of the art" in pretrial delay research had led us to several broad conclusions regarding this literature. There are few accepted truths in this field. Commentators seldom support theories or perceptions with data. Research often is inadequately designed or executed, and leads to inconclusive results. Moreover, research frequently is concentrated on courts solely as they exist on organization charts. More study should be devoted to the less formal aspects of courts, especially the network of relationships, motivations, and perceptions among court participants. [Church et al., 1978b:x]

Delay and the dynamics of courtroom work groups

The essential problem of the conventional wisdom is that it ignores the dynamics of courthouse justice. All too often the problems of case backlogs and trial delays are discussed in legalistic and mechanistic terms. The impression conveyed is that case flow management is somehow removed from other issues and problems in the criminal court process, with the result that the question is falsely viewed in apolitical, administrative terms. In short, the formal, the legal, and the structural have been stressed to the neglect of the informal pattern of discretionary relationships that exists.

Case backlogs, trial delay, and case management are intimately intertwined with the dynamics of courthouse justice. Typically proposals for reducing delay are based on a simple and straightforward analysis: cases produce delay; therefore better management of caseloads will reduce delay. But this equation is not as inherently logical as common sense may indicate. The evidence from an increasingly large number of studies shows that delay results from the voluntary actions of court participants (Oaks and Lehman; Banfield and Anderson; Levin). According to Levin, discussions of the causes and remedies of delay tend to take on an unreal and irrelevant air. Reformers approach the subject as if most defendants and most victims were middle-income persons, as if court officials considered their entire caseload to be composed of serious cases and thought many of the defendants innocent, and as if most of the accused spent the delay in jail (Levin:128). Such conditions simply do not exist in the real world.

Delay is tied not so much to caseload pressure as to the goals of the participants in the decisional process. Defense attorneys seek continuances to avoid harsh judges, to maximize their own goals (for example, fee collection and limiting court time), and to satisfy clients. Prosecutors use delay to increase the stakes of plea bargaining, or to postpone weak cases that they are likely to lose. Judges acquiesce in continuances to pursue their own goals of organization maintenance and enhancement. Viewed in this framework, delay is not simply a question of managing the court docket more efficiently and providing more resources.

Case scheduling

Waiting is one activity that people in the courthouse inevitably engage in: waiting for a defense attorney or prosecutor who is in another courtroom on another case, waiting for a vital witness to show up, waiting for the court reporter.

From an administrative perspective, the courts are extremely complex institutions. A hearing on a pretrial motion, accepting a guilty plea, or conducting a trial requires that numerous people come together at the same time and place. The disposition of a case often requires the presence of the following diverse people: judge, clerk, court reporter, bailiff, defendant, prosecutor, defense attorney, police officer, victim, and witness. Depending on the procedural stage, the appearance of jurors, a probation officer, a pretrial release representative, and an interpreter may also be necessary.

Many of these people have several different courts to appear in during a single day. Defense attorneys, prosecutors, the probation officer, and the translator may have several cases set for the same time. There can be administrative problems too. Heavy traffic can delay a juror or witness. Because of slow mail delivery, notices of court appearances may arrive the day after the scheduled hearing. An illegible address means the defendant never receives a notice. Or the jailer may inadvertently forget to include the needed defendant on the day's list. If just one person is late, the others must wait. And if one person never shows up at all, the hearing must be rescheduled.

To complicate further the administrative complexity of the courts, judges have only limited authority to control the other agencies. The court is actually a collection of separate and independent organizations: judge, police department(s), prosecutor, sheriff, clerk, probation officer, and court reporter. Most of these organizations in state court are headed by elected officials or, like the police, report to elected officials. They have their own base of power and their own separate legal mandates. Judges, then, have only limited administrative control (although they are often held responsible when something goes wrong). When a group of Minnesota district judges was asked to state the major organizational and administrative problem facing the trial courts, 36 percent chose "inadequate" control by the courts of the services or functions required to support court operations (Beerhalter and Gainey:14).

In turn, each of these separate organizations has scheduling problems. Typically each tries to establish a schedule of court appearances that is best for them. But such schedules often inconvenience other agencies. The sheriff, for example, may decide to bring prisoners to court only once a day. If a defendant is inadvertently left off the day's list, the case must be set for another day.

A major study of the federal courts concluded that most of the best-run district courts held regular meetings of top officials of the various organizations to iron out administrative problems. In the other, less well-run courts, each agency head was critical of operating procedures of the others for causing delay and inconvenience. But they never met to work out a coordinated plan (Flanders). A report on the success of four state trial courts in reducing delay pointed to improved communications between the principal agencies as a chief factor. Meeting periodically, the heads of the court agencies were able to share information and work out common problems (Ryan et al.:72).

Trial schedules

case scheduling

Case scheduling is a juggling act. A profusion of cases involving numerous different people must constantly be rearranged in order to accommodate conflicts in schedules. For example, at the last minute a prosecutor cannot make a scheduled trial because a trial in another court has taken longer than expected.

A key ingredient in effective court management is the ability to set a certain date for trial. The District Courts Studies Project (Flanders) reported that courts with low backlogs and little delay were ones that set a date for trial early in the history of a case. Lawyers knew they must be prepared by that date. The key is that the date must be certain. Often dates are set, but lawyers, knowing the case will not be reached by then, do not prepare.

Judges vary both in their authority and willingness to enforce the certainty of trial settings. In some jurisdictions only the judge can grant a request for *continuance*

continuance

ance. In others, however, the judge has no legal power to deny a request from both parties for a continuance. Even when judges have this authority, though, they are often reluctant to use it. Many do not wish to antagonize the local lawyers. Judges are understandably reluctant to force a case to trial when one party states they are not prepared. To complicate matters further, in some areas prosecutors—not judges—determine trial settings.

There are two principal methods courts use in scheduling cases: individual and master calendars.

individual calendar

Individual Calendar. The simplest procedure is the *individual calendar*. A case is assigned to one judge for all matters—arraignment, pretrial motions, and trial. A central advantage is continuity. All parties know that a single judge is responsible. Judge shopping is minimal. Administrative responsibility is fixed. One can easily compare judges' dockets to determine who is moving the cases and who is not.

Where the individual calendar system is used, there are often major differences in the dockets, though. Some judges are speedy, others slow. The speed of disposition is tied to the luck of the draw. For example, if a judge is assigned a difficult and complex case that takes a long time to try, all the other cases are delayed.

The main difficulty in setting certain trial dates is that there are potentially more cases to try than dates available. Thus cases must be stacked—more than one case set on a given day. Because most cases will plead out, such stacking can work. But there are dual dangers. Some judges set too many. As a result, when two cases do not plead out, only one can be tried; the other must be rescheduled. If this happens too often, the certainty of the trial date is eroded. The opposite can also happen. Fearful of not being able to try a case that is ready, the judge stacks too few cases. When they all settle, a trial date is vacant. This often leads to a situation in which judges with large backlogs have little to do on a given day.

master cal-endar

Master Calendar. The *master calendar* is a more recent development. Judges specialize (typically on a rotating basis) on given stages of a case—arraignment, motions, bargaining, and trial. The central advantage is that judges who are good in one aspect of litigation (settling cases, for example) but feel less comfortable in other areas (jury trials, for instance) can be assigned what they do best. The disadvantage is that it is hard to locate responsibility for delay. Cases move to the top of the list in each section of court and when they are finally reached, the case goes on the next list. Judges have less incentive to try to keep their docket current because when they dispose of one case, another appears. Say three judges handle pretrial motions. If two work hard but the third does not, the hard-working judges are penalized because they end up with more cases.

Under a master calendar system a case is set on the trial docket and when it reaches the top of the list, it is supposed to be tried. Flexibility is a clear advantage. If there is a single long case, one judge is available to handle it. However, the master calendar is less able to establish firm trial dates. Cases that reach the top of the list may not be able to be tried on that date; a lawyer may be busy on another case in another court, or the case may require witnesses who are not available.

IN THE NEWS: KILLER IS RELEASED THROUGH LEGAL SNAFU

New Orleans police have put out a nationwide alert for a convicted killer released from Louisiana State Penitentiary at Angola through a legal snafu.

Prison officials and District Attorney Harry Connick's office were blaming each other for the release of Kester Lee Hall, 31, an armed robber and slayer who was a rodeo champ at Angola.

Hall was under a 198-year sentence for armed robbery, but was freed with no legal action after the Louisiana Supreme Court ruled his conviction illegal.

He was convicted in June of 1967 of the 1966 armed robbery of the Li'l General Food Store at 6229 N. Claiborne.

Since he had a previous murder conviction on his record, Criminal District Judge Matthew Braniff imposed the lengthy term. But the high court on July 1 of this year reversed the conviction on grounds that the DA in his trial made reference to the fact that

Hall did not take the stand, a defendant's right under the constitution.

Normally, the case is then set for retrial. But Angola Warden Murray Henderson said he was forced to order Hall's release Aug. 13 because he got no new trial notice from Connick's office.

"I can't do their job," said Henderson of Connick's office. "His sentence was set aside July 1. He was here illegally from that day on."

He said he sent notices to both Connick and Criminal Sheriff Charles Foti of Hall's impending release unless charges were filed. But Assistant DA William Wessel said the office got no such notice.

Police have been looking for Hall since Monday and have entered his name on the national crime data computer, showing he is wanted for trial for armed robbery.

New Orleans States-Item, August 17, 1977.

An evaluation

There is a running debate over which calendaring system is best. Which system is "best" depends partly on the nature of the court. Small courts, such as U.S. district courts, use the individual calendar system successfully. Because of the complexity of their dockets, big city and state courts almost uniformly use master calendars. While both the individual and master calendars have advantages as well as drawbacks, research indicates that courts using the master calendar experience the greatest difficulty. Typical are problems identified in Detroit and Las Vegas: (1) some judges refused to take their fair share of cases; (2) the administrative burden on the chief judge was too great; (3) as a result a significant backlog of cases developed. In these courts when the master calendar was scrapped in favor of the individual calendar, major reductions in delay were achieved (Neubauer et al.).

The role of technology

paperwork

Courts are paperwork bureaucracies. Even the simplest case requires stacks of papers: charging document, bail papers, pretrial motions and responses, appearance of counsel, and so on. Courts have been slow to adopt modern management techniques or equipment to process this *paperwork*. Papers are processed by hand, which is both cumbersome and time-consuming. Papers get lost, thus delaying the case. Moreover, there is no ability to generate the type of statistical data vital for managing the courts. Chief Justice Burger put it this way:

> In terms of methods, machinery, and equipment, the flow of papers—and we know [that] the business of courts depends on the flow of papers—most courts have changed very little fundamentally in a hundred years or more. . . .
> As litigation has grown and multiple-judge courts have steadily enlarged, the continued use of the old equipment and old methods has brought about a virtual

breakdown in many places and a slowdown everywhere in the efficiency and functioning of courts.

technology   The adoption of modern data management *technology* like the computer offers many advantages. It can organize, index, and docket information so that it is useful to all the parties—judge, prosecutor, clerk, defense, probation, sheriff—who need to know about what is currently happening in a specific case. It can help schedule cases and aid in avoiding conflicts in court appearances. It can account for the large sums of money handled by courts and related agencies. By centralizing information it can generate data on the extent of case backlog and bottlenecks in the system. Finally, it can provide the documentation needed to evaluate the effectiveness of court operations (Blaine).

For a number of reasons, courts have been slower than virtually all other major organizations in America to adopt such techniques. One factor is cost. Courts are short of funds to finance new equipment and hire the skilled personnel to utilize them. Because the courts are decentralized, disseminating accurate knowledge about the benefits of new technology has been slow. But more fundamentally, many court officials are not prone to innovate. Some judges falsely fear that a computer will replace them altogether. At times the benefits of the computer have been greatly oversold. For example, St. Louis County courts attempted to computerize many of their operations, but after several years—and substantial expenditures—the computer was able to produce only limited information. Such failures are partially the product of the fact that many court docket systems are so primitive. The old methods used are not systematic enough to be incorporated into a modern management system. Finally, small and medium-sized courts correctly perceive that expensive computer hardware is best suited for large courts. Some of these courts have successfully adopted less sophisticated but equally effective methods.

In short, courts require better statistical information than most currently possess if they are to successfully tackle their administrative and management problems. But the specifics of the technology, the computer in this case, must be viewed not as an end in itself but as a means to an end—the more effective management of the courts.

Managing the courts

A constant complaint is that the courts are mismanaged. The attorney general of Massachusetts characterized the court system in his state as "ineffective, inaccessible, chaotic, archaic, ponderously slow, and beginning to fall almost by its own weight" ("Bellotti"). In most states there are three distinct sets of court managers: court clerks, chief judges, and court administrators.

Clerks of court

clerks of court   The *clerks of court*, variously referred to as prothonotaries, registers of probate, and clerks, are pivotal in the administration of local judiciaries. They are responsible for docketing cases, collecting court fees and costs, overseeing jury selection, and maintaining court records. Although these local officials often have enormous power, they have been overlooked by academics and reformers alike (Gertz). They have traditionally competed with judges for control over judicial administration. Given that they are elected officials in all but six states, they can operate semiautonomously from the judge. Typically clerks have not been associated with effective management. The reasons are summarized thus:

> Generally they are conservative in nature and reflect the attitudes and culture of the community. Their parochial backgrounds coupled with their conservative orientation, in part accounts for this resistance to change. This resistance often compels judicial systems to retain archaic procedures and managerial techniques. [Berkson, Hays, and Carbon:164]

Although there are notable exceptions, most clerks are not trained to manage the local courts.

Chief judges

Although judges are responsible for court administration, they have historically been ineffective managers. This fact is primarily the result of the unique environment in which the courts operate. For example, while judges may be held responsible, they seldom have the necessary authority. Moreover they are not trained in management. The skills of the lawyer center on treating each case individually, and most practicing attorneys handle only a few cases at any one time. The end result is that the lawyers who become judges are not accustomed to analyzing patterns of case dispositions or to managing large dockets. Yet those are the essential skills a manager needs.

chief judge   These problems are reflected in the position of *chief judge*. While the chief judge has general administrative responsibilities, the position is really one of first among equals with the other judges. Particularly when the chief judge assumes the position by seniority, as many do, there is no guarantee that the person will be interested in management or will be effective at it. Election by the other judges sometimes does result in selecting a powerful and effective manager. But election can also produce a candidate who will not rock the boat.

Court administrators

One of the most innovative approaches to the solution of court problems has been the creation of a professional group of trained administrators to assist judges in their administrative duties. The guiding theory is that well-trained managers can infuse the courts with managerial talent they often have lacked.

> "Management—like law—is a profession" today. Few judges or lawyers with severe chest pains would attempt to treat themselves. There would be slight hesitation about consulting the medical profession. Congested dockets and long delays are symptoms that court systems need the help of professionals. Those professionals are managers. If court administration is to be effective, judicial recognition that managerial skill and knowledge are necessary to efficient performance is vital. [Meyer:234]

Underlying this theory is the assumption that the managers can perform administrative tasks (case management, budgeting, personnel) without interfering with the judges' primary task of adjudicating (deciding specific cases).

court ad-
ministrator
The development of the professional position of *court administrator* has been sporadic. In 1937 Connecticut established the first centralized office of court administrator. It was not until after World War II, however, that many other states followed; by 1978, every state except Mississippi had established a statewide court administrator. The primary duties of these officials are to prepare annual reports summarizing caseload data, preparing budgets, and trouble-shooting. Typically they report to the state supreme court or the chief justice of the state supreme court. Increasingly trial courts are also employing court administrators. Few, if any, major metropolitan areas are without professional judicial employees.

Because the position is so new, several aspects of the court administrator's role are still being debated. Arguments among advocates of professional court executives center around two topics: qualifications and administrative relations with other agencies.

Qualifications.   In the past, it was common for the court administrator to be merely another patronage position. Moreover, there was no agreed-upon body of knowledge or set of skills court administrators needed. To counter these factors reformers have sought to professionalize the position. The creation of the Institute for Court Management in 1970 was a landmark. By creating the mechanism for training court administrators, it legitimized their standing within the legal establishment. But there is still no agreement as to the skills and qualifications the court administrator should possess. Many reformers believed that managerial expertise was needed and a law degree was unnecessary. On the other hand, many judges contend that a law degree is essential. For example, some complain that some court administrators hired for their background in business techniques have been ineffective because they know too little about courts and the common law.

Administrative Relationships.   A second area of concern is the proper relationship between the court administrator and other agencies of the judiciary. For example, what supervisory powers should the court administrator have over the clerk's office? Often clerks view the position as a threat and resent any intrusion. Yet to be an effective executive, the court administrator requires the type of data on cases that only the clerk can provide. This means many potential conflicts are associated with creating the new position of court executive. Court clerks have assumed a central role in resisting the creation of court executive. If the position is created, they can greatly reduce the administrator's effectiveness by not cooperating.

Tension between judges and the court administrator may arise too. Some judges are reluctant to delegate responsibility over important aspects of the court's work—case scheduling, for example.

In practice, the distinction between administration and adjudication is not clear-cut. A court administrator's proposal to streamline court procedures may be viewed by the judges as an intrusion on how they decide cases. For example, deciding whether the power to transfer the judge from one assignment to another is a judicial or nonjudicial responsibility is not an easy task.

An evaluation

Despite their potential ability to improve the efficiency of the court, court administrators have encountered opposition from both clerks and judges. Most have not been given full responsibility over most aspects of the court's nonjudicial duties. A survey in Florida, for instance, found that most court administrators handle only relatively minor tasks (Berkson). In other areas, however, judicial administrators have been able to fulfill the reformers' expectations that they would be able to innovate. As is typical of emerging positions, substantial confusion still exists over the role of the court administrator (Stott).

Speedy trial acts

Although the Sixth Amendment guarantees the right to a speedy trial, the Supreme Court has refused to give this rather vague concept any precise time frame (*Barker* v. *Wingo*, 407 U.S. 514, 1972). Likewise, thirty-five state constitutions have speedy trial guarantees but these provisions apply only when the delay has been "extensive." In the last few years, though, there has been considerable interest in putting some teeth into the guarantee of a speedy trial. The best known and most comprehensive such effort is the *Speedy Trial Act* of 1974 (18 USC §3161). Congress mandated that all defendants in federal court must be indicted within thirty days of arrest, arraigned within ten days of indictment, and tried within sixty days of arraignment.

speedy trial act

Speedy trial statutes exist in all fifty states. These laws, however, have a different orientation than their federal counterpart. Most state laws are defendant-centered; that is, they are designed to protect defendants from suffering extensive delay, particularly if they are incarcerated prior to trial. By contrast the federal law is designed to protect the interests of society; that is, a speedy trial is viewed as an important objective irrespective of whether the defendant's interests are in jeopardy.

Substantial variation is evident in the statutory requirements of speedy trial laws. The length of the time period varies from thirty days for a misdemeanor in California to 180 days for a felony in Pennsylvania. A number of states have different periods for defendants in custody than for those released on bail.

Most striking about efforts to mandate speedy trials is their generality. These laws are not based on an analysis of why delay occurs; they incorporate none of the conflicting explanations of why courts are too slow. Moreover they do not provide for any additional resources (more judges, court reporters, and so on) to aid the courts in complying. This can produce some unforeseen consequences. A number of federal courts have had great difficulty in complying. Often compliance has come at the price of delaying civil cases. Speedy trial acts, because they reduce flexibility in scheduling, can also result in courts expending greater effort per case.

Potential difficulties also arise because not all cases easily fit into the mandated time frames. A major case or a complex drug conspiracy case take longer to prepare than an ordinary burglary case. State laws generally allow trial judges wide discretion in deciding that in the interests of justice the time frames can be waived. These laws also specify general periods that can be excluded.

Common grounds for exclusion is the congestion of the trial docket, as in Texas, Indiana, and Kansas. But given the general and extreme congestion so prevalent throughout some American courts, this exception has the potential to undermine the purpose of speedy trial provisions. The federal Speedy Trial Act sought to limit such discretion by specifying excludable time. But to some such specifications fail to allow for needed flexibility.

reprosecu-
tion

Finally, enforcement is a problem. Ten states provide that the case must be dismissed. This can result in a guilty defendant's going free because of an administrative problem. It can also allow the prosecutor not to proceed deliberately because there is no case and then later blame the judge when the case is dismissed. Other states permit dismissal but allow *reprosecution*. This latter approach can undermine the effectiveness of speedy trial provisions by subjecting defendants to a series of reprosecutions. Dismissal with or without the right for reprosecution at the discretion of the judge is provided for in other state provisions and in the federal act as well.

Overall, speedy trial laws have had only a limited impact in speeding up the flow of cases through the criminal court process (Nimmer). The primary reason is that most state laws fail to provide the court with adequate and effective enforcement mechanisms. As a result, time limits specified by speedy trial laws are seldom a guide to actual practice.

> Like most big-city court administrators, I have been locked continuously in a struggle with calendar delay, and I have utilized every device and contrivance I could copy to speed the disposition of cases. I now fear that in doing so we may have done the courts a great disservice. For, while in many cases justice delayed is justice denied, it does not follow that the prompt administration of justice, in and of itself, is adequate justice. It is a prime ingredient, no doubt, but there are others. We, judges and lawyers alike, have lost sight of the fact that while a speedy disposition of a case is usually essential to a fully appropriate disposition, it is a means, not an end.
>
> Too many judges have become caught up in a consuming campaign against that Old Debbil Calendar—in the obsessive delusion that rapid disposition of cases is the be-all and end-all of the judicial process—and without thought to the calibre of the disposition.
>
> Bernard Botein, "The Case Against Instant Justice," *American Bar Association Journal* (August 1966):713–716.

Conclusion

The central theme of most reform proposals is the elimination of court delay. The National Advisory Commission, for example, assigned first priority to ensuring "speed and efficiency in achieving final determination of guilt or innocence of a defendant" (7).

The passage of time needed for case preparation must be distinguished from unnecessary delay. Many of the recommendations are directly aimed at this objective: imposition of a sixty-day period for commencing trial; abolition of the grand jury; priority case scheduling; limitations on *voir dire*; and upgrading court administration. In addition, several recommendations are indirectly aimed at improving speed and efficiency through reduced dockets; namely, case screening and diversion.

The courts are in need of better management. It is interesting that the traditional concern for the incarcerated defendant awaiting trial has now been supplemented with a realization that delay works a disservice to jurors and witnesses as well. Thus upgrading management by improved docketing, record keeping, and selective incorporation of computerized systems will help reduce needless delay and provide data to monitor other inequities in the system.

Although the courts need to concentrate on more effective management of their dockets, the National Advisory Commission overestimates the improvements that are likely to result from speedier and more efficient procedures. Well-run courts, staffed by capable persons using modern management techniques, will continue to be confronted with the same conditions—large volume of cases, sentencing disparities, and overcrowded jails—that plague the courts now (Neubauer and Cole).

For discussion

1. What advantages would result from greater centralized administration of state courts? What disadvantages?
2. Examine docket sheets, analyze news accounts of criminal cases, and talk to court officials. Try to develop an estimate of how long it takes to dispose of criminal cases in your community. Is the time too long or too short? Why? Using the same sources develop an estimate of the case backlog.
3. Why do you think delay is a problem? Which of the four perspectives comes closest to your own? Why?
4. What procedural steps do you think contribute to unnecessary delay? What might be done?
5. In chapter 1 we argued that the criminal justice system is fragmented. How does this fragmentation contribute to delay? What can be done to overcome the problem?
6. Examine the court files in several cases. Do they seem to be complete? Are notations made in pen, typewritten, or by computer? Are the courts able to provide accurate data on the number of cases pending, what stages the cases are at, and the average length of delay? Interview a professor from your department of business. Ask about the types of modern paper-flow management techniques that might be successfully used in the courts.
7. What advantages do you see to the Speedy Trial Act? What disadvantages? To be effective the law must have enforcement provisions, but typically these involve dismissing the case. Do you favor case dismissal? What other enforcement mechanisms might be considered?
8. Interview a judge, prosecutor, defense attorney, and court clerk about delay. Do

they think the local court has a problem? Do they agree or disagree on what might be done to speed up case dispositions?

9. In designing and implementing programs to reduce case backlog and delay, why is it important to consider the dynamics of courtroom work groups?

References

Banfield, L., and C. David Anderson. "Continuances in the Cook County Criminal Courts." *University of Chicago Law Review* 35 (Winter 1968):259–316.

Beerhalter, Susan, and James Gainey. *Minnesota District Court Survey.* Denver: National Center for State Courts, 1974.

"Bellotti Calls Judicial System Inaccessible, Archaic, Chaotic." *Boston Globe,* February 1, 1976, C1.

Berkson, Larry. "Delay and Congestion in State Court Systems: An Overview." In Larry Berkson, Steven Hays, and Susan Carbon, eds., *Managing the State Courts: Text and Readings.* St. Paul, Minn.: West Publishing, 1977.

Blaine, Gerald. "Computer-Based Information Systems Can Help Solve Urban Court Problems." *Judicature* 54 (November 1970):149–153.

Casper, Jonathan. *American Criminal Justice: The Defendant's Perspective.* Englewood Cliffs, N.J.: Prentice-Hall, 1972.

Church, Thomas, Alan Carlson, Jo-Lynne Lee, and Teresa Tan. *Justice Delayed: The Pace of Litigation in Urban Trial Courts.* Williamsburg, Va.: National Center for State Courts, 1978a.

———, Jo-Lynne Lee, Teresa Tan, Alan Carlson, and Virginia McConnell. *Pretrial Delay: A Review and Bibliography.* Williamsburg, Va.: National Center for State Courts, 1978b.

Flanders, Steven. *Case Management and Court Management in United States District Courts.* Washington, D.C.: Federal Judicial Center, 1977.

Gertz, Marc. "Influence in Court Systems: The Clerk as Interface," *Justice Systems Journal* (Fall 1977):30–37.

Levin, Martin. "Delay in 'Five Criminal Courts.'" *Journal of Legal Studies* 4 (1972):83.

Luskin, Mary. "Building a Theory of Case-Processing Time." *Judicature* 62 (September 1978):114–127.

Meyer, Bernadine. "Court Administration: The Newest Profession." *Duquesne Law Review* 10 (Winter 1971):220–235.

National Advisory Commission on Criminal Justice Standards and Goals. *Courts.* Washington, D.C.: Government Printing Office, 1973.

Neubauer, David W., and George F. Cole. "A Political Critique of the Court Recommendations of the National Advisory Commission on Criminal Justice Standards and Goals." *Emory Law Journal* 24 (Fall 1975).

———, Marcia Lipetz, Mary Luskin, and John Paul Ryan. *Managing the Pace of Justice: An Evaluation of LEAA's Court Delay Reduction Programs.* Washington, D.C.: Government Printing Office, 1981.

Nimmer, Raymond. *The Nature of System Change: Reform Impact in the Criminal Courts.* Chicago: American Bar Foundation, 1978.

Oaks, D., and W. Lehman. *A Criminal Justice System and the Indigent.* Chicago: University of Chicago Press, 1968.

Ryan, John Paul, Marcia Lipetz, Mary Luskin, and David Neubauer. "Analyzing Court Delay-Reduction Programs: Why Do Some Succeed?" *Judicature* 65 (August 1981):58–75.

Stott, E. Keith. "The Judicial Executive: Toward Greater Congruence in an Emerging Profession." *Justice System Journal* 7 (Summer 1982):152–179.

Wheeler, Russell, and Howard R. Whitcomb. *Judicial Administration: Text and Reading.* Englewood Cliffs, N.J.: Prentice-Hall, 1977.

Yankelovich, Shelly and White, Inc. *The Public Image of Courts: Highlights of a National Survey of the General Public, Judges, Lawyers and Community Leaders.* Williamsburg, Va.: National Center for State Courts, 1978.

For further reading

Berkson, Larry, Steven Hays, and Susan Carbon, eds. *Managing the State Courts: Text and Readings.* St. Paul, Minn.: West Publishing, 1977.

Church, Thomas, Alan Carlson, Jo-Lynne Lee, and Teresa Tan. *Justice Delayed: The Pace of Litigation in Urban Trial Courts.* Williamsburg, Va.: National Center for State Courts, 1978.

Nimmer, Raymond. *The Nature of System Change: Reform Impact in the Criminal Courts.* Chicago: American Bar Foundation, 1978.

Ryan, John Paul, Marcia Lipetz, Mary Luskin, and David Neubauer. "Analyzing Court Delay-Reduction Programs: Why Do Some Succeed?" *Judicature* 65 (August 1981):58–75.

Wheeler, Russell, and Howard Whitcomb. *Judicial Administration: Text and Reading.* Englewood Cliffs, N.J.: Prentice-Hall, 1977.

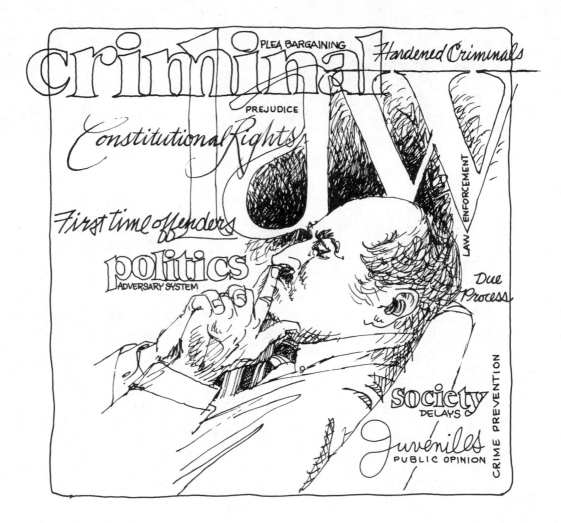

Epilogue:
The Troubled Courthouse

The problems

Clearly, the criminal courts face serious problems. Rising crime rates swell the court dockets. Arrestees often languish in overcrowded jails. Cases may take months or years to wind through the process. Plea bargaining practices are questioned. Witnesses meet with indifference. Victims often feel mistreated. Prisons are filled to overflowing.

The problems of the courthouse are real. But acknowledging these problems does not mean they are on the brink of collapse. Exaggerated assertions about the "crisis" facing the courts detract from realistic assessments about what the problems are and what can be done to solve them. The primary problems of the courts are not the result of external calamities, such as increased crime rates and expanded case loads. Rather they are due to increased attention and raised standards. (Feeley, 1983).

Historical perspective

Exaggerated statements about the problems of the courts stem from the lack of a historical perspective. What many label as "new" problems have actually been around for a long time. The last few years are not the only time Americans have discovered the problem of crime—it only seems that way. In an often-cited speech given in 1906, "The Causes of Dissatisfaction with the Administration of Justice," legal scholar Roscoe Pound warned that a legal system created within the framework of a rural, agrarian America could not meet the needs of an urban, industrialized society. Pound's warnings went largely unheeded until the turmoil of prohibition and the rise of modern gangsters like Al Capone focused attention on the state of the courts. In 1931 the *Wickersham Reports* labeled the court system inefficient and called for major overhauls. But the nation's interest in the sorry state of the criminal courts was soon replaced by more pressing matters—the Great Depression and, later, World War II. It was not until the 1960s that national attention again returned to criminal justice. To study the crime problem, President Lyndon Johnson created the *President's Commission on Law Enforcement and Administration of Justice*, which probed the entire spectrum of the criminal justice process, identified problems, and made general suggestions for improvements.

In 1971, President Nixon created the *National Advisory Commission on Criminal Justice Standards and Goals*. Funded by the Law Enforcement Assistance Administration (LEAA), it was given a mandate to "formulate for the first time national criminal justice standards and goals for crime reduction and prevention." By and large these standards and goals express the agreement within the legal community about the direction of reform. The work of these prestigious national commissions has been supplemented by the activities of a diverse array of citizen groups, business associations, ex-offenders, and court officials themselves.

The result has been a period of unprecedented activity aimed at improving the criminal justice system. While most early concern focused on the police and corrections, in the last few years the problems of the courts have come to occupy a more equal footing.

Increased expectations

This increased attention to the troubled courthouse has contributed to an exaggeration of the problems in a second important way–expectations have increased. This tide of rising expectations is clearly legitimate. Confronted with cases that take years to be processed or misdemeanor courts that provide only rough justice, society can reasonably expect more. What is of concern, though, is that some of these increased expectations are unrealistic. Unrealistic expectations create frustration when lofty goals are not met. We need to ask hard headed questions: How much delay is too much? how much due process can the lower courts reasonably be expected to provide?

The troubled history of the Law Enforcement Assistance Administration provides a case in point. Initially created by President Johnson, showcased by President Nixon and later abolished by Presidents Carter and Reagan, LEAA was plagued with difficulty. Crime rates did not fall.

Hopes for far reaching changes in police, courts, and prisons did not materialize. Why? The typical criticisms of LEAA centered on a rigid bureaucracy, the lack of firm leadership, too much partisan politics and at times just plain ineptitude. In their thoughtful review, however, Malcolm Feeley and Austin Sarat point to more fundamental problems. The Congressional Act itself was flawed. Congress had no clear idea about what needed to be done, only a general sense that change was necessary. Instead of providing policy direction, the act created a planning process. But this left unclear what was to be planned. Overall the stated goals were overly ambitious.

LEAA did foster important changes and some much needed improvements. But unrealistic expectations distracted attention from these achievements and contributed to a sense of frustration about reform.

Sorting out where the courts have been and where they are going is obviously a difficult task. The purpose of this epilogue is to offer a realistic assessment of the troubled courthouse. The attempt is to walk the line between two extremes: the rhetoric of crisis and the endorsement of the status quo. The core concerns of this epilogue are several. The nature of the problems facing the criminal courts are not always self-evident. Expectations of reformers have been set unrealistically high. The nation must learn to live with inevitable tensions in the court process. We must acknowledge that fundamental social changes are outside the capacity of the courts. Much reform activity places too much emphasis on legalistic and mechanistic matters and gives too little attention to the dynamics of the courthouse justice.

> My thesis is that, because our understanding of the courts is flawed and our expectations about what the courts can do are unrealistic, many innovations fail. Some fail because we try to impose bureaucratic structures on a protean if imperfect adversary process. Some fail because we mistake discretion for arbitrariness. Some are misdirected because we focus on isolated horror stories. Others respond to the symbols of legal formalism and ignore actual practices. Some strive to extend the courts beyond their capacities.
>
> Conversely, many concerned observers have unrealistic expectations about what courts can do, while others fail to appreciate that some of their concern stems from increased standards and expectations; as a result, they underestimate the significance of changes that have taken place.
>
> Malcolm Feeley, *Court Reform on Trial: Why Simple Solutions Fail.* NY: Basic Books, 1983. p. XIV.

Disagreement over goals

The starting point in constructing realistic expectations is the realization that there is a lack of agreement on the fundamental goals of the courts. Like beauty, statements of the problems of the courthouse often lie in the eye of the beholder. What one person applauds as progress, another denounces as a step backwards. Are pretrial release practices too limited or not restrictive enough? Are sentences too lenient or unduly harsh? Reasonable persons disagree over issues like these. The disagreements need to be recognized. The essential difficulty is that reform efforts mask these areas of disagreement.

Consider, for example, the National Advisory Commission on Criminal Justice Standards and Goals recommendations on the Courts. The primacy given to procedural improvements comes at the expense of substantive policy issues. Examination of different governmental reform movements suggests that while they purport to be neutral ways of doing the same thing better, they actually disguise policy alternatives. Thus, it is necessary to separate the reformers' rhetoric from their underlying and sometimes unarticulated concerns.

For example, at several points the report indicates displeasure with such fundamental policies of prosecutors as non-filing of certain cases because they are low on the D.A.'s list of priorities and charge reductions during plea bargaining to avoid harsh sentences. In each instance the Commission discusses changing these procedures when it is really quarreling with the policies themselves. Not only does the emphasis on procedure mask substantive policy issues, it diverts attention from questions about the fairness of the system and protection of defendants' rights (Cole and Neubauer). We thus need to consider efforts to improve court efficiency in substantive terms.

Efficiency

Clearly the criminal court process needs better management. Reformers are certainly correct in stressing the need for improved efficiency. All too often poor management prevents actors in the system from focusing on priorities, at times resulting in truly dangerous criminals somehow falling between the cracks. But a realistic appraisal of the court process indicates that increased efficiency will not solve many of the basic difficulties. Well-run courts staffed by capable persons using modern management techniques will face the same conditions—large volume of cases, sentencing disparities, and over-crowded jails—as the courts do now (Cole and Neubauer).

Efficiency for whose benefit we may also ask. The failure to confront directly conflicts over goals of the court process can blind us to the fact that some reforms may make the process harsher. This was the conclusion of a recent study that probed the effects of the no plea bargaining policy in Alaska. The study found that the strongest negative impact was on middle class defendants charged with property crimes (Rubinstein and White). We must always be mindful that reforms based on the goal of efficiency may involve hidden political agendas. (Ryan). A stress on improving efficiency that does not take into account important substantive concerns serves to promote unrealistic expectations. Justice must be considered as well.

Evenhandedness

In considering what the courts can do better, one must keep in mind the overriding criteria; justice must be served. The process by which justice is administered, as well as the results achieved, must be perceived to be fair and impartial. Alas, the public rhetoric concerning the criminal courts all too often neglects to consider evenhandedness.

There are clear areas where evenhandedness is a major concern. Disparities in treatment based on race, or poverty do not conform to the ideals of equal justice under the law. Likewise harsher penalties for those who go to trial rather than plead guilty raise questions. Perceptions that the rich receive undue leniency in white-collar crimes prompt attention.

Recent studies indicate that these factors operate in a more indirect fashion than was often thought. Rather than being direct, and blatant, research indicates that the influences are actually subtle. To apply the old cliche, issues of disparity emerge as shades of gray rather than stark contrasts of black and white.

At the same time recent studies indicate that courthouse officials do wrestle with important issues of doing justice. Judges, prosecutors and defense attorneys are not preprogrammed computers who merely examine a few immediately obvious factors and crank out a decision. Rather they consider various nuances: the true nature of the crime; and the individual nature of the defendant. Court actors attempt to produce substantive justice rather than merely following the book (procedural justice) (Feeley, 1979).

But where justice ends and expediency begins is difficult to decipher. Courthouse officials are expected to both do justice and move cases. As Rosett and Cressey write "When Steve Ohler the [hypothetical] public defender exercises his discretionary power to settle a case, no one is able to tell whether the settlement is made in the interests of justice rather than in the interests of bureaucratic efficiency. Even Steve himself is not certain." (131).

Settling cases in the interest of justice reflects a group sense of justice. Each courthouse has a "going rate"–a typical penalty applied to a crime category, based on the defendant's background.

To properly assess how substantive justice is meted out in the courthouse requires an understanding of the courtroom work group.

The dynamics of courthouse justice

A flawed understanding of the court process contributes to unrealistic expectations (Feeley, 1983). Reformers focus on individual problems in isolation from the broader process. They stress the formal dimensions of the process to the neglect of the informal ways that discretionary power is controlled and channeled.

The courts are a community of actors. Throughout this book we have stressed the central role of the courtroom work group. Judges, prosecutors, defense attorneys, juries, and in some cases the police are tied together by more than a shared workplace. Because these actors appear daily on the same judicial stage, their interactions combine to create what is best described as a social organization.

Unfortunately the reform efforts as typified by the National Advisory Commission on Criminal Justice Standards and Goals do not recognize the dynamics of the process. Much the same criticism was made about the 1967 report: "The President's Commission reports deal with the formal, the legal, the structural—and virtually ignore the reality of the criminal court as a social system, as a community of human beings who are engaged in doing certain things with, to, and for each other" (Blumberg:viii-ix).

The inattention paid by the *Report on Courts* to the existence of a social control network necessarily limits its analysis of discretion. The recommendations to formalize the standards that guide discretion are substantially off target for they fail to grapple with the real source of limitations: the courtroom work group.

The limited and partial knowledge about the dynamics of courthouse justice explains why numerous reform efforts have not been successful. Efforts to limit or control discretion at one point in the process typically result in increased discretion elsewhere. Our discussions of efforts to abolish plea bargaining (Chapter 13), alter sentencing (Chapter 16) and reduce delay are cases in point.

Once we recognize that the courtroom work groups set standards that structure discretion, we can proceed to the central task of examining and analyzing these standards. Typically the screening criteria employed by one young assistant prosecutor differs from another. The same variation occurs between sections of courts on sentencing. We need to confront these differences in order to achieve more consistency. But at the same time, we must recognize that uniformity that is the product of the lowest common denominator must also be avoided.

> A reform is an external variable, and the systemic reaction to it is determined in large part by the preexisting relationships and personal interests of the participants in the judicial process. If it is to produce system impact, a reform must disrupt the prior balance and accommodation of interests sufficiently to induce the participants to engage in a new pattern of behavior. . . .
>
> A basic fallacy of most current reform planning is that it ignores these factors. Reformers plan the enterprise as if the sole relevant activity were to enable practitioners to act more correctly from the reform perspective. . . .
>
> The idea that participants in the judicial process desire change is, at best, naive. In part, it is perpetuated by the absence of systematic attention to the process of reform. However, there is also a seeming desire to displace attention from the behavior of judicial professionals to alleged artificial barriers and constraints. This amounts to an implicit unwillingness to recognize the true nature of most judicial problems. These problems are typically not the product of artificial barriers or constraints but of conscious behavioral choices made both individually and as a group by professionals within the system. These choices may be related in complex ways to various environmental influences. However, it is to these conscious choices and the resulting behavior that a reform must be directed and not merely to removing a seemingly undesirable influence in the environment, such as caseload pressure. Environmental reforms can succeed only to the extent that they supply incentives to participants to change their behavior. To the extent that they do not, other measures designed to induce change and to manipulate behavior are necessary.

Raymond Nimmer, *The Nature of System Change: Reform Impact in the Criminal Courts,* Chicago: American Bar Foundation, 1978:pp. 175–176.

Crime reduction

A realistic assessment indicates that the courts cannot be expected to solve the problems of crime. This perspective stands in sharp contrast to political rhetoric that lashes out at the criminal courts for their failure to protect the community.

As America entered the decade of the 80s, the nation remained troubled by increasing crime rates. Compared to other industrialized nations of the world, the American crime rate is indeed high in both absolute and relative terms. Just as disturbing are the indications that violent crime is on the increase (Radzinowicz and King). The American public remains very fearful of crime, and demands that something be done. What can be done, of course, is unclear to politicians, and court officials alike.

Despite these public concerns, however, it is unrealistic to expect that the courts can have much impact upon the crime rate. Consider for example the facts discussed in Chapters 9 and 10 on case attrition. Putting these numbers together indicates that roughly only about 5% of crimes ever make it as far as sentencing. It is not realistic to expect that how the courts sentence this small percentage of wrong doers will have much impact on the overall crime problem (Feeley, 1983; Miller, 1981). Proper sentencing will have at best a marginal impact.

Conclusion

Throughout this book we have discussed a number of major reform efforts. We have suggested that some of these reform efforts require a healthy dose of skepticism. But at the same time one needs to note that in a number of important ways the court process is fairer and more focused than in earlier times. Future efforts require the establishment of realistic expectations about the nature of the court process, how change occurs and what can be done to make courts better.

It is appropriate to conclude that reform efforts must avoid the trap of perceiving that nothing works. As part of the increased attention to the court process a number of works have suggested the futility of reform. Evaluations of sentencing reforms, pretrial release programs and diversion efforts have shown that the reformers' claims of success have been greatly over inflated. These evaluations indicate that programs have been poorly implemented or not implemented at all; expectations for success were unduly optimistic; and measures of actual success are hard to come by (Feeley, 1983). Concluding that nothing works though is unduly pessimistic. Part of the difficulty is that these evaluations have themselves suffered from important limitations.

The last decade has been a period marked by a great deal of experimentation. While some of the programs have not necessarily shown a direct impact, they have often had important indirect affects. Pretrial release practices have been liberalized. Alternatives to incarceration have gained legitimacy (Feeley, 1983). Court delay has been reduced in some, but certainly not all, jurisdictions (Neubauer, et al.).

The message to be drawn from reform efforts is a better sense of how changes actually occur in complex organizational entities like the criminal courts.

Patterns of behavior, once established and routinized, become hard to change, because the participants often see no need to act any differently. Moreover, some reform efforts resemble thunder bolts from a far off Mount Olympus. Outsiders proclaim that a problem exists and reform is needed to correct the problem. But those on the working level either fail to see the problem or if they perceive the problem find that the proposed solution bears little resemblance to how their court system actually operates. When the reform fails because it was poorly tailored to local conditions the sense that nothing works gains greater momentum. In short, reform efforts need to refocus by taking into account the legitimate practices reflected in the courtroom work group.

The recommendations of the two presidential commissions exemplify the lawyer's approach to reform: reform procedure. If decisions are being made poorly or badly, the lawyer's solution is to create a better procedural structure. But the fundamental problems of justice cannot be solved by imposing more adversarial due process, for such efforts ignore the fact that the exercise of discretion is a response to the need for flexibility. The inevitability of trying to regularize discretion in this way is that it simply reappears elsewhere. To be successful, reforms must recognize the fundamental role of the courtroom work group. Of course, there are important disagreements over the direction of these reforms. Some argue that the central task is to improve the ability of courts to reduce crime. Others doubt that the courts can ever play a role in crime reduction; they stress instead the need to improve the fairness of justice that defendants receive or to upgrade the public's confidence in the courts by working more effectively with jurors, witnesses, and so on. In short, the public dialogue surrounding the courts continues.

References

Blumberg, Abraham. *Criminal Justice.* Chicago: Quadrangle Books, 1967.

Cole, George and David Neubauer. "The Living Courtroom: A Critique of the National Advisory Commission Recommendations." *Judicature* 59 (January, 1979):293–299.

Feeley, Malcolm. *The Process is the Punishment: Handling Cases in Lower Criminal Court.* New York: Russell Sage Foundation, 1979.

Feeley, Malcolm. *Court Reform on Trial: Why Simple Solutions Fail.* New York: Basic Books, 1983.

Feeley, Malcolm and Austin Sarat. *The Policy Dilemma: Federal Crime Policy and the Law Enforcement Assistance Administration, 1968–1978.* Minneapolis: University of Minnesota Press, 1980.

Gallas, Geoff. "Court Reform: Has it Been Built on an Adequate Foundation?" *Judicature* 63 (June-July, 1979): 28–38.

Miller, J. L., Marilyn Roberts and Charlotte Carter. *Sentencing Reform: A Review and Annotated Bibliography.* Williamsburg, Va.: National Center for State Courts, 1981.

National Advisory Commission on Criminal Justice Standards and Goals. *Report on Courts.* Washington, D.C.: Government Printing Office, 1973.

Neubauer, David *et. al. Managing the Pace of Justice: An Evaluation of LEAA's Court Delay-Reduction Programs.* Washington, D.C.: Government Printing Office, 1981.

Nimmer, Raymond. *The Nature of System Change: Reform Impact in the Criminal Courts.* Chicago: American Bar Foundation, 1978.

Pound, Roscoe. "The Causes of Popular Dissatisfaction With the Administration of Justice." *American Bar Association Reports* 29 (1906):395.

President's Commission on Law Enforcement and Administration of Justice. *Task Force Report: The Courts.* Washington, D.C.: Government Printing Office, 1967.

Radzinowicz, Sir Leon and Joan King. *The Growth of Crime: An International Experience.* New York: Basic Books, 1977.

Rosett, Arthur and Donald Cressey. *Justice by Consent: Plea Bargains in the American Courthouse.* Philadelphia: J. B. Lippincott, 1976.

Rubinstein, Michael and Teresa White. "Plea Bargaining: Can Alaska Live Without It?" *Judicature* 62 (December-January, 1979):270.

Ryan, John Paul. "Management Science in the Real World of Courts." *Judicature*, 62 (September, 1978):144–146.

For further reading

Downie, Leonard. *Justice Denied: The Case for Reform of the Courts.* Baltimore: Penguin Books, 1971.

Fleming, Macklin. *The Price of Perfect Justice.* New York: Basic Books, 1974.

Jacob, Herbert. *The Potential for Reform of Criminal Justice.* Beverly Hills: Sage Publications, 1974.

James, Howard. *Crisis in the Courts.* New York: David McKay, 1971.

Weinreb, Lloyd. *Denial of Justice: Criminal Process in the United States.* New York: The Free Press, 1977.

Index